Foreword by
ALASTAIR COOK

Editor
JO HARMAN

Compiled by
ED DAVIS, VITHUSHAN EHANTHARAJAH, ED KEMP, JAMES SCRAGG, SAM STOW, MATT THACKER & PHIL WALKER

Design
JOE PROVIS & ROB WHITEHOUSE

This edition first published in the UK by All Out Cricket Ltd

www.alloutcricket.com

ISBN: 978-1-909178-61-8

 A CIP Catalogue record for this book is available from the British Library.

Published under the imprint Pitch Publishing Ltd, A2 Yeoman Gate, Yeoman Way, Worthing, BN13 3QZ.
www.pitchpublishing.co.uk

Editor: *Jo Harman;* Research and editorial: *Ed Davis, Vithushan Ehantharajah, Ed Kemp, James Scragg, Sam Stow, Matt Thacker, Phil Walker;*
Design: *Joe Provis, Rob Whitehouse;* Images: *Getty Images unless stated;*
Print: *Jellyfish Print Solutions*

Acknowledgements
The publishers would like to thank the county clubs, the Professional Cricketers' Association and the players for their assistance in helping to put together this book. Additional information has been gathered from espncricinfo.com and cricketarchive.com. Thanks also to Donald MacLeod and SW Pix for providing photographs and Tom Graham for editorial assistance.

CONTENTS

The
Cricketers'
Who's Who
2013

Openers

FOREWORD

by Alastair Cook

Welcome to the 2013 edition of The Cricketers' Who's Who. I'm delighted to write the foreword to a book that has been enjoyed by players and fans alike for so many years. I can tell you it's as popular as ever in county dressing rooms up and down the country and it gives supporters the chance to learn a little more about the players they are watching, as personalities as well as cricketers.

It's a misconception that once players break through into the England set-up they are no longer part of the county cricket bubble. Having worked my way up through the age-groups at Essex, the Chelmsford dressing room is still like a second home to me and I always jump at the chance to represent my county. The demands of the international fixture schedule mean that regular members of the England squad can't do that quite as much as they might wish, but we all keenly follow our counties – hopefully Essex can put on a good show this season and get back into Division One of the County Championship.

It's that excellent early grounding in county cricket with Essex that led to me having the great privilege of being named Test captain last August, and this is such an exciting time to be leading my country. Straussy left the team in great shape and to go and do what we did in India – to end such a long wait for a series win over there – showed what we are capable of achieving as a group and we're determined to build on that this summer against New Zealand and Australia.

I've always tried to meet every challenge head on, to never take a backward step, and this season will be no different. New Zealand have shown over the last couple of years with Test match wins in Australia and Sri Lanka that they're not a side to take lightly.

Several of our current team were fortunate enough to be part of the last Ashes series in Australia, and those of us that were have wonderful memories from that incredible tour. But while we can look back to that series for inspiration, it's crucial that we focus on the here and now. Make no mistake, Australia will be out for revenge this summer. They will come at us hard and we will be doing our very best to ensure we're ready for everything the Aussies have to throw at us. There really is no greater thrill for an England cricketer than playing in the Ashes.

We also have the ICC Champions Trophy to look forward to in June and it's important that we continue to progress in the 50-over format. I've been really pleased with our

development over the last 18 months but we're well aware there's still plenty of work to do ahead of the 2015 World Cup in Australia and New Zealand. With the top eight nations going up against each other in an action-packed 17-day tournament, the Champions Trophy is sure to provide plenty of entertainment.

Away from the international game, we have another exciting domestic campaign to look forward to. Warwickshire ran out deserved County Championship winners in 2012 and the chasing pack will be hot on their heels in this campaign, while Hampshire will be hunting for more silverware after claiming two limited overs trophies last season. In my view the county game continues to go from strength to strength and that's been reflected in England's performances over the last few years. It promises to be fascinating viewing once again in 2013.

Enjoy the summer!

Alastair Cook
England Test and ODI captain

EDITOR'S NOTES

The release of the 34th edition of The Cricketers' Who's Who comes at a testing but also an exciting time for the future of county cricket. Individual sports are fighting harder than ever for exposure and funding, and cricket is no exception. The commercialisation of the game worldwide has led some to question whether our 18-county first-class structure is a sustainable business model, but in February the ECB signalled their intent by giving each of the counties £1m, with one of the provisos being that these "soft loans" – as they are described by the ECB's managing director of county business, Gordon Hollins – are used to create a more customer-centric business. "We believe £1m can make a significant difference and offers a real opportunity for counties to become a robust future force," says Hollins.

In spite of the tough economic climate, county cricket has remained resilient and grounds up and down the country are expanding. Encouraged and supported by the ECB, clubs are shifting from an outdated and unsustainable six-month business model into a 365-day dynamic enterprise fit for the times we live in. Essex's three-phase development of four large residential tower blocks overlooking the Ford County Ground in Chelmsford, Gloucestershire's £10m refurbishment of Nevil Road and Kent's partnership with Sainsbury's are just three examples of clubs building for the future. This can only be a good thing for those of us who passionately follow the domestic game.

Next year will see the introduction of a new-look county programme – the Yorkshire Bank 40 changing to a 50-over competition with a reduction in the number of group games; the first 14 rounds of County Championship fixtures starting on a Sunday; and an increase in the number of Friends Life t20 group games, with the majority being played on Friday evenings. Again, the opinions of the fans are at the heart of the changes following the biggest survey ever conducted in English cricket. "What came out of the research that hit us between the eyes was the fans' request for a predictable schedule – they need to know when games are on," says Hollins. The ECB have listened and reacted.

The domestic game is doing its best to strike a balance: protecting the values and traditions of the game, while showing a willingness to move with the times and make the most of every opportunity to expand its reach. We've tried to reflect this metamorphosis within The Cricketers' Who's Who. The introduction last year of a new questionnaire, which we distribute to all professional cricketers in the UK, was greeted with a positive response from readers and while we received the odd bit of criticism for including players' Twitter feeds and some of the more light-hearted questions, by and large the feedback suggested we're moving in the right direction. The players too have reacted positively and we received more responses to the questionnaire this year than ever before. It's heartening to know that The Cricketers' Who's Who is still a fixture in dressing rooms across the country.

The replies from the players never fail to amuse and inform us. For instance, who knew that Joe Root had a childhood brush with fame by getting down to the last three in an audition to become the new Milkybar Kid? Or that Surrey's totemic seamer Chris Tremlett is able to fit an entire tennis ball inside his mouth? It's little nuggets such as these that help to humanise the players and hopefully make the game more accessible.

We've made an overdue addition to this year's issue with the inclusion of the England Women's squad. The women's game continues to go from strength to strength and that was reflected in February at the World Cup, which received more press attention than ever before and threw up some thrilling cricket. England were bitterly disappointed to return from India empty-handed but they will have the opportunity to exact revenge over tournament winners Australia this summer, with a one-off Ashes Test as well as ODI and T20I series. With that in mind, there seemed no better opportunity to include Charlotte Edwards and her team. Thanks to the players for responding so enthusiastically.

With the majority of counties beginning their season with warm-up fixtures in the first week of April, we were keen to make this book available as early as possible to give readers a chance to swot up on their team before the County Championship campaign begins on April 10. Unfortunately this meant we went to print before the Unicorns had finalised their squad for this season's Yorkshire Bank 40 competition, and as a result we were unable to include the team's player profiles. The Unicorns 2013 squad list should be confirmed in early April and you'll be able to find it at www.unicorns40.co.uk.

With England's men and women competing for the Ashes, an ICC Champions Trophy plus three domestic trophies to be fought over, 2013 promises to be a season to remember. We hope this publication provides a fitting accompaniment to it.

As ever, we would appreciate any feedback you may have on this year's edition. Please drop me a line at cwweditor@alloutcricket.co.uk with any comments.

Jo Harman
March 24, 2012

IN SICKNESS AND IN HEALTH

All Out Cricket's editor-at-large John Stern on the complex and changeable relationship between club and country that lies at the heart of English cricket.

Fifteen years ago this February England won the Under 19 World Cup for the first and, so far, only time. The team contained a number of players to be found in this book, and a few others whose qualification to appear lapsed relatively soon after that memorable day in Johannesburg.

Graeme Swann was there at the finish, scrambling the winning run with Owais Shah. Stephen Peters, newly appointed as Northamptonshire's captain, scored a match-winning hundred, having shared a century opening stand with Rob Key, who recently stood down as Kent captain. Nottinghamshire's Paul Franks and Essex's Graham Napier make up the six still playing the game professionally, while Chris Schofield was with Surrey in 2011.

This tournament, which had been staged in 1988 but not again until 1998, took place at a time when English cricket was at a low ebb. The closest England were getting to the Ashes was a tour round the Lord's museum and the national team was a convenient butt of every sporting joke. The consequences of this malaise was an endless bout of soul-searching and a severe discrediting of the county game. As the ECB came into being at the start of 1997, charged with bringing together the professional and recreational elements of the national game, the view was that England's next Ashes-winners would come not from the ranks of established players at the 18 first-class counties but from a hand-picked band of likely lads who had yet to be tainted by the bad habits and corner-cutting cynicism of the county circuit.

These players were a couple of injuries or one stellar performance away from international recognition. "One good game on the telly," is how Swann has described it to me in the past. And sure enough in 2000, when the first dozen central contracts were handed out, one of the recipients was Schofield, a leg spinner with negligible first-class experience behind him. He played his only two Tests that summer against Zimbabwe. It would be wildly inaccurate to say that he was never heard of again but his career since then was a fraught tale of fleeting first-team opportunities, departure from his home county of Lancashire and a relentlessly determined effort to reinvent himself as a limited overs specialist, which he did with some considerable success.

Swann went on Duncan Fletcher's first England tour to South Africa in 1999/2000, did not display the right kind of attitude and was cast aside. It looked unlikely he would ever return to the top until Peter Moores picked him for a one-day tour of Sri Lanka in 2007. A year later he had usurped his old Northants teammate Monty Panesar as England's No.1 spinner.

These were desperate times and perhaps they called for desperate measures but the last 15 years have shown us just how misguided some of them were.

Ever since May 1898 when Lord Hawke suggested that MCC take control of England's Test matches against Australia – rather than the private enterprises they had been up to that point – there has been an uneasy tension between the England team and the first-class counties. The same arguments that you hear today about resources, player availability and prioritising international over domestic cricket, have been conducted in committee rooms, bars and clubs up and down the country for well over a century.

England's success over the past decade is down to many things but it certainly isn't down to absurd fast-tracking of youngsters and just letting them sink or swim. Lessons were learnt pretty quickly at the turn of the millennium. England could not operate despite the county clubs, it had to work with them to produce quality players. Development sides, performance programmes and the Lions are all integral parts of an aspiring player's education, but so is the cut and thrust of the County Championship. Statistics do lie, they always have, and only a fool would select an England XI based solely on the first-class averages but things like resilience, consistency and match-awareness are things that can only be learned in the domestic first-class programme.

This past winter has been a good one for the England selectors and also been a good advert for the county game. Nick Compton was heralded – since birth with a name like that – through England under 19s and then moved counties from Middlesex to Somerset. But after stacking up 2,500 runs in the past two seasons he made his Test debut in India at the age of 29. A few months later, he had back-to-back Test centuries in New Zealand. At the other end of the age spectrum is Joe Root, 22 going on 14, who has already shown many of the attributes to succeed for England. Andy Flower has warned that "everyone should keep a little calm about his prospects" and it would not be a major shock if Root were to return to the Yorkshire ranks, ready to reappear when opportunity next presents itself. There are few players with their talents so ready-made and fully-formed that they arrive in international cricket never to depart, except in retirement. It would not be a failure, simply the natural order of things. And thankfully, there is a lot more understanding of this process these days.

One final footnote to the too-much-too-young debate: one of England under 19s' opponents in their World Cup final against New Zealand all those years ago was a left-arm spinner called Bruce Martin who, aged 32, made his Test debut in the first Test against England at Dunedin in March. Patience, as they say, is a selector.

KEY

EXAMPLE

RHB LB R1 W1 MVP2

R – 1,000 or more first-class runs in an English season (the number next to 'R' denotes how many times the player has achieved this feat)
W – 50 or more first-class wickets in an English season (the number next to 'W' denotes how many times the player has achieved this feat)
MVP – Denotes a player's presence in the top 100 places of the 2011 Overall FTI MVP Points (the number next to 'MVP' denotes the player's specific placing)

---

* – Not out innings (e.g. 137*)
(s) – A competition has been shared between two or more winners
CB40 – Clydesdale Bank 40 (English domestic 40-over competition, 2010-2012)
CC1/CC2 – County Championship Division One/County Championship Division Two
FL t20 – Friends Life t20 (English domestic 20-over competition)
LB – Leg break bowler
LF – Left-arm fast bowler
LFM – Left-arm fast-medium bowler
LHB – Left-hand batsman
LM – Left-arm medium
LMF – Left-arm medium-fast bowler
MCCU – Marylebone Cricket Club University
OB – Off break bowler
ODI – One-Day International
RF – Right-arm fast bowler
RFM – Right-arm fast-medium bowler
RHB – Right-hand batsman
RM – Right-arm medium bowler
RMF – Right-arm medium-fast bowler
SLA – Slow left-arm orthodox
SLC – Slow left-arm Chinaman
T20/T20I – Twenty20/Twenty20 International
UCCE – University Centre of Cricketing Excellence
WK – Wicketkeeper
YB40 – Yorkshire Bank 40 (English domestic 40-over competition for 2013)

NOTES: The stats given for a player's best batting and best bowling performance are limited to first-class cricket. If a field within a player's career statistics is left blank then the record for that particular statistic is incomplete, e.g. there is no record for how many balls a player has faced in first-class cricket. An '-' indicates that a particular statistic is inapplicable, e.g. a player has never bowled a ball in first-class cricket. All stats correct as of March 1, 2013

The Teams

DERBYSHIRE

FORMED: 1870
HOME GROUND: County Ground, Derby
ONE-DAY NAME: Falcons
CAPTAIN: Wayne Madsen
2012 RESULTS: CC2: 1/9; CB40: 4/7 in Group C; FL t20: 5/6 in North Group
HONOURS: Championship: 1936; Gillette/NatWest/C&G/FP Trophy: 1981; Benson & Hedges Cup: 1993; Sunday League: 1990

THE LOWDOWN

One of Derbyshire's best seasons in both the score and accounting books, 2012 put a line under a period of upheaval and consolidation with promotion to Division One of the County Championship, as the club announced a cash surplus for the sixth time in seven years. Seamer Tony Palladino bettered his impressive 2011 wicket haul by four, finishing the campaign with 56 first-class wickets; while left-arm spinner David Wainwright also reached a half-century of four-day wickets, his permanent move to the County Ground from Yorkshire paying dividends for both himself and Derbyshire. Captain Wayne Madsen, Wes Durston and Dan Redfern's consistency with the bat – aided and abetted by half-season cameos from the Antipodean pair of Martin Guptill (New Zealand) and Usman Khawaja (Australia) – ensured runs were never an issue. The pre-season signings of West Indian legend Shivnarine Chanderpaul and the talented yet mercurial Billy Godleman from Essex will bolster an already impressive unit of run-getters.

HEAD COACH: KARL KRIKKEN

Krikken enjoyed 16 years out in the middle for Derbyshire as a reliable wicketkeeper-batsman. Retirement was followed by his appointment as the club's academy director, a role which allowed him to nurture a new generation of players, many of whom are now excelling in the 1st XI. Krikken took on the role of head coach in 2011 following John Morris' departure and he went on to lead the county into Division One in his first full season in charge, while still maintaining his aptitude for spotting and fostering young talents.

FIRST-CLASS AVERAGES 2012

	Mat	Inns	NO	Runs	HS	Ave	SR	100	50	4s	6s
MJ Guptill	8	14	2	594	137	49.50	67.27	2	2	74	8
UT Khawaja	8	14	3	537	110*	48.81	49.63	1	6	66	8
DJ Redfern	17	25	3	848	133	38.54	62.62	2	6	108	2
WL Madsen	17	27	2	928	231*	37.12	51.84	3	3	109	0
WJ Durston	17	27	3	878	121	36.58	63.43	2	4	108	13
T Poynton	14	17	4	393	106	30.23	44.40	1	2	45	3
RA Whiteley	15	21	3	509	83	28.27	41.44	0	3	61	12
CF Hughes	1	1	0	28	28	28.00	58.33	0	0	5	0
PM Borrington	10	18	3	321	98	21.40	31.65	0	1	37	1
JL Clare	11	13	1	247	48	20.58	78.41	0	0	37	3
TD Groenewald	14	15	4	225	42	20.45	61.47	0	0	31	3
MS Lineker	7	11	0	219	45	19.90	43.88	0	0	31	0
AP Palladino	16	21	3	344	106	19.11	60.24	1	1	44	3
DJ Wainwright	17	23	4	350	51*	18.42	37.07	0	2	34	1
RM Johnson	2	3	1	20	15*	10.00	33.89	0	0	2	0
ML Turner	7	7	2	43	13	8.60	62.31	0	0	8	0
MHA Footitt	5	6	3	11	8*	3.66	25.00	0	0	1	0
CM Durham	1	1	1	12	12*	-	54.54	0	0	1	0

Batting

	Overs	Mdns	Runs	Wkts	BBI	BBM	Ave	Econ	SR	5w	10w
JL Clare	204.3	40	642	30	6/40	11/57	21.40	3.13	40.9	2	1
AP Palladino	499.4	107	1431	56	7/53	9/118	25.55	2.86	53.5	3	0
TD Groenewald	399.4	89	1086	42	5/29	5/29	25.85	2.71	57.0	1	0
WJ Durston	177.3	25	574	22	5/34	5/34	26.09	3.23	48.4	1	0
MHA Footitt	108.2	21	332	11	3/43	5/79	30.18	3.06	59.0	0	0
DJ Wainwright	565.5	141	1542	50	6/33	8/134	30.84	2.72	67.9	3	0
RA Whiteley	177.1	23	736	20	2/6	4/43	36.80	4.15	53.1	0	0
ML Turner	140.5	12	619	15	3/53	4/98	41.26	4.39	56.3	0	0
DJ Redfern	19.0	3	72	1	1/25	1/25	72.00	3.78	114.0	0	0
PM Borrington	1.0	0	2	0	-	-	-	2.00	-	0	0
MJ Guptill	3.0	0	6	0	-	-	-	2.00	-	0	0
UT Khawaja	4.0	1	15	0	-	-	-	3.75	-	0	0
MS Lineker	2.0	0	2	0	-	-	-	1.00	-	0	0
WL Madsen	1.0	0	1	0	-	-	-	1.00	-	0	0

Bowling

Catches/Stumpings:
43 Poynton (inc 1st), 26 Durston, 13 Guptill, 11 Wainwright, 10 Khawaja, 8 Redfern, 7 Lineker, Madsen, Turner, 5 Whiteley, 4 Johnson, 3 Borrington, 2 Clare, Durham (inc 1st) Footitt

LIST A AVERAGES 2012

Batting

	Mat	Inns	NO	Runs	HS	Ave	SR	100	50	4s	6s
RM Johnson	3	2	1	80	79	80.00	105.26	0	1	6	2
MJ Guptill	3	3	0	217	125	72.33	112.43	1	1	15	9
DJ Wainwright	9	4	3	38	16	38.00	80.85	0	0	1	2
WJ Durston	12	10	1	288	120*	32.00	89.16	1	0	28	5
WL Madsen	11	10	3	186	64*	26.57	72.65	0	1	17	1
AL Hughes	7	4	2	52	37*	26.00	85.24	0	0	5	0
UT Khawaja	7	6	1	124	104	24.80	77.98	1	0	11	2
JL Clare	7	5	1	88	57	22.00	112.82	0	1	7	4
CF Hughes	12	10	0	209	66	20.90	79.16	0	2	27	2
TD Groenewald	10	2	1	15	13*	15.00	65.21	0	0	1	1
DJ Redfern	12	8	0	106	49	13.25	72.10	0	0	12	0
RA Whiteley	8	6	1	50	20	10.00	45.04	0	0	3	0
T Poynton	7	4	0	28	16	7.00	75.67	0	0	2	0
GT Park	4	3	0	15	13	5.00	36.58	0	0	0	0
ML Turner	10	3	0	9	7	3.00	47.36	0	0	0	0
PI Burgoyne	2	1	1	24	24*	-	120.00	0	0	4	0
AP Palladino	1	1	1	9	9*	-	300.00	0	0	2	0
TC Knight	1	1	1	2	2*	-	11.76	0	0	0	0

Bowling

	Overs	Mdns	Runs	Wkts	BBI	Ave	Econ	SR	4w	5w
PI Burgoyne	14.0	0	63	5	3/31	12.60	4.50	16.8	0	0
AC Evans	7.0	0	34	2	2/34	17.00	4.85	21.0	0	0
TD Groenewald	70.0	7	320	15	3/30	21.33	4.57	28.0	0	0
ML Turner	65.1	0	408	17	4/38	24.00	6.26	23.0	2	0
WJ Durston	48.0	1	240	8	2/30	30.00	5.00	36.0	0	0
CF Hughes	38.1	1	215	6	5/29	35.83	5.63	38.1	0	1
RA Whiteley	12.0	0	74	2	1/17	37.00	6.16	36.0	0	0
AL Hughes	33.0	0	151	3	1/23	50.33	4.57	66.0	0	0
JL Clare	32.0	1	160	3	2/51	53.33	5.00	64.0	0	0
TC Knight	8.0	0	54	1	1/54	54.00	6.75	48.0	0	0
DJ Wainwright	51.5	0	246	4	1/9	61.50	4.74	77.7	0	0
GT Park	18.0	0	122	1	1/5	122.00	6.77	108.0	0	0
M Higginbottom	5.0	1	43	0	-	-	8.60	-	0	0
Naved-ul-Hasan	4.0	0	21	0	-	-	5.25	-	0	0
AP Palladino	6.0	0	29	0	-	-	4.83	-	0	0
DJ Redfern	1.0	0	5	0	-	-	5.00	-	0	0

Catches/Stumpings:

7 Durston, 5 Madsen, Poynton (inc 1st), 4 Redfern, 3 Johnson (inc 2st), Wainwright, 2 Burgoyne, Durham, Groenewald, Khawaja, Whiteley, 1 Guptill, A Hughes, Park

T20 AVERAGES 2012

Batting

	Mat	Inns	NO	Runs	HS	Ave	SR	100	50	4s	6s
GT Park	5	4	2	83	29*	41.50	136.06	0	0	6	2
Naved-ul-Hasan	8	7	4	91	40*	30.33	149.18	0	0	6	4
WJ Durston	8	8	1	201	56	28.71	127.21	0	2	25	4
CF Hughes	8	8	2	160	48	26.66	129.03	0	0	12	4
JL Clare	5	4	1	52	17*	17.33	173.33	0	0	5	2
WL Madsen	8	8	0	135	33	16.87	106.29	0	0	14	2
UT Khawaja	8	8	0	131	36	16.37	94.24	0	0	15	0
RA Whiteley	5	5	0	51	24	10.20	96.22	0	0	5	2
T Poynton	7	4	2	17	8*	8.50	85.00	0	0	1	1
DJ Redfern	3	3	0	15	13	5.00	75.00	0	0	1	0
ML Turner	5	1	0	3	3	3.00	50.00	0	0	0	0
AL Hughes	3	2	0	2	2	1.00	40.00	0	0	0	0
TD Groenewald	6	2	0	1	1	0.50	25.00	0	0	0	0
CM Durham	1	1	0	0	0	0.00	0.00	0	0	0	0
DJ Wainwright	5	1	1	15	15*	-	83.33	0	0	1	0
TC Knight	3	1	1	1	1*	-	33.33	0	0	0	0

Bowling

	Overs	Mdns	Runs	Wkts	BBI	Ave	Econ	SR	4w	5w
GT Park	1.0	0	5	1	1/5	5.00	5.00	6.0	0	0
DJ Wainwright	17.0	0	95	5	2/14	19.00	5.58	20.4	0	0
TC Knight	8.0	0	69	3	1/13	23.00	8.62	16.0	0	0
WJ Durston	14.0	0	73	3	2/16	24.33	5.21	28.0	0	0
Naved-ul-Hasan	28.0	0	245	10	3/20	24.50	8.75	16.8	0	0
ML Turner	16.0	0	113	4	2/18	28.25	7.06	24.0	0	0
TD Groenewald	22.0	0	172	6	2/25	28.66	7.81	22.0	0	0
CF Hughes	21.0	0	186	4	1/14	46.50	8.85	31.5	0	0
JL Clare	10.0	0	93	1	1/12	93.00	9.30	60.0	0	0
AL Hughes	7.0	0	66	0	-	-	9.42	-	0	0

Catches/Stumpings:
9 Poynton (inc 3st), 5 Durston, 3 Naved-ul-Hasan, 2 Knight, Clare, Park, Khawaja, Madsen, 1 A Hughes, Redfern, Whiteley, Groenewald, C Hughes

DURHAM

FORMED: 1882
HOME GROUND: Emirates Durham International Cricket Ground
ONE-DAY NAME: Dynamos
CAPTAIN: Paul Collingwood (Championship), Dale Benkenstein (YB40 and FL t20)
2012 RESULTS: CC1: 6/9; CB40: 5/7 in Group B; FL t20 3/6 in North Group
HONOURS: Championship: (2) 2008, 2009; Gillette/Natwest/C&G/FP Trophy: 2007

THE LOWDOWN

At around the halfway point of their 2012 campaign, Durham's bubble looked set to burst. Without a single Championship win in their first 10 games – a fact compounded by the Dynamos failing to reach the quarter-finals of the FL t20 – and with Phil Mustard having resigned the four-day captaincy, the club were teetering on the brink. Enter Paul Collingwood. The former England man's appointment as Championship captain coincided with the club's surge back to form, and following four successive Championship wins, a Collingwood century at Aigburth against fellow relegation candidates Lancashire in the penultimate fixture of the season all but confirmed their top-flight status. With a triumphant win in their final match against Sussex making it five wins from six, Durham were safe. If Collingwood was the catalyst last year, then Graham Onions was the enforcer. Taking 68 first-class wickets at 14.30 for the club, the seamer held Durham's campaign together, and they will be looking to their star man to produce the goods again this term. The top order will be weakened by the absence of Michael Di Venuto – the Aussie retiring with immediate effect last July – and the departure of Liam Plunkett to Yorkshire trims the bowling stocks. But with Steve Harmison back to full fitness and enjoying the fruits of a Benefit year in the final season of his contract, expect him to have a big say in Durham's four-day fortunes. And watch out for the batting allrounder Ben Stokes. Hugely talented, but sent home prematurely from the England Lions tour of Australia in February for disciplinary reasons, he will feel he has a point to prove.

HEAD COACH: GEOFF COOK

A doughty opening batsman for Northants, Durham, Eastern Province and seven Tests for England, following his retirement in 1992 the Middlesbrough man took charge of Durham's youth academy before being promoted to head coach in 2007. He subsequently guided the club to their first silverware, the 2007 Friends Provident Trophy, before delivering back-to-back County Championship crowns in 2008 and 2009.

FIRST-CLASS AVERAGES 2012

Batting

	Mat	Inns	NO	Runs	HS	Ave	SR	100	50	4s	6s
PD Collingwood	14	25	3	744	114	33.81	50.20	1	4	96	2
P Coughlin	1	2	1	32	29*	32.00	58.18	0	0	4	1
BA Stokes	15	27	0	801	121	29.66	73.08	1	5	99	9
MJ Di Venuto	5	10	0	291	96	29.10	70.12	0	1	48	2
DM Benkenstein	14	25	3	583	69	26.50	46.41	0	3	82	1
MD Stoneman	14	26	1	661	114	26.44	51.96	1	2	94	2
C Rushworth	9	11	7	93	24*	23.25	75.60	0	0	9	2
MJ Richardson	5	8	0	184	58	23.00	37.47	0	1	19	0
P Mustard	15	25	3	482	80	21.90	55.46	0	1	72	4
SG Borthwick	14	22	4	380	60	21.11	47.79	0	2	51	3
KK Jennings	5	8	0	168	70	21.00	44.56	0	1	23	0
JG Myburgh	1	2	0	42	34	21.00	45.65	0	0	7	0
G Onions	13	18	7	216	36	19.63	60.67	0	0	32	1
WR Smith	14	27	1	509	100	19.57	39.42	1	1	67	4
MA Wood	2	4	0	76	34	19.00	41.30	0	0	9	0
ID Blackwell	7	14	1	229	62	17.61	58.56	0	1	28	4
Ramanpreet Singh	1	2	0	34	22	17.00	73.91	0	0	6	0
ME Claydon	8	13	2	139	55	12.63	60.17	0	1	20	1
J Harrison	3	6	1	60	23	12.00	43.16	0	0	8	0
LE Plunkett	1	2	0	24	24	12.00	40.67	0	0	4	0
CD Thorp	14	21	2	221	36	11.63	70.60	0	0	32	3
RMR Brathwaite	3	5	2	29	16	9.66	49.15	0	0	5	0
GJ Muchall	7	13	0	125	25	9.61	40.32	0	0	16	0
SJ Harmison	3	5	3	6	3*	3.00	24.00	0	0	0	0

Bowling

	Overs	Mdns	Runs	Wkts	BBI	BBM	Ave	Econ	SR	5w	10w
G Onions	385.4	107	973	68	9/67	11/95	14.30	2.52	34.0	5	3
RMR Brathwaite	33.3	4	137	9	3/32	5/74	15.22	4.08	22.3	0	0
MA Wood	46.4	6	147	9	5/78	5/97	16.33	3.15	31.1	1	0
C Rushworth	210.5	51	623	38	5/38	7/83	16.39	2.95	33.2	3	0
CD Thorp	320.3	90	818	44	5/59	8/73	18.59	2.55	43.7	1	0
ID Blackwell	107.0	26	331	17	7/52	8/63	19.47	3.09	37.7	1	0
BA Stokes	241.4	49	800	37	4/3	6/65	21.62	3.31	39.1	0	0
J Harrison	68.0	10	260	10	4/112	5/131	26.00	3.82	40.8	0	0
SG Borthwick	130.4	12	446	15	4/37	4/37	29.73	3.41	52.2	0	0
ME Claydon	126.2	23	495	16	4/84	7/117	30.93	3.91	47.3	0	0
WR Smith	7.2	1	35	1	1/32	1/32	35.00	4.77	44.0	0	0
SJ Harmison	56.2	11	229	6	2/38	2/49	38.16	4.06	56.3	0	0
P Coughlin	10.0	0	46	1	1/26	1/46	46.00	4.60	60.0	0	0
PD Collingwood	19.0	3	60	1	1/8	1/8	60.00	3.15	114.0	0	0
DM Benkenstein	1.0	0	2	0	-	-	-	2.00	-	0	0
KK Jennings	5.0	2	9	0	-	-	-	1.80	-	0	0
LE Plunkett	12.0	0	69	0	-	-	-	5.75	-	0	0

Catches/Stumpings:
46 Mustard, 21 Borthwick, 19 Collingwood, 13 Richardson, 11 Di Venuto, 9 Stoneman, Thorp, 8 Stokes, 5 Muchall, Smith, 4 Wood, Benkenstein, 3 Blackwell, 1 Coughlin, Singh, Brathwaite, Harmison, Rushworth, Onions

LIST A AVERAGES 2012

DURHAM DYNAMOS

Batting

	Mat	Inns	NO	Runs	HS	Ave	SR	100	50	4s	6s
MD Stoneman	11	10	2	558	136*	69.75	98.23	3	2	62	4
P Mustard	11	10	0	475	143	47.50	143.07	3	1	49	14
GJ Muchall	11	10	2	395	96*	49.37	84.94	0	3	27	4
BA Stokes	10	8	0	155	45	19.37	101.97	0	0	16	3
DM Benkenstein	7	6	1	141	39*	28.20	100.00	0	0	12	3
PD Collingwood	9	7	1	124	32	20.66	80.51	0	0	7	3
WR Smith	5	3	0	79	55	26.33	68.10	0	1	3	2
GR Breese	8	6	2	60	31*	15.00	70.58	0	0	6	0
ME Claydon	11	6	3	49	18*	16.33	76.56	0	0	3	2
MJ Richardson	2	1	0	45	45	45.00	70.31	0	0	2	1
SG Borthwick	11	7	1	30	15	5.00	73.17	0	0	2	0
JG Myburgh	4	3	0	24	15	8.00	68.57	0	0	0	1
LE Plunkett	5	3	1	18	11*	9.00	75.00	0	0	0	1
C Rushworth	7	4	0	17	8	4.25	58.62	0	0	1	0
G Onions	3	1	0	8	8	8.00	80.00	0	0	1	0
J Harrison	2	1	1	7	7*	-	140.00	0	0	1	0
MA Wood	2	1	1	1	1*	-	100.00	0	0	0	0

Bowling

	Overs	Mdns	Runs	Wkts	BBI	Ave	Econ	SR	4w	5w
WR Smith	4.0	0	22	2	2/22	11.00	5.50	12.0	0	0
BA Stokes	23.3	4	124	8	3/24	15.50	5.27	17.6	0	0
MA Wood	12.0	1	63	4	3/32	15.75	5.25	18.0	0	0
C Rushworth	47.3	1	280	15	5/31	18.66	5.89	19.0	0	1
GR Breese	42.0	1	200	10	4/50	20.00	4.76	25.2	1	0
SG Borthwick	56.2	0	351	13	4/51	27.00	6.23	26.0	1	0
LE Plunkett	31.0	2	190	7	4/33	27.14	6.12	26.5	1	0
ME Claydon	69.4	0	474	12	3/58	39.50	6.80	34.8	0	0
J Harrison	12.0	0	83	2	2/51	41.50	6.91	36.0	0	0
JG Myburgh	9.0	0	50	1	1/21	50.00	5.55	54.0	0	0
G Onions	23.0	2	117	2	1/27	58.50	5.08	69.0	0	0
PD Collingwood	31.0	0	161	1	1/37	161.00	5.19	186.0	0	0
P Coughlin	1.0	0	15	0	-	-	15.00	-	0	0

Catches/Stumpings:
16 Mustard (inc 5st), 5 Muchall, 4 Benkenstein, 3 Wood, Collingwood, Stokes, Borthwick, 2 Smith, Stoneman, 1 Myburgh, Plunkett, Breese, Claydon, Richardson

T20 AVERAGES 2012

DURHAM DYNAMOS

	Mat	Inns	NO	Runs	HS	Ave	SR	100	50	4s	6s
HH Gibbs	9	9	2	277	83*	39.57	124.21	0	2	31	8
GJ Muchall	9	7	4	111	25*	37.00	97.36	0	0	5	2
JG Myburgh	9	8	1	171	46	24.42	103.63	0	0	16	3
BA Stokes	9	8	1	159	56	22.71	117.77	0	1	12	6
P Mustard	9	9	0	201	51	22.33	117.54	0	1	26	3
LE Plunkett	9	5	3	43	19*	21.50	138.70	0	0	5	0
SG Borthwick	9	5	3	35	17*	17.50	106.06	0	0	1	0
GR Breese	7	5	1	66	33	16.50	132.00	0	0	8	0
DM Benkenstein	9	8	0	87	28	10.87	108.75	0	0	6	2
G Onions	9	2	0	7	7	3.50	77.77	0	0	0	1
ME Claydon	6	2	0	0	0	0.00	0.00	0	0	0	0

Batting

	Overs	Mdns	Runs	Wkts	BBI	Ave	Econ	SR	4w	5w
ME Claydon	19.0	0	151	9	3/34	16.77	7.94	12.6	0	0
C Rushworth	15.0	2	110	6	2/19	18.33	7.33	15.0	0	0
SG Borthwick	31.0	0	240	12	2/19	20.00	7.74	15.5	0	0
GR Breese	21.0	0	127	6	2/15	21.16	6.04	21.0	0	0
BA Stokes	19.0	0	153	6	2/14	25.50	8.05	19.0	0	0
G Onions	35.0	0	240	6	2/24	40.00	6.85	35.0	0	0
LE Plunkett	25.1	0	181	3	2/22	60.33	7.19	50.3	0	0
DM Benkenstein	1.0	0	13	0	-	-	13.00	-	0	0
JG Myburgh	4.1	0	27	0	-	-	6.48	-	0	0

Bowling

Catches/Stumpings:
9 Mustard (inc 2st), 6 Stokes, 3 Muchall, Myburgh, Onions, 2 Rushworth, Gibbs, 1 Breese, Benkenstein, Plunkett

ESSEX

FORMED: 1876
HOME GROUND: The Ford County Ground, Chelmsford
ONE-DAY NAME: Eagles
CAPTAIN: James Foster
2012 RESULTS: CC2: 5/9; CB40: 5/7 in Group A; FL t20: Quarter-finalists
HONOURS: Championship: (6) 1979, 1983, 1984, 1986, 1991, 1992; Gillette/ NatWest/C&G/FP Trophy: (3) 1985, 1997, 2008; Benson & Hedges Cup: (2) 1979, 1998; Pro40/National League/CB40: (2) 2005, 2006; Sunday League: (3) 1981, 1984, 1985

THE LOWDOWN

After an indifferent campaign last term which bore little relation to the rich seam of talent in their ranks, the management at Chelmsford's sleeping giant have been hard at work in the off-season. New contracts have been signed by their batting matchwinners Ryan ten Doeschate and Owais Shah, along with new deals for the young leg spinner Tom Craddock and the highly rated 6ft 7in left-arm seamer Reece Topley, whose 19 wickets at 9.10 put him head and shoulders above his counterparts in last August's U19 World Cup. In the overseas department, the left-hander Rob Quiney has been signed for at least the first half of the season to add some Australian grit to their top order, while Shaun Tait will bring his unique brand of ultra-fast toe-crunchers to Essex's FL t20 campaign. With the southpaw seamer Tymal Mills another from the 'genuine quick' bracket, Essex will pack a serious punch in the shortest format, in which James Foster, the club captain, will once again be showcasing his virtuosity behind the stumps. But ultimately the club will be desperate to return to the top-flight of the Championship. Since the split to two divisions in 2000, Essex have competed in the top tier on just three occasions. Last year genuinely high hopes of promotion were dashed by – in particular – a string of misfiring batsmen, as no player managed to break 800 runs for the Championship season. This year, with Ravi Bopara likely to be available for a full season and Ben Foakes, the brilliant 20-year-old batsman-keeper, also available, they will go into 2013 loaded with genuine belief that this, finally, could be their year.

HEAD COACH: PAUL GRAYSON

As a native of Yorkshire, Essex's coach enjoyed a decent career with his home county before moving to Chelmsford where – as a one-day specialist left-arm spinner and flinty batsman – he flourished over an eight-year period that culminated in two ODIs in 2000-2001. After retiring from the first-class game in 2005, he returned to Essex as coach in 2008.

FIRST-CLASS AVERAGES 2012

Batting

	Mat	Inns	NO	Runs	HS	Ave	SR	100	50	4s	6s
TJ Phillips	2	2	1	80	73*	80.00	66.11	0	1	12	0
RS Bopara	5	7	2	331	174	66.20	51.15	2	0	45	2
JS Foster	16	19	4	769	135	51.26	53.58	2	4	87	10
OA Shah	8	13	1	589	161	49.08	54.73	2	2	73	8
RN ten Doeschate	9	12	3	412	69	45.77	71.77	0	4	45	10
BA Godleman	8	13	1	437	130	36.41	38.98	1	2	48	2
AJ Wheater	12	15	2	462	98	35.53	83.39	0	4	62	9
T Westley	17	25	2	786	185	34.17	51.71	2	3	112	0
ML Pettini	16	23	4	644	92	33.89	44.94	0	7	63	5
GR Napier	12	12	2	335	100*	33.50	78.63	1	0	38	9
GM Smith	9	10	0	318	160	31.80	82.59	1	0	44	3
Harbhajan Singh	5	3	1	58	40	29.00	69.04	0	0	7	2
BT Foakes	4	4	0	114	93	28.50	55.88	0	1	17	0
JC Mickleburgh	9	14	1	359	126	27.61	41.12	1	2	44	2
AN Petersen	7	11	0	235	145	21.36	54.77	1	0	26	1
DD Masters	14	12	0	165	52	13.75	36.91	0	1	14	1
TR Craddock	6	8	3	46	16	9.20	23.35	0	0	4	0
TS Mills	8	10	4	30	20*	5.00	25.42	0	0	0	2
AN Cook	2	3	0	15	9	5.00	20.00	0	0	2	0
CM Willoughby	8	6	4	2	1*	1.00	9.09	0	0	0	0
MA Chambers	7	7	1	2	2	0.33	4.08	0	0	0	0
RJW Topley	3	4	1	1	1	0.33	5.55	0	0	0	0

Bowling

	Overs	Mdns	Runs	Wkts	BBI	BBM	Ave	Econ	SR	5w	10w
DD Masters	395.3	119	941	53	7/60	7/60	17.75	2.37	44.7	4	0
GR Napier	317.2	56	1033	45	5/58	9/119	22.95	3.25	42.3	2	0
MA Chambers	163.1	29	567	20	4/31	7/96	28.35	3.47	48.9	0	0
TR Craddock	125.5	23	438	15	5/96	6/90	29.20	3.48	50.3	1	0
TS Mills	129.2	19	425	14	4/25	4/34	30.35	3.28	55.4	0	0
RJW Topley	112.1	24	350	11	3/59	6/154	31.81	3.12	61.1	0	0
CM Willoughby	180.0	34	621	19	5/70	5/74	32.68	3.45	56.8	1	0
Harbhajan Singh	176.3	38	431	13	4/91	7/153	33.15	2.44	81.4	0	0
T Westley	152.3	24	504	10	3/5	4/34	50.40	3.30	91.5	0	0
RN ten Doeschate	86.0	11	332	6	3/39	4/68	55.33	3.86	86.0	0	0
GM Smith	122.0	22	407	6	2/31	2/45	67.83	3.33	122.0	0	0
ML Pettini	3.1	0	72	1	1/72	1/72	72.00	22.73	19.0	0	0
AJ Wheater	4.0	0	86	1	1/86	1/86	86.00	21.50	24.0	0	0
TJ Phillips	19.4	0	95	1	1/49	1/95	95.00	4.83	118.0	0	0
RS Bopara	2.0	0	5	0	-	-	-	2.50	-	0	0
AN Petersen	1.0	0	4	0	-	-	-	4.00	-	0	0

Catches/Stumpings:
46 Foster (inc 3st), 10 Harbhajan, 9 Westley, 8 Petersen, 7 Wheater, ten Doeschate, Mickleburgh, 5 Godleman, Mills, Pettini, 4 Chambers, Smith, Napier, 3 Shah, Masters, 2 Craddock, Willoughby, 1 Cook, Phillips, Foakes

LIST A AVERAGES 2012

Batting

	Mat	Inns	NO	Runs	HS	Ave	SR	100	50	4s	6s
RS Bopara	4	4	1	162	120*	54.00	95.29	1	0	18	2
OA Shah	7	7	2	209	53	41.80	87.08	0	1	15	5
T Westley	10	10	0	400	82	40.00	85.28	0	4	45	4
RN ten Doeschate	8	7	2	173	52	34.60	118.49	0	2	11	6
JS Foster	9	7	0	221	79	31.57	106.25	0	1	17	2
ML Pettini	11	11	0	321	111	29.18	85.37	1	1	27	7
AN Cook	2	2	0	52	47	26.00	71.23	0	0	9	0
Harbhajan Singh	5	3	1	47	22*	23.50	123.68	0	0	2	2
GR Napier	9	6	0	137	51	22.83	129.24	0	1	15	5
DD Masters	5	3	2	16	15*	16.00	80.00	0	0	1	0
TJ Phillips	10	7	3	60	25	15.00	57.69	0	0	4	0
GM Smith	10	9	2	93	44	13.28	75.00	0	0	7	1
AJ Wheater	8	7	0	84	33	12.00	89.36	0	0	3	3
AN Petersen	3	3	0	33	24	11.00	71.73	0	0	3	0
JEC Franklin	1	1	0	4	4	4.00	33.33	0	0	0	0
MA Comber	2	2	0	6	6	3.00	50.00	0	0	0	0
TS Mills	9	4	3	3	2*	3.00	25.00	0	0	0	0
MA Chambers	3	1	0	2	2	2.00	33.33	0	0	0	0
RJW Topley	1	1	0	2	2	2.00	15.38	0	0	0	0
CM Willoughby	1	1	0	0	0	0.00	0.00	0	0	0	0
JC Mickleburgh	2	1	1	22	22*	-	146.66	0	0	1	1
TR Craddock	1	1	1	4	4*	-	40.00	0	0	0	0

Bowling

	Overs	Mdns	Runs	Wkts	BBI	Ave	Econ	SR	4w	5w
RJW Topley	8.0	0	46	4	4/46	11.50	5.75	12.0	1	0
RS Bopara	17.2	0	89	6	3/19	14.83	5.13	17.3	0	0
Harbhajan Singh	35.0	0	222	11	5/37	20.18	6.34	19.0	0	1
T Westley	7.0	0	41	2	1/9	20.50	5.85	21.0	0	0
AN Petersen	3.5	0	22	1	1/22	22.00	5.73	23.0	0	0
DD Masters	30.0	1	172	5	4/41	34.40	5.73	36.0	1	0
GR Napier	58.1	1	382	11	3/57	34.72	6.56	31.7	0	0
TJ Phillips	57.3	3	319	9	3/34	35.44	5.54	38.3	0	0
TR Craddock	6.0	0	38	1	1/38	38.00	6.33	36.0	0	0
MA Chambers	15.0	1	86	2	1/21	43.00	5.73	45.0	0	0
GM Smith	52.0	0	292	5	2/32	58.40	5.61	62.4	0	0
TS Mills	51.3	1	293	5	2/40	58.60	5.68	61.8	0	0
RN ten Doeschate	32.0	0	203	2	1/20	101.50	6.34	96.0	0	0
MA Comber	3.0	0	26	0	-	-	8.66	-	0	0
JEC Franklin	3.0	0	17	0	-	-	5.66	-	0	0
CM Willoughby	3.0	0	14	0	-	-	4.66	-	0	0

Catches/Stumpings:
10 Foster (inc 2st), 7 Shah, 5 Smith, 3 Harbhajan, Napier, Pettini, 2 Wheater, ten Doeschate, Phillips, Westley, 1 Cook, Chambers, Petersen, Bopara, Masters

T20 AVERAGES 2012

Batting

	Mat	Inns	NO	Runs	HS	Ave	SR	100	50	4s	6s
JS Foster	10	10	2	270	65*	33.75	165.64	0	2	18	15
AN Cook	1	1	0	28	28	28.00	103.70	0	0	2	0
JEC Franklin	10	10	1	248	78	27.55	110.71	0	2	20	8
TJ Phillips	10	6	4	50	16*	25.00	138.88	0	0	2	3
ML Pettini	10	10	0	242	59	24.20	125.38	0	2	19	10
GM Smith	9	7	0	142	39	20.28	110.93	0	0	8	4
OA Shah	4	4	1	55	25*	18.33	127.90	0	0	4	2
RN ten Doeschate	10	10	0	175	47	17.50	121.52	0	0	11	8
AJ Wheater	8	6	3	42	12*	14.00	107.69	0	0	3	1
RS Bopara	2	2	0	28	28	14.00	90.32	0	0	3	0
T Westley	4	2	1	13	13	13.00	130.00	0	0	1	1
GR Napier	10	10	1	111	32	12.33	118.08	0	0	13	3
MA Comber	2	2	1	12	12	12.00	60.00	0	0	0	0
DD Masters	10	4	1	13	6	4.33	54.16	0	0	1	0
TS Mills	1	1	1	3	3*	-	60.00	0	0	0	0
RJW Topley	9	2	2	1	1*	-	50.00	0	0	0	0

Bowling

	Overs	Mdns	Runs	Wkts	BBI	Ave	Econ	SR	4w	5w
RJW Topley	32.0	0	246	17	3/19	14.47	7.68	11.2	0	0
GM Smith	18.0	0	146	10	5/17	14.60	8.11	10.8	0	1
RN ten Doeschate	23.5	0	181	10	2/7	18.10	7.59	14.3	0	0
TJ Phillips	31.0	0	227	10	3/27	22.70	7.32	18.6	0	0
GR Napier	37.5	0	273	10	3/16	27.30	7.21	22.7	0	0
DD Masters	32.0	0	238	6	2/18	39.66	7.43	32.0	0	0
RS Bopara	5.0	0	46	1	1/22	46.00	9.20	30.0	0	0
JEC Franklin	17.0	0	145	3	2/13	48.33	8.52	34.0	0	0
TS Mills	1.0	0	8	0	-	-	8.00	-	0	0

Catches/Stumpings:
11 Foster (inc 4st), 6 Phillips, ten Doeschate, 3 Cook, Smith, Napier, 2 Topley, Franklin, Pettini, 1 Comber, Shah, Westley, Wheater, Masters

GLAMORGAN

FORMED: 1888
HOME GROUND: SWALEC Stadium, Cardiff
CAPTAIN: Mark Wallace (Championship), Marcus North (YB40 and FL t20)
2012 RESULTS: CC2: 6/9; CB40: 6/7 in Group B; FL t20: 5/6 in Midlands/Wales/ West Group
HONOURS: Championship: (3) 1948, 1969, 1997; Pro40/National League/CB40: (2) 2002, 2004; Sunday League: 1993

THE LOWDOWN

An indifferent 2012 campaign for Glamorgan – sixth in the second tier of the Championship and nowhere in the cup competitions – was an anti-climactic way for Robert Croft to depart the scene after one of the all-time great county careers. The club, with Croft now on the coaching staff, will be desperate to improve their performances in 2013, though they will have to soldier on without their gifted homegrown talent James Harris, who has departed for Middlesex. The impressively assured wicketkeeper-batsman Mark Wallace remains the club captain, while Australian Marcus North has been appointed as the limited overs skipper, a task made easier by the fact he'll be captaining the maverick Australian left-arm seamer Dirk Nannes in the FL t20. Much will be expected again of their Aussie-born allrounder Jim Allenby, and all eyes will be watching Simon Jones, who has agreed a new deal to play six first-class matches in 2013. Off the pitch, former Somerset director of cricket Brian Rose has been appointed to conduct an independent review of Glamorgan cricket with a view to getting the playing staff up to a standard that matches the excellence of the club's Test-quality ground.

HEAD OF ELITE PERFORMANCE: MATTHEW MOTT

The much-travelled Queenslander was appointed as Glamorgan coach in 2011 on a three-year contract but he has yet to deliver significant success, with a pair of sixth-place finishes in his two County Championship Division Two campaigns to date. A left-handed batsman who played for Victoria and Queensland, as well as a short time for the Netherlands, he became New South Wales coach in 2007 and has had a stint as John Buchanan's assistant coach for Kolkata Knight Riders in the IPL.

www.glamorgancricket.com / tel: 029 2041 9380

FIRST-CLASS AVERAGES 2012

Batting

	Mat	Inns	NO	Runs	HS	Ave	SR	100	50	4s	6s
HT Waters	13	14	12	106	39	53.00	41.24	0	0	13	0
MJ North	9	13	0	577	116	44.38	57.35	1	5	75	2
MA Wallace	16	24	5	775	122*	40.78	64.47	3	1	87	3
J Allenby	15	22	4	733	125*	40.72	57.85	2	3	76	11
SJ Walters	14	23	2	813	159	38.71	51.06	1	7	105	1
BJ Wright	16	27	3	661	104	27.54	46.71	1	1	81	1
WD Bragg	15	25	0	648	92	25.92	54.68	0	5	92	0
GP Rees	12	20	0	413	66	20.65	41.38	0	1	57	2
GG Wagg	9	13	0	263	60	20.23	70.13	0	2	27	5
NA James	9	17	0	327	83	19.23	40.17	0	1	49	0
JAR Harris	4	3	0	56	48	18.66	67.46	0	0	7	0
JC Glover	7	10	3	125	55	17.85	41.94	0	1	13	1
DA Cosker	15	17	3	243	49*	17.35	51.37	0	0	27	0
RDB Croft	7	9	2	89	23	12.71	59.33	0	0	14	0
WT Owen	3	3	1	20	13*	10.00	46.51	0	0	4	0
MC Henriques	5	8	0	64	28	8.00	44.13	0	0	8	0
DL Lloyd	2	4	1	11	11*	3.66	29.72	0	0	2	0
MT Reed	4	7	2	18	5*	3.60	18.75	0	0	1	0
SP Jones	1	2	0	5	4	2.50	35.71	0	0	1	0

Bowling

	Overs	Mdns	Runs	Wkts	BBI	BBM	Ave	Econ	SR	5w	10w
RDB Croft	141.3	27	403	23	5/31	8/104	17.52	2.84	36.9	2	0
MC Henriques	95.0	18	323	16	4/54	6/94	20.18	3.40	35.6	0	0
HT Waters	304.2	79	798	39	7/53	9/98	20.46	2.62	46.8	2	0
J Allenby	359.3	80	992	42	4/39	5/54	23.61	2.75	51.3	0	0
GG Wagg	246.3	45	769	32	6/44	8/65	24.03	3.11	46.2	1	0
JC Glover	176.4	40	585	19	4/76	7/121	30.78	3.31	55.7	0	0
MJ North	73.0	8	223	7	3/40	3/40	31.85	3.05	62.5	0	0
WT Owen	56.2	5	238	7	4/87	6/141	34.00	4.22	48.2	0	0
SP Jones	22.0	2	70	2	2/70	2/70	35.00	3.18	66.0	0	0
MT Reed	88.0	10	310	8	3/39	4/91	38.75	3.52	66.0	0	0
JAR Harris	129.0	19	402	10	5/118	5/127	40.20	3.11	77.4	1	0
DA Cosker	361.3	83	991	16	4/22	5/46	61.93	2.74	135.5	0	0
WD Bragg	26.1	2	107	1	1/10	1/10	107.00	4.08	157.0	0	0
NA James	17.0	0	68	0	-	-	-	4.00	-	0	0
GP Rees	4.1	0	22	0	-	-	-	5.28	-	0	0
SJ Walters	1.0	0	6	0	-	-	-	6.00	-	0	0
BJ Wright	13.0	2	30	0	-	-	-	2.30	-	0	0

Catches/Stumpings:
46 Wallace (inc 4st), 13 Walters, 11 Allenby, 10 Rees, Cosker, 8 Bragg, 5 Waters, 3 Glover, James, Wagg, Wright, 2 Owen, Croft, North, 1 S Jones, Henriques

LIST A AVERAGES 2012

Batting

	Mat	Inns	NO	Runs	HS	Ave	SR	100	50	4s	6s
CB Cooke	11	9	1	249	137*	31.12	102.04	1	0	20	4
SJ Walters	11	8	1	183	68	26.14	74.08	0	1	17	1
GP Rees	11	10	2	194	60*	24.25	67.12	0	1	22	3
MA Wallace	11	10	1	212	105	23.55	95.49	1	0	26	0
J Allenby	7	7	1	130	39*	21.66	73.86	0	0	14	1
MJ North	8	6	0	125	59	20.83	65.78	0	1	7	1
BJ Wright	9	6	0	116	62	19.33	82.85	0	1	7	2
NA James	4	2	0	38	37	19.00	95.00	0	0	2	0
M van Jaarsveld	2	2	0	35	25	17.50	79.54	0	0	4	0
GG Wagg	5	4	0	62	28	15.50	76.54	0	0	5	1
WT Owen	4	2	1	15	10*	15.00	100.00	0	0	1	1
DA Cosker	10	8	2	51	25	8.50	76.11	0	0	4	1
JC Glover	5	3	1	16	10	8.00	94.11	0	0	1	1
AG Salter	2	1	0	3	3	3.00	50.00	0	0	0	0
SP Jones	11	6	4	5	3	2.50	26.31	0	0	0	0
MP O'Shea	1	1	0	2	2	2.00	40.00	0	0	0	0
JAR Harris	5	3	0	4	4	1.33	25.00	0	0	0	0
AJ Norman	1	1	0	1	1	1.00	25.00	0	0	0	0
AJ Jones	1	1	1	1	1*	-	100.00	0	0	0	0

Bowling

	Overs	Mdns	Runs	Wkts	BBI	Ave	Econ	SR	4w	5w
RDB Croft	4.0	0	15	1	1/15	15.00	3.75	24.0	0	0
J Allenby	49.5	5	183	12	3/16	15.25	3.67	24.9	0	0
WT Owen	17.3	0	80	4	2/38	20.00	4.57	26.2	0	0
GG Wagg	34.0	0	229	10	4/45	22.90	6.73	20.4	1	0
AG Salter	16.0	0	90	3	2/41	30.00	5.62	32.0	0	0
AJ Jones	4.0	0	31	1	1/31	31.00	7.75	24.0	0	0
DA Cosker	68.0	5	295	9	3/26	32.77	4.33	45.3	0	0
JC Glover	36.0	0	230	7	3/34	32.85	6.38	30.8	0	0
SP Jones	71.0	0	443	13	4/23	34.07	6.23	32.7	1	0
NA James	7.0	0	41	1	1/33	41.00	5.85	42.0	0	0
JAR Harris	35.0	1	217	4	2/36	54.25	6.20	52.5	0	0
AJ Norman	4.0	0	27	0	-	-	6.75	-	0	0
MJ North	13.0	0	64	0	-	-	4.92	-	0	0
MP O'Shea	5.0	0	30	0	-	-	6.00	-	0	0
HT Waters	3.0	0	8	0	-	-	2.66	-	0	0

Catches/Stumpings:
10 Wallace (inc 2st), 5 North, 4 Allenby, Walters, 3 Harris, Cosker, 2 van Jaarsveld, S Jones, Rees, 1 Glover, Cooke

T20 AVERAGES 2012

Batting

	Mat	Inns	NO	Runs	HS	Ave	SR	100	50	4s	6s
SE Marsh	6	5	1	209	85	52.25	129.81	0	2	21	8
J Allenby	6	5	1	94	33	23.50	125.33	0	0	9	4
M van Jaarsveld	6	4	0	87	36	21.75	119.17	0	0	9	2
MA Wallace	6	3	0	47	25	15.66	142.42	0	0	7	2
DA Cosker	5	1	0	13	13	13.00	100.00	0	0	1	0
JAR Harris	5	2	1	13	13*	13.00	86.66	0	0	1	0
MJ North	6	5	1	47	17	11.75	77.04	0	0	4	1
CB Cooke	5	4	0	42	32	10.50	168.00	0	0	3	3
RDB Croft	6	1	0	3	3	3.00	21.42	0	0	0	0
SJ Walters	6	3	3	75	40*	-	129.31	0	0	6	1
SP Jones	6	1	1	1	1*	-	100.00	0	0	0	0

Bowling

	Overs	Mdns	Runs	Wkts	BBI	Ave	Econ	SR	4w	5w
SP Jones	19.0	0	128	7	3/29	18.28	6.73	16.2	0	0
MJ North	4.0	0	21	1	1/5	21.00	5.25	24.0	0	0
RDB Croft	18.0	1	131	4	2/27	32.75	7.27	27.0	0	0
DA Cosker	13.1	0	104	3	2/23	34.66	7.89	26.3	0	0
JAR Harris	15.0	2	146	4	2/48	36.50	9.73	22.5	0	0
J Allenby	15.2	0	125	3	1/1	41.66	8.15	30.6	0	0
WT Owen	5.0	0	59	1	1/20	59.00	11.80	30.0	0	0

Catches/Stumpings:
6 Wallace (inc 1st), 4 Walters, 3 Marsh, 1 Cooke, Cosker, Harris, Croft, North

GLOUCESTERSHIRE

FORMED: 1871
HOME GROUND: County Ground, Bristol
ONE-DAY NAME: Gladiators
CAPTAIN: Michael Klinger
2012 RESULTS: CC2: 9/9; CB40: 3/7 in Group A; FL t20: Quarter-finalists
HONOURS: Gillette/NatWest/C&G/FP Trophy: (5) 1973, 1999, 2000, 2003, 2004; Benson & Hedges Cup: (3) 1977, 1999, 2000; Pro40/National League/CB40: 2000

THE LOWDOWN

After the optimism that surrounded their four-day performances in 2011, finishing bottom of the County Championship for the ninth time in their history emphasised the lack of experience in Gloucestershire's squad. Jon Batty's retirement at the end of last summer compounds the issue, but the off-season has seen grizzled Australian top order batsman Michael Klinger drafted in. Klinger, who is available for the entirety of the 2013 campaign, will also take over the captaincy, allowing Alex Gidman to step down from the role he has occupied since 2008 to concentrate on his batting in the hope of recapturing the form of his early career. Decent displays in the shorter forms, particularly in the Friends Life t20 where they reached the last eight, gave Gloucestershire fans and players some relief last term, but consistent improvement is needed if they are to make the most of Nevil Road's recent expansion and garner greater support in the Bristol area.

DIRECTOR OF CRICKET: JOHN BRACEWELL

Bracewell's first stint as coach at Gloucestershire began in 1998 and ended in 2003 when he took charge of New Zealand. In that time the Kiwi led the club to unprecedented success in one-day competitions, winning five trophies in the space of two seasons between 1999 and 2000. He returned to Bristol in 2009 once his turbulent tenure with the Black Caps came to an end, charged with reviving the fortunes of a talented but inexperienced squad. The Gladiators remain a work in progress, but there are signs that their limited overs form is returning.

FIRST-CLASS AVERAGES 2012

Batting

	Mat	Inns	NO	Runs	HS	Ave	SR	100	50	4s	6s
KS Williamson	4	7	0	366	128	52.28	48.41	2	1	42	1
JMR Taylor	3	5	1	151	63	37.75	93.20	0	1	18	4
HJH Marshall	15	25	3	822	117*	37.36	54.80	1	5	96	2
IA Cockbain	15	24	2	764	112	34.72	44.70	1	5	102	1
CDJ Dent	8	15	1	424	114	30.28	47.21	1	2	64	0
EJM Cowan	3	5	0	147	103	29.40	37.98	1	0	19	1
JN Batty	8	11	2	256	55	28.44	38.09	0	1	33	1
DM Housego	10	16	0	450	62	28.12	43.73	0	4	40	3
WRS Gidman	11	17	1	447	72	27.93	43.99	0	3	53	1
RJ Nicol	4	7	2	128	75*	25.60	56.38	0	1	17	3
APR Gidman	13	22	1	528	129	25.14	59.86	1	3	61	3
BAC Howell	13	24	3	497	83*	23.66	53.32	0	3	69	5
AJ Ireland	2	3	1	47	25*	23.50	43.51	0	0	5	1
ID Saxelby	11	16	7	200	30	22.22	44.74	0	0	21	1
EGC Young	8	12	2	186	55*	18.60	49.33	0	1	20	1
PB Muchall	4	7	2	82	23	16.40	38.49	0	0	4	0
JK Fuller	8	12	1	134	57	12.18	71.27	0	1	21	1
DA Payne	8	10	3	75	16	10.71	39.47	0	0	10	0
RG Coughtrie	7	12	0	125	40	10.41	27.05	0	0	10	0
LC Norwell	9	11	4	37	18	5.28	16.37	0	0	3	0
GJ McCarter	1	1	1	29	29*	-	207.14	0	0	4	2

Bowling

	Overs	Mdns	Runs	Wkts	BBI	BBM	Ave	Econ	SR	5w	10w
RJ Nicol	38.5	2	129	7	4/53	5/76	18.42	3.32	33.2	0	0
WRS Gidman	318.0	58	943	44	5/43	9/114	21.43	2.96	43.3	2	0
DA Payne	147.0	24	504	22	4/89	7/112	22.90	3.42	40.0	0	0
KS Williamson	34.3	4	121	5	3/58	4/76	24.20	3.50	41.4	0	0
APR Gidman	14.0	3	50	2	2/50	2/50	25.00	3.57	42.0	0	0
ID Saxelby	293.3	58	897	35	6/48	7/107	25.62	3.05	50.3	1	0
JK Fuller	174.2	27	653	24	5/29	7/126	27.20	3.74	43.5	1	0
LC Norwell	194.1	25	632	22	5/51	8/74	28.72	3.25	52.9	1	0
JMR Taylor	87.0	15	277	8	2/28	4/103	34.62	3.18	65.2	0	0
AJ Ireland	39.0	2	159	4	2/20	3/54	39.75	4.07	58.5	0	0
EGC Young	137.5	28	414	10	2/23	3/41	41.40	3.00	82.7	0	0
BAC Howell	93.4	14	266	6	2/37	2/37	44.33	2.83	93.6	0	0
PB Muchall	39.2	3	218	2	2/60	2/60	109.00	5.54	118.0	0	0
CDJ Dent	11.0	0	32	0	-	-	-	2.90	-	0	0
GJ McCarter	19.0	3	67	0	-	-	-	3.52	-	0	0

Catches/Stumpings:
25 Batty (inc 1st), 17 Coughtrie, 12 Cockbain, 11 Dent, 10 A Gidman, 7 Housego, 6 Nicol, Marshall, 5 Howell, 4 Saxelby, 3 Williamson, Young, Fuller, Norwell, 2 Payne, W Gidman, 1 McCarter, Muchall, J Taylor

LIST A AVERAGES 2012

Batting

	Mat	Inns	NO	Runs	HS	Ave	SR	100	50	4s	6s
KS Williamson	5	5	0	232	112	46.40	102.20	1	1	19	1
DM Housego	7	7	1	269	132	44.83	83.80	1	1	21	5
BAC Howell	11	10	2	286	88	35.75	84.61	0	2	18	6
APR Gidman	12	11	2	317	59	35.22	93.23	0	1	27	5
JK Fuller	8	6	2	138	43	34.50	98.57	0	0	8	5
RJ Nicol	6	6	1	165	133	33.00	94.28	1	0	10	8
EJM Cowan	1	1	0	29	29	29.00	82.85	0	0	2	0
WRS Gidman	8	5	0	139	76	27.80	72.02	0	1	8	0
IA Cockbain	12	11	2	240	58	26.66	100.00	0	2	13	8
HJH Marshall	12	12	0	244	47	20.33	91.04	0	0	29	1
CDJ Dent	4	4	0	76	36	19.00	86.36	0	0	5	0
EGC Young	12	8	2	75	28	12.50	97.40	0	0	6	1
JN Batty	12	6	3	22	6*	7.33	88.00	0	0	1	0
RS Bopara	1	1	0	3	3	3.00	21.42	0	0	0	0
PB Muchall	1	1	0	0	0	0.00	0.00	0	0	0	0
JMR Taylor	2	2	2	35	22*	-	159.09	0	0	4	0
ID Saxelby	7	1	1	3	3*	-	50.00	0	0	0	0
DA Payne	6	2	2	2	2*	-	66.66	0	0	0	0
LC Norwell	3	1	1	1	1*	-	33.33	0	0	0	0

Bowling

	Overs	Mdns	Runs	Wkts	BBI	Ave	Econ	SR	4w	5w
GJ McCarter	9.3	0	56	6	3/15	9.33	5.89	9.5	0	0
RS Bopara	10.0	0	43	3	3/43	14.33	4.30	20.0	0	0
LC Norwell	19.0	1	129	8	6/52	16.12	6.78	14.2	0	1
KS Williamson	4.0	0	17	1	1/17	17.00	4.25	24.0	0	0
JK Fuller	54.1	1	285	15	6/35	19.00	5.26	21.6	0	1
CDJ Dent	27.0	0	132	6	4/43	22.00	4.88	27.0	1	0
DA Payne	38.5	0	238	10	3/39	23.80	6.12	23.3	0	0
APR Gidman	21.0	1	74	3	3/20	24.66	3.52	42.0	0	0
JMR Taylor	16.0	0	56	2	2/21	28.00	3.50	48.0	0	0
EGC Young	82.1	1	424	15	3/25	28.26	5.16	32.8	0	0
BAC Howell	25.0	0	122	4	2/26	30.50	4.88	37.5	0	0
ID Saxelby	39.3	1	234	7	2/25	33.42	5.92	33.8	0	0
WRS Gidman	51.0	6	235	4	2/10	58.75	4.60	76.5	0	0
RJ Nicol	32.0	0	178	1	1/26	178.00	5.56	192.0	0	0
PB Muchall	2.0	0	24	0	-	-	12.00	-	0	0

Catches/Stumpings:
20 Batty (inc 4st), 8 Cockbain, 6 Marshall, 5 Howell, A Gidman, 3 Nicol, Payne, 2 Williamson, Housego, Fuller, W Gidman, Young, 1 Bopara, Muchall, Dent

T20 AVERAGES 2012

	Mat	Inns	NO	Runs	HS	Ave	SR	100	50	4s	6s
DM Housego	4	4	2	127	59*	63.50	125.74	0	1	10	4
KS Williamson	2	2	0	76	39	38.00	118.75	0	0	10	0
EJM Cowan	2	2	0	74	70	37.00	139.62	0	1	10	2
HJH Marshall	7	7	0	239	72	34.14	146.62	0	2	26	6
JN Batty	7	4	3	25	12*	25.00	86.20	0	0	1	0
JK Fuller	7	4	0	84	36	21.00	168.00	0	0	5	6
APR Gidman	7	5	1	81	44	20.25	155.76	0	0	5	4
BAC Howell	6	6	2	77	55*	19.25	120.31	0	1	11	1
IA Cockbain	7	6	2	64	36	16.00	92.75	0	0	2	1
ID Saxelby	6	2	1	9	7*	9.00	150.00	0	0	1	0
EGC Young	7	4	0	25	19	6.25	131.57	0	0	0	1
M Muralitharan	7	2	1	2	2*	2.00	66.66	0	0	0	0
DA Payne	1	1	0	2	2	2.00	66.66	0	0	0	0
JMR Taylor	3	3	0	2	1	0.66	33.33	0	0	0	0
LC Norwell	4	1	1	1	1*	-	50.00	0	0	0	0

Batting

	Overs	Mdns	Runs	Wkts	BBI	Ave	Econ	SR	4w	5w
ID Saxelby	22.0	0	160	11	4/16	14.54	7.27	12.0	1	0
M Muralitharan	25.3	0	135	5	2/20	27.00	5.29	30.6	0	0
EGC Young	20.0	0	116	4	1/16	29.00	5.80	30.0	0	0
LC Norwell	13.0	0	123	4	2/41	30.75	9.46	19.5	0	0
KS Williamson	7.0	0	63	2	1/25	31.50	9.00	21.0	0	0
JK Fuller	25.1	0	265	8	2/40	33.12	10.52	18.8	0	0
APR Gidman	1.0	0	11	0	-	-	11.00	-	0	0
BAC Howell	2.0	0	24	0	-	-	12.00	-	0	0
DA Payne	4.0	0	51	0	-	-	12.75	-	0	0
JMR Taylor	7.0	0	60	0	-	-	8.57	-	0	0

Bowling

Catches/Stumpings:
8 Marshall, 6 Batty (inc 1st), 3 Muralitharan, 2 Housego, Howell, Cockbain, 1 Cowan, J Taylor, Saxelby, Fuller

HAMPSHIRE

FORMED: 1863
HOME GROUND: The Ageas Bowl
ONE-DAY NAME: Royals
CAPTAIN: Jimmy Adams (Championship and YB40), Dimitri Mascarenhas (FL t20)
2012 RESULTS: CC2 4/9; CB40: Winners; FL t20: Winners
HONOURS: Championship: (2) 1961, 1973; Gillette/NatWest/C&G/FP Trophy: (2) 1991, 2005; Benson & Hedges Cup: (2) 1988, 1992; Pro40/National League/CB40: 2012; Sunday League: (3) 1975, 1978, 1986; Twenty20 Cup: (2) 2010, 2012

THE LOWDOWN

Hampshire lifted two limited overs trophies in thrilling fashion in 2012. The CB40 final against Warwickshire went down to the very last ball before being settled by virtue of the Royals losing fewer wickets, while the Friends Life t20 final victory over Yorkshire was another nail-biter. Old pros like captain Dimitri Mascarenhas, Simon Katich and Neil McKenzie dovetailed nicely with emerging youngsters Danny Briggs, Chris Wood and James Vince to produce a winning formula. However, the club will have been disappointed having failed to return to Division One of the County Championship at the first attempt and that will be the primary goal this time around. Their main undoing was inconsistency in the batting, with the division's leading run-scorer Jimmy Adams receiving only sporadic support, although the arrival of Australian Twenty20 captain George Bailey and Essex keeper-batsman Adam Wheater could go some way to solving that problem. The bowling was more reliable, with David Balcombe and James Tomlinson hoping to build on fine 2012 campaigns, and the arrival of Saeed Ajmal for the latter part of the season is sure to delight the Hampshire faithful and aid the development of tyro twirler Briggs.

TEAM MANAGER: GILES WHITE

Originally appointed on a caretaker basis in 2008, White was placed in charge of the first team at the beginning of the 2009 season. His tenure has been one of ups and downs, with one-day success tempered by 2011's County Championship relegation. A player for both Somerset and Hampshire in his day, White averaged 30 with the bat in first-class cricket before deciding to retire in 2002 at the age of 30. His support staff includes former England allrounder Craig White and Hants stalwart Tony Middleton.

FIRST-CLASS AVERAGES 2012

Batting

	Mat	Inns	NO	Runs	HS	Ave	SR	100	50	4s	6s
ND McKenzie	5	9	3	403	139	67.16	53.94	1	2	55	2
JHK Adams	15	27	6	1024	149	48.76	44.69	3	4	141	3
SM Ervine	17	25	4	763	109*	36.33	61.73	1	4	84	4
SM Katich	15	23	2	738	196	35.14	63.40	1	5	95	2
JM Vince	12	19	1	545	128	30.27	67.87	2	0	88	3
BM Shafayat	8	10	0	289	93	28.90	51.42	0	2	41	1
LA Dawson	17	27	2	684	134*	27.36	48.71	1	2	88	2
MA Carberry	11	20	2	468	84*	26.00	47.32	0	3	68	7
H Riazuddin	5	7	2	123	55*	24.60	64.73	0	1	17	1
SP Terry	4	5	1	93	59*	23.25	52.84	0	1	11	0
CP Wood	10	15	1	324	105*	23.14	65.58	1	1	44	3
MD Bates	17	23	0	530	103	23.04	49.71	1	2	82	0
DJ Balcombe	17	22	7	299	73	19.93	71.02	0	1	45	2
Kabir Ali	8	9	1	140	31	17.50	49.29	0	0	16	1
AD Mascarenhas	5	5	0	79	27	15.80	39.50	0	0	12	0
DR Briggs	4	6	2	49	20*	12.25	41.52	0	0	6	0
JA Tomlinson	12	14	7	45	11	6.42	18.59	0	0	4	0
DA Griffiths	5	6	1	27	21	5.40	30.00	0	0	6	0

Bowling

	Overs	Mdns	Runs	Wkts	BBI	BBM	Ave	Econ	SR	5w	10w
JHK Adams	3.0	2	4	1	1/4	1/4	4.00	1.33	18.0	0	0
MA Carberry	6.0	2	19	1	1/1	1/19	19.00	3.16	36.0	0	0
H Riazuddin	92.0	23	269	12	5/61	6/81	22.41	2.92	46.0	1	0
DJ Balcombe	533.1	111	1671	64	8/71	11/119	26.10	3.13	49.9	3	1
JA Tomlinson	376.1	82	1131	43	5/69	6/105	26.30	3.00	52.4	2	0
SM Ervine	232.2	59	716	27	4/96	5/64	26.51	3.08	51.6	0	0
CP Wood	273.5	73	732	26	5/41	7/49	28.15	2.67	63.1	1	0
LA Dawson	265.2	62	837	26	5/29	5/29	32.19	3.15	61.2	1	0
AD Mascarenhas	104.0	36	241	7	2/40	2/40	34.42	2.31	89.1	0	0
DA Griffiths	110.3	18	382	11	3/40	3/136	34.72	3.45	60.2	0	0
Kabir Ali	216.3	36	769	22	3/42	4/107	34.95	3.55	59.0	0	0
SM Katich	33.0	4	93	2	1/22	1/22	46.50	2.81	99.0	0	0
DR Briggs	82.1	15	249	5	2/79	2/64	49.80	3.03	98.6	0	0
BM Shafayat	2.0	0	15	0	-	-	-	7.50	-	0	0
JM Vince	3.0	0	6	0	-	-	-	2.00	-	0	0

Catches/Stumpings:
57 Bates (inc 1st), 37 Dawson, 15 Adams, 13 Vince, 10 Ervine, 8 Katich, 6 McKenzie, 4 Carberry, Tomlinson, Balcombe, 3 Terry, 2 Briggs, Mascarenhas, Griffiths, 1 Riazuddin, Wood

LIST A AVERAGES 2012

Batting

	Mat	Inns	NO	Runs	HS	Ave	SR	100	50	4s	6s
MA Carberry	10	9	2	598	148*	85.42	104.72	2	5	68	16
JM Vince	14	13	3	555	102*	55.50	101.64	1	3	69	3
JHK Adams	13	12	2	333	66	33.30	98.23	0	3	41	5
SM Katich	14	11	4	213	59*	30.42	86.93	0	1	17	3
ND McKenzie	7	6	0	181	88	30.16	79.03	0	1	16	0
AD Mascarenhas	6	3	0	89	48	29.66	132.83	0	0	6	5
SM Ervine	14	10	2	218	68	27.25	84.49	0	2	20	1
Kabir Ali	7	4	1	58	32	19.33	89.23	0	0	5	2
LA Dawson	14	9	2	117	36	16.71	74.05	0	0	7	0
DR Briggs	13	4	1	42	25	14.00	102.43	0	0	2	2
MD Bates	14	5	1	37	16	9.25	59.67	0	0	0	1
CP Wood	14	5	1	30	16	7.50	76.92	0	0	3	0
H Riazuddin	2	2	0	8	8	4.00	36.36	0	0	0	0
DA Griffiths	10	3	3	5	4*	-	100.00	0	0	0	0

Bowling

	Overs	Mdns	Runs	Wkts	BBI	Ave	Econ	SR	4w	5w
MA Carberry	2.0	0	8	1	1/8	8.00	4.00	12.0	0	0
DR Briggs	84.0	1	410	19	4/32	21.57	4.88	26.5	1	0
Kabir Ali	40.0	1	256	10	3/39	25.60	6.40	24.0	0	0
DA Griffiths	55.0	4	318	12	3/29	26.50	5.78	27.5	0	0
SM Ervine	54.0	3	292	11	3/35	26.54	5.40	29.4	0	0
CP Wood	92.5	2	511	19	5/22	26.89	5.50	29.3	0	1
AD Mascarenhas	38.0	2	172	6	2/17	28.66	4.52	38.0	0	0
SM Katich	10.1	0	51	1	1/9	51.00	5.01	61.0	0	0
LA Dawson	82.0	3	381	7	2/26	54.42	4.64	70.2	0	0
H Riazuddin	7.0	0	53	0	-	-	7.57	-	0	0

Catches/Stumpings:
10 Bates, 9 Dawson, 7 Adams, 6 Katich, 4 Ervine, 3 Ali, Vince, Wood, 2 McKenzie, Carberry, Briggs, 1 Griffiths

T20 AVERAGES 2012

Batting

	Mat	Inns	NO	Runs	HS	Ave	SR	100	50	4s	6s
GJ Maxwell	9	7	3	179	66*	44.75	175.49	0	2	14	13
SM Katich	7	6	2	165	42*	41.25	127.90	0	0	16	2
SM Ervine	11	8	3	190	75*	38.00	125.00	0	1	13	6
JM Vince	11	10	2	254	64*	31.75	118.69	0	1	28	3
AD Mascarenhas	11	4	2	54	21	27.00	142.10	0	0	6	1
LA Dawson	9	3	1	47	30	23.50	156.66	0	0	6	0
ND McKenzie	11	9	3	140	79*	23.33	117.64	0	1	11	3
JHK Adams	11	10	1	195	43	21.66	114.70	0	0	21	5
MA Carberry	5	5	0	83	33	16.60	91.20	0	0	13	0
Kabir Ali	4	2	2	25	13*	-	208.33	0	0	2	1

Bowling

	Overs	Mdns	Runs	Wkts	BBI	Ave	Econ	SR	4w	5w
AD Mascarenhas	38.0	1	247	15	2/11	16.46	6.50	15.2	0	0
LA Dawson	31.0	0	218	9	2/10	24.22	7.03	20.6	0	0
GJ Maxwell	24.0	1	182	7	3/36	26.00	7.58	20.5	0	0
CP Wood	36.4	0	282	9	3/26	31.33	7.69	24.4	0	0
SM Ervine	25.0	0	201	6	2/22	33.50	8.04	25.0	0	0
DA Griffiths	4.0	0	40	1	1/40	40.00	10.00	24.0	0	0
DR Briggs	36.0	0	261	6	2/28	43.50	7.25	36.0	0	0
Kabir Ali	12.2	0	122	1	1/31	122.00	9.89	74.0	0	0

Catches/Stumpings:
7 Vince, 5 Briggs, Ervine, 3 Bates (inc 1st), Katich, Wood, 2 Dawson, Maxwell, Adams, 1 Ali, Carberry

KENT

FORMED: 1870
HOME GROUND: St Lawrence Ground, Canterbury
ONE-DAY NAME: Spitfires
CAPTAIN: James Tredwell
2012 RESULTS: CC2: 3/9; CB40: 3/7 in Group C; FL t20: 4/6 in South Division
HONOURS: Championship: (7) 1906, 1909, 1910, 1913, 1970, 1977(s), 1978; Gillette/NatWest/C&G/FP Trophy: (2) 1967, 1974; Pro40/National League/CB40: 2001; Benson & Hedges Cup: (3) 1973, 1976, 1978; Sunday League: (4) 1972, 1973, 1976, 1995; Twenty20 Cup: 2007

THE LOWDOWN

After several seasons of financial turmoil, Kent can look back on 2012 with justifiable pride. A summer of quiet achievement saw them push hard for promotion in the County Championship and narrowly miss qualification for the knockout stages in the shorter formats. With that foundation to build on and promising batting tyros Sam Northeast, Daniel Bell-Drummond and Sam Billings all a season older and wiser, 2013 could be a huge year for the club. Long-standing skipper Rob Key has stood down after eight years at the helm, allowing James Tredwell to take over the reins. Key's shoes will be tough ones to fill, and the situation may be complicated by Graeme Swann's long-standing elbow condition – should England's No.1 off spinner retire from one-day cricket to prolong his Test career, the St Lawrence faithful will probably be seeing far less of their captain than they would like. If Tredwell is required by England for much of the season a great deal of responsibility will rest on the shoulders of Matt Coles, Charlie Shreck and Mark Davies, who took a combined total of 147 first-class wickets in 2012. If they are all fit and firing, Kent's seam attack looks among the strongest in the country; throw in Tredwell or promising young tweaker Adam Riley and the Spitfires look a side that can give anyone a run for their money.

HEAD COACH: JIMMY ADAMS

The ex-West Indies captain begins his second season in charge of Kent, having been appointed in January 2012. Adams made a sublime start to his Test career, averaging 87 after 12 matches, but was – unsurprisingly – unable to continue in the same vein, eventually bowing out in 2001 with a batting average of a jot over 40. He moved into a role working with the West Indies U19s before making the move to England to lead Kent. The Spitfires' success in 2012 has only added to his growing reputation as one of the game's most promising coaches.

FIRST-CLASS AVERAGES 2012

	Mat	Inns	NO	Runs	HS	Ave	SR	100	50	4s	6s
SA Northeast	12	19	2	969	165	57.00	53.00	3	6	112	3
BP Nash	16	24	5	908	132*	47.78	57.14	3	4	98	1
GO Jones	16	20	4	677	88	42.31	52.03	0	7	74	3
DJ Bell-Drummond	2	4	1	123	48*	41.00	51.89	0	0	19	0
MJ Powell	17	21	4	695	134	40.88	44.38	2	3	87	1
RWT Key	15	24	3	797	119	37.95	47.04	1	5	92	0
DI Stevens	16	20	0	619	123	30.95	61.71	2	2	89	2
Azhar Mahmood	1	2	0	49	49	24.50	63.63	0	0	5	0
SA Newman	6	9	0	215	64	23.88	49.53	0	1	34	0
AJ Blake	5	8	1	164	73	23.42	44.56	0	1	24	0
MT Coles	15	18	1	392	103*	23.05	72.45	1	1	47	9
JC Tredwell	13	13	2	227	87	20.63	43.48	0	1	25	0
BW Harmison	12	17	1	325	46	20.31	40.72	0	0	36	1
M Davies	15	16	4	227	58	18.91	47.48	0	1	30	2
CE Shreck	17	17	11	86	16	14.33	55.84	0	0	13	3
SJ Cook	2	2	0	28	15	14.00	51.85	0	0	4	0
SW Billings	1	1	0	13	13	13.00	46.42	0	0	1	0
AEN Riley	6	6	0	20	8	3.33	13.69	0	0	0	0
IAA Thomas	2	2	1	0	0*	0.00	0.00	0	0	0	0

Batting

	Overs	Mdns	Runs	Wkts	BBI	BBM	Ave	Econ	SR	5w	10w
BP Nash	28.5	1	72	4	1/2	1/2	18.00	2.49	43.2	0	0
SJ Cook	12.0	5	19	1	1/19	1/19	19.00	1.58	72.0	0	0
M Davies	368.3	129	699	36	5/27	7/58	19.41	1.89	61.4	1	0
MT Coles	357.4	46	1197	53	6/51	9/83	22.58	3.34	40.4	2	0
DI Stevens	304.3	63	840	35	5/35	6/46	24.00	2.75	52.2	1	0
CE Shreck	526.3	112	1544	58	5/41	9/140	26.62	2.93	54.4	2	0
IAA Thomas	35.0	11	88	3	2/29	2/29	29.33	2.51	70.0	0	0
Azhar Mahmood	21.0	5	71	2	2/25	2/71	35.50	3.38	63.0	0	0
JC Tredwell	301.0	78	752	19	3/38	5/118	39.57	2.49	95.0	0	0
AEN Riley	81.4	19	301	7	2/43	3/111	43.00	3.68	70.0	0	0
AJ Blake	1.0	0	1	0	-	-	-	1.00	-	0	0
BW Harmison	19.0	2	66	0	-	-	-	3.47	-	0	0
RWT Key	4.0	1	27	0	-	-	-	6.75	-	0	0
SA Newman	6.0	0	31	0	-	-	-	5.16	-	0	0

Bowling

Catches/Stumpings:
52 Jones, 15 Tredwell, 7 Key, Stevens, 6 Northeast, Nash, Powell, 5 Blake, 4 Davies, Coles, 3 Newman, Riley, Harmison, 1 Mahmood, Bell-Drummond, Billings

LIST A AVERAGES 2012

Batting	Mat	Inns	NO	Runs	HS	Ave	SR	100	50	4s	6s
GO Jones	11	6	5	152	52*	152.00	117.82	0	1	11	2
BP Nash	9	5	3	189	70*	94.50	95.45	0	2	12	0
SW Billings	11	11	4	315	143	45.00	100.00	1	1	44	1
RWT Key	11	11	3	283	101	35.37	73.50	1	0	26	2
SA Northeast	11	8	1	198	69	28.28	71.48	0	1	12	1
DI Stevens	11	7	0	197	59	28.14	80.08	0	1	23	0
Azhar Mahmood	4	2	1	28	20*	28.00	93.33	0	0	3	1
JC Tredwell	10	3	2	19	14	19.00	73.07	0	0	2	0
AJ Blake	8	7	1	77	18*	12.83	68.75	0	0	12	0
MT Coles	9	1	0	2	2	2.00	28.57	0	0	0	0
AJ Ball	5	1	0	1	1	1.00	33.33	0	0	0	0
M Davies	9	1	1	3	3*	-	25.00	0	0	0	0

Bowling	Overs	Mdns	Runs	Wkts	BBI	Ave	Econ	SR	4w	5w
DI Stevens	74.1	2	326	20	5/36	16.30	4.39	22.2	1	1
MT Coles	52.2	3	281	17	6/32	16.52	5.36	18.4	0	1
JC Tredwell	61.4	1	300	13	4/24	23.07	4.86	28.4	1	0
M Davies	69.0	12	255	10	3/10	25.50	3.69	41.4	0	0
Azhar Mahmood	17.0	0	83	3	2/14	27.66	4.88	34.0	0	0
AJ Ball	27.0	2	142	4	2/39	35.50	5.25	40.5	0	0
SJ Cook	39.0	0	187	5	2/30	37.40	4.79	46.8	0	0
BP Nash	18.0	0	75	2	2/14	37.50	4.16	54.0	0	0
AEN Riley	4.0	0	19	0	-	-	4.75	-	0	0

Catches/Stumpings:
16 Jones (inc 2st), 7 Tredwell, Stevens, 5 Blake, 4 Northeast, 3 Coles, Billings, 2 Davies, Key, 1 Mahmood, Ball

T20 AVERAGES 2012

	Mat	Inns	NO	Runs	HS	Ave	SR	100	50	4s	6s
SJ Cook	4	4	3	30	19*	30.00	115.38	0	0	1	1
SA Northeast	9	8	1	192	60	27.42	122.29	0	1	19	4
DI Stevens	9	9	1	207	60	25.87	135.29	0	1	11	12
SW Billings	9	9	0	216	59	24.00	101.88	0	1	17	4
AJ Blake	4	4	0	70	35	17.50	127.27	0	0	3	4
BP Nash	6	5	1	69	26	17.25	106.15	0	0	7	0
RWT Key	8	8	1	116	51*	16.57	91.33	0	1	12	2
GO Jones	9	7	3	64	24*	16.00	101.58	0	0	2	2
Azhar Mahmood	8	8	0	110	30	13.75	98.21	0	0	7	3
MT Coles	6	5	2	31	14*	10.33	124.00	0	0	6	0
AJ Ball	9	6	2	39	18	9.75	130.00	0	0	4	1
M Davies	9	4	1	15	13	5.00	83.33	0	0	1	0
JC Tredwell	6	2	0	3	2	1.50	60.00	0	0	0	0
AEN Riley	3	1	1	5	5*	-	125.00	0	0	0	0

Batting

	Overs	Mdns	Runs	Wkts	BBI	Ave	Econ	SR	4w	5w
AJ Ball	28.3	0	217	12	2/18	18.08	7.61	14.2	0	0
DI Stevens	22.0	0	135	7	3/13	19.28	6.13	18.8	0	0
Azhar Mahmood	24.2	0	212	10	3/12	21.20	8.71	14.6	0	0
SJ Cook	14.0	0	103	4	3/41	25.75	7.35	21.0	0	0
M Davies	36.0	0	206	7	2/18	29.42	5.72	30.8	0	0
AEN Riley	9.0	0	61	2	2/15	30.50	6.77	27.0	0	0
BP Nash	3.0	0	32	1	1/32	32.00	10.66	18.0	0	0
JC Tredwell	23.0	0	149	4	2/27	37.25	6.47	34.5	0	0
MT Coles	16.0	0	192	4	2/46	48.00	12.00	24.0	0	0

Bowling

Catches/Stumpings:
9 Jones (inc 3st), 5 Key, 4 Coles, Billings, 3 Ball, 2 Davies, Northeast, Stevens, 1 Blake, Cook, Mahmood

LANCASHIRE

FORMED: 1864
HOME GROUND: Emirates Old Trafford
ONE-DAY NAME: Lightning
CAPTAIN: Glen Chapple
2012 RESULTS: CC1: 8/9; CB40: Semi-finalists; FL t20: 4/6 in North Division
HONOURS: Championship: (9) 1897, 1904, 1926, 1927, 1928, 1930, 1950(s), 2011; Gillette/NatWest/C&G/FP Trophy: (7) 1970, 1971, 1972, 1985, 1990, 1996, 1998; Benson & Hedges Cup: (4) 1984, 1990, 1995, 1996; Pro40/National League/CB40: 1999; Sunday League: (4) 1969, 1970, 1989, 1998

THE LOWDOWN

Despite reaching the semi-finals of the CB40, 2012 will not be remembered fondly by the Lancashire faithful. Relegation in the Championship the season after being crowned four-day champions will have stung considering the level of talent at the club, and the desire to set things right will mean they start this year among the promotion favourites. Lancashire's well-publicised financial struggles have eased somewhat of late, helped in part by the recent landmark 10-year partnership with airline firm Emirates, and consequently the squad has been bolstered by the arrival of experienced campaigners Simon Katich, Kabir Ali and Wayne White. Katich will provide the gritty top order runs that the team failed to produce last term, Ali – fitness permitting – remains one of the finest new ball bowlers on the county circuit, while White is a dynamic allrounder who could help transform the club from one-day nearly men to a side able to consistently deliver the silverware their ability deserves. Key to their fortunes will be Glen Chapple – can the evergreen skipper continue his outstanding form from the last few seasons? If so, and the likes of Katich, Stephen Moore and Paul Horton can pile on the runs, Lancashire will take some stopping in 2013.

HEAD COACH: PETER MOORES

The former England coach must have watched Kevin Pietersen's summer travails with great interest. A fall-out with Pietersen led to Moores losing his job, but his spell in charge of the national side didn't do anything to worsen his reputation; he remains in the eyes of many one of the world's leading coaches. In 2003 he made history for Sussex as he brought them Championship glory, and Lancashire's title success in 2011 provided another feather in his cap. The 2012 campaign will have disappointed him, but few people will be betting against Moores leading his charges back into the top tier.

FIRST-CLASS AVERAGES 2012

Batting

	Mat	Inns	NO	Runs	HS	Ave	SR	100	50	4s	6s
AG Prince	15	24	1	1008	144	43.82	49.65	2	8	84	5
TC Smith	7	11	1	352	91	35.20	53.41	0	4	50	1
KW Hogg	14	19	9	336	61*	33.60	48.34	0	2	37	0
PJ Horton	17	27	4	742	137*	32.26	41.36	2	2	95	0
SJ Croft	17	25	1	749	154*	31.20	53.57	2	3	76	8
LA Procter	14	21	3	491	77	27.27	36.83	0	1	53	1
KR Brown	17	27	2	636	78	25.44	50.15	0	3	79	3
GD Cross	16	25	3	547	75*	24.86	61.73	0	3	65	2
G Chapple	15	23	0	381	46	16.56	60.66	0	0	42	9
SC Moore	13	22	0	363	47	16.50	47.45	0	0	45	2
A Shahzad	10	15	5	134	28*	13.40	45.11	0	0	14	0
AP Agathangelou	3	3	0	36	24	12.00	32.43	0	0	6	0
SC Kerrigan	16	19	7	96	34*	8.00	29.17	0	0	9	1
SI Mahmood	4	4	0	18	14	4.50	48.64	0	0	1	0
G Keedy	5	4	0	8	5	2.00	10.66	0	0	1	0
JM Anderson	1	2	0	0	0	0.00	0.00	0	0	0	0

Bowling

	Overs	Mdns	Runs	Wkts	BBI	BBM	Ave	Econ	SR	5w	10w
JM Anderson	36.2	7	105	5	5/82	5/105	21.00	2.88	43.6	1	0
LA Procter	190.1	33	631	28	7/71	8/79	22.53	3.31	40.7	2	0
G Chapple	394.5	101	1010	42	5/47	10/133	24.04	2.55	56.4	2	1
SJ Croft	96.4	13	289	12	6/41	9/105	24.08	2.98	48.3	1	0
SI Mahmood	53.4	7	247	8	4/38	4/67	30.87	4.60	40.2	0	0
A Shahzad	216.3	50	709	20	4/40	4/59	35.45	3.27	64.9	0	0
SC Kerrigan	530.5	88	1562	44	4/45	7/122	35.50	2.94	72.3	0	0
TC Smith	66.0	7	248	6	2/12	2/12	41.33	3.75	66.0	0	0
KW Hogg	262.4	62	795	19	3/23	4/89	41.84	3.02	82.9	0	0
G Keedy	139.5	18	421	8	3/101	3/101	52.62	3.01	104.8	0	0
OJ Newby	13.0	0	59	1	1/59	1/59	59.00	4.53	78.0	0	0
TE Bailey	17.0	2	67	1	1/67	1/67	67.00	3.94	102.0	0	0
KR Brown	3.0	0	5	0	-	-	-	1.66	-	0	0
AG Prince	2.0	1	5	0	-	-	-	2.50	-	0	0

Catches/Stumpings:
34 Cross (inc 3st), 18 Horton, 15 Prince, Croft, 7 Moore, 6 Smith, 5 Brown, 4 Kerrigan, 3 Chapple, 2 Davies, 1 Anderson, Agathangelou, Shahzad, Hogg

LIST A AVERAGES 2012

Batting

	Mat	Inns	NO	Runs	HS	Ave	SR	100	50	4s	6s
SJ Croft	13	13	4	513	82	57.00	92.93	0	6	35	10
SC Moore	13	13	2	581	113	52.81	103.93	1	6	70	5
KR Brown	13	11	4	319	87*	45.57	86.21	0	2	26	7
TC Smith	4	4	1	131	106	43.66	179.45	1	0	13	10
PJ Horton	13	10	2	250	78	31.25	102.88	0	2	17	0
AG Prince	12	11	0	317	85	28.81	88.54	0	2	29	3
G Chapple	7	3	1	31	16	15.50	63.26	0	0	2	0
SI Mahmood	5	3	0	41	29	13.66	78.84	0	0	3	0
GD Cross	13	6	1	64	19	12.80	78.04	0	0	5	0
A Shahzad	11	6	0	68	29	11.33	89.47	0	0	5	1
SD Parry	12	5	0	54	17	10.80	84.37	0	0	4	0
SC Kerrigan	3	1	0	10	10	10.00	76.92	0	0	1	0
LA Procter	2	1	0	8	8	8.00	80.00	0	0	0	0
OJ Newby	7	2	2	43	36*	-	93.47	0	0	4	1
G Keedy	11	5	5	7	3*	-	46.66	0	0	0	0

Bowling

	Overs	Mdns	Runs	Wkts	BBI	Ave	Econ	SR	4w	5w
OJ Newby	31.1	1	176	10	5/35	17.60	5.64	18.7	0	1
G Keedy	76.2	1	401	20	5/55	20.05	5.25	22.9	0	1
G Chapple	45.0	5	204	10	5/26	20.40	4.53	27.0	1	1
A Shahzad	70.5	1	431	21	4/51	20.52	6.08	20.2	1	0
TC Smith	15.0	0	92	3	1/13	30.66	6.13	30.0	0	0
SC Kerrigan	15.0	0	100	3	3/44	33.33	6.66	30.0	0	0
SD Parry	86.0	2	474	14	4/21	33.85	5.51	36.8	2	0
NS Tahir	8.0	0	48	1	1/48	48.00	6.00	48.0	0	0
SI Mahmood	39.0	0	309	6	2/50	51.50	7.92	39.0	0	0
SJ Croft	33.0	0	176	3	2/46	58.66	5.33	66.0	0	0
LA Procter	8.0	0	75	0	-	-	9.37	-	0	0

Catches/Stumpings:
19 Cross (inc 6st), 13 Croft, 7 Horton, 6 Moore, 5 Prince, 4 Parry, 3 Chapple, Brown, 2 Mahmood, Shahzad, 1 Smith, Keedy

T20 AVERAGES 2012

Batting

	Mat	Inns	NO	Runs	HS	Ave	SR	100	50	4s	6s
SJ Croft	8	8	3	313	65*	62.60	129.33	0	2	17	11
SC Moore	8	8	0	249	80	31.12	139.88	0	3	26	7
TC Smith	8	8	0	227	56	28.37	122.70	0	1	20	10
KR Brown	8	8	2	145	46	24.16	117.88	0	0	13	2
Yasir Arafat	8	5	3	43	20*	21.50	126.47	0	0	3	0
PJ Horton	8	6	2	65	27*	16.25	100.00	0	0	3	0
GD Cross	8	6	1	74	26	14.80	105.71	0	0	2	2
G Chapple	6	3	2	7	5*	7.00	77.77	0	0	1	0
A Shahzad	2	1	0	4	4	4.00	44.44	0	0	0	0
OJ Newby	3	1	0	1	1	1.00	50.00	0	0	0	0
SI Mahmood	1	1	1	3	3*	-	100.00	0	0	0	0
SD Parry	8	1	1	1	1*	-	50.00	0	0	0	0

Bowling

	Overs	Mdns	Runs	Wkts	BBI	Ave	Econ	SR	4w	5w
G Chapple	23.5	1	118	9	2/10	13.11	4.95	15.8	0	0
LA Procter	8.2	0	82	4	2/15	20.50	9.84	12.5	0	0
G Keedy	24.0	0	186	9	4/25	20.66	7.75	16.0	1	0
OJ Newby	2.4	0	22	1	1/17	22.00	8.25	16.0	0	0
Yasir Arafat	24.0	0	224	10	3/21	22.40	9.33	14.4	0	0
SD Parry	27.0	0	190	6	2/31	31.66	7.03	27.0	0	0
SJ Croft	4.0	0	32	1	1/32	32.00	8.00	24.0	0	0
A Shahzad	5.0	0	36	1	1/29	36.00	7.20	30.0	0	0
SI Mahmood	2.3	0	42	1	1/42	42.00	16.80	15.0	0	0
TC Smith	13.0	0	92	1	1/13	92.00	7.07	78.0	0	0

Catches/Stumpings:
9 Croft, 8 Cross (inc 2st), 5 Smith, 4 Horton, 3 Keedy, 1 Brown, Moore, Arafat

LEICESTERSHIRE

FORMED: 1879
HOME GROUND: County Ground, Grace Road
ONE-DAY NAME: Foxes
CAPTAIN: Ramnaresh Sarwan (Championship), Josh Cobb (YB40 and FL t20)
2012 RESULTS: CC2: 7/9; CB40: 6/7 in Group A; FL t20: 6/6 in North Group
HONOURS: Championship: (3) 1975, 1996, 1998; Benson & Hedges Cup: (3) 1972, 1975, 1985; Sunday League: (2) 1974, 1977; Twenty20 Cup: (3) 2004, 2006, 2011

THE LOWDOWN

Leicestershire endured another difficult season in the Championship in 2012, but did at least avoid a repeat of the previous year when they finished bottom of the pile. Ramnaresh Sarwan was their stand-out performer with the bat, finishing as Division Two's second highest run-scorer, and he will lead the side in four-day cricket in 2013 when not on duty with the West Indies, with Josh Cobb taking charge in the shorter formats. When the Windies come calling in the middle part of the campaign, promising Australian batsman Joe Burns will step in as their overseas player. England U19 captain Shiv Thakor showed just what an exciting talent he is by scoring four half-centuries in just 10 innings at the back-end of the season and the highly-rated allrounder will have a lead role to play this season, particularly in the absence of last season's leading wicket-taker Wayne White, who swapped Grace Road for Old Trafford over the winter. Young seamers Nathan Buck and Alex Wyatt will be expected to step up and fill the void in the bowling department, with veteran Matthew Hoggard – who relinquished the four-day captaincy last December – acting as the spearhead of the attack. The Foxes' performances in the Friends Life t20 – a competition they won in 2011 – were particularly disappointing as they lost seven from 10 matches and finished bottom of their group. Twenty20 is a format they have excelled in since its conception and they will be anxious to make up for last year's setback this time around.

HEAD COACH/ACADEMY DIRECTOR: PHIL WHITTICASE

Whitticase is Leicestershire through and through, having spent the entirety of his playing career at Grace Road before moving in to a coaching role at the club. He took the reins in 2010 after Tim Boon left the club, and by combining the roles of head coach and academy chief he is responsible for nurturing the talented youngsters that come through Leicestershire's acclaimed academy and promoting them to the first team when the time is right.

FIRST-CLASS AVERAGES 2012

	Mat	Inns	NO	Runs	HS	Ave	SR	100	50	4s	6s
SJ Thakor	6	10	3	427	85*	61.00	51.07	0	4	47	1
RR Sarwan	14	25	2	941	117	40.91	55.35	2	5	128	3
JJ Cobb	14	23	1	752	105	34.18	53.37	1	5	110	9
MA Thornely	9	16	0	514	131	32.12	42.58	2	1	57	7
MAG Boyce	14	25	2	733	122	31.86	41.62	2	4	88	0
EJH Eckersley	16	28	4	739	137*	30.79	45.75	1	3	93	2
WA White	16	26	5	616	67	29.33	50.53	0	4	82	7
WS Jones	3	6	0	138	48	23.00	48.76	0	0	20	0
CW Henderson	12	19	4	296	57*	19.73	46.90	0	2	35	3
WI Jefferson	2	4	0	75	49	18.75	46.01	0	0	10	0
GP Smith	13	23	0	429	77	18.65	41.01	0	2	55	0
PL Mommsen	2	3	0	49	35	16.33	39.51	0	0	5	0
MJ Hoggard	10	12	7	81	28	16.20	32.01	0	0	9	1
Kadeer Ali	3	4	0	63	48	15.75	42.56	0	0	5	1
JKH Naik	2	3	0	40	33	13.33	56.33	0	0	3	0
J du Toit	6	10	0	127	48	12.70	36.49	0	0	13	1
NL Buck	11	15	2	119	27	9.15	36.39	0	0	16	0
RH Joseph	9	13	4	79	29	8.77	40.10	0	0	10	0
MN Malik	5	7	1	51	21*	8.50	32.07	0	0	5	0
PG Dixey	3	5	1	30	13	7.50	34.88	0	0	3	0
ACF Wyatt	5	6	2	14	8	3.50	31.11	0	0	1	0
RML Taylor	1	1	0	1	1	1.00	12.50	0	0	0	0

Batting

	Overs	Mdns	Runs	Wkts	BBI	BBM	Ave	Econ	SR	5w	10w
RML Taylor	19.0	2	91	5	5/91	5/91	18.20	4.78	22.8	1	0
WS Jones	26.0	2	129	5	3/71	3/78	25.80	4.96	31.2	0	0
MJ Hoggard	220.4	42	691	24	4/27	6/76	28.79	3.13	55.1	0	0
WA White	349.0	41	1286	43	5/54	5/69	29.90	3.68	48.6	3	0
RH Joseph	202.3	36	762	24	6/47	12/111	31.75	3.76	50.6	2	1
CW Henderson	390.1	82	1110	30	5/116	6/104	37.00	2.84	78.0	1	0
ACF Wyatt	100.0	22	333	9	3/35	4/97	37.00	3.33	66.6	0	0
SJ Thakor	34.0	3	159	4	2/24	2/24	39.75	4.67	51.0	0	0
NL Buck	292.0	58	955	20	3/50	4/128	47.75	3.27	87.6	0	0
MA Thornely	40.0	3	150	3	2/29	2/51	50.00	3.75	80.0	0	0
MN Malik	87.0	10	309	6	2/22	2/40	51.50	3.55	87.0	0	0
JKH Naik	56.2	5	205	3	2/36	2/127	68.33	3.63	112.6	0	0
JJ Cobb	56.0	4	208	3	1/5	1/8	69.33	3.71	112.0	0	0
Kadeer Ali	11.0	2	33	0	-	-	-	3.00	-	0	0
MAG Boyce	2.0	1	9	0	-	-	-	4.50	-	0	0
J du Toit	18.0	1	54	0	-	-	-	3.00	-	0	0
PL Mommsen	10.0	0	43	0	-	-	-	4.30	-	0	0
RR Sarwan	16.1	0	75	0	-	-	-	4.63	-	0	0
GP Smith	1.0	0	9	0	-	-	-	9.00	-	0	0

Bowling

Catches/Stumpings:
46 Eckersley (inc 3st), 13 Smith, 9 Boyce, 7 Sarwan, 6 Thornely, Cobb, 5 Dixey (inc 1st) 4 du Toit, 2 Mommsen, Naik, Jones, Thakor, Joseph, 1 Jefferson, Ali, Wyatt, White

LIST A AVERAGES 2012

Batting

	Mat	Inns	NO	Runs	HS	Ave	SR	100	50	4s	6s
SJ Thakor	4	4	1	165	83*	55.00	100.00	0	2	10	1
RR Sarwan	9	9	0	318	115	35.33	93.52	2	0	28	3
EJH Eckersley	8	8	2	183	72*	30.50	127.97	0	1	9	10
JJ Cobb	9	9	0	262	137	29.11	103.96	1	1	29	6
MA Thornely	8	8	0	230	86	28.75	98.71	0	2	21	8
MAG Boyce	10	10	0	252	64	25.20	96.92	0	3	20	0
GP Smith	9	9	0	180	44	20.00	71.14	0	0	13	3
WA White	8	8	0	159	38	19.87	71.62	0	0	4	5
J du Toit	5	5	0	96	48	19.20	76.80	0	0	10	2
WS Jones	4	4	1	56	44	18.66	96.55	0	0	6	0
RML Taylor	9	9	3	106	29*	17.66	108.16	0	0	9	2
JS Sykes	7	3	2	15	12*	15.00	68.18	0	0	2	0
MJ Hoggard	3	1	0	14	14	14.00	140.00	0	0	2	0
MN Malik	3	3	1	27	27*	13.50	96.42	0	0	2	0
PG Dixey	3	3	1	25	17	12.50	71.42	0	0	0	0
CW Henderson	4	4	0	43	22	10.75	102.38	0	0	6	0
ACF Wyatt	3	2	1	9	9*	9.00	90.00	0	0	1	0
Abdul Razzaq	1	1	0	6	6	6.00	60.00	0	0	1	0
TJ Wells	1	1	0	4	4	4.00	133.33	0	0	0	0
RH Joseph	4	3	1	1	1	0.50	33.33	0	0	0	0
PL Mommsen	1	1	0	0	0	0.00	0.00	0	0	0	0
NL Buck	7	3	3	14	7*	-	58.33	0	0	0	0

Bowling

	Overs	Mdns	Runs	Wkts	BBI	Ave	Econ	SR	4w	5w
Abdul Razzaq	9.0	0	39	3	3/39	13.00	4.33	18.0	0	0
RML Taylor	55.4	1	291	11	2/26	26.45	5.22	30.3	0	0
MJ Hoggard	16.1	0	109	4	3/26	27.25	6.74	24.2	0	0
JS Sykes	39.0	2	194	7	3/39	27.71	4.97	33.4	0	0
WA White	37.0	0	251	6	2/17	41.83	6.78	37.0	0	0
ACF Wyatt	18.0	1	126	3	2/47	42.00	7.00	36.0	0	0
MA Thornely	19.0	0	140	3	1/20	46.66	7.36	38.0	0	0
NL Buck	50.3	3	357	6	3/49	59.50	7.06	50.5	0	0
JJ Cobb	48.0	0	299	5	1/35	59.80	6.22	57.6	0	0
MN Malik	23.0	1	136	2	1/42	68.00	5.91	69.0	0	0
CW Henderson	26.0	0	201	2	1/48	100.50	7.73	78.0	0	0
WS Jones	3.0	0	14	0	-	-	4.66	-	0	0
RH Joseph	17.0	0	121	0	-	-	7.11	-	0	0
JKH Naik	3.0	0	23	0	-	-	7.66	-	0	0
SJ Thakor	3.0	0	26	0	-	-	8.66	-	0	0

Catches/Stumpings:
8 Eckersely (inc 1st), 5 Smith, 3 Joseph, Buck, 2 Jones, Thornely, White, Cobb, Taylor, 1 Sykes, Sarwan, Boyce

T20 AVERAGES 2012

Batting

	Mat	Inns	NO	Runs	HS	Ave	SR	100	50	4s	6s
Abdul Razzaq	9	9	0	266	69	29.55	112.23	0	2	28	7
MAG Boyce	9	9	2	175	63*	25.00	119.04	0	1	15	4
JJ Cobb	9	9	0	187	46	20.77	135.50	0	0	21	5
WA White	9	9	3	114	22	19.00	109.61	0	0	6	2
RR Sarwan	9	8	0	138	45	17.25	103.75	0	0	8	2
GP Smith	8	8	0	115	23	14.37	115.00	0	0	11	2
RML Taylor	8	6	1	39	18*	7.80	105.40	0	0	1	2
EJH Eckersley	9	7	2	38	13	7.60	88.37	0	0	1	0
CW Henderson	8	5	4	7	4*	7.00	63.63	0	0	0	0
Kadeer Ali	1	1	0	6	6	6.00	54.54	0	0	0	0
NL Buck	4	2	1	5	5*	5.00	55.55	0	0	0	0
J du Toit	3	3	0	14	11	4.66	70.00	0	0	1	0
MJ Hoggard	9	3	0	0	0	0.00	0.00	0	0	0	0
JS Sykes	1	1	1	2	2*	-	50.00	0	0	0	0
MA Thornely	1	1	1	1	1*	-	100.00	0	0	0	0

Bowling

	Overs	Mdns	Runs	Wkts	BBI	Ave	Econ	SR	4w	5w
JS Sykes	4.0	0	24	2	2/24	12.00	6.00	12.0	0	0
RML Taylor	23.0	0	159	7	2/7	22.71	6.91	19.7	0	0
Abdul Razzaq	28.0	0	252	9	3/20	28.00	9.00	18.6	0	0
NL Buck	13.2	1	117	4	3/28	29.25	8.77	20.0	0	0
WA White	13.0	0	162	5	2/25	32.40	12.46	15.6	0	0
MJ Hoggard	28.0	1	213	5	2/25	42.60	7.60	33.6	0	0
CW Henderson	21.0	0	152	2	1/26	76.00	7.23	63.0	0	0
JJ Cobb	19.0	0	153	2	1/20	76.50	8.05	57.0	0	0
PL Mommsen	3.0	0	28	0	-	-	9.33	-	0	0
MA Thornely	1.0	0	8	0	-	-	8.00	-	0	0

Catches/Stumpings:
4 Taylor, Cobb, 3 du Toit, 2 Buck, Boyce, Eckersley, Sarwan, White, 1 Mommsen, Henderson, Smith, Razzaq, Hoggard

MIDDLESEX

FORMED: 1864
HOME GROUND: Lord's
ONE-DAY NAME: Panthers
CAPTAIN: Chris Rogers (Championship), Neil Dexter (YB40 and FL t20)
2012 RESULTS: CC1: 3/9; CB40: 2/7 in Group A; FL t20: 5/6 in South Group
HONOURS: Championship: (12) 1903, 1920, 1921, 1947, 1949(s), 1976, 1977(s), 1980, 1982, 1985, 1990, 1993; Gillette/NatWest/C&G/FP Trophy: (4) 1977, 1980, 1984, 1988; Benson & Hedges Cup: (2) 1983, 1986; Sunday League: 1992; Twenty20 Cup: 2008

THE LOWDOWN

Middlesex enjoyed an impressive season on their return to the top-flight of the County Championship, finishing the 2012 campaign in third place. Seam duo Toby Roland-Jones and Tim Murtagh were key to their success, sharing 125 first-class wickets between them, while the ever-reliable Australian batsman Chris Rogers finished as the division's second highest run-scorer. Rogers – who took over as four-day captain last April when Neil Dexter stood down – will continue to lead the side in Championship cricket and be able to call upon the services of England Lions paceman James Harris, who arrived from Glamorgan in the off-season. In the batting department Rogers will hope for more support from a crop of talented strokemakers that includes Joe Denly, Eoin Morgan and Dawid Malan. In 2012 each of them showed flashes of brilliance but lacked consistency. Dexter remains skipper in the limited over competitions, and he will no doubt have identified the Friends Life t20 as an area in need of improvement. Since winning the competition in 2008, the Panthers have failed to progress past the group stage and they will be hoping the addition of Aussie Twenty20 supremo Adam Voges – who performed superbly for Nottinghamshire in the same competition in 2012 – can bring a change in fortunes.

HEAD COACH: RICHARD SCOTT

Scott had a six-year county career with Hampshire and Gloucestershire, as well as playing some 2nd XI matches for Middlesex. After a spell as Dorset's director of cricket he returned to Lord's in 2007 to take charge of the 2nd XI before being elevated to head coach midway through the 2009 season when Toby Radford stepped down unexpectedly. He was given the role on a permanent basis after impressing in difficult circumstances and, alongside managing director of cricket Angus Fraser, he has helped rejuvenate the club in recent seasons.

www.middlesexccc.com / tel: 0207 289 1300

FIRST-CLASS AVERAGES 2012

	Mat	Inns	NO	Runs	HS	Ave	SR	100	50	4s	6s
AJ Strauss	4	7	2	277	127*	55.40	52.66	1	1	31	2
AB London	1	2	1	40	30	40.00	39.21	0	0	6	0
CJL Rogers	17	31	2	1108	173	38.20	57.58	3	6	134	5
JL Denly	16	28	4	840	134*	35.00	49.18	2	4	112	5
NJ Dexter	13	23	2	701	125	33.38	50.00	2	4	89	2
DJ Malan	17	27	0	897	140	33.22	50.44	2	4	110	2
SD Robson	16	29	2	814	117	30.14	44.65	1	4	95	0
SP Crook	6	10	0	285	67	28.50	81.89	0	2	34	5
OP Rayner	11	15	2	359	143*	27.61	45.73	1	1	42	3
TJ Murtagh	16	22	7	391	45	26.06	59.78	0	0	49	4
GK Berg	16	24	1	526	83	22.86	54.90	0	3	53	2
TS Roland-Jones	15	21	6	296	52	19.73	48.20	0	1	35	2
EJG Morgan	5	7	1	109	71	18.16	40.07	0	1	9	2
JA Simpson	14	21	2	343	49*	18.05	47.11	0	0	36	2
TMJ Smith	1	2	0	31	31	15.50	30.39	0	0	4	0
RH Patel	3	5	2	46	20	15.33	57.50	0	0	7	0
AM Rossington	3	5	0	62	29	12.40	30.69	0	0	5	0
A Balbirnie	1	2	0	17	14	8.50	44.73	0	0	3	0
CD Collymore	7	10	6	29	8	7.25	22.30	0	0	1	0
ST Finn	5	6	4	1	1*	0.50	4.54	0	0	0	0

Batting

	Overs	Mdns	Runs	Wkts	BBI	BBM	Ave	Econ	SR	5w	10w
ST Finn	170.0	39	538	28	4/43	7/98	19.21	3.16	36.4	0	0
TS Roland-Jones	405.0	87	1245	64	6/66	10/118	19.45	3.07	37.9	4	1
TJ Murtagh	526.3	127	1455	61	5/37	6/68	23.85	2.76	51.7	2	0
RH Patel	104.0	12	356	14	4/72	8/198	25.42	3.42	44.5	0	0
NJ Dexter	115.0	25	332	12	3/23	3/37	27.66	2.88	57.5	0	0
GK Berg	329.4	73	1014	35	3/25	5/85	28.97	3.07	56.5	0	0
SP Crook	158.3	25	534	18	5/48	7/136	29.66	3.36	52.8	1	0
DJ Malan	63.2	13	227	7	5/61	5/61	32.42	3.58	54.2	1	0
OP Rayner	240.5	38	590	18	4/67	5/130	32.77	2.44	80.2	0	0
CD Collymore	187.1	44	540	11	3/66	3/66	49.09	2.88	102.0	0	0
TMJ Smith	27.3	3	71	1	1/71	1/71	71.00	2.58	165.0	0	0
JL Denly	27.0	2	104	1	1/18	1/18	104.00	3.85	162.0	0	0
A Balbirnie	8.0	0	24	0	-	-	-	3.00	-	0	0
SD Robson	4.5	0	17	0	-	-	-	3.51	-	0	0

Bowling

Catches/Stumpings:
48 Simpson (inc 5st), 25 Malan, 13 Berg, 12 Rayner, Robson, 10 Rossington (inc 1st), Dexter, 7 Strauss, Finn, Denly, Rogers, 6 Morgan, 5 Murtagh, 3 Patel, Roland-Jones, 2 Crook

LIST A AVERAGES 2012

Batting

	Mat	Inns	NO	Runs	HS	Ave	SR	100	50	4s	6s
JH Davey	3	3	2	88	53*	88.00	84.61	0	1	6	0
EJG Morgan	6	4	1	263	120*	87.66	146.92	2	0	19	17
CJL Rogers	8	8	4	335	122*	83.75	101.20	1	2	35	3
DJ Malan	11	11	2	466	134	51.77	99.36	1	2	43	11
JL Denly	8	8	1	267	96*	38.14	80.18	0	2	26	2
PR Stirling	9	8	0	256	119	32.00	110.34	1	0	28	6
GK Berg	10	6	0	165	61	27.50	105.09	0	1	13	2
TMJ Smith	8	2	1	23	16	23.00	52.27	0	0	1	0
JA Simpson	9	5	2	55	29	18.33	107.84	0	0	4	0
NJ Dexter	11	8	1	106	54*	15.14	86.17	0	1	13	0
OP Rayner	6	3	1	27	14	13.50	142.10	0	0	1	0
AM Rossington	2	2	0	22	17	11.00	91.66	0	0	3	0
SP Crook	10	4	1	17	9*	5.66	89.47	0	0	0	1
ST Finn	3	1	0	4	4	4.00	133.33	0	0	1	0
AB London	1	1	0	3	3	3.00	30.00	0	0	0	0
SD Robson	1	1	0	3	3	3.00	23.07	0	0	0	0
CD Collymore	4	1	0	1	1	1.00	50.00	0	0	0	0
AJ Ireland	1	1	0	0	0	0.00	0.00	0	0	0	0
TJ Murtagh	2	2	1	0	0*	0.00	0.00	0	0	0	0
GS Sandhu	1	1	0	0	0	0.00	0.00	0	0	0	0
TE Scollay	1	1	1	2	2*	-	28.57	0	0	0	0

Bowling

	Overs	Mdns	Runs	Wkts	BBI	Ave	Econ	SR	4w	5w
GS Sandhu	6.0	0	28	3	3/28	9.33	4.66	12.0	0	0
JL Denly	1.2	0	10	1	1/6	10.00	7.50	8.0	0	0
TS Roland-Jones	29.0	2	136	11	3/24	12.36	4.68	15.8	0	0
PR Stirling	33.0	0	178	9	4/27	19.77	5.39	22.0	1	0
SP Crook	54.0	0	303	14	3/26	21.64	5.61	23.1	0	0
ST Finn	24.0	2	109	5	3/30	21.80	4.54	28.8	0	0
OP Rayner	21.0	0	128	3	2/29	42.66	6.09	42.0	0	0
JH Davey	21.0	0	136	3	2/35	45.33	6.47	42.0	0	0
TMJ Smith	33.0	1	186	4	3/30	46.50	5.63	49.5	0	0
DJ Malan	6.0	0	47	1	1/3	47.00	7.83	36.0	0	0
NJ Dexter	45.0	0	308	6	2/45	51.33	6.84	45.0	0	0
CD Collymore	25.0	2	104	2	1/20	52.00	4.16	75.0	0	0
TJ Murtagh	14.0	0	109	2	1/34	54.50	7.78	42.0	0	0
GK Berg	49.1	0	287	4	2/33	71.75	5.83	73.7	0	0
AJ Ireland	10.0	0	74	1	1/74	74.00	7.40	60.0	0	0
REM Williams	4.0	1	20	0	-	-	5.00	-	0	0

Catches/Stumpings:
6 Smith, 5 Stirling, Berg, Malan, 4 Simpson, Rogers, 3 Rayner, 2 Rossington (inc 1st), Morgan, Denly, 1 Davey, Collymore, Crook, Dexter

T20 AVERAGES 2012

	Mat	Inns	NO	Runs	HS	Ave	SR	100	50	4s	6s
PR Stirling	7	7	1	271	82*	45.16	142.63	0	3	32	8
EJG Morgan	1	1	0	36	36	36.00	200.00	0	0	1	3
JL Denly	8	8	1	199	90*	28.42	101.01	0	2	18	2
DJ Malan	10	10	2	188	46	23.50	115.33	0	0	19	2
NJ Dexter	10	8	1	155	42	22.14	101.30	0	0	16	1
GK Berg	9	7	2	98	39	19.60	97.02	0	0	9	1
OP Rayner	10	7	3	76	39*	19.00	131.03	0	0	5	2
O Wilkin	3	3	1	38	28	19.00	122.58	0	0	3	1
TE Scollay	1	1	0	19	19	19.00	86.36	0	0	0	1
SP Crook	8	7	1	90	25	15.00	173.07	0	0	6	7
JA Simpson	10	7	0	75	32	10.71	93.75	0	0	4	1
AM Rossington	6	6	0	57	22	9.50	93.44	0	0	5	1
TS Roland-Jones	8	4	2	13	7*	6.50	86.66	0	0	1	0
CJL Rogers	4	4	0	18	11	4.50	75.00	0	0	2	0
TJ Murtagh	3	2	1	2	1*	2.00	50.00	0	0	0	0
TMJ Smith	10	3	3	11	5*	-	183.33	0	0	2	0

Batting

	Overs	Mdns	Runs	Wkts	BBI	Ave	Econ	SR	4w	5w
O Wilkin	4.0	0	20	4	3/12	5.00	5.00	6.0	0	0
GK Berg	26.0	0	205	10	3/17	20.50	7.88	15.6	0	0
TS Roland-Jones	28.0	0	228	11	4/25	20.72	8.14	15.2	1	0
SP Crook	22.0	0	168	7	2/21	24.00	7.63	18.8	0	0
TJ Murtagh	8.2	0	50	2	1/13	25.00	6.00	25.0	0	0
DJ Malan	3.0	0	26	1	1/17	26.00	8.66	18.0	0	0
NJ Dexter	23.0	0	195	7	3/22	27.85	8.47	19.7	0	0
TMJ Smith	34.0	0	245	8	3/24	30.62	7.20	25.5	0	0
PR Stirling	12.0	0	89	2	1/24	44.50	7.41	36.0	0	0
OP Rayner	31.4	0	192	3	2/16	64.00	6.06	63.3	0	0
ST Finn	4.0	0	15	0	-	-	3.75	-	0	0

Bowling

Catches/Stumpings:
5 Simpson (inc 1st), Dexter, 4 Wilkin, Denly, 3 Crook, Malan, Smith, 2 Davey, Morgan, Rossington, Rayner, 1 Murtagh, Rogers, Stirling, Berg

NORTHAMPTONSHIRE

FORMED: 1878
HOME GROUND: County Ground, Wantage Road
ONE-DAY NAME: Steelbacks
CAPTAIN: Stephen Peters (Championship), Alex Wakely (YB40 and FL t20)
2012 RESULTS: CC2: 8/9; CB40: 6/7 in Group C; FL t20: 6/6 in Midlands/Wales/West Group
HONOURS: Gillette/NatWest/C&G/FP Trophy: (2) 1976, 1992; Benson & Hedges Cup: 1980

THE LOWDOWN

Fans and players had to endure terrible weather across much of the country last year but the inclement conditions affected Northants more than most. Losing over 52 hours of cricket to bad weather, the county were only able to muster four victories across all competitions in 2012. Newly appointed Championship captain Stephen Peters topped their run-scoring charts in four-day cricket but the standout performer with the bat was Rob Newton, who added to his growing reputation with three Championship tons, including a century in each innings against Division Two champions Derbyshire in August. Former England U19 skipper Alex Wakely will share captaincy duties with Peters, leading the side in the Yorkshire Bank 40 and Friends Life t20 after Andrew Hall decided to focus on his own form midway through last season. The loss of Jack Brooks to Yorkshire and the release of Chaminda Vaas has left a gaping hole in the seam department, but the re-signing of Steven Crook from Middlesex and the capture of Australian Test paceman Trent Copeland for the first half of the season should go some way to remedying that. In the Friends Life t20 the Steelbacks will be buoyed by the return of hard-hitting Aussie allrounder Cameron White. Having skippered his country in Twenty20 cricket, White has a wealth of short-format experience and he made it count in last year's competition by smashing 228 runs at an average of 57.

HEAD COACH: DAVID RIPLEY

Ripley has been a loyal servant of Northamptonshire both as a player and coach throughout his cricketing career. He represented Northants in 307 first-class matches and 281 one-day matches, scoring over 10,000 runs and claiming over 1,000 dismissals as wicketkeeper during his 17-year career. Ripley left his position as 2nd XI coach and took charge of the first team in July 2012 when David Capel parted company with the club.

FIRST-CLASS AVERAGES 2012

Batting

	Mat	Inns	NO	Runs	HS	Ave	SR	100	50	4s	6s
CD de Lange	4	5	4	156	40*	156.00	39.29	0	0	19	0
RI Newton	13	20	3	751	119*	44.17	69.02	3	2	91	9
JD Middlebrook	15	22	4	714	121	39.66	45.47	2	4	82	5
DJG Sales	14	21	3	706	140	39.22	50.79	2	3	91	0
NJ O'Brien	11	17	2	580	182	38.66	41.22	1	3	60	0
SD Peters	15	23	2	763	148	36.33	45.88	2	3	82	2
AG Wakely	14	21	2	690	96	36.31	47.06	0	5	74	4
DJ Willey	15	18	4	489	76	34.92	71.70	0	4	53	6
RA White	2	3	1	62	42	31.00	84.93	0	0	10	0
KJ Coetzer	13	19	0	563	120	29.63	44.40	1	2	76	2
D Murphy	10	11	1	252	54	25.20	38.18	0	1	33	4
OP Stone	3	3	1	47	26*	23.50	65.27	0	0	8	0
AJ Hall	12	19	1	343	79	19.05	41.82	0	3	38	0
LM Daggett	14	14	5	110	26*	12.22	33.23	0	0	15	0
DA Burton	1	1	0	11	11	11.00	29.72	0	0	1	0
JA Brooks	10	10	3	54	22	7.71	43.90	0	0	4	2
WPUJC Vaas	6	4	1	19	13*	6.33	22.61	0	0	2	0
RI Keogh	1	1	0	6	6	6.00	21.42	0	0	1	0
L Evans	2	3	0	5	5	1.66	17.24	0	0	0	0
BHN Howgego	1	1	0	1	1	1.00	3.70	0	0	0	0

Bowling

	Overs	Mdns	Runs	Wkts	BBI	BBM	Ave	Econ	SR	5w	10w
L Evans	65.0	16	214	12	4/38	6/101	17.83	3.29	32.5	0	0
AJ Hall	293.5	73	812	34	5/50	8/87	23.88	2.76	51.8	1	0
DJ Willey	440.1	90	1474	43	5/39	8/92	34.27	3.34	61.4	1	0
JA Brooks	259.4	66	821	23	5/61	7/137	35.69	3.16	67.7	2	0
JD Middlebrook	346.2	100	883	24	5/63	6/110	36.79	2.54	86.5	1	0
OP Stone	64.0	13	202	5	1/6	2/41	40.40	3.15	76.8	0	0
LM Daggett	372.1	95	1218	27	4/76	4/67	45.11	3.27	82.7	0	0
WPUJC Vaas	107.0	28	280	6	2/4	2/4	46.66	2.61	107.0	0	0
DA Burton	13.0	1	52	1	1/44	1/52	52.00	4.00	78.0	0	0
CD de Lange	54.0	11	176	3	1/11	2/86	58.66	3.25	108.0	0	0
RI Keogh	20.0	5	69	1	1/69	1/69	69.00	3.45	120.0	0	0
KJ Coetzer	19.0	1	74	1	1/9	1/9	74.00	3.89	114.0	0	0
NJ O'Brien	1.0	0	3	0	-	-	-	3.00	-	0	0
AG Wakely	7.0	0	35	0	-	-	-	5.00	-	0	0

Catches/Stumpings:
25 Murphy (inc 2st), 10 Peters, 9 O'Brien (inc 1st), Wakely, 6 Sales, Middlebrook, 5 Coetzer, Daggett, 4 Hall, 3 Stone, Newton, Willey

LIST A AVERAGES 2012

Batting

	Mat	Inns	NO	Runs	HS	Ave	SR	100	50	4s	6s
AG Wakely	10	9	1	366	85	45.75	81.87	0	4	27	6
DJG Sales	9	8	1	313	74	44.71	91.25	0	4	25	4
AJ Hall	5	4	1	102	52*	34.00	79.06	0	1	4	1
SD Peters	2	2	0	61	39	30.50	54.46	0	0	3	2
CAL Davis	2	2	0	57	54	28.50	90.47	0	1	7	0
RI Newton	7	7	0	160	45	22.85	99.37	0	0	18	3
KJ Coetzer	10	10	1	190	68	21.11	89.62	0	1	29	2
RI Keogh	6	5	1	82	30	20.50	63.07	0	0	7	0
CD de Lange	9	7	3	78	27*	19.50	79.59	0	0	4	2
NJ O'Brien	7	7	1	115	46	19.16	61.49	0	0	7	1
RA White	2	2	0	38	29	19.00	59.37	0	0	1	2
D Murphy	7	6	2	67	18*	16.75	95.71	0	0	7	1
DJ Willey	7	6	0	75	24	12.50	92.59	0	0	10	0
DA Burton	5	4	3	12	5*	12.00	92.30	0	0	0	0
JD Middlebrook	9	7	2	56	37	11.20	57.73	0	0	2	0
JA Brooks	3	1	0	5	5	5.00	62.50	0	0	0	0
OP Stone	8	6	3	10	7*	3.33	30.30	0	0	0	0
LM Daggett	6	2	0	1	1	0.50	11.11	0	0	0	0
L Evans	2	1	0	0	0	0.00	0.00	0	0	0	0

Bowling

	Overs	Mdns	Runs	Wkts	BBI	Ave	Econ	SR	4w	5w
LM Daggett	28.0	1	136	12	4/31	11.33	4.85	14.0	3	0
CD de Lange	44.0	1	191	12	3/31	15.91	4.34	22.0	0	0
AG Wakely	2.0	0	17	1	1/17	17.00	8.50	12.0	0	0
L Evans	8.0	0	46	2	2/46	23.00	5.75	24.0	0	0
WPUJC Vaas	11.0	2	51	2	1/12	25.50	4.63	33.0	0	0
JD Middlebrook	42.0	1	182	7	3/14	26.00	4.33	36.0	0	0
KJ Coetzer	6.0	0	38	1	1/25	38.00	6.33	36.0	0	0
AJ Hall	15.1	0	106	2	1/22	53.00	6.98	45.5	0	0
DJ Willey	27.1	0	138	2	1/7	69.00	5.07	81.5	0	0
DA Burton	17.1	0	90	1	1/48	90.00	5.24	103.0	0	0
OP Stone	31.4	2	184	2	1/12	92.00	5.81	95.0	0	0
JA Brooks	12.0	0	73	0	-	-	6.08	-	0	0
RI Keogh	18.0	0	109	0	-	-	6.05	-	0	0
SA Sweeney	2.0	0	17	0	-	-	8.50	-	0	0
RA White	2.0	0	12	0	-	-	6.00	-	0	0

Catches/Stumpings:
3 Murphy (inc 1st), O'Brien, Stone, de Lange, 2 Burton, Willey, Coetzer, 1 Peters, Daggett, Newton, Sales, Wakely

N

T20 AVERAGES 2012

Batting

	Mat	Inns	NO	Runs	HS	Ave	SR	100	50	4s	6s
CL White	9	8	4	228	62*	57.00	131.03	0	2	11	10
JD Middlebrook	9	4	2	63	23	31.50	87.50	0	0	1	1
KJ Coetzer	8	8	1	198	44	28.28	117.85	0	0	20	5
DJ Willey	9	8	3	105	30*	21.00	100.96	0	0	12	0
NJ O'Brien	3	3	0	58	38	19.33	82.85	0	0	5	0
RI Newton	7	6	0	107	38	17.83	127.38	0	0	7	3
AG Wakely	9	9	2	121	54*	17.28	93.07	0	1	13	0
D Murphy	6	4	2	33	18*	16.50	117.85	0	0	4	0
WPUJC Vaas	7	3	1	29	11*	14.50	111.53	0	0	5	0
CD de Lange	9	3	2	12	6*	12.00	75.00	0	0	0	0
RA White	3	3	0	14	5	4.66	58.33	0	0	1	0
RI Keogh	5	1	0	1	1	1.00	50.00	0	0	0	0
BM Duckett	1	1	1	5	5*	-	41.66	0	0	0	0

Bowling

	Overs	Mdns	Runs	Wkts	BBI	Ave	Econ	SR	4w	5w
WPUJC Vaas	21.0	0	131	7	2/15	18.71	6.23	18.0	0	0
CD de Lange	24.1	0	150	8	3/15	18.75	6.20	18.1	0	0
OP Stone	5.0	0	38	2	2/26	19.00	7.60	15.0	0	0
JA Brooks	12.0	0	97	5	2/23	19.40	8.08	14.4	0	0
LM Daggett	6.2	0	43	2	2/22	21.50	6.78	19.0	0	0
JD Middlebrook	26.4	1	206	8	3/16	25.75	7.72	20.0	0	0
DJ Willey	23.5	0	195	5	1/5	39.00	8.18	28.6	0	0
DA Burton	3.0	0	24	0	-	-	8.00	-	0	0
RI Keogh	4.0	0	27	0	-	-	6.75	-	0	0
CL White	5.0	0	41	0	-	-	8.20	-	0	0

Catches/Stumpings:
4 Coetzer, 3 Keogh, de Lange, 2 O'Brien, White, Wakely, White, 1 Stone, Willey, Murphy (inc 1st)

NOTTINGHAMSHIRE

FORMED: 1841
HOME GROUND: Trent Bridge, Nottingham
ONE-DAY NAME: Outlaws
CAPTAIN: Chris Read (Championship and YB40), David Hussey (FL t20)
2012 RESULTS: CC1: 5/9; CB40: 4/7 in Group B; FL t20: Quarter-finalists
HONOURS: Championship: (6) 1907, 1929, 1981, 1987, 2005, 2010; Gillette/NatWest/C&G/FP Trophy: 1987; Benson & Hedges Cup: 1989; Sunday League: 1991

THE LOWDOWN

One of the country's most consistent sides in recent years, Nottinghamshire have been in the top division of the County Championship for six years and won the trophy as recently as 2010. But they frequently find themselves without the services of their best English players. Stuart Broad and Graeme Swann are barely around, while the likes of James Taylor, Samit Patel and Alex Hales are frequently involved in international cricket of some kind. Promising youngsters such as Sam Wood and Sam Kelsall can expect further opportunities as a result. Meanwhile, Notts have recruited shrewdly for 2013. Middlesex-bound Adam Voges will not return, but in the first part of the season Aussie opener Ed Cowan will try to solve the Outlaws' troublesome top order problem, while club stalwart David Hussey will take over overseas duties later in the season and captain the side in the Friends Life t20. His experience could prove invaluable. The other notable signing is that of Yorkshireman Ajmal Shahzad, who will add firepower to a steady bowling line-up. Unlikely to be called upon by England in the short-term, it will be fascinating to see how Shahzad fares at seam-friendly Trent Bridge this year.

DIRECTOR OF CRICKET: MICK NEWELL

Newell was heavily linked with the Bangladesh coach's role when it came up last summer, but eventually decided not to apply for the position because the timing wasn't right. But there's no doubting he's an ambitious and highly respected coach. Newell spent eight years with Nottinghamshire as a player, opening the batting for the county between 1984 and 1992. Ten years later he took control of team affairs and since then has guided Notts to two Championship titles and two second-place finishes. As well as regaining the four-day trophy, a first one-day trophy for 22 years must surely be on Newell's wishlist before he looks to move on.

FIRST-CLASS AVERAGES 2012

Batting

	Mat	Inns	NO	Runs	HS	Ave	SR	100	50	4s	6s
CMW Read	17	26	4	1014	104*	46.09	57.54	1	8	130	8
MH Wessels	13	20	0	905	199	45.25	71.37	3	1	131	4
SJ Mullaney	6	10	1	391	94	43.44	55.14	0	4	43	10
MJ Lumb	15	25	0	971	171	38.84	46.88	3	3	137	2
JWA Taylor	15	24	4	709	163*	35.45	47.14	2	1	85	2
AD Hales	16	26	1	857	155*	34.28	57.28	2	4	128	1
NJ Edwards	9	16	1	512	195	34.13	46.84	1	1	68	5
PJ Franks	11	19	7	389	86*	32.41	52.85	0	3	47	3
AC Voges	9	12	2	313	105	31.30	43.35	1	2	32	0
SR Patel	9	14	2	329	69	27.41	47.88	0	2	41	1
SKW Wood	1	2	0	47	45	23.50	39.83	0	0	5	0
BJ Phillips	14	20	4	286	47	17.87	51.34	0	0	44	1
S Kelsall	1	2	0	35	35	17.50	46.05	0	0	3	0
LJ Fletcher	9	14	5	116	42*	12.88	52.96	0	0	19	1
GG White	6	11	2	109	30*	12.11	40.22	0	0	18	0
AR Adams	12	14	0	151	29	10.78	100.66	0	0	17	7
SCJ Broad	2	4	1	30	12	10.00	85.71	0	0	4	1
A Carter	10	9	4	36	17*	7.20	45.00	0	0	3	1
GP Swann	3	5	0	23	12	4.60	79.31	0	0	4	0
HF Gurney	10	9	1	10	6	1.25	13.33	0	0	2	0

Bowling

	Overs	Mdns	Runs	Wkts	BBI	BBM	Ave	Econ	SR	5w	10w
AC Voges	7.0	2	6	1	1/2	1/2	6.00	0.85	42.0	0	0
GP Swann	87.2	21	188	10	3/26	5/56	18.80	2.15	52.4	0	0
AR Adams	344.3	63	1035	54	7/32	10/50	19.16	3.00	38.2	4	1
LJ Fletcher	266.5	77	708	28	4/21	7/98	25.28	2.65	57.1	0	0
BJ Phillips	345.3	105	841	32	4/33	5/62	26.28	2.43	64.7	0	0
SKW Wood	28.0	2	84	3	3/64	3/84	28.00	3.00	56.0	0	0
HF Gurney	234.3	52	713	21	4/40	4/40	33.95	3.04	67.0	0	0
GG White	157.4	34	532	15	4/97	6/175	35.46	3.37	63.0	0	0
A Carter	261.2	43	938	26	4/55	4/97	36.07	3.58	60.3	0	0
SR Patel	164.4	30	536	14	4/67	7/154	38.28	3.25	70.5	0	0
PJ Franks	204.5	32	667	16	4/47	6/90	41.68	3.25	76.8	0	0
MH Wessels	15.0	3	43	1	1/40	1/40	43.00	2.86	90.0	0	0
SCJ Broad	62.0	8	225	4	3/67	3/127	56.25	3.62	93.0	0	0
MJ Lumb	2.0	0	13	0	-	-	-	6.50	-	0	0
SJ Mullaney	16.0	2	41	0	-	-	-	2.56	-	0	0
JWA Taylor	2.0	0	16	0	-	-	-	8.00	-	0	0

Catches/Stumpings:
46 Read (inc 1st), 18 Hales, 12 Voges, 9 Wessels (inc 1st), 8 Adams, Taylor, 7 Patel, Lumb, 6 Edwards, 5 Mullaney, Phillips, 2 White, Fletcher, Carter, 1 Broad, Swann, Franks

LIST A AVERAGES 2012

Batting

	Mat	Inns	NO	Runs	HS	Ave	SR	100	50	4s	6s
JWA Taylor	8	8	2	385	115*	64.16	91.88	1	2	30	7
CMW Read	11	10	6	236	71*	59.00	98.33	0	2	15	6
NJ Edwards	1	1	0	58	58	58.00	105.45	0	1	7	1
AC Voges	10	10	4	232	74	38.66	90.27	0	2	15	3
PJ Franks	3	2	0	65	57	32.50	110.16	0	1	5	3
SR Patel	11	11	0	340	82	30.90	77.80	0	2	29	4
AD Hales	12	12	0	356	94	29.66	92.46	0	2	40	3
GG White	8	5	3	57	39*	28.50	93.44	0	0	6	1
MH Wessels	12	12	0	312	55	26.00	113.45	0	2	29	12
MJ Lumb	10	10	0	240	84	24.00	96.38	0	2	30	3
SJ Mullaney	11	6	2	75	26*	18.75	70.75	0	0	2	1
SL Elstone	3	3	1	33	16	16.50	89.18	0	0	2	0
A Carter	7	2	1	10	7*	10.00	47.61	0	0	0	0
JT Ball	8	3	0	19	11	6.33	67.85	0	0	1	0
LJ Fletcher	3	2	0	2	1	1.00	16.66	0	0	0	0
HF Gurney	7	2	2	15	13*	-	125.00	0	0	0	2
DJ Pattinson	7	1	1	7	7*	-	100.00	0	0	1	0

Bowling

	Overs	Mdns	Runs	Wkts	BBI	Ave	Econ	SR	4w	5w
GG White	45.3	2	232	12	3/28	19.33	5.09	22.7	0	0
DJ Pattinson	36.4	1	239	12	3/27	19.91	6.51	18.3	0	0
A Carter	46.3	0	307	12	4/45	25.58	6.60	23.2	1	0
SR Patel	80.0	1	428	15	3/47	28.53	5.35	32.0	0	0
HF Gurney	44.0	3	214	7	4/22	30.57	4.86	37.7	1	0
JT Ball	32.4	0	156	5	3/38	31.20	4.77	39.2	0	0
AC Voges	25.4	0	132	3	3/37	44.00	5.14	51.3	0	0
SJ Mullaney	64.0	2	287	6	3/44	47.83	4.48	64.0	0	0
PJ Franks	15.0	0	118	1	1/44	118.00	7.86	90.0	0	0
SL Elstone	2.0	0	10	0	-	-	5.00	-	0	0
LJ Fletcher	10.0	0	59	0	-	-	5.90	-	0	0

Catches/Stumpings:

12 Read (inc 3st), 10 Wessels, 9 Voges, 5 Lumb, Mullaney, 3 Carter, 2 White, Patel, 1 Elstone, Pattinson, Taylor, Hales

T20 AVERAGES 2012

	Mat	Inns	NO	Runs	HS	Ave	SR	100	50	4s	6s
CMW Read	8	4	3	60	21*	60.00	146.34	0	0	5	2
AC Voges	8	8	4	209	70	52.25	120.11	0	1	20	0
JWA Taylor	8	5	2	127	45	42.33	129.59	0	0	11	3
SR Patel	6	5	2	109	60	36.33	149.31	0	1	13	1
MJ Lumb	8	8	1	252	62	36.00	138.46	0	1	25	11
AD Hales	5	5	0	127	88	25.40	139.56	0	1	12	4
MH Wessels	8	8	1	150	53	21.42	153.06	0	1	20	4
SJ Mullaney	8	2	1	16	12*	16.00	133.33	0	0	2	0
GG White	3	1	1	4	4*	-	133.33	0	0	0	0

Batting

	Overs	Mdns	Runs	Wkts	BBI	Ave	Econ	SR	4w	5w
AC Voges	4.3	0	23	4	2/6	5.75	5.11	6.7	0	0
A Carter	23.0	0	173	9	3/12	19.22	7.52	15.3	0	0
GG White	7.4	0	58	3	2/19	19.33	7.56	15.3	0	0
SJ Mullaney	26.0	0	194	9	4/19	21.55	7.46	17.3	1	0
SR Patel	24.0	0	170	7	3/26	24.28	7.08	20.5	0	0
DJ Pattinson	22.0	0	167	6	2/21	27.83	7.59	22.0	0	0
HF Gurney	25.0	0	179	6	2/26	29.83	7.16	25.0	0	0
JT Ball	3.0	0	33	0	-	-	11.00	-	0	0

Bowling

Catches/Stumpings:
7 Voges, 4 Read (inc 2st), Patel, 3 Mullaney, Wessels, 1 Ball, Elstone, White, Hales, Pattinson, Carter, Gurney, Lumb, Taylor

SOMERSET

FORMED: 1875
HOME GROUND: County Ground, Taunton
CAPTAIN: Marcus Trescothick
2012 RESULTS: CC1: 2/9; CB40: 3/7 in Group B; FL t20: Semi-finalists
HONOURS: Gillette/NatWest/C&G/FP Trophy: (3) 1979, 1983, 2001; Benson & Hedges Cup: (2) 1981, 1982; Sunday League: 1979; Twenty20 Cup: 2005

THE LOWDOWN

Marcus Trescothick's side may have ditched their pyjama moniker several years ago, but you could have been forgiven for calling them the 'Somerset Bridesmaids' after a frustrating string of near misses in the last few years. Despite a strong showing in four-day cricket they never really looked like overhauling Warwickshire, while 12 months on from a brace of showpiece defeats they fell at the penultimate hurdle in the FL t20. On the bright side, it was another impressive season across all three competitions, and had the skipper not been injured for much of the summer it seems likely that they may finally have broken their sequence of near misses. With very few changes to the squad over the winter there remains a wealth of talent at Taunton, and the desire to get over the finish line will be burning stronger than ever. There are high hopes that some of the club's young talent – including the gifted Overton twins – will really come of age this year, and if Somerset's frontline seamers can provide a little more support for the impressive Pete Trego all the ingredients are there for an assault on that elusive Championship pennant.

HEAD COACH: ANDY HURRY

An ex-Royal Marine, Hurry is not hampered by the fact that he never played first-class cricket, and having worked for free when he first linked up with Somerset's youth system, his time at Taunton has been characterised by continual progression. Appointed to the top job in 2006, he has lifted the first team from the foot of the Championship's second tier to regular title contenders, and three consecutive trips to Finals Day are proof of Somerset's status as one of the finest limited overs sides in the country. The challenge now is to turn consistency into silverware. In 2012, Hurry took charge of the England side that competed in the Hong Kong Sixes.

FIRST-CLASS AVERAGES 2012

Batting

	Mat	Inns	NO	Runs	HS	Ave	SR	100	50	4s	6s
NRD Compton	12	19	6	1427	236	109.76	47.22	5	7	137	7
JC Hildreth	17	26	3	1214	268	52.78	68.08	4	5	164	2
C Kieswetter	11	17	4	654	152	50.30	67.84	1	2	89	11
ME Trescothick	9	13	0	506	146	38.92	53.09	2	1	77	0
PD Trego	17	22	4	630	92	35.00	77.30	0	4	86	10
AV Suppiah	17	26	0	769	124	29.57	56.92	2	5	107	9
CAJ Meschede	7	7	1	172	62	28.66	67.18	0	1	30	1
J Overton	3	4	2	55	34*	27.50	91.66	0	0	11	0
JC Buttler	12	16	1	400	93	26.66	60.42	0	2	60	4
AJ Dibble	1	2	0	44	43	22.00	89.79	0	0	6	1
CR Jones	5	7	0	150	50	21.42	38.86	0	1	23	0
GM Hussain	6	7	4	55	29	18.33	39.00	0	0	9	0
AWR Barrow	9	15	0	186	47	12.40	41.05	0	0	29	0
C Overton	7	8	1	75	50	10.71	52.08	0	1	12	0
VD Philander	5	6	0	62	38	10.33	49.20	0	0	6	2
L Gregory	4	4	0	40	18	10.00	49.38	0	0	6	0
AC Thomas	9	11	1	96	39*	9.60	40.00	0	0	16	0
GH Dockrell	11	10	4	54	13*	9.00	18.06	0	0	7	0
SD Snell	2	2	0	18	10	9.00	42.85	0	0	2	0
Abdur Rehman	4	5	0	43	17	8.60	37.39	0	0	4	1
SI Mahmood	3	4	1	25	13	8.33	58.13	0	0	2	1
MTC Waller	3	3	0	24	17	8.00	38.09	0	0	3	0
SP Kirby	9	11	5	20	6*	3.33	27.77	0	0	3	0
MJ Leach	2	1	1	0	0*	-	0.00	0	0	0	0

Bowling

	Overs	Mdns	Runs	Wkts	BBI	BBM	Ave	Econ	SR	5w	10w
C Kieswetter	3.0	0	3	2	2/3	2/3	1.50	1.00	9.0	0	0
AJ Dibble	13.0	2	42	3	3/42	3/42	14.00	3.23	26.0	0	0
Abdur Rehman	174.0	50	383	27	9/65	14/101	14.18	2.20	38.6	3	1
CR Jones	2.0	0	17	1	1/17	1/17	17.00	8.50	12.0	0	0
VD Philander	181.1	42	491	23	5/43	7/81	21.34	2.71	47.2	2	0
MJ Leach	20.0	4	43	2	2/37	2/39	21.50	2.15	60.0	0	0
AC Thomas	252.4	50	740	33	6/60	9/108	22.42	2.92	45.9	2	0
GH Dockrell	340.5	80	996	35	6/27	8/62	28.45	2.92	58.4	2	0
GM Hussain	101.4	17	385	13	5/48	5/118	29.61	3.78	46.9	1	0
SI Mahmood	66.1	10	241	8	4/62	6/107	30.12	3.64	49.6	0	0
C Overton	113.1	23	363	12	4/38	6/87	30.25	3.20	56.5	0	0
SP Kirby	225.1	47	735	24	3/34	4/73	30.62	3.26	56.2	0	0
L Gregory	24.0	2	127	4	2/22	2/22	31.75	5.29	36.0	0	0
PD Trego	523.5	125	1609	50	5/53	7/115	32.18	3.07	62.8	2	0
JE Burke	18.0	3	68	2	2/51	2/68	34.00	3.77	54.0	0	0
CAJ Meschede	119.0	22	418	12	3/26	6/64	34.83	3.51	59.5	0	0
MTC Waller	52.0	14	145	4	3/33	3/62	36.25	2.78	78.0	0	0
J Overton	66.0	7	229	6	2/61	3/106	38.16	3.46	66.0	0	0
AP Sutton	30.0	6	99	2	1/31	2/99	49.50	3.30	90.0	0	0
AV Suppiah	80.0	18	232	3	1/8	2/41	77.33	2.90	160.0	0	0
JC Buttler	2.0	0	11	0	-	-	-	5.50	-	0	0
JC Hildreth	2.0	0	30	0	-	-	-	15.00	-	0	0

Catches/Stumpings:
29 Kieswetter (inc 1st), 26 Trescothick, 17 Hildreth, 14 Barrow, 13 Buttler (inc 1st), Trego, 9 Suppiah, 8 Compton, Snell, 5 Dockrell, 4 Waller, C Overton, Kirby, 3 Meschede, 2 Rehman, Philander, Jones, 1 Mahmood, J Overton, Thomas

LIST A AVERAGES 2012

Batting

	Mat	Inns	NO	Runs	HS	Ave	SR	100	50	4s	6s
AWR Barrow	5	3	1	108	72	54.00	87.09	0	1	8	1
NRD Compton	6	6	1	237	81	47.40	77.45	0	3	19	1
JC Buttler	10	8	1	289	71	41.28	90.59	0	2	36	1
ME Trescothick	5	4	1	118	87*	39.33	108.25	0	1	14	1
C Kieswetter	7	7	0	236	103	33.71	122.91	1	1	29	9
PD Trego	11	9	0	245	81	27.22	130.31	0	2	34	6
CAJ Meschede	6	5	1	102	33	25.50	87.17	0	0	8	4
AV Suppiah	7	7	1	144	56	24.00	85.20	0	1	14	2
CR Jones	3	2	0	48	24	24.00	65.75	0	0	4	1
AC Thomas	5	3	2	23	16*	23.00	79.31	0	0	2	0
J Overton	3	3	2	19	10	19.00	63.33	0	0	2	0
L Gregory	10	6	0	103	39	17.16	75.18	0	0	8	0
JC Hildreth	11	10	2	102	26	12.75	70.83	0	0	10	0
C Overton	2	2	0	25	20	12.50	119.04	0	0	2	0
MTC Waller	8	4	1	30	13	10.00	66.66	0	0	1	0
Abdur Rehman	3	2	0	17	9	8.50	73.91	0	0	2	0
GH Dockrell	6	4	1	21	18	7.00	58.33	0	0	1	0
MJ Leach	3	1	0	2	2	2.00	20.00	0	0	0	0
GM Hussain	3	2	2	19	18*	-	135.71	0	0	1	2

Bowling

	Overs	Mdns	Runs	Wkts	BBI	Ave	Econ	SR	4w	5w
Abdur Rehman	20.5	2	73	9	6/16	8.11	3.50	13.8	0	1
J Overton	17.0	1	100	6	4/42	16.66	5.88	17.0	1	0
C Kieswetter	2.0	0	19	1	1/19	19.00	9.50	12.0	0	0
SP Kirby	40.3	1	175	8	3/19	21.87	4.32	30.3	0	0
CAJ Meschede	35.0	0	198	9	4/27	22.00	5.65	23.3	1	0
AC Thomas	27.0	3	112	5	2/13	22.40	4.14	32.4	0	0
RG Mutch	8.0	0	46	2	2/46	23.00	5.75	24.0	0	0
PD Trego	61.4	2	372	15	3/26	24.80	6.03	24.6	0	0
GM Hussain	18.2	0	104	4	2/29	26.00	5.67	27.5	0	0
L Gregory	28.4	0	195	6	2/25	32.50	6.80	28.6	0	0
MTC Waller	34.0	1	180	4	2/29	45.00	5.29	51.0	0	0
AV Suppiah	18.0	0	99	2	1/32	49.50	5.50	54.0	0	0
C Overton	11.0	0	72	1	1/35	72.00	6.54	66.0	0	0
GH Dockrell	28.0	1	168	2	2/32	84.00	6.00	84.0	0	0
MJ Leach	19.0	0	90	1	1/30	90.00	4.73	114.0	0	0

Catches/Stumpings:
7 Kieswetter, 5 Trescothick, Waller, 4 Buttler, Hildreth, 3 C Overton, Dockrell, Suppiah, Gregory, Trego, 2 Barrow, Meschede, 1 Compton, Kirby

T20 AVERAGES 2012

SOMERSET
CRICKET CLUB

	Mat	Inns	NO	Runs	HS	Ave	SR	100	50	4s	6s
C Kieswetter	4	4	1	134	63*	44.66	120.72	0	2	12	4
JC Hildreth	9	8	3	223	107*	44.60	133.53	1	1	30	2
AC Thomas	10	3	2	28	11*	28.00	93.33	0	0	3	0
JC Buttler	10	9	2	195	58*	27.85	116.07	0	1	19	3
L Gregory	7	5	2	83	22	27.66	127.69	0	0	7	2
RE Levi	7	7	0	179	69	25.57	161.26	0	1	18	11
NRD Compton	8	7	2	120	42*	24.00	97.56	0	0	10	2
JA Morkel	5	4	0	81	38	20.25	112.50	0	0	6	3
AV Suppiah	7	5	2	55	18	18.33	114.58	0	0	5	0
KJ O'Brien	6	4	1	52	22	17.33	101.96	0	0	6	1
ME Trescothick	2	2	0	31	19	15.50	140.90	0	0	4	1
CAJ Meschede	3	3	1	19	19*	9.50	118.75	0	0	2	1
PD Trego	8	8	1	52	16	7.42	67.53	0	0	3	0
SD Snell	2	1	0	4	4	4.00	100.00	0	0	0	0
GH Dockrell	7	2	1	2	1*	2.00	22.22	0	0	0	0
SP Kirby	8	1	1	4	4*	-	400.00	0	0	1	0

Batting

	Overs	Mdns	Runs	Wkts	BBI	Ave	Econ	SR	4w	5w
JA Morkel	11.5	0	89	5	3/30	17.80	7.52	14.2	0	0
GH Dockrell	26.0	0	169	9	2/17	18.77	6.50	17.3	0	0
L Gregory	17.3	0	120	6	4/39	20.00	6.85	17.5	1	0
MTC Waller	21.0	0	148	7	4/16	21.14	7.04	18.0	1	0
SP Kirby	26.4	0	171	8	3/37	21.37	6.41	20.0	0	0
AV Suppiah	12.0	0	88	4	2/10	22.00	7.33	18.0	0	0
AC Thomas	33.0	0	282	8	3/17	35.25	8.54	24.7	0	0
PD Trego	11.0	0	72	2	2/23	36.00	6.54	33.0	0	0
KJ O'Brien	8.0	0	63	1	1/15	63.00	7.87	48.0	0	0
CAJ Meschede	4.0	0	39	0	-	-	9.75	-	0	0

Bowling

Catches/Stumpings:
5 Buttler (inc 1st), 4 O'Brien, Waller, Dockrell, Trego, 3 Kieswetter (inc 3st), Levi, Hildreth, Thomas, 2 Compton, 1 Meschede, Trescothick, Morkel, Suppiah

SURREY

FORMED: 1845
GROUND: The Kia Oval
CAPTAIN: Graeme Smith
2012 RESULTS: CC1: 7/9; CB40: 2/7 in Group B; FL t20: 6/6 in South Group
HONOURS: Championship: (19) 1890, 1891, 1892, 1894, 1895, 1899, 1914, 1950, 1952, 1953, 1954, 1955, 1956, 1957, 1958, 1971, 1999, 2000, 2002; Gillette/NatWest/C&G/FP Trophy: 1982; Benson & Hedges Cup: (3) 1974, 1997, 2001; Pro40/National League/CB40: (2) 2003, 2011; Sunday League: 1996; Twenty20 Cup: 2003

THE LOWDOWN

The tragic passing of young batsman Tom Maynard cast a pall over Surrey's 2012 season – a year of promise sadly turning into an exercise in survival – and it is a credit to stand-in skipper Gareth Batty and his side that they were able to rouse themselves to preserve their top-flight Championship status and put in consistent performances in the CB40. In terms of individual achievements, emerging young opener Rory Burns and rapid seamer Stuart Meaker can both be extremely satisfied with their efforts – topping the county's batting and bowling charts respectively – and showing plenty of raw talent that should serve Surrey well for years to come. Of course, the county hopes for a much happier 2013, and the whole club will have been cheered by the signing of two of the most successful captains in the history of the game. South Africa's skipper Graeme Smith will lead the team in between international commitments, while Ricky Ponting will bring experience and excitement to the Twenty20 team. With Vikram Solanki and Gary Keedy also added to the ranks, there's a great mix of youth and experience and – on paper at least – Surrey should be challenging on all fronts.

TEAM DIRECTOR: CHRIS ADAMS

Considerable success as Sussex's skipper (he masterminded the Martlets' maiden, second and third Championship titles between 2003 and 2007) highlighted Adams' leadership credentials, and the former England international doesn't lack the courage of his convictions. Having already championed the development of Surrey's young talent, he has now added plenty of experience to his team, both on and off the pitch, and having dealt impressively with both deficiency and disaster, it is now time to see if 'Grizz' can restore the glory days to The Oval.

FIRST-CLASS AVERAGES 2012

Batting

	Mat	Inns	NO	Runs	HS	Ave	SR	100	50	4s	6s
KP Pietersen	4	7	1	572	234*	95.33	97.27	2	2	71	16
RJ Burns	10	17	2	741	121	49.40	50.16	2	4	98	0
TL Maynard	8	16	2	635	143	45.35	69.62	1	3	91	3
TM Jewell	2	2	0	88	70	44.00	47.82	0	1	9	0
GC Wilson	3	6	1	206	68	41.20	48.47	0	2	26	1
A Harinath	6	11	1	368	109	36.80	40.93	2	0	38	0
RJ Hamilton-Brown	9	18	1	577	115	33.94	58.87	1	4	68	5
JJ Roy	13	23	2	644	83	30.66	75.94	0	3	90	9
GA Edwards	2	2	1	27	17	27.00	45.00	0	0	5	0
Z de Bruyn	15	27	0	709	125	26.25	47.04	1	5	80	5
J Lewis	13	19	6	326	42	25.07	64.55	0	0	39	1
JA Rudolph	5	10	0	229	68	22.90	42.25	0	1	30	1
SM Davies	12	20	0	438	104	21.90	55.44	1	1	48	2
ZS Ansari	8	13	1	234	83*	19.50	34.31	0	1	30	0
M Kartik	7	8	2	113	23*	18.83	67.66	0	0	15	2
SC Meaker	10	14	4	177	41	17.70	35.90	0	0	21	0
CJ Jordan	8	14	1	213	54	16.38	39.96	0	1	26	2
MNW Spriegel	3	5	0	73	25	14.60	45.91	0	0	14	0
GJ Batty	14	24	2	287	36	13.04	39.20	0	0	34	1
MR Ramprakash	5	10	0	107	37	10.70	27.29	0	0	13	0
TE Linley	8	11	4	43	15	6.14	25.59	0	0	5	0
JW Dernbach	7	14	4	55	22	5.50	50.45	0	0	11	1
FOE van den Bergh	1	1	1	16	16*	-	53.33	0	0	3	0
MP Dunn	2	1	1	0	0*	-	0.00	0	0	0	0

Bowling

	Overs	Mdns	Runs	Wkts	BBI	BBM	Ave	Econ	SR	5w	10w
KP Pietersen	11.0	3	27	2	2/24	2/24	13.50	2.45	33.0	0	0
TM Jewell	39.0	11	114	6	3/39	5/90	19.00	2.92	39.0	0	0
M Kartik	251.1	58	597	27	5/69	8/160	22.11	2.37	55.8	1	0
SC Meaker	284.3	51	993	44	8/52	11/167	22.56	3.49	38.7	3	1
TE Linley	188.5	39	570	22	5/45	6/90	25.90	3.01	51.5	2	0
GJ Batty	305.0	71	789	30	6/73	10/142	26.30	2.58	61.0	2	1
JW Dernbach	172.0	39	522	19	3/39	5/73	27.47	3.03	54.3	0	0
J Lewis	335.0	77	980	31	5/41	7/97	31.61	2.92	64.8	1	0
MP Dunn	24.1	1	136	4	3/41	3/86	34.00	5.62	36.2	0	0
GA Edwards	44.5	6	184	5	4/44	5/92	36.80	4.10	53.8	0	0
RJ Hamilton-Brown	13.0	0	38	1	1/14	1/38	38.00	2.92	78.0	0	0
CJ Jordan	160.3	23	599	15	3/29	5/82	39.93	3.73	64.2	0	0
Z de Bruyn	130.0	24	383	6	2/16	2/25	63.83	2.94	130.0	0	0
FOE van den Bergh	23.0	5	69	1	1/69	1/69	69.00	3.00	138.0	0	0
CT Tremlett	27.0	6	82	1	1/82	1/82	82.00	3.03	162.0	0	0
ZS Ansari	16.0	2	55	0	-	-	-	3.43	-	0	0
JJ Roy	1.0	0	1	0	-	-	-	1.00	-	0	0
MNW Spriegel	12.0	2	36	0	-	-	-	3.00	-	0	0

Catches/Stumpings:
25 Davies (inc 1st), 15 Batty, 12 Maynard, 11 Roy, 8 Wilson, 7 Burns, 5 de Bruyn, 4 Linley, Jordan, Hamilton-Brown, 3 Ansari, Kartik, Lewis, 2 Jewell, Ramprakash, Rudolph, Dernbach, 1 Pietersen, Meaker

LIST A AVERAGES 2012

Batting

	Mat	Inns	NO	Runs	HS	Ave	SR	100	50	4s	6s
JA Rudolph	1	1	0	69	69	69.00	77.52	0	1	1	0
ZS Ansari	7	6	2	160	60*	40.00	91.42	0	1	12	4
TL Maynard	5	3	0	118	77	39.33	77.12	0	1	10	0
MNW Spriegel	12	9	1	220	51	27.50	58.82	0	1	9	2
KP Pietersen	3	3	1	54	43	27.00	108.00	0	0	7	0
RJ Hamilton-Brown	10	9	1	204	101	25.50	106.80	1	0	29	2
SM Davies	12	11	0	260	72	23.63	97.37	0	2	39	0
Z de Bruyn	12	9	0	210	57	23.33	65.62	0	2	16	0
RJ Burns	2	2	0	35	32	17.50	74.46	0	0	3	0
GC Wilson	5	4	0	65	29	16.25	60.74	0	0	5	0
GJ Batty	12	9	3	93	24	15.50	72.65	0	0	6	2
J Lewis	9	4	1	39	16	13.00	121.87	0	0	5	0
JJ Roy	12	11	2	115	43	12.77	100.87	0	0	17	1
JW Dernbach	10	3	2	12	10	12.00	100.00	0	0	0	1
M Kartik	9	5	1	23	8	5.75	69.69	0	0	3	0
SC Meaker	11	4	4	27	21*	-	100.00	0	0	3	0

Bowling

	Overs	Mdns	Runs	Wkts	BBI	Ave	Econ	SR	4w	5w
Z de Bruyn	7.4	0	48	5	5/46	9.60	6.26	9.2	0	1
GJ Batty	55.0	0	247	14	3/4	17.64	4.49	23.5	0	0
M Kartik	46.3	2	212	11	4/27	19.27	4.55	25.3	1	0
SC Meaker	39.5	1	189	9	3/24	21.00	4.74	26.5	0	0
MNW Spriegel	46.5	2	190	9	2/14	21.11	4.05	31.2	0	0
JW Dernbach	56.1	3	299	13	3/39	23.00	5.32	25.9	0	0
ZS Ansari	32.0	2	148	6	3/28	24.66	4.62	32.0	0	0
J Lewis	39.0	1	197	4	1/19	49.25	5.05	58.5	0	0
RJ Hamilton-Brown	1.0	0	10	0	-	-	10.00	-	0	0

Catches/Stumpings:
17 Davies (inc 8st), 5 Ansari, 3 Batty, de Bruyn, Spriegel, 2 Wilson, Kartik, Lewis, Hamilton-Brown, Roy, 1 Burns, Maynard, Dernbach, Meaker

T20 AVERAGES 2012

	Mat	Inns	NO	Runs	HS	Ave	SR	100	50	4s	6s
GC Wilson	6	6	3	182	54*	60.66	118.95	0	2	14	4
ZS Ansari	10	9	3	144	38*	24.00	102.85	0	0	13	1
KP Pietersen	5	5	1	93	42	23.25	120.77	0	0	5	4
MNW Spriegel	10	8	2	130	53*	21.66	88.43	0	1	4	3
SM Davies	10	10	0	184	37	18.40	143.75	0	0	28	2
Z de Bruyn	8	6	1	80	30*	16.00	73.39	0	0	5	0
RJ Burns	3	3	0	41	23	13.66	95.34	0	0	2	1
JJ Roy	10	10	0	120	40	12.00	122.44	0	0	11	5
GJ Batty	10	6	2	40	23*	10.00	70.17	0	0	2	0
TL Maynard	1	1	0	7	7	7.00	41.17	0	0	0	0
RJ Hamilton-Brown	4	4	0	23	9	5.75	85.18	0	0	3	0
CT Tremlett	6	2	1	5	5	5.00	55.55	0	0	0	0
M Kartik	9	4	1	8	8*	2.66	100.00	0	0	1	0
SC Meaker	6	1	0	0	0	0.00	-	0	0	0	0
DP Nannes	9	2	2	2	1*	-	100.00	0	0	0	0
JW Dernbach	2	1	1	1	1*	-	100.00	0	0	0	0

Batting

	Overs	Mdns	Runs	Wkts	BBI	Ave	Econ	SR	4w	5w
RJ Hamilton-Brown	1.0	0	5	2	2/5	2.50	5.00	3.0	0	0
JW Dernbach	6.0	0	39	3	2/17	13.00	6.50	12.0	0	0
GJ Batty	31.0	0	162	11	4/13	14.72	5.22	16.9	1	0
CT Tremlett	16.0	0	113	7	3/19	16.14	7.06	13.7	0	0
SC Meaker	10.4	0	101	4	2/20	25.25	9.46	16.0	0	0
M Kartik	31.0	0	179	7	3/16	25.57	5.77	26.5	0	0
ZS Ansari	20.0	0	171	6	2/26	28.50	8.55	20.0	0	0
Z de Bruyn	3.0	0	32	1	1/16	32.00	10.66	18.0	0	0
MNW Spriegel	13.0	0	89	2	1/15	44.50	6.84	39.0	0	0
DP Nannes	21.2	0	205	4	2/23	51.25	9.60	32.0	0	0
CJ Jordan	1.0	0	14	0	-	-	14.00	-	0	0

Bowling

Catches/Stumpings:
9 Davies (inc 6st), 6 Roy, 5 Pietersen, Batty, 2 Burns, Meaker, Spriegel, 1 Hamilton-Brown, de Bruyn

SUSSEX

FORMED: 1839
HOME GROUND: The BrightonandHoveJobs.com County Ground, Hove
ONE-DAY NAME: Sharks
CAPTAIN: Ed Joyce
2012 RESULTS: CC1: 4/9; CB40: Semi-finalists; FL t20: Semi-finalists
HONOURS: Championship: (3) 2003, 2006, 2007; Gillette/NatWest/C&G/FP Trophy: (5) 1963, 1964, 1978, 1986, 2006; Pro40/ National League/CB40: (2) 2008, 2009; Sunday League: 1982; Twenty20 Cup: 2009

THE LOWDOWN

Incremental changes abound at Hove after a respectable if unfulfilling 2012 season. Their Championship form was solid but lacked the cutting edge required to really challenge: five wins – only one fewer than the winners – was set against five defeats, while excellent showings in the group stages of both cup competitions couldn't be translated into knockout success. The club has said goodbye to the great middle-order man Murray Goodwin, while handing Ed Joyce overall captaincy of the club with the highly regarded Chris Nash installed as his deputy. But perhaps the most intriguing new development is the return of Rory Hamilton-Brown for a second stint at the club. It was at Hove that the London-born allrounder initially made his name, before deciding to head back to Surrey, where he'd grown up, as club captain. Now he is back on the south coast with a point to prove. Other notable developments will see the strapping Australian John Hastings come in to buttress an already formidable Twenty20 team, meaning the Sharks be approaching 2013 in a positive frame of mind. If Monty Panesar turns it on again this year, they could be well placed to be back amongst the silverware.

HEAD COACH: MARK ROBINSON

Robinson has been in post at Hove since October 2005 following Peter Moores' move to become the ECB's academy director. His links with the club were already well established, having spent the latter part of his 15-year playing career with the south coast club following profitable spells at Northants and the county of his birth, Yorkshire. In all he took 584 first-class wickets with his nagging right-arm seamers.

FIRST-CLASS AVERAGES 2012

	Mat	Inns	NO	Runs	HS	Ave	SR	100	50	4s	6s
EC Joyce	14	24	3	829	108*	39.47	44.83	2	5	110	4
CD Nash	17	28	2	984	162	37.84	64.35	3	2	132	5
LWP Wells	15	21	2	713	127	37.52	40.41	2	3	102	0
A Khan	8	7	3	142	57*	35.50	64.84	0	1	17	2
JE Anyon	15	19	8	316	64*	28.72	52.23	0	2	33	2
BC Brown	14	22	3	521	76*	27.42	49.80	0	5	70	0
LJ Wright	9	14	1	356	81	27.38	54.68	0	3	45	2
MH Yardy	16	25	2	574	110	24.95	49.74	1	3	63	1
MJ Prior	5	5	0	114	86	22.80	78.62	0	1	10	4
SJ Magoffin	15	19	3	363	41*	22.68	53.53	0	0	47	2
JS Gatting	11	16	3	279	72*	21.46	51.95	0	1	28	8
Naved Arif	8	10	0	184	46	18.40	34.01	0	0	19	1
MW Goodwin	14	23	1	360	77	16.36	36.54	0	2	44	0
KO Wernars	3	4	0	65	50	16.25	43.91	0	1	7	0
LJ Hatchett	3	6	3	32	18*	10.66	26.01	0	0	4	0
WA Adkin	1	2	0	15	9	7.50	37.50	0	0	1	0
MS Panesar	16	16	4	88	31	7.33	53.98	0	0	14	1
MW Machan	2	2	0	10	6	5.00	37.03	0	0	1	0

Batting

	Overs	Mdns	Runs	Wkts	BBI	BBM	Ave	Econ	SR	5w	10w
CJ Liddle	6.0	2	10	1	1/10	1/10	10.00	1.66	36.0	0	0
SJ Magoffin	480.1	161	1143	57	7/34	9/50	20.05	2.38	50.5	2	0
CD Nash	135.2	23	446	21	3/23	5/67	21.23	3.29	38.6	0	0
MS Panesar	514.1	157	1227	53	7/60	13/137	23.15	2.38	58.2	2	1
KO Wernars	44.0	14	121	5	2/16	2/48	24.20	2.75	52.8	0	0
A Khan	167.4	30	564	22	5/25	8/64	25.63	3.36	45.7	2	0
Naved Arif	160.0	26	528	18	3/34	6/116	29.33	3.30	53.3	0	0
MH Yardy	12.0	1	68	2	1/12	1/12	34.00	5.66	36.0	0	0
LJ Hatchett	64.5	12	280	8	3/25	4/113	35.00	4.31	48.6	0	0
LWP Wells	10.0	4	37	1	1/24	1/24	37.00	3.70	60.0	0	0
JE Anyon	429.5	73	1646	42	5/36	6/134	39.19	3.82	61.4	2	0
LJ Wright	79.0	6	327	5	1/14	2/61	65.40	4.13	94.8	0	0
WA Adkin	5.0	1	20	0	-	-	-	4.00	-	0	0
JS Gatting	12.0	0	56	0	-	-	-	4.66	-	0	0

Bowling

Catches/Stumpings:
41 Brown (inc 3st), 32 Yardy, 12 Wells, 9 Joyce, Nash, 8 Prior, 7 Wright, 6 Anyon, 5 Gatting, Goodwin, 4 Magoffin, 3 Panesar, 2 Arif, 1 Adkin, Wernars, Hatchett

LIST A AVERAGES 2012

Batting

	Mat	Inns	NO	Runs	HS	Ave	SR	100	50	4s	6s
MJ Prior	2	2	1	106	78*	106.00	87.60	0	1	6	3
LJ Wright	8	8	1	418	122	59.71	106.90	3	1	52	6
MW Machan	4	4	1	161	126*	53.66	107.33	1	0	14	4
KO Wernars	5	3	1	73	37*	36.50	83.90	0	0	4	0
MH Yardy	9	6	1	158	61	31.60	75.59	0	1	14	0
EC Joyce	10	9	1	249	102	31.12	81.37	1	1	32	1
CD Nash	9	9	0	240	53	26.66	102.12	0	1	35	3
MW Goodwin	9	8	1	183	67*	26.14	88.83	0	1	18	2
CJ Liddle	10	3	2	24	15	24.00	77.41	0	0	3	0
JS Gatting	8	7	1	112	45	18.66	83.58	0	0	6	4
WAT Beer	7	5	3	30	11*	15.00	71.42	0	0	3	0
BC Brown	10	7	2	52	20	10.40	83.87	0	0	4	1
A Khan	8	4	1	26	16*	8.66	104.00	0	0	2	1
MS Panesar	5	2	1	5	5	5.00	45.45	0	0	0	0
SB Styris	2	1	0	5	5	5.00	27.77	0	0	0	0
SJ Magoffin	2	1	1	9	9*	-	56.25	0	0	0	0

Bowling

	Overs	Mdns	Runs	Wkts	BBI	Ave	Econ	SR	4w	5w
SB Styris	6.0	1	12	2	2/12	6.00	2.00	18.0	0	0
Naved Arif	4.0	0	14	1	1/14	14.00	3.50	24.0	0	0
CD Nash	39.4	1	187	10	3/27	18.70	4.71	23.8	0	0
CJ Liddle	61.5	1	330	14	4/21	23.57	5.33	26.5	1	0
WAT Beer	42.0	1	213	9	3/27	23.66	5.07	28.0	0	0
A Khan	53.0	2	238	10	3/51	23.80	4.49	31.8	0	0
LJ Wright	7.0	0	50	2	1/14	25.00	7.14	21.0	0	0
KO Wernars	26.0	1	114	3	2/24	38.00	4.38	52.0	0	0
MH Yardy	52.4	1	227	5	2/20	45.40	4.31	63.2	0	0
MS Panesar	34.0	0	165	3	1/29	55.00	4.85	68.0	0	0
SJ Magoffin	12.0	0	83	1	1/36	83.00	6.91	72.0	0	0

Catches/Stumpings:
17 Brown (inc 3st), 5 Joyce, 3 Liddle, 2 Arif, Wernars, Gatting, Nash, 1 Prior, Machan, Panesar, Beer, Khan

T20 AVERAGES 2012

	Mat	Inns	NO	Runs	HS	Ave	SR	100	50	4s	6s
SB Styris	8	7	3	204	100*	51.00	190.65	1	0	10	13
MJ Prior	7	6	0	249	81	41.50	196.06	0	2	28	11
CD Nash	10	10	2	319	80*	39.87	131.27	0	3	32	8
LJ Wright	10	10	1	312	91	34.66	160.00	0	2	32	11
MW Goodwin	10	9	1	262	68*	32.75	129.70	0	2	31	3
JS Gatting	10	7	3	131	45*	32.75	139.36	0	0	11	3
WAT Beer	10	3	2	20	12*	20.00	181.81	0	0	2	0
MW Machan	4	4	0	47	22	11.75	100.00	0	0	5	0
BC Brown	5	4	1	18	9	6.00	94.73	0	0	2	0
MH Yardy	10	6	2	19	12*	4.75	70.37	0	0	0	1
A Khan	9	1	1	5	5*	-	100.00	0	0	0	0
J Theron	1	1	1	1	1*	-	100.00	0	0	0	0

Batting

	Overs	Mdns	Runs	Wkts	BBI	Ave	Econ	SR	4w	5w
CJ Liddle	27.4	0	203	17	5/17	11.94	7.33	9.7	0	1
SB Styris	16.5	1	111	7	3/22	15.85	6.59	14.4	0	0
MJ Rippon	11.0	0	96	5	4/23	19.20	8.72	13.2	1	0
A Khan	23.2	0	188	8	2/32	23.50	8.05	17.5	0	0
WAT Beer	26.0	0	222	8	2/26	27.75	8.53	19.5	0	0
MH Yardy	32.0	0	209	7	2/15	29.85	6.53	27.4	0	0
J Theron	4.0	0	43	1	1/43	43.00	10.75	24.0	0	0
LJ Wright	10.4	0	104	2	1/16	52.00	9.75	32.0	0	0
CD Nash	7.1	0	72	1	1/20	72.00	10.04	43.0	0	0
Naved Arif	2.0	0	16	0	-	-	8.00	-	0	0

Bowling

Catches/Stumpings:
8 Gatting, 5 Liddle, Nash, 4 Machan, Brown (inc 2st), 3 Goodwin, Wright, 2 Styris, Beer, Yardy, 1 Prior

WARWICKSHIRE

FORMED: 1882
HOME GROUND: Edgbaston
ONE-DAY NAME: Bears
CAPTAIN: Jim Troughton
2012 RESULTS: CC1: Champions; CB40: Runners-up; FL t20: 4/6 in Midlands/Wales/West Group
HONOURS: Championship: (7) 1911, 1951, 1972, 1994, 1995, 2004, 2012; Gillette/NatWest/C&G/FP Trophy: (5) 1966, 1968, 1989, 1993, 1995; Benson & Hedges Cup: (2) 1994, 2002; Pro40/National League/CB40: 2010; Sunday League: (3) 1980, 1994, 1997

THE LOWDOWN

That a team largely shorn of their two gun batsmen in Ian Bell and Jonathan Trott should so emphatically romp to the Championship title says much about Warwickshire's strength in reserve and the ability of their bowling attack to consistently take 20 wickets. Whereas their previous Championship in 2004 was built on a rock-solid batting line-up, this win – the seventh in their history – was achieved on the back of three bowlers enjoying the season of their lives. It wasn't just that new-ball pair Chris Wright and Keith Barker shared 123 first-class wickets between them; backing them up was the New Zealander Jeetan Patel, whose off spin delivered 51 wickets. In all, Warwickshire won six of their 16 matches but, crucially, only once did they go down to defeat. With Rikki Clarke chipping in with runs and wickets and Varun Chopra showing his class to enjoy a 1,000 run first-class campaign, this was truly a team triumph. The mastermind who oversaw last year's campaign has moved on and up. Ashley Giles is now England's limited overs coach, meaning that Dougie Brown – an Edgbaston old boy himself – has moved in to the hotseat. The squad itself remains largely intact – only Neil Carter of Warwickshire's established stars has gone; it was Carter's misfortune to be swatting at mid-air against Hampshire at Lord's in the final match of last season as the Bears finished one hit short of a league and cup double.

DIRECTOR OF CRICKET: DOUGIE BROWN

After achieving legendary status at Warwickshire over a lengthy first-class career with the club, the affable Scot – who represented both Scotland and England at ODI level – was a natural choice to head up Edgbaston's academy as the club's assistant coach, and now to take the reins as director of cricket. "Dougie has been an integral part of the club's success over many years and there really isn't anyone more committed to the club than him," said chief executive Colin Povey when Brown's promotion was announced. "It is hard to define exactly what 'a Bear' is, but whatever it is, he epitomises it."

FIRST-CLASS AVERAGES 2012

Batting

	Mat	Inns	NO	Runs	HS	Ave	SR	100	50	4s	6s
IJL Trott	2	2	0	180	178	90.00	54.71	1	0	27	0
CR Woakes	8	10	4	431	118*	71.83	59.69	2	1	62	2
ID Blackwell	4	6	1	265	84	53.00	81.03	0	2	27	9
R Clarke	17	22	4	826	140	45.88	64.18	3	3	97	14
TR Ambrose	14	19	4	660	151*	44.00	54.14	1	3	86	1
IR Bell	4	6	1	215	120	43.00	55.55	1	1	28	2
IJ Westwood	13	20	1	771	120	40.57	40.94	2	5	94	0
V Chopra	17	27	1	1052	195	40.46	48.88	3	5	138	1
JO Troughton	16	25	3	800	132	36.36	44.69	2	5	79	7
A Javid	1	1	0	31	31	31.00	36.90	0	0	5	0
WTS Porterfield	15	23	2	558	84	26.57	48.43	0	3	77	2
DL Maddy	15	22	2	478	112	23.90	45.52	1	0	58	3
KHD Barker	15	17	4	304	46	23.38	57.90	0	0	39	3
JS Patel	13	14	3	221	76	20.09	91.32	0	1	29	6
TP Milnes	4	3	1	40	24	20.00	58.82	0	0	5	1
CJC Wright	16	16	5	201	53	18.27	48.66	0	1	24	2
RM Johnson	3	4	0	72	49	18.00	40.67	0	0	9	1
NM Carter	2	4	0	51	26	12.75	66.23	0	0	6	1
LJ Evans	1	2	0	13	9	6.50	33.33	0	0	2	0
WB Rankin	6	4	2	9	5	4.50	31.03	0	0	0	0
AS Miller	1	1	1	0	0*	-	-	0	0	0	0

Bowling

	Overs	Mdns	Runs	Wkts	BBI	BBM	Ave	Econ	SR	5w	10w
KHD Barker	392.1	94	1166	56	6/40	10/70	20.82	2.97	42.0	5	1
R Clarke	204.0	54	569	26	4/46	6/15	21.88	2.78	47.0	0	0
JS Patel	395.1	87	1161	51	7/75	8/114	22.76	2.93	46.4	4	0
CJC Wright	471.3	77	1562	67	5/24	9/89	23.31	3.31	42.2	2	0
CR Woakes	225.5	47	681	27	4/67	7/103	25.22	3.01	50.1	0	0
DL Maddy	147.0	50	354	14	4/39	4/39	25.28	2.40	63.0	0	0
WB Rankin	138.1	15	515	16	5/78	8/150	32.18	3.72	51.8	1	0
TP Milnes	49.0	5	202	5	2/31	3/60	40.40	4.12	58.8	0	0
AS Miller	16.0	3	46	1	1/24	1/46	46.00	2.87	96.0	0	0
ID Blackwell	90.2	15	279	6	4/47	4/145	46.50	3.08	90.3	0	0
NM Carter	36.0	4	149	2	2/86	2/127	74.50	4.13	108.0	0	0
V Chopra	2.0	0	5	0	-	-	-	2.50	-	0	0
IJ Westwood	9.0	4	26	0	-	-	-	2.88	-	0	0

Catches/Stumpings:
47 Ambrose (inc 1st), 31 Clarke, 27 Chopra, 21 Porterfield, 12 Maddy, 9 Troughton, 6 Bell, Johnson, 5 Westwood, Barker, 3 Woakes, Patel, 2 Carter, Rankin, Wright, 1 Evans, Miller, Trott

LIST A AVERAGES 2012

Batting

	Mat	Inns	NO	Runs	HS	Ave	SR	100	50	4s	6s
IR Bell	2	2	1	163	82*	163.00	98.78	0	2	14	2
TR Ambrose	11	9	3	321	87*	53.50	91.45	0	3	32	1
V Chopra	11	11	2	472	110	52.44	78.27	1	3	45	4
IJL Trott	2	2	1	51	41*	51.00	63.75	0	0	5	0
WTS Porterfield	12	12	2	395	100*	39.50	95.18	1	2	52	5
DL Maddy	12	9	1	258	79*	32.25	99.61	0	1	23	4
R Clarke	12	9	2	225	54*	32.14	90.72	0	1	19	5
SA Piolet	6	4	2	59	28	29.50	137.20	0	0	2	4
CR Woakes	8	5	2	65	25*	21.66	85.52	0	0	8	0
JO Troughton	13	11	0	178	61	16.18	79.11	0	1	21	0
PM Best	7	5	2	42	16*	14.00	107.69	0	0	5	1
LJ Evans	3	3	0	35	22	11.66	53.03	0	0	1	0
CJC Wright	13	3	2	9	7*	9.00	90.00	0	0	1	0
KHD Barker	9	6	1	41	26	8.20	83.67	0	0	3	0
ID Blackwell	4	3	2	5	2*	5.00	71.42	0	0	0	0
A Javid	1	1	0	4	4	4.00	25.00	0	0	0	0
JS Patel	10	3	0	11	5	3.66	137.50	0	0	2	0
NM Carter	3	1	1	4	4*	-	133.33	0	0	1	0

Bowling

	Overs	Mdns	Runs	Wkts	BBI	Ave	Econ	SR	4w	5w
NM Carter	22.0	1	117	9	4/16	13.00	5.31	14.6	2	0
R Clarke	16.0	2	72	4	3/22	18.00	4.50	24.0	0	0
CR Woakes	56.0	4	279	14	4/24	19.92	4.98	24.0	1	0
CJC Wright	82.0	3	416	20	3/43	20.80	5.07	24.6	0	0
KHD Barker	54.5	1	258	12	3/27	21.50	4.70	27.4	0	0
JS Patel	64.0	1	241	11	4/27	21.90	3.76	34.9	1	0
DL Maddy	26.3	1	156	6	2/30	26.00	5.88	26.5	0	0
PM Best	31.5	1	183	6	3/43	30.50	5.74	31.8	0	0
ID Blackwell	29.0	1	134	4	2/36	33.50	4.62	43.5	0	0
SA Piolet	38.0	1	193	5	4/31	38.60	5.07	45.6	1	0
WB Rankin	6.0	0	47	1	1/47	47.00	7.83	36.0	0	0
AS Miller	8.0	0	48	1	1/48	48.00	6.00	48.0	0	0

Catches/Stumpings:
12 Clarke, 9 Ambrose (inc 1st), Troughton, 6 Patel, Porterfield, 4 Chopra, Maddy, 2 Evans, 1 Bell, Blackwell, 1 Best, Johnson

T20 AVERAGES 2012

	Mat	Inns	NO	Runs	HS	Ave	SR	100	50	4s	6s
LJ Evans	8	6	4	146	68*	73.00	171.76	0	1	15	4
V Chopra	8	7	2	240	56*	48.00	107.62	0	2	20	5
CR Woakes	6	4	3	47	23*	47.00	127.02	0	0	3	0
JO Troughton	5	4	1	123	68*	41.00	119.41	0	1	17	0
DL Maddy	8	7	1	125	49	20.83	109.64	0	0	11	3
RM Johnson	8	1	0	14	14	14.00	107.69	0	0	1	0
R Clarke	8	7	0	86	48	12.28	122.85	0	0	9	1
KHD Barker	8	2	1	11	8*	11.00	78.57	0	0	0	0
CJC Wright	5	1	0	6	6	6.00	150.00	0	0	1	0
WTS Porterfield	3	3	0	15	7	5.00	83.33	0	0	2	0
JS Patel	8	1	0	1	1	1.00	50.00	0	0	0	0
SA Piolet	8	1	1	26	26*	-	185.71	0	0	3	1

Batting

	Overs	Mdns	Runs	Wkts	BBI	Ave	Econ	SR	4w	5w
DL Maddy	6.0	0	47	5	2/13	9.40	7.83	7.2	0	0
PM Best	10.0	0	61	4	3/19	15.25	6.10	15.0	0	0
CR Woakes	23.0	1	170	9	3/27	18.88	7.39	15.3	0	0
JS Patel	23.1	0	176	5	1/15	35.20	7.59	27.8	0	0
CJC Wright	17.0	0	147	4	2/43	36.75	8.64	25.5	0	0
SA Piolet	23.0	0	140	3	2/21	46.66	6.08	46.0	0	0
KHD Barker	29.0	0	217	4	1/17	54.25	7.48	43.5	0	0
NM Carter	4.0	0	37	0	-	-	9.25	-	0	0

Bowling

Catches/Stumpings:
3 Johnson, Wright, Woakes, Patel, 2 Clarke, Evans, Maddy, 1 Carter, Best, Troughton, Barker, Chopra, Piolet

WORCESTERSHIRE

FORMED: 1865
HOME GROUND: New Road, Worcester
ONE-DAY NAME: Royals
CAPTAIN: Daryl Mitchell
2012 RESULTS: CC1: 9/9; CB40: 7/7 in Group A; FL t20: Quarter-finalists
HONOURS: Championship: (5) 1964, 1965, 1974, 1988, 1989; Gillette/NatWest/C&G/FP Trophy: 1994; Benson & Hedges Cup: 1991; Pro40/National League/CB40: 2007; Sunday League: (3) 1971, 1987, 1988

THE LOWDOWN

After defying the odds and avoiding relegation in 2011, Worcestershire were unable to conjure a repeat performance last season and finished bottom of Division One as they were relegated to the Championship's second tier. Australian overseas player Phil Hughes scored prolifically in the limited overs competitions, but the fact that captain Daryl Mitchell topped their run-scoring charts in Championship cricket despite averaging just 27.76 reveals the problems they had in putting totals on the board in the four-day format. The evergreen Alan Richardson led from the front with the ball, and his parsimonious bowling earned him 57 first-class wickets. However, aside from solid contributions from Moeen Ali's off breaks and paceman Richard Jones, the bowling department lacked the bite to make up for the shortfall in runs from their batsmen. The Royals put in an encouraging showing in the Friends Life t20 by reaching the quarter-finals before losing to eventual finalists Yorkshire, but the Clydesdale Bank 40 proved to be a disappointment as they finished rock bottom of their group. The signing of RAF corporal Graeme Cessford should help to bolster the pace ranks, and experienced Sri Lankan middle order batsman Thilan Samaraweera – joining as their overseas player for 2013 – should fill the void left by Vikram Solanki, who ended his long association with the club and moved to Surrey in the off-season.

DIRECTOR OF CRICKET: STEVE RHODES

Rhodes began his career with his home county Yorkshire before making the move to New Road in 1985, where he became a Worcestershire institution. A talented wicketkeeper and nuggety batsman, Rhodes was named as one of Wisden's five Cricketers of the Year in 1995 having made his Test debut the previous year against New Zealand at Trent Bridge. He went on to represent England a further 10 times in Test matches and played in nine ODIs.

FIRST-CLASS AVERAGES 2012

Batting

	Mat	Inns	NO	Runs	HS	Ave	SR	100	50	4s	6s
M Klinger	7	12	1	413	120	37.54	49.46	1	2	51	4
PJ Hughes	9	17	1	560	135*	35.00	62.43	2	2	88	2
DKH Mitchell	17	32	2	833	133*	27.76	35.00	2	2	90	0
JG Cameron	12	19	4	399	88	26.60	46.23	0	2	42	4
MM Ali	17	30	4	672	94	25.84	45.71	0	4	72	7
AN Kervezee	7	12	1	283	76	25.72	58.71	0	3	36	0
VS Solanki	14	25	3	556	106	25.27	51.57	1	3	71	4
JD Shantry	5	5	2	67	22*	22.33	37.85	0	0	9	0
MG Pardoe	12	22	2	407	55	20.35	38.10	0	1	55	1
ND Pinner	4	7	0	132	82	18.85	38.26	0	1	16	0
A Kapil	4	6	1	93	41	18.60	44.07	0	0	11	0
RA Jones	10	15	5	151	32	15.10	44.15	0	0	16	4
BJM Scott	14	21	1	301	106	15.05	50.00	1	1	35	0
OB Cox	3	6	1	67	25*	13.40	40.60	0	0	6	1
GM Andrew	10	17	3	161	29	11.50	44.10	0	0	17	2
CJ Russell	6	10	2	83	22	10.37	41.91	0	0	9	1
J Leach	5	9	0	93	46	10.33	33.81	0	0	12	0
BL D'Oliveira	3	6	0	62	19	10.33	42.46	0	0	5	0
DS Lucas	7	9	0	74	19	8.22	47.43	0	0	11	0
A Richardson	14	21	9	79	18	6.58	54.48	0	0	12	0
SH Choudhry	4	7	1	31	20	5.16	17.91	0	0	2	0
NL Harrison	3	4	0	12	10	3.00	20.68	0	0	2	0

Bowling

	Overs	Mdns	Runs	Wkts	BBI	BBM	Ave	Econ	SR	5w	10w
SH Choudhry	70.4	13	165	10	4/38	6/54	16.50	2.33	42.4	0	0
A Richardson	461.3	137	1113	57	6/47	10/128	19.52	2.41	48.5	4	1
RA Jones	200.1	26	857	31	6/32	8/171	27.64	4.28	38.7	1	0
JD Shantry	135.0	24	423	15	5/58	5/58	28.20	3.13	54.0	1	0
MM Ali	296.1	42	957	33	6/29	12/96	29.00	3.23	53.8	2	1
J Leach	40.0	8	127	4	2/49	2/49	31.75	3.17	60.0	0	0
CJ Russell	134.4	23	563	17	4/43	6/117	33.11	4.18	47.5	0	0
A Kapil	35.0	4	136	4	3/17	3/28	34.00	3.88	52.5	0	0
DS Lucas	239.0	40	852	22	4/37	6/147	38.72	3.56	65.1	0	0
GM Andrew	194.0	28	745	19	5/86	5/127	39.21	3.84	61.2	1	0
NL Harrison	46.0	8	176	3	2/78	2/78	58.66	3.82	92.0	0	0
JG Cameron	48.0	3	192	2	1/19	1/21	96.00	4.00	144.0	0	0
BL D'Oliveira	43.0	2	198	0	-	-	-	4.60	-	0	0
DKH Mitchell	9.0	0	27	0	-	-	-	3.00	-	0	0
ND Pinner	4.0	0	13	0	-	-	-	3.25	-	0	0

Catches/Stumpings:
34 Scott (inc 5st), 23 Mitchell, 18 Solanki, 10 Pardoe, 8 Klinger, 7 Kervezee, Ali, 5 Cox, Jones, 3 Choudhry, Andrew, Cameron, Richardson, 2 Shantry, Russell, Lucas, Hughes, 1 Harrison, Pinner

LIST A AVERAGES 2012

Batting

	Mat	Inns	NO	Runs	HS	Ave	SR	100	50	4s	6s
PJ Hughes	10	9	3	498	111	83.00	84.98	2	4	40	6
BL D'Oliveira	6	4	3	41	16*	41.00	117.14	0	0	3	0
VS Solanki	12	11	1	401	121	40.10	82.85	1	1	38	6
M Klinger	2	2	1	29	27*	29.00	55.76	0	0	2	0
MM Ali	12	11	0	259	99	23.54	88.09	0	1	27	4
DKH Mitchell	12	10	2	182	48	22.75	93.33	0	0	14	1
ND Pinner	5	4	0	80	31	20.00	75.47	0	0	3	1
GM Andrew	9	8	0	157	42	19.62	106.80	0	0	11	7
JG Cameron	8	7	0	134	38	19.14	78.82	0	0	7	3
BJM Scott	11	6	1	91	29*	18.20	97.84	0	0	2	4
DS Lucas	9	3	2	17	17	17.00	73.91	0	0	2	0
MG Pardoe	1	1	0	16	16	16.00	133.33	0	0	1	0
AN Kervezee	8	5	2	36	16	12.00	80.00	0	0	3	1
SH Choudhry	6	2	0	17	16	8.50	70.83	0	0	1	0
JD Shantry	12	2	2	9	7*	-	60.00	0	0	0	0
NL Harrison	3	1	1	5	5*	-	166.66	0	0	1	0
A Kapil	4	2	2	2	2*	-	66.66	0	0	0	0

Bowling

	Overs	Mdns	Runs	Wkts	BBI	Ave	Econ	SR	4w	5w
JD Shantry	78.3	3	490	20	4/32	24.50	6.24	23.5	2	0
MM Ali	65.0	2	374	12	3/33	31.16	5.75	32.5	0	0
DKH Mitchell	46.0	0	248	7	2/10	35.42	5.39	39.4	0	0
NL Harrison	22.0	1	184	5	2/54	36.80	8.36	26.4	0	0
SH Choudhry	23.0	0	122	3	2/37	40.66	5.30	46.0	0	0
GM Andrew	39.1	3	210	5	3/9	42.00	5.36	47.0	0	0
DS Lucas	49.3	1	295	7	2/11	42.14	5.95	42.4	0	0
BL D'Oliveira	41.0	0	211	5	2/35	42.20	5.14	49.2	0	0
JG Cameron	1.0	0	11	0	-	-	11.00	-	0	0
A Kapil	8.5	0	65	0	-	-	7.35	-	0	0
J Leach	4.0	0	47	0	-	-	11.75	-	0	0
ND Pinner	1.0	0	7	0	-	-	7.00	-	0	0

Catches/Stumpings:
8 Solanki, 5 Andrew, Lucas, 4 Scott (inc 1st), Hughes, Mitchell, 3 Kervezee, Shantry, 2 D'Oliveira, Ali, 1 Kapil, Pinner, Choudhry, Cameron, Cox (inc 1st)

T20 AVERAGES 2012

Batting	Mat	Inns	NO	Runs	HS	Ave	SR	100	50	4s	6s
PJ Hughes	8	8	4	402	87*	100.50	126.81	0	4	37	7
GM Andrew	8	8	2	148	43	24.66	154.16	0	0	9	8
MM Ali	8	8	0	195	82	24.37	142.33	0	1	24	7
JG Cameron	8	7	0	166	57	23.71	114.48	0	1	15	3
DKH Mitchell	8	7	1	102	31	17.00	143.66	0	0	15	0
BJM Scott	8	5	3	31	19	15.50	119.23	0	0	2	1
VS Solanki	8	8	0	123	33	15.37	89.13	0	0	12	2
AN Kervezee	7	6	3	17	8	5.66	77.27	0	0	1	0
A Kapil	1	1	0	4	4	4.00	66.66	0	0	0	0
BL D'Oliveira	8	3	3	8	6*	-	114.28	0	0	1	0

Bowling	Overs	Mdns	Runs	Wkts	BBI	Ave	Econ	SR	4w	5w
DKH Mitchell	25.0	0	171	11	3/13	15.54	6.84	13.6	0	0
A Kapil	1.0	0	18	1	1/18	18.00	18.00	6.0	0	0
JD Shantry	31.0	0	248	9	4/33	27.55	8.00	20.6	1	0
DS Lucas	26.5	2	173	6	2/9	28.83	6.44	26.8	0	0
GM Andrew	25.5	0	211	7	3/20	30.14	8.16	22.1	0	0
BL D'Oliveira	12.0	0	104	3	3/20	34.66	8.66	24.0	0	0
MM Ali	28.4	0	201	5	2/14	40.20	7.01	34.4	0	0
JG Cameron	1.0	0	13	0	-	-	13.00	-	0	0

Catches/Stumpings:
7 Scott (inc 2st), 5 Cameron, 4 Ali, Solanki, 3 Kervezee, Mitchell, 2 Lucas, 1 Kapil, Andrew, D'Oliveira, Hughes

YORKSHIRE

FORMED: 1863
HOME GROUND: Headingley Carnegie
ONE-DAY NAME: Vikings
CAPTAIN: Andrew Gale
2012 RESULTS: CC2: 2/9; CB40: 5/7 in Group C; FL t20: Runners-up
HONOURS: County Championship: (31) 1893, 1896, 1898, 1900, 1901, 1902, 1905, 1908, 1912, 1919, 1922, 1923, 1924, 1925, 1931, 1932, 1933, 1935, 1937, 1938, 1939, 1946, 1949, 1959, 1960, 1962, 1963, 1966, 1967, 1968, 2001; Gillette/NatWest/C&G/FP Trophy: (3) 1965, 1969, 2002; Benson & Hedges Cup: 1987; Sunday League: 1983

THE LOWDOWN

In the year of their 150th anniversary, Yorkshire find themselves back at the top table of county cricket following promotion from Division Two of the Championship. Jason Gillespie oversaw a hugely successful campaign in his first year in charge, as Andrew Gale's side also qualified for the Champions League T20. Yorkshire's second-place finish in the Championship's second tier was very much a team effort, with no batsman passing 1,000 first-class runs. Veteran Australian opener Phil Jaques was the county's leading scorer, while 29-year-old seamer Steven Patterson enjoyed his most impressive season to date, taking 53 first-class wickets. Success was harder to come by in the Clydesdale Bank 40 as the Tykes finished fifth in their group, but they enjoyed a fine Friends Life t20 campaign, falling just short in the final against Hampshire. Gillespie has bolstered the ranks for 2013 by bringing in some high-profile recruits. England Lions seamer Jack Brooks has swapped Wantage Road for Headingley, while ex-England man Liam Plunkett has joined from Durham in a bid to reignite his career and wicketkeeper Andrew Hodd, who impressed during a loan spell last year, made his move from Sussex a permanent one during the off-season.

FIRST TEAM COACH: JASON GILLESPIE

Expectations were high when Gillespie was appointed at the beginning of the 2012 season. Promotion was the goal and, despite missing out on the title, Dizzy saw to it that his side delivered on that aim. The Twenty20 campaign was something of a bonus, and the way in which Joe Root, Jonny Bairstow, Azeem Rafiq and Gary Ballance have prospered of late suggests an encouraging future. It will be interesting to see how much cricket Yorkshire's England contingent are able to play for their county this summer, but their strongest XI is capable of mixing it with the very best in the country.

FIRST-CLASS AVERAGES 2012

Batting

	Mat	Inns	NO	Runs	HS	Ave	SR	100	50	4s	6s
JM Bairstow	9	12	1	588	182	53.45	66.66	3	1	77	6
A Lyth	13	16	1	751	248*	50.06	62.22	1	5	99	3
A McGrath	14	17	3	648	106*	46.28	49.24	2	3	81	4
PA Jaques	15	19	1	792	160	44.00	56.57	2	4	104	3
JE Root	15	21	2	746	222*	39.26	59.06	2	2	91	3
GS Ballance	17	20	4	617	121*	38.56	48.92	1	2	79	4
I Wardlaw	3	3	2	31	17*	31.00	58.49	0	0	6	0
AW Gale	15	20	4	487	80	30.43	52.25	0	2	63	3
JJ Sayers	6	9	1	241	45	30.12	36.18	0	0	33	2
Azeem Rafiq	11	11	1	293	75*	29.30	58.48	0	2	31	0
GL Brophy	4	3	1	47	23	23.50	39.49	0	0	5	0
RJ Sidebottom	11	10	2	164	37	20.50	53.07	0	0	24	1
TT Bresnan	4	4	0	73	38	18.25	68.22	0	0	12	1
AJ Hodd	4	5	0	91	58	18.20	41.93	0	1	6	0
SA Patterson	16	15	5	180	37	18.00	38.37	0	0	22	0
AU Rashid	10	8	0	129	58	16.12	50.19	0	1	16	0
A Shahzad	3	3	0	34	25	11.33	43.58	0	0	4	0
SJ Harmison	3	3	0	25	23	8.33	78.12	0	0	3	1
MA Ashraf	8	6	4	14	6*	7.00	20.00	0	0	1	0
RM Pyrah	4	4	0	9	9	2.25	40.90	0	0	2	0
MA Starc	2	1	1	28	28*	-	90.32	0	0	4	0
OJ Hannon-Dalby	1	1	1	5	5*	-	31.25	0	0	0	0

Bowling

	Overs	Mdns	Runs	Wkts	BBI	BBM	Ave	Econ	SR	5w	10w
OJ Hannon-Dalby	25.1	4	54	4	3/36	4/54	13.50	2.14	37.7	0	0
SA Patterson	427.2	125	1115	53	5/77	8/94	21.03	2.60	48.3	1	0
MA Starc	42.1	13	153	7	3/50	5/114	21.85	3.62	36.1	0	0
MA Ashraf	117.5	27	376	17	4/36	5/75	22.11	3.19	41.5	0	0
SJ Harmison	42.0	4	195	8	3/49	5/121	24.37	4.64	31.5	0	0
Azeem Rafiq	246.5	63	711	28	5/50	8/115	25.39	2.88	52.8	1	0
A McGrath	196.1	59	489	19	4/21	7/65	25.73	2.49	61.9	0	0
A Shahzad	68.1	14	210	8	3/86	3/70	26.25	3.08	51.1	0	0
TT Bresnan	130.2	31	397	14	5/81	5/81	28.35	3.04	55.8	1	0
RJ Sidebottom	297.0	72	798	24	5/30	5/45	33.25	2.68	74.2	1	0
AU Rashid	202.5	26	656	16	5/105	5/105	41.00	3.23	76.0	1	0
RM Pyrah	38.0	9	128	2	1/9	1/9	64.00	3.36	114.0	0	0
I Wardlaw	65.0	2	300	3	1/37	2/119	100.00	4.61	130.0	0	0
JE Root	48.0	14	130	1	1/39	1/59	130.00	2.70	288.0	0	0
GS Ballance	6.0	1	23	0	-	-	-	3.83	-	0	0
AW Gale	6.1	0	97	0	-	-	-	15.72	-	0	0
A Lyth	12.0	3	116	0	-	-	-	9.66	-	0	0

Catches/Stumpings:
18 Hodd, 16 Jaques, 14 Bairstow, 13 Lyth, 11 Ballance, 9 Root, 8 Brophy, 7 Rafiq, 5 McGrath, 4 Gale, 3 Sayers, 2 Wardlaw, Bresnan, 1 Hannon-Dalby, Harmison, Ashraf, Sidebottom, Patterson

LIST A AVERAGES 2012

Batting

	Mat	Inns	NO	Runs	HS	Ave	SR	100	50	4s	6s
GS Ballance	11	11	3	469	103*	58.62	105.15	1	3	38	17
AW Gale	10	10	0	393	76	39.30	73.45	0	3	40	5
JE Root	8	7	1	208	49	34.66	108.90	0	0	23	1
A Lyth	9	9	1	260	69	32.50	93.52	0	2	22	6
PA Jaques	10	10	0	299	87	29.90	93.73	0	1	36	1
TT Bresnan	1	1	0	27	27	27.00	117.39	0	0	2	1
A McGrath	3	1	0	26	26	26.00	113.04	0	0	3	0
AZ Lees	1	1	0	23	23	23.00	67.64	0	0	2	0
RM Pyrah	4	3	0	62	44	20.66	114.81	0	0	2	3
Azeem Rafiq	10	8	4	81	34*	20.25	84.37	0	0	5	1
DA Miller	3	3	0	45	44	15.00	77.58	0	0	1	1
JM Bairstow	2	2	0	28	25	14.00	71.79	0	0	0	2
SA Patterson	4	4	2	28	14	14.00	71.79	0	0	3	0
JA Leaning	1	1	0	11	11	11.00	50.00	0	0	1	0
AU Rashid	8	8	0	86	32	10.75	92.47	0	0	7	2
DM Hodgson	4	3	1	19	9	9.50	111.76	0	0	3	0
GL Brophy	5	3	0	24	19	8.00	109.09	0	0	2	0
I Wardlaw	7	4	2	10	6*	5.00	71.42	0	0	1	0
RJ Sidebottom	4	2	0	2	2	1.00	28.57	0	0	0	0
JJ Sayers	1	1	0	1	1	1.00	14.28	0	0	0	0
OJ Hannon-Dalby	1	1	1	21	21*	-	210.00	0	0	3	1
MA Starc	4	2	2	5	4*	-	71.42	0	0	0	0
MA Ashraf	10	3	3	3	3*	-	75.00	0	0	0	0

Bowling

	Overs	Mdns	Runs	Wkts	BBI	Ave	Econ	SR	4w	5w
A McGrath	16.0	0	65	3	2/24	21.66	4.06	32.0	0	0
MA Starc	31.4	1	181	8	3/28	22.62	5.71	23.7	0	0
JE Root	19.0	1	115	5	2/14	23.00	6.05	22.8	0	0
AU Rashid	56.0	0	302	12	4/38	25.16	5.39	28.0	1	0
SA Patterson	29.0	0	143	5	3/25	28.60	4.93	34.8	0	0
RJ Sidebottom	28.0	1	174	6	3/44	29.00	6.21	28.0	0	0
MA Ashraf	69.0	2	362	11	2/36	32.90	5.24	37.6	0	0
RM Pyrah	17.0	0	106	3	2/55	35.33	6.23	34.0	0	0
Azeem Rafiq	70.5	2	381	10	3/22	38.10	5.37	42.5	0	0
I Wardlaw	50.4	2	311	8	3/60	38.87	6.13	38.0	0	0
TT Bresnan	5.0	0	46	1	1/46	46.00	9.20	30.0	0	0
OJ Hannon-Dalby	6.0	0	58	0	-	-	9.66	-	0	0

Catches/Stumpings:
6 Ballance, 5 Root, 4 Hodgson (inc 1st), Brophy (inc 1st), 3 Miller, Pyrah, Rafiq, Gale, Jaques, 2 Rashid, 1 Patterson, Starc, Wardlaw, Lyth, Ashraf, Bairstow

T20 AVERAGES 2012

Batting

	Mat	Inns	NO	Runs	HS	Ave	SR	100	50	4s	6s
DA Miller	12	11	3	390	74*	48.75	153.54	0	4	30	21
A Lyth	6	5	0	154	78	30.80	141.28	0	1	19	5
AW Gale	6	6	0	165	70	27.50	144.73	0	1	23	3
JE Root	12	11	2	241	65	26.77	128.87	0	1	36	1
GL Brophy	5	4	2	53	32	26.50	115.21	0	0	6	0
PA Jaques	12	11	1	263	64	26.30	114.84	0	2	29	3
GS Ballance	12	11	3	209	47*	26.12	128.22	0	0	14	11
JM Bairstow	7	7	1	98	68*	16.33	115.29	0	1	2	4
RM Pyrah	12	9	3	94	35	15.66	134.28	0	0	9	4
Azeem Rafiq	12	5	3	25	21*	12.50	104.16	0	0	0	1
TT Bresnan	2	2	0	24	18	12.00	141.17	0	0	3	0
AU Rashid	4	1	0	4	4	4.00	200.00	0	0	1	0
MA Starc	10	2	1	0	0*	0.00	0.00	0	0	0	0
RJ Sidebottom	7	1	1	5	5*	-	71.42	0	0	0	0

Bowling

	Overs	Mdns	Runs	Wkts	BBI	Ave	Econ	SR	4w	5w
MA Starc	36.5	0	218	21	3/24	10.38	5.91	10.5	0	0
RJ Sidebottom	25.0	0	177	11	4/25	16.09	7.08	13.6	1	0
TT Bresnan	7.0	0	40	2	2/22	20.00	5.71	21.0	0	0
MA Ashraf	47.0	0	359	15	4/18	23.93	7.63	18.8	1	0
RM Pyrah	45.0	0	359	15	3/21	23.93	7.97	18.0	0	0
Azeem Rafiq	46.0	0	310	11	2/28	28.18	6.73	25.0	0	0
AU Rashid	12.0	0	101	2	1/19	50.50	8.41	36.0	0	0
JE Root	13.0	0	114	1	1/16	114.00	8.76	78.0	0	0
I Wardlaw	2.0	0	22	0	-	-	11.00	-	0	0

Catches/Stumpings:
13 Ballance, 6 Root, 5 Brophy (inc 1st), 4 Rafiq, Miller, 2 Bairstow, Lyth, Jaques, Pyrah, 1 Rashid, Starc, Ashraf

The
Players

TOM ABELL RHB RM

SOMERSET

FULL NAME: Thomas Benjamin Abell
BORN: March 5, 1994, Taunton, Somerset
SQUAD NO: 28
HEIGHT: 5ft 11in
NICKNAME: Tabez
EDUCATION: Taunton School; Exeter University
TEAMS: Somerset 2nd XI
CAREER: Yet to make first-team debut

WHO WOULD PLAY YOU IN A FILM OF YOUR LIFE? Russell Crowe
CAREER HIGHLIGHTS? Scoring 246* for Somerset U17 vs Sussex U17. Scoring over 1,000 runs for my school 1st XI. Being 12th man for the Somerset 1st XI
SUPERSTITIONS? I am quite superstitious when I bat. I have to make sure all my kit feels right, so I adjust everything after each ball, pads, gloves, etc
MOST MARKED CHARACTERISTIC? Probably my dodgy looking hair
BEST PLAYER IN COUNTY CRICKET? James Hildreth
TIPS FOR THE TOP? Jos Buttler, hopefully myself
IF YOU WEREN'T A CRICKETER? I am currently at university, so hopefully something in the sport/sports science field
DESERT ISLAND DISC? The Kooks – Naive
FAVOURITE TV? Geordie Shore
BIGGEST DRESSING DOWN YOU'VE RECEIVED? After our school team was bowled out for 54, that was a major reality check
CRICKETING HEROES? Brian Lara, Andrew Flintoff, Marcus Trescothick
NON-CRICKETING HEROES? Sonny Bill Williams, David Haye, Jonny Wilkinson
ACCOMPLISHMENTS? Hockey success with school team (four national finals). Runner-up in Aviva/Telegraph School Sport Matters Awards
SURPRISING FACT? I was Somerset U8 tennis champion
FANTASY SLIP CORDON? Keeper: James Corden, 1st: Lee Mack, 2nd: Jimmy Carr, 3rd: Jonny Wilkinson, Gully: Yohan Blake
TWITTER FEED: @tomabell1

ANDRE ADAMS RHB RMF W3 MVP41

FULL NAME: Andre Ryan Adams
BORN: July 17, 1975, Auckland, New Zealand
SQUAD NO: 41
HEIGHT: 5ft 11in
NICKNAME: Dre, Doctor, Dizzy
EDUCATION: West Lake Boys' High School, Auckland
TEAMS: New Zealand, Auckland, Essex, Herefordshire, Kolkata Tigers, Nottinghamshire
CAREER: Test: 2002; ODI: 2001; T20I: 2005; First-class: 1998; List A: 1997; T20: 2004

BEST BATTING: 124 Essex vs Leicestershire, Leicester, 2004
BEST BOWLING: 7-32 Nottinghamshire vs Lancashire, Manchester, 2012
COUNTY CAPS: 2004 (Essex); 2007 (Nottinghamshire)

CAREER HIGHLIGHTS? Winning the Championship, playing in a World Cup, playing a Test
CRICKETING HEROES? Michael Holding, Viv Richards
TIPS FOR THE TOP? Alex Hales, Jos Buttler
IF YOU WEREN'T A CRICKETER? Running a hunting lodge
WHEN RAIN STOPS PLAY? Xbox
FAVOURITE TV? True Blood
DREAM HOLIDAY? Rarotonga
SURPRISING FACTS? My grandfather is Corsican and my grandmother is Scottish. I like classical music
TWITTER FEED: @AndreAdams

Batting	Mat	Inns	NO	Runs	HS	Ave	SR	100	50	Ct	St
Tests	1	2	0	18	11	9.00	90.00	0	0	1	0
ODIs	42	34	10	419	45	17.45	100.47	0	0	8	0
T20Is	4	2	1	13	7	13.00	108.33	0	0	1	0
First-class	149	205	21	4067	124	22.10		3	18	99	0
List A	165	119	29	1504	90*	16.71		0	1	40	0
Twenty20	71	42	14	417	54*	14.89	131.96	0	1	21	0
Bowling	**Inns**	**Balls**	**Runs**	**Wkts**	**BBI**	**BBM**	**Ave**	**Econ**	**SR**	**5w**	**10**
Tests	1	190	105	6	3/44	6/105	17.50	3.31	31.6	0	0
ODIs	42	1885	1643	53	5/22	5/22	31.00	5.22	35.5	1	0
T20Is	4	77	105	3	2/20	2/20	35.00	8.18	25.6	0	0
First-class	149	28925	14215	614	7/32		23.15	2.94	47.1	31	6
List A	165	7561	5957	209	5/7	5/7	28.50	4.72	36.1	4	0
Twenty20	71	1498	1914	87	5/20	5/20	22.00	7.66	17.2	1	0

JIMMY ADAMS LHB LM R4 MVP33

FULL NAME: James Henry Kenneth Adams
BORN: September 23, 1980, Winchester, Hampshire
SQUAD NO: 4
HEIGHT: 6ft
NICKNAME: Bison
EDUCATION: Twyford; Sherborne; Loughborough University
TEAMS: Auckland, British Universities, England Lions, Hampshire, Hampshire 2nd XI, Loughborough MCCU
CAREER: First-class: 2002; List A: 2002; T20: 2005

BEST BATTING: 262* Hampshire vs Nottinghamshire, Nottingham, 2006
BEST BOWLING: 2-16 Hampshire vs Durham, Chester-le-Street, 2004
COUNTY CAP: 2006

CAREER HIGHLIGHTS? Batting on debut with Robin Smith who'd been my hero growing up. Being fortunate enough to play and win two finals at Lord's (2009 and then captaining in 2012), and being part of the teams that won the T20 (2010 and 2012), especially 2010 at our home ground. Changing next to Neil McKenzie
MOST MARKED CHARACTERISTIC? Indecisiveness and an over-sized big toe
TIPS FOR THE TOP? Of Hampshire's next batch of young players Tom Barber looks very exciting
DESERT ISLAND DISC? The Who – Live At Leeds
BIGGEST DRESSING DOWN YOU'VE RECEIVED? I've been fairly fortunate really. I remember Jimmy Cook not seeing the funny side of my 12th man efforts and you were never late for a second time for a session with Graham Dilley
CRICKETING HEROES? Robin Smith, Jimmy Adams
FANTASY SLIP CORDON? Keeper: Me (I'll give the gloves a go this time round), 1st: Bill Bailey (funny bloke and a bit random), 2nd: The Dude from The Big Lebowski (ditto first slip reason), 3rd: Jimmy Page (he's bound to have some good tales), Gully: Eddie Vedder (imagine he's had a pretty interesting life too)

Batting	Mat	Inns	NO	Runs	HS	Ave	SR	100	50	Ct	St
First-class	141	251	22	8797	262*	38.41		16	46	127	0
List A	70	66	7	2201	131	37.30	86.41	2	16	28	0
Twenty20	91	82	12	1787	101*	25.52	118.97	2	4	22	0
Bowling	**Inns**	**Balls**	**Runs**	**Wkts**	**BBI**	**BBM**	**Ave**	**Econ**	**SR**	**5w**	**10**
First-class	141	979	666	12	2/16		55.50	4.08	81.5	0	0
List A	70	79	105	1	1/34	1/34	105.00	7.97	79.0	0	0
Twenty20	91	36	60	0	-	-	-	10.00	-	0	0

ANDREA AGATHANGELOU RHB LB

FULL NAME: Andrea Peter Agathangelou
BORN: November 16, 1989, Rustenberg, South Africa
SQUAD NO: 11
HEIGHT: 6ft 3in
NICKNAME: Aggers
EDUCATION: UNISA
TEAMS: Lancashire, Lancashire 2nd XI, North West, North West Under-19s, South Africa Under-19s
CAREER: First-class: 2008; List A: 2008

LANCASHIRE

BEST BATTING: 158 North West vs KwaZulu-Natal, Potchefstroom, 2010
BEST BOWLING: 2-62 North West vs KwaZulu-Natal Inland, Potchefstroom, 2009

CAREER HIGHLIGHTS? Representing my province in all age-groups and South Africa at U19 level. Playing first-class cricket at 17. Representing Highveld Lions. Representing SA Amateurs. Signing a contract with Lancashire and being part of the Championship-winning squad in 2011
CRICKETING HEROES? Sachin Tendulkar, Rahul Dravid, Jacques Kallis, Matthew Hayden
NON-CRICKETING HEROES? My mother and father, my grandparents, John Openshaw (mentor)
BEST PLAYER IN COUNTY CRICKET? Marcus Trescothick
TIP FOR THE TOP? Simon Kerrigan
IF YOU WEREN'T A CRICKETER? I would be taking over the world!
WHEN RAIN STOPS PLAY? Relaxing and being part of the banter in the changing room
FAVOURITE FILM? The Replacements, The Warrior
FAVOURITE BOOK? Eagle In The Sky by Wilbur Smith
ACCOMPLISHMENTS? Head boy at primary and high school, and went 12 years without missing a single day from school. Provincial colours in cricket, squash and biathlon
SURPRISING FACTS? I speak three languages – English, Afrikaans and I'm bettering my hand at Greek. I was a provincial squash player
TWITTER FEED: @Agathangelou11

Batting	Mat	Inns	NO	Runs	HS	Ave	SR	100	50	Ct	St
First-class	30	56	2	1867	158	34.57	52.93	4	11	42	0
List A	23	22	2	654	94	32.70	78.13	0	5	9	1
Bowling	**Inns**	**Balls**	**Runs**	**Wkts**	**BBI**	**BBM**	**Ave**	**Econ**	**SR**	**5w**	**10**
First-class	30	465	311	6	2/62	3/66	51.83	4.01	77.5	0	0
List A	23	30	35	0	-	-	-	7.00	-	0	0

SAEED AJMAL

RHB OB

FULL NAME: Saeed Ajmal
BORN: October 14, 1977, Faisalabad, Pakistan
SQUAD NO: 50
HEIGHT: 5ft 8in
TEAMS: Pakistan, Dhaka Gladiators, Faisalabad, Islamabad Cricket Association, Khan Research Labs, Water and Power Development Authority, Worcestershire
CAREER: Test: 2009; ODI: 2008; T20I: 2009; First-class: 1996; List A: 1995; T20: 2005

BEST BATTING: 53 Faisalabad vs Quetta, Sargodha, 2004
BEST BOWLING: 7-55 Pakistan vs England, Dubai, 2012

NOTES: Ajmal joins Hampshire as their overseas player in August and September – a period when George Bailey is likely to be involved in Australia's T20 internationals against England. He took 24 wickets in three Tests against England in UAE in 2011. At 30, Ajmal came late into international cricket – he was 32 before he played a Test – but he has made up for lost time and become regarded by many as the world's leading spinner. Previously played county cricket for Worcestershire, in 2011

Batting	Mat	Inns	NO	Runs	HS	Ave	SR	100	50	Ct	St
Tests	26	38	10	318	50	11.35	40.30	0	1	9	0
ODIs	74	44	18	219	33	8.42	59.02	0	0	13	0
T20Is	50	17	10	63	21*	9.00	112.50	0	0	6	0
First-class	116	157	46	1322	53	11.90		0	3	38	0
List A	176	96	43	416	33	7.84		0	0	39	0
Twenty20	107	32	17	117	21*	7.80	102.63	0	0	16	0
Bowling	**Inns**	**Balls**	**Runs**	**Wkts**	**BBI**	**BBM**	**Ave**	**Econ**	**SR**	**5w**	**10**
Tests	26	8262	3671	133	7/55	11/111	27.60	2.66	62.1	7	3
ODIs	74	3846	2623	117	5/24	5/24	22.41	4.09	32.8	2	0
T20Is	50	1116	1159	71	4/19	4/19	16.32	6.23	15.7	0	0
First-class	116	25905	11777	438	7/55		26.88	2.72	59.1	28	4
List A	176	9117	6624	270	5/18	5/18	24.53	4.35	33.7	3	0
Twenty20	107	2357	2482	154	4/14	4/14	16.11	6.31	15.3	0	0

KABIR ALI

RHB RMF W5

FULL NAME: Kabir Ali
BORN: November 24, 1980, Moseley, Birmingham, Warwickshire
SQUAD NO: 23
HEIGHT: 6ft
NICKNAME: Kabby, Taxi
EDUCATION: Moseley School; Wolverhampton University
TEAMS: England, Barisal Burners, England A, England NCA XI, Hampshire, Rajasthan, Worcestershire, Lancashire
CAREER: Test: 2003; ODI: 2003; First-class: 1999; List A: 2000; T20: 2004

BEST BATTING: 84* Worcestershire vs Durham, Stockton-on-Tees, 2003
BEST BOWLING: 8-50 Worcestershire vs Lancashire, Manchester, 2007

FAMILY TIES? Father played club cricket. Cousin Moeen plays for Worcestershire and cousin Kadeer played for Gloucestershire
CRICKETING HEROES? Wasim Akram, Glenn McGrath
CAREER HIGHLIGHTS? Playing for England
TIP FOR THE TOP? Moeen Ali

Batting	Mat	Inns	NO	Runs	HS	Ave	SR	100	50	Ct	St
Tests	1	2	0	10	9	5.00	35.71	0	0	0	0
ODIs	14	9	3	93	39*	15.50	86.11	0	0	1	0
First-class	130	182	28	2621	84*	17.01		0	7	33	0
List A	164	102	27	1150	92	15.33		0	3	30	0
Twenty20	46	34	12	435	50	19.77	141.69	0	1	12	0
Bowling	**Inns**	**Balls**	**Runs**	**Wkts**	**BBI**	**BBM**	**Ave**	**Econ**	**SR**	**5w**	**10**
Tests	1	216	136	5	3/80	5/136	27.20	3.77	43.2	0	0
ODIs	14	673	682	20	4/45	4/45	34.10	6.08	33.6	0	0
First-class	130	22125	13214	483	8/50		27.35	3.58	45.8	23	4
List A	164	6923	6008	237	5/36	5/36	25.35	5.20	29.2	2	0
Twenty20	46	907	1296	48	4/44	4/44	27.00	8.57	18.8	0	0

MOEEN ALI

LHB OB R1 MVP3

WORCESTERSHIRE

FULL NAME: Moeen Munir Ali
BORN: June 18, 1987, Birmingham
SQUAD NO: 8
HEIGHT: 6ft
NICKNAME: Moe, Brother Mo
EDUCATION: Moseley School
TEAMS: Duronto Rajshahi, England Lions, England Under-19s, Matabeleland Tuskers, Moors Sports Club, Warwickshire, Worcestershire
CAREER: First-class: 2005; List A: 2006; T20: 2007

BEST BATTING: 158 Worcestershire vs Somerset, Worcester, 2011
BEST BOWLING: 6-29 Worcestershire vs Lancashire, Manchester, 2012
COUNTY CAP: 2007 (Worcestershire)

FAMILY TIES? Dad is a cricket coach. Kadeer Ali [former Leicestershire, Worcestershire, Gloucestershire] is my brother and Kabir Ali [Lancashire] is my cousin
CAREER HIGHLIGHTS? Captaining Worcestershire. Being promoted twice with Worcestershire. Winning the CB40. Scoring 136 against Sri Lankan tourists
CRICKETING HEROES? Brian Lara, Saeed Anwar, Marcus Trescothick, Saeed Ajmal
NON-CRICKETING HEROES? Prophet Muhammad (peace be upon him), Abu Bakr, Umar, Uthman, Ali (may Allah be pleased with them all)
TIPS FOR THE TOP? Aneesh Kapil, Ben Stokes
IF YOU WEREN'T A CRICKETER? I'd own and run a chippy called Big Mo's
FAVOURITE TV? Final Legacy on the Islam Channel
FAVOURITE FILM? The Message
FAVOURITE BOOK? Al-Quran (the recitation), Aurther-Allah (One true God)
DREAM HOLIDAY? Saudi Arabia or Palestine
ACCOMPLISHMENTS? Hajj, performing the fifth pillar of Islam
SURPRISING FACT? I wear my trousers above my ankles. My grandmother is a white English woman

Batting	Mat	Inns	NO	Runs	HS	Ave	SR	100	50	Ct	St
First-class	90	157	12	4968	158	34.26	53.21	8	30	47	0
List A	88	83	2	2426	158	29.95	98.13	6	10	24	0
Twenty20	64	61	3	1266	82	21.82	120.00	0	6	19	0
Bowling	**Inns**	**Balls**	**Runs**	**Wkts**	**BBI**	**BBM**	**Ave**	**Econ**	**SR**	**5w**	**10**
First-class	90	6942	4163	94	6/29	12/96	44.28	3.59	73.8	3	1
List A	88	1734	1662	36	3/32	3/32	46.16	5.75	48.1	0	0
Twenty20	64	731	894	34	3/19	3/19	26.29	7.33	21.5	0	0

JIM ALLENBY RHB RM MVP16

FULL NAME: James Allenby
BORN: September 12, 1982, Perth, Australia
SQUAD NO: 5
HEIGHT: 6ft
NICKNAME: Hank
EDUCATION: Christ Church Grammar School, Perth
TEAMS: Durham Cricket Board, Glamorgan, Leicestershire, Western Australia, Western Australia Under-19s
CAREER: First-class: 2006; List A: 2003; T20: 2005

GLAMORGAN

BEST BATTING: 138* Leicestershire vs Bangladesh A, Leicester, 2008
BEST BOWLING: 5-44 Glamorgan vs Derbyshire, Cardiff, 2011
COUNTY CAP: 2010 (Glamorgan)

WHO WOULD PLAY YOU IN A FILM OF YOUR LIFE? Jim Carrey
CAREER HIGHLIGHTS? Signing first pro contract in 2005 after three years trialling all over the country. Winning the T20 with Leicestershire in 2006 and playing at Finals Day in 2005. Century on County Championship debut. T20 century for Leicestershire
SUPERSTITIONS? Prepare for each ball in the same way and walk out on left hand side
MOST MARKED CHARACTERISTIC? Too many to even begin to start!
IF YOU WEREN'T A CRICKETER? Lawn mowing
DESERT ISLAND DISC? Triple J Hottest 100
FAVOURITE TV? The Simpsons
BIGGEST DRESSING DOWN YOU'VE RECEIVED? Once again, far too many to mention!
CRICKETING HEROES? Dean Jones, Steve Waugh, Matt and Tom Maynard
TWITTER FEED: @jimallenby

Batting	Mat	Inns	NO	Runs	HS	Ave	SR	100	50	Ct	St
First-class	87	135	20	4425	138*	38.47	57.00	7	32	77	0
List A	75	70	8	1488	91*	24.00	82.07	0	6	23	0
Twenty20	73	67	11	1504	110	26.85	118.33	1	9	22	0
Bowling	**Inns**	**Balls**	**Runs**	**Wkts**	**BBI**	**BBM**	**Ave**	**Econ**	**SR**	**5w**	**10**
First-class	87	9587	4423	166	5/44	6/86	26.64	2.76	57.7	3	0
List A	75	2262	1886	66	5/43	5/43	28.57	5.00	34.2	1	0
Twenty20	73	912	1208	43	5/21	5/21	28.09	7.94	21.2	2	0

TOM ALLIN RHB RMF

WARWICKSHIRE

FULL NAME: Thomas William Allin
BORN: November 27, 1987, Devon
SQUAD NO: 87
HEIGHT: 5ft 11in
NICKNAME: Muscles, Guetta, TA
EDUCATION: Bideford College; UWIC
TEAMS: Cardiff MCCU, Devon, Warwickshire
CAREER: List A: 2011

FAMILY TIES? Dad [Tony] used to play professionally for Glamorgan
CAREER HIGHLIGHTS? Signing for Warwickshire and subsequently making my debut
SUPERSTITIONS? Three practice balls to mid on, left pad on first, lucky socks
CRICKETING HEROES? Sachin Tendulkar
NON-CRICKETING HEROES? Kauto Star
BEST PLAYER IN COUNTY CRICKET? Chris Woakes
TIP FOR THE TOP? Tom Milnes
IF YOU WEREN'T A CRICKETER? Involved in horse racing or a teacher
WHEN RAIN STOPS PLAY? iPhone
FAVOURITE TV? Channel 4 Racing or Hustle
FAVOURITE FILM? The Next Three Days
FAVOURITE BOOK? Lucky Break by Paul Nicholls
DREAM HOLIDAY? Sydney
ACCOMPLISHMENTS? Degree
SURPRISING SKILL? I'm class at Mario Kart on N64, lost once in 10 years!
SURPRISING FACTS? I want to be a jockey, I love rain, I only hit my first six when I was 16
TWITTER FEED: @tommya87

Batting	Mat	Inns	NO	Runs	HS	Ave	SR	100	50	Ct	St
List A	1	1	1	2	2*	-	16.66	0	0	0	0
Bowling	**Inns**	**Balls**	**Runs**	**Wkts**	**BBI**	**BBM**	**Ave**	**Econ**	**SR**	**5w**	**10**
List A	1	12	29	0	-	-	-	14.50	-	0	0

TIM AMBROSE

RHB WK MVP78

FULL NAME: Timothy Raymond Ambrose
BORN: December 1, 1982, Newcastle, Australia
SQUAD NO: 11
HEIGHT: 5ft 7in
NICKNAME: Freak
EDUCATION: Merewether Selective High, New South Wales
TEAMS: England, Sussex, Warwickshire
CAREER: Test: 2008; ODI: 2008; T20I: 2008; First-class: 2001; List A: 2001; T20: 2003

WARWICKSHIRE

BEST BATTING: 251* Warwickshire vs Worcestershire, Worcester, 2007
COUNTY CAPS: 2003 (Sussex); 2007 (Warwickshire)

FAMILY TIES? Father played for Nelson Bay
CAREER HIGHLIGHTS? Winning the Championship with Sussex in 2003, any time I've played for England
SUPERSTITIONS? Left pad before right
CRICKETING HEROES? Steve Waugh, Adam Gilchrist, Mushtaq Ahmed
NON-CRICKETING HEROES? Peter Griffin, Eric Cantona
BEST PLAYER IN COUNTY CRICKET? Marcus Trescothick
TIP FOR THE TOP? Laurie Evans
FAVOURITE TV? Dexter, Family Guy
FAVOURITE FILM? Cool Hand Luke
FAVOURITE BOOK? Bravo Two Zero
DREAM HOLIDAY? Nelson Bay

Batting	Mat	Inns	NO	Runs	HS	Ave	SR	100	50	Ct	St
Tests	11	16	1	447	102	29.80	46.41	1	3	31	0
ODIs	5	5	1	10	6	2.50	29.41	0	0	3	0
T20Is	1	-	-	-	-	-	-	-	-	1	1
First-class	150	226	22	6937	251*	34.00	51.79	10	42	364	22
List A	131	108	17	2672	135	29.36	74.72	3	11	128	23
Twenty20	55	43	13	800	77	26.66	114.77	0	2	32	17
Bowling	**Inns**	**Balls**	**Runs**	**Wkts**	**BBI**	**BBM**	**Ave**	**Econ**	**SR**	**5w**	**10**
Tests	11	-	-	-	-	-	-	-	-	-	-
ODIs	5	-	-	-	-	-	-	-	-	-	-
T20Is	1	-	-	-	-	-	-	-	-	-	-
First-class	150	6	1	0	-	-	-	1.00	-	0	0
List A	131	-	-	-	-	-	-	-	-	-	-
Twenty20	55	-	-	-	-	-	-	-	-	-	-

JAMES ANDERSON — LHB RFM W2

LANCASHIRE

FULL NAME: James Michael Anderson
BORN: July 30, 1982, Burnley, Lancashire
SQUAD NO: 9
HEIGHT: 6ft 2in
NICKNAME: Jimmy, Jimbo, Jimbob
EDUCATION: St Theodore's RC High School; St Theodore's RC Sixth Form Centre, Burnley
TEAMS: England, Auckland, England Under-19s, Lancashire, Lancashire Cricket Board
CAREER: Test: 2003; ODI: 2002; T20I: 2007; First-class: 2002; List A: 2000; T20: 2004

BEST BATTING: 37* Lancashire vs Durham, Manchester, 2005
BEST BOWLING: 7-43 England vs New Zealand, Nottingham, 2008
COUNTY CAP: 2003; **BENEFIT YEAR:** 2012

FAMILY TIES? My dad played for Burnley and uncle and cousin still play club cricket
CAREER HIGHLIGHTS? Two Ashes wins
CRICKETING HEROES? Allan Donald, Peter Martin
NON-CRICKETING HEROES? Ian Wright, Steve Davis (ex Burnley FC), Boris Becker
IF YOU WEREN'T A CRICKETER? Busking with my recorder
WHEN RAIN STOPS PLAY? Cards, sleeping, singing a cappella with Swann, Cook and Bresnan
FAVOURITE FILM? Les Enfants Terribles (1950)
FAVOURITE BOOK? Birdsong
ACCOMPLISHMENTS? Marriage and kids, scaling Kilimanjaro
SURPRISING SKILL? I can peel a potato in 2.4 seconds
TWITTER FEED: @JimmyAnderson9

Batting	Mat	Inns	NO	Runs	HS	Ave	SR	100	50	Ct	St
Tests	77	103	38	709	34	10.90	37.97	0	0	43	0
ODIs	167	66	35	204	20*	6.58	41.80	0	0	45	0
T20Is	19	4	3	1	1*	1.00	50.00	0	0	3	0
First-class	144	173	65	1074	37*	9.94		0	0	76	0
List A	220	87	52	297	20*	8.48		0	0	54	0
Twenty20	40	9	6	23	16	7.66	92.00	0	0	8	0
Bowling	**Inns**	**Balls**	**Runs**	**Wkts**	**BBI**	**BBM**	**Ave**	**Econ**	**SR**	**5w**	**10**
Tests	77	16943	8754	288	7/43	11/71	30.39	3.10	58.8	12	1
ODIs	167	8273	6885	229	5/23	5/23	30.06	4.99	36.1	2	0
T20Is	19	422	552	18	3/23	3/23	30.66	7.84	23.4	0	0
First-class	144	28400	14799	540	7/43		27.40	3.12	52.5	25	3
List A	220	10683	8681	303	5/23	5/23	28.65	4.87	35.2	2	0
Twenty20	40	855	1190	37	3/23	3/23	32.16	8.35	23.1	0	0

GARETH ANDREW LHB RMF W1 MVP89

FULL NAME: Gareth Mark Andrew
BORN: December 27, 1983, Yeovil, Somerset
SQUAD NO: 14
HEIGHT: 6ft
NICKNAME: Gaz, Brad, Golden Gary
EDUCATION: Ansford Communtity School; Richard Huish College, Taunton
TEAMS: Canterbury, Somerset, Somerset Cricket Board, Worcestershire, Worcestershire 2nd XI
CAREER: First-class: 2003; List A: 2000; T20: 2003

BEST BATTING: 180* Canterbury vs Auckland, Auckland, 2012
BEST BOWLING: 5-58 Worcestershire vs Middlesex, Kidderminster, 2008

CAREER HIGHLIGHTS? Winning the 2005 T20 Cup with Somerset, getting promotion to Division One with Worcestershire in 2008 and 2010 and helping Worcestershire avoid relegation in 2011
MOST MARKED CHARACTERISTIC? Laid-back, organised and wanting to improve. I love a list
TIP FOR THE TOP? Brett D'Oliveira
IF YOU WEREN'T A CRICKETER? Archaeologist, like Indiana Jones
DESERT ISLAND DISC? Kings Of Leon – Only By The Night
FAVOURITE TV? Strike Back
BIGGEST DRESSING DOWN YOU'VE RECEIVED? A massive angry spray by our captain at the time Vikram Solanki after a one-day defeat to Glamorgan at the SWALEC
CRICKETING HEROES? Ian Botham, Keith Parsons, Ivan Short
NON-CRICKETING HEROES? Keith Lemon
SURPRISING FACT? I'm seriously colourblind
FANTASY SLIP CORDON? Keeper: Angelina Jolie, 1st: John Bishop, 2nd: Myself, 3rd: Keith Lemon, Gully: Dynamo
TWITTER FEED: @GAndrew14

Batting	Mat	Inns	NO	Runs	HS	Ave	SR	100	50	Ct	St
First-class	72	111	16	2338	180*	24.61	55.79	1	12	24	0
List A	102	70	14	973	104	17.37		1	1	35	0
Twenty20	92	61	20	725	65*	17.68	142.99	0	4	23	0
Bowling	**Inns**	**Balls**	**Runs**	**Wkts**	**BBI**	**BBM**	**Ave**	**Econ**	**SR**	**5w**	**10**
First-class	72	9696	6345	180	5/58		35.25	3.92	53.8	4	0
List A	102	3312	3445	99	5/31	5/31	34.79	6.24	33.4	1	0
Twenty20	92	1598	2276	81	4/22	4/22	28.09	8.54	19.7	0	0

ZAFAR ANSARI LHB SLA

SURREY

FULL NAME: Zafar Shahaan Ansari
BORN: December 10, 1991, Ascot, Berkshire
SQUAD NO: 22
HEIGHT: 5ft 11in
NICKNAME: Zaf, PM
EDUCATION: Hampton School; University of Cambridge
TEAMS: Cambridge MCCU, England Under-19s, Surrey, Surrey 2nd XI, Surrey Under-13s, Surrey Under-15s, Surrey Under-17s, Surrey Under-19s
CAREER: First-class: 2011; List A: 2010; T20: 2011

BEST BATTING: 83* Surrey vs Warwickshire, Birmingham, 2012
BEST BOWLING: 5-33 Cambridge MCCU vs Surrey, Cambridge, 2011

FAMILY TIES? My dad played three first-class matches in Pakistan. My brother [Akbar] has played a lot of county 2nd XI cricket (Surrey, Worcestershire, Nottinghamshire, Hampshire) and captained Cambridge Blues for two years
CAREER HIGHLIGHTS? T20 debut, winning the CB40 at Lord's
CRICKETING HEROES? Garry Sobers, Graham Thorpe, Wasim Akram, Chris Scott
NON-CRICKETING HEROES? Akbar Ansari, Costas Douzinas
BEST PLAYER IN COUNTY CRICKET? Steve Davies
TIPS FOR THE TOP? Jason Roy, Chris Jones, Aneesh Kapil
IF YOU WEREN'T A CRICKETER? Law or American footballer
WHEN RAIN STOPS PLAY? Reading, drinking tea
FAVOURITE TV? The West Wing
FAVOURITE FILM? Biutiful
FAVOURITE BOOK? Half Of A Yellow Sun by Chimamanda Adichie
ACCOMPLISHMENTS? Starred 1st in first-year Cambridge exams
GUILTY PLEASURES? Juicy Drop Pops, Mario Kart, and I love Nando's
FANTASY SLIP CORDON? Keeper: Malcolm X, 1st: Michael Vick, 2nd: Leon Trotsky, 3rd: Me, Gully: Mike Hussey

Batting	Mat	Inns	NO	Runs	HS	Ave	SR	100	50	Ct	St
First-class	15	25	2	408	83*	17.73	37.84	0	2	8	0
List A	16	13	6	236	60*	33.71	95.54	0	1	10	0
Twenty20	20	15	6	252	38*	28.00	117.75	0	0	2	0
Bowling	**Inns**	**Balls**	**Runs**	**Wkts**	**BBI**	**BBM**	**Ave**	**Econ**	**SR**	**5w**	**10**
First-class	15	1011	552	12	5/33	5/39	46.00	3.27	84.2	1	0
List A	16	402	373	12	3/28	3/28	31.08	5.56	33.5	0	0
Twenty20	20	306	392	10	2/26	2/26	39.20	7.68	30.6	0	0

JAMES ANYON LHB RFM W1 MVP96

FULL NAME: James Edward Anyon
BORN: May 5, 1983, Lancaster
SQUAD NO: 30
HEIGHT: 6ft 2in
NICKNAME: Jimmy
EDUCATION: Gorsbory High School; Preston College; Loughborough University
TEAMS: Cumberland, Loughborough MCCU, Surrey, Sussex, Warwickshire
CAREER: First-class: 2003; List A: 2003; T20: 2005

BEST BATTING: 64* Sussex vs Surrey, Horsham, 2012
BEST BOWLING: 6-82 Warwickshire vs Glamorgan, Cardiff, 2008
COUNTY CAP: 2011 (Sussex)

CAREER HIGHLIGHTS? My T20 hat-trick vs Somerset in 2005. My Man of the Match performance against Nottinghamshire in 2011
CRICKETING HEROES? Curtly Ambrose, Glenn McGrath, Darren Gough, Michael Atherton
NON-CRICKETING HEROES? Paul Scholes, Sir Alex Ferguson, Winston Churchill
TIP FOR THE TOP? Ben Brown
IF YOU WEREN'T A CRICKETER? A fitness instructor
WHEN RAIN STOPS PLAY? Reading
FAVOURITE TV? Anything on the History or Discovery channels
FAVOURITE FILM? The Godfather
DREAM HOLIDAY? Rome
ACCOMPLISHMENTS? Getting a degree
GUILTY PLEASURES? Basshunter – shocking!
FANTASY SLIP CORDON? Keeper: Andy Hodd (he used to crack me up all game and can keep pretty well), 1st: Brian Cox (when it gets boring, at least I could learn something), 2nd: Me, 3rd: Eva Mendes (so she would be stood in front of me), Gully: Winston Churchill (for some inspiration)

Batting	Mat	Inns	NO	Runs	HS	Ave	SR	100	50	Ct	St
First-class	88	115	36	1123	64*	14.21	37.43	0	4	29	0
List A	38	11	5	34	12	5.66	80.95	0	0	8	0
Twenty20	22	4	3	16	8*	16.00	69.56	0	0	3	0
Bowling	**Inns**	**Balls**	**Runs**	**Wkts**	**BBI**	**BBM**	**Ave**	**Econ**	**SR**	**5w**	**10**
First-class	88	14007	8707	238	6/82		36.58	3.72	58.8	5	0
List A	38	1375	1254	41	3/6	3/6	30.58	5.47	33.5	0	0
Twenty20	22	351	498	25	3/6	3/6	19.92	8.51	14.0	0	0

USMAN ARSHAD

RHB RMF

FULL NAME: Usman Arshad
BORN: January 9, 1993, Bradford, Yorkshire
SQUAD NO: 78
HEIGHT: 6ft 1in
NICKNAME: Benny
EDUCATION: Beckfoot Grammar School, Bingley, Bradford
TEAMS: Durham 2nd XI, Durham Academy, Durham Under-17s
CAREER: Yet to make first-team debut

BEST PLAYER IN COUNTY CRICKET? Ryan Pringle
TIP FOR THE TOP? Graham Clark
IF YOU WEREN'T A CRICKETER? Doctor
DESERT ISLAND DISC? Drake – Take Care
FAVOURITE TV? Family Guy
CRICKETING HEROES? Keaton Jennings, Chris Martin
NON-CRICKETING HEROES? My dad
ACCOMPLISHMENTS? Raising £2,000 for charity
WHEN YOU RETIRE? Become a coach
SURPRISING FACT? I only started playing cricket when I was 14
FANTASY SLIP CORDON? Keeper: Chris Martin, 1st: Ryan Buckley, 2nd: Keaton Jennings, 3rd: Waj from Four Lions, Gully: Faisal from Four Lions
TWITTER FEED: @usman_arshad65

MOIN ASHRAF

RHB RFM

FULL NAME: Moin Aqeeb Ashraf
BORN: January 5, 1992, Bradford, Yorkshire
SQUAD NO: 23
HEIGHT: 6ft 2in
NICKNAME: Mo, The Official
EDUCATION: Dixons City Academy; Leeds Metropolitan University
TEAMS: Yorkshire, Yorkshire 2nd XI, Yorkshire Academy, Yorkshire Under-17s
CAREER: First-class: 2010; List A: 2011; T20: 2012

YORKSHIRE

BEST BATTING: 10 Yorkshire vs Kent, Leeds, 2010
BEST BOWLING: 5-32 Yorkshire vs Kent, Leeds, 2010

WHO WOULD PLAY YOU IN A FILM OF YOUR LIFE? Tyrese or The Rock
CAREER HIGHLIGHTS? Taking 5-33 vs Kent at Headingley in my second first-class game. Beating Worcestershire in the quarter-final and Sussex in the semi-final of the 2012 T20. Qualifying for the main Champions League competition in South Africa
MOST MARKED CHARACTERISTIC? Bowling the yorker
BEST PLAYER IN COUNTY CRICKET? Marcus Trescothick
TIPS FOR THE TOP? Tymal Mills, Joe Root, Matt Coles
IF YOU WEREN'T A CRICKETER? I'd be a personal trainer
DESERT ISLAND DISC? Chris Brown – Champion
CRICKETING HEROES? Imran Khan, Darren Gough, Shoaib Akhtar, Waqar Younis
NON-CRICKETING HEROES? The Prophet Muhammad
WHEN YOU RETIRE? Personal trainer or journalist
SURPRISING FACT? I am not Official Moin Ashraf on Twitter!
FANTASY SLIP CORDON? Keeper: Cristiano Ronaldo, 1st: Imran Khan, 2nd: The Rock, 3rd: Kim Kardashian, 4th: Michelle Keegan, Gully: Lionel Messi
TWITTER FEED: @MoinA23

Batting	Mat	Inns	NO	Runs	HS	Ave	SR	100	50	Ct	St
First-class	19	19	5	56	10	4.00	18.66	0	0	2	0
List A	14	3	3	3	3*	-	75.00	0	0	2	0
Twenty20	16	-	-	-	-	-	-	-	-	1	0
Bowling	**Inns**	**Balls**	**Runs**	**Wkts**	**BBI**	**BBM**	**Ave**	**Econ**	**SR**	**5w**	**10**
First-class	19	2105	1149	39	5/32	6/45	29.46	3.27	53.9	1	0
List A	14	557	516	15	2/25	2/25	34.40	5.55	37.1	0	0
Twenty20	16	333	434	17	4/18	4/18	25.52	7.81	19.5	0	0

MUHAMMAD AZHAR ULLAH RHB RFM

NORTHAMPTONSHIRE

FULL NAME: Muhammad Azhar Ullah
BORN: December 25, 1983, Burewala, Pakistan
SQUAD NO: TBC
TEAMS: Multan Region, Multan Tigers, Quetta Bears, Water and Power Development Authority
CAREER: First-class: 2004; List A: 2005; T20: 2005

BEST BATTING: 41 Water and Power Development Authority vs Karachi Whites, Karachi, 2007
BEST BOWLING: 7-74 Quetta vs Lahore Ravi, Quetta, 2005

NOTES: Azhar Ullah has been signed by Northamptonshire on a one-year contract and qualifies as a non-overseas player through his UK residency. He learnt his trade playing first-class cricket in Pakistan and until last November was representing the Water and Power Development Authority. He was recommended to Northamptonshire by allrounder James Middlebrook after impressing in league cricket in the UK

Batting	Mat	Inns	NO	Runs	HS	Ave	SR	100	50	Ct	St
First-class	53	70	38	485	41	15.15		0	0	14	0
List A	27	14	8	57	9	9.50	58.76	0	0	9	0
Twenty20	8	5	4	6	5*	6.00	60.00	0	0	1	0
Bowling	**Inns**	**Balls**	**Runs**	**Wkts**	**BBI**	**BBM**	**Ave**	**Econ**	**SR**	**5w**	**10**
First-class	53	8492	5037	190	7/74		26.51	3.55	44.6	11	1
List A	27	1264	1111	40	5/56	5/56	27.77	5.27	31.6	1	0
Twenty20	8	152	193	1	1/15	1/15	193.00	7.61	152.0	0	0

GEORGE BAILEY RHB RM

FULL NAME: George John Bailey
BORN: September 7, 1982, Launceston, Tasmania, Australia
SQUAD NO: 5
HEIGHT: 5ft 9in
NICKNAME: Bails, Geronimo
TEAMS: Australia, Scotland, Australia A, Chennai Super Kings, Melbourne Stars, Tasmania
CAREER: ODI: 2012; T20I: 2012; First-class: 2004; List A: 2002; T20: 2006

BEST BATTING: 160* Tasmania vs Victoria, Hobart, 2011

FAMILY TIES? My great-great-grandfather toured the UK with the Australian team in the tour prior to the Ashes beginning. My father was an A-Grade club player
WHO WOULD PLAY YOU IN A FILM OF YOUR LIFE? Morgan Freeman
CAREER HIGHLIGHTS? Winning a Sheffield Shield with Tasmania. Debuting for Australia in T20 and ODI cricket
SUPERSTITIONS? Don't forget your box
MOST MARKED CHARACTERISTIC? My grin... and freckles
IF YOU WEREN'T A CRICKETER? Teaching
DESERT ISLAND DISC? Bon Iver
FAVOURITE TV? Grand Designs, Modern Family
CRICKETING HEROES? Ricky Ponting and David Boon
NON-CRICKETING HEROES? Stefan Edberg
SURPRISING FACT? I had a pet wombat growing up
FANTASY SLIP CORDON? Keeper: Karl Stefanovic, 1st: David Attenborough, 2nd: Thomas Cromwell, 3rd: Myself, Gully: Eddie Vedder

Batting	Mat	Inns	NO	Runs	HS	Ave	SR	100	50	Ct	St
ODIs	21	20	3	764	125*	44.94	84.04	1	4	15	0
T20Is	16	13	3	274	63	27.40	132.36	0	1	8	0
First-class	88	157	15	5617	160*	39.55	55.22	14	28	81	0
List A	153	143	16	4526	125*	35.63	84.09	6	26	71	0
Twenty20	63	53	10	1198	63	27.86	133.25	0	6	27	0
Bowling	**Inns**	**Balls**	**Runs**	**Wkts**	**BBI**	**BBM**	**Ave**	**Econ**	**SR**	**5w**	**10**
ODIs	21	-	-	-	-	-	-	-	-	-	-
T20Is	16	-	-	-	-	-	-	-	-	-	-
First-class	88	84	46	0	-	-	-	3.28	-	0	0
List A	153	53	40	1	1/19	1/19	40.00	4.52	53.0	0	0
Twenty20	63	12	24	0	-	-	-	12.00	-	0	0

YORKSHIRE

JONNY BAIRSTOW — RHB WK R1

FULL NAME: Jonathan Marc Bairstow
BORN: September 26, 1989, Bradford, Yorkshire
SQUAD NO: 21
HEIGHT: 6ft
NICKNAME: Bluey
EDUCATION: St. Peter's School, York; Leeds Metropolitan University
TEAMS: England, England Lions, Yorkshire, Yorkshire 2nd XI
CAREER: Test: 2012; ODI: 2011; T20I: 2011; First-class: 2009; List A: 2009; T20: 2010

BEST BATTING: 205 Yorkshire vs Nottinghamshire, Nottingham, 2011
COUNTY CAP: 2011

FAMILY TIES? My father David played for Yorkshire and England
CAREER HIGHLIGHTS? Making my Test debut and being named Man of the Match on my ODI debut
MOST MARKED CHARACTERISTIC? Blue eyes
BEST PLAYER IN COUNTY CRICKET? Andre Adams
TIP FOR THE TOP? Joe Root
DESERT ISLAND DISC? Vengaboys or David Guetta
NON-CRICKETING HEROES? Jonny Wilkinson and Steve Irwin
SURPRISING FACT? I played football for the Leeds United Academy for seven years
FANTASY SLIP CORDON? Keeper: David Bairstow, 1st: Me, 2nd: David Beckham, 3rd: Mila Kunis, 4th: Ray Mears, Gully: Elisha Cuthbert
TWITTER FEED: @jbairstow21

Batting	Mat	Inns	NO	Runs	HS	Ave	SR	100	50	Ct	St
Tests	5	7	1	196	95	32.66	56.00	0	2	5	0
ODIs	7	6	1	119	41*	23.80	76.77	0	0	3	0
T20Is	18	14	4	194	60*	19.40	108.37	0	1	21	0
First-class	62	103	19	3870	205	46.07		7	26	125	5
List A	49	44	5	1046	114	26.82	96.58	1	4	31	3
Twenty20	60	49	9	721	68*	18.02	115.36	0	2	33	4
Bowling	**Inns**	**Balls**	**Runs**	**Wkts**	**BBI**	**BBM**	**Ave**	**Econ**	**SR**	**5w**	**10**
Tests	5	-	-	-	-	-	-	-	-	-	-
ODIs	7	-	-	-	-	-	-	-	-	-	-
T20Is	18	-	-	-	-	-	-	-	-	-	-
First-class	62	-	-	-	-	-	-	-	-	-	-
List A	49	-	-	-	-	-	-	-	-	-	-
Twenty20	60	-	-	-	-	-	-	-	-	-	-

ANDREW BALBIRNIE RHB OB WK

FULL NAME: Andrew Balbirnie
BORN: December 28, 1990, Dublin
SQUAD NO: 15
HEIGHT: 6ft 1in
NICKNAME: Balbo
EDUCATION: St Andrew's College, Dublin; Cardiff Metropolitan University
TEAMS: Ireland, Cardiff MCCU, Ireland Under-13s, Ireland Under-15s, Ireland Under-17s, Ireland Under-19s, Middlesex, Middlesex 2nd XI
CAREER: ODI: 2010; First-class: 2012; List A: 2010

MIDDLESEX

BEST BATTING: 36* Ireland vs South Africa A, Oak Hill, 2012

FAMILY TIES? My grandfather played for the YMCA club in Dublin
WHO WOULD PLAY YOU IN A FILM OF YOUR LIFE? Ben Affleck or Christian Bale
CAREER HIGHLIGHTS? My Ireland debut in 2010 and my Middlesex debut in 2012
SUPERSTITIONS? Left sock, shoe and pad on first
MOST MARKED CHARACTERISTIC? I'm told I have a massive head
BEST PLAYER IN COUNTY CRICKET? Marcus Trescothick
TIPS FOR THE TOP? Paul Stirling, Toby Roland-Jones
IF YOU WEREN'T A CRICKETER? A photographer, teacher or coach
DESERT ISLAND DISC? Mumford And Sons – Babel
FAVOURITE TV? Homeland
BIGGEST DRESSING DOWN YOU'VE RECEIVED? Mark Alleyne while playing for the MCC Young Cricketers following a horrendous day in the field against Notts in 2010
CRICKETING HEROES? Michael Vaughan
NON-CRICKETING HEROES? Nelson Mandela, Barack Obama
WHEN YOU RETIRE? Coaching at grassroots level
SURPRISING FACT? I put a square leg umpire in hospital by pulling a short ball straight at his head
TWITTER FEED: @balbo90

Batting	Mat	Inns	NO	Runs	HS	Ave	SR	100	50	Ct	St
ODIs	4	4	0	29	17	7.25	33.72	0	0	1	0
First-class	5	8	1	99	36*	14.14	48.29	0	0	2	0
List A	6	5	0	30	17	6.00	31.57	0	0	3	0
Bowling	**Inns**	**Balls**	**Runs**	**Wkts**	**BBI**	**BBM**	**Ave**	**Econ**	**SR**	**5w**	**10**
ODIs	4	-	-	-	-	-	-	-	-	-	-
First-class	5	48	24	0	-	-	-	3.00	-	0	0
List A	6	24	27	0	-	-	-	6.75	-	0	0

DAVID BALCOMBE RHB RMF W1 MVP73

FULL NAME: David John Balcombe
BORN: December 24, 1984, London
SQUAD NO: 84
HEIGHT: 6ft 3in
NICKNAME: Balcs, Snowman, Polar
EDUCATION: St John's School, Leatherhead; Durham University
TEAMS: Durham MCCU, Hampshire, Kent, Surrey 2nd XI
CAREER: First-class: 2005; List A: 2007; T20: 2006

BEST BATTING: 73 Durham UCCE vs Leicestershire, Leicester, 2005
BEST BOWLING: 8-71 Hampshire vs Gloucestershire, Southampton, 2012

WHO WOULD PLAY YOU IN A FILM OF YOUR LIFE? Bradley Cooper!
CAREER HIGHLIGHTS? My maiden County Championship five-wicket haul for Kent against Surrey at The Oval, taking 5-63. My best first-class bowling figures of 8-71 vs Gloucestershire at the Ageas Bowl, which was a ground record. Equalling my highest first-class score of 73, which was the highest score by a Hampshire No.11
TIPS FOR THE TOP? Daniel Bell-Drummond, Sam Billings
DESERT ISLAND DISC? Oasis
FAVOURITE TV? Downton Abbey
CRICKETING HEROES? Shane Warne, Glenn McGrath, Alec Stewart
ACCOMPLISHMENTS? My degree and my Durham Palatinate for achievements in and contributions to university sport
WHEN YOU RETIRE? Undecided, still exploring options and open to offers!
FANTASY SLIP CORDON? Keeper: Michael McIntyre, 1st: Jack Whitehall (they'd both add some humour to the field of play and in the changing room), 2nd: Berenice Marlohe (you've got to have someone nice to look at!), 3rd: Jessica Ennis (Olympic champion, enough said), Gully: Dave Brailsford (brilliant strategist)
TWITTER FEED: @DavidBalcombe1

Batting	Mat	Inns	NO	Runs	HS	Ave	SR	100	50	Ct	St
First-class	51	66	16	761	73	15.22	53.70	0	2	13	0
List A	12	5	0	10	6	2.00	32.25	0	0	4	0
Twenty20	3	2	1	3	3	3.00	60.00	0	0	0	0

Bowling	Inns	Balls	Runs	Wkts	BBI	BBM	Ave	Econ	SR	5w	10
First-class	51	8806	5091	169	8/71		30.12	3.46	52.1	8	2
List A	12	483	464	16	4/38	4/38	29.00	5.76	30.1	0	0
Twenty20	3	49	61	1	1/23	1/23	61.00	7.46	49.0	0	0

ADAM BALL RHB LFM

FULL NAME: Adam James Ball
BORN: March 1, 1993, Greenwich, London
SQUAD NO: 24
HEIGHT: 6ft 2in
NICKNAME: Bally
EDUCATION: Beths Grammar School, Bexley
TEAMS: England Under-19s, Kent, Kent 2nd XI, Kent Academy XI, Kent Under-13s, Kent Under-15s, Kent Under-17s
CAREER: First-class: 2011; List A: 2010; T20: 2011

BEST BATTING: 46 Kent vs Gloucestershire, Canterbury, 2011
BEST BOWLING: 3-36 Kent vs Leicestershire, Leicester, 2011

CRICKETING HEROES? Andrew Flintoff
FAVOURITE MUSICIAN? Taio Cruz
FAVOURITE FOOD? Nando's
FAVOURITE FILM? Ali G Indahouse
BEST CRICKETING MOMENT? Playing in the T20 quarter-finals
CAREER HIGHLIGHTS? Signing my first professional contract with Kent and being named as England U19 captain
TWITTER FEED: @AdamBall2

Batting	Mat	Inns	NO	Runs	HS	Ave	SR	100	50	Ct	St
First-class	9	15	1	184	46	13.14	35.24	0	0	5	0
List A	15	10	6	68	19	17.00	89.47	0	0	1	0
Twenty20	22	9	2	61	18	8.71	115.09	0	0	12	0
Bowling	Inns	Balls	Runs	Wkts	BBI	BBM	Ave	Econ	SR	5w	10
First-class	9	858	560	15	3/36	3/45	37.33	3.91	57.2	0	0
List A	15	507	441	17	2/31	2/31	25.94	5.21	29.8	0	0
Twenty20	22	399	497	22	2/18	2/18	22.59	7.47	18.1	0	0

JAKE BALL

RHB RMF

FULL NAME: Jacob Timothy Ball
BORN: March 14, 1991, Mansfield, Nottinghamshire
SQUAD NO: 28
HEIGHT: 6ft 1in
NICKNAME: Bally
EDUCATION: Meden School, Mansfield
TEAMS: England Under-19s, Nottinghamshire, Nottinghamshire 2nd XI
CAREER: First-class: 2011; List A: 2009; T20: 2011

BEST BATTING: 4 Nottinghamshire vs MCC, Abu Dhabi, 2011
BEST BOWLING: 3-72 Nottinghamshire vs MCC, Abu Dhabi, 2011

FAMILY TIES? My brother played for Lincolnshire and Notts U15, U17 and 2nd XI
WHO WOULD PLAY YOU IN A FILM OF YOUR LIFE? Jude Law
CAREER HIGHLIGHTS? Playing for England U19. Signing pro contract
SUPERSTITIONS? Kiss the ball before every over
MOST MARKED CHARACTERISTIC? My body
BEST PLAYER IN COUNTY CRICKET? Paul Franks
TIPS FOR THE TOP? Alex Hales, Adam Tillcock
IF YOU WEREN'T A CRICKETER? Male model
DESERT ISLAND DISC? Justin Bieber – My World
FAVOURITE TV? The Valleys
CRICKETING HEROES? Dominic Cork, Darren Gough
NON-CRICKETING HEROES? Ted Grewcock, Geoff Whittington
WHEN YOU RETIRE? Drive an ice cream van
SURPRISING FACT? I do the best impression of Paul Franks
FANTASY SLIP CORDON? Keeper: Cheryl Cole, 1st: Alex Hales, 2nd: Luke Fletcher, 3rd: Keeley Hazell, Gully: Daniel Kitson
TWITTER FEED: @JakeBall30

Batting	Mat	Inns	NO	Runs	HS	Ave	SR	100	50	Ct	St
First-class	1	2	1	4	4	4.00	57.14	0	0	0	0
List A	15	8	3	60	19*	12.00	101.69	0	0	0	0
Twenty20	2	-	-	-	-	-	-	-	-	1	0
Bowling	**Inns**	**Balls**	**Runs**	**Wkts**	**BBI**	**BBM**	**Ave**	**Econ**	**SR**	**5w**	**10**
First-class	1	126	106	3	3/72	3/106	35.33	5.04	42.0	0	0
List A	15	442	410	11	3/32	3/32	37.27	5.56	40.1	0	0
Twenty20	2	24	44	0	-	-	-	11.00	-	0	0

GARY BALLANCE LHB LB MVP53

FULL NAME: Gary Simon Ballance
BORN: November 22, 1989, Harare, Zimbabwe
SQUAD NO: 19
HEIGHT: 6ft
NICKNAME: Gazza, GB
EDUCATION: Peterhouse, Zimbabwe; Harrow School
TEAMS: Derbyshire, Derbyshire 2nd XI, England Lions, Mid West Rhinos, Yorkshire, Zimbabwe Under-19s
CAREER: First-class: 2008; List A: 2006; T20: 2010

YORKSHIRE

BEST BATTING: 210 Mid West Rhinos vs Southern Rocks, Masvingo, 2011
COUNTY CAP: 2012

NOTES: Nephew of former Zimbabwe skipper David Houghton, Ballance signed for Derbyshire at 16 before joining the Yorkshire Academy in 2008. He played for Zimbabwe U19 at the World Cup in 2006 but has now qualified for England, and toured Australia with the England Lions squad this February. Ballance played for the Mid West Rhinos in Zimbabwe under Jason Gillespie during the winters of 2010/11 and 2011/12, and scored four first-class hundreds for them before his first for Yorkshire in 2011. Last year he scored an undefeated 121 to help Yorkshire chase down 400 to beat Gloucestershire at Bristol. He also appeared in the Champions League 2012, hitting two half centuries

Batting	Mat	Inns	NO	Runs	HS	Ave	SR	100	50	Ct	St
First-class	50	79	13	3380	210	51.21	51.72	12	16	50	0
List A	45	44	10	1841	135*	54.14	90.11	4	10	21	0
Twenty20	46	41	7	889	67	26.14	121.78	0	4	25	0
Bowling	**Inns**	**Balls**	**Runs**	**Wkts**	**BBI**	**BBM**	**Ave**	**Econ**	**SR**	**5w**	**10**
First-class	50	60	40	0	-	-	-	4.00	-	0	0
List A	45	-	-	-	-	-	-	-	-	-	-
Twenty20	46	-	-	-	-	-	-	-	-	-	-

KEITH BARKER

LHB LFM W1 MVP5

FULL NAME: Keith Hubert Douglas Barker
BORN: October 21, 1986, Manchester, Lancashire
SQUAD NO: 13
HEIGHT: 6ft 2in
NICKNAME: Barksy
EDUCATION: Moorhead High School
TEAMS: Warwickshire, Warwickshire 2nd XI
CAREER: First-class: 2009; List A: 2009; T20: 2009

BEST BATTING: 118 Warwickshire vs Sussex, Birmingham, 2011
BEST BOWLING: 6-40 Warwickshire vs Somerset, Taunton, 2012

FAMILY TIES? My father Keith Barker Snr played for British Guinea, and my godfather Clive Lloyd is a West Indies legend
NON-CRICKETING HEROES? Lewis Hamilton
BEST PLAYER IN COUNTY CRICKET? Marcus Trescothick
TIP FOR THE TOP? Chris Woakes
WHEN RAIN STOPS PLAY? Resting or playing cricket inside with a tennis ball
FAVOURITE TV? Family Guy, Man vs Food
FAVOURITE FILM? The Dark Knight
FAVOURITE BOOK? Twilight
DREAM HOLIDAY? Barbados
ACCOMPLISHMENTS? Playing international football at age-group level
SURPRISING FACTS? My heart stopped beating during an operation when I was 15 and I was brought back to life. I played football in the UEFA Cup for Blackburn Rovers
FANTASY SLIP CORDON? Keeper: James Corden, 1st: Karl Pilkington, 2nd: Keith Barker Jnr, 3rd: Keith Barker Snr, Gully: Chris Tucker
TWITTER FEED: @KBarks13

Batting	Mat	Inns	NO	Runs	HS	Ave	SR	100	50	Ct	St
First-class	32	38	6	862	118	26.93	58.00	2	2	11	0
List A	43	30	7	397	56	17.26	89.01	0	1	8	0
Twenty20	48	23	4	285	46	15.00	109.61	0	0	12	0
Bowling	**Inns**	**Balls**	**Runs**	**Wkts**	**BBI**	**BBM**	**Ave**	**Econ**	**SR**	**5w**	**10**
First-class	32	4388	2279	84	6/40	10/70	27.13	3.11	52.2	6	1
List A	43	1498	1468	48	4/33	4/33	30.58	5.87	31.2	0	0
Twenty20	48	919	1178	55	4/19	4/19	21.41	7.69	16.7	0	0

ALEX BARROW RHB OB

FULL NAME: Alexander William Rogerson Barrow
BORN: May 6, 1992, Bath, Somerset
SQUAD NO: 18
HEIGHT: 5ft 7in
NICKNAME: Baz, Wheels, Pocket Rocket
EDUCATION: King's College, Taunton
TEAMS: England Under-19s, Somerset, Somerset 2nd XI, Somerset Under-17s
CAREER: First-class: 2011; List A: 2012

BEST BATTING: 69 Somerset vs Yorkshire, Leeds, 2011
BEST BOWLING: 1-4 Somerset vs Hampshire, Southampton, 2011

FAMILY TIES? My dad played first-class cricket
WHO WOULD PLAY YOU IN A FILM OF YOUR LIFE? Patrick J Adams
CAREER HIGHLIGHTS? Playing in the Champions League and my first-class and List A debuts
SUPERSTITIONS? Just the order that I pad up. It's not really superstition, just routine
BEST PLAYER IN COUNTY CRICKET? Marcus Trescothick
TIPS FOR THE TOP? Joe Root, Jos Buttler
IF YOU WEREN'T A CRICKETER? Anything… but not working in an office!
DESERT ISLAND DISC? The Verve – Bitter Sweet Symphony
FAVOURITE TV? Suits
CRICKETING HEROES? Jonty Rhodes, Ian Bell, Michael Clarke
NON-CRICKETING HEROES? Jonny Wilkinson
SURPRISING FACT? My mum is half Maltese
FANTASY SLIP CORDON? Keeper: Meghan Markle, 1st: Jonny Wilkinson, 2nd: James Corden, 3rd: Rihanna, Gully: George Dockrell
TWITTER FEED: @Alex_Barrow5

Batting	Mat	Inns	NO	Runs	HS	Ave	SR	100	50	Ct	St
First-class	16	26	0	404	69	15.53	44.39	0	1	18	0
List A	5	3	1	108	72	54.00	87.09	0	1	2	0
Bowling	**Inns**	**Balls**	**Runs**	**Wkts**	**BBI**	**BBM**	**Ave**	**Econ**	**SR**	**5w**	**10**
First-class	16	42	36	1	1/4	1/4	36.00	5.14	42.0	0	0
List A	5	-	-	-	-	-	-	-	-	-	-

MICHAEL BATES

RHB WK

HAMPSHIRE

FULL NAME: Michael David Bates
BORN: October 10, 1990, Frimley
SQUAD NO: 16
HEIGHT: 5ft 8in
NICKNAME: Batesy
EDUCATION: Yateley Manor; Lord Wandsworth College
TEAMS: England Under-19s, Hampshire, Hampshire 2nd XI
CAREER: First-class: 2010; List A: 2010; T20: 2010

BEST BATTING: 103 Hampshire vs Yorkshire, Leeds, 2012

CAREER HIGHLIGHTS? Winning at T20 Finals Day in 2010
CRICKETING HEROES? Alec Stewart
TIPS FOR THE TOP? Jos Buttler, James Vince, Danny Briggs, Ben Stokes
IF YOU WEREN'T A CRICKETER? I don't know!
FAVOURITE TV? Scrubs
FAVOURITE FILM? Blood Diamond
DREAM HOLIDAY? Greece
NOTES: Represented England at U15, U17, U18 and U10 level. Played in the U19 World Cup in New Zealand in 2010
TWITTER FEED: @batesy10_16

Batting	Mat	Inns	NO	Runs	HS	Ave	SR	100	50	Ct	St
First-class	33	46	4	826	103	19.66	44.76	1	3	102	5
List A	31	13	4	73	24*	8.11	62.93	0	0	20	4
Twenty20	29	4	1	25	10	8.33	80.64	0	0	12	6
Bowling	**Inns**	**Balls**	**Runs**	**Wkts**	**BBI**	**BBM**	**Ave**	**Econ**	**SR**	**5w**	**10**
First-class	33	-	-	-	-	-	-	-	-	-	-
List A	31	-	-	-	-	-	-	-	-	-	-
Twenty20	29	-	-	-	-	-	-	-	-	-	-

GARETH BATTY RHB OB W2 MVP18

FULL NAME: Gareth Jon Batty
BORN: October 13, 1977, Bradford, Yorkshire
SQUAD NO: 13
HEIGHT: 5ft 11in
NICKNAME: Bats, Mick, Boom Boom, Jack
EDUCATION: Bingley Grammar
TEAMS: England, Worcestershire, Yorkshire
CAREER: Test: 2003; ODI: 2002; T20I: 2009; First-class: 1997; List A: 1998; T20: 2003

BEST BATTING: 133 Worcestershire vs Surrey, The Oval, 2004
BEST BOWLING: 7-52 Worcestershire vs Northamptonshire, Northampton, 2004
COUNTY CAP: 2011 (Surrey)

FAMILY TIES? My brother [Jeremy] played for Yorkshire and Somerset and my dad still plays as well as coaching on the Yorkshire Academy
CAREER HIGHLIGHTS? Playing for England and getting my county cap
MOST MARKED CHARACTERISTIC? Ginger (well, strawberry blonde) hair
TIPS FOR THE TOP? Jason Roy, Matt Dunn, Rory Burns
DESERT ISLAND DISC? Rick Astley
BIGGEST DRESSING DOWN YOU'VE RECEIVED? I've had a few but the one that sticks in my mind was from Alan Butcher. I had gotten out four out of five times caught on the hook and he left it very clear what he would do to me if it happened again. I can't remember doing it again...
WHEN YOU RETIRE? Hopefully keep on with some property ventures

Batting	Mat	Inns	NO	Runs	HS	Ave	SR	100	50	Ct	St
Tests	7	8	1	144	38	20.57	27.01	0	0	3	0
ODIs	10	8	2	30	17	5.00	41.09	0	0	4	0
T20Is	1	1	0	4	4	4.00	57.14	0	0	0	0
First-class	181	278	44	5677	133	24.26		2	28	139	0
List A	216	167	35	2172	83*	16.45		0	5	74	0
Twenty20	82	60	16	521	87	11.84	105.46	0	1	30	0
Bowling	**Inns**	**Balls**	**Runs**	**Wkts**	**BBI**	**BBM**	**Ave**	**Econ**	**SR**	**5w**	**10**
Tests	7	1394	733	11	3/55	5/153	66.63	3.15	126.7	0	0
ODIs	10	440	366	5	2/40	2/40	73.20	4.99	88.0	0	0
T20Is	1	18	17	0	-	-	-	5.66	-	0	0
First-class	181	32741	16130	478	7/52		33.74	2.95	68.4	19	2
List A	216	8315	6339	199	5/35	5/35	31.85	4.57	41.7	1	0
Twenty20	82	1440	1758	67	4/13	4/13	26.23	7.32	21.4	0	0

WILL BEER RHB LB

FULL NAME: William Andrew Thomas Beer
BORN: October 8, 1988, Crawley, Sussex
SQUAD NO: 18
HEIGHT: 5ft 10in
NICKNAME: Beery
EDUCATION: Reigate Grammar
TEAMS: Sussex, Sussex 2nd XI
CAREER: First-class: 2008; List A: 2009; T20: 2008

BEST BATTING: 37* Sussex vs Worcestershire, Worcester, 2010
BEST BOWLING: 3-31 Sussex vs Worcestershire, Worcester, 2010

FAMILY TIES? My dad played for Sussex 2nd XI
CAREER HIGHLIGHTS? Winning the T20 domestic tournament in 2009 and going to the Champions League
CRICKETING HEROES? Shane Warne, Michael Yardy
NON-CRICKETING HEROES? David Beckham, Joey Essex
BEST PLAYER IN COUNTY CRICKET? Marcus Trescothick
TIPS FOR THE TOP? Matt Machan, Luke Wells
IF YOU WEREN'T A CRICKETER? Professional golfer
WHEN RAIN STOPS PLAY? Play Monopoly with teammates on my iPad – it can get very competitive! Dressing room golf
FAVOURITE FILM? Snakes On A Plane
FAVOURITE TV? The Only Way Is Essex
FAVOURITE BOOK? Harry Potter series
DREAM HOLIDAY? New York
ACCOMPLISHMENTS? Swimming badge for 25m. Orange belt in judo
GUILTY PLEASURES? Dairy Milk Buttons
TWITTER FEED: @willbeer18

Batting	Mat	Inns	NO	Runs	HS	Ave	SR	100	50	Ct	St
First-class	5	4	2	76	37*	38.00	38.97	0	0	1	0
List A	23	11	4	93	27*	13.28	77.50	0	0	5	0
Twenty20	41	19	7	106	22	8.83	117.77	0	0	7	0
Bowling	**Inns**	**Balls**	**Runs**	**Wkts**	**BBI**	**BBM**	**Ave**	**Econ**	**SR**	**5w**	**10**
First-class	5	388	228	9	3/31	3/36	25.33	3.52	43.1	0	0
List A	23	894	729	17	3/27	3/27	42.88	4.89	52.5	0	0
Twenty20	41	744	897	31	3/19	3/19	28.93	7.23	24.0	0	0

IAN BELL RHB RM R4

FULL NAME: Ian Ronald Bell
BORN: April 11, 1982, Walsgrave, Coventry, Warwickshire
SQUAD NO: 4
HEIGHT: 5ft 10in
NICKNAME: Belly
EDUCATION: Princethorpe College, Rugby
TEAMS: England, England Lions, England Under-19s, Marylebone Cricket Club, Warwickshire, Warwickshire Cricket Board
CAREER: Test: 2004; ODI: 2004; T20I: 2006; First-class: 1999; List A: 1999; T20: 2003

BEST BATTING: 262* Warwickshire vs Sussex, Horsham, 2004
BEST BOWLING: 4-4 Warwickshire vs Middlesex, Lord's, 2004
COUNTY CAP: 2001; BENEFIT YEAR: 2011

CAREER HIGHLIGHTS? Winning the County Championship with Warwickshire. Ashes victories
CRICKETING HEROES? Ricky Ponting, Dominic Ostler, Jeetan Patel
NON-CRICKETING HEROES? Gary Shaw, Gordon Cowans
BEST PLAYER IN COUNTY CRICKET? Marcus Trescothick
TIP FOR THE TOP? Chris Woakes
IF YOU WEREN'T A CRICKETER? I'd be sitting at the Holte End watching the Villa
DREAM HOLIDAY? Maldives
ACCOMPLISHMENTS? Honorary doctorate at Coventry University

Batting	Mat	Inns	NO	Runs	HS	Ave	SR	100	50	Ct	St
Tests	83	141	19	5699	235	46.71	50.76	17	34	64	0
ODIs	127	123	11	4149	126*	37.04	74.70	3	25	43	0
T20Is	7	7	1	175	60*	29.16	119.86	0	1	4	0
First-class	215	360	41	14478	262*	45.38		40	75	154	0
List A	255	244	24	8814	158	40.06		10	62	91	0
Twenty20	44	43	6	926	85	25.02	114.60	0	4	16	0
Bowling	**Inns**	**Balls**	**Runs**	**Wkts**	**BBI**	**BBM**	**Ave**	**Econ**	**SR**	**5w**	**10**
Tests	83	108	76	1	1/33	1/33	76.00	4.22	108.0	0	0
ODIs	127	88	88	6	3/9	3/9	14.66	6.00	14.6	0	0
T20Is	7	-	-	-	-	-	-	-	-	-	-
First-class	215	2827	1598	47	4/4		34.00	3.39	60.1	0	0
List A	255	1290	1138	33	5/41	5/41	34.48	5.29	39.0	1	0
Twenty20	44	132	186	3	1/12	1/12	62.00	8.45	44.0	0	0

DANIEL BELL-DRUMMOND RHB RM

FULL NAME: Daniel James Bell-Drummond
BORN: August 4, 1993, Lewisham, London
SQUAD NO: 23
HEIGHT: 5ft 11in
NICKNAME: DBD, Deebs
EDUCATION: Millfield School
TEAMS: England Under-19s, Kent, Kent 2nd XI
CAREER: First-class: 2011; List A: 2011; T20: 2011

BEST BATTING: 80 Kent vs Loughborough MCCU, Canterbury, 2011

WHY CRICKET? My father got me into it and I've always really enjoyed spending time at my local club Catford Wanderers CC
CAREER HIGHLIGHTS? Making my first-class debut
CRICKETING HEROES? Brian Lara, Kevin Pietersen, Chris Gayle
NON-CRICKETING HEROES? Nelson Mandela, Muhammad Ali
BEST PLAYER IN COUNTY CRICKET? Marcus Trescothick
TIPS FOR THE TOP? Adam Ball, Ben Foakes, Sam Northeast
IF YOU WEREN'T A CRICKETER? I'd be a musician
WHEN RAIN STOPS PLAY? I listen to my iPod, read magazines or watch TV
FAVOURITE TV? EastEnders
FAVOURITE FILM? Coach Carter
FAVOURITE BOOK? Animal Farm
DREAM HOLIDAY? The Caribbean
FANTASY SLIP CORDON? Keeper: Floyd Mayweather Jr, 1st: Me, 2nd: Robin van Persie, 3rd: Lee Evans, Gully: Brian Lara
TWITTER FEED: @deebzz23

Batting	Mat	Inns	NO	Runs	HS	Ave	SR	100	50	Ct	St
First-class	6	11	1	270	80	27.00	56.48	0	1	4	0
List A	5	5	0	111	42	22.20	98.23	0	0	0	0
Twenty20	1	1	0	11	11	11.00	183.33	0	0	0	0
Bowling	**Inns**	**Balls**	**Runs**	**Wkts**	**BBI**	**BBM**	**Ave**	**Econ**	**SR**	**5w**	**10**
First-class	6	-	-	-	-	-	-	-	-	-	-
List A	5	-	-	-	-	-	-	-	-	-	-
Twenty20	1	-	-	-	-	-	-	-	-	-	-

DALE BENKENSTEIN

RHB RM R5

FULL NAME: Dale Martin Benkenstein
BORN: June 9, 1974, Harare, Zimbabwe
SQUAD NO: 44
HEIGHT: 5ft 7in
NICKNAME: Benki
EDUCATION: Michaelhouse School
TEAMS: South Africa, Delhi Giants, Dolphins, Durham, KwaZulu-Natal, Natal
CAREER: ODI: 1998; First-class: 1993; List A: 1992; T20: 2004

BEST BATTING: 259 KwaZulu-Natal vs Northerns, Durban, 2002
BEST BOWLING: 4-16 Dolphins vs Warriors, Durban, 2005
COUNTY CAP: 2005

FAMILY TIES? My father Martin, uncle Des and twin brothers, Boyd and Brett, all played first-class cricket
CAREER HIGHLIGHTS? Playing for South Africa, winning the double with the Dolphins in 1997, winning the FP Trophy final at Lord's with Durham in 2007 and our first Championship in 2008
NON-CRICKETING HEROES? Seb Coe, Bjorn Borg, Christian Cullen
BEST PLAYER IN COUNTY CRICKET? Marcus Trescothick
TIPS FOR THE TOP? Ben Stokes, Scott Borthwick
FAVOURITE TV? Hawaii Five-O
FAVOURITE FILM? Hall Pass
ACCOMPLISHMENTS? My family, and beating Jansher Khan at squash
FANTASY SLIP CORDON? Keeper: Sir Alex Ferguson, 1st: Arsene Wenger (just so they have to stand next to each other all day), 2nd: Garry Sobers, 3rd: Roger Federer, Gully: Nelson Mandela

Batting	Mat	Inns	NO	Runs	HS	Ave	SR	100	50	Ct	St
ODIs	23	20	3	305	69	17.94	65.87	0	1	3	0
First-class	257	395	45	15690	259	44.82		38	84	164	0
List A	297	268	61	7275	107*	35.14		1	44	111	0
Twenty20	99	89	16	1769	60	24.23	128.18	0	6	32	0
Bowling	**Inns**	**Balls**	**Runs**	**Wkts**	**BBI**	**BBM**	**Ave**	**Econ**	**SR**	**5w**	**10**
ODIs	23	65	44	4	3/5	3/5	11.00	4.06	16.2	0	0
First-class	257	7523	3570	100	4/16		35.70	2.84	75.2	0	0
List A	297	3197	2681	87	4/16	4/16	30.81	5.03	36.7	0	0
Twenty20	99	468	579	21	3/10	3/10	27.57	7.42	22.2	0	0

GARETH BERG

RHB RMF MVP24

FULL NAME: Gareth Kyle Berg
BORN: January 18, 1981, Cape Town, South Africa
SQUAD NO: 8
HEIGHT: 6ft
NICKNAME: Ice, Bergy, Ford
EDUCATION: South African College School
TEAMS: Italy, Middlesex, Western Province
CAREER: First-class: 2008; List A: 2008; T20: 2009

BEST BATTING: 130* Middlesex vs Leicestershire, Leicester, 2011
BEST BOWLING: 6-58 Middlesex vs Glamorgan, Cardiff, 2011
COUNTY CAP: 2010

WHO WOULD PLAY YOU IN A FILM OF YOUR LIFE? Some might say I live a boring life, but far from it. People know very little of who I actually am and what I enjoy doing. Perhaps someone like Matt Damon – he's a great actor and seems to be quite a genuine down-to-earth guy who lives life outside of the limelight
CAREER HIGHLIGHTS? Winning promotion to Division One in 2011, my first five-fer and maiden hundred both coming at the Home of Cricket, and getting capped by Middlesex in 2010
SUPERSTITIONS? I like to stare into the sun when crossing the ropes before batting
BEST PLAYER IN COUNTY CRICKET? I admire the skills of Andre Adams
TIP FOR THE TOP? Tom Helm
WHEN YOU RETIRE? I would love to end up coaching cricket in Italy and playing for Italy for a couple of years before making the next big step in my life
SURPRISING FACT? I really enjoy playing the piano. It's my go-to place where I can switch off from the world
TWITTER FEED: @Bergy646

Batting	Mat	Inns	NO	Runs	HS	Ave	SR	100	50	Ct	St
First-class	55	89	10	2479	130*	31.37	65.18	2	15	37	0
List A	49	39	6	844	65	25.57	89.12	0	4	16	0
Twenty20	38	31	10	583	60*	27.76	121.96	0	1	11	0
Bowling	**Inns**	**Balls**	**Runs**	**Wkts**	**BBI**	**BBM**	**Ave**	**Econ**	**SR**	**5w**	**10**
First-class	55	6250	3512	115	6/58	7/90	30.53	3.37	54.3	3	0
List A	49	1249	1163	35	4/24	4/24	33.22	5.58	35.6	0	0
Twenty20	38	661	809	29	4/20	4/20	27.89	7.34	22.7	0	0

PAUL BEST LHB SLA

FULL NAME: Paul Merwood Best
BORN: March 8, 1991, Nuneaton
SQUAD NO: 15
HEIGHT: 5ft 10in
NICKNAME: Besty
EDUCATION: Bablake School, Coventry; Cambridge University
TEAMS: Cambridge MCCU, Cambridge University, England Under-19s, Northamptonshire, Warwickshire, Warwickshire 2nd XI
CAREER: First-class: 2011; List A: 2011; T20: 2012

BEST BATTING: 150 Cambridge MCCU vs Warwickshire, Cambridge, 2011
BEST BOWLING: 6-86 Cambridge University vs Oxford University, Cambridge, 2011

CAREER HIGHLIGHTS? Captaining England U19 in 2009 and 2010. Scoring 150* for Cambridge MCCU vs Surrey in 2011 and winning the game. Getting a six-fer vs Middlesex for Cambridge MCCU in 2011. Making my Warwickshire Championship debut. Being in the Cambridge team that won the treble vs Oxford in 2011
CRICKETING HEROES? Daniel Vettori
NON-CRICKETING HEROES? Hugh Laurie
BEST PLAYER IN COUNTY CRICKET? Marcus Trescothick
TIPS FOR THE TOP? Mark Best, Zafar Ansari, Charlie Taylor
IF YOU WEREN'T A CRICKETER? Either in the City or owning my own set of delicatessens
FAVOURITE TV? The Wire
FAVOURITE FILM? The Shawshank Redemption
FAVOURITE BOOK? Beowulf
DREAM HOLIDAY? Tanzania
SURPRISING FACT? The subjects I am studying at university are Anglo Saxon, Norse and Celtic
FANTASY SLIP CORDON? Keeper: Frankie Boyle, 1st: Shakespeare, 2nd: King Aethelred the Unready, 3rd: Me, Gully: Jamie Oliver

Batting	Mat	Inns	NO	Runs	HS	Ave	SR	100	50	Ct	St
First-class	9	12	2	378	150	37.80	49.15	1	1	5	0
List A	13	9	4	57	16*	11.40	75.00	0	0	3	0
Twenty20	3	-	-	-	-	-	-	-	-	1	0
Bowling	**Inns**	**Balls**	**Runs**	**Wkts**	**BBI**	**BBM**	**Ave**	**Econ**	**SR**	**5w**	**10**
First-class	9	2299	1340	31	6/86	9/131	43.22	3.49	74.1	2	0
List A	13	443	463	11	3/43	3/43	42.09	6.27	40.2	0	0
Twenty20	3	60	61	4	3/19	3/19	15.25	6.10	15.0	0	0

KENT

SAM BILLINGS RHB WK

FULL NAME: Samuel William Billings
BORN: June 15, 1991, Pembury, Kent
SQUAD NO: 20
HEIGHT: 5ft 11in
NICKNAME: Bilbo, Doug
EDUCATION: Haileybury College
TEAMS: England Under-19s, Kent, Kent 2nd XI, Loughborough MCCU
CAREER: First-class: 2011; List A: 2011; T20: 2011

BEST BATTING: 131 Loughborough MCCU vs Northamptonshire, Loughborough, 2011

FAVOURITE MUSICIAN? Tinie Tempah
FAVOURITE FOOD? Roast lamb or steak and chips
FAVOURITE QUOTE? "What you do in life, echoes in eternity"
FAVOURITE FILM? The Blindside
BEST CRICKETING MEMORY? Seeing England win the Ashes in Australia in 2010/11
PROUDEST MOMENT? Making my debuts for Kent and England U19
WORST HABIT? Playing too much FIFA
LOOKALIKE? Alex Pettyfer
TWITTER FEED: @sambillings

Batting	Mat	Inns	NO	Runs	HS	Ave	SR	100	50	Ct	St
First-class	6	9	0	353	131	39.22	52.68	1	1	6	0
List A	14	14	4	369	143	36.90	100.00	1	1	6	2
Twenty20	13	11	0	219	59	19.90	100.92	0	1	5	0
Bowling	**Inns**	**Balls**	**Runs**	**Wkts**	**BBI**	**BBM**	**Ave**	**Econ**	**SR**	**5w**	**10**
First-class	6	-	-	-	-	-	-	-	-	-	-
List A	14	-	-	-	-	-	-	-	-	-	-
Twenty20	13	-	-	-	-	-	-	-	-	-	-

ALEX BLAKE LHB RM

FULL NAME: Alexander James Blake
BORN: January 25, 1989, Farnborough, Kent
SQUAD NO: 18
HEIGHT: 6ft 2in
NICKNAME: Blakey, Butler, TS
EDUCATION: Hayes Secondary School; Leeds Metropolitan University
TEAMS: Kent, Kent 2nd XI, Leeds/Bradford MCCU
CAREER: First-class: 2008; List A: 2007; T20: 2010

BEST BATTING: 105* Kent vs Yorkshire, Leeds, 2010
BEST BOWLING: 2-9 Kent vs Pakistanis, Canterbury, 2010

CAREER HIGHLIGHTS? Maiden first-class century at Headingley. Representing England U19
CRICKETING HEROES? Graham Thorpe, Freddie Flintoff
NON-CRICKETING HEROES? David Beckham
BEST PLAYER IN COUNTY CRICKET? Marcus Trescothick
TIPS FOR THE TOP? Ben Stokes, Matt Coles, Jonny Bairstow
WHEN RAIN STOPS PLAY? Winding up Matt Coles or Fabian Cowdrey
FAVOURITE FILM? Moulin Rouge
FAVOURITE BOOK? The Game
DREAM HOLIDAY? Magaluf
SURPRISING SKILL? I'm a gourmet chef
GUILTY PLEASURES? Domino's pizza
SURPRISING FACTS? I lived with Jonny Bairstow at university, I can name all the countries of the world and I have a pet budgie
FANTASY SLIP CORDON? Keeper: Calvin Harris (to bust out some beats), 1st: Karl Pilkington (to entertain us all day by not having a clue), 2nd: Me, 3rd: Joey Barton (chief sledger), Gully: Joey Essex
TWITTER FEED: @aj_blake10

Batting	Mat	Inns	NO	Runs	HS	Ave	SR	100	50	Ct	St
First-class	28	47	2	993	105*	22.06	56.80	1	4	17	0
List A	33	25	6	434	81*	22.84	91.94	0	2	15	0
Twenty20	25	19	2	197	35	11.58	121.60	0	0	14	0
Bowling	**Inns**	**Balls**	**Runs**	**Wkts**	**BBI**	**BBM**	**Ave**	**Econ**	**SR**	**5w**	**10**
First-class	28	204	129	3	2/9	2/9	43.00	3.79	68.0	0	0
List A	33	84	74	3	2/13	2/13	24.66	5.28	28.0	0	0
Twenty20	25	-	-	-	-	-	-	-	-	-	-

RAVI BOPARA RHB RM R1

FULL NAME: Ravinder Singh Bopara
BORN: May 4, 1985, Forest Gate, London
SQUAD NO: 25
HEIGHT: 5ft 10in
NICKNAME: Puppy
EDUCATION: Brampton Manor School
TEAMS: England, Chittagong Kings, Dolphins, England Lions, England Under-19s, Essex, Essex Cricket Board, Gloucestershire, Kings XI Punjab, Marylebone Cricket Club
CAREER: Test: 2007; ODI: 2007; T20I: 2008; First-class: 2002; List A: 2002; T20: 2003

BEST BATTING: 229 Essex vs Northamptonshire, Chelmsford, 2007
BEST BOWLING: 5-75 Essex vs Surrey, Colchester, 2006
COUNTY CAP: 2005

CAREER HIGHLIGHTS? Playing for England, playing for Essex, scoring 201* vs Leicestershire in a one-day match, playing in the IPL and BPL, and scoring three centuries in a row for England
MOST MARKED CHARACTERISTIC? I'm chilled out
BEST PLAYER IN COUNTY CRICKET? Marcus Trescothick
DESERT ISLAND DISC? A Drake or Jay-Z album
CRICKETING HEROES? Sachin Tendulkar
SURPRISING FACT? I have a fast food business
FANTASY SLIP CORDON? Keeper: Robert De Niro, 1st: Ronnie Kray, 2nd: Reggie Kray, Gully: Sachin Tendulkar. They all achieved great things in their respective fields
TWITTER FEED: @ravibopara

Batting	Mat	Inns	NO	Runs	HS	Ave	SR	100	50	Ct	St
Tests	13	19	1	575	143	31.94	52.89	3	0	6	0
ODIs	83	77	15	1899	96	30.62	75.68	0	10	25	0
T20Is	22	20	2	365	59	20.27	98.11	0	2	5	0
First-class	129	215	27	7895	229	41.99	53.20	22	30	74	0
List A	216	202	41	6100	201*	37.88		7	36	64	0
Twenty20	130	119	14	2494	105*	23.75	113.26	1	13	41	0
Bowling	**Inns**	**Balls**	**Runs**	**Wkts**	**BBI**	**BBM**	**Ave**	**Econ**	**SR**	**5w**	**10**
Tests	13	434	290	1	1/39	1/39	290.00	4.00	434.0	0	0
ODIs	83	965	745	20	4/38	4/38	37.25	4.63	48.2	0	0
T20Is	22	130	141	9	4/10	4/10	15.66	6.50	14.4	0	0
First-class	129	9088	5836	134	5/75		43.55	3.85	67.8	1	0
List A	216	4699	4105	160	5/63	5/63	25.65	5.24	29.3	1	0
Twenty20	130	1589	2002	82	4/10	4/10	24.41	7.55	19.3	0	0

PAUL BORRINGTON

RHB RM

FULL NAME: Paul Michael Borrington
BORN: May 24, 1988, Nottingham
SQUAD NO: 17
HEIGHT: 5ft 11in
NICKNAME: Bozza, Boz
EDUCATION: Chellaston School; Repton School; Loughborough University
TEAMS: Derbyshire, Loughborough UCCE
CAREER: First-class: 2005; List A: 2009

BEST BATTING: 105 Loughborough UCCE vs Hampshire, Southampton, 2005

FAMILY TIES? My father played for Derbyshire between 1970 and 1982
WHO WOULD PLAY YOU IN A FILM OF YOUR LIFE? Will Smith
CAREER HIGHLIGHTS? Captaining the Midlands to victory in the Bunbury Festival in 2003. First-class debut against Leicestershire at Grace Road in 2005. Winning County Championship Division Two title in 2012
BEST PLAYER IN COUNTY CRICKET? Marcus Trescothick
FAVOURITE TV? An Idiot Abroad, 24, The X Factor
CRICKETING HEROES? Michael Vaughan
NON-CRICKETING HEROES? Dario Gradi, Jack Bauer
FANTASY SLIP CORDON? Keeper: Karl Pilkington, 1st: Me, 2nd: Nick Powell, 3rd: Jack Bauer, Gully: David Beckham
TWITTER FEED: @pborrington

Batting	Mat	Inns	NO	Runs	HS	Ave	SR	100	50	Ct	St
First-class	38	64	8	1544	105	27.57	35.64	2	7	22	0
List A	2	1	0	25	25	25.00	67.56	0	0	0	0
Bowling	**Inns**	**Balls**	**Runs**	**Wkts**	**BBI**	**BBM**	**Ave**	**Econ**	**SR**	**5w**	**10**
First-class	38	12	7	0	-	-	-	3.50	-	0	0
List A	2	-	-	-	-	-	-	-	-	-	-

SCOTT BORTHWICK LHB LB MVP75

DURHAM

FULL NAME: Scott George Borthwick
BORN: April 19, 1990, Sunderland, County Durham
SQUAD NO: 16
TEAMS: England, Durham, Durham 2nd XI, England Lions, England Under-19s
CAREER: ODI: 2011; T20I: 2011; First-class 2009; List A: 2009; T20: 2008

BEST BATTING: 101 Durham vs Sri Lanka A, Chester-le-Street, 2011
BEST BOWLING: 5-80 Durham vs Sussex, Hove, 2011

FAMILY TIES? Uncle [David] played for Northumberland
NOTES: Toured South Africa with England U19 in 2009, following selection for the Elite England Player Development XI in 2008. He was awarded the NBC Denis Compton Award for Durham's most promising young player in 2009. In the course of taking 35 first-class wickets in 2011, he made his ODI debut for England against Ireland in August, his T20I bow in September at The Oval vs the West Indies, and his overseas senior debut in India in October 2011. He spent the 2011/12 winter with the England Lions in Bangladesh and toured Australia with the Lions in early 2013

Batting	Mat	Inns	NO	Runs	HS	Ave	SR	100	50	Ct	St
ODIs	2	2	0	18	15	9.00	112.50	0	0	0	0
T20Is	1	1	0	14	14	14.00	87.50	0	0	1	0
First-class	42	61	13	1201	101	25.02	51.90	1	6	44	0
List A	40	25	7	209	44	11.61	69.20	0	0	12	0
Twenty20	27	12	7	114	30	22.80	95.79	0	0	5	0
Bowling	**Inns**	**Balls**	**Runs**	**Wkts**	**BBI**	**BBM**	**Ave**	**Econ**	**SR**	**5w**	**10**
ODIs	2	54	72	0	-	-	-	8.00	-	0	0
T20Is	1	24	15	1	1/15	1/15	15.00	3.75	24.0	0	0
First-class	42	3794	2302	76	5/80	8/84	30.28	3.64	49.9	1	0
List A	40	1266	1217	31	4/51	4/51	39.25	5.76	40.8	0	0
Twenty20	27	368	482	22	3/19	3/19	21.90	7.85	16.7	0	0

MATTHEW BOYCE LHB RM

FULL NAME: Matthew Andrew Golding Boyce
BORN: August 13, 1985, Cheltenham
SQUAD NO: 11
HEIGHT: 5ft 9in
NICKNAME: Boycey, Weasel
EDUCATION: Oakham School; Nottingham University
TEAMS: Leicestershire, Leicestershire 2nd XI
CAREER: First-class: 2006; List A: 2007; T20: 2008

BEST BATTING: 122 Leicestershire vs Yorkshire, Scarborough, 2012

WHO WOULD PLAY YOU IN A FILM OF YOUR LIFE? Tom Cruise
CAREER HIGHLIGHTS? My first first-class hundred and winning the T20 Cup in 2011
MOST MARKED CHARACTERISTIC? I have the thinnest face in world cricket
BEST PLAYER IN COUNTY CRICKET? Marcus Trescothick
TIPS FOR THE TOP? Shiv Thakor, Alex Wyatt
IF YOU WEREN'T A CRICKETER? I would be in the City trading things I know nothing about!
DESERT ISLAND DISC? Any power ballad compilation!
FAVOURITE TV? Scrubs
CRICKETING HEROES? Brian Lara, Graham Thorpe
NON-CRICKETING HEROES? Jonny Wilkinson
ACCOMPLISHMENTS? Playing rugby at Twickenham twice and walking from John O'Groats to Land's End off-road in 2012 for charity
FANTASY SLIP CORDON? Keeper: Brian Lara, 1st: Myself, 2nd: Muhammad Ali, 3rd: Michael McIntyre
TWITTER FEED: @Boycey85

Batting	Mat	Inns	NO	Runs	HS	Ave	SR	100	50	Ct	St
First-class	78	140	8	3736	122	28.30	40.90	5	19	48	0
List A	51	46	3	1116	80	25.95	82.85	0	7	13	0
Twenty20	35	24	6	426	63*	23.66	112.99	0	1	5	0
Bowling	**Inns**	**Balls**	**Runs**	**Wkts**	**BBI**	**BBM**	**Ave**	**Econ**	**SR**	**5w**	**10**
First-class	78	54	72	0	-	-	-	8.00	-	0	0
List A	51	-	-	-	-	-	-	-	-	-	-
Twenty20	35	-	-	-	-	-	-	-	-	-	-

WILL BRAGG

LHB RM WK R1

FULL NAME: William David Bragg
BORN: October 24, 1986, Newport
SQUAD NO: 22
HEIGHT: 5ft 10in
NICKNAME: BPOT, Shelf
EDUCATION: Rougemont School, Newport; University of Wales Institute, Cardiff
TEAMS: Glamorgan, Glamorgan 2nd XI, Wales Minor Counties
CAREER: First-class 2007; List A: 2005; T20: 2010

BEST BATTING: 110 Glamorgan vs Leicestershire, Colwyn Bay, 2011
BEST BOWLING: 1-4 Glamorgan vs Kent, Canterbury, 2010

FAMILY TIES? Dad played club cricket in South Wales League
CAREER HIGHLIGHTS? Scoring 1,000 runs in my first full season in 2011
SUPERSTITIONS? Always go to the toilet before batting!
CRICKETING HEROES? Herschelle Gibbs, Brian Lara, Daryll Cullinan
NON-CRICKETING HEROES? Kenny Powers, Ricky Gervais
BEST PLAYER IN COUNTY CRICKET? Marcus Trescothick
TIPS FOR THE TOP? James Harris, Scott Murphy
IF YOU WEREN'T A CRICKETER? Working abroad in some kind of financial environment
FAVOURITE TV? The Office
FAVOURITE FILM? See No Evil, Hear No Evil
FAVOURITE BOOK? Financial Times
ACCOMPLISHMENTS? Getting a BSc degree in Civil Engineering
SURPRISING SKILL? Acoustic guitar
GUILTY PLEASURES? Feeding the ducks whilst eating chocolate
FANTASY SLIP CORDON? Keeper: Ricky Gervais, 1st: Karl Pilkington, 2nd: Piers Morgan, 3rd: Britney Spears, Gully: Peggy Mitchell
TWITTER FEED: @WDBragg22

Batting	Mat	Inns	NO	Runs	HS	Ave	SR	100	50	Ct	St
First-class	45	77	0	2155	110	27.98	53.44	1	15	21	1
List A	14	13	1	283	78	23.58	70.57	0	1	2	0
Twenty20	1	1	0	15	15	15.00	68.18	0	0	0	0
Bowling	**Inns**	**Balls**	**Runs**	**Wkts**	**BBI**	**BBM**	**Ave**	**Econ**	**SR**	**5w**	**10**
First-class	45	247	157	2	1/4	1/5	78.50	3.81	123.5	0	0
List A	14	12	17	0	-	-	-	8.50	-	0	0
Twenty20	1	-	-	-	-	-	-	-	-	-	-

RUEL BRATHWAITE RHB RFM

FULL NAME: Ruel Marlon Ricardo Brathwaite
BORN: September 6, 1985, Barbados
SQUAD NO: 8
HEIGHT: 6ft 3in
NICKNAME: Brath
EDUCATION: Queen's College, Barbados; Dulwich College; Loughborough University
TEAMS: Cambridge MCCU, Combined Campuses and Colleges, Durham, Loughborough MCCU, Marylebone Cricket Club, Surrey 2nd XI, West Indies A
CAREER: First-class: 2006; List A: 2007; T20: 2010

BEST BATTING: 76* Loughborough UCCE vs Worcestershire, Worcester, 2007
BEST BOWLING: 5-54 Cambridge University vs Oxford University, Cambridge, 2009

WHY CRICKET? The passion and skill levels of two great West Indian fast bowlers Courtney Walsh and Curtly Ambrose first attracted me to the game
CAREER HIGHLIGHTS? Taking five wickets in an innings in the first two Championship matches I played as a professional cricketer. Playing for a West Indies A team, captained by Chris Gayle, in a warm-up match against the England Lions. Scoring 75* to see an MCC Universities team to victory over Ireland A in Ireland
CRICKETING HEROES? Malcolm Marshall, Michael Holding, Courtney Walsh, Curtly Ambrose, Brian Lara, Sir Vivian Richards, George Headley, Andrew Flintoff
NON-CRICKETING HEROES? The late Stephen Alleyne
TIP FOR THE TOP? Ben Stokes
IF YOU WEREN'T A CRICKETER? I have two degrees in Engineering and I am interested in investment management so I would pursue a career in one of those fields
FAVOURITE TV? Criminal Minds, An Idiot Abroad
ACCOMPLISHMENTS? Outside of cricket my greatest achievement was graduating from Cambridge University with a Masters
FANTASY SLIP CORDON? Keeper: Michael McIntyre, 1st: Charlie Sheen, 2nd: Myself, 3rd: Martin Lawrence, Gully: Will Smith

Batting	Mat	Inns	NO	Runs	HS	Ave	SR	100	50	Ct	St
First-class	23	26	10	200	76*	12.50	55.24	0	1	2	0
List A	2	-	-	-	-	-	-	-	-	0	0
Twenty20	1	1	0	0	0	0.00	0.00	0	0	0	0
Bowling	**Inns**	**Balls**	**Runs**	**Wkts**	**BBI**	**BBM**	**Ave**	**Econ**	**SR**	**5w**	**10**
First-class	23	3430	2087	65	5/54	8/130	32.10	3.65	52.7	3	0
List A	2	54	68	1	1/19	1/19	68.00	7.55	54.0	0	0
Twenty20	1	18	33	1	1/33	1/33	33.00	11.00	18.0	0	0

GARETH BREESE RHB OB

FULL NAME: Gareth Rohan Breese
BORN: January 9, 1976, Montego Bay, St James, Jamaica
SQUAD NO: 70
HEIGHT: 5ft 7in
NICKNAME: Briggy
EDUCATION: Wolmer's Boys School, Kingston; University of Technology, Jamaica
TEAMS: West Indies, Durham, Jamaica
CAREER: Test: 2002; First-class: 1995; List A: 1996; T20: 2004

BEST BATTING: 165* Durham vs Somerset, Taunton, 2004
BEST BOWLING: 7-60 Jamaica vs Barbados, Bridgetown, 2004

FAMILY TIES? My father played league cricket and is a cricket administrator
WHO WOULD PLAY YOU IN A FILM OF YOUR LIFE? Me. Film stars make a lot of money
CAREER HIGHLIGHTS? Winning the FP Trophy with Durham in the Lord's final. Being part of Durham's back-to-back County Championship titles and playing Test cricket
SUPERSTITIONS? No, I just love to fiddle with my kit
MOST MARKED CHARACTERISTIC? Being easy to talk to
BEST PLAYER IN COUNTY CRICKET? As a batsman Marcus Trescothick has to be up there
TIP FOR THE TOP? I've been really impressed with Joe Root. I think he will be a fantastic player for England
DESERT ISLAND DISC? You can't get better island music than Bob Marley
FAVOURITE TV? Cricket, Arrow, Chicago Fire, Suits, Last Resort
CRICKETING HEROES? Jimmy Adams, Courtney Walsh
NON-CRICKETING HEROES? My father, my mother, my wife
ACCOMPLISHMENTS? My children Savannah and Max
SURPRISING FACT? I loved to spear fish as a hobby when I lived in Jamaica

Batting	Mat	Inns	NO	Runs	HS	Ave	SR	100	50	Ct	St
Tests	1	2	0	5	5	2.50	19.23	0	0	1	0
First-class	117	187	20	4401	165*	26.35		4	27	99	0
List A	169	128	33	1959	68*	20.62		0	3	65	0
Twenty20	84	56	14	572	37	13.61	117.69	0	0	36	0
Bowling	**Inns**	**Balls**	**Runs**	**Wkts**	**BBI**	**BBM**	**Ave**	**Econ**	**SR**	**5w**	**10**
Tests	1	188	135	2	2/108	2/135	67.50	4.30	94.0	0	0
First-class	117	18165	8390	281	7/60		29.85	2.77	64.6	12	3
List A	169	6315	4950	178	5/41	5/41	27.80	4.70	35.4	2	0
Twenty20	84	1386	1566	73	4/14	4/14	21.45	6.77	18.9	0	0

TIM BRESNAN RHB RFM

FULL NAME: Timothy Thomas Bresnan
BORN: February 28, 1985, Pontefract, Yorkshire
SQUAD NO: 16
HEIGHT: 6ft 1in
NICKNAME: Brez
EDUCATION: Castleford High School; Pontefract New College
TEAMS: England, England Lions, England Under-19s, Marylebone Cricket Club, Yorkshire
CAREER: Test: 2009; ODI: 2006; T20I: 2006; First-class: 2003; List A: 2001; T20: 2003

BEST BATTING: 126* England Lions vs Indians, Chelmsford, 2007
BEST BOWLING: 5-42 Yorkshire vs Worcestershire, Worcester, 2005
COUNTY CAP: 2006

WHO WOULD PLAY YOU IN A FILM OF YOUR LIFE? Jimmy Anderson
CAREER HIGHLIGHTS? The Ashes in 2010/11
MOST MARKED CHARACTERISTIC? Curly hair
TIP FOR THE TOP? Joe Root
IF YOU WEREN'T A CRICKETER? Secret agent
DESERT ISLAND DISC? Alex Clare
FAVOURITE TV? Homeland
CRICKETING HEROES? Jacques Kallis
NON-CRICKETING HEROES? Sir Steve Redgrave
ACCOMPLISHMENTS? I'm saving them for retirement
TWITTER FEED: @timbresnan

Batting	Mat	Inns	NO	Runs	HS	Ave	SR	100	50	Ct	St
Tests	18	17	3	438	91	31.28	41.83	0	3	7	0
ODIs	69	49	13	719	80	19.97	91.12	0	1	19	0
T20Is	25	14	6	80	23*	10.00	100.00	0	0	6	0
First-class	121	156	27	3562	126*	27.61	47.55	3	17	49	0
List A	208	144	40	1952	80	18.76	90.83	0	4	55	0
Twenty20	77	51	19	510	42	15.93	114.09	0	0	21	0
Bowling	**Inns**	**Balls**	**Runs**	**Wkts**	**BBI**	**BBM**	**Ave**	**Econ**	**SR**	**5w**	**10**
Tests	18	3753	1855	57	5/48	8/141	32.54	2.96	65.8	1	0
ODIs	69	3439	3099	88	5/48	5/48	35.21	5.40	39.0	1	0
T20Is	25	490	610	19	3/10	3/10	32.10	7.46	25.7	0	0
First-class	121	20760	10606	337	5/42		31.47	3.06	61.6	6	0
List A	208	9195	7901	233	5/48	5/48	33.90	5.15	39.4	1	0
Twenty20	77	1533	1883	70	3/10	3/10	26.90	7.36	21.9	0	0

DANNY BRIGGS RHB SLA

HAMPSHIRE

FULL NAME: Danny Richard Briggs
BORN: April 30, 1991, Newport, Isle of Wight
SQUAD NO: 19
HEIGHT: 6ft 2in
NICKNAME: Briggsy
EDUCATION: Carisbrooke High School
TEAMS: England, Berkshire, England Lions, England Under-19s, Hampshire, Hampshire 2nd XI
CAREER: ODI: 2012; T20I: 2012; First-class: 2009; List A: 2009; T20: 2010

BEST BATTING: 38* England Lions vs Barbados, Bridgetown, 2011
BEST BOWLING: 6-45 England Lions vs Windward Islands, Roseau, 2011
COUNTY CAP: 2012

CAREER HIGHLIGHTS? Winning the T20 Cup in 2010
CRICKETING HEROES? Daniel Vettori
BEST PLAYER IN COUNTY CRICKET? James Tomlinson
TIP FOR THE TOP? Jos Buttler
IF YOU WEREN'T A CRICKETER? Anything to do with sport
WHEN RAIN STOPS PLAY? Very bored, sleeping or listening to music
FAVOURITE TV? Any comedy
FAVOURITE FILM? The Shawshank Redemption
DREAM HOLIDAY? Caribbean
GUILTY PLEASURES? 80s music
FANTASY SLIP CORDON? Keeper: Happy Gilmore, 1st: Viv Richards, 2nd: James Tomlinson, 3rd: Pele
TWITTER FEED: @DannyBriggs19

Batting	Mat	Inns	NO	Runs	HS	Ave	SR	100	50	Ct	St
ODIs	1	-	-	-	-	-	-	-	-	0	0
T20Is	3	-	-	-	-	-	-	-	-	0	0
First-class	37	46	9	371	38*	10.02		0	0	11	0
List A	42	19	5	138	25	9.85	85.18	0	0	13	0
Twenty20	56	10	5	27	10	5.40	103.84	0	0	11	0
Bowling	**Inns**	**Balls**	**Runs**	**Wkts**	**BBI**	**BBM**	**Ave**	**Econ**	**SR**	**5w**	**10**
ODIs	1	60	39	2	2/39	2/39	19.50	3.90	30.0	0	0
T20Is	3	42	70	2	1/16	1/16	35.00	10.00	21.0	0	0
First-class	37	7328	3854	118	6/45	9/96	32.66	3.15	62.1	5	0
List A	42	1926	1534	52	4/32	4/32	29.50	4.77	37.0	0	0
Twenty20	56	1135	1293	69	5/19	5/19	18.73	6.83	16.4	1	0

STUART BROAD LHB RFM

FULL NAME: Stuart Christopher John Broad
BORN: June 24, 1986, Nottingham
SQUAD NO: 16
HEIGHT: 6ft 5in
NICKNAME: Broady
EDUCATION: Oakham School
TEAMS: England, Leicestershire, Nottinghamshire
CAREER: Test: 2007; ODI: 2006; T20I: 2006; First-class: 2005; List A: 2005; T20: 2006

BEST BATTING: 169 England vs Pakistan, Lord's, 2010
BEST BOWLING: 8-52 Nottinghamshire vs Warwickshire, Birmingham, 2010
COUNTY CAP: 2007 (Leicestershire)

FAMILY TIES? My father [Chris] played for England, Nottinghamshire and Gloucestershire and is now an ICC match official
SUPERSTITIONS? Three warm-up balls before I bowl a new spell
BEST PLAYER IN COUNTY CRICKET? Graeme Swann
TIP FOR THE TOP? Joe Root
BIGGEST DRESSING DOWN YOU'VE RECEIVED? I've upset most international referees
CRICKETING HEROES? Glenn McGrath, Shaun Pollock
NON-CRICKETING HEROES? Brian Clough, Lewis Hamilton
ACCOMPLISHMENTS? Setting up the Broad Appeal [www.thebroadappeal.org]
SURPRISING FACT? I often dream in French
TWITTER FEED: @StuartBroad8

Batting	Mat	Inns	NO	Runs	HS	Ave	SR	100	50	Ct	St
Tests	52	71	9	1612	169	26.00	64.37	1	9	14	0
ODIs	96	51	17	416	45*	12.23	73.23	0	0	20	0
T20Is	46	19	7	71	18*	5.91	95.94	0	0	20	0
First-class	102	134	24	2669	169	24.26	59.23	1	16	30	0
List A	113	57	18	462	45*	11.84	71.96	0	0	22	0
Twenty20	64	21	8	80	18*	6.15	91.95	0	0	23	0
Bowling	**Inns**	**Balls**	**Runs**	**Wkts**	**BBI**	**BBM**	**Ave**	**Econ**	**SR**	**5w**	**10**
Tests	52	10824	5493	172	7/72	11/165	31.93	3.04	62.9	6	1
ODIs	96	4897	4242	152	5/23	5/23	27.90	5.19	32.2	1	0
T20Is	46	981	1205	55	4/24	4/24	21.90	7.37	17.8	0	0
First-class	102	19223	10402	360	8/52		28.89	3.24	53.3	16	2
List A	113	5679	4930	177	5/23	5/23	27.85	5.20	32.0	1	0
Twenty20	64	1383	1577	81	4/24	4/24	19.46	6.84	17.0	0	0

JACK BROOKS

RHB RFM

FULL NAME: Jack Alexander Brooks
BORN: June 4, 1984, Oxford
SQUAD NO: 70
HEIGHT: 6ft 2in
NICKNAME: Brooksy, Ferret, Animal, Gianluigi Von Burgernips, Scrumpy, Subo, Headband Warrior
EDUCATION: Wheatley Park School, Oxford
TEAMS: England Lions, Northamptonshire, Northamptonshire 2nd XI, Oxfordshire
CAREER: First-class: 2009; List A: 2009; T20: 2010

BEST BATTING: 53 Northamptonshire vs Gloucestershire, Bristol, 2010
BEST BOWLING: 5-23 Northamptonshire vs Leicestershire, Leicester, 2011
COUNTY CAP: 2012 (Northamptonshire)

FAMILY TIES? Father Don played and captained local village side Tiddington for 100 years, brother Nathan also plays for Tiddington and has represented Oxfordshire Development XI
SUPERSTITIONS? Always scratch my bowling marker with a J and change the headband now and then
CRICKETING HEROES? Dennis Lillee, Curtly Ambrose, Colin Milburn
NON-CRICKETING HEROES? Vincent Chase, John Malkovich and Rambo
BEST PLAYER IN COUNTY CRICKET? Batsman: Marcus Trescothick. Bowler: David Masters is an annoyingly good English seamer who is never injured!
FAVOURITE TV? Entourage
FAVOURITE FILM? Rambo or The Goonies
FAVOURITE BOOK? 4,000 Days
DREAM HOLIDAY? Oxfordshire
SURPRISING SKILL? Damn good salesman and I can drive a tractor
GUILTY PLEASURES? Skittles
TWITTER FEED: @BrooksyFerret

Batting	Mat	Inns	NO	Runs	HS	Ave	SR	100	50	Ct	St
First-class	37	42	14	327	53	11.67	47.39	0	1	8	0
List A	23	10	4	34	10	5.66	64.15	0	0	0	0
Twenty20	33	10	6	59	33*	14.75	134.09	0	0	5	0
Bowling	**Inns**	**Balls**	**Runs**	**Wkts**	**BBI**	**BBM**	**Ave**	**Econ**	**SR**	**5w**	**10**
First-class	37	6235	3417	118	5/23	7/97	28.95	3.28	52.8	4	0
List A	23	918	760	19	3/35	3/35	40.00	4.96	48.3	0	0
Twenty20	33	594	700	25	3/24	3/24	28.00	7.07	23.7	0	0

BEN BROWN RHB WK

FULL NAME: Ben Christopher Brown
BORN: November 23, 1988, Crawley, Sussex
SQUAD NO: 26
HEIGHT: 5ft 8in
NICKNAME: Brownie
EDUCATION: Balcombe Primary; Ardingly College
TEAMS: England Under-19s, Sussex, Sussex 2nd XI
CAREER: First-class: 2007; List A: 2007; T20: 2008

SUSSEX

BEST BATTING: 112 Sussex vs Derbyshire, Horsham, 2010

CAREER HIGHLIGHTS? Scoring my maiden Championship century, Sussex winning the T20 Cup in 2009
CRICKETING HEROES? Alec Stewart and Adam Gilchrist
BEST PLAYER IN COUNTY CRICKET? Chris Nash
TIPS FOR THE TOP? Luke Wells, Will Beer and Matt Machan
WHEN RAIN STOPS PLAY? Talking rubbish in the dressing room and trying to irritate anybody attempting to do a crossword or Sudoku!
FAVOURITE TV? Match Of The Day
FAVOURITE FILM? Gladiator
FAVOURITE BOOK? One Day by David Nicholls
DREAM HOLIDAY? Rome
ACCOMPLISHMENTS? School exam results
GUILTY PLEASURES? Ben and Jerry's Chocolate Fudge Brownie (preferably the whole tub)
FANTASY SLIP CORDON? Keeper: Me, 1st: Julius Caesar (commanding leader), 2nd: Jesus (must be a good fielder), 3rd: Russell Brand, Gully: David Beckham
TWITTER FEED: @Ben_Brown26

Batting	Mat	Inns	NO	Runs	HS	Ave	SR	100	50	Ct	St
First-class	35	56	7	1586	112	32.36	59.09	4	9	61	7
List A	30	21	8	351	60	27.00	107.33	0	3	30	6
Twenty20	27	22	2	282	68	14.10	103.29	0	1	11	3
Bowling	**Inns**	**Balls**	**Runs**	**Wkts**	**BBI**	**BBM**	**Ave**	**Econ**	**SR**	**5w**	**10**
First-class	35	-	-	-	-	-	-	-	-	-	-
List A	30	-	-	-	-	-	-	-	-	-	-
Twenty20	27	-	-	-	-	-	-	-	-	-	-

KARL BROWN RHB RM

FULL NAME: Karl Robert Brown
BORN: May 17, 1988, Bolton, Lancashire
SQUAD NO: 14
HEIGHT: 5ft 10in
NICKNAME: Browny, Charlie
EDUCATION: Hesketh Fletcher CE, Atherton, Lancashire
TEAMS: Lancashire, Lancashire 2nd XI, Moors Sports Club
CAREER: First-class: 2006; List A: 2007; T20: 2011

BEST BATTING: 114 Lancashire vs Sussex, Liverpool, 2011
BEST BOWLING: 2-30 Lancashire vs Nottinghamshire, Nottingham, 2009

FAMILY TIES? My dad played league cricket for Atherton CC and was the professional for Clifton CC
CAREER HIGHLIGHTS? Scoring my maiden first-class and one-day hundreds, playing for England U19
CRICKETING HEROES? Andrew Flintoff, Stuart Law
NON-CRICKETING HEROES? Kevin Davies, Lionel Messi, Ronnie O'Sullivan, Phil Taylor, Sergio Garcia
BEST PLAYER IN COUNTY CRICKET? Marcus Trescothick
TIP FOR THE TOP? Simon Kerrigan
WHEN RAIN STOPS PLAY? Playing cards or watching TV
FAVOURITE TV? Celebrity Juice
FAVOURITE FILM? Snatch, Layer Cake
DREAM HOLIDAY? Anywhere with a golf course
ACCOMPLISHMENTS? Playing football for Wigan Athletic
GUILTY PLEASURES? Sweets
TWITTER FEED: @karlos173

Batting	Mat	Inns	NO	Runs	HS	Ave	SR	100	50	Ct	St
First-class	45	76	5	1862	114	26.22	48.83	1	10	20	0
List A	36	34	7	1006	101*	37.25	84.75	1	5	7	0
Twenty20	19	17	3	385	51	27.50	124.59	0	2	4	0
Bowling	**Inns**	**Balls**	**Runs**	**Wkts**	**BBI**	**BBM**	**Ave**	**Econ**	**SR**	**5w**	**10**
First-class	45	84	49	2	2/30	2/37	24.50	3.50	42.0	0	0
List A	36	-	-	-	-	-	-	-	-	-	-
Twenty20	19	-	-	-	-	-	-	-	-	-	-

NATHAN BUCK

RHB RFM

FULL NAME: Nathan Liam Buck
BORN: April 26, 1991, Leicester
SQUAD NO: 9
HEIGHT: 6ft 3in
NICKNAME: Bucky
EDUCATION: Ashby School
TEAMS: England Lions, England Under-17s, England Under-19s, Leicestershire, Leicestershire 2nd XI
CAREER: First-class: 2009; List A: 2009; T20: 2010

BEST BATTING: 27 Leicestershire vs Kent, Canterbury, 2012
BEST BOWLING: 5-99 Leicestershire vs Gloucestershire, Bristol, 2011
COUNTY CAP: 2011

WHO WOULD PLAY YOU IN A FILM OF YOUR LIFE? Bart Simpson
CAREER HIGHLIGHTS? Playing for England at the U19 World Cup, England Lions tour of the West Indies in 2011, England Lions tour of Bangladesh and Sri Lanka in 2012 and Leicestershire county cap in 2011
BEST PLAYER IN COUNTY CRICKET? Graham Onions
TIP FOR THE TOP? Shiv Thakor
IF YOU WEREN'T A CRICKETER? I'd be trying to graduate from Loughborough University
FAVOURITE TV? The Inbetweeners, Facejacker
WHEN YOU RETIRE? I'd like to be a pilot
SURPRISING FACT? I gained seven A-stars, three A's and one B at GCSE
TWITTER FEED: @NathanBuck17

Batting	Mat	Inns	NO	Runs	HS	Ave	SR	100	50	Ct	St
First-class	47	64	16	384	27	8.00		0	0	6	0
List A	28	12	5	71	21	10.14	63.96	0	0	6	0
Twenty20	15	3	2	8	5*	8.00	66.66	0	0	4	0
Bowling	**Inns**	**Balls**	**Runs**	**Wkts**	**BBI**	**BBM**	**Ave**	**Econ**	**SR**	**5w**	**10**
First-class	47	7129	4012	102	5/99	7/79	39.33	3.37	69.8	1	0
List A	28	1159	1124	32	4/39	4/39	35.12	5.81	36.2	0	0
Twenty20	15	308	406	20	3/16	3/16	20.30	7.90	15.4	0	0

PETER BURGOYNE RHB OB

FULL NAME: Peter Ian Burgoyne
BORN: November 11, 1993, Nottingham
SQUAD NO: 11
HEIGHT: 6ft 2in
NICKNAME: Pie Man, Burgy, Stench
EDUCATION: St John Houghton School, Ilkeston; Derby Sixth Form College
TEAMS: Derbyshire, Derbyshire 2nd XI, England Under-19s, Southern Rocks
CAREER: First-class: 2012; List A: 2011; T20: 2012

BEST BATTING: 104 Southern Rocks vs Mid West Rhinos, Kwekwe, 2013
BEST BOWLING: 3-27 Southern Rocks vs Mid West Rhinos, Kwekwe, 2013

FAMILY TIES? My dad and brother play club cricket, but that's about it
CAREER HIGHLIGHTS? Making my Derbyshire 1st XI debut, playing for England U19, and making my first-class debut in Zimbabwe and getting my maiden first-class hundred
SUPERSTITIONS? Just make sure I have some toast before playing
MOST MARKED CHARACTERISTIC? Being a funny sort of character. I'm a bit of a nutter
BEST PLAYER IN COUNTY CRICKET? Wes Durston, easily
TIPS FOR THE TOP? Matt Pardoe, Dan Redfern
IF YOU WEREN'T A CRICKETER? As I'm not the brightest spark in the world, most probably working in a shop
DESERT ISLAND DISC? Right Said Fred – You're My Mate. Unreal song!
FAVOURITE TV? Premier League Darts, Two And A Half Men, The Powerpuff Girls
ACCOMPLISHMENTS? I won a few competitions playing golf for Derbyshire and I used to play in goal for Notts County FC
WHEN YOU RETIRE? I'd like to be an umpire in Zimbabwe
SURPRISING FACT? I absolutely love Marmite with any food. Even with cookies
TWITTER FEED: @PeterBurgoyne1

Batting	Mat	Inns	NO	Runs	HS	Ave	SR	100	50	Ct	St
First-class	7	12	1	370	104	33.63	36.70	2	0	6	0
List A	11	9	2	125	43	17.85	70.22	0	0	4	0
Twenty20	6	5	0	98	38	19.60	116.66	0	0	0	0
Bowling	**Inns**	**Balls**	**Runs**	**Wkts**	**BBI**	**BBM**	**Ave**	**Econ**	**SR**	**5w**	**10**
First-class	7	482	327	10	3/27	6/113	32.70	4.07	48.2	0	0
List A	11	417	351	11	3/31	3/31	31.90	5.05	37.9	0	0
Twenty20	6	96	89	2	1/17	1/17	44.50	5.56	48.0	0	0

JOE BURNS RHB RM

FULL NAME: Joseph Anthony Burns
BORN: September 6, 1989, Herston, Brisbane, Australia
SQUAD NO: TBC
TEAMS: Australia A, Queensland, Queensland Under-19s, Queensland Under-23s, Sussex 2nd XI
CAREER: First-class: 2011; List A: 2010; T20: 2012

BEST BATTING: 140* Queensland vs South Australia, Adelaide, 2011

NOTES: Burns will stand in for Leicestershire's four-day skipper Ramnaresh Sarwan when the West Indian leaves for international duty. He is scheduled to arrive on May 15 and leave on August 30 and his spell will comprise seven County Championship fixtures, the whole of the Friends Life t20 and 11 YB40 matches. He was voted the Bradman Young Cricketer of the Year by his fellow Australian players for his performances for Queensland in the 2012/13 season and scored 114 against the touring England Lions for Australia A in an unofficial 'ODI' in Hobart in February. He had a short stint with Sussex 2nd XI in 2010, scoring 54* against Somerset 2nd XI in a 2nd XI Trophy match at Birdham. His late great-uncle Harold Burns was a former wicketkeeper for Queensland, playing five first-class matches between 1930 and 1932

Batting	Mat	Inns	NO	Runs	HS	Ave	SR	100	50	Ct	St
First-class	24	41	4	1503	140*	40.62	53.14	4	7	15	0
List A	17	17	2	533	114	35.53	73.92	1	3	6	0
Twenty20	9	9	1	248	44	31.00	129.16	0	0	1	0
Bowling	**Inns**	**Balls**	**Runs**	**Wkts**	**BBI**	**BBM**	**Ave**	**Econ**	**SR**	**5w**	**10**
First-class	24	-	-	-	-	-	-	-	-	-	-
List A	17	-	-	-	-	-	-	-	-	-	-
Twenty20	9	-	-	-	-	-	-	-	-	-	-

RORY BURNS

LHB WK

SURREY

FULL NAME: Rory Joseph Burns
BORN: August 26, 1990, Epsom, Surrey
SQUAD NO: 17
HEIGHT: 5ft 9in
NICKNAME: Biebs, Fong, Chinese
EDUCATION: City of London Freemen's School; UWIC
TEAMS: Cardiff MCCU, Hampshire 2nd XI, Surrey, Surrey 2nd XI, Surrey Under-19s
CAREER: First-class: 2011; List A: 2012; T20: 2012

BEST BATTING: 121 Surrey vs Middlesex, The Oval, 2012

WHO WOULD PLAY YOU IN A FILM OF YOUR LIFE? Leonardo DiCaprio
CAREER HIGHLIGHTS? My first-class, List A, and T20 debuts and my first-class hundreds. Winning the Walter Lawrence Trophy. Becoming a professional cricketer
SUPERSTITIONS? I always walk out on the left of the other batter and I love taking first ball
BEST PLAYER IN COUNTY CRICKET? Marcus Trescothick
TIPS FOR THE TOP? Jason Roy, Matthew Dunn
IF YOU WEREN'T A CRICKETER? I'd be a student
DESERT ISLAND DISC? Justin Bieber or maybe Skrillex. Depends on my mood!
FAVOURITE TV? Any teen drama!
CRICKETING HEROES? Alec Stewart, Graham Thorpe, Kumar Sangakkara, Brian Lara
NON-CRICKETING HEROES? Jonny Wilkinson
ACCOMPLISHMENTS? Being able to play the saxophone and getting a place at university
SURPRISING FACT? I am an outstanding dancer
FANTASY SLIP CORDON? Keeper: Alec Stewart, 1st: Brian Lara, 2nd: Me, 3rd: Superman, 4th: Hayden Panettiere, Gully: Russell Howard
TWITTER FEED: @roryburns17

Batting	Mat	Inns	NO	Runs	HS	Ave	SR	100	50	Ct	St
First-class	11	19	2	776	121	45.64	49.93	2	4	9	0
List A	2	2	0	35	32	17.50	74.46	0	0	1	0
Twenty20	3	3	0	41	23	13.66	95.34	0	0	2	0
Bowling	**Inns**	**Balls**	**Runs**	**Wkts**	**BBI**	**BBM**	**Ave**	**Econ**	**SR**	**5w**	**10**
First-class	11	-	-	-	-	-	-	-	-	-	-
List A	2	-	-	-	-	-	-	-	-	-	-
Twenty20	3	-	-	-	-	-	-	-	-	-	-

JOS BUTTLER RHB WK

FULL NAME: Joseph Charles Buttler
BORN: September 8, 1990, Taunton, Somerset
SQUAD NO: 15
HEIGHT: 6ft
EDUCATION: King's College, Taunton
TEAMS: England, England Lions, England Under-19s, Somerset, Somerset 2nd XI
CAREER: ODI: 2012; T20I: 2011; First-class: 2009; List A: 2009; T20: 2009

BEST BATTING: 144 Somerset vs Hampshire, Southampton, 2010

TWITTER FEED: @josbuttler
NOTES: Came to prominence after scoring 55 from just 25 balls in the 2010 FP t20 semi between Somerset and Notts. Scored 440 runs at 55 in the 2010 CB40 and 411 runs at 137 in 2011, including 86 from 72 balls in the final. A successful tour with England Lions to Sri Lanka in early 2012 (262 runs at 87.33) led to a call-up for England's limited overs squads for the series against Pakistan in the UAE. Replaced Somerset teammate Craig Kieswetter as England's first choice ODI and T20I wicketkeeper in early 2012. Made his maiden international half-century (54 from just 30 balls) during the T20I against New Zealand at Hamilton in February

Batting	Mat	Inns	NO	Runs	HS	Ave	SR	100	50	Ct	St
ODIs	6	4	0	38	21	9.50	135.71	0	0	7	0
T20Is	21	16	7	242	54	26.88	147.56	0	1	5	0
First-class	39	55	5	1523	144	30.46	59.79	2	7	66	2
List A	56	47	16	1674	119	54.00	119.40	2	11	36	4
Twenty20	80	65	20	1203	72*	26.73	140.37	0	6	43	10
Bowling	**Inns**	**Balls**	**Runs**	**Wkts**	**BBI**	**BBM**	**Ave**	**Econ**	**SR**	**5w**	**10**
ODIs	6	-	-	-	-	-	-	-	-	-	-
T20Is	21	-	-	-	-	-	-	-	-	-	-
First-class	39	12	11	0	-	-	-	5.50	-	0	0
List A	56	-	-	-	-	-	-	-	-	-	-
Twenty20	80	-	-	-	-	-	-	-	-	-	-

MICHAEL CARBERRY

LHB OB R3 MVP80

FULL NAME: Michael Alexander Carberry
BORN: September 29, 1980, Croydon, Surrey
SQUAD NO: 15
HEIGHT: 5ft 11in
NICKNAME: Carbs
EDUCATION: St John Rigby College
TEAMS: England, England Lions, Hampshire, Kent, Marylebone Cricket Club, Surrey, Surrey Cricket Board
CAREER: Test: 2010; First-class: 2001; List A: 1999; T20: 2003

BEST BATTING: 300* Hampshire vs Yorkshire, Southampton, 2011
BEST BOWLING: 2-85 Hampshire vs Durham, Chester-le-Street, 2006
COUNTY CAP: 2006 (Hampshire)

FAMILY TIES? My dad played club cricket
CAREER HIGHLIGHTS? Every day is a highlight
CRICKETERS PARTICULARLY ADMIRED? Ricky Ponting, Brian Lara
RELAXATIONS? Sleeping
NOTES: Toured India with England Lions in 2008. Member of the England Performance Programme squad 2009/10. Opened the batting on Test debut for England against Bangladesh in 2010, scored 30 and 34, and has not played since. Helped Hampshire to two titles – the FL t20 and the CB40 – in 2012

Batting	Mat	Inns	NO	Runs	HS	Ave	SR	100	50	Ct	St
Tests	1	2	0	64	34	32.00	45.71	0	0	1	0
First-class	133	235	22	9197	300*	43.17	52.12	26	41	60	0
List A	134	124	13	3528	148*	31.78		4	26	52	0
Twenty20	73	68	9	1600	90	27.11	112.28	0	11	31	0
Bowling	**Inns**	**Balls**	**Runs**	**Wkts**	**BBI**	**BBM**	**Ave**	**Econ**	**SR**	**5w**	**10**
Tests	1	-	-	-	-	-	-	-	-	-	-
First-class	133	1288	910	14	2/85		65.00	4.23	92.0	0	0
List A	134	228	214	5	2/11	2/11	42.80	5.63	45.6	0	0
Twenty20	73	18	19	1	1/16	1/16	19.00	6.33	18.0	0	0

ANDY CARTER RHB RMF

FULL NAME: Andrew Carter
BORN: August 27, 1988, Lincoln
SQUAD NO: 37
HEIGHT: 6ft 5in
NICKNAME: Carts
EDUCATION: Lincoln College
TEAMS: Essex, Essex 2nd XI, Lincolnshire, Nottinghamshire, Nottinghamshire 2nd XI
CAREER: First-class: 2009; List A: 2009; T20: 2010

BEST BATTING: 17* Nottinghamshire vs Sussex, Hove, 2012
BEST BOWLING: 5-40 Essex vs Kent, Canterbury, 2010

WHO WOULD PLAY YOU IN A FILM OF YOUR LIFE? Keith Lemon
CAREER HIGHLIGHTS? Staying fit
SUPERSTITIONS? Always carry a rabbit's foot
MOST MARKED CHARACTERISTIC? I'm ginger
BEST PLAYER IN COUNTY CRICKET? Ben Phillips
TIPS FOR THE TOP? Brett Hutton, Sam Kelsall
IF YOU WEREN'T A CRICKETER? Plumber
DESERT ISLAND DISC? Iron Maiden – The Number Of The Beast
FAVOURITE TV? Jimmy's Farm
CRICKETING HEROES? Mike Hendrick, Luke Fletcher, Matthew Hoggard
NON-CRICKETING HEROES? Ted Nugent, butchers
ACCOMPLISHMENTS? My charity work
WHEN YOU RETIRE? Be a farmer or butcher
SURPRISING FACT? I was Lincolnshire trampoline junior champion
FANTASY SLIP CORDON? Keeper: My dog, 1st: Luke Fletcher, 2nd and 3rd: The Hairy Bikers, 4th: Lisa Riley, Gully: Nigel Dennis
TWITTER FEED: @andy_carter2011

Batting	Mat	Inns	NO	Runs	HS	Ave	SR	100	50	Ct	St
First-class	17	17	5	107	17*	8.91		0	0	4	0
List A	17	8	2	35	12	5.83	52.23	0	0	6	0
Twenty20	18	-	-	-	-	-	-	-	-	4	0
Bowling	**Inns**	**Balls**	**Runs**	**Wkts**	**BBI**	**BBM**	**Ave**	**Econ**	**SR**	**5w**	**10**
First-class	17	2737	1509	47	5/40	7/121	32.10	3.30	58.2	1	0
List A	17	573	586	24	4/45	4/45	24.41	6.13	23.8	0	0
Twenty20	18	341	471	18	4/20	4/20	26.16	8.28	18.9	0	0

GRAEME CESSFORD RHB RFM

FULL NAME: Graeme Cessford
BORN: October 4, 1983, Hexham, Northumberland
SQUAD NO: 16
HEIGHT: 6ft 1in
EDUCATION: Queen Elizabeth High School, Hexham
TEAMS: Northumberland, Worcestershire 2nd XI
CAREER: Yet to make first-team debut

NOTES: A Royal Air Force corporal, Cessford has been granted Elite Athlete Status by the RAF. Made three appearances for Worcestershire 2nd XI during the 2012 season as well as appearing for Northumberland. Last August, his 4-59 off 15 overs helped secure a 71-run victory over the MCC Young Cricketers at New Road. After signing Cessford, Worcestershire's director of cricket Steve Rhodes said: "Cess has the ability to bowl with pace and this will be a valuable asset in our 2013 campaign."

MAURICE CHAMBERS RHB RFM

FULL NAME: Maurice Anthony Chambers
BORN: September 14, 1987, Port Antonio, Portland, Jamaica
SQUAD NO: 29
HEIGHT: 6ft 3in
NICKNAME: Mozza, Mauri
EDUCATION: Homerton College of Technology; Sir George Monoux College
TEAMS: England Lions, Essex, Essex 2nd XI
CAREER: First-class: 2005; List A: 2008; T20: 2008

BEST BATTING: 30 Essex vs Leicestershire, Leicester, 2011
BEST BOWLING: 6-68 Essex vs Nottinghamshire, Chelmsford, 2010

WHO WOULD PLAY YOU IN A FILM OF YOUR LIFE? Will Smith
CAREER HIGHLIGHTS? Getting selected for the England Lions tour to Australia in 2010 and the tour to the West Indies in 2011
SUPERSTITIONS? No sexy time before cricket
MOST MARKED CHARACTERISTIC? Calm and steadfast in the face of adversity
BEST PLAYER IN COUNTY CRICKET? Ravi Bopara
TIPS FOR THE TOP? Reece Topley, Tymal Mills, Kishen Velani
DESERT ISLAND DISC? Ne-Yo – Year Of The Gentleman
FAVOURITE TV? The Big Bang Theory
CRICKETING HEROES? Courtney Walsh and Curtly Ambrose
NON-CRICKETING HEROES? Usain Bolt
ACCOMPLISHMENTS? Getting through college and passing my driving test
WHEN YOU RETIRE? Fast bowling coach, carpenter or electrician
FANTASY SLIP CORDON? Keeper: James Foster (fantastic man and the best keeper in the country), 1st: Usain Bolt, 2nd: Will Smith, 3rd: Chris Gayle (Will and him will make me laugh until my belly hurts), Gully: Me
TWITTER FEED: @Maurice29chamb

Batting	Mat	Inns	NO	Runs	HS	Ave	SR	100	50	Ct	St
First-class	43	56	21	197	30	5.62		0	0	12	0
List A	6	2	1	3	2	3.00	42.85	0	0	2	0
Twenty20	18	8	5	28	10*	9.33	96.55	0	0	6	0
Bowling	**Inns**	**Balls**	**Runs**	**Wkts**	**BBI**	**BBM**	**Ave**	**Econ**	**SR**	**5w**	**10**
First-class	43	5967	3573	110	6/68		32.48	3.59	54.2	2	1
List A	6	180	179	5	1/21	1/21	35.80	5.96	36.0	0	0
Twenty20	18	312	461	17	3/31	3/31	27.11	8.86	18.3	0	0

SHIVNARINE CHANDERPAUL LHB LB R1

FULL NAME: Shivnarine Chanderpaul
BORN: August 16, 1974, Unity Village, East Coast, Demerara, Guyana
SQUAD NO: 11
TEAMS: West Indies, Durham, Guyana, Khulna Royal Bengals, Lancashire, Royal Challengers Bangalore, Stanford Superstars, Uva Next, Warwickshire, Warwickshire 2nd XI
CAREER: Test: 1994; ODI: 1994; T20I: 2006; First-class: 1992; List A: 1992; T20: 2006

BEST BATTING: 303* Guyana vs Jamaica, Kingston, 1996
BEST BOWLING: 4-48 Guyana vs Leeward Islands, Basseterre, 1993
COUNTY CAP: 2010 (Lancashire)

NOTES: Chanderpaul signed a two-year deal with Derbyshire in January, with the club retaining first-option for a third season. He will be available across all formats in 2013. At the time of writing he sits ninth on the list of all-time leading Test run-scorers, and is only the second West Indian to score in excess of 10,000 Test runs. He had a short stint as West Indies skipper in 2005/06 but gave up the role to focus on his batting. Chanderpaul has a wealth of experience in county cricket, having previously represented Durham, Lancashire and Warwickshire. Named one of Wisden's five Cricketers of the Year in 2008 and won the ICC Player of the Year award in the same year

Batting	Mat	Inns	NO	Runs	HS	Ave	SR	100	50	Ct	St
Tests	146	249	42	10696	203*	51.67	42.97	27	61	62	0
ODIs	268	251	40	8778	150	41.60	70.74	11	59	73	0
T20Is	22	22	5	343	41	20.17	98.84	0	0	7	0
First-class	292	474	89	21686	303*	56.32		64	108	163	0
List A	385	358	63	12293	150	41.67		12	88	109	0
Twenty20	71	68	10	1358	87*	23.41	106.01	0	7	22	0
Bowling	**Inns**	**Balls**	**Runs**	**Wkts**	**BBI**	**BBM**	**Ave**	**Econ**	**SR**	**5w**	**10**
Tests	146	1740	883	9	1/2	1/2	98.11	3.04	193.3	0	0
ODIs	268	740	636	14	3/18	3/18	45.42	5.15	52.8	0	0
T20Is	22	-	-	-	-	-	-	-	-	-	-
First-class	292	4694	2491	57	4/48		43.70	3.18	82.3	0	0
List A	385	1681	1388	56	4/22	4/22	24.78	4.95	30.0	0	0
Twenty20	71	-	-	-	-	-	-	-	-	-	-

GLEN CHAPPLE RHB RMF W6 MVP10

FULL NAME: Glen Chapple
BORN: January 23, 1974, Skipton, Yorkshire
SQUAD NO: 3
HEIGHT: 6ft 2in
NICKNAME: Chappie, Boris
EDUCATION: West Craven High School; Nelson and Colne College
TEAMS: England, Lancashire
CAREER: ODI: 2006; First-class: 1992; List A: 1993; T20: 2003

BEST BATTING: 155 Lancashire vs Somerset, Manchester, 2001
BEST BOWLING: 7-53 Lancashire vs Durham, Blackpool, 2007
COUNTY CAP: 1994; BENEFIT YEAR: 2004

FAMILY TIES? Father played in Lancashire League for Nelson CC and was a professional for Darwen and Earby
SUPERSTITIONS? None
CRICKETING HEROES? Dennis Lillee, Robin Smith
FAVOURITE BAND? U2, Oasis, Stone Roses
RELAXATIONS? Golf
OTHER SPORTS FOLLOWED? Football (Liverpool)
TWITTER FEED: @chappie03

Batting	Mat	Inns	NO	Runs	HS	Ave	SR	100	50	Ct	St
ODIs	1	1	0	14	14	14.00	200.00	0	0	0	0
First-class	281	392	67	7907	155	24.32		6	34	89	0
List A	278	158	42	2035	81*	17.54		0	9	63	0
Twenty20	59	33	13	294	55*	14.70	110.94	0	1	14	0
Bowling	**Inns**	**Balls**	**Runs**	**Wkts**	**BBI**	**BBM**	**Ave**	**Econ**	**SR**	**5w**	**10**
ODIs	1	24	14	0	-	-	-	3.50	-	0	0
First-class	281	47865	23311	883	7/53		26.39	2.92	54.2	36	3
List A	278	11931	8974	312	6/18	6/18	28.76	4.51	38.2	5	0
Twenty20	59	1144	1395	62	3/36	3/36	22.50	7.31	18.4	0	0

VARUN CHOPRA RHB OB R2 MVP14

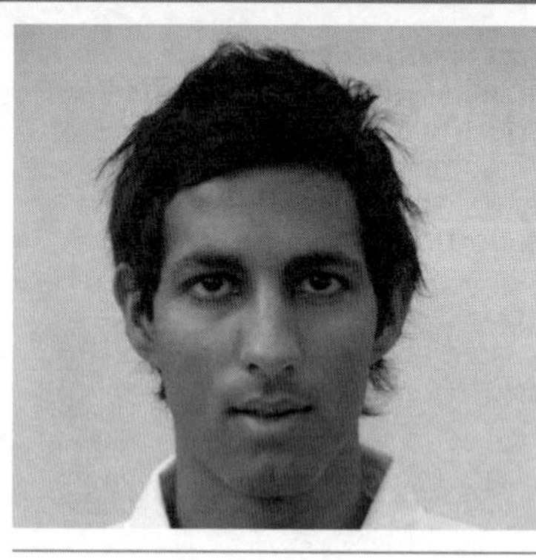

FULL NAME: Varun Chopra
BORN: June 21, 1987, Barking, Essex
SQUAD NO: 3
HEIGHT: 6ft 1in
NICKNAME: Tidz, Chops
EDUCATION: Ilford County High School
TEAMS: England Lions, England Under-19s, Essex, Essex 2nd XI, Tamil Union Cricket and Athletic Club, Warwickshire
CAREER: First-class: 2006; List A: 2006; T20: 2006

BEST BATTING: 233* Tamil Union vs Sinhalese Sports Club, Colombo, 2012

WHO WOULD PLAY YOU IN A FILM OF YOUR LIFE? Will Smith
CAREER HIGHLIGHTS? Winning the Championship with Warwickshire in 2012 and back-to-back double hundreds in 2011
MOST MARKED CHARACTERISTIC? My two birth marks
BEST PLAYER IN COUNTY CRICKET? Chris Woakes
TIPS FOR THE TOP? Tom Milnes, Richard Johnson
IF YOU WEREN'T A CRICKETER? Working in a bank
DESERT ISLAND DISC? Kanye West
FAVOURITE TV? Entourage
BIGGEST DRESSING DOWN YOU'VE RECEIVED? Too many to choose from!
CRICKETING HEROES? Sachin Tendulkar, Shane Warne
NON-CRICKETING HEROES? Roger Federer, Usain Bolt
FANTASY SLIP CORDON? Keeper: Russell Peters, 1st: Me, 2nd: Mila Kunis, 3rd: Usain Bolt, Gully: Chris Gayle
TWITTER FEED: @vchops3

Batting	Mat	Inns	NO	Runs	HS	Ave	SR	100	50	Ct	St
First-class	96	160	9	5380	233*	35.62	50.65	10	26	96	0
List A	66	64	3	2466	115	40.42	75.94	5	18	20	0
Twenty20	38	36	6	592	56*	19.73	103.85	0	3	4	0
Bowling	**Inns**	**Balls**	**Runs**	**Wkts**	**BBI**	**BBM**	**Ave**	**Econ**	**SR**	**5w**	**10**
First-class	96	149	95	0	-	-	-	3.82	-	0	0
List A	66	18	18	0	-	-	-	6.00	-	0	0
Twenty20	38	-	-	-	-	-	-	-	-	-	-

SHAAIQ CHOUDHRY RHB SLA

FULL NAME: Shaaiq Hussain Choudhry
BORN: November 3, 1985, Rotherham, Yorkshire
SQUAD NO: 28
HEIGHT: 5ft 11in
NICKNAME: Shak, Chouds
EDUCATION: Fire Vale School; Rotherham College of Arts and Technology; University of Bradford
TEAMS: Leeds-Bradford UCCE, Marylebone Cricket Club, Warwickshire, Worcestershire
CAREER: First-class: 2007; List A: 2010; T20: 2010

BEST BATTING: 75 Warwickshire vs Durham UCCE, Durham University, 2009
BEST BOWLING: 4-38 Worcestershire vs Lancashire, Manchester, 2012

CAREER HIGHLIGHTS? First-class debut against West Indies and scoring 54*. Championship debut for Worcestershire against Sussex, scoring 63 and taking 1-30. Taking 4-54 in a CB40 game against Surrey
SUPERSTITIONS? I tend to blink four times before facing each ball
CRICKETING HEROES? Muttiah Muralitharan, Jacques Kallis, Sachin Tendulkar
BEST PLAYER IN COUNTY CRICKET? Marcus Trescothick, Alan Richardson
TIP FOR THE TOP? Aneesh Kapil
IF YOU WEREN'T A CRICKETER? I would be working in graphics and photography
WHEN RAIN STOPS PLAY? Play games on my iPhone and eating
FAVOURITE FILM? Scarface
FANTASY SLIP CORDON? Keeper: Charlie Sheen, 1st: Mario Balotelli, 2nd: Rihanna, 3rd: Me, Gully: Muhammad Ali
TWITTER FEED: @ShaaiqChoudhry

Batting	Mat	Inns	NO	Runs	HS	Ave	SR	100	50	Ct	St
First-class	9	15	3	253	75	21.08	33.07	0	3	5	0
List A	22	16	7	163	39	18.11	87.16	0	0	7	0
Twenty20	11	10	8	61	26*	30.50	112.96	0	0	0	0
Bowling	**Inns**	**Balls**	**Runs**	**Wkts**	**BBI**	**BBM**	**Ave**	**Econ**	**SR**	**5w**	**10**
First-class	9	628	321	12	4/38	6/54	26.75	3.06	52.3	0	0
List A	22	618	646	14	4/54	4/54	46.14	6.27	44.1	0	0
Twenty20	11	156	182	6	2/24	2/24	30.33	7.00	26.0	0	0

DANIEL CHRISTIAN

RHB RFM

FULL NAME: Daniel Trevor Christian
BORN: May 4, 1983, Camperdown, Sydney, New South Wales
SQUAD NO: TBC
HEIGHT: 5ft 10in
TEAMS: Australia, Brisbane Heat, Deccan Chargers, Hampshire, New South Wales, South Australia
CAREER: ODI: 2012; T20I: 2010; First-class: 2008; List A: 2006; T20: 2006

BEST BATTING: 131* South Australia vs New South Wales, Adelaide, 2011
BEST BOWLING: 5-24 South Australia vs Western Australia, Perth, 2010

NOTES: Christian, who has previous county cricket experience with Hampshire, has signed with Gloucestershire for the 2013 Friends Life t20 and will be available for the entirety of the competition. In 2010 he helped Hampshire win the domestic T20 competition and was at the crease when the Royals claimed a dramatic last ball win over Somerset in the final. He has a wealth of experience in the format having played for Deccan Chargers in the IPL and Brisbane Heat in the Big Bash League. He was part of the Heat team that won the 2013 Big Bash, scoring 37 off 21 balls in the final against Perth Scorchers, and in February he secured a contract with Royal Challengers Bangalore for the 2013 edition of the IPL, attracting US$100,000 at auction. He has an ODI hat-trick to his name, taken against Sri Lanka in March 2012

Batting	Mat	Inns	NO	Runs	HS	Ave	SR	100	50	Ct	St
ODIs	17	17	5	250	39	20.83	86.80	0	0	7	0
T20Is	11	4	2	12	4*	6.00	109.09	0	0	5	0
First-class	37	64	5	1708	131*	28.94	54.06	3	8	38	0
List A	74	70	17	1704	100	32.15	96.27	1	6	30	0
Twenty20	100	83	21	1296	75*	20.90	131.57	0	2	44	0
Bowling	**Inns**	**Balls**	**Runs**	**Wkts**	**BBI**	**BBM**	**Ave**	**Econ**	**SR**	**5w**	**10**
ODIs	17	655	528	17	5/31	5/31	31.05	4.83	38.5	1	0
T20Is	11	168	240	10	3/27	3/27	24.00	8.57	16.8	0	0
First-class	37	6389	3494	98	5/24	9/87	35.65	3.28	65.1	2	0
List A	74	2667	2416	72	6/48	6/48	33.55	5.43	37.0	2	0
Twenty20	100	1765	2391	94	5/26	5/26	25.43	8.12	18.7	1	0

JONATHAN CLARE RHB RMF

FULL NAME: Jonathan Luke Clare
BORN: June 14, 1986, Burnley, Lancashire
SQUAD NO: 13
HEIGHT: 6ft 3in
NICKNAME: JC, Sidewinder, Scream
EDUCATION: St Theodore's RC High School and Sixth Form
TEAMS: Derbyshire, Derbyshire 2nd XI, Lancashire 2nd XI, Surrey 2nd XI
CAREER: First-class: 2007; List A: 2007; T20: 2008

BEST BATTING: 130 Derbyshire vs Glamorgan, Derby, 2011
BEST BOWLING: 7-74 Derbyshire vs Northamptonshire, Northampton, 2008

CAREER HIGHLIGHTS? County Championship Division Two champions in 2012. Taking 7-77 and scoring my maiden first-class century in the same match vs Northants. Taking match figures of 11-57 against Glamorgan in 2012
SUPERSTITIONS? None. My shirt number is 13!
MOST MARKED CHARACTERISTIC? Turning from a quite laid-back character to a raving lunatic when bowling!
TIP FOR THE TOP? Pete Burgoyne
IF YOU WEREN'T A CRICKETER? Being a football referee as the current crop are a disgrace!
DESERT ISLAND DISC? Arctic Monkeys – Whatever People Say I Am, That's What I'm Not
FAVOURITE TV? Newsroom
NON-CRICKETING HEROES? Michael Jordan, Jimmy Mullen (ex-Burnley manager)
ACCOMPLISHMENTS? Watching Burnley FC week in week out! Putting up with Mark Footitt on a daily basis
SURPRISING FACT? I play golf to a nine handicap, I can play a couple of songs on the steel drums and I played in a Burnley U17 game containing three first-class players: Michael Brown, James Anderson, David Brown
TWITTER FEED: @jcfalcons13

Batting	Mat	Inns	NO	Runs	HS	Ave	SR	100	50	Ct	St
First-class	49	68	8	1590	130	26.50	69.52	2	8	19	0
List A	39	30	3	313	57	11.59	96.01	0	1	11	0
Twenty20	31	20	6	163	18	11.64	118.11	0	0	12	0
Bowling	**Inns**	**Balls**	**Runs**	**Wkts**	**BBI**	**BBM**	**Ave**	**Econ**	**SR**	**5w**	**10**
First-class	49	6130	3612	135	7/74	11/57	26.75	3.53	45.4	5	1
List A	39	1256	1157	28	3/39	3/39	41.32	5.52	44.8	0	0
Twenty20	31	298	426	7	2/20	2/20	60.85	8.57	42.5	0	0

JORDAN CLARK

RHB WK

LANCASHIRE

FULL NAME: Jordan Clark
BORN: October 14, 1990, Whitehaven, Cumbria
SQUAD NO: 16
HEIGHT: 6ft 4in
NICKNAME: Clarky
EDUCATION: Sedbergh School
TEAMS: Cumberland, England Under-15s, Lancashire, Lancashire 2nd XI
CAREER: List A: 2010; T20: 2011

CAREER HIGHLIGHTS? Taking part in T20 Finals Day and being part of the squad that won the County Championship title in 2011
SUPERSTITIONS? I put my right pad on first
CRICKETING HEROES? Andrew Flintoff
NON-CRICKETING HEROES? Steven Cheetham
TIP FOR THE TOP? Ben Stokes
IF YOU WEREN'T A CRICKETER? I'd be at university
FAVOURITE TV? Geordie Shore
FAVOURITE FILM? I Love You Man
DREAM HOLIDAY? Barbados
GUILTY PLEASURES? Nicki Minaj

Batting	Mat	Inns	NO	Runs	HS	Ave	SR	100	50	Ct	St
List A	5	2	0	40	32	20.00	75.47	0	0	0	0
Twenty20	9	8	2	127	38	21.16	138.04	0	0	4	0
Bowling	**Inns**	**Balls**	**Runs**	**Wkts**	**BBI**	**BBM**	**Ave**	**Econ**	**SR**	**5w**	**10**
List A	5	-	-	-	-	-	-	-	-	-	-
Twenty20	9	-	-	-	-	-	-	-	-	-	-

RIKKI CLARKE

RHB RMF R1 MVP12

FULL NAME: Rikki Clarke
BORN: September 29, 1981, Orsett, Essex
SQUAD NO: 81
HEIGHT: 6ft 4in
NICKNAME: Clarkey, Bad Lad
EDUCATION: Broadwater Secondary; Godalming College
TEAMS: England, Derbyshire, Marylebone Cricket Club, Surrey, Warwickshire
CAREER: Test: 2003; ODI: 2003; First-class: 2002; List A: 2001; T20: 2003

BEST BATTING: 214 Surrey vs Somerset, Guildford, 2006
BEST BOWLING: 6-63 Warwickshire vs Kent, Canterbury, 2010
COUNTY CAPS: 2005 (Surrey); 2011 (Warwickshire)

CAREER HIGHLIGHTS? Making my Test and ODI debuts. Winning the County Championship with Surrey and Warwickshire
SUPERSTITIONS? No, not anymore. I got those out of my game about two years ago
BEST PLAYER IN COUNTY CRICKET? Marcus Trescothick, without a doubt. Serious player. Pity his sledging isn't up there with his batting!
TIPS FOR THE TOP? Laurie Evans, Tom Milnes, Sam Billings
DESERT ISLAND DISC? Flo Rida, Akon, Example and David Guetta, all on one disc
FAVOURITE TV? TOWIE, Match Of The Day, Celebrity Juice and EastEnders
CRICKETING HEROES? Freddie Flintoff, Darren Gough and Graham Thorpe
WHEN YOU RETIRE? Become a sports master at a private school
SURPRISING FACT? That I was named after Ricky Villa, who scored the FA Cup winning final goal in 1981 – the year I was born
TWITTER FEED: @RikkiClarke81

Batting	Mat	Inns	NO	Runs	HS	Ave	SR	100	50	Ct	St
Tests	2	3	0	96	55	32.00	37.94	0	1	1	0
ODIs	20	13	0	144	39	11.07	62.06	0	0	11	0
First-class	150	232	24	7407	214	35.61		16	33	231	0
List A	180	149	21	3297	98*	25.75		0	16	86	0
Twenty20	87	81	23	1169	79*	20.15	121.64	0	3	42	0
Bowling	**Inns**	**Balls**	**Runs**	**Wkts**	**BBI**	**BBM**	**Ave**	**Econ**	**SR**	**5w**	**10**
Tests	2	174	60	4	2/7	3/11	15.00	2.06	43.5	0	0
ODIs	20	469	415	11	2/28	2/28	37.72	5.30	42.6	0	0
First-class	150	13541	8392	240	6/63		34.96	3.71	56.4	2	0
List A	180	4175	3913	101	4/28	4/28	38.74	5.62	41.3	0	0
Twenty20	87	822	1127	42	3/11	3/11	26.83	8.22	19.5	0	0

MITCHELL CLAYDON LHB RFM

DURHAM

FULL NAME: Mitchell Eric Claydon
BORN: November 25, 1982, Fairfield, New South Wales, Australia
SQUAD NO: 25
HEIGHT: 6ft 4in
NICKNAME: Lips, Ellen, Precious, Big Fella
EDUCATION: Robert Townson Primary School; West Fields Sports High School, Sydney
TEAMS: Canterbury, Durham, Durham 2nd XI, Yorkshire, Yorkshire 2nd XI
CAREER: First-class: 2005; List A: 2006; T20: 2006

BEST BATTING: 55 Durham vs Nottinghamshire, Chester-le-Street, 2012
BEST BOWLING: 6-104 Durham vs Somerset, Taunton, 2011

FAMILY TIES? Father played Yorkshire league cricket
CAREER HIGHLIGHTS? Being a part of two Championship winning teams. Every game I play for Durham is a highlight. Playing T20 cricket in New Zealand for the Canterbury Wizards for the last three years as their overseas player
BEST PLAYER IN COUNTY CRICKET? Graham Onions
TIPS FOR THE TOP? Ben Stokes, Scott Borthwick
IF YOU WEREN'T A CRICKETER? Working in a factory
DESERT ISLAND DISC? Powderfinger – Happiness
FAVOURITE TV? Mrs Brown's Boys
CRICKETING HEROES? Ricky Ponting
SURPRISING FACT? I am a part-time magician
FANTASY SLIP CORDON? Keeper: Shane Warne, 1st: Tiger Woods, 2nd: Me, 3rd: Michael Jordan
TWITTER FEED: @mitchellclaydon

Batting	Mat	Inns	NO	Runs	HS	Ave	SR	100	50	Ct	St
First-class	49	61	12	693	55	14.14	56.89	0	1	6	0
List A	62	31	9	179	19	8.13	81.73	0	0	3	0
Twenty20	66	18	11	91	19	13.00	124.65	0	0	15	0
Bowling	**Inns**	**Balls**	**Runs**	**Wkts**	**BBI**	**BBM**	**Ave**	**Econ**	**SR**	**5w**	**10**
First-class	49	6387	3867	120	6/104		32.22	3.63	53.2	2	0
List A	62	2628	2327	78	4/39	4/39	29.83	5.31	33.6	0	0
Twenty20	66	1289	1710	67	5/26	5/26	25.52	7.95	19.2	1	0

JOSH COBB RHB OB MVP64

FULL NAME: Joshua James Cobb
BORN: August 17, 1990, Leicester
SQUAD NO: 5
HEIGHT: 6ft
NICKNAME: Cobby, Cobblet
EDUCATION: Bosworth College; Oakham School
TEAMS: Dhaka Gladiators, England Under-19s, Leicestershire, Leicestershire 2nd XI
CAREER: First-class: 2007; List A: 2008; T20: 2008

BEST BATTING: 148* Leicestershire vs Middlesex, Lord's, 2008
BEST BOWLING: 2-11 Leicestershire vs Gloucestershire, Leicester, 2011

FAMILY TIES? My dad [Russell] played for Leicestershire and my uncle played minor counties
WHY CRICKET? I had no choice. My dad arrived at my birth during a game in his whites so I've literally been born into it
CAREER HIGHLIGHTS? Scoring 148* at Lord's to become Leicestershire's youngest Championship century-maker, playing in T20 Finals Day
SUPERSTITIONS? Left shoe and pad on first, when gardening down the wicket I try and keep my taps to even numbers
CRICKETING HEROES? Paul Nixon, Darren Stevens, Chris Gayle
BEST PLAYER IN COUNTY CRICKET? Marcus Trescothick or Darren Stevens
TIPS FOR THE TOP? Jason Roy, Shiv Thakor, Jos Buttler
SURPRISING SKILL? I play the violin in my spare time
SURPRISING FACT? I used to be a Next model. I know, don't laugh…
FANTASY SLIP CORDON? Keeper: Paul Nixon, 1st: Cheryl Cole, 2nd: Myself, 3rd: Jessica-Jane Clement, Gully: Liam Kinch
TWITTER FEED: @cobby24

Batting	Mat	Inns	NO	Runs	HS	Ave	SR	100	50	Ct	St
First-class	51	89	6	2072	148*	24.96	46.67	2	12	24	0
List A	38	35	3	1004	137	31.37	99.50	1	6	14	0
Twenty20	52	47	6	798	60	19.46	143.52	0	2	23	0
Bowling	**Inns**	**Balls**	**Runs**	**Wkts**	**BBI**	**BBM**	**Ave**	**Econ**	**SR**	**5w**	**10**
First-class	51	816	530	9	2/11	2/11	58.88	3.89	90.6	0	0
List A	38	672	691	13	2/35	2/35	53.15	6.16	51.6	0	0
Twenty20	52	354	506	17	4/22	4/22	29.76	8.57	20.8	0	0

IAN COCKBAIN RHB

GLOUCESTERSHIRE

FULL NAME: Ian Andrew Cockbain
BORN: February 17, 1987, Liverpool, Lancashire
SQUAD NO: 28
HEIGHT: 6ft
NICKNAME: Coey
EDUCATION: Maghull High School; Liverpool John Moores University
TEAMS: Gloucestershire, Gloucestershire 2nd XI, Lancashire 2nd XI, Marylebone Cricket Club Young Cricketers
CAREER: First-class: 2011; List A: 2011; T20: 2011

BEST BATTING: 127 Gloucestershire vs Middlesex, Uxbridge, 2011
COUNTY CAP: 2011

FAMILY TIES? My dad [Ian] played for Lancashire CCC back in the day
WHO WOULD PLAY YOU IN A FILM OF YOUR LIFE? Will Ferrell
CAREER HIGHLIGHTS? Making my maiden first-class hundred vs Middlesex
MOST MARKED CHARACTERISTIC? My annoying habit of trying to wind the lads up
BEST PLAYER IN COUNTY CRICKET? Marcus Trescothick
TIP FOR THE TOP? Chris Dent – great opening batsman and if he keeps fit he will hopefully have further honours
IF YOU WEREN'T A CRICKETER? Hopefully working with my old man in Wealth Management for St James' Place
DESERT ISLAND DISC? Luciano Pavarotti's Greatest Hits – brilliant for all moods
BIGGEST DRESSING DOWN YOU'VE RECEIVED? Probably most weekends when I was playing cricket with my dad for Bootle CC. He loves having a go at me!
CRICKETING HEROES? Shane Warne, Ricky Ponting, AB de Villiers
NON-CRICKETING HEROES? Roger Federer, Tiger Woods
FANTASY SLIP CORDON? Keeper: Will Ferrell (he would provide hours of entertainment), 1st: Tiger Woods (I'm sure he would have some great stories), 2nd: Me, 3rd: Blake Lively
TWITTER FEED: @IanCoey

Batting	Mat	Inns	NO	Runs	HS	Ave	SR	100	50	Ct	St
First-class	27	45	3	1306	127	31.09	45.05	2	8	22	0
List A	24	22	4	549	79	30.50	93.68	0	5	16	0
Twenty20	19	18	3	345	78	23.00	111.29	0	1	8	0
Bowling	**Inns**	**Balls**	**Runs**	**Wkts**	**BBI**	**BBM**	**Ave**	**Econ**	**SR**	**5w**	**10**
First-class	27	-	-	-	-	-	-	-	-	-	-
List A	24	-	-	-	-	-	-	-	-	-	-
Twenty20	19	-	-	-	-	-	-	-	-	-	-

KYLE COETZER RHB RM

FULL NAME: Kyle James Coetzer
BORN: April 14, 1984, Aberdeen
SQUAD NO: 30
HEIGHT: 5ft 11in
NICKNAME: Costa, Meerkat, Shortbread
EDUCATION: Aberdeen Grammar School
TEAMS: Scotland, Durham, Northamptonshire, Scotland Under-19s, Western Province
CAREER: ODI: 2008; T20I: 2008; First-class: 2004; List A: 2003; T20: 2007

BEST BATTING: 172 Durham vs MCC, Sheikh Zayed Stadium, 2010
BEST BOWLING: 2-16 Scotland vs Kenya, Gymkhana Club Ground, 2009

FAMILY TIES? Elder brothers Shaun and Stuart both played some level of cricket for Scotland. Grandfather Sid Dugmore played for Eastern Province and so did my uncle Grant Dugmore, who has coached and played for Argentina. He is now the development officer for the Americas
SUPERSTITIONS? I touch my bat in the crease after each ball
BEST PLAYER IN COUNTY CRICKET? Graham Onions
TIP FOR THE TOP? Olly Stone
DESERT ISLAND DISC? Kenny Rogers – The Gambler
FAVOURITE TV? You've Been Framed
NON-CRICKETING HEROES? Andy Murray
WHEN YOU RETIRE? I'd like to get involved in coaching in some way
SURPRISING FACT? I was given a Meerkat toy by my ex-teammate Paul Wiseman who claimed I looked like it. It has never left my kitbag since, hence the nickname
TWITTER FEED: @MeerGoose11

Batting	Mat	Inns	NO	Runs	HS	Ave	SR	100	50	Ct	St
ODIs	10	10	1	388	89*	43.11	82.02	0	4	6	0
T20Is	14	14	1	383	62	29.46	103.23	0	1	6	0
First-class	63	107	10	3238	172	33.38	48.01	6	14	33	0
List A	87	85	11	2505	127	33.85	79.57	3	17	33	0
Twenty20	42	40	4	892	64	24.77	105.56	0	2	13	0
Bowling	**Inns**	**Balls**	**Runs**	**Wkts**	**BBI**	**BBM**	**Ave**	**Econ**	**SR**	**5w**	**10**
ODIs	10	114	125	1	1/35	1/35	125.00	6.57	114.0	0	0
T20Is	14	66	71	5	3/25	3/25	14.20	6.45	13.2	0	0
First-class	63	372	231	4	2/16	2/16	57.75	3.72	93.0	0	0
List A	87	294	291	2	1/25	1/25	145.50	5.93	147.0	0	0
Twenty20	42	102	116	6	3/25	3/25	19.33	6.82	17.0	0	0

FREDDIE COLEMAN RHB OB

FULL NAME: Frederick Robert John Coleman
BORN: December 15, 1991, Edinburgh, Midlothian
SQUAD NO: 21
HEIGHT: 6ft
EDUCATION: Strathallan School; Oxford Brookes University
TEAMS: Oxford MCCU, Scotland, Scotland Under-13s, Scotland Under-15s, Scotland Under-17s, Scotland Under-19s, Warwickshire 2nd XI
CAREER: First-class: 2012; List A: 2010

BEST BATTING: 110 Oxford MCCU vs Worcestershire, Oxford, 2012

NOTES: Coleman signed a summer contract with Warwickshire after graduating from the county's academy and will be available after completing his summer examinations at Oxford Brookes University. Made 110 on first-class debut against Worcestershire. On a retainer with Cricket Scotland

Batting	Mat	Inns	NO	Runs	HS	Ave	SR	100	50	Ct	St
First-class	2	2	0	130	110	65.00	54.39	1	0	2	0
List A	3	2	0	5	5	2.50	33.33	0	0	0	0
Bowling	**Inns**	**Balls**	**Runs**	**Wkts**	**BBI**	**BBM**	**Ave**	**Econ**	**SR**	**5w**	**10**
First-class	2	-	-	-	-	-	-	-	-	-	-
List A	3	-	-	-	-	-	-	-	-	-	-

MATT COLES

LHB RFM W1 MVP30

FULL NAME: Matthew Thomas Coles
BORN: May 26, 1990, Maidstone, Kent
SQUAD NO: 26
HEIGHT: 6ft 3in
NICKNAME: Colesy
EDUCATION: Maplesden Noakes Secondary School
TEAMS: England Lions, Kent, Kent 2nd XI
CAREER: First-class: 2009; List A: 2009; T20: 2010

BEST BATTING: 103* Kent vs Yorkshire, Leeds, 2012
BEST BOWLING: 6-51 Kent vs Northamptonshire, Northampton, 2012
COUNTY CAP: 2012

FAVOURITE SPORTSMAN? Andrew Flintoff or Stephen Jack Rigg
FAVOURITE BAND? Red Hot Chili Peppers
FAVOURITE FOOD? Roast lamb
FAVOURITE FILM? Anchorman
FAVOURITE CAR? Land Rover Defender
FAVOURITE QUOTE? "Powerful dreams inspire powerful action"
PROUDEST MOMENT? Walking out onto pitch for the first time in a Kent shirt
MOST ANNOYING HABIT? Talking when I shouldn't
TWITTER FEED: @MattColes_90

Batting	Mat	Inns	NO	Runs	HS	Ave	SR	100	50	Ct	St
First-class	43	60	11	1042	103*	21.26	67.39	1	3	11	0
List A	26	10	0	83	47	8.30	91.20	0	0	7	0
Twenty20	23	15	3	96	16*	8.00	124.67	0	0	9	0
Bowling	Inns	Balls	Runs	Wkts	BBI	BBM	Ave	Econ	SR	5w	10
First-class	43	5894	3531	120	6/51	9/83	29.42	3.59	49.1	4	0
List A	26	851	873	40	6/32	6/32	21.82	6.15	21.2	1	0
Twenty20	23	368	576	19	3/30	3/30	30.31	9.39	19.3	0	0

PAUL COLLINGWOOD RHB RM R2

DURHAM

FULL NAME: Paul David Collingwood
BORN: May 26, 1976, Shotley Bridge, County Durham
SQUAD NO: 5
HEIGHT: 5ft 11in
NICKNAME: Colly, Weed, Wobbles
EDUCATION: Blackfyne Comprehensive School; Derwentside College
TEAMS: England, Delhi Daredevils, Durham, Impi, Perth Scorchers, Rajasthan Royals
CAREER: Test: 2003; ODI: 2001; T20I: 2005; First-class: 1996; List A: 1995; T20:2005

BEST BATTING: 206 England vs Australia, Adelaide, 2006
BEST BOWLING: 5-52 Durham vs Somerset, Grangefield Road, 2005
BENEFIT YEAR: 2007

CAREER HIGHLIGHTS? Playing for England, winning the World T20 and the three Ashes wins
SUPERSTITIONS? Left pad on first and a little jig as I walk out to bat but it's getting harder as it involves squatting three times
MOST MARKED CHARACTERISTIC? Tenacious
TIPS FOR THE TOP? Ben Stokes, Joe Root, Scott Borthwick
DESERT ISLAND DISC? Snow Patrol – Chasing Cars
ACCOMPLISHMENTS? Beating Brezzie in the final of the table-tennis masters in Bloemfontein during the 2010 South Africa tour. Also taking down Geoff Miller (he brought his own bat) emphatically in the 'exhibition' match straight after the final
SURPRISING FACT? I'm an artist
TWITTER FEED: @Colly622

Batting	Mat	Inns	NO	Runs	HS	Ave	SR	100	50	Ct	St
Tests	68	115	10	4259	206	40.56	46.44	10	20	96	0
ODIs	197	181	37	5092	120*	35.36	76.98	5	26	108	0
T20Is	35	33	2	583	79	18.80	127.01	0	3	14	0
First-class	218	375	31	12493	206	36.31		26	64	251	0
List A	382	358	63	9950	120*	33.72		8	56	195	0
Twenty20	89	77	6	1330	79	18.73	121.68	0	6	24	0
Bowling	**Inns**	**Balls**	**Runs**	**Wkts**	**BBI**	**BBM**	**Ave**	**Econ**	**SR**	**5w**	**10**
Tests	68	1905	1018	17	3/23	3/35	59.88	3.20	112.0	0	0
ODIs	197	5186	4294	111	6/31	6/31	38.68	4.96	46.7	1	0
T20Is	35	222	329	16	4/22	4/22	20.56	8.89	13.8	0	0
First-class	218	10360	5244	133	5/52		39.42	3.03	77.8	1	0
List A	382	9996	8087	230	6/31	6/31	35.16	4.85	43.4	1	0
Twenty20	89	799	975	58	5/6	5/6	16.81	7.32	13.7	2	0

COREY COLLYMORE RHB RMF W1

FULL NAME: Corey Dalanelo Collymore
BORN: December 21, 1977, Boscobelle, St Peter, Barbados
SQUAD NO: 32
HEIGHT: 6ft
NICKNAME: Legend
EDUCATION: Boscobelle Boys' School; Alexandra Secondary School
TEAMS: West Indies, Barbados, Middlesex, Sussex, Warwickshire
CAREER: Test: 1999; ODI: 1999; First-class: 1999; List A: 1999; T20: 2006

BEST BATTING: 23 Sussex vs Nottinghamshire, Horsham, 2009
BEST BOWLING: 7-57 West Indies vs Sri Lanka, Kingston, 2003
COUNTY CAPS: 2008 (Sussex); 2011 (Middlesex)

WHO WOULD PLAY YOU IN A FILM OF YOUR LIFE? Me!
CAREER HIGHLIGHTS? Representing Barbados and the West Indies
MOST MARKED CHARACTERISTIC? Humbleness
BEST PLAYER IN COUNTY CRICKET? Marcus Trescothick
TIPS FOR THE TOP? Christopher Jordan, Luke Wells, Dawid Malan, Sam Robson, Jonny Bairstow
IF YOU WEREN'T A CRICKETER? Trying to be a footballer
DESERT ISLAND DISC? Sizzla – Be Strong
FAVOURITE TV? Sky Sports
CRICKETING HEROES? Courtney Walsh, Malcolm Marshall, Vasbert Drakes
NON-CRICKETING HEROES? Ian Wright, Michael Johnson
WHEN YOU RETIRE? Coach cricketers, especially fast bowlers
SURPRISING FACT? I haven't been to the beach in Barbados in two years

Batting	Mat	Inns	NO	Runs	HS	Ave	SR	100	50	Ct	St
Tests	30	52	27	197	16*	7.88	30.68	0	0	6	0
ODIs	84	35	17	104	13*	5.77	39.84	0	0	12	0
First-class	157	212	98	891	23	7.81		0	0	46	0
List A	140	53	27	155	13*	5.96		0	0	22	0
Twenty20	6	2	1	5	4	5.00	45.45	0	0	4	0
Bowling	**Inns**	**Balls**	**Runs**	**Wkts**	**BBI**	**BBM**	**Ave**	**Econ**	**SR**	**5w**	**10**
Tests	30	6337	3004	93	7/57	11/134	32.30	2.84	68.1	4	1
ODIs	84	4074	2924	83	5/51	5/51	35.22	4.30	49.0	1	0
First-class	157	26831	12546	466	7/57		26.92	2.80	57.5	12	2
List A	140	6498	4653	149	5/27	5/27	31.22	4.29	43.6	2	0
Twenty20	6	95	133	3	1/21	1/21	44.33	8.40	31.6	0	0

NICK COMPTON RHB OB R3 MVP34

FULL NAME: Nicholas Richard Denis Compton
BORN: June 26, 1983, Durban, South Africa
SQUAD NO: 3
HEIGHT: 6ft 2in
NICKNAME: Compo, Ledge, Cheser, Comp Dog
EDUCATION: Hilton College, South Africa; Harrow School; Durham University
TEAMS: England, England Lions, Mashonaland Eagles, Middlesex, Somerset
CAREER: Test: 2012; First-class: 2004; List A: 2001; T20: 2004

BEST BATTING: 254* Somerset vs Durham, Chester-le-Street, 2011
BEST BOWLING: 1-1 Somerset vs Hampshire, Southampton, 2010
COUNTY CAPS: 2006 (Middlesex); 2011 (Somerset)

FAMILY TIES? Grandfather Denis played cricket for Middlesex and England. Great uncle Leslie played cricket for Middlesex. Father Richard played first-class cricket in South Africa and uncle Patrick played a few games too
SUPERSTITIONS? I only walk over the white line after my batting partner – I like to feel like I've given them the respect!
CRICKETING HEROES? Jacques Kallis, Rahul Dravid and Brian Lara
NON-CRICKETING HEROES? Arsene Wenger, Muhammad Ali
BEST PLAYER IN COUNTY CRICKET? Marcus Trescothick
TIPS FOR THE TOP? Jos Buttler, Craig Meschede and James Vince
FAVOURITE FILM? The Matrix, Gladiator, Lock Stock And Two Smoking Barrels
FAVOURITE BOOK? Bounce
ACCOMPLISHMENTS? PCA Benevolent Fund charity walk to Mount Everest Base Camp
SURPRISING SKILL? I'm not bad at oil painting
TWITTER FEED: @thecompdog

Batting	Mat	Inns	NO	Runs	HS	Ave	SR	100	50	Ct	St
Tests	4	8	2	208	57	34.66	33.93	0	1	1	0
First-class	103	177	25	6637	254*	43.66	47.59	16	30	52	0
List A	92	84	17	2678	131	39.97	80.42	6	16	42	0
Twenty20	64	55	6	966	74	19.71	109.02	0	5	23	0
Bowling	**Inns**	**Balls**	**Runs**	**Wkts**	**BBI**	**BBM**	**Ave**	**Econ**	**SR**	**5w**	**10**
Tests	4	-	-	-	-	-	-	-	-	-	-
First-class	103	164	215	3	1/1	1/1	71.66	7.86	54.6	0	0
List A	92	61	53	1	1/0	1/0	53.00	5.21	61.0	0	0
Twenty20	64	-	-	-	-	-	-	-	-	-	-

ALASTAIR COOK

LHB OB R5

FULL NAME: Alastair Nathan Cook
BORN: December 25, 1984, Gloucester
SQUAD NO: 26
HEIGHT: 6ft 2in
NICKNAME: Cookie, Chef
EDUCATION: Bedford School
TEAMS: England, Bedfordshire, England Lions, England Under-19s, Essex, Marylebone Cricket Club
CAREER: Test: 2006; ODI: 2006; T20I: 2007; First-class: 2003; List A: 2003; T20: 2005

BEST BATTING: 294 England vs India, Birmingham, 2011
BEST BOWLING: 3-13 Essex vs Northamptonshire, Chelmsford, 2005
COUNTY CAP: 2005

FAMILY TIES? My dad played for the local club side and was a very good opening bat, while my mum made the teas. Brothers played for Maldon Cricket Club
CAREER HIGHLIGHTS? Ashes wins home and away, becoming world No.1 Test team, Essex winning the 50-over comp, making England debut
CRICKETING HEROES? Graham Gooch – watched him playing for Essex at the County Ground as a kid
BEST PLAYER IN COUNTY CRICKET? Ryan ten Doeschate and James Foster
TIP FOR THE TOP? Ben Foakes
IF YOU WEREN'T A CRICKETER? Farmer
FAVOURITE BOOK? The Girl With The Dragon Tattoo
GUILTY PLEASURES? Shooting, beer and darts

Batting	Mat	Inns	NO	Runs	HS	Ave	SR	100	50	Ct	St
Tests	87	154	10	7117	294	49.42	47.63	23	29	75	0
ODIs	64	64	3	2456	137	40.26	78.44	5	16	20	0
T20Is	4	4	0	61	26	15.25	112.96	0	0	1	0
First-class	179	317	26	14058	294	48.30	52.30	42	66	163	0
List A	120	118	9	4331	137	39.73	79.36	9	26	45	0
Twenty20	30	28	2	862	100*	33.15	128.84	1	5	12	0
Bowling	**Inns**	**Balls**	**Runs**	**Wkts**	**BBI**	**BBM**	**Ave**	**Econ**	**SR**	**5w**	**10**
Tests	87	6	1	0	-	-	-	1.00	-	0	0
ODIs	64	-	-	-	-	-	-	-	-	-	-
T20Is	4	-	-	-	-	-	-	-	-	-	-
First-class	179	270	205	6	3/13		34.16	4.55	45.0	0	0
List A	120	18	10	0	-	-	-	3.33	-	0	0
Twenty20	30	-	-	-	-	-	-	-	-	-	-

CHRIS COOKE RHB WK

FULL NAME: Christopher Barry Cooke
BORN: May 30, 1986, Johannesburg, South Africa
SQUAD NO: 24
HEIGHT: 5ft 11in
NICKNAME: Minty, Shapeless, Cooky
EDUCATION: Bishops; University of Cape Town (UCT)
TEAMS: Glamorgan, Glamorgan 2nd XI, Hampshire 2nd XI, Western Province
CAREER: First-class: 2009; List A: 2009; T20: 2011

BEST BATTING: 44* Western Province vs Eastern Province, Newlands, 2010

FAMILY TIES? I grew up watching my old man and two big brothers playing cricket. I seemed to always be attracted to the game and must have copied them as they were all also keeper-batters
CAREER HIGHLIGHTS? Scoring my maiden List A hundred at Newlands. Hitting my second, third and fourth balls for six on my Glamorgan T20 debut. Scoring my first hundred for the county in a 40-over match at Taunton and it becoming the fourth highest one-day score for Glamorgan
SUPERSTITIONS? Batting: left pad on first. Keeping: right pad on first
MOST MARKED CHARACTERISTIC? My back-lift probably!
BEST PLAYER IN COUNTY CRICKET? Matt Prior
TIPS FOR THE TOP? Aneurin Donald, Rory Smith, Andrew Salter, Dave Lloyd
IF YOU WEREN'T A CRICKETER? International DJ
DESERT ISLAND DISC? Surely an iPod would be easier to take!? At the moment I'm loving Phantogram, so probably that if I had to
CRICKETING HEROES? Kevin Pietersen, Hylton Ackerman
ACCOMPLISHMENTS? A degree in Psychology and Media from UCT
SURPRISING FACTS? I have to have the volume on an even number!
TWITTER FEED: @Cooky_24

Batting	Mat	Inns	NO	Runs	HS	Ave	SR	100	50	Ct	St
First-class	6	11	1	186	44*	18.60	36.97	0	0	12	1
List A	32	29	5	790	137*	32.91	101.28	2	2	11	2
Twenty20	21	18	2	266	47	16.62	143.78	0	0	9	0
Bowling	**Inns**	**Balls**	**Runs**	**Wkts**	**BBI**	**BBM**	**Ave**	**Econ**	**SR**	**5w**	**10**
First-class	6	-	-	-	-	-	-	-	-	-	-
List A	32	-	-	-	-	-	-	-	-	-	-
Twenty20	21	-	-	-	-	-	-	-	-	-	-

TRENT COPELAND RHB RFM

FULL NAME: Trent Aaron Copeland
BORN: March 14, 1986, Gosford, Australia
SQUAD NO: 18
HEIGHT: 6ft 5in
TEAMS: Australia, Australia A, New South Wales, New South Wales 2nd XI, St George, Sydney Thunder
CAREER: Test: 2011; First-class: 2010; List A: 2010; T20: 2011

BEST BATTING: 106 New South Wales vs Tasmania, Hobart, 2013
BEST BOWLING: 8-92 New South Wales vs Queensland, Sydney, 2010

TWITTER FEED: @copes9
NOTES: Copeland worked his way up to the national team by excelling at grade level and then state cricket. His made his debut for New South Wales in the Sheffield Shield during the 2009/10 season, aged 23. However, up until four years before his first-class debut he was a wicketkeeper. Copeland will be available for Northants' opening match in the County Championship against Glamorgan on April 10 and will be with the county until June 8

Batting	Mat	Inns	NO	Runs	HS	Ave	SR	100	50	Ct	St
Tests	3	4	1	39	23*	13.00	50.64	0	0	2	0
First-class	35	44	7	655	106	17.70	55.36	1	2	27	0
List A	16	8	3	52	21	10.40	81.25	0	0	2	0
Twenty20	2	1	0	1	1	1.00	33.33	0	0	0	0
Bowling	**Inns**	**Balls**	**Runs**	**Wkts**	**BBI**	**BBM**	**Ave**	**Econ**	**SR**	**5w**	**10**
Tests	3	648	227	6	2/24	3/87	37.83	2.10	108.0	0	0
First-class	35	8461	3498	135	8/92	10/149	25.91	2.48	62.6	5	1
List A	16	885	732	15	5/44	5/44	48.80	4.96	59.0	1	0
Twenty20	2	24	46	0	-	-	-	11.50	-	0	0

DEAN COSKER RHB SLA W1

FULL NAME: Dean Andrew Cosker
BORN: January 7, 1978, Weymouth, Dorset
SQUAD NO: 23
HEIGHT: 5ft 11in
NICKNAME: Lurks
EDUCATION: Millfield School
TEAMS: England A, Glamorgan
CAREER: First-class: 1996; List A: 1996; T20: 2003

BEST BATTING: 52 Glamorgan vs Gloucestershire, Bristol, 2005
BEST BOWLING: 6-91 Glamorgan vs Essex, Cardiff, 2009
COUNTY CAP: 2000; BENEFIT YEAR: 2010

CAREER HIGHLIGHTS? Debut at Glamorgan in 1996, Championship medal in 1997, England A caps, trophies with Glamorgan
CRICKET MOMENTS TO FORGET? Every time I bowl from the Taff End at the SWALEC Stadium in the T20 when the wind is with the batsman
FAVOURITE BAND? Bananarama
CRICKETERS PARTICULARLY ADMIRED? Mike Kasprowicz, Matt Elliott, Matt Maynard, Robert Croft, Steve Watkin, Graham Thorpe
NOTES: Leading wicket-taker on England A tour of Zimbabwe and South Africa 1998/99. Third youngest Glamorgan player to receive his county cap. Passed 500 first-class wickets in 2012
TWITTER FEED: @DCosker23

Batting	Mat	Inns	NO	Runs	HS	Ave	SR	100	50	Ct	St
First-class	209	273	78	2731	52	14.00		0	1	126	0
List A	222	119	53	748	50*	11.33		0	1	84	0
Twenty20	80	26	19	118	21*	16.85	90.07	0	0	23	0
Bowling	**Inns**	**Balls**	**Runs**	**Wkts**	**BBI**	**BBM**	**Ave**	**Econ**	**SR**	**5w**	**10**
First-class	209	38965	18531	510	6/91		36.33	2.85	76.4	8	1
List A	222	9283	7393	225	5/54	5/54	32.85	4.77	41.2	1	0
Twenty20	80	1385	1816	61	3/11	3/11	29.77	7.86	22.7	0	0

PAUL COUGHLIN RHB RM

FULL NAME: Paul Coughlin
BORN: October 23, 1992, Sunderland, County Durham
SQUAD NO: 29
EDUCATION: St Robert of Newminster Catholic Comprehensive School, Washington, County Durham
TEAMS: Durham, Durham 2nd XI, Durham Academy, Durham Under-17s
CAREER: First-class: 2012; List A: 2012

DURHAM

BEST BATTING: 29* Durham vs Australia A, Chester-le-Street, 2012
BEST BOWLING: 1-26 Durham vs Australia A, Chester-le-Street, 2012

TWITTER FEED: @Coughlin92
NOTES: A bowling allrounder who graduated from Durham Academy to make his first-class debut against Australia A in August 2012. Coughlin has also appeared for Northumberland in the Minor Counties Championship

Batting	Mat	Inns	NO	Runs	HS	Ave	SR	100	50	Ct	St
First-class	1	2	1	32	29*	32.00	58.18	0	0	1	0
List A	1	-	-	-	-	-	-	-	-	0	0
Bowling	**Inns**	**Balls**	**Runs**	**Wkts**	**BBI**	**BBM**	**Ave**	**Econ**	**SR**	**5w**	**10**
First-class	1	60	46	1	1/26	1/46	46.00	4.60	60.0	0	0
List A	1	6	15	0	-	-	-	15.00	-	0	0

RICHARD COUGHTRIE RHB WK

FULL NAME: Richard George Coughtrie
BORN: September 1, 1988, North Shields, Northumberland
SQUAD NO: 12
HEIGHT: 5ft 9in
NICKNAME: Coffers
EDUCATION: Royal Grammar School, Newcastle; Oxford Brookes University
TEAMS: Durham 2nd XI, Gloucestershire, Gloucestershire 2nd XI, Northumberland, Oxford MCCU
CAREER: First-class: 2009; T20: 2011

BEST BATTING: 54*Gloucestershire vs Derbyshire, Derby, 2011
COUNTY CAP: 2011

WHO WOULD PLAY YOU IN A FILM OF YOUR LIFE? Apparently I look like Daniel Radcliffe, so I guess it would have to be him
CAREER HIGHLIGHTS? First-class debut for Oxford. County Championship debut vs Derbyshire. Hitting the winning runs with Murali at the other end in a T20 vs Somerset in 2011. Being selected to tour South Africa with Scotland
SUPERSTITIONS? I used to have a few lucky car park spaces, hopefully the ground redevelopment at Bristol hasn't moved them! I might have to go hunting for some more during pre-season if so
BEST PLAYER IN COUNTY CRICKET? Graham Onions
TIP FOR THE TOP? Ben Stokes
IF YOU WEREN'T A CRICKETER? I'd start up a business with my brother James
DESERT ISLAND DISC? Lionel Richie – Dancing On The Ceiling
CRICKETING HEROES? Jack Russell, Alec Stewart, Mark Butcher
NON-CRICKETING HEROES? Nelson Mandela, Winston Churchill, Abraham Lincoln
ACCOMPLISHMENTS? Beating Jon Lewis at golf a couple of years ago
SURPRISING FACT? I've been teaching myself the guitar and piano for the last couple of years
TWITTER FEED: @rgcoughtrie

Batting	Mat	Inns	NO	Runs	HS	Ave	SR	100	50	Ct	St
First-class	30	52	6	909	54*	19.76	33.61	0	2	59	1
Twenty20	13	10	2	54	18	6.75	83.07	0	0	6	5
Bowling	**Inns**	**Balls**	**Runs**	**Wkts**	**BBI**	**BBM**	**Ave**	**Econ**	**SR**	**5w**	**10**
First-class	30	-	-	-	-	-	-	-	-	-	-
Twenty20	13	-	-	-	-	-	-	-	-	-	-

ED COWAN LHB LB

FULL NAME: Edward James McKenzie Cowan
BORN: June 16, 1982, Paddington, Australia
SQUAD NO: 3
HEIGHT: 5ft 10in
NICKNAME: Fred
EDUCATION: Tudor House School; Cranbrook School
TEAMS: Australia, Australia A, British Universities, Gloucestershire, New South Wales, Oxford MCCU, Sydney Sixers, Tasmania
CAREER: Test: 2011; First-class: 2003; List A: 2005; T20: 2007

BEST BATTING: 225 Tasmania vs South Australia, Hobart, 2009

FAMILY TIES? My wife [Virginia Lette] works on Fox Sports TV
SUPERSTITIONS? Yellow socks and red pants
BEST PLAYER IN COUNTY CRICKET? Rikki Clarke
DESERT ISLAND DISC? Kasabian
CRICKETING HEROES? Paul Johnson
TWITTER FEED: @eddiecowan

Batting	Mat	Inns	NO	Runs	HS	Ave	SR	100	50	Ct	St
Tests	14	24	0	783	136	32.62	43.09	1	5	19	0
First-class	86	153	9	5732	225	39.80	46.99	16	22	68	0
List A	61	58	8	1857	131*	37.14	69.78	3	13	20	0
Twenty20	10	9	0	162	70	18.00	127.55	0	1	2	0
Bowling	**Inns**	**Balls**	**Runs**	**Wkts**	**BBI**	**BBM**	**Ave**	**Econ**	**SR**	**5w**	**10**
Tests	14	-	-	-	-	-	-	-	-	-	-
First-class	86	18	33	0	-	-	-	11.00	-	0	0
List A	61	-	-	-	-	-	-	-	-	-	-
Twenty20	10	-	-	-	-	-	-	-	-	-	-

FABIAN COWDREY RHB SLA

FULL NAME: Fabian Kruuse Cowdrey
BORN: January 30, 1993, Canterbury
SQUAD NO: 30
HEIGHT: 6ft
NICKNAME: Cow, Fabs, Fabes, Calf
EDUCATION: Tonbridge School; Cardiff Metropolitan University
TEAMS: Kent 2nd XI
CAREER: Yet to make first-team debut

FAMILY TIES? My grandfather [Colin], father [Chris] and uncle [Graham] all played for Kent, with my grandfather and father both captaining England
WHO WOULD PLAY YOU IN A FILM OF YOUR LIFE? I'd like to play myself one day. You've got to shoot for the stars!
CAREER HIGHLIGHTS? Winning the 2nd XI Championship by one wicket at Grace Road and becoming a professional in late 2011
SUPERSTITIONS? No, I try not to engage in that
MOST MARKED CHARACTERISTIC? I'm comical and occasionally lacking the odd bit of intuitiveness...
BEST PLAYER IN COUNTY CRICKET? Nick Compton – stunning 2012 season
TIPS FOR THE TOP? I'll stick with the Kent boys! Daniel Bell-Drummond and Adam Ball
IF YOU WEREN'T A CRICKETER? Writing songs, cleaning the dishes and probably studying harder!
DESERT ISLAND DISC? Passenger – Let Her Go
FAVOURITE TV? Two And A Half Men
CRICKETING HEROES? Sir Vivian Richards, Kevin Pietersen
NON-CRICKETING HEROES? Will Smith, Mike Tyson
ACCOMPLISHMENTS? Getting into university, playing first-team hockey and rackets at school
WHEN YOU RETIRE? I'd like to be a motivator, own a business and be a renowned songwriter
SURPRISING FACT? I am unbelievably scared of heights!
FANTASY SLIP CORDON? Keeper: Bugs Bunny, 1st: Charlie Sheen, 2nd: David Lloyd, 3rd: Me, Gully: Forrest Gump
TWITTER FEED: @fkcowdrey

BEN COX

RHB WK

FULL NAME: Oliver Benjamin Cox
BORN: February 2, 1992, Wordsley, Stourbridge, Worcestershire
SQUAD NO: 10
HEIGHT: 5ft 10in
EDUCATION: Bromsgrove School, Bromsgrove
TEAMS: Worcestershire, Worcestershire 2nd XI
CAREER: First-class: 2009; List A: 2010; T20: 2010

BEST BATTING: 61 Worcestershire vs Somerset, Taunton, 2009

CAREER HIGHLIGHTS? My debut vs Somerset whilst I was still at school in 2009
SUPERSTITIONS? Left pad first and not washing keeping inners!
CRICKETING HEROES? Steve Rhodes and Steve Davies
NON-CRICKETING HEROES? Jonny Wilkinson for his determination to succeed
BEST PLAYER IN COUNTY CRICKET? Marcus Trescothick
TIPS FOR THE TOP? Christian Davies, Aneesh Kapil, Ross Whiteley
IF YOU WEREN'T A CRICKETER? Hopefully playing rugby for Worcester Warriors after a couple of hard years in the gym!
WHEN RAIN STOPS PLAY? Sleep, Football Manager, iPad, receiving abuse about my hairline
FAVOURITE TV? Friday Night Lights
FAVOURITE FILM? The Blind Side, Transformers
DREAM HOLIDAY? Cape Town
ACCOMPLISHMENTS? England U18 rugby trials and beating Millfield School 25-20
SURPRISING FACTS? I was close to quitting cricket to play rugby. I was once on the books at West Bromwich Albion. I trialled with Manu Tuilagi
FANTASY SLIP CORDON? Keeper: Owen Farrell, 1st: David Beckham, 2nd: Will Beer, 3rd: Lee Evans, Gully: Mila Kunis
TWITTER FEED: @BenCox10

Batting	Mat	Inns	NO	Runs	HS	Ave	SR	100	50	Ct	St
First-class	17	31	6	432	61	17.28	48.10	0	2	42	2
List A	13	6	3	25	9*	8.33	62.50	0	0	9	3
Twenty20	8	5	3	13	6*	6.50	108.33	0	0	2	2
Bowling	**Inns**	**Balls**	**Runs**	**Wkts**	**BBI**	**BBM**	**Ave**	**Econ**	**SR**	**5w**	**10**
First-class	17	-	-	-	-	-	-	-	-	-	-
List A	13	-	-	-	-	-	-	-	-	-	-
Twenty20	8	-	-	-	-	-	-	-	-	-	-

TOM CRADDOCK RHB LB

FULL NAME: Thomas Richard Craddock
BORN: July 13, 1989, Huddersfield
SQUAD NO: 20
HEIGHT: 5ft 9in
NICKNAME: Crads
EDUCATION: Holmfith High School; Huddersfield New College; Leeds Metropolitan University
TEAMS: Essex, Essex 2nd XI, Gloucestershire 2nd XI, Leeds/Bradford MCCU, Marylebone Cricket Club Universities, Unicorns
CAREER: First-class: 2011; List A: 2011; T20: 2011

BEST BATTING: 21 Essex vs Leicestershire, Southend, 2011
BEST BOWLING: 5-96 Essex vs Derbyshire, Chelmsford, 2012

FAMILY TIES? My mother's side of the family all played. My grandfather was a league umpire and my mum's cousin played for Yorkshire
WHO WOULD PLAY YOU IN A FILM OF YOUR LIFE? Brad Pitt
CAREER HIGHLIGHTS? Making my first-class debut against Sri Lanka, my County Championship debut against Northamptonshire and my first first-class five-fer against Derbyshire last season
SUPERSTITIONS? I always wear football socks when playing cricket
MOST MARKED CHARACTERISTIC? I like to think I have a good sense of humour
BEST PLAYER IN COUNTY CRICKET? Chris Woakes
TIP FOR THE TOP? Ben Foakes
DESERT ISLAND DISC? Drake – Take Care
FAVOURITE TV? Lost
CRICKETING HEROES? Shane Warne, Ricky Ponting
NON-CRICKETING HEROES? Parents
SURPRISING FACT? I didn't start playing cricket until I was 15
TWITTER FEED: @tcradd20

Batting	Mat	Inns	NO	Runs	HS	Ave	SR	100	50	Ct	St
First-class	14	19	7	111	21	9.25	27.68	0	0	3	0
List A	7	5	5	13	5*	-	32.50	0	0	2	0
Twenty20	2	-	-	-	-	-	-	-	-	3	0
Bowling	**Inns**	**Balls**	**Runs**	**Wkts**	**BBI**	**BBM**	**Ave**	**Econ**	**SR**	**5w**	**10**
First-class	14	1981	1066	37	5/96	6/71	28.81	3.22	53.5	1	0
List A	7	282	220	5	2/38	2/38	44.00	4.68	56.4	0	0
Twenty20	2	12	23	0	-	-	-	11.50	-	0	0

STEVEN CROFT RHB RMF/OB MVP9

FULL NAME: Steven John Croft
BORN: October 11, 1984, Blackpool, Lancashire
SQUAD NO: 15
HEIGHT: 5ft 11in
NICKNAME: Crofty
EDUCATION: Highfield High, Blackpool; Myerscough College
TEAMS: Auckland, Lancashire, Lancashire Cricket Board, Northern Districts
CAREER: First-class: 2005; List A: 2003; T20: 2006

BEST BATTING: 154* Lancashire vs Surrey, Guildford, 2012
BEST BOWLING: 6-41 Lancashire vs Worcestershire, Manchester, 2012
COUNTY CAP: 2010

FAMILY TIES? My father was a very poor leg spinner, so I got plenty of practice hitting sixes!
CAREER HIGHLIGHTS? Winning the County Championship with Lancashire in 2011. Captaining the county
CRICKETING HEROES? Andrew Flintoff, Stuart Law, Jacques Kallis
NON-CRICKETING HEROES? Alan Shearer
BEST PLAYER IN COUNTY CRICKET? Glen Chapple
TIPS FOR THE TOP? Jos Buttler, Simon Kerrigan
FAVOURITE TV? Modern Family
FAVOURITE FILM? Step Brothers or The Shawshank Redemption
FAVOURITE BOOK? Alan Partridge
SURPRISING SKILL? Being the best PS3 player in the Lancashire team
GUILTY PLEASURES? Rioja and pizza
SURPRISING FACT? I'm the first person from the Fylde Coast to play for Lancashire
FANTASY SLIP CORDON? Keeper: Alan Partridge, 1st: Mila Kunis, 2nd: Myself, 3rd: David Brent, Gully: Adam Sandler
TWITTER FEED: @Stevenjcroft

Batting	Mat	Inns	NO	Runs	HS	Ave	SR	100	50	Ct	St
First-class	94	146	12	4128	154*	30.80	51.54	5	25	84	0
List A	101	92	20	2670	107	37.08		1	20	47	0
Twenty20	93	86	15	2193	88	30.88	123.41	0	13	55	0
Bowling	**Inns**	**Balls**	**Runs**	**Wkts**	**BBI**	**BBM**	**Ave**	**Econ**	**SR**	**5w**	**10**
First-class	94	3245	1915	50	6/41	9/105	38.30	3.54	64.9	1	0
List A	101	1699	1529	43	4/24	4/24	35.55	5.39	39.5	0	0
Twenty20	93	543	771	27	3/6	3/6	28.55	8.51	20.1	0	0

STEVEN CROOK RHB RFM MVP86

FULL NAME: Steven Paul Crook
BORN: May 28, 1983, Adelaide, Australia
SQUAD NO: 25
HEIGHT: 5ft 11in
NICKNAME: Crookster, Crooky, Weirdo
EDUCATION: Rostrevor College, Adelaide
TEAMS: Lancashire, Middlesex, Northamptonshire, South Australia Under-17s, South Australia Under-19s
CAREER: First-class: 2003; List A: 2003; T20: 2004

BEST BATTING: 97 Northamptonshire vs Yorkshire, Northampton, 2005
BEST BOWLING: 5-48 Middlesex vs Lancashire, Lord's, 2012

FAMILY TIES? Brother [Andrew] played for South Australia, Lancashire and Northants
CAREER HIGHLIGHTS? Division Two County Championship winners with Middlesex in 2011
CRICKETING HEROES? Chris Rogers
NON-CRICKETING HEROES? Chris Martin from Coldplay
BEST PLAYER IN COUNTY CRICKET? Jack Brooks
TIP FOR THE TOP? Adam Rossington
WHEN RAIN STOPS PLAY? Sleeping
FAVOURITE TV? CSI
FAVOURITE FILM? Point Break
FAVOURITE BOOK? Where's Wally?
DREAM HOLIDAY? Phuket
ACCOMPLISHMENTS? Starting my own business
SURPRISING SKILL? I sing opera
GUILTY PLEASURES? Rick Astley
SURPRISING FACT? My dad had a No.1 hit in Australia

Batting	Mat	Inns	NO	Runs	HS	Ave	SR	100	50	Ct	St
First-class	52	66	8	1610	97	27.75	70.76	0	11	18	0
List A	46	28	3	369	72	14.76	96.59	0	2	12	0
Twenty20	56	35	6	370	29	12.75	126.71	0	0	11	0
Bowling	**Inns**	**Balls**	**Runs**	**Wkts**	**BBI**	**BBM**	**Ave**	**Econ**	**SR**	**5w**	**10**
First-class	52	6291	4188	103	5/48		40.66	3.99	61.0	3	0
List A	46	1611	1584	41	4/20	4/20	38.63	5.89	39.2	0	0
Twenty20	56	619	885	33	3/21	3/21	26.81	8.57	18.7	0	0

GARETH CROSS

RHB RM WK

FULL NAME: Gareth David Cross
BORN: June 20, 1984, Bury, Lancashire
SQUAD NO: 7
HEIGHT: 5ft 9in
NICKNAME: Crossy, Squirrel, Manc
EDUCATION: Moorside High School; Eccles College
TEAMS: Lancashire, Lancashire Cricket Board
CAREER: First-class: 2005; List A: 2003; T20: 2006

BEST BATTING: 125 Lancashire vs Sussex, Hove, 2011

FAMILY TIES? My dad played for Prestwich where I grew up watching and playing
WHO WOULD PLAY YOU IN A FILM OF YOUR LIFE? Mr Bean
CAREER HIGHLIGHTS? Winning the County Championship. Getting to T20 Finals Day twice, but not making the final on both occasions was disappointing
SUPERSTITIONS? I put my left pad on first but that's about it
MOST MARKED CHARACTERISTIC? I'm up for a challenge on the pitch
TIPS FOR THE TOP? Simon Kerrigan, Arron Lilley
IF YOU WEREN'T A CRICKETER? I'd be a bin man
DESERT ISLAND DISC? Arctic Monkeys – Favourite Worst Nightmare
FAVOURITE TV? An Idiot Abroad
CRICKETING HEROES? Adam Gilchrist
NON-CRICKETING HEROES? Eric Cantona, Roy Keane, Floyd Mayweather Jr
SURPRISING FACT? I'm a Meat Loaf fan
FANTASY SLIP CORDON? Keeper: Myself, 1st: Karl Pilkington, 2nd: George Best, 3rd: Eva Mendes, Gully: Eric Cantona
TWITTER FEED: @gazcross07

Batting	Mat	Inns	NO	Runs	HS	Ave	SR	100	50	Ct	St
First-class	49	77	5	1787	125	24.81	62.07	2	9	120	21
List A	66	49	6	898	76	20.88		0	3	45	21
Twenty20	76	57	11	727	65*	15.80	125.56	0	2	48	22
Bowling	**Inns**	**Balls**	**Runs**	**Wkts**	**BBI**	**BBM**	**Ave**	**Econ**	**SR**	**5w**	**10**
First-class	49	-	-	-	-	-	-	-	-	-	-
List A	66	36	26	2	2/26	2/26	13.00	4.33	18.0	0	0
Twenty20	76	-	-	-	-	-	-	-	-	-	-

BRETT D'OLIVEIRA RHB LB

FULL NAME: Brett Louis D'Oliveira
BORN: February 28, 1992, Worcester
SQUAD NO: 15
HEIGHT: 5ft 8in
NICKNAME: Dolly, Bdoll
EDUCATION: Blessed Edwards High School; Worcestershire Sixth Form College
TEAMS: Worcestershire, Worcestershire 2nd XI
CAREER: First-class: 2012; List A: 2011; T20: 2012

BEST BATTING: 19 Worcestershire vs Warwickshire, Birmingham, 2012

FAMILY TIES? My dad Damian played for Worcestershire and is the current academy and 2nd XI director. My grandfather Basil played for Worcestershire and England
WHO WOULD PLAY YOU IN A FILM OF YOUR LIFE? Denzel Washington (no chance!)
CAREER HIGHLIGHTS? Signing a professional contract with Worcestershire, making my debut in all forms for Worcestershire and playing in the T20 quarter-finals last year
MOST MARKED CHARACTERISTIC? Enthusiasm
BEST PLAYER IN COUNTY CRICKET? Marcus Trescothick
TIP FOR THE TOP? Aneesh Kapil
IF YOU WEREN'T A CRICKETER? Trying to get involved in the coaching side of things
DESERT ISLAND DISC? Drake – Take Care
FAVOURITE TV? The Fresh Prince Of Bel-Air
CRICKETING HEROES? Shane Warne, Sachin Tendulkar
ACCOMPLISHMENTS? My national diploma in Sport and Exercise Science. Currently trying to get involved in some charity work in aid of my grandfather and other patients
FANTASY SLIP CORDON? Keeper: Drake, 1st: Myself, 2nd: Nelson Mandela, 3rd: Lil Wayne, Gully: Shane Warne
TWITTER FEED: @Bdolly09

Batting	Mat	Inns	NO	Runs	HS	Ave	SR	100	50	Ct	St
First-class	3	6	0	62	19	10.33	42.46	0	0	0	0
List A	7	4	3	41	16*	41.00	117.14	0	0	3	0
Twenty20	8	3	3	8	6*	-	114.28	0	0	1	0
Bowling	**Inns**	**Balls**	**Runs**	**Wkts**	**BBI**	**BBM**	**Ave**	**Econ**	**SR**	**5w**	**10**
First-class	3	258	198	0	-	-	-	4.60	-	0	0
List A	7	282	251	6	2/35	2/35	41.83	5.34	47.0	0	0
Twenty20	8	72	104	3	3/20	3/20	34.66	8.66	24.0	0	0

LEE DAGGETT RHB RMF

FULL NAME: Lee Martin Daggett
BORN: October 1, 1982, Bury, Lancashire
SQUAD NO: 10
HEIGHT: 6ft
NICKNAME: Dags, Von Daggentooth
EDUCATION: Woodhey High School, Bury; Holy Cross College; Durham University; Salford University
TEAMS: Durham UCCE, Lancashire Cricket Board, Leicestershire, Northamptonshire, Warwickshire
CAREER: First-class: 2003; List A: 2006; T20: 2007

BEST BATTING: 50* Northamptonshire vs Leicestershire, Grace Road, 2011
BEST BOWLING: 8-94 Durham UCCE vs Durham, Chester-le-Street, 2004

CAREER HIGHLIGHTS? Taking eight wickets for Durham University whilst I didn't have a contract, six wickets against Durham for Warwickshire in 2006, T20 quarter-final win against Hampshire in 2009
SUPERSTITIONS? I don't like my bowling marker being moved and I never shave during a game
CRICKETING HEROES? Allan Donald, Brett Lee
BEST PLAYER IN COUNTY CRICKET? Marcus Trescothick
TIPS FOR THE TOP? Alex Wakely, Olly Stone
IF YOU WEREN'T A CRICKETER? Physiotherapist
WHEN RAIN STOPS PLAY? Drinking tea, eating biscuits, darts, catching up with emails, loitering in the physio room
FAVOURITE TV? An Idiot Abroad, Modern Family, Family Guy
FAVOURITE FILM? Gladiator, Anchorman, Dumb And Dumber, Bronson
FAVOURITE BOOK? Anything written by Lee Child
DREAM HOLIDAY? Mauritius
GUILTY PLEASURES? Fig rolls and Glee
TWITTER FEED: @LeeDaggett

Batting	Mat	Inns	NO	Runs	HS	Ave	SR	100	50	Ct	St
First-class	68	81	35	601	50*	13.06	33.16	0	1	12	0
List A	55	16	11	79	14*	15.80	66.38	0	0	9	0
Twenty20	43	9	5	8	3*	2.00	44.44	0	0	10	0
Bowling	**Inns**	**Balls**	**Runs**	**Wkts**	**BBI**	**BBM**	**Ave**	**Econ**	**SR**	**5w**	**10**
First-class	68	10617	6097	164	8/94		37.17	3.44	64.7	2	0
List A	55	2192	1826	72	4/17	4/17	25.36	4.99	30.4	0	0
Twenty20	43	535	701	22	2/17	2/17	31.86	7.86	24.3	0	0

JOSH DAVEY

RHB RM

FULL NAME: Joshua Henry Davey
BORN: August 3, 1990, Aberdeen
SQUAD NO: 24
EDUCATION: Culford School; Oxford Brookes University
TEAMS: Scotland, Middlesex, Middlesex 2nd XI, Suffolk
CAREER: ODI: 2010; T20I: 2012; First-class: 2010; List A: 2010; T20: 2010

BEST BATTING: 72 Middlesex vs Oxford MCCU, Oxford, 2010
BEST BOWLING: 2-41 Middlesex vs Oxford MCCU, Oxford, 2010

NOTES: Davey signed a new one-year contract extension with Middlesex last October after featuring in three one-day fixtures in 2012. Made his highest first-class score of 72 on his debut for Middlesex against Oxford MCCU in 2010. Hit unbeaten 48 and took 3-41 for Scotland against Ireland at Edinburgh in the 2011 Tri-Nation Tournament to help his country to a five-wicket win. Attended the Darren Lehmann Cricket Academy in Adelaide in 2009. Holds the record for the best ever ODI bowling figures for Scotland of 5-9 against Afghanistan at Ayr in 2010. At the time of writing, has scored three half-centuries in seven first-class innings for Middlesex

Batting	Mat	Inns	NO	Runs	HS	Ave	SR	100	50	Ct	St
ODIs	9	9	1	170	48*	21.25	55.73	0	0	4	0
T20Is	1	1	0	7	7	7.00	116.66	0	0	1	0
First-class	5	9	1	269	72	33.62	41.77	0	3	3	0
List A	39	38	6	783	91	24.46	63.71	0	3	13	0
Twenty20	8	6	3	45	18*	15.00	109.75	0	0	5	0
Bowling	**Inns**	**Balls**	**Runs**	**Wkts**	**BBI**	**BBM**	**Ave**	**Econ**	**SR**	**5w**	**10**
ODIs	9	320	257	14	5/9	5/9	18.35	4.81	22.8	1	0
T20Is	1	24	23	3	3/23	3/23	7.66	5.75	8.0	0	0
First-class	5	198	133	3	2/41	2/65	44.33	4.03	66.0	0	0
List A	39	1058	1024	36	5/9	5/9	28.44	5.80	29.3	1	0
Twenty20	8	54	71	3	3/23	3/23	23.66	7.88	18.0	0	0

ALEX DAVIES RHB WK

FULL NAME: Alexander Luke Davies
BORN: August 23, 1994, Darwen, Lancashire
SQUAD NO: 17
HEIGHT: 5ft 7in
NICKNAME: Al, Davo, AD, Harry
EDUCATION: QEGS Blackburn
TEAMS: England Under-19s, Lancashire, Lancashire 2nd XI, Lancashire Cricket Academy, Lancashire Under-13s, Lancashire Under-14s, Lancashire Under-15s, Lancashire Under-17s
CAREER: First-class: 2012; List A: 2011

WHO WOULD PLAY YOU IN A FILM OF YOUR LIFE? Prince Harry
CAREER HIGHLIGHTS? Making my first-class and List A debuts for Lancashire, playing in the U19 World Cup for England, representing England at U15 and U17 level
SUPERSTITIONS? I always put my left foot on and off the field first and I always put my gear on and prepare in the same order
MOST MARKED CHARACTERISTIC? Leaving everything until the last minute
BEST PLAYER IN COUNTY CRICKET? Simon Kerrigan, Steven Croft, Jos Buttler
TIPS FOR THE TOP? Ben Foakes, Reece Topley, Joe Root
DESERT ISLAND DISC? Eminem or Avicii
FAVOURITE TV? Phoenix Nights, Family Guy
CRICKETING HEROES? Sachin Tendulkar, Mark Boucher, James Foster, AB de Villiers
NON-CRICKETING HEROES? Michael Owen, Jonny Wilkinson, Mario Balotelli, my granddad
ACCOMPLISHMENTS? Playing football for Blackburn Rovers
WHEN YOU RETIRE? Play lots of golf and travel the world
SURPRISING FACT? I bowled left-arm spin as a kid, then changed to right-arm, then became a keeper! I'm still a class bowler though!
FANTASY SLIP CORDON? Keeper: Me, 1st: Brian Potter, 2nd: Lachie Mason, 3rd: Happy Gilmore, Gully: Ted
TWITTER FEED: @aldavies23

Batting	Mat	Inns	NO	Runs	HS	Ave	SR	100	50	Ct	St
First-class	1	-	-	-	-	-	-	-	-	2	0
List A	1	1	1	6	6*	-	85.71	0	0	0	0
Bowling	**Inns**	**Balls**	**Runs**	**Wkts**	**BBI**	**BBM**	**Ave**	**Econ**	**SR**	**5w**	**10**
First-class	1	-	-	-	-	-	-	-	-	-	-
List A	1	-	-	-	-	-	-	-	-	-	-

MARK DAVIES RHB RMF W1 MVP26

FULL NAME: Anthony Mark Davies
BORN: October 4, 1980, Stockton-on-Tees, County Durham
SQUAD NO: 31
HEIGHT: 6ft 2in
NICKNAME: Davo, Bob
EDUCATION: Northfield School, Billingham
TEAMS: Durham, Durham 2nd XI, Durham Cricket Board, Kent
CAREER: First-class: 2002; List A: 1998; T20: 2003

BEST BATTING: 62 Durham vs Somerset, Stockton-on-Tees, 2005
BEST BOWLING: 8-24 Durham vs Hampshire, Basingstoke, 2008
COUNTY CAP: 2005 (Durham)

FAMILY TIES? My uncle Paul played for Yorkshire's 2nd XI
CAREER HIGHLIGHTS? Winning back-to-back Championships with Durham. Also being picked for the England Lions tour to New Zealand was a special time for me
CRICKETING HEROES? My uncle Paul in the early years and then Glenn McGrath
NON-CRICKETING HEROES? Oasis
BEST PLAYER IN COUNTY CRICKET? Marcus Trescothick
TIP FOR THE TOP? Ben Stokes
IF YOU WEREN'T A CRICKETER? Anything to do with sport
FAVOURITE TV? This Is England
FAVOURITE FILM? Wedding Crashers
FAVOURITE BOOK? Racing Through The Dark by David Millar
DREAM HOLIDAY? Marbella
ACCOMPLISHMENTS? Becoming a dad in 2008
GUILTY PLEASURES? Curries and lager
FANTASY SLIP CORDON? Keeper: Noel Gallagher, 1st: Liam Gallagher, 2nd: Gazza, 3rd: Myself, Gully: Floyd Mayweather Jr

Batting	Mat	Inns	NO	Runs	HS	Ave	SR	100	50	Ct	St
First-class	98	123	45	960	62	12.30	35.58	0	2	21	0
List A	82	37	15	169	31*	7.68		0	0	12	0
Twenty20	18	8	4	26	13	6.50	81.25	0	0	4	0
Bowling	**Inns**	**Balls**	**Runs**	**Wkts**	**BBI**	**BBM**	**Ave**	**Econ**	**SR**	**5w**	**10**
First-class	98	14751	6425	289	8/24		22.23	2.61	51.0	13	2
List A	82	3396	2342	78	4/13	4/13	30.02	4.13	43.5	0	0
Twenty20	18	420	447	15	2/14	2/14	29.80	6.38	28.0	0	0

STEVE DAVIES LHB WK R4 MVP45

FULL NAME: Steven Michael Davies
BORN: June 17, 1986, Bromsgrove, Worcestershire
SQUAD NO: 9
HEIGHT: 5ft 11in
NICKNAME: Davo
EDUCATION: King Charles High School, Kidderminster
TEAMS: England, England Lions, Marylebone Cricket Club, Surrey, Worcestershire, Worcestershire Cricket Board
CAREER: ODI: 2009; T20I: 2009; First-class: 2005; List A: 2003; T20: 2006

BEST BATTING: 192 Worcestershire vs Gloucestershire, Bristol, 2006
COUNTY CAP: 2011 (Surrey)

WHO WOULD PLAY YOU IN A FILM OF YOUR LIFE? Daniel Craig
CAREER HIGHLIGHTS? Getting my first professional contract, my debuts for Worcestershire, Surrey and England. Winning the CB40 with both Worcestershire and Surrey and being part of the Ashes squad that won in Australia in 2010/11
BEST PLAYER IN COUNTY CRICKET? Graham Onions
TIPS FOR THE TOP? Arun Harinath, Rory Burns, Matthew Dunn, George Edwards
DESERT ISLAND DISC? Elton John's Greatest Hits
FAVOURITE TV? An Idiot Abroad
CRICKETING HEROES? Adam Gilchrist, Brian Lara
NON-CRICKETING HEROES? Roger Federer
ACCOMPLISHMENTS? Playing tennis on the grass at Wimbledon
SURPRISING FACT? I can serve both left- and right-handed at tennis
TWITTER FEED: @SteveDavies43

Batting	Mat	Inns	NO	Runs	HS	Ave	SR	100	50	Ct	St
ODIs	8	8	0	244	87	30.50	105.62	0	1	8	0
T20Is	5	5	0	102	33	20.40	124.39	0	0	2	1
First-class	122	204	20	7005	192	38.07	62.50	11	35	360	17
List A	134	123	12	3880	119	34.95		5	23	118	39
Twenty20	80	73	7	1571	99*	23.80	143.60	0	8	43	15
Bowling	**Inns**	**Balls**	**Runs**	**Wkts**	**BBI**	**BBM**	**Ave**	**Econ**	**SR**	**5w**	**10**
ODIs	8	-	-	-	-	-	-	-	-	-	-
T20Is	5	-	-	-	-	-	-	-	-	-	-
First-class	122	-	-	-	-	-	-	-	-	-	-
List A	134	-	-	-	-	-	-	-	-	-	-
Twenty20	80	-	-	-	-	-	-	-	-	-	-

CHRISTIAN DAVIS RHB LFM

FULL NAME: Christian Arthur Linghorne Davis
BORN: October 11, 1992, Milton Keynes, Buckinghamshire
SQUAD NO: 2
HEIGHT: 6ft 2in
NICKNAME: Davo
EDUCATION: Bedford School
TEAMS: Bedfordshire, England Under-19s, Northamptonshire 2nd XI
CAREER: List A: 2010

FAMILY TIES? My dad played minor counties for Bedfordshire
WHO WOULD PLAY YOU IN A FILM OF YOUR LIFE? I would like to say Russell Crowe, but looks-wise I think Gareth (from The Office) would get the call up
CAREER HIGHLIGHTS? Representing England U19 in Sri Lanka and playing for Northamptonshire 1st XI
MOST MARKED CHARACTERISTIC? General bad haircut and love of Arsenal FC
BEST PLAYER IN COUNTY CRICKET? Chris Woakes
TIPS FOR THE TOP? Ben Duckett and Shiv Thakor
FAVOURITE TV? Homeland, The X Factor, Dragons' Den
BIGGEST DRESSING DOWN YOU'VE RECEIVED? Getting in an argument with a leg spinner, then next over hitting a low full toss back to him for a caught and bowled. He walked me halfway off the pitch
CRICKETING HEROES? Shane Watson, Ricky Ponting, Sir Garry Sobers
NON-CRICKETING HEROES? Thierry Henry, Dennis Bergkamp, James Dyson, Arsene Wenger, Steve Jobs
WHEN YOU RETIRE? Move somewhere sunny and chill out
SURPRISING FACT? I'm passionate about product design and art. I like the work of Jonathan Ive, Klimt and Van Gogh
FANTASY SLIP CORDON? Keeper: Ricky Gervais (plenty of gags and he'd be an unbelievable sledger), 1st: Me, 2nd: Thierry Henry (to chat all things Arsenal), 3rd: Karl Pilkington (because he is the most stupid man in the world and will help fuel Ricky's jokes), Gully: Usain Bolt (so he can sprint and get the ball when it goes down to third man!)
TWITTER FEED: @daviscal123

Batting	Mat	Inns	NO	Runs	HS	Ave	SR	100	50	Ct	St
List A	3	2	0	57	54	28.50	90.47	0	1	0	0
Bowling	**Inns**	**Balls**	**Runs**	**Wkts**	**BBI**	**BBM**	**Ave**	**Econ**	**SR**	**5w**	**10**
List A	3	45	44	0	-	-	-	5.86	-	0	0

LIAM DAWSON RHB SLA MVP22

FULL NAME: Liam Andrew Dawson
BORN: March 1, 1990, Swindon, Wiltshire
SQUAD NO: 8
HEIGHT: 5ft 10in
NICKNAME: Daws, Leemo, Stomper
EDUCATION: John Bentley School
TEAMS: England Lions, England Under-19s, Hampshire, Hampshire 2nd XI, Mountaineers
CAREER: First-class: 2007; List A: 2007; T20: 2008

BEST BATTING: 169 Hampshire vs Somerset, Southampton, 2011
BEST BOWLING: 7-51 Mountaineers vs Mashonaland Eagles, Mutare Sports Club, 2011

FAMILY TIES? My dad and brother play for Goatacre CC
WHO WOULD PLAY YOU IN A FILM OF YOUR LIFE? Adam Sandler
CAREER HIGHLIGHTS? Winning a Lord's final and two T20 finals. Also winning Man of the Match at Lord's in the CB40
MOST MARKED CHARACTERISTIC? My stomping around the outfield
BEST PLAYER IN COUNTY CRICKET? Michael Carberry
TIP FOR THE TOP? Sean Terry
DESERT ISLAND DISC? Wiley – Heatwave
FAVOURITE TV? Crimewatch
CRICKETING HEROES? Shane Warne, Shaun Udal, Simon Katich
WHEN YOU RETIRE? Sit and watch my kids play sport professionally
SURPRISING FACT? I turned down a career in football
FANTASY SLIP CORDON? Keeper: Alan Garner, 1st: Rihanna, 2nd: Me, 3rd: David Beckham, Gully: Cheryl Cole
TWITTER FEED: @daws128

Batting	Mat	Inns	NO	Runs	HS	Ave	SR	100	50	Ct	St
First-class	62	99	10	2829	169	31.78	48.97	5	14	72	0
List A	64	51	11	1031	70	25.77	93.55	0	3	35	0
Twenty20	47	29	8	267	30	12.71	105.53	0	0	21	0
Bowling	**Inns**	**Balls**	**Runs**	**Wkts**	**BBI**	**BBM**	**Ave**	**Econ**	**SR**	**5w**	**10**
First-class	62	3239	1893	53	7/51	7/84	35.71	3.50	61.1	2	0
List A	64	1677	1458	35	4/45	4/45	41.65	5.21	47.9	0	0
Twenty20	47	466	601	18	3/25	3/25	33.38	7.73	25.8	0	0

ZANDER DE BRUYN RHB RM R1 MVP74

FULL NAME: Zander de Bruyn
BORN: July 5, 1975, Johannesburg, South Africa
SQUAD NO: 58
HEIGHT: 6ft 1in
NICKNAME: Zed
EDUCATION: Randburg High School; University of Johannesburg
TEAMS: South Africa, Gauteng, Lions, Marylebone Cricket Club, Somerset, Surrey, Titans, Transvaal, Warriors, Worcestershire
CAREER: Test: 2004; First-class: 2005; List A: 1996; T20: 2005

BEST BATTING: 266* Easterns vs Griqualand West, Kimberley, 2003
BEST BOWLING: 7-67 Warriors vs Titans, Port Elizabeth, 2007
COUNTY CAP: 2008 (Somerset)

WHO WOULD PLAY YOU IN A FILM OF YOUR LIFE? Hugh Jackman
CAREER HIGHLIGHTS? Playing for South Africa
SUPERSTITIONS? I chew a particular sort of gum every time I bat and I always strap my wrist
MOST MARKED CHARACTERISTIC? My competitiveness
BEST PLAYER IN COUNTY CRICKET? Marcus Trescothick
TIPS FOR THE TOP? Rory Burns, Jos Buttler
IF YOU WEREN'T A CRICKETER? I'd be an entrepreneur
DESERT ISLAND DISC? AC/DC – Thunderstruck
FAVOURITE TV? CBeebies. And when I'm not watching that with my son then Top Gear
BIGGEST DRESSING DOWN YOU'VE RECEIVED? Ray Jennings after a bad game
CRICKETING HEROES? Steve Waugh, Clive Rice
SURPRISING FACT? I have an addiction to cricket bats
FANTASY SLIP CORDON? Keeper: Mr Elastic (to take all the nicks), 1st: Michael McIntyre, 2nd: Me, 3rd: Eminem (to abuse the batsmen), Gully: Sienna Miller

Batting	Mat	Inns	NO	Runs	HS	Ave	SR	100	50	Ct	St
Tests	3	5	1	155	83	38.75	37.89	0	1	0	0
First-class	223	376	35	13583	266*	39.83		28	77	135	0
List A	231	208	44	5896	122*	35.95		6	36	56	0
Twenty20	114	97	27	2049	95*	29.27	106.33	0	9	22	0
Bowling	**Inns**	**Balls**	**Runs**	**Wkts**	**BBI**	**BBM**	**Ave**	**Econ**	**SR**	**5w**	**10**
Tests	3	216	92	3	2/32	2/32	30.66	2.55	72.0	0	0
First-class	223	18063	10123	263	7/67		38.49	3.36	68.6	4	0
List A	231	5147	4741	156	5/44	5/44	30.39	5.52	32.9	2	0
Twenty20	114	977	1441	49	4/18	4/18	29.40	8.84	19.9	0	0

CON DE LANGE RHB SLA

FULL NAME: Con de Wet de Lange
BORN: February 11, 1981, Bellville, South Africa
SQUAD NO: 31
HEIGHT: 5ft 8in
NICKNAME: Goose, Conaldo
EDUCATION: Worcester Gymnasium High School; UNISA
TEAMS: South Africa A, Boland, Cape Cobras, Eagles, Free State, Knights, Northamptonshire, Western Province
CAREER: First-class: 1998; List A: 2000; T20: 2007

BEST BATTING: 109 Boland vs Easterns, Paarl, 2003
BEST BOWLING: 7-48 Gauteng vs Boland, Randjesfontein, 2004

FAMILY TIES? My father and uncle played provincial cricket
WHO WOULD PLAY YOU IN A FILM OF YOUR LIFE? Russell Crowe
CAREER HIGHLIGHTS? Playing for South Africa A and winning three limited overs trophies
MOST MARKED CHARACTERISTIC? I'm a hard worker and will fight to the end
BEST PLAYER IN COUNTY CRICKET? Jos Buttler
TIPS FOR THE TOP? Oliver Stone, Christian Davis
IF YOU WEREN'T A CRICKETER? Pro golfer
DESERT ISLAND DISC? U2's Greatest Hits
FAVOURITE TV? Anger Management, Friends, Two And A Half Men
CRICKETING HEROES? My father and Jacques Kallis
WHEN YOU RETIRE? I'd like to coach cricket and study Sports Psychology
TWITTER FEED: @cdwdelange

Batting	Mat	Inns	NO	Runs	HS	Ave	SR	100	50	Ct	St
First-class	87	139	16	2879	109	23.40		1	13	45	0
List A	127	84	21	1451	66	23.03		0	7	39	0
Twenty20	25	10	4	35	8	5.83	83.33	0	0	13	0
Bowling	**Inns**	**Balls**	**Runs**	**Wkts**	**BBI**	**BBM**	**Ave**	**Econ**	**SR**	**5w**	**10**
First-class	87	14953	6923	178	7/48		38.89	2.77	84.0	5	1
List A	127	5170	3780	130	4/8	4/8	29.07	4.38	39.7	0	0
Twenty20	25	451	510	22	3/15	3/15	23.18	6.78	20.5	0	0

JOE DENLY RHB LB R2 MVP70

FULL NAME: Joseph Liam Denly
BORN: March 16, 1986, Canterbury, Kent
SQUAD NO: 10
HEIGHT: 6ft
NICKNAME: JD, Denners
EDUCATION: Chaucer Technology College, Canterbury
TEAMS: England, England Lions, England Performance Programme, England Under-19s, Kent, Kent 2nd XI, Middlesex
CAREER: ODI: 2009; T20I: 2009; First-class: 2004; List A: 2004; T20: 2004

BEST BATTING: 199 Kent vs Derbyshire, Derby, 2011
BEST BOWLING: 3-43 Kent vs Surrey, The Oval, 2011
COUNTY CAPS: 2008 (Kent); 2012 (Middlesex)

WHO WOULD PLAY YOU IN A FILM OF YOUR LIFE? Brad Pitt
CAREER HIGHLIGHTS? Representing England at ODI and T20I and winning the domestic T20 Cup
SUPERSTITIONS? Left pad on first
MOST MARKED CHARACTERISTIC? Big… ears
BEST PLAYER IN COUNTY CRICKET? Marcus Trescothick
TIPS FOR THE TOP? Ravi Patel, Jaydn Denly
DESERT ISLAND DISC? Michael Buble
FAVOURITE TV? The X Factor (auditions)
BIGGEST DRESSING DOWN YOU'VE RECEIVED? Rob Key often spat his dummy when I kept getting the golden boot at Kent
CRICKETING HEROES? Sachin Tendulkar, Ricky Ponting
TWITTER FEED: @joed1986

Batting	Mat	Inns	NO	Runs	HS	Ave	SR	100	50	Ct	St
ODIs	9	9	0	268	67	29.77	65.52	0	2	5	0
T20Is	5	5	0	20	14	4.00	68.96	0	0	1	0
First-class	100	177	10	5770	199	34.55	57.42	14	28	44	0
List A	91	89	8	2686	115	33.16	73.04	4	13	27	0
Twenty20	93	90	6	2083	100	24.79	110.97	1	12	35	0
Bowling	**Inns**	**Balls**	**Runs**	**Wkts**	**BBI**	**BBM**	**Ave**	**Econ**	**SR**	**5w**	**10**
ODIs	9	-	-	-	-	-	-	-	-	-	-
T20Is	5	6	9	1	1/9	1/9	9.00	9.00	6.0	0	0
First-class	100	1909	1071	21	3/43	6/114	51.00	3.36	90.9	0	0
List A	91	128	132	5	3/42	3/42	26.40	6.18	25.6	0	0
Twenty20	93	48	76	1	1/9	1/9	76.00	9.50	48.0	0	0

CHRIS DENT

LHB SLA WK

FULL NAME: Christopher David James Dent
BORN: January 20, 1991, Bristol
SQUAD NO: 15
HEIGHT: 5ft 10in
NICKNAME: Denty, Maggot, Weezle, Harry
EDUCATION: Filton College
TEAMS: England Under-19s, Gloucestershire, Gloucestershire 2nd XI
CAREER: First-class: 2010; List A: 2009; T20: 2010

BEST BATTING: 114 Gloucestershire vs Hampshire, Southampton, 2012
COUNTY CAP: 2010

CAREER HIGHLIGHTS? Maiden first-class hundred
CRICKETING HEROES? Brian Lara, Chris Taylor, Jack Russell
NON-CRICKETING HEROES? Tiger Woods
BEST PLAYER IN COUNTY CRICKET? Marcus Trescothick
TIP FOR THE TOP? Jos Buttler
IF YOU WEREN'T A CRICKETER? I'd be working in Mbargos in Bristol
WHEN RAIN STOPS PLAY? On my phone or sleeping
FAVOURITE TV? The Joy Of Teen Sex
FAVOURITE FILM? The Girl With The Dragon Tattoo
FAVOURITE BOOK? The Game
DREAM HOLIDAY? Las Vegas
ACCOMPLISHMENTS? Tonning up on the leaderboard and getting through college
GUILTY PLEASURES? Night out and bubble bath in the changing rooms
FANTASY SLIP CORDON? Keeper: Rihanna, 1st: Megan Fox, 2nd: Me, 3rd: Tiger Woods, Gully: Jessica Alba
TWITTER FEED: @Cdent15

Batting	Mat	Inns	NO	Runs	HS	Ave	SR	100	50	Ct	St
First-class	36	67	6	1798	114	29.47	50.46	2	9	52	0
List A	12	9	0	125	36	13.88	83.33	0	0	3	0
Twenty20	8	7	0	169	63	24.14	118.18	0	1	0	0
Bowling	**Inns**	**Balls**	**Runs**	**Wkts**	**BBI**	**BBM**	**Ave**	**Econ**	**SR**	**5w**	**10**
First-class	36	144	83	0	-	-	-	3.45	-	0	0
List A	12	174	149	7	4/43	4/43	21.28	5.13	24.8	0	0
Twenty20	8	-	-	-	-	-	-	-	-	-	-

JADE DERNBACH

RHB RFM W1

FULL NAME: Jade Winston Dernbach
BORN: March 3, 1986, Johannesburg, South Africa
SQUAD NO: 16
HEIGHT: 6ft 2in
NICKNAME: Dirtbag
EDUCATION: St John The Baptist, Johannesburg
TEAMS: England, England Lions, Surrey, Surrey 2nd XI
CAREER: ODI: 2011; T20I: 2011; First-class: 2003; List A: 2005; T20: 2005

BEST BATTING: 56* Surrey vs Northamptonshire, Northampton, 2011
BEST BOWLING: 6-47 Surrey vs Leicestershire, Leicester, 2010
COUNTY CAP: 2011

NOTES: Leading wicket-taker in the 2008 Pro40, with 24 wickets at 13.08. Took 51 first-class wickets at 27.75 in 2010. Replaced the injured Ajmal Shahzad for the knockout stages of the 2011 World Cup. Made his ODI and T20I debuts against Sri Lanka in 2011. Impressed in the 2012 T20I series against Pakistan, claiming four wickets at 17 with an economy of 6.18. Claimed six wickets in February's T20I series win against New Zealand

Batting	Mat	Inns	NO	Runs	HS	Ave	SR	100	50	Ct	St
ODIs	22	7	1	17	5	2.83	50.00	0	0	5	0
T20Is	21	4	1	17	12	5.66	121.42	0	0	7	0
First-class	73	93	34	561	56*	9.50		0	1	10	0
List A	106	39	15	184	31	7.66	81.05	0	0	22	0
Twenty20	68	16	5	58	12	5.27	89.23	0	0	15	0
Bowling	**Inns**	**Balls**	**Runs**	**Wkts**	**BBI**	**BBM**	**Ave**	**Econ**	**SR**	**5w**	**10**
ODIs	22	1114	1166	30	4/45	4/45	38.86	6.28	37.1	0	0
T20Is	21	444	588	26	4/22	4/22	22.61	7.94	17.0	0	0
First-class	73	11537	6538	203	6/47		32.20	3.40	56.8	9	0
List A	106	4523	4590	167	5/31	5/31	27.48	6.08	27.0	2	0
Twenty20	68	1305	1828	68	4/22	4/22	26.88	8.40	19.1	0	0

NEIL DEXTER

RHB RM MVP44

FULL NAME: Neil John Dexter
BORN: August 21, 1984, Johannesburg, South Africa
SQUAD NO: 8
HEIGHT: 6ft
NICKNAME: Ted, Dex, Sexy Dexy
EDUCATION: Northwood School, Durban; UNISA
TEAMS: Essex, Essex 2nd XI, Kent, Kent 2nd XI, Middlesex
CAREER: First-class: 2005; List A: 2005; T20: 2006

BEST BATTING: 146 Middlesex vs Kent, Uxbridge, 2009
BEST BOWLING: 3-23 Middlesex vs Surrey, Lord's, 2012
COUNTY CAP: 2010 (Middlesex)

CRICKETING HEROES? Steve Waugh, Brett Lee
OTHER SPORTS PLAYED? Golf, tennis
FAVOURITE BAND? Simple Plan, Goo Goo Dolls
NOTES: Resigned as Middlesex's Championship captain in April 2012, passing the responsibility to Chris Rogers, but he remains club skipper and leads the team in limited overs competitions. Initially appointed to the role in June 2010 when Shaun Udal stood down, becoming the third youngest captain in Middlesex's history, and led the side to the Championship Division Two title in 2011. Signed for the club in 2008 after rejecting a three-year contract extension with Kent, whom he joined as a Kolpak player in 2005. Had a loan spell with Essex in 2008. Played for Natal U13-19, Natal Academy and Natal A in his native South Africa

Batting	Mat	Inns	NO	Runs	HS	Ave	SR	100	50	Ct	St
First-class	77	126	17	4217	146	38.68	54.37	10	22	65	0
List A	73	63	13	1570	135*	31.40	81.85	2	7	16	0
Twenty20	77	67	7	1261	73	21.01	109.65	0	2	31	0
Bowling	**Inns**	**Balls**	**Runs**	**Wkts**	**BBI**	**BBM**	**Ave**	**Econ**	**SR**	**5w**	**10**
First-class	77	3463	1910	49	3/23		38.97	3.30	70.6	0	0
List A	73	1619	1495	30	3/17	3/17	49.83	5.54	53.9	0	0
Twenty20	77	803	1031	38	4/21	4/21	27.13	7.70	21.1	0	0

ADAM DIBBLE

RHB RMF

FULL NAME: Adam John Dibble
BORN: March 9, 1991, Exeter, Devon
SQUAD NO: 16
HEIGHT: 6ft 4in
NICKNAME: Dibbs, Officer
EDUCATION: St John's School, Sidmouth; Taunton School
TEAMS: Devon, Somerset, Somerset 2nd XI
CAREER: First-class: 2011; List A: 2011; T20: 2011

BEST BATTING: 43 Somerset vs Warwickshire, Birmingham, 2012
BEST BOWLING: 3-42 Somerset vs Warwickshire, Birmingham, 2012

FAMILY TIES? My dad played cricket for Sidmouth CC. Sister [Jodie] is in England Women's Academy
WHO WOULD PLAY YOU IN A FILM OF YOUR LIFE? Ryan Reynolds
CAREER HIGHLIGHTS? Somerset debut and Champions League T20 semi-final in 2011
BEST PLAYER IN COUNTY CRICKET? James Hildreth
TIP FOR THE TOP? Tom Abell
DESERT ISLAND DISC? Coldplay – Viva La Vida
FAVOURITE TV? Sherlock
CRICKETING HEROES? Chris Gayle
NON-CRICKETING HEROES? David Beckham, Jonny Wilkinson, Will Smith, Jay-Z, Eminem
WHEN YOU RETIRE? Travel
FANTASY SLIP CORDON? Keeper: David Beckham, 1st: Ricky Gervais, 2nd: Will Smith, 3rd: Jay-Z, Gully: Steve Jobs
TWITTER FEED: @adam_dibble

Batting	Mat	Inns	NO	Runs	HS	Ave	SR	100	50	Ct	St
First-class	3	6	2	84	43	21.00	72.41	0	0	0	0
List A	4	-	-	-	-	-	-	-	-	0	0
Twenty20	2	-	-	-	-	-	-	-	-	0	0
Bowling	**Inns**	**Balls**	**Runs**	**Wkts**	**BBI**	**BBM**	**Ave**	**Econ**	**SR**	**5w**	**10**
First-class	3	294	184	5	3/42	3/42	36.80	3.75	58.8	0	0
List A	4	156	170	5	3/52	3/52	34.00	6.53	31.2	0	0
Twenty20	2	48	44	2	1/20	1/20	22.00	5.50	24.0	0	0

GEORGE DOCKRELL RHB SLA MVP100

FULL NAME: George Henry Dockrell
BORN: July 22, 1992, Dublin
SQUAD NO: 20
HEIGHT: 6ft 4in
NICKNAME: Doc
EDUCATION: Gonzaga College, Dublin; Trinity College, Dublin
TEAMS: Ireland, Ireland Under-13s, Ireland Under-15s, Ireland Under-19s, Somerset, Somerset 2nd XI
CAREER: ODI: 2010; T20I: 2010; First-class: 2010; List A: 2010; T20: 2010

BEST BATTING: 53 Ireland vs Namibia, Belfast, 2011
BEST BOWLING: 6-27 Somerset vs Middlesex, Taunton, 2012

CAREER HIGHLIGHTS? Beating England in the 2011 World Cup with Ireland and taking six wickets vs Middlesex and Durham at Taunton in 2012
MOST MARKED CHARACTERISTIC? I'm a thinker
BEST PLAYER IN COUNTY CRICKET? Kevin Pietersen – impossible to bowl to
TIP FOR THE TOP? Lewis Gregory
IF YOU WEREN'T A CRICKETER? Something science related
DESERT ISLAND DISC? G-Eazy – The Endless Summer
FAVOURITE TV? Any kind of sport
CRICKETING HEROES? Daniel Vettori – consistent performances at the top level year after year
NON-CRICKETING HEROES? Brian O'Driscoll, Rob Dyrdek
ACCOMPLISHMENTS? Making the Irish U16 hockey squad
SURPRISING FACT? I've never had a cup of tea or coffee in my life
TWITTER FEED: @georgedockrell

Batting	Mat	Inns	NO	Runs	HS	Ave	SR	100	50	Ct	St
ODIs	30	16	8	80	19	10.00	65.57	0	0	13	0
T20Is	19	3	2	2	2*	2.00	25.00	0	0	4	0
First-class	19	19	5	171	53	12.21	28.26	0	1	9	0
List A	45	23	11	135	22*	11.25	69.94	0	0	20	0
Twenty20	43	7	5	4	2*	2.00	22.22	0	0	20	0
Bowling	**Inns**	**Balls**	**Runs**	**Wkts**	**BBI**	**BBM**	**Ave**	**Econ**	**SR**	**5w**	**10**
ODIs	30	1353	940	37	4/35	4/35	25.40	4.16	36.5	0	0
T20Is	19	388	372	27	4/20	4/20	13.77	5.75	14.3	0	0
First-class	19	3188	1641	64	6/27	9/87	25.64	3.08	49.8	4	0
List A	45	1917	1395	48	4/35	4/35	29.06	4.36	39.9	0	0
Twenty20	43	837	889	51	4/20	4/20	17.43	6.37	16.4	0	0

BEN DUCKETT LHB OB WK

FULL NAME: Ben Matthew Duckett
BORN: October 17, 1994, Farnborough, Kent
SQUAD NO: 24
HEIGHT: 5ft 9in
NICKNAME: Ducky
EDUCATION: Millfield; Stowe School
TEAMS: England Under-19s, Northamptonshire, Northamptonshire 2nd XI
CAREER: T20: 2012

FAMILY TIES? My dad was on the Surrey staff for a few years. My grandfather Tom Duckett played and was then a successful umpire
WHO WOULD PLAY YOU IN A FILM OF YOUR LIFE? Adam Sandler
CAREER HIGHLIGHTS? Winning the 2nd XI T20 competition with England U19 and getting Man of the Match in the final with 73 not out. Getting picked for the U19 World Cup in Australia two years later. Making my debut for Northants last summer in a T20 game
MOST MARKED CHARACTERISTIC? My hair
BEST PLAYER IN COUNTY CRICKET? Kevin Pietersen
TIPS FOR THE TOP? Dom Sibley, Shiv Thakor, Olly Stone, Ben Collins
IF YOU WEREN'T A CRICKETER? I'd just be at school this year but I would look into some sort of coaching after that
DESERT ISLAND DISC? Mac Miller
FAVOURITE TV? The Only Way Is Essex
BIGGEST DRESSING DOWN YOU'VE RECEIVED? Two-match ban from my school last year
CRICKETING HEROES? Chris Gayle, Brian Lara
NON-CRICKETING HEROES? Jonny Wilkinson, Joey Essex
ACCOMPLISHMENTS? I came second in the nationals for tennis when I was 13
FANTASY SLIP CORDON? Keeper: Me, 1st: Jack Chaplin (one of my best friends at school and never fails to amuse me), 2nd: Cheryl Cole (wouldn't mind having her near me all day), 3rd: Chris Gayle (I just think he's one of the coolest cricketers there's ever been), Gully: Mario Balotelli (he will keep us entertained throughout the day and will give good chat to the batsmen)
TWITTER FEED: @BenDuckett1

Batting	Mat	Inns	NO	Runs	HS	Ave	SR	100	50	Ct	St
Twenty20	1	1	1	5	5*	-	41.66	0	0	0	0
Bowling	**Inns**	**Balls**	**Runs**	**Wkts**	**BBI**	**BBM**	**Ave**	**Econ**	**SR**	**5w**	**10**
Twenty20	1	-	-	-	-	-	-	-	-	-	-

MATT DUNN — LHB RFM

FULL NAME: Matthew Peter Dunn
BORN: May 5, 1992, Egham, Surrey
SQUAD NO: 4
HEIGHT: 6ft 1in
NICKNAME: Dunny
EDUCATION: Bishopsgate School; Bearwood College
TEAMS: England Under-15s, England Under-19s, Surrey, Surrey Under-15s, Surrey Under-17s, Surrey Under-19s
CAREER: First-class: 2010; List A: 2011

BEST BATTING: 2* Surrey vs Cambridge MCCU, Cambridge, 2011
BEST BOWLING: 5-56 Surrey vs Derbyshire, Derby, 2011

WHO WOULD PLAY YOU IN A FILM OF YOUR LIFE? Tom Hardy
CAREER HIGHLIGHTS? Taking five wickets on debut for Surrey against Derbyshire and having the chance to represent my country at U19 level
MOST MARKED CHARACTERISTIC? My smile
BEST PLAYER IN COUNTY CRICKET? Steve Davies
TIP FOR THE TOP? Dominic Sibley
IF YOU WEREN'T A CRICKETER? I'd be at university
DESERT ISLAND DISC? Drake – Take Care
FAVOURITE TV? The Office
BIGGEST DRESSING DOWN YOU'VE RECEIVED? Getting told off by the umpire for cursing all the way from finishing my over to my position at fine leg!
CRICKETING HEROES? Brett Lee, Dale Steyn, Dirk Nannes
NON-CRICKETING HEROES? Tom Hardy, Mario Balotelli, Channing Tatum, David Beckham
ACCOMPLISHMENTS? Completing my A-Levels
WHEN YOU RETIRE? Travel the world with a backpack!
SURPRISING FACT? I lived in Norway for a bit of my childhood
FANTASY SLIP CORDON? Keeper: Tom Hardy, 1st: Myself; 2nd: Karl Pilkington, 3rd: Jack Whitehall, Gully: James Corden
TWITTER FEED: @MatthewDunn05

Batting	Mat	Inns	NO	Runs	HS	Ave	SR	100	50	Ct	St
First-class	6	6	6	3	2*	-	8.57	0	0	0	0
List A	1	-	-	-	-	-	-	-	-	1	0
Bowling	**Inns**	**Balls**	**Runs**	**Wkts**	**BBI**	**BBM**	**Ave**	**Econ**	**SR**	**5w**	**10**
First-class	6	469	377	13	5/56	5/68	29.00	4.82	36.0	1	0
List A	1	36	32	2	2/32	2/32	16.00	5.33	18.0	0	0

CHRIS DURHAM RHB WK

FULL NAME: Christopher Michael Durham
BORN: March 4, 1992, Stockport, Cheshire
SQUAD NO: 33
TEAMS: Derbyshire, Derbyshire 2nd XI, Derbyshire Under-13s, Derbyshire Under-14s, Derbyshire Under-15s, Derbyshire Under-17s
CAREER: First-class: 2012; List A: 2012; T20: 2012

BEST BATTING: 12* Derbyshire vs Australia A, Derby, 2012

NOTES: Wicketkeeper whose first-class debut came in 2012, when he played in a three-day game for Derbyshire against a touring Australia A. He also featured in two CB40 matches, both against Northamptonshire, and a T20 fixture against Yorkshire

Batting	Mat	Inns	NO	Runs	HS	Ave	SR	100	50	Ct	St
First-class	1	1	1	12	12*	-	54.54	0	0	1	1
List A	2	-	-	-	-	-	-	-	-	2	0
Twenty20	1	1	0	0	0	0.00	0.00	0	0	0	0
Bowling	**Inns**	**Balls**	**Runs**	**Wkts**	**BBI**	**BBM**	**Ave**	**Econ**	**SR**	**5w**	**10**
First-class	1	-	-	-	-	-	-	-	-	-	-
List A	2	-	-	-	-	-	-	-	-	-	-
Twenty20	1	-	-	-	-	-	-	-	-	-	-

WES DURSTON

RHB OB R1 MVP8

FULL NAME: Wesley John Durston
BORN: October 6, 1980, Taunton, Somerset
SQUAD NO: 3
HEIGHT: 5ft 9in
NICKNAME: Bestie, Durst, Ace, Pringles
EDUCATION: Millfield School, Glastonbury; University of Worcester
TEAMS: Derbyshire, Somerset, Somerset Cricket Board, Unicorns
CAREER: First-class: 2002; List A: 2000; T20: 2003

BEST BATTING: 151 Derbyshire vs Gloucestershire, Derby, 2011
BEST BOWLING: 5-34 Derbyshire vs Yorkshire, Leeds, 2012

WHO WOULD PLAY YOU IN A FILM OF YOUR LIFE? Is Harrison Ford any good at cricket?
CAREER HIGHLIGHTS? Winning trophies as a team will always leave me with very fond memories. Twenty20 Cup in 2005 with Somerset, County Championship Division Two title in 2007 with Somerset and Division Two title with Derbyshire in 2012. Besides that, scoring 117 for the Unicorns in the CB40 and 111 in Twenty20 for Derbyshire were two of my more dynamic and exciting innings to date
SUPERSTITIONS? I always salute magpies, cross the lines with my right foot first and tap my forehead with my index finger before every ball I face!
BEST PLAYER IN COUNTY CRICKET? Marcus Trescothick is still the best player in county cricket but Kevin Pietersen possesses the x-factor and I love watching them both bat
TIPS FOR THE TOP? Dan Redfern and Jos Buttler are two rising talents that I think will have long and successful careers
IF YOU WEREN'T A CRICKETER? I would love to be a professional golfer
DESERT ISLAND DISC? Barenaked Ladies – $1,000,000
CRICKETING HEROES? Viv Richards, Graham Gooch, Shane Warne, Keith Parsons
NON-CRICKETING HEROES? Eric Cantona, Sir Alex Ferguson, Tiger Woods, Roger Federer
TWITTER FEED: @Wjdurston3

Batting	Mat	Inns	NO	Runs	HS	Ave	SR	100	50	Ct	St
First-class	73	126	18	3982	151	36.87	59.56	6	24	76	0
List A	92	80	18	2121	120*	34.20		2	12	29	0
Twenty20	76	67	11	1314	111	23.46	121.32	1	7	31	0
Bowling	**Inns**	**Balls**	**Runs**	**Wkts**	**BBI**	**BBM**	**Ave**	**Econ**	**SR**	**5w**	**10**
First-class	73	3902	2415	55	5/34		43.90	3.71	70.9	1	0
List A	92	1533	1432	40	3/7	3/7	35.80	5.60	38.3	0	0
Twenty20	76	558	751	35	3/25	3/25	21.45	8.07	15.9	0	0

NED ECKERSLEY RHB WK

FULL NAME: Edmund James Holden Eckersley
BORN: August 9, 1989, Oxford
SQUAD NO: 33
HEIGHT: 6ft
EDUCATION: St Benedict's School, Ealing
TEAMS: Leicestershire, Leicestershire 2nd XI, Marylebone Cricket Club, Marylebone Cricket Club Young Cricketers, Middlesex 2nd XI, Mountaineers
CAREER: First-class: 2011; List A: 2008; T20: 2011

BEST BATTING: 137* Leicestershire vs Glamorgan, Cardiff, 2012

CAREER HIGHLIGHTS? Scoring my maiden first-class hundred in the last game of the 2011 season
CRICKETING HEROES? Alec Stewart
BEST PLAYER IN COUNTY CRICKET? Marcus Trescothick
TIP FOR THE TOP? Alex Hales
IF YOU WEREN'T A CRICKETER? Studying at university
WHEN RAIN STOPS PLAY? Cards, listening to iPod
FAVOURITE TV? 24
FAVOURITE FILM? Blood Diamond
DREAM HOLIDAY? Cuba or the Maldives
GUILTY PLEASURES? Westlife
FANTASY SLIP CORDON? Keeper: Nelson Mandela, 1st: Michael McIntyre, 2nd: Freddie Flintoff, 3rd: Myself, Gully: David Beckham
TWITTER FEED: @nedeckersley

Batting	Mat	Inns	NO	Runs	HS	Ave	SR	100	50	Ct	St
First-class	23	40	4	1186	137*	32.94	45.49	2	6	71	3
List A	12	11	3	211	72*	26.37	117.87	0	1	13	1
Twenty20	14	12	5	67	13	9.57	82.71	0	0	4	1
Bowling	**Inns**	**Balls**	**Runs**	**Wkts**	**BBI**	**BBM**	**Ave**	**Econ**	**SR**	**5w**	**10**
First-class	23	-	-	-	-	-	-	-	-	-	-
List A	12	-	-	-	-	-	-	-	-	-	-
Twenty20	14	-	-	-	-	-	-	-	-	-	-

GEORGE EDWARDS RHB RFM

FULL NAME: George Alexander Edwards
BORN: July 29, 1992, King's College Hospital, Lambeth, London
SQUAD NO: 56
HEIGHT: 6ft 4in
NICKNAME: Chicken
EDUCATION: St Joseph's College, Upper Norwood
TEAMS: Surrey, Surrey 2nd XI
CAREER: First-class: 2011

BEST BATTING: 19 Surrey vs Cambridge MCCU, Cambridge, 2011
BEST BOWLING: 4-44 Surrey vs Worcestershire, Worcester, 2012

WHO WOULD PLAY YOU IN A FILM OF YOUR LIFE? Will Smith
CAREER HIGHLIGHTS? My Championship debut against Worcestershire
MOST MARKED CHARACTERISTIC? My height
BEST PLAYER IN COUNTY CRICKET? Marcus Trescothick
TIPS FOR THE TOP? Rory Burns, Matthew Dunn, Dominic Sibley
IF YOU WEREN'T A CRICKETER? Working on Dave Chappelle's Show
DESERT ISLAND DISC? Kid Cudi – Man On The Moon Part II
FAVOURITE TV? Breaking Bad
CRICKETING HEROES? The West Indies team
FANTASY SLIP CORDON? Keeper: Kevin Garnett, 1st: Myself, 2nd: Alicia Keys, 3rd: Carmelo Anthony, Gully: Eva Mendes
TWITTER FEED: @GEdwards29

Batting	Mat	Inns	NO	Runs	HS	Ave	SR	100	50	Ct	St
First-class	3	4	1	56	19	18.66	38.62	0	0	1	0
Bowling	**Inns**	**Balls**	**Runs**	**Wkts**	**BBI**	**BBM**	**Ave**	**Econ**	**SR**	**5w**	**10**
First-class	3	380	266	5	4/44	5/92	53.20	4.20	76.0	0	0

SEAN ERVINE LHB RM MVP15

FULL NAME: Sean Michael Ervine
BORN: December 6, 1982, Harare, Zimbabwe
SQUAD NO: 7
HEIGHT: 6ft 2in
NICKNAME: Slug, Lion
EDUCATION: Lomagundi College
TEAMS: Zimbabwe, Duronto Rajshahi, Hampshire, Midlands, Southern Rocks, Western Australia, Matabeleland Tuskers
CAREER: Test: 2003; ODI: 2001; First-class: 2001; List A: 2001; T20: 2005

BEST BATTING: 237* Hampshire vs Somerset, Southampton, 2010
BEST BOWLING: 6-82 Midlands vs Mashonaland, Kwekwe, 2003
COUNTY CAP: 2005

FAMILY TIES? Father Rory played first-class cricket in Zimbabwe. Brother Craig plays for the current Zimbabwe team. Brother Ryan plays for the franchise Southern Rocks in Zimbabwe. Uncle Neil played first-class cricket in Zimbabwe
CAREER HIGHLIGHTS? Scoring 100 vs India at Adelaide Oval in the 2004/05 VB series. Hundreds and Man of the Match in both the semi-final and final of the C&G Trophy in 2005. Four wickets vs Australia in the first Test match in Perth in 2003 for Zimbabwe. Scoring 208 and 160 in the same game for the Southern Rocks in 2010. Playing in the 2003 World Cup in South Africa. Playing with Shane Warne at Hampshire
CRICKETING HEROES? Andy Flower, Shane Warne, Neil McKenzie
TIPS FOR THE TOP? James Vince, Chris Wood, Ben Stokes
FAVOURITE BOOK? Mukiwa – about a white boy growing up in Africa
GUILTY PLEASURES? Biltong, Bounty chocolate, sticky toffee pudding
TWITTER FEED: @slug_7

Batting	Mat	Inns	NO	Runs	HS	Ave	SR	100	50	Ct	St
Tests	5	8	0	261	86	32.62	55.41	0	3	7	0
ODIs	42	34	7	698	100	25.85	85.53	1	2	5	0
First-class	153	243	28	7681	237*	35.72		14	39	122	0
List A	201	178	28	4722	167*	31.48		7	20	55	0
Twenty20	123	112	26	2166	82	25.18	128.24	0	8	42	0
Bowling	**Inns**	**Balls**	**Runs**	**Wkts**	**BBI**	**BBM**	**Ave**	**Econ**	**SR**	**5w**	**10**
Tests	5	570	388	9	4/146	4/146	43.11	4.08	63.3	0	0
ODIs	42	1649	1561	41	3/29	3/29	38.07	5.67	40.2	0	0
First-class	153	15999	9544	226	6/82		42.23	3.57	70.7	5	0
List A	201	6799	6299	192	5/50	5/50	32.80	5.55	35.4	2	0
Twenty20	123	1296	1877	65	4/12	4/12	28.87	8.68	19.9	0	0

ALASDAIR EVANS

RHB RMF

FULL NAME: Alasdair Campbell Evans
BORN: January 12, 1989, Kent
SQUAD NO: 45
HEIGHT: 6ft 5in
NICKNAME: Pipe, Evo, Melman, Llama
EDUCATION: George Watson's College; Loughborough University
TEAMS: Scotland, Loughborough UCCE, Scotland Under-13s, Scotland Under-15s, Scotland Under-17s, Scotland Under-19s
CAREER: ODI: 2009; First-class: 2009; List A: 2009

BEST BATTING: 2 Scotland vs Ireland, Aberdeen, 2009
BEST BOWLING: 2-41 Loughborough UCCE vs Leicestershire, Leicester, 2009

WHO WOULD PLAY YOU IN A FILM OF YOUR LIFE? Samuel L Jackson
CAREER HIGHLIGHTS? Gaining my first full cap for Scotland vs Canada in 2009. Being a member of the 2012 County Championship Division Two winning squad with Derbyshire
MOST MARKED CHARACTERISTIC? Moaning at fielders
BEST PLAYER IN COUNTY CRICKET? Chris Wright
TIP FOR THE TOP? Peter Burgoyne
DESERT ISLAND DISC? Westlife's Greatest Hits
FAVOURITE TV? 24, Prison Break, TheWest Wing, Game Of Thrones
BIGGEST DRESSING DOWN YOU'VE RECEIVED? While at Loughborough University my coach – the late, great Graham Dilley – had a great passion for winning. After a number of poor performances each player was given an individual meeting. Once we had finished that meeting we certainly knew where we stood
ACCOMPLISHMENTS? Playing for Scotland at hockey until U18 level. I gained a 2:1 honours degree in Psychology from Loughborough University
WHEN YOU RETIRE? I'd like to become good at golf and travel the world
SURPRISING FACT? When I was young I performed in Shakespeare and musical productions
TWITTER FEED: @AliEvans647

Batting	Mat	Inns	NO	Runs	HS	Ave	SR	100	50	Ct	St
ODIs	3	-	-	-	-	-	-	-	-	1	0
First-class	4	2	0	3	2	1.50	18.75	0	0	1	0
List A	13	4	2	4	2*	2.00	36.36	0	0	2	0
Bowling	**Inns**	**Balls**	**Runs**	**Wkts**	**BBI**	**BBM**	**Ave**	**Econ**	**SR**	**5w**	**10**
ODIs	3	139	112	2	1/13	1/13	56.00	4.83	69.5	0	0
First-class	4	318	247	4	2/41	2/41	61.75	4.66	79.5	0	0
List A	13	433	387	7	2/34	2/34	55.28	5.36	61.8	0	0

LAURIE EVANS RHB RM

WARWICKSHIRE

FULL NAME: Laurie John Evans
BORN: October 12, 1987, Lambeth, London
SQUAD NO: 32
HEIGHT: 6ft 1in
NICKNAME: LJ, Loz
EDUCATION: Whitgift School; The John Fisher School; Durham University
TEAMS: Durham UCCE, ECB Centre of Excellence XI, Malden Wanderers, Marylebone Cricket Club, Surrey, Surrey 2nd XI, Warwickshire
CAREER: First-class: 2007; List A: 2009; T20: 2009

BEST BATTING: 133* Durham UCCE vs Lancashire, Durham University, 2007
BEST BOWLING: 1-30 Surrey vs Bangladeshis, The Oval, 2010

CAREER HIGHLIGHTS? Maiden first-class hundred
CRICKETING HEROES? Viv Richards
NON-CRICKETING HEROES? Mick Skinner
BEST PLAYER IN COUNTY CRICKET? Ian Bell
IF YOU WEREN'T A CRICKETER? Rugby player
WHEN RAIN STOPS PLAY? I'm bored
FAVOURITE FILM? The Boat That Rocked
DREAM HOLIDAY? Barbados
ACCOMPLISHMENTS? Golf handicap of eight, going down. Won Daily Mail rugby competition. Played in Harlequins Academy
SURPRISING SKILL? I play piano and guitar, and work as a part-time chef
GUILTY PLEASURES? Clothes, trainers and accessories
SURPRISING FACT? My uncle Greg Searle is an Olympic gold medallist
FANTASY SLIP CORDON? Keeper: Justin Timberlake, 1st: Mick Jagger, 2nd: Peter Kay, 3rd: David Attenborough
TWITTER FEED: @LaurieEvans32

Batting	Mat	Inns	NO	Runs	HS	Ave	SR	100	50	Ct	St
First-class	13	24	1	680	133*	29.56	45.82	1	4	8	0
List A	5	5	1	74	36*	18.50	69.15	0	0	4	0
Twenty20	9	7	4	153	68*	51.00	164.51	0	1	2	0
Bowling	**Inns**	**Balls**	**Runs**	**Wkts**	**BBI**	**BBM**	**Ave**	**Econ**	**SR**	**5w**	**10**
First-class	13	36	30	1	1/30	1/30	30.00	5.00	36.0	0	0
List A	5	-	-	-	-	-	-	-	-	-	-
Twenty20	9	-	-	-	-	-	-	-	-	-	-

LUKE EVANS RHB RMF

FULL NAME: Luke Evans
BORN: April 26, 1987, Sunderland, County Durham
SQUAD NO: 26
HEIGHT: 6ft 7in
NICKNAME: Evo, Big Luke, Goose, Foghorn Leghorn
EDUCATION: St Aidan's RC School and Sixth Form, Sunderland
TEAMS: Durham, Durham 2nd XI, Northamptonshire
CAREER: First-class: 2007; List A: 2009; T20: 2011

BEST BATTING: 8* Northamptonshire vs Gloucestershire, Bristol, 2010
BEST BOWLING: 4-38 Northamptonshire vs Gloucestershire, Bristol, 2012

WHO WOULD PLAY YOU IN A FILM OF YOUR LIFE? Ryan Gosling but only if Verne Troyer wasn't available
CAREER HIGHLIGHTS? I think the real highlights are yet to come but I was delighted with the way I recovered from my back operation last year and the way I bowled in the last two County Championship games of the season
MOST MARKED CHARACTERISTIC? I'm a very long human
TIPS FOR THE TOP? Olly Stone, Ben Duckett, Rob Keogh, Christian Davis and James Kettleborough have all recently joined the squad at Northants. Hopefully the forthcoming season brings them great success
IF YOU WEREN'T A CRICKETER? Flying passenger jets and teaching guitar in my spare time
CRICKETING HEROES? Everyone associated with Chester-le-Street CC, Curtly Ambrose, Courtney Walsh, Steve Harmison, Shane Bond, Dale Steyn, Morne Morkel and my good mate Ben Drummond
ACCOMPLISHMENTS? Gaining my pilot's licence in 2011 and teaching myself guitar, bass guitar and a few piano tunes
WHEN YOU RETIRE? I'll hopefully be in a position to explore my career in aviation, preferably flying for an airline

Batting	Mat	Inns	NO	Runs	HS	Ave	SR	100	50	Ct	St
First-class	8	10	4	31	8*	5.16	26.27	0	0	1	0
List A	9	4	1	19	18	6.33	33.33	0	0	2	0
Twenty20	3	-	-	-	-	-	-	-	-	0	0
Bowling	**Inns**	**Balls**	**Runs**	**Wkts**	**BBI**	**BBM**	**Ave**	**Econ**	**SR**	**5w**	**10**
First-class	8	1075	666	26	4/38	6/101	25.61	3.71	41.3	0	0
List A	9	240	273	7	2/46	2/46	39.00	6.82	34.2	0	0
Twenty20	3	54	70	3	1/15	1/15	23.33	7.77	18.0	0	0

TOM FELL

RHB WK

WORCESTERSHIRE

FULL NAME: Thomas Charles Fell
BORN: October 17, 1993, Hillingdon, Middlesex
SQUAD NO: 29
HEIGHT: 6ft 1in
NICKNAME: Felly
EDUCATION: Oakham School
TEAMS: Staffordshire Under-17s, Worcestershire 2nd XI, Worcestershire Academy
CAREER: Yet to make first-team debut

CAREER HIGHLIGHTS? Playing for the MCC Schools at Lord's last year. Breaking the school record for most runs scored in a season. Scoring a double century for Staffs U17
SUPERSTITIONS? I tread on the rope as I go out to bat
CRICKETING HEROES? Sachin Tendulkar
NON-CRICKETING HEROES? Lionel Messi, Gareth Bale, Matt Hampson
BEST PLAYER IN COUNTY CRICKET? Marcus Trescothick
TIPS FOR THE TOP? Worcestershire's Aneesh Kapil and Shiv Thakor from Leicestershire
WHEN RAIN STOPS PLAY? Listening to music or playing one hand-one bounce in the changing room
FAVOURITE TV? Sky Sports News and Top Gear
FAVOURITE FILM? Gladiator
FAVOURITE BOOK? Holes by Louis Sachar
DREAM HOLIDAY? Anywhere hot where they play cricket – the Caribbean probably
FANTASY SLIP CORDON? Keeper: Me, 1st: Jeff Stelling, 2nd: Jeremy Clarkson, 3rd: Harry Redknapp, Gully: David Lloyd (Bumble)

STEVEN FINN RHB RF W2

FULL NAME: Steven Thomas Finn
BORN: April 4, 1989, Watford, Hertfordshire
SQUAD NO: 9
HEIGHT: 6ft 7in
NICKNAME: Finny, Gonzo, Cyril
EDUCATION: Parmiter's School, Watford
TEAMS: England, England Lions, England Under-19s, Middlesex, Middlesex 2nd XI, Otago
CAREER: Test: 2010; ODI: 2011; T20I: 2011; First-class: 2005; List A: 2007; T20: 2008

BEST BATTING: 32 Middlesex vs Essex, Lord's, 2011
BEST BOWLING: 9-37 Middlesex vs Worcestershire, Worcester, 2010
COUNTY CAP: 2009

FAMILY TIES? My father [Terry] played minor counties, my granddad played club cricket and I grew up at cricket grounds
CAREER HIGHLIGHTS? Test debut, winning the Ashes, and the 2012 Test series win in India
BEST PLAYER IN COUNTY CRICKET? Tim Murtagh
TIPS FOR THE TOP? Billy Godleman (Derbyshire), Sam Robson (Middlesex), Joe Root (Yorkshire), Jos Buttler (Somerset)
DESERT ISLAND DISC? Pink Floyd – The Wall
FAVOURITE TV? Come Dine With Me
BIGGEST DRESSING DOWN YOU'VE RECEIVED? Angus Fraser in a pub in 2012
CRICKETING HEROES? Glenn McGrath
TWITTER FEED: @finnysteve

Batting	Mat	Inns	NO	Runs	HS	Ave	SR	100	50	Ct	St
Tests	17	19	13	51	19	8.50	25.50	0	0	4	0
ODIs	33	12	6	80	35	13.33	89.88	0	0	8	0
T20Is	16	3	3	14	8*	-	73.68	0	0	4	0
First-class	79	93	32	419	32	6.86	31.26	0	0	25	0
List A	77	25	8	150	35	8.82	70.42	0	0	12	0
Twenty20	43	8	6	32	8*	16.00	82.05	0	0	8	0
Bowling	**Inns**	**Balls**	**Runs**	**Wkts**	**BBI**	**BBM**	**Ave**	**Econ**	**SR**	**5w**	**10**
Tests	17	3273	1976	70	6/125	9/187	28.22	3.62	46.7	3	0
ODIs	33	1799	1380	52	4/34	4/34	26.53	4.60	34.5	0	0
T20Is	16	360	412	23	3/16	3/16	17.91	6.86	15.6	0	0
First-class	79	13995	7995	289	9/37		27.66	3.42	48.4	7	1
List A	77	3575	2896	107	5/33	5/33	27.06	4.86	33.4	1	0
Twenty20	43	902	1099	46	3/16	3/16	23.89	7.31	19.6	0	0

LUKE FLETCHER RHB RFM

NOTTINGHAMSHIRE

FULL NAME: Luke Jack Fletcher
BORN: September 18, 1988, Nottingham
SQUAD NO: 19
HEIGHT: 6ft 6in
NICKNAME: Fletch
EDUCATION: Henry Mellish Comprehensive School
TEAMS: England Under-19s, Nottinghamshire, Nottinghamshire 2nd XI
CAREER: First-class: 2008; List A: 2008; T20: 2009

BEST BATTING: 92 Nottinghamshire vs Hampshire, Southampton, 2009
BEST BOWLING: 5-82 Nottinghamshire vs Lancashire, Nottingham, 2011

CAREER HIGHLIGHTS? Making my debut for Notts, winning the Championship and playing in the T20 quarter-finals
SUPERSTITIONS? I like to receive the ball from mid off when bowling
CRICKETING HEROES? Freddie Flintoff
BEST PLAYER IN COUNTY CRICKET? Marcus Trescothick, Andre Adams
TIPS FOR THE TOP? George Bacon, Sam Wood
WHEN RAIN STOPS PLAY? Abuse senior/veteran players
FAVOURITE TV? Take Me Out
FAVOURITE FILM? The Shawshank Redemption
DREAM HOLIDAY? Las Vegas
GUILTY PLEASURES? Chick flicks
SURPRISING FACTS? I played football at Wembley and Old Trafford as a youngster, I enjoy helping out my good friend Johnny Thrower with his groundsman duties at Papplewick and Linby CC and I'm an ex-chef at Hooters
TWITTER FEED: @fletcherluke

Batting	Mat	Inns	NO	Runs	HS	Ave	SR	100	50	Ct	St
First-class	38	54	16	522	92	13.73	56.55	0	1	7	0
List A	30	16	5	99	40*	9.00	86.08	0	0	3	0
Twenty20	24	5	3	7	5	3.50	46.66	0	0	7	0
Bowling	**Inns**	**Balls**	**Runs**	**Wkts**	**BBI**	**BBM**	**Ave**	**Econ**	**SR**	**5w**	**10**
First-class	38	6946	3519	118	5/82	8/131	29.82	3.03	58.8	1	0
List A	30	1172	1088	28	3/27	3/27	38.85	5.56	41.8	0	0
Twenty20	24	498	638	26	4/30	4/30	24.53	7.68	19.1	0	0

BEN FOAKES RHB WK

FULL NAME: Benjamin Thomas Foakes
BORN: February 15, 1993, Colchester, Essex
SQUAD NO: 4
HEIGHT: 6ft 1in
NICKNAME: Brad, Scarface
EDUCATION: Tendring Technology College
TEAMS: England Lions, England Under-17s, England Under-19s, Essex, Essex 2nd XI
CAREER: First-class: 2011; List A: 2013

BEST BATTING: 93 Essex vs Leicestershire, Leicester, 2012

CAREER HIGHLIGHTS? Making 93 on debut in the Championship against Leicestershire. Scoring 111 in the third U19 ODI in Chittagong. Being named Man of the Tournament in an U19 quadrangular tournament against Australia, India and New Zealand
SUPERSTITIONS? I have to touch my lip and my belly button whilst waiting to face the next delivery
MOST MARKED CHARACTERISTIC? A lot of people say I'm slightly camp
BEST PLAYER IN COUNTY CRICKET? Nick Compton
TIPS FOR THE TOP? Tymal Mills, Reece Topley, Sam Wood, Daniel Bell-Drummond
DESERT ISLAND DISC? Adele's album 21 is absolute class!
FAVOURITE TV? Lost. Tymal Mills, Tom Craddock and I were on a Lost marathon until Crads decided to leave us to go to Australia for the winter
CRICKETING HEROES? James Foster was unbelievable to watch when I was a youngster, especially with the gloves
ACCOMPLISHMENTS? Nothing significant but I banged in a few goals for Ipswich Town when I played in their elite squad as a kid
WHEN YOU RETIRE? It would be good to work for Gray-Nicolls as a kit designer
SURPRISING FACT? When I was young my two front teeth were both completely black for three years after my brother pushed me and I hit my face on the bathtub

Batting	Mat	Inns	NO	Runs	HS	Ave	SR	100	50	Ct	St
First-class	5	5	0	119	93	23.80	53.60	0	1	4	0
List A	6	6	0	80	56	13.33	86.95	0	1	1	1
Bowling	**Inns**	**Balls**	**Runs**	**Wkts**	**BBI**	**BBM**	**Ave**	**Econ**	**SR**	**5w**	**10**
First-class	5	-	-	-	-	-	-	-	-	-	-
List A	6	-	-	-	-	-	-	-	-	-	-

MARK FOOTITT RHB LFM

DERBYSHIRE

FULL NAME: Mark Harold Alan Footitt
BORN: November 25, 1985, Nottingham
SQUAD NO: 4
HEIGHT: 6ft 2in
NICKNAME: Footy
EDUCATION: Carlton le Willows School
TEAMS: Derbyshire, England Under-19s, Marylebone Cricket Club, Nottinghamshire, Nottinghamshire Cricket Board
CAREER: First-class: 2005; List A: 2002; T20: 2005

BEST BATTING: 30 Derbyshire vs Surrey, The Oval, 2010
BEST BOWLING: 5-45 Nottinghamshire vs West Indies A, Nottingham, 2006

CAREER HIGHLIGHTS? My first game for Notts and taking five wickets for Derbyshire
CRICKETING HEROES? Brett Lee
NON-CRICKETING HEROES? Adam Sandler
TIP FOR THE TOP? Ross Whiteley
WHEN RAIN STOPS PLAY? Reading newspapers and playing games on my phone
FAVOURITE TV? The Simpsons
DREAM HOLIDAY? The Maldives
ACCOMPLISHMENTS? Being a dad to Heidi Footitt
GUILTY PLEASURES? Cheese, garlic pizza bread, cookies
SURPRISING FACT? I started off bowling right-arm then changed to left-arm

Batting	Mat	Inns	NO	Runs	HS	Ave	SR	100	50	Ct	St
First-class	27	32	12	165	30	8.25	47.96	0	0	9	0
List A	11	3	1	5	4	2.50	83.33	0	0	1	0
Twenty20	2	-	-	-	-	-	-	-	-	0	0
Bowling	**Inns**	**Balls**	**Runs**	**Wkts**	**BBI**	**BBM**	**Ave**	**Econ**	**SR**	**5w**	**10**
First-class	27	3592	2234	72	5/45		31.02	3.73	49.8	3	0
List A	11	348	363	10	3/20	3/20	36.30	6.25	34.8	0	0
Twenty20	2	24	56	0	-	-	-	14.00	-	0	0

JAMES FOSTER RHB WK R1 MVP39

FULL NAME: James Savin Foster
BORN: April 15, 1980, Whipps Cross, Leytonstone, Essex
SQUAD NO: 7
HEIGHT: 6ft
NICKNAME: Fozzy, Chief
EDUCATION: Forest School; Durham University
TEAMS: England, Durham UCCE, Essex, Marylebone Cricket Club, Northern Districts
CAREER: Test: 2001; ODI: 2001; T20I: 2009; First-class: 2000; List A: 2000; T20: 2003

BEST BATTING: 212 Essex vs Leicestershire, Chelmsford, 2004
BEST BOWLING: 1-122 Essex vs Northamptonshire, Northampton, 2008
COUNTY CAP: 2001; BENEFIT YEAR: 2011

FAMILY TIES? Dad played for Essex Amateurs
CAREER HIGHLIGHTS? Playing for my country
CRICKETERS PARTICULARLY ADMIRED? Nasser Hussain, Stuart Law, Robert Rollins, Ian Healy, Jack Russell, Alec Stewart, Adam Gilchrist
OTHER SPORTS PLAYED? Hockey (Essex U21), tennis (played for GB U14 vs Sweden U14)
OTHER SPORTS FOLLOWED? Football
NOTES: Current Essex captain. Achieved the 'double' of 1,037 runs and 51 dismissals in 2004. In a Pro40 match against Durham in September 2009, he hit five sixes in consecutive balls from Scott Borthwick

Batting	Mat	Inns	NO	Runs	HS	Ave	SR	100	50	Ct	St
Tests	7	12	3	226	48	25.11	34.55	0	0	17	1
ODIs	11	6	3	41	13	13.66	57.74	0	0	13	7
T20Is	5	5	2	37	14*	12.33	115.62	0	0	3	3
First-class	206	310	41	9946	212	36.97		18	49	575	51
List A	181	134	35	2843	83*	28.71		0	15	206	55
Twenty20	108	92	25	1589	65*	23.71	140.74	0	6	46	39
Bowling	**Inns**	**Balls**	**Runs**	**Wkts**	**BBI**	**BBM**	**Ave**	**Econ**	**SR**	**5w**	**10**
Tests	7	-	-	-	-	-	-	-	-	-	-
ODIs	11	-	-	-	-	-	-	-	-	-	-
T20Is	5	-	-	-	-	-	-	-	-	-	-
First-class	206	84	128	1	1/122	1/122	128.00	9.14	84.0	0	0
List A	181	-	-	-	-	-	-	-	-	-	-
Twenty20	108	-	-	-	-	-	-	-	-	-	-

PAUL FRANKS LHB RFM W2

NOTTINGHAMSHIRE

FULL NAME: Paul John Franks
BORN: February 3, 1979, Mansfield, Nottinghamshire
SQUAD NO: 8
HEIGHT: 6ft 2in
NICKNAME: Franksie, Pike, The General
EDUCATION: Minster School, Southwell
TEAMS: England, Mid West Rhinos, Nottinghamshire
CAREER: ODI: 2000; First-class: 1996; List A: 1997; T20: 2003

BEST BATTING: 123* Nottinghamshire vs Leicestershire, Leicester, 2003
BEST BOWLING: 7-56 Nottinghamshire vs Middlesex, Lord's, 2000
COUNTY CAP: 1999; BENEFIT YEAR: 2007

CAREER HIGHLIGHTS? England debut, County Championship wins in 2005 and 2010, T20 Finals Day
CRICKETING HEROES? Ian Botham, Andrew Flintoff, Graeme Swann
NON-CRICKETING HEROES? Eric Cantona, Seve Ballesteros
BEST PLAYER IN COUNTY CRICKET? Marcus Trescothick, Dale Benkenstein
TIPS FOR THE TOP? Alex Hales, Jos Buttler
WHEN RAIN STOPS PLAY? Changing room banter or catching up on sleep
FAVOURITE FILM? Top Gun, Major League
DREAM HOLIDAY? Bali
FANTASY SLIP CORDON? Keeper: Paul Gascoigne, 1st: Me, 2nd: Elle Macpherson, 3rd: David Beckham, Gully: Luke Fletcher
TWITTER FEED: @thegeneral_8

Batting	Mat	Inns	NO	Runs	HS	Ave	SR	100	50	Ct	St
ODIs	1	1	0	4	4	4.00	23.52	0	0	1	0
First-class	206	301	56	6862	123*	28.00		4	38	66	0
List A	183	134	41	1964	84*	21.11		0	6	28	0
Twenty20	50	30	13	287	29*	16.88	117.62	0	0	8	0
Bowling	**Inns**	**Balls**	**Runs**	**Wkts**	**BBI**	**BBM**	**Ave**	**Econ**	**SR**	**5w**	**10**
ODIs	1	54	48	0	-	-	-	5.33	-	0	0
First-class	206	30693	16828	512	7/56		32.86	3.28	59.9	11	0
List A	183	6697	5645	195	6/27	6/27	28.94	5.05	34.3	3	0
Twenty20	50	479	687	20	2/12	2/12	34.35	8.60	23.9	0	0

OLLIE FRECKINGHAM RHB RMF

FULL NAME: Oliver Henry Freckingham
BORN: November 12, 1988, Oakham, Rutland, England
SQUAD NO: 24
HEIGHT: 6ft
NICKNAME: Frecky
EDUCATION: King Edward School, Melton Mowbray
TEAMS: Leicestershire 2nd XI
CAREER: Yet to make first-team debut

WHO WOULD PLAY YOU IN A FILM OF YOUR LIFE? Liam Neeson
CAREER HIGHLIGHTS? Taking five wickets in my first 2nd XI game against Durham and signing my first professional contract at Leicestershire
MOST MARKED CHARACTERISTIC? I'm very easy going
BEST PLAYER IN COUNTY CRICKET? Marcus Trescothick
TIP FOR THE TOP? Shiv Thakor
IF YOU WEREN'T A CRICKETER? PGA professional golfer or something in golf
DESERT ISLAND DISC? Calvin Harris featuring Example – We'll Be Coming Back
FAVOURITE TV? Eastenders followed closely by The Inbetweeners
BIGGEST DRESSING DOWN YOU'VE RECEIVED? Many from Dips Patel who is the captain of my club side Loughborough Town
CRICKETING HEROES? Andrew Flintoff, Brett Lee, James Anderson
NON-CRICKETING HEROES? Tiger Woods, Frank Lampard
ACCOMPLISHMENTS? My only real achievements outside of cricket have come in golf. Winning six club championships at Rutland County Golf Club. Being cut to scratch after a course record 65, again at Rutland County Golf Club. Representing Leicestershire and Rutland Golf Union
WHEN YOU RETIRE? A dream of mine is to play golf at Augusta so I would look at doing that. And as a job, something within cricket or golf
FANTASY SLIP CORDON? Keeper: Kelly Brook (for viewing purposes), 1st: James Corden (entertainment value, jokes, banter and stories), 2nd: David Beckham (to hear stories from the world's most famous person), 3rd: Me, Gully: Jimmy Carr (I think his banter would be outrageous)
TWITTER FEED: @olliefreck

JAMES FULLER

RHB RFM MVP90

FULL NAME: James Kerr Fuller
BORN: January 24, 1990, Cape Town, South Africa
SQUAD NO: 26
HEIGHT: 6ft 3in
NICKNAME: Foz, Fozza, Fuller
EDUCATION: Westlake High School; Otago University
TEAMS: Gloucestershire, Gloucestershire 2nd XI, New Zealand Under-19s, Otago, Otago Under-19s
CAREER: First-class: 2010; List A: 2011; T20: 2011

BEST BATTING: 57 Gloucestershire vs Leicestershire, Cheltenham, 2012
BEST BOWLING: 6-24 Otago vs Wellington, Dunedin, 2013
COUNTY CAP: 2011

WHO WOULD PLAY YOU IN A FILM OF YOUR LIFE? Hugh Jackman – close enough to the Kiwi accent
CAREER HIGHLIGHTS? Playing as an overseas player for Otago and winning the New Zealand T20 competition. Taking six wickets in the CB40 vs the Netherlands. Taking my first 10-wicket haul in a first-class match vs Wellington
SUPERSTITIONS? Always putting my left pad on first before going out to bat
MOST MARKED CHARACTERISTIC? Tall with a big fast bowler's bum
BEST PLAYER IN COUNTY CRICKET? Darren Stevens
TIP FOR THE TOP? Ed Young
IF YOU WEREN'T A CRICKETER? An engineer or a professional golfer
DESERT ISLAND DISC? Coldplay Live 2012
CRICKETING HEROES? Glenn McGrath, Brett Lee, Chris Cairns
ACCOMPLISHMENTS? Going even through nine holes. Four over through 18
WHEN YOU RETIRE? Undecided at the moment
SURPRISING FACT? I studied Neuroscience at university
TWITTER FEED: @James_Fuller246

Batting	Mat	Inns	NO	Runs	HS	Ave	SR	100	50	Ct	St
First-class	12	17	2	177	57	11.80	66.29	0	1	5	0
List A	16	13	5	224	43	28.00	98.24	0	0	4	0
Twenty20	17	8	4	133	36	33.25	172.72	0	0	9	0
Bowling	**Inns**	**Balls**	**Runs**	**Wkts**	**BBI**	**BBM**	**Ave**	**Econ**	**SR**	**5w**	**10**
First-class	12	1699	1025	37	6/24	10/79	27.70	3.61	45.9	2	1
List A	16	661	611	31	6/35	6/35	19.70	5.54	21.3	1	0
Twenty20	17	371	575	21	4/24	4/24	27.38	9.29	17.6	0	0

ANDREW GALE LHB LB

FULL NAME: Andrew William Gale
BORN: November 28, 1983, Dewsbury, Yorkshire
SQUAD NO: 26
HEIGHT: 6ft 2in
NICKNAME: Galey, Bobby
EDUCATION: Heckmondwike Grammar School
TEAMS: England Lions, England Under-19s, Yorkshire, Yorkshire Cricket Board
CAREER: First-class: 2004; List A: 2002; T20: 2004

BEST BATTING: 151* Yorkshire vs Nottinghamshire, Nottingham, 2010
BEST BOWLING: 1-33 Yorkshire vs Leeds/Bradford UCCE, Leeds, 2007
COUNTY CAP: 2008

WHO WOULD PLAY YOU IN A FILM OF YOUR LIFE? Sean Bean
CAREER HIGHLIGHTS? Captaining Yorkshire, promotion back to Division One in 2012, playing in the Champions League T20 and captaining England Lions
SUPERSTITIONS? I don't like odd numbers
MOST MARKED CHARACTERISTIC? Commitment
BEST PLAYER IN COUNTY CRICKET? Marcus Trescothick
TIPS FOR THE TOP? Gary Ballance and Jack Leaning
DESERT ISLAND DISC? Fleetwood Mac's Greatest Hits
CRICKETING HEROES? Marcus Trescothick, Matthew Hayden, Ricky Ponting, Darren Lehmann, Anthony McGrath
WHEN YOU RETIRE? Coach or run one of my businesses
SURPRISING FACT? I love to play the piano – I have Grade 3!
FANTASY SLIP CORDON? Keeper: David Beckham (coolest man on earth), 1st: John Bishop (good for a few gags), 2nd: Steve Patterson (just in case I need 40 winks), 3rd: Me (I can't catch but I need to be close to hear the chat)
TWITTER FEED: @GaleyLad

Batting	Mat	Inns	NO	Runs	HS	Ave	SR	100	50	Ct	St
First-class	94	149	13	4963	151*	36.49		12	22	37	0
List A	111	103	10	2994	125*	32.19		2	17	23	0
Twenty20	83	75	9	1822	91	27.60	123.35	0	14	28	0

Bowling	Inns	Balls	Runs	Wkts	BBI	BBM	Ave	Econ	SR	5w	10
First-class	94	61	144	1	1/33	1/33	144.00	14.16	61.0	0	0
List A	111	-	-	-	-	-	-	-	-	-	-
Twenty20	83	-	-	-	-	-	-	-	-	-	-

JOE GATTING RHB OB

FULL NAME: Joe Stephen Gatting
BORN: November 25, 1987, Brighton, Sussex
SQUAD NO: 25
HEIGHT: 5ft 11in
EDUCATION: Brighton College
TEAMS: Sussex, Sussex 2nd XI
CAREER: First-class: 2009; List A: 2009; T20: 2009

BEST BATTING: 152 Sussex vs Cambridge UCCE, Cambridge, 2009
BEST BOWLING: 1-8 Sussex vs Nottinghamshire, Nottingham, 2011

FAMILY TIES? My uncle [Mike of England and Middlesex] and dad [Steve of Middlesex 2nd XI] played
CAREER HIGHLIGHTS? Champions League in India. First centuries in first-class and List A cricket
SUPERSTITIONS? Left pad first
CRICKETING HEROES? Brian Lara, Andrew Symonds and my uncle
NON-CRICKETING HEROES? Tiger Woods
BEST PLAYER IN COUNTY CRICKET? Marcus Trescothick
TIP FOR THE TOP? Luke Wells
IF YOU WEREN'T A CRICKETER? Footballer
WHEN RAIN STOPS PLAY? I look at the internet and drink tea
FAVOURITE TV? Celebrity Juice
FAVOURITE FILM? The Next Three Days
FAVOURITE BOOK? Bounce
ACCOMPLISHMENTS? Playing Championship football for Brighton and Hove Albion
GUILTY PLEASURES? The X Factor
SURPRISING FACT? I'm colour blind (green and red)

Batting	Mat	Inns	NO	Runs	HS	Ave	SR	100	50	Ct	St
First-class	30	44	4	1257	152	31.42	59.85	3	5	14	0
List A	39	37	4	944	122	28.60	86.76	1	4	11	0
Twenty20	48	38	8	468	45*	15.60	116.12	0	0	20	0
Bowling	**Inns**	**Balls**	**Runs**	**Wkts**	**BBI**	**BBM**	**Ave**	**Econ**	**SR**	**5w**	**10**
First-class	30	174	111	2	1/8	1/8	55.50	3.82	87.0	0	0
List A	39	20	22	0	-	-	-	6.60	-	0	0
Twenty20	48	10	14	1	1/12	1/12	14.00	8.40	10.0	0	0

JAKE GEORGE RHB OB

FULL NAME: Jacob George
BORN: May 5, 1994, Ealing, Middlesex
SQUAD NO: 24
EDUCATION: Ventnor Middle School; Portsmouth Grammar School
TEAMS: Hampshire 2nd XI, Hampshire Cricket Academy, Hampshire Under-15s, Hampshire Under-17s
CAREER: Yet to make first-team debut

NOTES: Isle of Wight-based batsman. Spent the winter playing at North Sydney but returned early after being hit on the foot by a yorker batting in a Second Grade match. Hit 51 from 74 balls in his final 2nd XI Trophy match of 2012 vs Somerset 2nd XI at Taunton

ALEX GIDMAN

RHB RM R4

FULL NAME: Alexander Peter Richard Gidman
BORN: June 22, 1981, High Wycombe, Buckinghamshire
SQUAD NO: 5
HEIGHT: 6ft 2in
NICKNAME: Giddo
EDUCATION: Wycliffe College, Stonehouse
TEAMS: England A, England Lions, Gloucestershire, Gloucestershire 2nd XI, Marylebone Cricket Club, Otago
CAREER: First-class: 2002; List A: 2001; T20: 2003

BEST BATTING: 176 Gloucestershire vs Surrey, Bristol, 2009
BEST BOWLING: 4-47 Gloucestershire vs Glamorgan, Cardiff, 2009
BENEFIT YEAR: 2012

FAMILY TIES? I play with my brother Will at Gloucestershire
WHO WOULD PLAY YOU IN A FILM OF YOUR LIFE? Gerard Butler
CAREER HIGHLIGHTS? Winning the 2003 and 2004 one-day trophies. Representing England A on three tours
MOST MARKED CHARACTERISTIC? My ears
TIP FOR THE TOP? Dan Housego
BIGGEST DRESSING DOWN YOU'VE RECEIVED? Our coach John Bracewell has given us plenty of dressing downs! All deserved!
CRICKETING HEROES? Steve Waugh
NON-CRICKETING HEROES? Jonny Wilkinson, Michael Jordan
ACCOMPLISHMENTS? Bringing up children is pretty challenging!
SURPRISING FACT? I taught myself how to play the guitar
FANTASY SLIP CORDON? Keeper: Jack Russell, 1st: Eric Clapton, 2nd: Jonny Wilkinson, 3rd: Myself, Gully: Steve Waugh
TWITTER FEED: @agiddo

Batting	Mat	Inns	NO	Runs	HS	Ave	SR	100	50	Ct	St
First-class	158	276	24	8779	176	34.83	57.30	17	49	102	0
List A	178	168	18	4200	116	28.00		5	21	59	0
Twenty20	71	62	11	1072	64	21.01	118.45	0	3	12	0
Bowling	**Inns**	**Balls**	**Runs**	**Wkts**	**BBI**	**BBM**	**Ave**	**Econ**	**SR**	**5w**	**10**
First-class	158	7133	4428	101	4/47		43.84	3.72	70.6	0	0
List A	178	3172	2710	68	5/42	5/42	39.85	5.12	46.6	1	0
Twenty20	71	268	371	8	2/24	2/24	46.37	8.30	33.5	0	0

WILL GIDMAN LHB RMF R1 W1 MVP54

FULL NAME: William Robert Simon Gidman
BORN: February 14, 1985, High Wycombe, Buckinghamshire
SQUAD NO: 23
HEIGHT: 6ft 2in
NICKNAME: Gidders, Giddo, Wilbur, PT
EDUCATION: Wycliffe College, Stonehouse; Berkshire College of Agriculture
TEAMS: Durham, Gloucestershire, Marylebone Cricket Club, Marylebone Cricket Club Young Cricketers
CAREER: First-class: 2007; List A: 2003; T20: 2011

BEST BATTING: 116* Gloucestershire vs Northamptonshire, Bristol, 2011
BEST BOWLING: 6-92 Gloucestershire vs Derbyshire, Derby, 2011
COUNTY CAP: 2011 (Gloucestershire)

FAMILY TIES? My brother Alex also plays for Gloucestershire
WHO WOULD PLAY YOU IN A FILM OF YOUR LIFE? Any actor with a big nose
CAREER HIGHLIGHTS? Maiden Championship hundred and any five-fer
BEST PLAYER IN COUNTY CRICKET? Marcus Trescothick
TIP FOR THE TOP? David Payne
IF YOU WEREN'T A CRICKETER? Running a coffee shop
DESERT ISLAND DISC? Meat Loaf – Greatest Hits
FAVOURITE TV? Friends
CRICKETING HEROES? Garry Sobers
NON-CRICKETING HEROES? Muhammad Ali
FANTASY SLIP CORDON? Keeper: Michael McIntyre, 1st: James Corden, 2nd: Peter Kay, 3rd: Jennifer Aniston, Gully: Natalie Portman
TWITTER FEED: @wgiddo

Batting	Mat	Inns	NO	Runs	HS	Ave	SR	100	50	Ct	St
First-class	28	47	7	1461	116*	36.52	48.57	1	11	6	0
List A	34	21	4	352	76	20.70		0	1	10	0
Twenty20	8	7	1	78	40*	13.00	86.66	0	0	2	0
Bowling	**Inns**	**Balls**	**Runs**	**Wkts**	**BBI**	**BBM**	**Ave**	**Econ**	**SR**	**5w**	**10**
First-class	28	4298	2117	99	6/92	9/114	21.38	2.95	43.4	5	0
List A	34	1122	888	27	4/36	4/36	32.88	4.74	41.5	0	0
Twenty20	8	48	76	1	1/18	1/18	76.00	9.50	48.0	0	0

JOHN GLOVER RHB RMF

GLAMORGAN

FULL NAME: John Charles Glover
BORN: August 29, 1989, Cardiff
SQUAD NO: 36
HEIGHT: 6ft 4in
NICKNAME: Gloves, Glovebox, MC
EDUCATION: Llantarnam Comprehensive School; Durham University
TEAMS: Durham MCCU, Durham UCCE, Glamorgan, Wales Minor Counties
CAREER: First-class: 2008; List A: 2012

BEST BATTING: 55 Glamorgan vs Kent, Cardiff, 2012
BEST BOWLING: 5-38 Durham UCCE vs Durham, Durham University, 2009

WHY CRICKET? My father played for Panteg Cricket Club so I grew up watching and playing
CAREER HIGHLIGHTS? Glamorgan debut in 2011, playing in the first County Championship game under floodlights
SUPERSTITIONS? Always put left pad on first
CRICKETING HEROES? Courtney Walsh
NON-CRICKETING HEROES? Graeme McDowell, Martyn Williams, Kevin McNaughton
IF YOU WEREN'T A CRICKETER? I would probably be trying to find a job in sport development
WHEN RAIN STOPS PLAY? Either reading books or watching films
FAVOURITE TV? Friends
FAVOURITE FILM? Pulp Fiction, Gladiator, Inception
FAVOURITE BOOK? 1984 by George Orwell
DREAM HOLIDAY? Barry Island
ACCOMPLISHMENTS? Getting a 2:1 from Durham University
GUILTY PLEASURES? Standing on the terraces at Cardiff City FC, football accumulators on a Saturday afternoon
SURPRISING FACTS? 1. Played football at Ninian Park in a schools cup final 2. Wrestled with lion cubs in Potchefstroom 3. Took part in salsa dancing for my dissertation
TWITTER FEED: @John_Gloves

Batting	Mat	Inns	NO	Runs	HS	Ave	SR	100	50	Ct	St
First-class	18	24	7	201	55	11.82	33.72	0	1	6	0
List A	5	3	1	16	10	8.00	94.11	0	0	1	0
Bowling	**Inns**	**Balls**	**Runs**	**Wkts**	**BBI**	**BBM**	**Ave**	**Econ**	**SR**	**5w**	**10**
First-class	18	2396	1387	39	5/38	7/121	35.56	3.47	61.4	1	0
List A	5	216	230	7	3/34	3/34	32.85	6.38	30.8	0	0

BILLY GODLEMAN LHB LB

FULL NAME: Billy Ashley Godleman
BORN: February 11, 1989, Camden, London
SQUAD NO: 1
HEIGHT: 6ft 3in
EDUCATION: Islington Green School
TEAMS: England Under-19s, Essex, Middlesex, Middlesex 2nd XI
CAREER: First-class: 2005; List A: 2007; T20: 2006

BEST BATTING: 130 Essex vs Leicestershire, Leicester, 2011

NOTES: A first-class debut for Middlesex against Cambridge UCCE at 16, in which he scored a second innings 69, was soon followed by a professional contract at 17. Touted as a future international, 2007 was a breakthrough season for Godleman, as he amassed 842 first-class runs, and scored an unbeaten 149 for England U19 against Pakistan – still the highest Youth ODI innings for England. He found it difficult to recreate this form in the following season and was unable to hold down his place in the Middlesex 1st XI, prompting a move to Essex in 2009. After another couple of disappointing seasons – averaging 25.86 in 2010 and 26.41 in 2011 – he looked to have rediscovered his form with 130 against Gloucestershire at the beginning of 2012. However, he struggled for the remainder of the season before being released by Essex and picked up by newly promoted Derbyshire

Batting	Mat	Inns	NO	Runs	HS	Ave	SR	100	50	Ct	St
First-class	69	118	4	3447	130	30.23	41.37	5	17	52	0
List A	17	17	1	342	82	21.37	70.80	0	1	4	0
Twenty20	24	23	0	419	69	18.21	107.43	0	3	11	0
Bowling	**Inns**	**Balls**	**Runs**	**Wkts**	**BBI**	**BBM**	**Ave**	**Econ**	**SR**	**5w**	**10**
First-class	69	30	35	0	-	-	-	7.00	-	0	0
List A	17	-	-	-	-	-	-	-	-	-	-
Twenty20	24	-	-	-	-	-	-	-	-	-	-

MURRAY GOODWIN

RHB LB R9

FULL NAME: Murray William Goodwin
BORN: December 11, 1972, Harare, Zimbabwe
SQUAD NO: 40
HEIGHT: 5ft 9in
NICKNAME: Muzza, Fuzz, Goodie
EDUCATION: St John's, Zimbabwe; Newtonmoore Senior High, Australia
TEAMS: Netherlands, Zimbabwe, Mashonaland, Subiaco-Floreat, Sussex, Warriors, Western Australia
CAREER: Test: 1998; ODI: 1998; First-class: 1994; List A: 1994; T20: 2003

BEST BATTING: 344* Sussex vs Somerset, Taunton, 2009
BEST BOWLING: 2-23 Zimbabweans vs Lahore City, Lahore, 1998
COUNTY CAP: 2001 (Sussex); BENEFIT YEAR: 2009 (Sussex)

FAMILY TIES? Dad is a coach. Eldest brother [Darrell] played for Zimbabwe
CAREER HIGHLIGHTS? Becoming the highest individual scorer in Sussex's history – 335* vs Leicestershire, September 2003 at Hove. Broke Duleepsinhji's record of 333 from 1930
CRICKETERS PARTICULARLY ADMIRED? Allan Border, Steve Waugh, Curtly Ambrose, Sachin Tendulkar
OTHER SPORTS PLAYED? Hockey, golf, tennis

Batting	Mat	Inns	NO	Runs	HS	Ave	SR	100	50	Ct	St
Tests	19	37	4	1414	166*	42.84	46.31	3	8	10	0
ODIs	71	70	3	1818	112*	27.13	68.50	2	8	20	0
First-class	296	513	42	22113	344*	46.94		67	90	155	0
List A	362	344	41	10837	167	35.76		14	67	108	0
Twenty20	98	91	12	2265	102*	28.67	122.43	2	12	19	0
Bowling	**Inns**	**Balls**	**Runs**	**Wkts**	**BBI**	**BBM**	**Ave**	**Econ**	**SR**	**5w**	**10**
Tests	19	119	69	0	-	-	-	3.47	-	0	0
ODIs	71	248	210	4	1/12	1/12	52.50	5.08	62.0	0	0
First-class	296	713	376	7	2/23		53.71	3.16	101.8	0	0
List A	362	351	306	7	1/9	1/9	43.71	5.23	50.1	0	0
Twenty20	98	-	-	-	-	-	-	-	-	-	-

RECORDO GORDON

RHB RFM

FULL NAME: Recordo Olton Gordon
BORN: October 12, 1991, St Elizabeth's, Jamaica
SQUAD NO: 44
HEIGHT: 6 ft
NICKNAME: Ricky, Flash
EDUCATION: Aston Manor Academy; Hamstead Hall Sixth Form
TEAMS: Herefordshire, Warwickshire 2nd XI, Warwickshire Under-15s, Warwickshire Under-17s
CAREER: Yet to make first-team debut

CAREER HIGHLIGHTS? Taking 4-4 in a T20 game, and gaining a contract
CRICKETING HEROES? Courtney Walsh and Curtly Ambrose
NON-CRICKETING HEROES? My father
BEST PLAYER IN COUNTY CRICKET? There are a lot of good players but I really rate Alfonso Thomas as a bowler
TIPS FOR THE TOP? Jos Buttler, Ben Stokes
IF YOU WEREN'T A CRICKETER? I'd be at universiy
WHEN RAIN STOPS PLAY? Putting my feet up, getting them out of my bowling boots
FAVOURITE TV? The Big Bang Theory
FAVOURITE BOOK? The Tomb
DREAM HOLIDAY? Jamaica
ACCOMPLISHMENTS? Being head boy of my school
SURPRISING SKILL? I'm a good cook and baker
TWITTER FEED: @recordogordon

LEWIS GREGORY RHB RFM

SOMERSET

FULL NAME: Lewis Gregory
BORN: May 24, 1992, Plymouth
SQUAD NO: 24
EDUCATION: Hele's School, Plymouth
TEAMS: Devon, England Under-19s, Somerset, Somerset 2nd XI
CAREER: First-class: 2011; List A: 2010; T20: 2011

BEST BATTING: 48 Somerset vs Warwickshire, Birmingham, 2011
BEST BOWLING: 2-22 Somerset vs Nottinghamshire, Taunton, 2012

TWITTER FEED: @lewisgregory23
NOTES: Former England U19 skipper. Took a hat-trick for Somerset's 2nd XI against Essex in 2010. Claimed 4-49 on his List A debut against the touring Pakistanis. Somerset's leading wicket-taker in the 2011 FL t20, claiming 18 wickets at 17. Claimed 4-39 in last year's FL t20 quarter-final win against Essex

Batting	Mat	Inns	NO	Runs	HS	Ave	SR	100	50	Ct	St
First-class	10	14	2	141	48	11.75	43.51	0	0	0	0
List A	18	9	0	115	39	12.77	70.55	0	0	5	0
Twenty20	22	10	3	110	22	15.71	105.76	0	0	7	0
Bowling	**Inns**	**Balls**	**Runs**	**Wkts**	**BBI**	**BBM**	**Ave**	**Econ**	**SR**	**5w**	**10**
First-class	10	522	412	11	2/22	3/63	37.45	4.73	47.4	0	0
List A	18	424	433	23	4/27	4/27	18.82	6.12	18.4	0	0
Twenty20	22	345	444	26	4/15	4/15	17.07	7.72	13.2	0	0

DAVID GRIFFITHS LHB RFM

FULL NAME: David Andrew Griffiths
BORN: September 10, 1985, Newport, Isle of Wight
SQUAD NO: 18
HEIGHT: 6ft 1in
NICKNAME: Griff, Griffta, Chozza, Sog
EDUCATION: Sandown High School
TEAMS: Hampshire, Hampshire 2nd XI
CAREER: First-class: 2006; List A: 2008; T20: 2007

BEST BATTING: 31* Hampshire vs Surrey, Southampton, 2007
BEST BOWLING: 6-85 Hampshire vs Nottinghamshire, Nottingham, 2011

FAMILY TIES? My father captained Wales, my step-dad captained Isle of Wight and my uncles all played for the Isle of Wight too
WHO WOULD PLAY YOU IN A FILM OF YOUR LIFE? Jim Carrey
CAREER HIGHLIGHTS? Playing for England U19 and getting my first wicket for Hampshire, which Warnie caught
SUPERSTITIONS? I always turn right at the end of my run-up and always put my right boot on first
MOST MARKED CHARACTERISTIC? My lovely teeth
BEST PLAYER IN COUNTY CRICKET? Michael Carberry
TIPS FOR THE TOP? Jake George, Kieran Griffiths
IF YOU WEREN'T A CRICKETER? Handyman or coaching sport
DESERT ISLAND DISC? Tracy Chapman album
BIGGEST DRESSING DOWN YOU'VE RECEIVED? From Paul Terry after I pulled his shorts down at Worcester
CRICKETING HEROES? Darren Gough, Brett Lee, Graham Thorpe
NON-CRICKETING HEROES? David Beckham
TWITTER FEED: @griffta18

Batting	Mat	Inns	NO	Runs	HS	Ave	SR	100	50	Ct	St
First-class	33	48	19	187	31*	6.44	25.00	0	0	4	0
List A	18	5	4	15	7	15.00	50.00	0	0	3	0
Twenty20	5	1	1	4	4*	-	36.36	0	0	0	0
Bowling	**Inns**	**Balls**	**Runs**	**Wkts**	**BBI**	**BBM**	**Ave**	**Econ**	**SR**	**5w**	**10**
First-class	33	5203	3292	94	6/85	7/102	35.02	3.79	55.3	2	0
List A	18	648	631	22	4/29	4/29	28.68	5.84	29.4	0	0
Twenty20	5	90	121	5	3/13	3/13	24.20	8.06	18.0	0	0

GAVIN GRIFFITHS RHB RFM

FULL NAME: Gavin Timothy Griffiths
BORN: November 19, 1993, Ormskirk, Lancashire
SQUAD NO: 18
HEIGHT: 6ft 3in
NICKNAME: Gavvlar, Griff
EDUCATION: St Michael's Church of England High School, Chorley; St Mary's College, Crosby
TEAMS: England Under-19s, Lancashire 2nd XI
CAREER: Yet to make first-team debut

WHO WOULD PLAY YOU IN A FILM OF YOUR LIFE? Gerard Butler
CAREER HIGHLIGHTS? Playing for England U19 and becoming a professional for Lancashire
MOST MARKED CHARACTERISTIC? Military-style hair cut
BEST PLAYER IN COUNTY CRICKET? Marcus Trescothick
TIPS FOR THE TOP? Shiv Thakor, Ben Duckett, Olly Stone
IF YOU WEREN'T A CRICKETER? I'd be at university
DESERT ISLAND DISC? Coldplay – The Scientist
FAVOURITE TV? The Royle Family
CRICKETING HEROES? Allan Donald, Andrew Flintoff, Dale Steyn
NON-CRICKETING HEROES? Tim Cahill, Jonny Wilkinson
ACCOMPLISHMENTS? I played for Lancashire at rugby and Everton and Liverpool FC Academies
WHEN YOU RETIRE? Physiotherapist
SURPRISING FACT? I once played chess at national level
FANTASY SLIP CORDON? Keeper: Duncan Ferguson (hard man), 1st: Me, 2nd: Ricky Tomlinson (hilarious), 3rd: Peter Kay (hilarious), Gully: Stacey Solomon
TWITTER FEED: @gavvlar

TIM GROENEWALD RHB RFM MVP38

FULL NAME: Timothy Duncan Groenewald
BORN: January 10, 1984, Pietermaritzburg, South Africa
SQUAD NO: 12
HEIGHT: 6ft 2in
NICKNAME: TG, Groeners
EDUCATION: Maritzburg College, Natal; University of South Africa
TEAMS: Derbyshire, Warwickshire, Warwickshire 2nd XI
CAREER: First-class: 2006; List A: 2006; T20: 2006

BEST BATTING: 78 Warwickshire vs Bangladesh A, Birmingham, 2008
BEST BOWLING: 6-50 Derbyshire vs Surrey, Croydon, 2009
COUNTY CAP: 2011 (Derbyshire)

CAREER HIGHLIGHTS? Playing in FP Trophy semi-final for Warwickshire against Hampshire in 2007. My two eight-wicket hauls have been special as well. Defending six runs off the last over against Lancashire in the T20 last year
SUPERSTITIONS? I don't enjoy watching whilst we bat, I'd rather do other things like listen to music or get in the gym until I'm required
CRICKETING HEROES? Hansie Cronje and Allan Donald while growing up, and after playing with Dale Steyn, I admire him massively
NON-CRICKETING HEROES? Being from South Africa, Nelson Mandela is a huge inspiration
BEST PLAYER IN COUNTY CRICKET? Marcus Trescothick
FAVOURITE TV? The Apprentice, Two And A Half Men
FAVOURITE FILM? Lincoln Lawyer, Law Abiding Citizen, Taken
FAVOURITE BOOK? The Kite Runner, The Street Lawyer
FANTASY SLIP CORDON? Keeper: Adam Gilchrist (all-round good guy of cricket), 1st: Will Ferrell (hilarious, would keep us going all day), 2nd: Karl Pilkington (just laugh looking at him), 3rd: Me, Gully: Jennifer Aniston (to improve the scenery)
TWITTER FEED: @timmyg12

Batting	Mat	Inns	NO	Runs	HS	Ave	SR	100	50	Ct	St
First-class	67	87	26	1284	78	21.04	47.89	0	4	22	0
List A	65	38	11	360	36	13.33	94.73	0	0	15	0
Twenty20	63	24	11	265	41	20.38	125.59	0	0	15	0
Bowling	**Inns**	**Balls**	**Runs**	**Wkts**	**BBI**	**BBM**	**Ave**	**Econ**	**SR**	**5w**	**10**
First-class	67	11384	5853	188	6/50	8/97	31.13	3.08	60.5	6	0
List A	65	2342	2102	65	4/22	4/22	32.33	5.38	36.0	0	0
Twenty20	63	1097	1472	53	3/18	3/18	27.77	8.05	20.6	0	0

NICK GUBBINS

LHB LB

FULL NAME: Nicholas Richard Trail Gubbins
BORN: December 31, 1993, Richmond, Surrey
SQUAD NO: 18
HEIGHT: 6ft
NICKNAME: Gubbo
EDUCATION: Radley College; Leeds University
TEAMS: Middlesex 2nd XI, Middlesex Under-15s, Middlesex Under-17s
CAREER: Yet to make first-team debut

FAMILY TIES? None significant but my dad did play an 'ODI' for Singapore Cricket Club against Malaysia
WHO WOULD PLAY YOU IN A FILM OF YOUR LIFE? Johnny Depp
CAREER HIGHLIGHTS? My first contract for Middlesex and representing England at age-group levels
SUPERSTITIONS? I put my right pad on before my left. I always put my box and thigh pad on first. I always wear my bracelets outside of my gloves on my wrist (never on the inside). I have the same throwdown routine before each game
MOST MARKED CHARACTERISTIC? My ability to make people laugh even when I don't mean to
BEST PLAYER IN COUNTY CRICKET? Shivnarine Chanderpaul at Derbyshire
TIPS FOR THE TOP? Harry Podmore and Tom Helm will go a long way (around the park)
IF YOU WEREN'T A CRICKETER? Reserve goalkeeper for Chelsea. If Ross Turnbull can do it, anyone can
BIGGEST DRESSING DOWN YOU'VE RECEIVED? After a game against Lancashire 2nd XI and being given out lbw. My reaction got me a ticket into the umpires' room after the match
CRICKETING HEROES? Andrew Strauss
ACCOMPLISHMENTS? Handicap of 13 in golf and an A*, A, B, B in my A-Levels
WHEN YOU RETIRE? I'll go and live by the sea somewhere hot
SURPRISING FACT? When I get new clothes I usually don't take them off for at least a week
FANTASY SLIP CORDON? Keeper: David Attenborough (just because of his voice), 1st: Pokemon (gotta catch 'em all), 2nd: Michael McIntyre (I would not stop laughing), 3rd: Me (no other captain would put me in the slips), Gully: Liam Neeson (just for his role in Taken… not so much Taken 2)
TWITTER FEED: @ngubbins18

HARRY GURNEY RHB LFM

FULL NAME: Harry Frederick Gurney
BORN: October 25, 1986, Nottingham
SQUAD NO: 11
HEIGHT: 6ft 1in
NICKNAME: Gurns, Sicknote, Contract, Chicken Legs
EDUCATION: Garendon High School; Loughborough Grammar School; University of Leeds
TEAMS: Leeds/Bradford MCCU, Leicestershire, Nottinghamshire
CAREER: First-class: 2007; ODI: 2009; T20: 2009

BEST BATTING: 24* Leicestershire vs Middlesex, Leicester, 2009
BEST BOWLING: 5-82 Leicestershire vs Surrey, Leicester, 2009

CAREER HIGHLIGHTS? Signing first professional contract, Championship and Pro40 five-wicket hauls
CRICKETING HEROES? Ryan Sidebottom, Dale Steyn
NON-CRICKETING HEROES? Peter Jones, Richard Branson, Alan Sugar
BEST PLAYER IN COUNTY CRICKET? Marcus Trescothick
TIP FOR THE TOP? Joe Root
IF YOU WEREN'T A CRICKETER? Probably something in the financial sector in London
WHEN RAIN STOPS PLAY? Poker, reading, and drinking coffee
FAVOURITE TV? Frozen Planet
FAVOURITE BOOK? Bounce by Matthew Syed
DREAM HOLIDAY? St Anton, Austria
SURPRISING SKILL? I play the piano and speak pretty good French
GUILTY PLEASURES? Westlife, they are amazing
SURPRISING FACTS? I was once a sponsored poker player
FANTASY SLIP CORDON? Keeper: Ricky Gervais, 1st: Alan Sugar, 2nd: Natalie Portman, 3rd: Me, 4th: Harry Redknapp, Gully: Tony Blair/Margaret Thatcher
TWITTER FEED: @gurneyhf

Batting	Mat	Inns	NO	Runs	HS	Ave	SR	100	50	Ct	St
First-class	27	27	9	73	24*	4.05	26.64	0	0	2	0
List A	26	7	2	24	13*	4.80	72.72	0	0	1	0
Twenty20	38	2	2	5	5*	-	100.00	0	0	5	0
Bowling	**Inns**	**Balls**	**Runs**	**Wkts**	**BBI**	**BBM**	**Ave**	**Econ**	**SR**	**5w**	**10**
First-class	27	3785	2160	52	5/82	5/82	41.53	3.42	72.7	1	0
List A	26	973	859	22	5/24	5/24	39.04	5.29	44.2	1	0
Twenty20	38	743	920	44	3/21	3/21	20.90	7.42	16.8	0	0

CALUM HAGGETT LHB RM

KENT

FULL NAME: Calum John Haggett
BORN: October 30, 1990, Taunton, Somerset
SQUAD NO: TBC
HEIGHT: 6ft 5in
TEAMS: England Under-19s, Kent, Somerset, Somerset 2nd XI
CAREER: T20: 2011

NOTES: A highly-rated former England U19 international, Haggett began his career with Somerset but his development was significantly disrupted when it was discovered during a routine screening at Loughborough at the start of 2010 that he had aortic root dilatation and a leaking heart valve. He was withdrawn from the England U19 squad to tour New Zealand that winter and underwent open-heart surgery. He spent the majority of the 2012 summer playing for Kent's 2nd XI, and impressed sufficiently to be offered a deal for the 2013 campaign, with Simon Willis, Kent's high performance director, commenting: "Calum has impressed with consistent performances for the 2nd XI, finishing the season with a major contribution against Leicestershire with both bat and ball."

Batting	Mat	Inns	NO	Runs	HS	Ave	SR	100	50	Ct	St
Twenty20	3	2	0	3	2	1.50	75.00	0	0	0	0
Bowling	**Inns**	**Balls**	**Runs**	**Wkts**	**BBI**	**BBM**	**Ave**	**Econ**	**SR**	**5w**	**10**
Twenty20	3	30	32	1	1/15	1/15	32.00	6.40	30.0	0	0

SAM HAIN RHB OB

FULL NAME: Samuel Robert Hain
BORN: July 16, 1995, Hong Kong
SQUAD NO: 16
HEIGHT: 5ft 10in
EDUCATION: The Southport School, Gold Coast, Queensland
TEAMS: Australia Under-19s, Queensland Under-19s, Warwickshire 2nd XI
CAREER: Yet to make first-team debut

TWITTER FEED: @SammieHain
NOTES: Hain signed for the Bears last year having first been spotted by former club skipper Michael Powell while on an exchange scheme at Loretto School in Edinburgh at the age of 14. He will represent Warwickshire in the 2013 season having concluded his studies in Australia last year. Hain made his first appearance for Australia U19 at the age of 16 but both his parents are British

ALEX HALES

RHB RM R1 MVP63

NOTTINGHAMSHIRE

FULL NAME: Alexander Daniel Hales
BORN: January 3, 1989, Hillingdon, Middlesex
SQUAD NO: 10
HEIGHT: 6ft 5in
NICKNAME: Baz, Halesy, Trigg
EDUCATION: Chesham High School
TEAMS: England, Buckinghamshire, Duronto Rajshahi, England Lions, Melbourne Renegades, Nottinghamshire, Nottinghamshire 2nd XI
CAREER: T20I: 2011; First-class: 2008; List A: 2008; T20: 2009

BEST BATTING: 184 Nottinghamshire vs Somerset, Nottingham, 2011
BEST BOWLING: 2-63 Nottinghamshire vs Yorkshire, Nottingham, 2009
COUNTY CAP: 2011

WHO WOULD PLAY YOU IN A FILM OF YOUR LIFE? Daniel Radcliffe
CAREER HIGHLIGHTS? England debut
MOST MARKED CHARACTERISTIC? Patience
BEST PLAYER IN COUNTY CRICKET? Jonny Bairstow
TIPS FOR THE TOP? Jake Ball, George Bacon
IF YOU WEREN'T A CRICKETER? Groundsman
DESERT ISLAND DISC? Nicki Minaj – Pound The Alarm
CRICKETING HEROES? Ian Bell, Nick Lines, Vinnie Fazio
NON-CRICKETING HEROES? Steve Jobs, Paul Merson
ACCOMPLISHMENTS? I rowed across the English Channel in an old tin bath
WHEN YOU RETIRE? Professional poker player
FANTASY SLIP CORDON? Keeper: Bilal Shafayat, 1st: Maria Sharapova, 2nd: Arsene Wenger, 3rd: Kirstie Edwards, Gully: Jimmy Carr
TWITTER FEED: @AlexHales1

Batting	Mat	Inns	NO	Runs	HS	Ave	SR	100	50	Ct	St
T20Is	17	17	3	524	99	37.42	134.35	0	5	7	0
First-class	51	86	5	3116	184	38.46	58.51	6	20	47	0
List A	58	56	2	1771	150*	32.79	98.77	3	9	20	0
Twenty20	69	68	5	1837	99	29.15	137.60	0	16	25	0
Bowling	**Inns**	**Balls**	**Runs**	**Wkts**	**BBI**	**BBM**	**Ave**	**Econ**	**SR**	**5w**	**10**
T20Is	17	-	-	-	-	-	-	-	-	-	-
First-class	51	281	167	3	2/63	2/63	55.66	3.56	93.6	0	0
List A	58	4	10	0	-	-	-	15.00	-	0	0
Twenty20	69	3	7	0	-	-	-	14.00	-	0	0

ANDREW HALL

RHB RMF R1

FULL NAME: Andrew James Hall
BORN: July 31, 1975, Johannesburg, South Africa
SQUAD NO: 1
HEIGHT: 6ft
NICKNAME: HB, HBomb, Hancock
EDUCATION: Alberton High
TEAMS: South Africa, Chandigarh Lions, Dolphins, Easterns, Gauteng, Kent, Mashonaland Eagles, Northamptonshire, Transvaal, Worcestershire
CAREER: Test: 2002; ODI: 1999; T20I: 2006; First-class: 1995; List A: 1995; T20: 2003

BEST BATTING: 163 South Africa vs India, Kanpur, 2004
BEST BOWLING: 6-77 Easterns vs Western Province, Benoni, 2002
COUNTY CAPS: 2005 (Kent); 2009 (Northamptonshire)

WHO WOULD PLAY YOU IN A FILM OF YOUR LIFE? A younger Bruce Willis
CAREER HIGHLIGHTS? The ODI against Australia when we chased down 438 to win. Scoring 163 vs India in Kanpur and taking 5-18 vs England in the 2007 World Cup
SUPERSTITIONS? More like habits but I always pad up the same way and like to keep whites for batting and bowling if I've done well in them. I always cross the boundary with my left foot first
BEST PLAYER IN COUNTY CRICKET? Alastair Cook
TIPS FOR THE TOP? Olly Stone and David Willey
CRICKETING HEROES? Ray Jennings, Clive Rice, Jimmy Cook
WHEN YOU RETIRE? I always wanted to be a coach and help future players
TWITTER FEED: @AndrewHall99

Batting	Mat	Inns	NO	Runs	HS	Ave	SR	100	50	Ct	St
Tests	21	33	4	760	163	26.20	46.06	1	3	16	0
ODIs	88	56	13	905	81	21.04	75.04	0	3	29	0
T20Is	2	1	0	11	11	11.00	110.00	0	0	0	0
First-class	210	311	40	9443	163	34.84		12	57	200	0
List A	308	243	46	5833	129*	29.60		6	32	90	1
Twenty20	98	85	20	1404	66*	21.60	118.98	0	4	27	0
Bowling	**Inns**	**Balls**	**Runs**	**Wkts**	**BBI**	**BBM**	**Ave**	**Econ**	**SR**	**5w**	**10**
Tests	21	3001	1617	45	3/1	5/20	35.93	3.23	66.6	0	0
ODIs	88	3341	2515	95	5/18	5/18	26.47	4.51	35.1	1	0
T20Is	2	48	60	3	3/22	3/22	20.00	7.50	16.0	0	0
First-class	210	31695	15400	567	6/77		27.16	2.91	55.8	16	1
List A	308	12211	9722	354	5/18	5/18	27.46	4.77	34.4	2	0
Twenty20	98	1894	2398	118	6/21	6/21	20.32	7.59	16.0	2	0

RORY HAMILTON-BROWN

RHB OB R1

FULL NAME: Rory James Hamilton-Brown
BORN: September 3, 1987, Wellington Hospital, London
SQUAD NO: 27
HEIGHT: 6ft
NICKNAME: Razza, HB
EDUCATION: Dulwich Prep; Millfield School
TEAMS: England Under-19s, Mashonaland Eagles, Surrey, Surrey 2nd XI, Sussex
CAREER: First-class: 2005; List A: 2005; T20: 2008

BEST BATTING: 171* Sussex vs Yorkshire, Hove, 2009
BEST BOWLING: 2-49 Sussex vs Yorkshire, Hove, 2009
COUNTY CAP: 2011 (Surrey)

CAREER HIGHLIGHTS? Being appointed Surrey captain and winning the CB40 in 2011
CRICKETING HEROES? Jacques Kallis and Herschelle Gibbs
NON-CRICKETING HEROES? Joel Stransky and Mark Wright
BEST PLAYER IN COUNTY CRICKET? Marcus Trescothick
TIPS FOR THE TOP? Daniel Bell-Drummond, Billy Godleman
IF YOU WEREN'T A CRICKETER? I would like to be working in the City, depending on grades
FAVOURITE TV? An Idiot Abroad
FAVOURITE FILM? The Other Guys
FAVOURITE BOOK? The Innocent Man by John Grisham
DREAM HOLIDAY? Las Vegas
GUILTY PLEASURES? A love of the commentary style of Bob Willis

Batting	Mat	Inns	NO	Runs	HS	Ave	SR	100	50	Ct	St
First-class	51	91	6	2893	171*	34.03	73.65	6	13	36	0
List A	72	64	3	1617	115	26.50	112.84	2	7	23	0
Twenty20	73	67	3	1107	87*	17.29	118.14	0	4	22	0
Bowling	**Inns**	**Balls**	**Runs**	**Wkts**	**BBI**	**BBM**	**Ave**	**Econ**	**SR**	**5w**	**10**
First-class	51	895	542	9	2/49	3/85	60.22	3.63	99.4	0	0
List A	72	1242	1164	32	3/28	3/28	36.37	5.62	38.8	0	0
Twenty20	73	526	667	36	4/15	4/15	18.52	7.60	14.6	0	0

OLIVER HANNON-DALBY LHB RMF

FULL NAME: Oliver James Hannon-Dalby
BORN: June 20, 1989, Halifax, Yorkshire
SQUAD NO: 20
HEIGHT: 6ft 8in
NICKNAME: Bunse, Dave, OHD, Shaggy
EDUCATION: Brooksbank School, Elland
TEAMS: Yorkshire, Yorkshire 2nd XI
CAREER: First-class: 2008; List A: 2011; T20: 2012

BEST BATTING: 11* Yorkshire vs Lancashire, Manchester, 2010
BEST BOWLING: 5-68 Yorkshire vs Somerset, Leeds, 2010

CAREER HIGHLIGHTS? Debut and first five-fer
CRICKETING HEROES? Glenn McGrath, Brett Lee
BEST PLAYER IN COUNTY CRICKET? Marcus Trescothick
TIPS FOR THE TOP? Jonny Bairstow, Azeem Rafiq
IF YOU WEREN'T A CRICKETER? Teacher
WHEN RAIN STOPS PLAY? Eating or crosswords
FAVOURITE TV? Top Gear, Family Guy
FAVOURITE FILM? Blades Of Glory
FAVOURITE BOOK? Guinness World Records
DREAM HOLIDAY? Barbados
ACCOMPLISHMENTS? Buying my first house
SURPRISING SKILL? I can juggle
SURPRISING FACTS? Local high jump champion aged 12, Yorkshire CCC Scrabble champion in 2011, Cyril Sneer impressionist
TWITTER FEED: @OHD12

Batting	Mat	Inns	NO	Runs	HS	Ave	SR	100	50	Ct	St
First-class	24	25	10	45	11*	3.00	11.42	0	0	2	0
List A	5	1	1	21	21*	-	210.00	0	0	3	0
Twenty20	2	-	-	-	-	-	-	-	-	0	0
Bowling	**Inns**	**Balls**	**Runs**	**Wkts**	**BBI**	**BBM**	**Ave**	**Econ**	**SR**	**5w**	**10**
First-class	24	3347	1938	43	5/68	7/122	45.06	3.47	77.8	2	0
List A	5	166	202	5	2/22	2/22	40.40	7.30	33.2	0	0
Twenty20	2	48	58	3	2/23	2/23	19.33	7.25	16.0	0	0

ARUN HARINATH LHB OB

FULL NAME: Arun Harinath
BORN: March 26, 1987, Sutton, Surrey
SQUAD NO: 10
HEIGHT: 5ft 10in
NICKNAME: The Baron
EDUCATION: Tiffin Boys' Grammar School; Loughborough University
TEAMS: Loughborough MCCU, Marylebone Cricket Club, Surrey, Surrey 2nd XI
CAREER: First-class: 2007; List A: 2009

BEST BATTING: 109 Surrey vs Middlesex, The Oval, 2012

FAMILY TIES? My father played cricket in Sri Lanka and my brother Muhunthan Harinath was on the staff at Surrey
WHO WOULD PLAY YOU IN A FILM OF YOUR LIFE? My brother – he would do a very good impression of me!
CAREER HIGHLIGHTS? Making my Surrey debut and getting my maiden first-class hundred in 2012
BEST PLAYER IN COUNTY CRICKET? Chris Rogers, Marcus Trescothick
TIP FOR THE TOP? Dom Sibley
DESERT ISLAND DISC? The Strokes – Is This It?
FAVOURITE TV? The West Wing
BIGGEST DRESSING DOWN YOU'VE RECEIVED? From Dil [Graham Dilley] after losing one of our UCCE games!
CRICKETING HEROES? Brian Lara, Graham Thorpe, Mark Ramprakash
NON-CRICKETING HEROES? Tom Hanks, Roger Federer
ACCOMPLISHMENTS? Obtaining my degree
FANTASY SLIP CORDON? Keeper: Frank Sinatra, 1st: Russell Brand, 2nd: Barack Obama, 3rd: Me, 4th: Roger Federer, Gully: Spider-Man
TWITTER FEED: @arunharinath

Batting	Mat	Inns	NO	Runs	HS	Ave	SR	100	50	Ct	St
First-class	32	55	2	1497	109	28.24	41.13	2	8	7	0
List A	1	1	1	21	21*	-	80.76	0	0	0	0
Bowling	**Inns**	**Balls**	**Runs**	**Wkts**	**BBI**	**BBM**	**Ave**	**Econ**	**SR**	**5w**	**10**
First-class	32	36	30	0	-	-	-	5.00	-	0	0
List A	1	-	-	-	-	-	-	-	-	-	-

BEN HARMISON LHB RM

FULL NAME: Ben William Harmison
BORN: January 9, 1986, Ashington, Northumberland
SQUAD NO: 21
HEIGHT: 6ft 5in
NICKNAME: Harmy
EDUCATION: Ashington High School
TEAMS: Durham, Durham 2nd XI, Kent, Northumberland
CAREER: First-class: 2006; List A: 2005; T20: 2006

BEST BATTING: 110 Durham vs Oxford UCCE, Oxford, 2006
BEST BOWLING: 4-27 Durham vs Surrey, Guildford, 2008

CAREER HIGHLIGHTS? Signing my first professional contract at the age of 18. Consecutive hundreds in my first two first-class games for Durham
CRICKET MOMENT TO FORGET? Getting a first-baller vs Bangladesh in a one-dayer
CRICKETERS PARTICULARLY ADMIRED? Andrew Flintoff
FAVOURITE FILM? Armageddon
FAVOURITE BAND? Take That
OTHER SPORTS PLAYED? Golf, fishing, football
OTHER SPORTS FOLLOWED? Football (Newcastle United)
RELAXATIONS? Fishing, listening to music
FAMILY TIES? Brother Steve plays for Durham and England. Father Jim and brother James play league cricket for Ashington CC

Batting	Mat	Inns	NO	Runs	HS	Ave	SR	100	50	Ct	St
First-class	49	79	6	1813	110	24.83	43.72	3	7	26	0
List A	54	44	5	953	67	24.43	71.65	0	3	18	0
Twenty20	30	17	7	117	24	11.70	107.33	0	0	9	0
Bowling	**Inns**	**Balls**	**Runs**	**Wkts**	**BBI**	**BBM**	**Ave**	**Econ**	**SR**	**5w**	**10**
First-class	49	1671	1210	33	4/27	6/98	36.66	4.34	50.6	0	0
List A	54	865	855	24	3/43	3/43	35.62	5.93	36.0	0	0
Twenty20	30	348	471	23	3/20	3/20	20.47	8.12	15.1	0	0

STEVE HARMISON RHB RFM W6

DURHAM

FULL NAME: Stephen James Harmison
BORN: October 23, 1978, Ashington, Northumberland
SQUAD NO: 10
HEIGHT: 6ft 4in
NICKNAME: Harmy
EDUCATION: Ashington High School
TEAMS: England, Durham, Durham 2nd XI, ICC World XI, Lions
CAREER: Test: 2002; ODI: 2002; T20I: 2005; First-class: 1996; List A: 1998; T20: 2004

BEST BATTING: 49* England vs South Africa, The Oval, 2008
BEST BOWLING: 7-12 England vs West Indies, Kingston, 2004
BENEFIT YEAR: 2013 (Durham)

FAMILY TIES? Brother James played for Northumberland and younger brother Ben plays for Kent
CRICKETERS PARTICULARLY ADMIRED? David Boon, Courtney Walsh
RELAXATIONS? Spending time with the family
OTHER SPORTS FOLLOWED? Football (Newcastle United)
NOTES: Made his Test debut in 2002 against India at Trent Bridge. At The Oval in 2003 he took four second-innings wickets to help England draw a series against South Africa. In early 2004 he demolished West Indies with 7-12 at Jamaica and 6-61 at Trinidad, taking 23 wickets in the series. After eight wickets in a day against West indies at The Oval in September 2004, he went to No.1 in the Test rankings for bowlers. An Ashes winner in 2005 and 2009, he became an MBE in the 2006 New Year's Honours List

Batting	Mat	Inns	NO	Runs	HS	Ave	SR	100	50	Ct	St
Tests	63	86	23	743	49*	11.79	57.19	0	0	7	0
ODIs	58	25	14	91	18*	8.27	64.53	0	0	10	0
T20Is	2	-	-	-	-	-	-	-	-	1	0
First-class	211	270	77	1888	49*	9.78		0	0	31	0
List A	143	67	34	267	25*	8.09		0	0	23	0
Twenty20	28	6	1	11	6	2.20	84.61	0	0	3	0
Bowling	**Inns**	**Balls**	**Runs**	**Wkts**	**BBI**	**BBM**	**Ave**	**Econ**	**SR**	**5w**	**10**
Tests	63	13375	7192	226	7/12	11/76	31.82	3.22	59.1	8	1
ODIs	58	2899	2481	76	5/33	5/33	32.64	5.13	38.1	1	0
T20Is	2	39	42	1	1/13	1/13	42.00	6.46	39.0	0	0
First-class	211	39374	20805	744	7/12		27.96	3.17	52.9	27	1
List A	143	6838	5658	184	5/33	5/33	30.75	4.96	37.1	1	0
Twenty20	28	505	668	29	5/41	5/41	23.03	7.93	17.4	1	0

JAMES HARRIS

RHB RFM W1

FULL NAME: James Alexander Russell Harris
BORN: May 16, 1990, Morriston, Swansea
SQUAD NO: 5
HEIGHT: 6ft 1in
NICKNAME: Rolf, Bones, Lloyd Christmas, LC
EDUCATION: Pontarddulais Comprehensive; Gorseinon College
TEAMS: England Lions, England Under-19s, Glamorgan, Glamorgan 2nd XI, Wales Minor Counties
CAREER: First-class: 2007; List A: 2007; T20: 2008

BEST BATTING: 87* Glamorgan vs Nottinghamshire, Swansea, 2007
BEST BOWLING: 7-66 Glamorgan vs Gloucestershire, Bristol, 2007
COUNTY CAP: 2010 (Glamorgan)

FAMILY TIES? Father played British Universities
CAREER HIGHLIGHTS? Taking 12 wickets in my second first-class game on my 17th birthday. County cap in 2010. Lions tour to the West Indies in 2011
SUPERSTITIONS? Left pad before right
CRICKETING HEROES? Glenn McGrath, Jacques Kallis
NON-CRICKETING HEROES? Tiger Woods
BEST PLAYER IN COUNTY CRICKET? Marcus Trescothick
TIPS FOR THE TOP? James Taylor, Ben Stokes, Jos Buttler
IF YOU WEREN'T A CRICKETER? Attempting to play golf most probably
WHEN RAIN STOPS PLAY? Time on the iPad
FAVOURITE TV? Entourage (highly recommended)
FAVOURITE FILM? The Shawshank Redemption, Anchorman
FAVOURITE BOOK? The Da Vinci Code, Angels And Demons
DREAM HOLIDAY? Barbados
TWITTER FEED: @James_Harris9

Batting	Mat	Inns	NO	Runs	HS	Ave	SR	100	50	Ct	St
First-class	65	89	17	1532	87*	21.27		0	7	16	0
List A	35	23	5	179	29	9.94	71.03	0	0	8	0
Twenty20	28	16	8	100	18	12.50	114.94	0	0	3	0
Bowling	**Inns**	**Balls**	**Runs**	**Wkts**	**BBI**	**BBM**	**Ave**	**Econ**	**SR**	**5w**	**10**
First-class	65	11829	6297	228	7/66	12/118	27.61	3.19	51.8	9	1
List A	35	1338	1222	44	4/48	4/48	27.77	5.47	30.4	0	0
Twenty20	28	494	723	24	4/23	4/23	30.12	8.78	20.5	0	0

JAMIE HARRISON RHB LMF

FULL NAME: Jamie Harrison
BORN: November 19, 1990, Whiston, Knowsley, Lancashire
SQUAD NO: 13
HEIGHT: 6ft
NICKNAME: Jay, Bieber, JB
EDUCATION: Sedbergh School
TEAMS: Durham, Durham 2nd XI, Durham Academy, Gloucestershire 2nd XI, Sedbergh School
CAREER: First-class: 2012; List A: 2012

BEST BATTING: 23 Durham vs Warwickshire, Chester-le-Street, 2012
BEST BOWLING: 4-112 Durham vs Somerset, Taunton, 2012

FAMILY TIES? Step-father [Simon] played in the Cumbria cricket league for Egremont and Cleator. Cousin [Matthew] plays for Cleator Cricket Club U13
WHO WOULD PLAY YOU IN A FILM OF YOUR LIFE? Frankie Boyle
SUPERSTITIONS? The night before each game I go for a swim and stretch. Also I pack my bag the night before, packing my training/warm-up gear in the left of the bag and playing whites to the right. The morning before the game I swim and stretch
MOST MARKED CHARACTERISTIC? Reliability
BEST PLAYER IN COUNTY CRICKET? Graham Onions
TIPS FOR THE TOP? Paul Coughlin, Rammy Singh, Graham Clark
IF YOU WEREN'T A CRICKETER? Being involved within some kind of social work by day and performing as a DJ somewhere by night
DESERT ISLAND DISC? Drake – Take Care
FAVOURITE TV? Shameless
CRICKETING HEROES? Glenn McGrath, Wasim Akram, Graham Onions
NON-CRICKETING HEROES? Sean Long, Keiron Cunningham
ACCOMPLISHMENTS? I became a part-time Justin Bieber lookalike
WHEN YOU RETIRE? Work within social work, helping young offenders and disadvantaged children
TWITTER FEED: @jayharrison13

Batting	Mat	Inns	NO	Runs	HS	Ave	SR	100	50	Ct	St
First-class	3	6	1	60	23	12.00	43.16	0	0	0	0
List A	2	1	1	7	7*	-	140.00	0	0	0	0
Bowling	**Inns**	**Balls**	**Runs**	**Wkts**	**BBI**	**BBM**	**Ave**	**Econ**	**SR**	**5w**	**10**
First-class	3	408	260	10	4/112	5/131	26.00	3.82	40.8	0	0
List A	2	72	83	2	2/51	2/51	41.50	6.91	36.0	0	0

NICK HARRISON RHB RM

FULL NAME: Nicholas Luke Harrison
BORN: February 3, 1992, Bath, Somerset
SQUAD NO: 12
HEIGHT: 6ft 4in
NICKNAME: Trigger, Pablo
EDUCATION: Hardenhuish School, Chippenham
TEAMS: Wiltshire, Worcestershire, Worcestershire 2nd XI
CAREER: First-class: 2012; List A: 2011

BEST BATTING: 10 Worcestershire vs Somerset, Taunton, 2012
BEST BOWLING: 2-78 Worcestershire vs Oxford MCCU, Oxford, 2012

FAMILY TIES? My dad and brothers all played, as well as my uncle and my cousins. We all played together for Chippenham 3rd XI, where eight of us out of the 11 were related!
CAREER HIGHLIGHTS? Making my debut for the first team and playing on Sky in the same game. Taking three five-wicket hauls in two weeks. Taking my first wicket for the first team
CRICKETING HEROES? Glenn McGrath and Andrew Flintoff
BEST PLAYER IN COUNTY CRICKET? Marcus Trescothick or Alan Richardson
TIP FOR THE TOP? Aneesh Kapil
IF YOU WEREN'T A CRICKETER? I would try The X Factor! Or study to become a plumber or electrician
FAVOURITE TV? Two And A Half Men
FAVOURITE FILM? Good Will Hunting, Rise Of The Planet Of The Apes
FAVOURITE BOOK? Ross Kemp: Pirates, The Game by Neil Strauss
DREAM HOLIDAY? Miami beach holiday
ACCOMPLISHMENTS? I played basketball for my county
GUILTY PLEASURES? Ronan Keating, McDonald's cheeseburgers
SURPRISING FACTS? My toes are like fingers. I have produced a few music tracks that haven't quite made it into the business. I gave Katherine Jenkins a kiss on the cheek when working at a motorway services

Batting	Mat	Inns	NO	Runs	HS	Ave	SR	100	50	Ct	St
First-class	3	4	0	12	10	3.00	20.68	0	0	1	0
List A	7	2	2	7	5*	-	100.00	0	0	0	0
Bowling	**Inns**	**Balls**	**Runs**	**Wkts**	**BBI**	**BBM**	**Ave**	**Econ**	**SR**	**5w**	**10**
First-class	3	276	176	3	2/78	2/78	58.66	3.82	92.0	0	0
List A	7	306	364	8	2/43	2/43	45.50	7.13	38.2	0	0

JOHN HASTINGS RHB RFM

FULL NAME: John Wayne Hastings
BORN: November 4, 1985, Penrith, New South Wales, Australia
SQUAD NO: TBC
HEIGHT: 6ft 4in
NICKNAME: The Duke
TEAMS: Australia, Australia A, Kochi Tuskers Kerala, New South Wales 2nd XI, New South Wales Under-17s, New South Wales Under-19s, Victoria
CAREER: Test: 2012; ODI: 2010; T20I: 2010; First-class: 2007; List A: 2007; T20: 2007

BEST BATTING: 93 Victoria vs Tasmania, Hobart, 2010
BEST BOWLING: 5-30 Victoria vs Western Australia, Perth, 2012

NOTES: Hastings will represent Sussex in this season's FL t20 competition. The allrounder with one Test cap to his name was Victoria's leading wicket-taker in all competitions during his breakthrough season in 2009/10. He is a qualified PE teacher

Batting	Mat	Inns	NO	Runs	HS	Ave	SR	100	50	Ct	St
Tests	1	2	0	52	32	26.00	59.09	0	0	1	0
ODIs	11	9	4	82	21*	16.40	105.12	0	0	2	0
T20Is	3	3	2	32	15	32.00	177.77	0	0	0	0
First-class	27	35	3	792	93	24.75	48.49	0	3	14	0
List A	48	35	11	490	69*	20.41	98.59	0	1	15	0
Twenty20	30	23	5	150	23*	8.33	116.27	0	0	8	0
Bowling	**Inns**	**Balls**	**Runs**	**Wkts**	**BBI**	**BBM**	**Ave**	**Econ**	**SR**	**5w**	**10**
Tests	1	234	153	1	1/51	1/153	153.00	3.92	234.0	0	0
ODIs	11	546	410	8	2/35	2/35	51.25	4.50	68.2	0	0
T20Is	3	60	66	3	3/14	3/14	22.00	6.60	20.0	0	0
First-class	27	4825	2250	90	5/30	7/87	25.00	2.79	53.6	3	0
List A	48	2516	2061	75	4/28	4/28	27.48	4.91	33.5	0	0
Twenty20	30	584	758	25	3/14	3/14	30.32	7.78	23.3	0	0

LEWIS HATCHETT LHB LMF

FULL NAME: Lewis James Hatchett
BORN: January 21, 1990, Shoreham-by-Sea, Sussex
SQUAD NO: 5
HEIGHT: 6ft 3in
NICKNAME: Hatch
EDUCATION: Steyning Grammar School
TEAMS: Sussex, Sussex 2nd XI
CAREER: First-class: 2010

BEST BATTING: 20 Sussex vs Middlesex, Uxbridge, 2010
BEST BOWLING: 5-47 Sussex vs Leicestershire, Leicester, 2010

CAREER HIGHLIGHTS? First-class debut. Maiden first-class five-fer. Signing a contract with my home county Sussex. All of these happening in the same year!
SUPERSTITIONS? Try not to move places when the team are doing well. Sometimes shave my head before games! Always turn left at the top of my run-up
CRICKETING HEROES? Grew up watching the old West Indian bowlers such as Courtney Walsh and Curtly Ambrose. Watched a lot of Jason Lewry at Sussex, probably where I learnt my action from
NON-CRICKETING HEROES? My family. Our country's servicemen, past and present
BEST PLAYER IN COUNTY CRICKET? Batting: Marcus Trescothick. Bowling: Glen Chapple
TIPS FOR THE TOP? Jos Buttler and Alex Hales look super talented, those are two who stand out for me. I'd also back my mate Luke Wells to push on to higher things
IF YOU WEREN'T A CRICKETER? I would love to have been a Marine
FAVOURITE BOOK? I don't read often, but Steve Redgrave's book was a good read
DREAM HOLIDAY? Barbados – just to go and chill with friends out there
SURPRISING FACTS? I suffer from Poland Syndrome. I have my Sussex cap number tattooed under my left arm
FANTASY SLIP CORDON? Keeper: Will Ferrell, 1st: Jim Carrey, 2nd: Me, 3rd: Jonny Wilkinson, 4th: Tiger Woods, 5th: Nicki Minaj, Gully: Rihanna
TWITTER FEED: @lewis_hatchett

Batting	Mat	Inns	NO	Runs	HS	Ave	SR	100	50	Ct	St
First-class	8	10	3	62	20	8.85	26.83	0	0	2	0
Bowling	**Inns**	**Balls**	**Runs**	**Wkts**	**BBI**	**BBM**	**Ave**	**Econ**	**SR**	**5w**	**10**
First-class	8	909	581	22	5/47	6/92	26.40	3.83	41.3	1	0

TOM HELM RHB RMF

FULL NAME: Thomas George Helm
BORN: May 7, 1994, Stoke Mandeville Hospital, Buckinghamshire
SQUAD NO: 14
HEIGHT: 6ft 4in
NICKNAME: Ched, Helmet, Helmy
EDUCATION: Misbourne School
TEAMS: Buckinghamshire, Buckinghamshire Under-13s, Buckinghamshire Under-14s, Buckinghamshire Under-15s, Buckinghamshire Under-17s, Middlesex 2nd XI
CAREER: Yet to make first-team debut

FAMILY TIES? My dad and brother play for Ley Hill CC
WHO WOULD PLAY YOU IN A FILM OF YOUR LIFE? Daniel Craig
CAREER HIGHLIGHTS? England U19 T20 competition winners
SUPERSTITIONS? My taking guard routine
MOST MARKED CHARACTERISTIC? Bracelets
BEST PLAYER IN COUNTY CRICKET? Toby Roland-Jones
TIPS FOR THE TOP? Craig and Jamie Overton, Matt Dunn, Tymal Mills
IF YOU WEREN'T A CRICKETER? Studying at university
DESERT ISLAND DISC? Olly Murs – In Case You Didn't Know
FAVOURITE TV? Rules Of Engagement
CRICKETING HEROES? Andrew Flintoff, Stuart Broad
NON-CRICKETING HEROES? Frank Lampard, Ian Poulter, Tom Hardy
WHEN YOU RETIRE? I'd like to become a pundit
FANTASY SLIP CORDON? Keeper: Batman, 1st: Me, 2nd: Eidur Gudjohnsen, 3rd: Michael Jordan, Gully: Lee Mack
TWITTER FEED: @TomHelm14

CLAUDE HENDERSON RHB SLA W1

FULL NAME: Claude William Henderson
BORN: June 14, 1972, Worcester, Cape Province, South Africa
SQUAD NO: 15
HEIGHT: 6ft 2in
NICKNAME: Hendo
EDUCATION: Worcester High School, South Africa
TEAMS: South Africa, Boland, Cape Cobras, Leicestershire, Lions, Western Province, Worcestershire Cricket Board
CAREER: Test: 2001; ODI: 2001; First-class: 1990; List A: 1991; T20: 2004

BEST BATTING: 81 Leicestershire vs Gloucestershire, Leicester, 2001
BEST BOWLING: 7-57 Boland vs Eastern Province, Paarl, 1994
COUNTY CAP: 2004; TESTIMONIAL: 2011

FAMILY TIES? My brother James was a first-class opening batter for Boland and Transvaal
CAREER HIGHLIGHTS? All the trophies won in South Africa and for Leicestershire, and playing for South Africa
CRICKETING HEROES? Graeme Pollock, Shane Warne and Jacques Kallis
NON-CRICKETING HEROES? Ernie Els, Carel du Plessis
BEST PLAYER IN COUNTY CRICKET? Marcus Trescothick
TIP FOR THE TOP? James Taylor
IF YOU WEREN'T A CRICKETER? Spin bowling coach, commentator, restaurant owner
FAVOURITE FILM? Taken
FAVOURITE BOOK? The Long Walk To Freedom
GUILTY PLEASURES? I love red wine
FANTASY SLIP CORDON? Keeper: Marilyn Monroe, 1st: Lee Evans, 2nd: Elle Macpherson, 3rd: Shane Warne, Gully: Me

Batting	Mat	Inns	NO	Runs	HS	Ave	SR	100	50	Ct	St
Tests	7	7	0	65	30	9.28	32.17	0	0	2	0
ODIs	4	-	-	-	-	-	-	-	-	0	0
First-class	271	373	78	5589	81	18.94		0	20	88	0
List A	257	149	68	1203	45	14.85		0	0	57	0
Twenty20	105	41	18	186	32	8.08	97.89	0	0	27	0
Bowling	**Inns**	**Balls**	**Runs**	**Wkts**	**BBI**	**BBM**	**Ave**	**Econ**	**SR**	**5w**	**10**
Tests	7	1962	928	22	4/116	7/176	42.18	2.83	89.1	0	0
ODIs	4	217	132	7	4/17	4/17	18.85	3.64	31.0	0	0
First-class	271	64753	27707	899	7/57		30.81	2.56	72.0	34	2
List A	257	11384	8324	319	6/29	6/29	26.09	4.38	35.6	2	0
Twenty20	105	2062	2384	91	3/23	3/23	26.19	6.93	22.6	0	0

MATT HIGGINBOTTOM LHB RMF

FULL NAME: Matthew Higginbottom
BORN: October 20, 1990, Stockport, Cheshire
SQUAD NO: 20
HEIGHT: 6ft 2in
NICKNAME: Higgy
EDUCATION: New Mills Secondary School and Sixth Form College; Leeds Metropolitan University
TEAMS: Bradford/Leeds UCCE, Derbyshire, Derbyshire 2nd XI, Leeds/Bradford MCCU
CAREER: First-class: 2012; List A: 2012

BEST BATTING: 31* Leeds/Bradford MCCU vs Yorkshire, Leeds, 2012
BEST BOWLING: 2-22 Leeds/Bradford MCCU vs Surrey, The Oval, 2012

FAMILY TIES? My grandfather, father and brother all play or played for the local village club Hayfield
WHO WOULD PLAY YOU IN A FILM OF YOUR LIFE? Brad Pitt
CAREER HIGHLIGHTS? Playing against Australia and South Africa in two tour matches
BEST PLAYER IN COUNTY CRICKET? Wes Durston
TIPS FOR THE TOP? Pete Burgoyne, Dan Hodgson
IF YOU WEREN'T A CRICKETER? I'd like to be a pilot
DESERT ISLAND DISC? Ed Sheeran
FAVOURITE TV? How I Met Your Mother
CRICKETING HEROES? Darren Gough, Brian Lara
FANTASY SLIP CORDON? Keeper: David Walliams (funny guy who'd make a long session go much quicker), 1st: Glenn McGrath (to teach me how to bowl), 2nd: David Beckham (just a cool guy), 3rd: Me
TWITTER FEED: @matthigg12

Batting	Mat	Inns	NO	Runs	HS	Ave	SR	100	50	Ct	St
First-class	2	4	3	79	31*	79.00	52.31	0	0	0	0
List A	1	-	-	-	-	-	-	-	-	0	0
Bowling	**Inns**	**Balls**	**Runs**	**Wkts**	**BBI**	**BBM**	**Ave**	**Econ**	**SR**	**5w**	**10**
First-class	2	174	120	4	2/22	2/53	30.00	4.13	43.5	0	0
List A	1	30	43	0	-	-	-	8.60	-	0	0

JAMES HILDRETH RHB RM R3 MVP35

FULL NAME: James Charles Hildreth
BORN: September 9, 1984, Milton Keynes
SQUAD NO: 25
HEIGHT: 5ft 10in
NICKNAME: Hildy, Hildz, Drethpiece
EDUCATION: Millfield School, Glastonbury; Cardiff Metropolitan University
TEAMS: England Lions, Somerset
CAREER: First-class: 2003; List A: 2003; T20: 2004

BEST BATTING: 303* Somerset vs Warwickshire, Taunton, 2009
BEST BOWLING: 2-39 Somerset vs Hampshire, Taunton, 2009
COUNTY CAP: 2007

CAREER HIGHLIGHTS? Winning the T20 in 2005, captaining England Lions and captaining Somerset
BEST PLAYER IN COUNTY CRICKET? Marcus Trescothick
TIPS FOR THE TOP? Jamie and Craig Overton
IF YOU WEREN'T A CRICKETER? Travelling or on a beach somewhere
FAVOURITE TV? The Big Bang Theory
CRICKETING HEROES? Ricky Ponting
WHEN YOU RETIRE? Sport Psychology
SURPRISING FACT? I'm a big MK Dons fan
TWITTER FEED: @dreth25

Batting	Mat	Inns	NO	Runs	HS	Ave	SR	100	50	Ct	St
First-class	151	242	19	9866	303*	44.24		27	46	128	0
List A	149	141	23	3702	151	31.37		4	15	50	0
Twenty20	109	103	17	2056	107*	23.90	119.32	1	9	44	0
Bowling	**Inns**	**Balls**	**Runs**	**Wkts**	**BBI**	**BBM**	**Ave**	**Econ**	**SR**	**5w**	**10**
First-class	151	492	444	5	2/39		88.80	5.41	98.4	0	0
List A	149	150	185	6	2/26	2/26	30.83	7.40	25.0	0	0
Twenty20	109	169	247	10	3/24	3/24	24.70	8.76	16.9	0	0

ANDY HODD RHB WK

FULL NAME: Andrew John Hodd
BORN: January 12, 1984, Chichester, West Sussex
SQUAD NO: 4
HEIGHT: 5ft 9in
NICKNAME: Hoddy
EDUCATION: Bexhill High School; Bexhill College; Loughborough University
TEAMS: England Under-19s, Surrey, Sussex, Sussex Cricket Board, Yorkshire
CAREER: First-class: 2003; List A: 2002: T20: 2005

BEST BATTING: 123 Sussex vs Yorkshire, Hove, 2007

NOTES: Hodd began his career at Sussex, then moved to Surrey, but returned to Hove in 2006 to act as Matt Prior's understudy. He performed well for Sussex, including a career-best 123 against Yorkshire at Hove but the emergence of Ben Brown meant Hodd's chances became fewer and he joined Yorkshire in August 2012 on a temporary contract after Jonny Bairstow's call-up to England. His performances earned him a two-year contract, which he signed at the end of 2012

Batting	Mat	Inns	NO	Runs	HS	Ave	SR	100	50	Ct	St
First-class	61	89	15	2097	123	28.33	43.61	4	10	131	12
List A	42	33	9	566	91	23.58		0	1	34	8
Twenty20	47	25	4	253	26	12.04	103.26	0	0	22	10
Bowling	**Inns**	**Balls**	**Runs**	**Wkts**	**BBI**	**BBM**	**Ave**	**Econ**	**SR**	**5w**	**10**
First-class	61	10	7	0	-	-	-	4.20	-	0	0
List A	42	-	-	-	-	-	-	-	-	-	-
Twenty20	47	-	-	-	-	-	-	-	-	-	-

DAN HODGSON RHB WK

FULL NAME: Daniel Mark Hodgson
BORN: February 26, 1990, Northallerton, Yorkshire
SQUAD NO: 18
HEIGHT: 5ft 7in
NICKNAME: Hodgy
EDUCATION: Richmond School; Leeds University
TEAMS: Leeds/Bradford MCCU, Mountaineers, Yorkshire, Yorkshire 2nd XI
CAREER: First-class: 2012; List A: 2012; T20: 2012

BEST BATTING: 94* Mountaineers vs Southern Rocks, Mutare, 2013

CAREER HIGHLIGHTS? Signing for Yorkshire
CRICKETING HEROES? Shane Warne, Kumar Sangakkara
NON-CRICKETING HEROES? My parents, Alan Shearer, The Rock, Jay-Z
BEST PLAYER IN COUNTY CRICKET? Marcus Trescothick
TIPS FOR THE TOP? Ben Slater, Tom Craddock
FAVOURITE TV? Match Of The Day, One Tree Hill, House
FAVOURITE FILM? Man On Fire, Role Models, Inception
FAVOURITE BOOK? The Da Vinci Code
DREAM HOLIDAY? Anywhere with snow for skiing, or hot with a beach and windsurfing
SURPRISING SKILL? Fire juggling
FANTASY SLIP CORDON? Keeper: Me, 1st: Sonny Bill Williams, 2nd: P Diddy, 3rd: Peter Griffin, Gully: David Attenborough

Batting	Mat	Inns	NO	Runs	HS	Ave	SR	100	50	Ct	St
First-class	10	19	2	431	94*	25.35	48.48	0	4	31	2
List A	6	4	1	43	24	14.33	81.13	0	0	7	2
Twenty20	7	5	1	48	18	12.00	77.41	0	0	5	0
Bowling	**Inns**	**Balls**	**Runs**	**Wkts**	**BBI**	**BBM**	**Ave**	**Econ**	**SR**	**5w**	**10**
First-class	10	-	-	-	-	-	-	-	-	-	-
List A	6	-	-	-	-	-	-	-	-	-	-
Twenty20	7	-	-	-	-	-	-	-	-	-	-

MICHAEL HOGAN

RHB RFM

FULL NAME: Michael Garry Hogan
BORN: May 31, 1981, Newcastle, New South Wales, Australia
SQUAD NO: 31
TEAMS: New South Wales Country, New South Wales Second XI, Western Australia
CAREER: First-class: 2009; List A: 2009; T20: 2010

BEST BATTING: 43* Western Australia vs Queensland, Brisbane, 2013
BEST BOWLING: 6-70 Western Australia vs Tasmania, Hobart, 2010

TWITTER FEED: @Hoges31
NOTES: Hogan was initially due to join Glamorgan for the last two months of the 2012 season, but eventually saw out the final year of his contract with Western Australia. Now retired from cricket in Australia, he adds experience to the Glamorgan seam attack for 2013. Made his state debut for Western Australia in 2009 at the age of 28

Batting	Mat	Inns	NO	Runs	HS	Ave	SR	100	50	Ct	St
First-class	34	52	18	508	43*	14.94	99.41	0	0	13	0
List A	25	8	3	67	27	13.40	79.76	0	0	8	0
Twenty20	14	4	2	13	5*	6.50	72.22	0	0	4	0
Bowling	**Inns**	**Balls**	**Runs**	**Wkts**	**BBI**	**BBM**	**Ave**	**Econ**	**SR**	**5w**	**10**
First-class	34	7419	3440	120	6/70	9/86	28.66	2.78	61.8	4	0
List A	25	1450	1130	35	5/44	5/44	32.28	4.67	41.4	1	0
Twenty20	14	300	394	11	4/26	4/26	35.81	7.88	27.2	0	0

KYLE HOGG LHB RFM W1

FULL NAME: Kyle William Hogg
BORN: July 2, 1983, Birmingham, Warwickshire
SQUAD NO: 22
HEIGHT: 6ft 4in
NICKNAME: Hoggy, Boss
EDUCATION: Saddleworth High School
TEAMS: England Under-19s, Lancashire, Otago
CAREER: First-class: 2001; List A: 2001; T20: 2003

BEST BATTING: 88 Lancashire vs Yorkshire, Manchester, 2010
BEST BOWLING: 7-28 Lancashire vs Hampshire, Southampton, 2011
COUNTY CAPS: 2007 (Worcestershire); 2010 (Lancashire)

FAMILY TIES? My dad [Willie Hogg of Lancashire and Warwickshire] and granddad [Sonny Ramadhin of West Indies, Lancashire and Trinidad] played
WHO WOULD PLAY YOU IN A FILM OF YOUR LIFE? Denzel Washington
CAREER HIGHLIGHTS? County Championship win in 2011
MOST MARKED CHARACTERISTIC? I'm laid-back
BEST PLAYER IN COUNTY CRICKET? Marcus Trescothick
TIP FOR THE TOP? Simon Kerrigan
IF YOU WEREN'T A CRICKETER? Asking: "Would you like fries with that, sir?"
DESERT ISLAND DISC? Impossible to pick. Maybe The Smiths
FAVOURITE TV? The Crime Channel
CRICKETING HEROES? Andrew Flintoff, Curtly Ambrose, Brian Lara
NON-CRICKETING HEROES? Too many musicians to mention
ACCOMPLISHMENTS? Having a milk-round for five years at school
WHEN YOU RETIRE? Work in the music industry as a rep
SURPRISING FACT? I never get in lifts (after two bad experiences)
TWITTER FEED: @kylehogg22

Batting	Mat	Inns	NO	Runs	HS	Ave	SR	100	50	Ct	St
First-class	90	116	21	2355	88	24.78	58.14	0	15	19	0
List A	130	80	23	950	66*	16.66	69.44	0	1	22	0
Twenty20	28	18	4	226	44	16.14	137.80	0	0	5	0
Bowling	**Inns**	**Balls**	**Runs**	**Wkts**	**BBI**	**BBM**	**Ave**	**Econ**	**SR**	**5w**	**10**
First-class	90	11908	6154	193	7/28		31.88	3.10	61.6	4	1
List A	130	4902	3936	133	4/20	4/20	29.59	4.81	36.8	0	0
Twenty20	28	378	564	16	2/10	2/10	35.25	8.95	23.6	0	0

MATTHEW HOGGARD RHB RFM W3

FULL NAME: Matthew James Hoggard
BORN: December 31, 1976, Leeds, Yorkshire
SQUAD NO: 77
HEIGHT: 6ft 2in
NICKNAME: Oggie, Hoggy
EDUCATION: Pudsey Grangefield School
TEAMS: England, Free State, Leicestershire, Yorkshire
CAREER: Test: 2000; ODI: 2001; First-class: 1996; List A: 1998; T20: 2004

BEST BATTING: 89* Yorkshire vs Glamorgan, Leeds, 2004
BEST BOWLING: 7-49 Yorkshire vs Somerset, Leeds, 2003
COUNTY CAPS: 2000 (Yorkshire); 2010 (Leicestershire); BENEFIT YEAR: 2008 (Yorkshire)

TWITTER FEED: @Hoggy602
NOTES: Took 7-63 vs New Zealand in the first Test at Christchurch 2001/02, the best innings return by an England pace bowler in Tests vs New Zealand. Took a hat-trick in the third Test vs West Indies at Bridgetown 2003/04. His international awards include Man of the [Test] Series vs Bangladesh 2003/04 and Man of the Match in the fourth Test vs South Africa at Johannesburg 2004/05 (5-144/7-61) and in the first Test vs India at Nagpur 2005/06 (6-57). Appointed MBE in 2006 New Year Honours as part of the 2005 Ashes-winning England team. Took 200th Test wicket in the first Test vs Sri Lanka at Lord's 2006. Took 237th Test wicket in the fourth Test vs West Indies at Riverside 2007 to move into sixth place in the England list of Test wicket-takers, although he has since been passed by James Anderson. Having had his Yorkshire contract terminated in October 2009, he joined Leicestershire the following month as their new captain for 2010. He handed over the four-day captaincy to Ramnaresh Sarwan last December

Batting	Mat	Inns	NO	Runs	HS	Ave	SR	100	50	Ct	St
Tests	67	92	27	473	38	7.27	22.63	0	0	24	0
ODIs	26	6	2	17	7	4.25	56.66	0	0	5	0
First-class	232	294	91	1833	89*	9.02		0	4	62	0
List A	150	49	25	144	23	6.00		0	0	18	0
Twenty20	54	10	4	56	18	9.33	151.35	0	0	8	0
Bowling	**Inns**	**Balls**	**Runs**	**Wkts**	**BBI**	**BBM**	**Ave**	**Econ**	**SR**	**5w**	**10**
Tests	67	13909	7564	248	7/61	12/205	30.50	3.26	56.0	7	1
ODIs	26	1306	1152	32	5/49	5/49	36.00	5.29	40.8	1	0
First-class	232	41323	21194	770	7/49		27.52	3.07	53.6	25	1
List A	150	6932	5273	205	5/28	5/28	25.72	4.56	33.8	4	0
Twenty20	54	1073	1480	50	3/19	3/19	29.60	8.27	21.4	0	0

PAUL HORTON RHB RM R3

FULL NAME: Paul James Horton
BORN: September 20, 1982, Sydney, Australia
SQUAD NO: 20
HEIGHT: 5ft 10in
NICKNAME: Horts, Lefty, Aussie
EDUCATION: Colo High School, Sydney; Broadgreen Comp Liverpool; St Margaret's High School
TEAMS: Lancashire, Lancashire 2nd XI, Matabeleland Tuskers
CAREER: First-class: 2003; List A: 2003; T20: 2005

BEST BATTING: 209 Matabeleland Tuskers vs Southern Rocks, Masvingo, 2011
COUNTY CAP: 2007

CAREER HIGHLIGHTS? Nothing can top winning the County Championship in 2011 with Lancashire but every time I score a first-class hundred is pretty special. Back-to-back Logan Cup trophies with Matebeleland Tuskers in 2010/11 and 2011/12
CRICKETING HEROES? Mark Waugh, Dean Jones, Brian Lara
NON-CRICKETING HEROES? Roger Federer, Robbie Fowler
BEST PLAYER IN COUNTY CRICKET? Marcus Trescothick
TIPS FOR THE TOP? Simon Kerrigan, Ben Stokes
IF YOU WEREN'T A CRICKETER? Something in a suit!
WHEN RAIN STOPS PLAY? Ranges from hitting balls to talking rubbish in the dressing room
FAVOURITE TV? Location, Location, Location
FAVOURITE FILM? Notting Hill
ACCOMPLISHMENTS? Finished school in one piece!
SURPRISING FACT? I once stacked shelves in Sainsbury's. I was once held as an illegal immigrant!
FANTASY SLIP CORDON? Keeper: Tiger Woods, 1st: Myself, 2nd: Robbie Fowler, 3rd: Nelson Mandela, Gully: Wonder Woman
TWITTER FEED: @PJHorton20

Batting	Mat	Inns	NO	Runs	HS	Ave	SR	100	50	Ct	St
First-class	126	211	19	7375	209	38.41	48.54	15	40	135	1
List A	89	80	10	2148	111*	30.68		2	12	32	0
Twenty20	60	56	11	1037	71	23.04	105.06	0	2	22	0
Bowling	**Inns**	**Balls**	**Runs**	**Wkts**	**BBI**	**BBM**	**Ave**	**Econ**	**SR**	**5w**	**10**
First-class	126	18	16	0	-	-	-	5.33	-	0	0
List A	89	-	-	-	-	-	-	-	-	-	-
Twenty20	60	-	-	-	-	-	-	-	-	-	-

DAN HOUSEGO RHB LB

FULL NAME: Daniel Mark Housego
BORN: October 12, 1988, Windsor, Berkshire
SQUAD NO: 3
HEIGHT: 5ft 9in
NICKNAME: Housey
EDUCATION: The Oratory School, Reading; Moulsford Prep School
TEAMS: Berkshire, Gloucestershire, Gloucestershire 2nd XI, Middlesex, Middlesex 2nd XI
CAREER: First-class: 2008; List A: 2012; T20: 2008

BEST BATTING: 104 Middlesex vs Sri Lanka, Uxbridge, 2011

WHO WOULD PLAY YOU IN A FILM OF YOUR LIFE? Denzel Washington
CAREER HIGHLIGHTS? Scoring 132 against South Africa in August 2012. Hundred against Sri Lanka in July 2011. T20 victory over Somerset at Taunton in June 2012
SUPERSTITIONS? I have to drink a pint of water as soon as I wake up on game day
BEST PLAYER IN COUNTY CRICKET? Marcus Trescothick
TIPS FOR THE TOP? James Fuller, Chris Dent
IF YOU WEREN'T A CRICKETER? Personal trainer or cricket coach
DESERT ISLAND DISC? Emeli Sande – Clown
FAVOURITE TV? Only Fools And Horses
CRICKETING HEROES? Graeme Smith
NON-CRICKETING HEROES? It was Lance Armstrong but not anymore! Jose Mourinho, as he's fearless
ACCOMPLISHMENTS? My carp fishing record is 22lb 6oz
WHEN YOU RETIRE? Lots of fishing and golf
SURPRISING FACT? I don't drink fizzy or juice drinks, just water
FANTASY SLIP CORDON? Keeper: Peter Kay, 1st: Cheryl Cole, 2nd: Mila Kunis, 3rd: Alan Carr

Batting	Mat	Inns	NO	Runs	HS	Ave	SR	100	50	Ct	St
First-class	25	45	3	1153	104	27.45	45.62	2	4	12	0
List A	7	7	1	269	132	44.83	83.80	1	1	2	0
Twenty20	9	8	2	164	59*	27.33	114.68	0	1	2	0
Bowling	**Inns**	**Balls**	**Runs**	**Wkts**	**BBI**	**BBM**	**Ave**	**Econ**	**SR**	**5w**	**10**
First-class	25	7	17	0	-	-	-	14.57	-	0	0
List A	7	-	-	-	-	-	-	-	-	-	-
Twenty20	9	-	-	-	-	-	-	-	-	-	-

BENNY HOWELL RHB RM

FULL NAME: Benny Alexander Cameron Howell
BORN: October 5, 1988, Bordeaux, France
SQUAD NO: 16
HEIGHT: 5ft 11in
NICKNAME: Trowel, Max George
EDUCATION: Oratory School
TEAMS: Gloucestershire, Gloucestershire 2nd XI, Hampshire, Hampshire 2nd XI, Unicorns
CAREER: First-class: 2011; List A: 2010; T20: 2011

BEST BATTING: 83* Gloucestershire vs Yorkshire, Scarborough, 2012
BEST BOWLING: 2-37 Gloucestershire vs Northamptonshire, Bristol, 2012

FAMILY TIES? My dad John played for Warwickshire at a young age and my brother Nick played for Berkshire when he was young and hits a long ball
CAREER HIGHLIGHTS? Scoring 122 vs Surrey in the CB40. Hampshire and Gloucestershire first-class debuts
MOST MARKED CHARACTERISTIC? Eccentric
BEST PLAYER IN COUNTY CRICKET? Michael Carberry
TIPS FOR THE TOP? Chris Dent, James Fuller, Liam Norwell
IF YOU WEREN'T A CRICKETER? Real tennis or property
DESERT ISLAND DISC? David Gray
BIGGEST DRESSING DOWN YOU'VE RECEIVED? When I went on holiday mid/end season with Hampshire
CRICKETING HEROES? Steve Waugh, Sachin Tendulkar
NON-CRICKETING HEROES? Nelson Mandela, Mo Farah, my parents
SURPRISING FACT? I do magic
FANTASY SLIP CORDON? Keeper: Keith Lemon, 1st: Myself, 2nd: Megan Fox, 3rd: Derren Brown, Gully: Jesus

Batting	Mat	Inns	NO	Runs	HS	Ave	SR	100	50	Ct	St
First-class	14	26	3	568	83*	24.69	51.07	0	4	5	0
List A	24	20	4	643	122	40.18	88.56	1	4	8	0
Twenty20	19	16	8	200	55*	25.00	111.73	0	1	4	0
Bowling	**Inns**	**Balls**	**Runs**	**Wkts**	**BBI**	**BBM**	**Ave**	**Econ**	**SR**	**5w**	**10**
First-class	14	562	266	6	2/37	2/37	44.33	2.83	93.6	0	0
List A	24	252	217	6	2/26	2/26	36.16	5.16	42.0	0	0
Twenty20	19	53	80	3	2/14	2/14	26.66	9.05	17.6	0	0

ALEX HUGHES RHB RM

FULL NAME: Alex Lloyd Hughes
BORN: September 29, 1991, Wordsley, Staffordshire
SQUAD NO: 18
TEAMS: Derbyshire, Derbyshire 2nd XI, Staffordshire
CAREER: List A: 2012; T20: 2011

NOTES: A top order batsman who can bowl right-arm seam, Hughes made his first team debut for Derbyshire in their 2011 FL t20 fixture against Yorkshire. In 2012, he made seven CB40 appearances and played three more T20 games. At the end of the 2012 season, Derbyshire transferred his summer contract to a three-year deal. Yet to make his first-class debut

Batting	Mat	Inns	NO	Runs	HS	Ave	SR	100	50	Ct	St
List A	7	4	2	52	37*	26.00	85.24	0	0	1	0
Twenty20	4	3	1	13	11*	6.50	76.47	0	0	1	0
Bowling	**Inns**	**Balls**	**Runs**	**Wkts**	**BBI**	**BBM**	**Ave**	**Econ**	**SR**	**5w**	**10**
List A	7	198	151	3	1/23	1/23	50.33	4.57	66.0	0	0
Twenty20	4	60	90	0	-	-	-	9.00	-	0	0

CHESNEY HUGHES

LHB SLA

FULL NAME: Chesney Francis Hughes
BORN: January 20, 1991, Anguilla
SQUAD NO: 22
TEAMS: Anguilla, Derbyshire, Leeward Islands, West Indies Under-19s
CAREER: First-class: 2010; List A: 2007; T20: 2006

BEST BATTING: 167 Derbyshire vs Glamorgan, Derby, 2011
BEST BOWLING: 2-9 Derbyshire vs Middlesex, Derby, 2011

NOTES: After playing youth cricket for Leeward Islands, Hughes made his senior debut for Anguilla in the Stanford T20 competition in 2006. In 2009, he left for England, where he found a spot in Derbyshire's 2nd XI. His first-class debut came in 2010 against Middlesex – becoming only the third Anguillan to play county cricket – where he scored a gutsy 41. Four games later and he had his maiden first-class century, at the age of 19. In June of that year he was handed a three-year contract, and enjoyed good seasons in 2010 and 2011 before finding his chances limited last year

Batting	Mat	Inns	NO	Runs	HS	Ave	SR	100	50	Ct	St
First-class	27	49	2	1553	167	33.04	55.30	4	6	25	0
List A	52	49	1	1090	81	22.70		0	9	9	0
Twenty20	48	45	2	837	65	19.46	108.27	0	3	11	0
Bowling	**Inns**	**Balls**	**Runs**	**Wkts**	**BBI**	**BBM**	**Ave**	**Econ**	**SR**	**5w**	**10**
First-class	27	714	451	10	2/9	2/17	45.10	3.78	71.4	0	0
List A	52	877	754	22	5/29	5/29	34.27	5.15	39.8	1	0
Twenty20	48	528	642	23	4/23	4/23	27.91	7.29	22.9	0	0

GEMAAL HUSSAIN

RHB RMF W1

FULL NAME: Gemaal Maqsood Hussain
BORN: October 10, 1983, Waltham Forest, London
SQUAD NO: 27
HEIGHT: 6ft 4in
NICKNAME: G Man, Big G
EDUCATION: Top Valley Comprehensive, Nottingham; Leeds University
TEAMS: Essex 2nd XI, Gloucestershire, Leeds/Bradford MCCU, Somerset, Sussex 2nd XI, Worcestershire
CAREER: First-class: 2009; List A: 2009; T20: 2009

BEST BATTING: 42 Somerset vs Lancashire, Liverpool, 2011
BEST BOWLING: 6-33 Somerset vs Worcestershire, Taunton, 2011
COUNTY CAP: 2009 (Gloucestershire)

FAMILY TIES? My cousin is coach of the Singapore cricket team
CAREER HIGHLIGHTS? Finishing the 2010 season as highest wicket-taker for any English qualified player. It's a highlight because it was my first Championship season. Getting five wickets playing at Lord's for the first time
CRICKETING HEROES? Imran Khan, Wasim Akram, Shoaib Akhtar, Sachin Tendulkar, Saqlain Mushtaq, Sir Vivian Richards
NON-CRICKETING HEROES? Muhammad Ali
BEST PLAYER IN COUNTY CRICKET? Marcus Trescothick
TIP FOR THE TOP? Jos Buttler
IF YOU WEREN'T A CRICKETER? Working in the sports industry
WHEN RAIN STOPS PLAY? Go to the gym and pretend I'm working out, watch the boys play on their iPads
FAVOURITE TV? Top Gear, Friends, The Simpsons and, of course, The Inbetweeners
FAVOURITE FILM? The Pursuit Of Happyness

Batting	Mat	Inns	NO	Runs	HS	Ave	SR	100	50	Ct	St
First-class	31	49	16	299	42	9.06	27.81	0	0	4	0
List A	8	3	3	35	18*	-	125.00	0	0	2	0
Twenty20	18	12	4	35	8	4.37	57.37	0	0	4	0
Bowling	**Inns**	**Balls**	**Runs**	**Wkts**	**BBI**	**BBM**	**Ave**	**Econ**	**SR**	**5w**	**10**
First-class	31	4731	2976	104	6/33	9/98	28.61	3.77	45.4	4	0
List A	8	290	303	9	2/17	2/17	33.66	6.26	32.2	0	0
Twenty20	18	354	489	21	3/22	3/22	23.28	8.28	16.8	0	0

DAVID HUSSEY RHB OB R4

FULL NAME: David John Hussey
BORN: July 15, 1977, Mt Lawley, Perth, Australia
SQUAD NO: 29
HEIGHT: 5ft 9in
NICKNAME: Huss, Bomber
TEAMS: Australia, Australia A, Kings XI Punjab, Kolkata Knight Riders, Melbourne Stars, Northern Districts, Nottinghamshire, Sussex Cricket Board, Victoria
CAREER: ODI: 2008; T20I: 2008; First-class: 2003; List A: 2001; T20: 2004

BEST BATTING: 275 Nottinghamshire vs Essex, Nottingham, 2007
BEST BOWLING: 4-105 Nottinghamshire vs Hampshire, Nottingham, 2005
COUNTY CAP: 2004

FAMILY TIES? My brother Michael played for Australia
TWITTER FEED: @DHussey29
NOTES: Joins Notts for an eighth stint as overseas player, arriving in June to replace Ed Cowan who is likely to feature in the Ashes. Important one-day and T20 player for Australia in recent times – with busy middle order runs and useful off spin – but still no Test call-up

Batting	Mat	Inns	NO	Runs	HS	Ave	SR	100	50	Ct	St
ODIs	69	61	6	1796	111	32.65	90.70	1	14	29	0
T20Is	39	36	3	756	88*	22.90	121.34	0	3	24	0
First-class	167	262	26	12473	275	52.85	70.49	41	55	226	0
List A	242	224	32	7597	140*	39.56		10	52	115	0
Twenty20	198	190	34	4821	100*	30.90	135.11	1	26	108	0
Bowling	**Inns**	**Balls**	**Runs**	**Wkts**	**BBI**	**BBM**	**Ave**	**Econ**	**SR**	**5w**	**10**
ODIs	69	802	698	18	4/21	4/21	38.77	5.22	44.5	0	0
T20Is	39	361	392	19	3/25	3/25	20.63	6.51	19.0	0	0
First-class	167	2734	1674	28	4/105		59.78	3.67	97.6	0	0
List A	242	2203	1934	47	4/21	4/21	41.14	5.26	46.8	0	0
Twenty20	198	1247	1546	57	3/25	3/25	27.12	7.43	21.8	0	0

BRETT HUTTON RHB RM

FULL NAME: Brett Alan Hutton
BORN: February 6, 1993, Doncaster, Yorkshire
SQUAD NO: 26
HEIGHT: 6ft
NICKNAME: Hutts
EDUCATION: Worksop College
TEAMS: England Under-19s, Nottinghamshire, Nottinghamshire 2nd XI
CAREER: First-class: 2011; List A: 2011

BEST BATTING: 9 Nottinghamshire vs MCC, Abu Dhabi, 2011

WHO WOULD PLAY YOU IN A FILM OF YOUR LIFE? James McAvoy
CAREER HIGHLIGHTS? Playing for England U19, Notts debut vs MCC in Abu Dhabi
MOST MARKED CHARACTERISTIC? Stubble
BEST PLAYER IN COUNTY CRICKET? Andre Adams
TIPS FOR THE TOP? Sam Wood, Sam Kelsall
IF YOU WEREN'T A CRICKETER? Window cleaner
DESERT ISLAND DISC? Nicki Minaj – Pink Friday
FAVOURITE TV? Emmerdale
CRICKETING HEROES? Chris Tolley, Harold Larwood
NON-CRICKETING HEROES? Lee Westwood
SURPRISING FACT? I've got my own window cleaning round
FANTASY SLIP CORDON? Keeper: George Formby, 1st: Scarlett Johansson, 2nd: Tommy Johnson, 3rd: Stevie Wonder, 4th: Holly Willoughby

Batting	Mat	Inns	NO	Runs	HS	Ave	SR	100	50	Ct	St
First-class	1	2	0	9	9	4.50	50.00	0	0	1	0
List A	2	2	1	20	17*	20.00	117.64	0	0	1	0
Bowling	**Inns**	**Balls**	**Runs**	**Wkts**	**BBI**	**BBM**	**Ave**	**Econ**	**SR**	**5w**	**10**
First-class	1	108	69	0	-	-	-	3.83	-	0	0
List A	2	84	101	1	1/60	1/60	101.00	7.21	84.0	0	0

ANTHONY IRELAND RHB RMF

FULL NAME: Anthony John Ireland
BORN: August 30, 1984, Masvingo, Zimbabwe
SQUAD NO: 88
HEIGHT: 6ft 1in
EDUCATION: Plumtree High School, Matabeleland
TEAMS: Zimbabwe, Gloucestershire, Gloucestershire 2nd XI, Middlesex, Midlands, Southern Rocks
CAREER: ODI: 2005; T20I: 2006; First-class: 2003; List A: 2004; T20: 2006

BEST BATTING: 29 Middlesex vs Essex, Chelmsford, 2011
BEST BOWLING: 7-36 Zimbabwe A vs Bangladesh A, Mirpur, 2006
COUNTY CAP: 2007 (Gloucestershire)

NOTES: Leicestershire signed Ireland on a one-year contract in March following his release by Middlesex last summer. He arrived in England in 2004 to play club cricket after the player rebellion in Zimbabwe but returned to represent his homeland in the 2007 World Cup, taking the wicket of his new skipper Ramnaresh Sarwan against the West Indies in what proved to be his last ODI. He retired from international cricket after the tournament to take up a contract at Gloucestershire as a Kolpak player. He enjoyed his best season to date in 2010, taking 36 first-class wickets at 21.77, which prompted Middlesex to snap him up on a two-year deal. He featured only sporadically for them though, and after playing just three first-class matches in the space of two seasons he parted company with the club

Batting	Mat	Inns	NO	Runs	HS	Ave	SR	100	50	Ct	St
ODIs	26	13	5	30	8*	3.75	29.70	0	0	2	0
T20Is	1	1	1	2	2*	-	66.66	0	0	0	0
First-class	41	61	17	257	29	5.84	29.84	0	0	10	0
List A	71	34	16	116	22*	6.44	43.12	0	0	9	0
Twenty20	40	14	7	40	8*	5.71	65.57	0	0	10	0
Bowling	**Inns**	**Balls**	**Runs**	**Wkts**	**BBI**	**BBM**	**Ave**	**Econ**	**SR**	**5w**	**10**
ODIs	26	1326	1115	38	3/41	3/41	29.34	5.04	34.8	0	0
T20Is	1	18	33	1	1/33	1/33	33.00	11.00	18.0	0	0
First-class	41	6030	3715	122	7/36		30.45	3.69	49.4	4	1
List A	71	2995	2724	90	4/16	4/16	30.26	5.45	33.2	0	0
Twenty20	40	719	1075	42	3/7	3/7	25.59	8.97	17.1	0	0

NICK JAMES LHB SLA

FULL NAME: Nicholas Alexander James
BORN: September 17, 1986, Sandwell, West Midlands
SQUAD NO: 11
HEIGHT: 5ft 10in
NICKNAME: Jaymo
EDUCATION: King Edward VI Aston
TEAMS: England Under-19s, Glamorgan, Staffordshire, Wales Minor Counties, Warwickshire, Warwickshire 2nd XI
CAREER: First-class: 2008; List A: 2006; T20: 2007

BEST BATTING: 83 Glamorgan vs Oxford MCCU, Oxford, 2012
BEST BOWLING: 2-28 Glamorgan vs Kent, Canterbury, 2011

FAMILY TIES? My dad plays club cricket for Aldridge in the South Staffordshire Premier League
CAREER HIGHLIGHTS? Glamorgan 1st XI debut vs West Indies A
SUPERSTITIONS? Right pad on first, but I always forget
CRICKETING HEROES? Brian Lara, Chris Cooke, Nick Knight
NON-CRICKETING HEROES? Muhammad Ali, Remi Gaillard
BEST PLAYER IN COUNTY CRICKET? Marcus Trescothick
TIPS FOR THE TOP? James Harris, Will Owen
FAVOURITE TV? I'm Alan Partridge
FAVOURITE FILM? Dumb And Dumber
FAVOURITE BOOK? The Sun
DREAM HOLIDAY? Menorca
ACCOMPLISHMENTS? Top one per cent in the world on Call Of Duty

Batting	Mat	Inns	NO	Runs	HS	Ave	SR	100	50	Ct	St
First-class	15	27	1	622	83	23.92	40.49	0	2	4	0
List A	20	13	2	212	43	19.27	86.53	0	0	3	0
Twenty20	6	4	1	33	13	11.00	137.50	0	0	5	0
Bowling	**Inns**	**Balls**	**Runs**	**Wkts**	**BBI**	**BBM**	**Ave**	**Econ**	**SR**	**5w**	**10**
First-class	15	270	154	6	2/28	4/79	25.66	3.42	45.0	0	0
List A	20	396	324	15	3/36	3/36	21.60	4.90	26.4	0	0
Twenty20	6	90	92	4	2/22	2/22	23.00	6.13	22.5	0	0

PHIL JAQUES LHB LM R4 MVP68

FULL NAME: Philip Anthony Jaques
BORN: May 3, 1979, Wollongong, Australia
SQUAD NO: 2
HEIGHT: 6ft 1in
NICKNAME: Pro, Wingers
TEAMS: Australia, Hobart Hurriances, New South Wales, Northamptonshire, Worcestershire, Yorkshire
CAREER: Test: 2005; ODI: 2006; First-class: 2001; List A: 2000; T20: 2003

BEST BATTING: 244 Worcestershire vs Essex, Chelmsford, 2006
COUNTY CAPS: 2003 (Northamptonshire); 2005 (Yorkshire)

FAMILY TIES? My dad used to play league cricket in the UK
CAREER HIGHLIGHTS? Boxing Day Test match debut at the MCG. Being part of record-breaking side for the most Test match wins in a row
SUPERSTITIONS? I always put my gear on in a particular order and dislike people touching my bat before I go out to the middle
MOST MARKED CHARACTERISTIC? My chicken wing running style, I'm told
BEST PLAYER IN COUNTY CRICKET? Chris Rogers
TIP FOR THE TOP? Gary Ballance
DESERT ISLAND DISC? Some reggae to get me into the island mood
FAVOURITE TV? Dexter or Homeland
CRICKETING HEROES? Mike Hussey and Steve Waugh
NON-CRICKETING HEROES? Roger Federer
ACCOMPLISHMENTS? My wife and son, Samuel
TWITTER FEED: @philjaques

Batting	Mat	Inns	NO	Runs	HS	Ave	SR	100	50	Ct	St
Tests	11	19	0	902	150	47.47	54.23	3	6	7	0
ODIs	6	6	0	125	94	20.83	71.02	0	1	3	0
First-class	175	305	12	14371	244	49.04		40	67	141	0
List A	159	156	10	5969	171*	40.88	90.01	14	31	43	0
Twenty20	77	74	8	1929	92	29.22	125.17	0	12	17	0
Bowling	**Inns**	**Balls**	**Runs**	**Wkts**	**BBI**	**BBM**	**Ave**	**Econ**	**SR**	**5w**	**10**
Tests	11	-	-	-	-	-	-	-	-	-	-
ODIs	6	-	-	-	-	-	-	-	-	-	-
First-class	175	68	87	0	-	-	-	7.67	-	0	0
List A	159	18	19	0	-	-	-	6.33	-	0	0
Twenty20	77	6	15	0	-	-	-	15.00	-	0	0

ATEEQ JAVID RHB RM

WARWICKSHIRE

FULL NAME: Ateeq Javid
BORN: October 15, 1991, Birmingham, Warwickshire
SQUAD NO: 17
HEIGHT: 5ft 10in
EDUCATION: Aston Manor School, Birmingham
TEAMS: England Under-19s, Warwickshire, Warwickshire 2nd XI
CAREER: First-class: 2009; List A: 2011

BEST BATTING: 48 Warwickshire vs Yorkshire, Leeds, 2010

CAREER HIGHLIGHTS? Playing against England for Warwickshire ahead of the 2009 Ashes
CRICKETING HEROES? Sachin Tendulkar
DREAM HOLIDAY? Las Vegas
GUILTY PLEASURES? Coca-Cola
TWITTER FEED: @ateeqjavid2000

Batting	Mat	Inns	NO	Runs	HS	Ave	SR	100	50	Ct	St
First-class	8	14	0	177	48	12.64	30.30	0	0	6	0
List A	3	3	0	62	34	20.66	62.62	0	0	0	0
Bowling	**Inns**	**Balls**	**Runs**	**Wkts**	**BBI**	**BBM**	**Ave**	**Econ**	**SR**	**5w**	**10**
First-class	8	78	78	0	-	-	-	6.00	-	0	0
List A	3	24	27	0	-	-	-	6.75	-	0	0

KEATON JENNINGS LHB RMF

FULL NAME: Keaton Kent Jennings
BORN: June 19, 1992, Johannesburg, South Africa
SQUAD NO: 1
HEIGHT: 6ft 4in
NICKNAME: Jet
EDUCATION: King Edward VII School; University of South Africa
TEAMS: Durham, Durham 2nd XI, Gauteng, Gauteng Under-19s, South Africa Under-19s
CAREER: First-class: 2011; List A: 2012

BEST BATTING: 77 Gauteng vs KwaZulu-Natal Inland, Johannesburg, 2012
BEST BOWLING: 2-8 Gauteng vs Western Province, Cape Town, 2012

FAMILY TIES? My father, brother and uncle are all involved in cricket
WHO WOULD PLAY YOU IN A FILM OF YOUR LIFE? Chuck Norris
CAREER HIGHLIGHTS? Making my 1st XI debut for Durham
MOST MARKED CHARACTERISTIC? Strength of character
IF YOU WEREN'T A CRICKETER? I would be studying my Accountancy degree full-time
DESERT ISLAND DISC? U2 – The Joshua Tree
FAVOURITE TV? Family Guy
BIGGEST DRESSING DOWN YOU'VE RECEIVED? Our school 1st XI got a rude awakening from our coach Mr Spilhaus on a school tour. I have never seen so many 18 year olds with tears in their eyes before
CRICKETING HEROES? Michael Hussey, Jacques Kallis
NON-CRICKETING HEROES? Trevor Noah
ACCOMPLISHMENTS? Achieving six A grades in my final school year
WHEN YOU RETIRE? Play loads of golf and have a successful family life
SURPRISING FACT? I eat a huge amount of food for a skinny guy
TWITTER FEED: @JetJennings

Batting	Mat	Inns	NO	Runs	HS	Ave	SR	100	50	Ct	St
First-class	11	18	0	441	77	24.50	44.36	0	4	2	0
List A	6	6	1	286	71*	57.20	67.77	0	4	0	0
Bowling	**Inns**	**Balls**	**Runs**	**Wkts**	**BBI**	**BBM**	**Ave**	**Econ**	**SR**	**5w**	**10**
First-class	11	66	36	2	2/8	2/8	18.00	3.27	33.0	0	0
List A	6	18	11	0	-	-	-	3.66	-	0	0

TOM JEWELL RHB RFM

SURREY

FULL NAME: Thomas Melvin Jewell
BORN: January 13, 1991, Reading, Berkshire
SQUAD NO: 8
HEIGHT: 6ft 5in
NICKNAME: TJ, Jeweller, Jewellpig
EDUCATION: Bradfield College
TEAMS: Surrey, Surrey 2nd XI
CAREER: First-class: 2008; List A: 2009

BEST BATTING: 70 Surrey vs Lancashire, Liverpool, 2012
BEST BOWLING: 5-49 Surrey vs Cambridge MCCU, Cambridge, 2011

WHO WOULD PLAY YOU IN A FILM OF YOUR LIFE? Javier Bardem
CAREER HIGHLIGHTS? My first-class debut in 2007, fielding for England in Test cricket and my most recent County Championship game against Lancashire [70 and 1-24]
MOST MARKED CHARACTERISTIC? My nose
BEST PLAYER IN COUNTY CRICKET? Nick Compton
TIPS FOR THE TOP? Jason Roy, Rory Burns and Matt Dunn
IF YOU WEREN'T A CRICKETER? I would be finishing up a degree
DESERT ISLAND DISC? Macklemore – The Heist
FAVOURITE TV? Homes Under The Hammer
BIGGEST DRESSING DOWN YOU'VE RECEIVED? From Mick Powell in a Surrey U17 game. He never held back
CRICKETING HEROES? Viv Richards
NON-CRICKETING HEROES? Steve Jobs
WHEN YOU RETIRE? Commercial property/property development
FANTASY SLIP CORDON? Keeper: Micky Flanagan, 1st: Sean Lock, 2nd: Jimmy Carr, 3rd: Jon Richardson
TWITTER FEED: @TOMJEWELL8

Batting	Mat	Inns	NO	Runs	HS	Ave	SR	100	50	Ct	St
First-class	8	7	1	185	70	30.83	49.33	0	2	2	0
List A	2	2	1	1	1	1.00	11.11	0	0	0	0
Bowling	**Inns**	**Balls**	**Runs**	**Wkts**	**BBI**	**BBM**	**Ave**	**Econ**	**SR**	**5w**	**10**
First-class	8	700	374	16	5/49	5/49	23.37	3.20	43.7	1	0
List A	2	36	56	0	-	-	-	9.33	-	0	0

MICHAEL JOHNSON RHB WK

FULL NAME: Michael Anthony Johnson
BORN: August 11, 1988, Perth, Australia
SQUAD NO: 33
HEIGHT: 5ft 10in
TEAMS: Hampshire 2nd XI, Kent 2nd XI, Northamptonshire 2nd XI, Somerset 2nd XI, Surrey 2nd XI, Western Australia, Worcestershire
CAREER: First-class: 2009; List A: 2008; T20: 2008

BEST BATTING: 53 Western Australia vs Queensland, Perth, 2011

NOTES: Has played 2nd XI cricket for Somerset, Hampshire and most recently for Kent during the 2012 season. The former Australia U19 international holds a dual passport

Batting	Mat	Inns	NO	Runs	HS	Ave	SR	100	50	Ct	St
First-class	10	16	0	200	53	12.50	37.24	0	1	34	2
List A	2	2	0	16	14	8.00	76.19	0	0	2	0
Twenty20	2	2	1	11	8*	11.00	73.33	0	0	0	0
Bowling	**Inns**	**Balls**	**Runs**	**Wkts**	**BBI**	**BBM**	**Ave**	**Econ**	**SR**	**5w**	**10**
First-class	10	-	-	-	-	-	-	-	-	-	-
List A	2	-	-	-	-	-	-	-	-	-	-
Twenty20	2	-	-	-	-	-	-	-	-	-	-

RICHARD JOHNSON — RHB WK

FULL NAME: Richard Matthew Johnson
BORN: September 1, 1988, Solihull, West Midlands
SQUAD NO: 25
HEIGHT: 5ft 10in
NICKNAME: Johnno
EDUCATION: Solihull School
TEAMS: Derbyshire, Herefordshire, Warwickshire, Warwickshire 2nd XI
CAREER: First-class: 2008; List A: 2008; T20: 2009

BEST BATTING: 72 Warwickshire vs Cambridge UCCE, Cambridge, 2008

CAREER HIGHLIGHTS? Winning CB40 final vs Somerset in 2010
SUPERSTITIONS? Packing my bag the same way
CRICKETING HEROES? Keith Piper, Tony Frost, James Foster
NON-CRICKETING HEROES? Jamie Redknapp, Muhammad Ali
BEST PLAYER IN COUNTY CRICKET? Chris Woakes
TIP FOR THE TOP? Ateeq Javid
IF YOU WEREN'T A CRICKETER? Still a student
FAVOURITE TV? Take Me Out
FAVOURITE FILM? Enemy At The Gates
FAVOURITE BOOK? Bounce by Matthew Syed
DREAM HOLIDAY? Las Vegas
GUILTY PLEASURES? Chocolate
SURPRISING FACTS? Take That are my favourite group. I played football for Wolverhampton Wanderers U10 and U13 and like to believe I was quite good. I always listen to music whilst waiting to bat

Batting	Mat	Inns	NO	Runs	HS	Ave	SR	100	50	Ct	St
First-class	13	20	2	325	72	18.05	45.90	0	1	36	2
List A	16	8	3	126	79	25.20	94.73	0	1	11	4
Twenty20	18	5	3	21	14	10.50	100.00	0	0	5	3
Bowling	**Inns**	**Balls**	**Runs**	**Wkts**	**BBI**	**BBM**	**Ave**	**Econ**	**SR**	**5w**	**10**
First-class	13	-	-	-	-	-	-	-	-	-	-
List A	16	-	-	-	-	-	-	-	-	-	-
Twenty20	18	-	-	-	-	-	-	-	-	-	-

ALEX JONES

RHB LFM

FULL NAME: Alexander John Jones
BORN: November 10, 1988, Bridgend
SQUAD NO: 27
HEIGHT: 6ft 2in
NICKNAME: AJ, Spider, Magoo
EDUCATION: Cowbridge Comprehensive; UWIC
TEAMS: Cardiff MCCU, Cardiff UCCE, Glamorgan, Glamorgan 2nd XI, Marylebone Cricket Club Universities, Marylebone Cricket Club Young Cricketers,
CAREER: First-class: 2011; List A: 2010; T20: 2011

BEST BATTING: 26 Glamorgan vs Northamptonshire, Northampton, 2011
BEST BOWLING: 1-50 Glamorgan vs Surrey, The Oval, 2011

CAREER HIGHLIGHTS? Playing and winning at Lord's in the MCCU final for Cardiff
CRICKETING HEROES? Glenn McGrath, Andrew Flintoff, Kevin Pietersen
NON-CRICKETING HEROES? Muhammad Ali, Scott Gibbs
TIPS FOR THE TOP? James Harris, Andrew Salter
IF YOU WEREN'T A CRICKETER? I'd be trying to play rugby!
WHEN RAIN STOPS PLAY? Feet up with a cup of tea enjoying some drivel from the boys
FAVOURITE TV? Dirty Sanchez, Total Wipeout
FAVOURITE FILM? Snatch
FAVOURITE BOOK? The Game
DREAM HOLIDAY? Hawaii
ACCOMPLISHMENTS? Winning Glamorgan golf day 2011
SURPRISING SKILL? Represented Wales in rugby sevens in South Africa, partial to a karaoke night, used to play the trumpet
TWITTER FEED: @AJ_Jones27

Batting	Mat	Inns	NO	Runs	HS	Ave	SR	100	50	Ct	St
First-class	2	3	0	34	26	11.33	48.57	0	0	1	0
List A	5	4	2	9	5	4.50	56.25	0	0	2	0
Twenty20	14	5	3	9	4*	4.50	50.00	0	0	1	0
Bowling	**Inns**	**Balls**	**Runs**	**Wkts**	**BBI**	**BBM**	**Ave**	**Econ**	**SR**	**5w**	**10**
First-class	2	216	158	2	1/50	1/79	79.00	4.38	108.0	0	0
List A	5	180	233	4	1/31	1/31	58.25	7.76	45.0	0	0
Twenty20	14	192	256	15	3/16	3/16	17.06	8.00	12.8	0	0

CHRIS JONES

RHB OB

FULL NAME: Christopher Robert Jones
BORN: November 5, 1990, Harold Wood, Essex
SQUAD NO: 14
HEIGHT: 6ft 2in
NICKNAME: Jonesy, Nan
EDUCATION: Poole Grammar; Richard Huish College; Durham University
TEAMS: Dorset, Durham MCCU, Somerset, Somerset 2nd XI, Somerset Under-15s, Somerset Under-17s
CAREER: First-class: 2010; List A: 2011; T20: 2011

BEST BATTING: 69 Durham MCCU vs Yorkshire, Durham University, 2011
BEST BOWLING: 1-17 Somerset vs Surrey, Taunton, 2012

WHO WOULD PLAY YOU IN A FILM OF YOUR LIFE? Ryan Gosling
CAREER HIGHLIGHTS? Playing in the Champions League in India. Winning the universities competition at Lord's
MOST MARKED CHARACTERISTIC? Nose
BEST PLAYER IN COUNTY CRICKET? Marcus Trescothick
TIPS FOR THE TOP? Craig Overton, Daniel Bell-Drummond
IF YOU WEREN'T A CRICKETER? Lifelong student
DESERT ISLAND DISC? Ben Howard – Kingdom
FAVOURITE TV? QI
BIGGEST DRESSING DOWN YOU'VE RECEIVED? When we lost the U15 national semi-final the coach gave us a pretty hefty spray!
CRICKETING HEROES? Jacques Kallis and Ricky Ponting
NON-CRICKETING HEROES? John Maynard Keynes, Stephen Fry
ACCOMPLISHMENTS? Academic performances, including four A grades at A-Level
SURPRISING FACT? I am an avid supporter of the San Francisco 49ers NFL team
FANTASY SLIP CORDON? Keeper: Peter Schmeichel, 1st: Will Ferrell, 2nd: Jimmy Carr, 3rd: Colin Kaepernick, Gully: Jim Harbaugh

Batting	Mat	Inns	NO	Runs	HS	Ave	SR	100	50	Ct	St
First-class	19	29	1	489	69	17.46	38.05	0	4	10	0
List A	5	4	1	126	45*	42.00	78.75	0	0	0	0
Twenty20	3	3	0	36	16	12.00	138.46	0	0	1	0
Bowling	**Inns**	**Balls**	**Runs**	**Wkts**	**BBI**	**BBM**	**Ave**	**Econ**	**SR**	**5w**	**10**
First-class	19	12	17	1	1/17	1/17	17.00	8.50	12.0	0	0
List A	5	-	-	-	-	-	-	-	-	-	-
Twenty20	3	-	-	-	-	-	-	-	-	-	-

GERAINT JONES

RHB WK R2 MVP81

FULL NAME: Geraint Owen Jones
BORN: July 14, 1976, Kundiawa, Papua New Guinea
SQUAD NO: 9
HEIGHT: 5ft 10in
NICKNAME: Joner, Jonesy, G
EDUCATION: Harristown State, Queensland; Macgregor SHS, Brisbane
TEAMS: England, Papua New Guinea, Kent, Kent 2nd XI
CAREER: Test: 2004; ODI: 2004; T20I: 2005; First-class: 2001; List A: 2001; T20: 2003

BEST BATTING: 178 Kent vs Somerset, Canterbury, 2010
COUNTY CAP: 2003; BENEFIT YEAR: 2012

FAMILY TIES? James Tredwell is my brother-in-law, my father bowled off spin once for his region in North Wales and my sister bowls right-arm rapid (I'm still recovering from a blow to the family jewels aged 11!)
CAREER HIGHLIGHTS? My hundred against New Zealand in 2004, the 2005 Ashes, winning the T20 Cup and scoring 105 for Ash CC vs Walmer CC
SUPERSTITIONS? I use the same shower and toilet during a match. Left-sided dressing first
TIP FOR THE TOP? Sam Northeast
DESERT ISLAND DISC? Mumford And Sons – Babel
CRICKETING HEROES? Ian Healy, Jack Russell, Steve Waugh
SURPRISING FACT? I'm a qualified sheep shearer
FANTASY SLIP CORDON? Keeper: Me, 1st: Mother, 2nd: Tiger Woods, 3rd: Cheryl Cole
TWITTER FEED: @Gojones623

Batting	Mat	Inns	NO	Runs	HS	Ave	SR	100	50	Ct	St
Tests	34	53	4	1172	100	23.91	54.13	1	6	128	5
ODIs	49	41	8	815	80	24.69	78.21	0	4	68	4
T20Is	2	2	1	33	19	33.00	132.00	0	0	2	0
First-class	175	269	25	8075	178	33.09		15	43	540	35
List A	181	150	28	3013	86	24.69	81.08	0	12	197	41
Twenty20	95	74	15	1009	56	17.10	109.31	0	2	49	20
Bowling	**Inns**	**Balls**	**Runs**	**Wkts**	**BBI**	**BBM**	**Ave**	**Econ**	**SR**	**5w**	**10**
Tests	34	-	-	-	-	-	-	-	-	-	-
ODIs	49	-	-	-	-	-	-	-	-	-	-
T20Is	2	-	-	-	-	-	-	-	-	-	-
First-class	175	24	26	0	-	-	-	6.50	-	0	0
List A	181	-	-	-	-	-	-	-	-	-	-
Twenty20	95	-	-	-	-	-	-	-	-	-	-

RICHARD JONES

RHB RMF

FULL NAME: Richard Alan Jones
BORN: November 6, 1986, Stourbridge
SQUAD NO: 25
HEIGHT: 6ft 2in
NICKNAME: Jonah, Dick
EDUCATION: Grange School, Stourbridge; King Edward VI College, Stourbridge
TEAMS: England Under-19s, Loughborough MCCU, Matabeleland Tuskers, Worcestershire, Worcestershire 2nd XI
CAREER: First-class: 2007; List A: 2008; T20: 2010

BEST BATTING: 62 Matabeleland Tuskers vs Southern Rocks, Bulawayo, 2012
BEST BOWLING: 7-115 Worcestershire vs Sussex, Hove, 2010

CAREER HIGHLIGHTS? Signing my first professional contract with Worcestershire, the club I've been at since the age of nine, was a huge moment for me and my family. Getting selected for the England U19 tour of Bangladesh was also a huge honour.
SUPERSTITIONS? Only one – sit as far away from Jack Shantry as you can, else you run the risk of losing some of your kit amongst the atrocity that is his changing area
TIPS FOR THE TOP? Nottinghamshire's James Taylor looks as though he has a very big future for England. As does Jonny Bairstow, Alex Hales and Ben Stokes. Closer to home, young Aneesh Kapil is a huge talent
IF YOU WEREN'T A CRICKETER? I would have definitely gone to university, whether that would have been for better or worse I don't know! As for a job, I'd like to think I'd be a sports writer, which is something that I am going to study for in the near future
ACCOMPLISHMENTS? I was a senior prefect at high school. I went for head boy but they opted for Jimmy Martin, a quieter, more obedient student. The regime couldn't handle me, I knew it and they knew it! Other than that, I had my first sports article published in All Out Cricket magazine four years ago
TWITTER FEED: @richardjones441

Batting	Mat	Inns	NO	Runs	HS	Ave	SR	100	50	Ct	St
First-class	42	65	12	622	62	11.73	40.78	0	2	17	0
List A	10	5	2	23	11*	7.66	69.69	0	0	1	0
Twenty20	6	2	1	14	9	14.00	77.77	0	0	7	0
Bowling	**Inns**	**Balls**	**Runs**	**Wkts**	**BBI**	**BBM**	**Ave**	**Econ**	**SR**	**5w**	**10**
First-class	42	5780	4003	126	7/115	8/105	31.76	4.15	45.8	4	0
List A	10	333	380	3	1/25	1/25	126.66	6.84	111.0	0	0
Twenty20	6	66	119	2	1/17	1/17	59.50	10.81	33.0	0	0

SIMON JONES — LHB RFM

FULL NAME: Simon Philip Jones
BORN: December 25, 1978, Morriston, Swansea
SQUAD NO: 50
HEIGHT: 6ft 3in
NICKNAME: Horse
EDUCATION: Coedcae Comprehensive; Millfield
TEAMS: England, Glamorgan, Hampshire, Worcestershire
CAREER: Test: 2002; ODI: 2004; First-class: 1998; List A: 1999; T20: 2008

BEST BATTING: 46 Glamorgan vs Yorkshire, Scarborough, 2001
BEST BOWLING: 6-45 Glamorgan vs Derbyshire, 2002
COUNTY CAP: 2002 (Glamorgan)

FAMILY TIES? My father [Jeff] played for England and Glamorgan
CRICKET MOMENTS TO FORGET? Every injury
SUPERSTITIONS? Right boot on first
CRICKETERS PARTICULARLY ADMIRED? Allan Donald
OTHER SPORTS PLAYED? Football (trials with Leeds United)
FAVOURITE BAND? Eminem
CAREER HIGHLIGHTS? Winning the 2005 Ashes series

Batting	Mat	Inns	NO	Runs	HS	Ave	SR	100	50	Ct	St
Tests	18	18	5	205	44	15.76	51.89	0	0	4	0
ODIs	8	1	0	1	1	1.00	50.00	0	0	0	0
First-class	91	113	37	904	46	11.89		0	0	18	0
List A	54	22	15	82	26	11.71		0	0	4	0
Twenty20	34	8	5	28	11*	9.33	127.27	0	0	1	0
Bowling	**Inns**	**Balls**	**Runs**	**Wkts**	**BBI**	**BBM**	**Ave**	**Econ**	**SR**	**5w**	**10**
Tests	18	2821	1666	59	6/53	7/110	28.23	3.54	47.8	3	0
ODIs	8	348	275	7	2/43	2/43	39.28	4.74	49.7	0	0
First-class	91	13374	8142	267	6/45		30.49	3.65	50.0	15	1
List A	54	2193	1980	55	5/32	5/32	36.00	5.41	39.8	1	0
Twenty20	34	721	879	43	4/10	4/10	20.44	7.31	16.7	0	0

SUSSEX

CHRIS JORDAN RHB RFM

FULL NAME: Christopher James Jordan
BORN: October 4, 1988, Barbados
SQUAD NO: 8
HEIGHT: 6ft 2in
NICKNAME: CJ
EDUCATION: Dulwich College
TEAMS: Barbados, Surrey, Surrey 2nd XI, Sussex
CAREER: First-class: 2007; List A: 2007; T20: 2008

BEST BATTING: 79* Surrey vs Essex, Chelmsford, 2011
BEST BOWLING: 5-77 Barbados vs Guyana, Bridgetown, 2012

NOTES: Eligible to represent England through his grandmother. Took four wickets on first-class debut against Kent. Selected for the ECB Winter Performance Programme at the end of 2009. Missed the entire 2010 season due to a stress fracture. Claimed his maiden five-wicket haul last March, having registered a career best of 4-41 in Barbados' previous fixture against Guyana. Signed by Sussex on a two-year deal in December after being released by Surrey

Batting	Mat	Inns	NO	Runs	HS	Ave	SR	100	50	Ct	St
First-class	42	57	11	987	79*	21.45		0	4	27	0
List A	23	14	1	120	38	9.23		0	0	8	0
Twenty20	12	10	2	111	31	13.87	104.71	0	0	4	0
Bowling	**Inns**	**Balls**	**Runs**	**Wkts**	**BBI**	**BBM**	**Ave**	**Econ**	**SR**	**5w**	**10**
First-class	42	5779	3417	91	5/77	5/73	37.54	3.54	63.5	1	0
List A	23	937	846	31	3/24	3/24	27.29	5.41	30.2	0	0
Twenty20	12	180	273	5	2/34	2/34	54.60	9.10	36.0	0	0

ED JOYCE

LHB RM R6 MVP88

FULL NAME: Edmund Christopher Joyce
BORN: September 22, 1978, Dublin
SQUAD NO: 24
HEIGHT: 5ft 10in
NICKNAME: Joycey, Spud, Piece
EDUCATION: Presentation College, Bray; Trinity College, Dublin
TEAMS: England, Ireland, England Lions, Marylebone Cricket Club, Middlesex, Sussex
CAREER: ODI: 2006; T20I: 2006; First-class: 1997; List A: 1998; T20: 2003

BEST BATTING: 211 Middlesex vs Warwickshire, Birmingham, 2006
BEST BOWLING: 2-34 Middlesex vs Cambridge UCCE, Cambridge, 2004
COUNTY CAP: 2002 (Middlesex)

NOTES: Passed 1,000 first-class runs five English summers in a row between 2002-2006. Has represented both Ireland and England in ODI cricket. Scored his one ODI century for England against Australia in the 2007 Commonwealth Bank Series. Appointed Sussex club captain for the 2013 season

Batting	Mat	Inns	NO	Runs	HS	Ave	SR	100	50	Ct	St
ODIs	32	32	1	935	107	30.16	65.33	1	7	9	0
T20Is	13	10	2	262	78*	32.75	94.58	0	1	1	0
First-class	183	306	25	12522	211	44.56		28	71	157	0
List A	229	218	22	7293	146	37.20		11	44	79	0
Twenty20	76	70	12	1067	78*	18.39	94.34	0	1	21	0
Bowling	**Inns**	**Balls**	**Runs**	**Wkts**	**BBI**	**BBM**	**Ave**	**Econ**	**SR**	**5w**	**10**
ODIs	32	-	-	-	-	-	-	-	-	-	-
T20Is	13	-	-	-	-	-	-	-	-	-	-
First-class	183	1287	1025	11	2/34		93.18	4.77	117.0	0	0
List A	229	264	309	6	2/10	2/10	51.50	7.02	44.0	0	0
Twenty20	76	6	12	0	-	-	-	12.00	-	0	0

ANEESH KAPIL RHB RFM

FULL NAME: Aneesh Kapil
BORN: August 3, 1993, Wolverhampton
SQUAD NO: 22
HEIGHT: 5ft 9in
NICKNAME: Simba, Ponch
EDUCATION: Denstone College
TEAMS: England Under-19s, Worcestershire, Worcestershire 2nd XI
CAREER: First-class: 2011; List A: 2011; T20: 2011

BEST BATTING: 54 Worcestershire vs Sussex, Horsham, 2011
BEST BOWLING: 3-17 Worcestershire vs Nottinghamshire, Worcester, 2012

WHO WOULD PLAY YOU IN A FILM OF YOUR LIFE? Will Smith
CAREER HIGHLIGHTS? Playing in an U19 World Cup
SUPERSTITIONS? I've got to have my power-balance on!
BEST PLAYER IN COUNTY CRICKET? Nick Compton and Graham Onions
TIPS FOR THE TOP? Tom Fell, Neil Pinner and Nick Harrison
IF YOU WEREN'T A CRICKETER? Playing baseball for the New York Yankees
DESERT ISLAND DISC? Drake – Thank Me Later
FAVOURITE TV? Made In Chelsea, The X Factor
CRICKETING HEROES? Vikram Solanki, Virat Kohli, Jacques Kallis
NON-CRICKETING HEROES? Muhammad Ali, Roger Federer, Diego Maradona, Michael Jordan, Usain Bolt, James Bond
ACCOMPLISHMENTS? Winning a school dancing competition…
SURPRISING FACT? I can beat-box a little bit
FANTASY SLIP CORDON? Keeper: Alicia Keys, 1st: Alessandra Ambrosio, 2nd: Jessica Alba, 3rd: Eva Mendes, 4th: Nicole Scherzinger, 5th: Kim Kardashian, 6th: Eva Longoria, Gully: Me!
TWITTER FEED: @AneeshKapil22

Batting	Mat	Inns	NO	Runs	HS	Ave	SR	100	50	Ct	St
First-class	9	14	1	232	54	17.84	46.49	0	1	2	0
List A	10	8	3	107	44	21.40	74.30	0	0	3	0
Twenty20	7	5	2	30	13	10.00	96.77	0	0	3	0
Bowling	**Inns**	**Balls**	**Runs**	**Wkts**	**BBI**	**BBM**	**Ave**	**Econ**	**SR**	**5w**	**10**
First-class	9	392	274	8	3/17	3/28	34.25	4.19	49.0	0	0
List A	10	185	224	3	1/18	1/18	74.66	7.26	61.6	0	0
Twenty20	7	60	71	4	3/9	3/9	17.75	7.10	15.0	0	0

SIMON KATICH LHB SLC R3 MVP99

FULL NAME: Simon Mathew Katich
BORN: August 21, 1975, Middle Swan, Australia
SQUAD NO: 37
HEIGHT: 5ft 10in
EDUCATION: Trinity College Perth; University of WA
TEAMS: Australia, Derbyshire, Durham, Duronto Rajshahi, Hampshire, Kings XI Punjab, New South Wales, Perth Scorchers, Western Australia, Yorkshire, Lancashire
CAREER: Test: 2001; ODI: 2001; T20I: 2005; First-class: 1997; List A: 1995; T20: 2003

BEST BATTING: 306 New South Wales vs Queensland, Sydney, 2007
BEST BOWLING: 7-130 New South Wales vs Victoria, Melbourne, 2003
COUNTY CAP: 2007 (Derbyshire)

WHO WOULD PLAY YOU IN A FILM OF YOUR LIFE? Matt Damon
CAREER HIGHLIGHTS? Being presented my baggy green cap by Richie Benaud. To receive it from a legend of Australian cricket in front of my family and friends was very special. All the winning teams I have played in for Australia, WA, NSW and Hampshire
SUPERSTITIONS? I like to wear old gear
MOST MARKED CHARACTERISTIC? My competitiveness
BEST PLAYER IN COUNTY CRICKET? Graham Onions
TIPS FOR THE TOP? James Vince, Liam Dawson, Chris Wood, Michael Bates and Danny Briggs from Hampshire
CRICKETING HEROES? Sir Viv Richards
SURPRISING FACT? I have no sense of smell

Batting	Mat	Inns	NO	Runs	HS	Ave	SR	100	50	Ct	St
Tests	56	99	6	4188	157	45.03	49.36	10	25	39	0
ODIs	45	42	5	1324	107*	35.78	68.74	1	9	13	0
T20Is	3	2	0	69	39	34.50	146.80	0	0	2	0
First-class	254	432	51	19829	306	52.04		54	105	220	0
List A	240	226	26	7236	136*	36.18		7	56	108	0
Twenty20	94	79	16	1879	75	29.82	125.68	0	7	41	0
Bowling	**Inns**	**Balls**	**Runs**	**Wkts**	**BBI**	**BBM**	**Ave**	**Econ**	**SR**	**5w**	**10**
Tests	56	1039	635	21	6/65	6/90	30.23	3.66	49.4	1	0
ODIs	45	-	-	-	-	-	-	-	-	-	-
T20Is	3	-	-	-	-	-	-	-	-	-	-
First-class	254	6429	3778	107	7/130		35.30	3.52	60.0	3	0
List A	240	938	868	25	3/21	3/21	34.72	5.55	37.5	0	0
Twenty20	94	18	29	0	-	-	-	9.66	-	0	0

GARY KEEDY

LHB SLA W4

FULL NAME: Gary Keedy
BORN: November 27, 1974, Sandal, Wakefield, Yorkshire
SQUAD NO: TBC
HEIGHT: 5ft 11in
NICKNAME: Keeds
EDUCATION: Garforth Comprehensive; University of Salford
TEAMS: England Lions, Lancashire, Marylebone Cricket Club, Yorkshire
CAREER: First-class: 1994; List A: 1995; T20: 2004

BEST BATTING: 64 Lancashire vs Sussex, Hove, 2001
BEST BOWLING: 7-68 Lancashire vs Durham, Manchester, 2010
COUNTY CAP: 2000 (Lancashire); BENEFIT YEAR: 2009 (Lancashire)

WHO WOULD PLAY YOU IN A FILM OF YOUR LIFE? My twin brother
CAREER HIGHLIGHTS? Winning the Championship in 2011 with Lancashire, getting capped by Lancashire, playing for England Lions against Australia and T20 Finals Days
MOST MARKED CHARACTERISTIC? Baldness
BEST PLAYER IN COUNTY CRICKET? Marcus Trescothick
TIPS FOR THE TOP? Arron Lilley and George Edwards
DESERT ISLAND DISC? The Beatles – Help!
FAVOURITE TV? MasterChef
CRICKETING HEROES? Shane Warne and Graham Gooch
NON-CRICKETING HEROES? Jimmy Page
ACCOMPLISHMENTS? My degree
WHEN YOU RETIRE? I'd like to be a physiotherapist
SURPRISING FACT? I'm exceptionally good at playing the triangle
FANTASY SLIP CORDON? Keeper: Slash from Guns N' Roses, 1st: Gordon Ramsay, 2nd: Myself, 3rd: Karl Pilkington, Gully: Robert De Niro
TWITTER FEED: @keeds23

Batting	Mat	Inns	NO	Runs	HS	Ave	SR	100	50	Ct	St
First-class	217	250	121	1427	64	11.06		0	2	52	0
List A	90	32	16	150	33	9.37		0	0	14	0
Twenty20	71	11	6	27	9*	5.40	79.41	0	0	10	0
Bowling	**Inns**	**Balls**	**Runs**	**Wkts**	**BBI**	**BBM**	**Ave**	**Econ**	**SR**	**5w**	**10**
First-class	217	43855	20483	656	7/68		31.22	2.80	66.8	32	7
List A	90	3702	2935	114	5/30	5/30	25.74	4.75	32.4	2	0
Twenty20	71	1414	1541	72	4/15	4/15	21.40	6.53	19.6	0	0

SAM KELSALL RHB RM

FULL NAME: Samuel Kelsall
BORN: March 14, 1993, Stoke-on-Trent, Staffordshire
SQUAD NO: 18
HEIGHT: 5ft 7in
NICKNAME: Kels, Rugrat, Mouse
EDUCATION: Priory Primary School; Trentham High School; South Nottingham College
TEAMS: England Under-17s, England Under-19s, Nottinghamshire, Nottinghamshire 2nd XI
CAREER: First-class: 2011; List A: 2011

BEST BATTING: 35 Nottinghamshire vs Warwickshire, Nottingham, 2012

CAREER HIGHLIGHTS? Representing England at U15 and U19 level. Earning my first professional contract with Notts, having been a member since age 11
CRICKETING HEROES? Ian Bell has always been a role model to me
NON-CRICKETING HEROES? Phil Taylor
BEST PLAYER IN COUNTY CRICKET? Andre Adams and Marcus Trescothick
TIP FOR THE TOP? Thomas Rowe from Nottinghamshire
IF YOU WEREN'T A CRICKETER? Hopefully a PE teacher or coach of some sort
WHEN RAIN STOPS PLAY? Listening to music, resting, playing Doodle Jump
FAVOURITE TV? Eastenders, Emmerdale, MasterChef, TOWIE
FAVOURITE FILM? Billy Elliot
FAVOURITE BOOK? Andre Agassi – Open
DREAM HOLIDAY? Barbados
ACCOMPLISHMENTS? Completing my Level 2 coaching badge, completing my BTEC course
GUILTY PLEASURES? Watching Loose Women or crying at The Lion King
FANTASY SLIP CORDON? Keeper: Shaka Hislop, 1st: Rihanna, 2nd: Chris Kelsall, 3rd: James Corden, Gully: David English
TWITTER FEED: @kelsall93

Batting	Mat	Inns	NO	Runs	HS	Ave	SR	100	50	Ct	St
First-class	2	4	0	50	35	12.50	44.64	0	0	1	0
List A	1	1	0	40	40	40.00	64.51	0	0	0	0
Bowling	**Inns**	**Balls**	**Runs**	**Wkts**	**BBI**	**BBM**	**Ave**	**Econ**	**SR**	**5w**	**10**
First-class	2	-	-	-	-	-	-	-	-	-	-
List A	1	-	-	-	-	-	-	-	-	-	-

BEN KEMP RHB RFM

FULL NAME: Benedict William Kemp
BORN: May 26, 1993, Canterbury, Kent
SQUAD NO: 18
HEIGHT: 6ft 4in
NICKNAME: Kempy
EDUCATION: St Edmund's School, Canterbury; Oxford Brookes University
TEAMS: Kent 2nd XI, Kent Under-13s, Kent Under-15s, Kent Under-17s, Oxford MCCU
CAREER: First-class: 2012

BEST BATTING: 3 Oxford MCCU vs Worcestershire, Oxford, 2012
BEST BOWLING: 1-71 Oxford MCCU vs Worcestershire, Oxford, 2012

FAMILY TIES? The game has run through the family for years but my father played for Kent, Middlesex and Young England
WHO WOULD PLAY YOU IN A FILM OF YOUR LIFE? Leonardo DiCaprio
CAREER HIGHLIGHTS? Getting signed by Kent
MOST MARKED CHARACTERISTIC? I'm erratic
TIPS FOR THE TOP? Ivan Thomas, Daniel Bell-Drummond, Charlie Morris and Adam Ball
IF YOU WEREN'T A CRICKETER? I'd be running a business
DESERT ISLAND DISC? 50 Cent – Get Rich Or Die Tryin'
FAVOURITE TV? Prime Minister's Questions
CRICKETING HEROES? WG Grace
ACCOMPLISHMENTS? Keeping a clean sheet against St. Bede's School in the ISFA quarter-finals
WHEN YOU RETIRE? Nothing ideally or chairman of my own business
SURPRISING FACT? Even though I can sound smart at times, I'm actually really stupid. People probably already know that though
FANTASY SLIP CORDON? Keeper: 50 Cent, 1st: WG Grace, 2nd: Me, 3rd: Winston Churchill, 4th: Stephen Hawking, Gully: Boris Johnson, 2nd Gully: Ed Miliband
TWITTER FEED: @benkemp18

Batting	Mat	Inns	NO	Runs	HS	Ave	SR	100	50	Ct	St
First-class	1	1	0	3	3	3.00	27.27	0	0	1	0
Bowling	**Inns**	**Balls**	**Runs**	**Wkts**	**BBI**	**BBM**	**Ave**	**Econ**	**SR**	**5w**	**10**
First-class	1	120	81	1	1/71	1/81	81.00	4.05	120.0	0	0

ROB KEOGH RHB OB

FULL NAME: Robert Ian Keogh
BORN: October 21, 1991, Dunstable
SQUAD NO: 14
HEIGHT: 6ft 2in
NICKNAME: Keezy, Chav, Kellogs
EDUCATION: Queensbury School; Dunstable College
TEAMS: Bedfordshire, Northamptonshire, Northamptonshire 2nd XI
CAREER: First-class: 2012; List A: 2010; T20: 2011

BEST BATTING: 6 Northamptonshire vs Glamorgan, Cardiff, 2012
BEST BOWLING: 1-69 Northamptonshire vs Glamorgan, Cardiff, 2012

FAMILY TIES? My dad was a gun cricketer for Dunstable Town CC
WHO WOULD PLAY YOU IN A FILM OF YOUR LIFE? Sean William Scott or Vincent Chase
CAREER HIGHLIGHTS? Signing my first pro deal and making my debut in all formats for Northants
SUPERSTITIONS? I put kit on a certain way before batting. I can't take the first ball when opening. My bag has to be packed in a specific way
BEST PLAYER IN COUNTY CRICKET? Peter Trego
TIPS FOR THE TOP? Ben Duckett, Olly Stone, Christian Davis, James Kettleborough
IF YOU WEREN'T A CRICKETER? Fireman
DESERT ISLAND DISC? Wiz Khalifa – Rolling Papers
CRICKETING HEROES? Michael Clarke, AB de Villiers, Viv Richards
NON-CRICKETING HEROES? David Beckham, Muhammad Ali
ACCOMPLISHMENTS? I played for Luton Town FC as a junior from age seven-15
WHEN YOU RETIRE? Run my own bar, restaurant or nightclub
FANTASY SLIP CORDON? Keeper: Jimmy Carr, 1st: David Beckham, 2nd: Ted, 3rd: Cheryl Cole, Gully: Mario Balotelli
TWITTER FEED: @RobKeogh91

Batting	Mat	Inns	NO	Runs	HS	Ave	SR	100	50	Ct	St
First-class	1	1	0	6	6	6.00	21.42	0	0	0	0
List A	7	6	1	93	30	18.60	59.61	0	0	1	0
Twenty20	8	2	0	2	1	1.00	22.22	0	0	5	0
Bowling	**Inns**	**Balls**	**Runs**	**Wkts**	**BBI**	**BBM**	**Ave**	**Econ**	**SR**	**5w**	**10**
First-class	1	120	69	1	1/69	1/69	69.00	3.45	120.0	0	0
List A	7	108	109	0	-	-	-	6.05	-	0	0
Twenty20	8	36	45	0	-	-	-	7.50	-	0	0

SIMON KERRIGAN RHB SLA W1

FULL NAME: Simon Christopher Kerrigan
BORN: May 10, 1989, Preston, Lancashire
SQUAD NO: 10
HEIGHT: 5ft 9in
NICKNAME: Kegs, Kegsy, Kegger, Bish
EDUCATION: Corpus Christi High School; Preston College; Edge Hill University
TEAMS: England Lions, Lancashire, Lancashire 2nd XI
CAREER: First-class: 2010; List A: 2011; T20: 2010

BEST BATTING: 40 Lancashire vs Somerset, Taunton, 2010
BEST BOWLING: 9-51 Lancashire vs Hampshire, Liverpool, 2011

CAREER HIGHLIGHTS? Winning the Championship
SUPERSTITIONS? Not really, they come and go
CRICKETING HEROES? Andrew Flintoff, Darren Gough
NON-CRICKETING HEROES? Phil Ivey
BEST PLAYER IN COUNTY CRICKET? Marcus Trescothick
TIP FOR THE TOP? Karl Brown
IF YOU WEREN'T A CRICKETER? Jobless
WHEN RAIN STOPS PLAY? I sleep or make tea for everyone
FAVOURITE TV? Modern Family
FAVOURITE FILM? The Other Guys
DREAM HOLIDAY? Blackpool
GUILTY PLEASURES? All bad foods
TWITTER FEED: @Kegs10

Batting	Mat	Inns	NO	Runs	HS	Ave	SR	100	50	Ct	St
First-class	36	43	16	230	40	8.51	28.22	0	0	8	0
List A	24	11	3	23	10	2.87	43.39	0	0	4	0
Twenty20	19	2	2	4	4*	-	200.00	0	0	6	0
Bowling	**Inns**	**Balls**	**Runs**	**Wkts**	**BBI**	**BBM**	**Ave**	**Econ**	**SR**	**5w**	**10**
First-class	36	6814	3231	114	9/51	12/192	28.34	2.84	59.7	6	1
List A	24	980	841	19	3/21	3/21	44.26	5.14	51.5	0	0
Twenty20	19	408	469	15	3/17	3/17	31.26	6.89	27.2	0	0

ALEXEI KERVEZEE

RHB RM R1

FULL NAME: Alexei Nicolaas Kervezee
BORN: September 11, 1989, Walvis Bay, Namibia
SQUAD NO: 5
HEIGHT: 5ft 7in
NICKNAME: Cub, Rowdy
TEAMS: Netherlands, Netherlands Under-19s, Worcestershire, Worcestershire 2nd XI
CAREER: ODI: 2006; T20I: 2009; First-class: 2005; List A: 2006; T20: 2009

BEST BATTING: 155 Worcestershire vs Derbyshire, Derby, 2010
BEST BOWLING: 1-14 Netherlands vs Namibia, Windhoek, 2008

NOTES: Made his first-class debut for the Netherlands vs Scotland at Utrecht in the ICC Intercontinental Cup in 2005, aged 15. Made his ODI debut for the Netherlands vs Sri Lanka at Amstelveen in 2006, aged 16, scoring 47. One of five players to take part in a World Cup aged 17. His best season to date came in 2010 when he amassed 1,190 first-class runs at 44.07, including three centuries

Batting	Mat	Inns	NO	Runs	HS	Ave	SR	100	50	Ct	St
ODIs	39	36	3	924	92	28.00	73.15	0	4	18	0
T20Is	10	10	1	289	58*	32.11	110.30	0	2	4	0
First-class	59	103	7	3209	155	33.42		4	20	32	0
List A	78	72	6	1970	121*	29.84	76.38	2	8	31	0
Twenty20	58	54	8	837	58*	18.19	110.56	0	3	21	0
Bowling	**Inns**	**Balls**	**Runs**	**Wkts**	**BBI**	**BBM**	**Ave**	**Econ**	**SR**	**5w**	**10**
ODIs	39	24	34	0	-	-	-	8.50	-	0	0
T20Is	10	-	-	-	-	-	-	-	-	-	-
First-class	59	183	145	2	1/14	1/14	72.50	4.75	91.5	0	0
List A	78	48	73	0	-	-	-	9.12	-	0	0
Twenty20	58	12	13	0	-	-	-	6.50	-	0	0

JAMES KETTLEBOROUGH RHB OB

FULL NAME: James Michael Kettleborough
BORN: October 22, 1992, Huntingdon
SQUAD NO: 3
HEIGHT: 6ft
NICKNAME: Ketts, JK
EDUCATION: Bedford School
TEAMS: Bedfordshire, Middlesex 2nd XI, Northamptonshire 2nd XI
CAREER: Yet to make first-team debut

FAMILY TIES? My dad used to play for Bedfordshire and the MCC. I'm not overly sure if I'm related to Richard (the Test umpire)
WHO WOULD PLAY YOU IN A FILM OF YOUR LIFE? Either Arnold Schwarzenegger in his prime or Ricky Gervais playing a David Brent role
CAREER HIGHLIGHTS? Scoring hundreds on both my Middlesex 2nd XI debut and my Northants 2nd XI debut
SUPERSTITIONS? Not anymore. I used to always wear a jumper when I batted but when I first toured South Africa with my school I couldn't stand the heat so it had to come off
MOST MARKED CHARACTERISTIC? Hopefully hard-working yet game for a laugh
BEST PLAYER IN COUNTY CRICKET? Nick Compton
TIPS FOR THE TOP? Ben Duckett, Christian Davis, Olly Stone, Max Holden
IF YOU WEREN'T A CRICKETER? I'd like to be a personal trainer
DESERT ISLAND DISC? Professor Green (feat Emeli Sandé) – Read All About It
FAVOURITE TV? The Office
BIGGEST DRESSING DOWN YOU'VE RECEIVED? In an U17 one-day game against Essex at Billericay. We were 150-3 chasing 180 and lost. Our coach went ballistic and I still don't know how we lost
CRICKETING HEROES? Dan Housego, Stephen Peters, Ed Cowan
ACCOMPLISHMENTS? I've got a 180 in darts before
WHEN YOU RETIRE? Join Nasser in the commentary box
SURPRISING FACT? I'm a tattoo addict
FANTASY SLIP CORDON? Keeper: Tim Vine, 1st: Lee Evans, 2nd: Me, 3rd: Kelly Brook, Gully: Jesus
TWITTER FEED: @JKetts1305

ROB KEY

RHB OB R6

FULL NAME: Robert William Trevor Key
BORN: May 12, 1979, East Dulwich, London
SQUAD NO: 4
HEIGHT: 6ft 2in
NICKNAME: Keysy
EDUCATION: Colfe's School
TEAMS: England, England Lions, Kent, Marylebone Cricket Club
CAREER: Test: 2002; ODI: 2003; T20I: 2009; First-class: 1998; List A: 1998; T20: 2004

BEST BATTING: 270* Kent vs Glamorgan, Cardiff, 2009
BEST BOWLING: 2-31 Kent vs Somerset, Canterbury, 2010
COUNTY CAP: 2001; BENEFIT YEAR: 2011

WHO WOULD PLAY YOU IN A FILM OF YOUR LIFE? Russell Crowe
CAREER HIGHLIGHTS? Scoring 221 vs West Indies for England at Lord's
BEST PLAYER IN COUNTY CRICKET? Marcus Trescothick
TIP FOR THE TOP? Sam Northeast
DESERT ISLAND DISC? John Mayer – Free Fallin'
FAVOURITE TV? Newsroom
NON-CRICKETING HEROES? Will Ashby, George Digweed
ACCOMPLISHMENTS? Putting together a kids' trampoline
FANTASY SLIP CORDON? Keeper: George Digweed, 1st: Will Ashby, 2nd: James Fielding, 3rd: Glucka Wijesuriya, Gully: Andy Fussell
TWITTER FEED: @robkey612

Batting	Mat	Inns	NO	Runs	HS	Ave	SR	100	50	Ct	St
Tests	15	26	1	775	221	31.00	47.28	1	3	11	0
ODIs	5	5	0	54	19	10.80	40.00	0	0	0	0
T20Is	1	1	1	10	10*	-	125.00	0	0	1	0
First-class	253	438	33	16731	270*	41.31		46	66	146	0
List A	210	203	16	5876	120*	31.42		6	35	43	0
Twenty20	81	81	10	1775	98*	25.00	121.57	0	10	23	0
Bowling	**Inns**	**Balls**	**Runs**	**Wkts**	**BBI**	**BBM**	**Ave**	**Econ**	**SR**	**5w**	**10**
Tests	15	-	-	-	-	-	-	-	-	-	-
ODIs	5	-	-	-	-	-	-	-	-	-	-
T20Is	1	-	-	-	-	-	-	-	-	-	-
First-class	253	416	233	3	2/31	2/31	77.66	3.36	138.6	0	0
List A	210	-	-	-	-	-	-	-	-	-	-
Twenty20	81	-	-	-	-	-	-	-	-	-	-

AMJAD KHAN

RHB RFM W2

FULL NAME: Amjad Khan
BORN: October 14, 1980, Copenhagen, Denmark
SQUAD NO: 2
HEIGHT: 6ft
NICKNAME: Ammy
EDUCATION: Skolen pa Duevej, Copenhagen; Falkonergardens Gymnasium, Copenhagen
TEAMS: Denmark, England, Kent, Sussex, Sussex 2nd XI
CAREER: Test: 2009; T20I: 2009; First-class: 2001; List A: 1999; T20: 2004

BEST BATTING: 78 Kent vs Middlesex, Lord's, 2003
BEST BOWLING: 6-52 Kent vs Yorkshire, Canterbury, 2002

CAREER HIGHLIGHTS? My Test debut
CRICKETING HEROES? Wasim Akram, Dennis Lillee
NON-CRICKETING HEROES? Muhammad Ali
BEST PLAYER IN COUNTY CRICKET? Marcus Trescothick
TIPS FOR THE TOP? Matt Machan, Callum Jackson
IF YOU WEREN'T A CRICKETER? I'd be at university
WHEN RAIN STOPS PLAY? Music and iPad
FAVOURITE TV? Dexter
FAVOURITE FILM? The Godfather Part I and II
FAVOURITE BOOK? The Magus
DREAM HOLIDAY? Hawaii
SURPRISING SKILL? I speak five languages
GUILTY PLEASURES? Danish pastry
TWITTER FEED: @ammykhan1980

Batting	Mat	Inns	NO	Runs	HS	Ave	SR	100	50	Ct	St
Tests	1	-	-	-	-	-	-	-	-	0	0
T20Is	1	1	0	2	2	2.00	50.00	0	0	0	0
First-class	108	127	40	1466	78	16.85	49.22	0	6	26	0
List A	74	37	9	321	65*	11.46		0	1	17	0
Twenty20	38	15	8	52	15	7.42	94.54	0	0	7	0
Bowling	**Inns**	**Balls**	**Runs**	**Wkts**	**BBI**	**BBM**	**Ave**	**Econ**	**SR**	**5w**	**10**
Tests	1	174	122	1	1/111	1/122	122.00	4.20	174.0	0	0
T20Is	1	24	34	2	2/34	2/34	17.00	8.50	12.0	0	0
First-class	108	17949	10974	347	6/52		31.62	3.66	51.7	10	0
List A	74	2912	2504	76	4/26	4/26	32.94	5.15	38.3	0	0
Twenty20	38	641	949	39	3/11	3/11	24.33	8.88	16.4	0	0

CRAIG KIESWETTER RHB OB WK R1 MVP52

FULL NAME: Craig Kieswetter
BORN: November 28, 1987, Johannesburg, South Africa
SQUAD NO: 22
HEIGHT: 6ft
NICKNAME: Hobnob
EDUCATION: Bishops Diocesan College; Millfield School
TEAMS: England, England Lions, Somerset, South Africa Under-19s
CAREER: ODI: 2010; T20I: 2010; First-class: 2007; List A: 2007; T20: 2007

BEST BATTING: 164 Somerset vs Nottinghamshire, Nottingham, 2011
BEST BOWLING: 2-3 Somerset vs Worcestershire, Worcester, 2012
COUNTY CAP: 2009

CAREER HIGHLIGHTS? Man of the Match in World T20 final (Barbados 2010), second youngest ODI century scorer for England
CRICKETING HEROES? Jonty Rhodes, Adam Gilchrist, Justin Langer
NON-CRICKETING HEROES? Ayrton Senna, Jose Mourinho
BEST PLAYER IN COUNTY CRICKET? Marcus Trescothick
TIPS FOR THE TOP? Lewis Gregory, Joe Root
IF YOU WEREN'T A CRICKETER? I'd be studying Law
WHEN RAIN STOPS PLAY? iPod, PS3, TV, books
FAVOURITE TV? House, Lost, Made In Chelsea
FAVOURITE FILM? Sherlock Holmes
FAVOURITE BOOK? The Monk Who Sold His Ferrari by Robin Sharma
ACCOMPLISHMENTS? Helping charities with donations of cricket equipment
TWITTER FEED: @kiesy_22

Batting	Mat	Inns	NO	Runs	HS	Ave	SR	100	50	Ct	St
ODIs	46	40	5	1054	107	30.11	89.93	1	5	53	12
T20Is	25	25	1	526	63	21.91	111.91	0	3	17	3
First-class	89	131	19	4613	164	41.18		10	23	251	5
List A	127	118	15	3970	143	38.54	94.34	10	16	130	26
Twenty20	84	82	11	1962	84	27.63	120.59	0	14	50	16
Bowling	**Inns**	**Balls**	**Runs**	**Wkts**	**BBI**	**BBM**	**Ave**	**Econ**	**SR**	**5w**	**10**
ODIs	46	-	-	-	-	-	-	-	-	-	-
T20Is	25	-	-	-	-	-	-	-	-	-	-
First-class	89	18	3	2	2/3	2/3	1.50	1.00	9.0	0	0
List A	127	12	19	1	1/19	1/19	19.00	9.50	12.0	0	0
Twenty20	84	-	-	-	-	-	-	-	-	-	-

STEVE KIRBY RHB RFM W3

SOMERSET

FULL NAME: Steven Paul Kirby
BORN: October 4, 1977, Bury, Lancashire
SQUAD NO: 9
HEIGHT: 6ft 3in
NICKNAME: Tango
EDUCATION: Elton High School; Bury College
TEAMS: England Lions, Gloucestershire, Leicestershire, Marylebone Cricket Club, Somerset, Yorkshire
CAREER: First-class: 2001; List A: 2001; T20: 2004

BEST BATTING: 57 Yorkshire vs Hampshire, Leeds, 2002
BEST BOWLING: 8-80 Yorkshire vs Somerset, Taunton, 2003
COUNTY CAPS: 2003 (Yorkshire); 2005 (Gloucestershire)

NOTES: Signed with Leicestershire, but left for Yorkshire before making a first-class appearance. Claimed 7-50 on debut for the White Rose. Took match figures of 12-72 against his old club in just his third match. His best return in a first-class season came in 2003, when he claimed 67 wickets. Moved to Gloucestershire in 2005. Moved to Somerset ahead of the 2011 season and snared 53 wickets in his first year at Taunton. Dismissed Mike Atherton in both innings of the former England skipper's final Championship match

Batting	Mat	Inns	NO	Runs	HS	Ave	SR	100	50	Ct	St
First-class	156	217	66	1232	57	8.15	28.60	0	1	33	0
List A	92	34	13	88	15	4.19	42.51	0	0	16	0
Twenty20	68	24	8	70	25	4.37	74.46	0	0	12	0
Bowling	**Inns**	**Balls**	**Runs**	**Wkts**	**BBI**	**BBM**	**Ave**	**Econ**	**SR**	**5w**	**10**
First-class	156	27363	15444	546	8/80		28.28	3.38	50.1	17	4
List A	92	3728	3467	125	5/36	5/36	27.73	5.57	29.8	1	0
Twenty20	68	1289	1646	75	3/17	3/17	21.94	7.66	17.1	0	0

MICHAEL KLINGER RHB

FULL NAME: Michael Klinger
BORN: July 4, 1980, Kew, Melbourne, Australia
SQUAD NO: 2
HEIGHT: 5ft 9in
NICKNAME: Maxy
TEAMS: Adelaide Strikers, Australia A, Kochi Tuskers Kerala, South Australia, Victoria, Worcestershire
CAREER: First-class: 1999; List A: 1999; T20: 2006

BEST BATTING: 255 South Australia vs Western Australia, Adelaide, 2008

NOTES: Making his first-class debut for Victoria in 1999, Klinger had to wait seven years to register his maiden first-class century, which he achieved in the 2005/06 season. A former Australia U19 captain, Klinger was the youngest player to score a first grade century in Melbourne. A move to South Australia rejuvenated his career, where his performances for the next two seasons were so good that he was eventually appointed captain of the Redbacks. Last year he enjoyed a solid start to his first-class career in England with Worcestershire before agreeing to join Gloucestershire as their captain and overseas player for 2013

Batting	Mat	Inns	NO	Runs	HS	Ave	SR	100	50	Ct	St
First-class	100	179	18	5888	255	36.57	43.33	11	28	96	0
List A	104	104	11	3841	133*	41.30		9	25	34	0
Twenty20	49	47	5	1191	78	28.35	122.02	0	8	20	0
Bowling	**Inns**	**Balls**	**Runs**	**Wkts**	**BBI**	**BBM**	**Ave**	**Econ**	**SR**	**5w**	**10**
First-class	100	6	3	0	-	-	-	3.00	-	0	0
List A	104	-	-	-	-	-	-	-	-	-	-
Twenty20	49	-	-	-	-	-	-	-	-	-	-

TOM KNIGHT RHB SLA

DERBYSHIRE

FULL NAME: Thomas Craig Knight
BORN: June 28, 1993, Sheffield, Yorkshire
SQUAD NO: 27
HEIGHT: 6ft 2in
NICKNAME: Knighty
EDUCATION: Eckington School, Derbyshire
TEAMS: Derbyshire, Derbyshire 2nd XI, Derbyshire Under-15s, Derbyshire Under-17s, England Under-19s
CAREER: First-class: 2011; List A: 2011; T20: 2011

BEST BATTING: 14 Derbyshire vs Surrey, The Oval, 2011
BEST BOWLING: 2-32 Derbyshire vs Glamorgan, Cardiff, 2011

CAREER HIGHLIGHTS? Making my T20 debut at Trent Bridge, taking 3-16 for Derbyshire vs Worcestershire, playing for England U19. Also taking 3-27 for England U19 vs South Africa U19
CRICKETING HEROES? Shane Warne and Andrew Flintoff
NON-CRICKETING HEROES? Muhammad Ali, Tiger Woods, David Beckham
BEST PLAYER IN COUNTY CRICKET? Marcus Trescothick
TIPS FOR THE TOP? Alex Hughes, Paul Borrington
IF YOU WEREN'T A CRICKETER? I would have gone to university
WHEN RAIN STOPS PLAY? Do a crossword
FAVOURITE TV? Criminal Minds
FAVOURITE FILM? Saving Private Ryan
FAVOURITE BOOK? Holes
DREAM HOLIDAY? Caribbean
GUILTY PLEASURES? Chris Durham's fajitas
TWITTER FEED: @tomknight28

Batting	Mat	Inns	NO	Runs	HS	Ave	SR	100	50	Ct	St
First-class	2	3	1	15	14	7.50	39.47	0	0	1	0
List A	4	2	2	3	2*	-	16.66	0	0	0	0
Twenty20	13	2	2	3	2*	-	60.00	0	0	5	0
Bowling	**Inns**	**Balls**	**Runs**	**Wkts**	**BBI**	**BBM**	**Ave**	**Econ**	**SR**	**5w**	**10**
First-class	2	288	143	2	2/32	2/59	71.50	2.97	144.0	0	0
List A	4	192	167	6	2/27	2/27	27.83	5.21	32.0	0	0
Twenty20	13	228	270	12	3/16	3/16	22.50	7.10	19.0	0	0

TOM KOHLER-CADMORE RHB OB

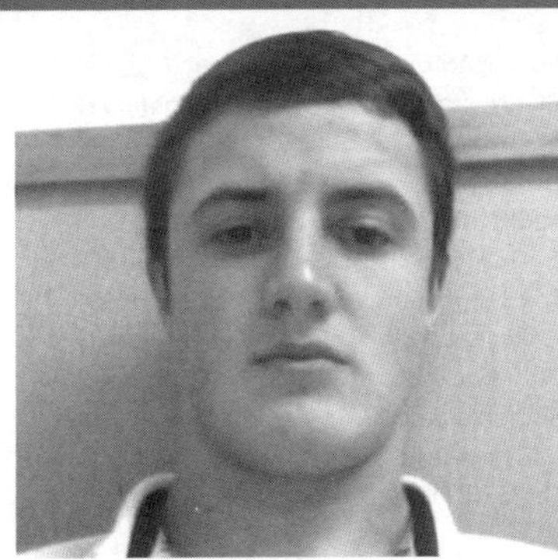

FULL NAME: Tom Kohler-Cadmore
BORN: August 19, 1994, Chatham, Kent
SQUAD NO: 32
HEIGHT: 6ft 2in
NICKNAME: Pepsi
EDUCATION: Malvern College
TEAMS: Worcestershire 2nd XI, Yorkshire Under-19s
CAREER: Yet to make first-team debut

FAMILY TIES? My father has played club cricket for most of his life and my brother plays in Yorkshire for Driffield CC
CAREER HIGHLIGHTS? Winning the U15 County Championship with Yorkshire, making my Worcestershire 2nd XI debut against Gloucestershire aged 15 and making 36*
MOST MARKED CHARACTERISTIC? My large feet. When I was five or six I had size 11 feet, so I looked a bit funny
CRICKETING HEROES? Michael Vaughan
NON-CRICKETING HEROES? Usain Bolt and Dwayne 'The Rock' Johnson
BEST PLAYER IN COUNTY CRICKET? Alan Richardson for bowling and Nick Compton for batting
TIPS FOR THE TOP? Ben Twohig (Worcestershire Academy). He bowls great left-arm spin
IF YOU WEREN'T A CRICKETER? I would have most probably joined the Navy like my elder brother
FAVOURITE TV? Family Guy
WHEN YOU RETIRE? Cricker or racket ball pro at a private school (ideally back at Malvern)
DESERT ISLAND DISC? Drake – Headlines
ACCOMPLISHMENTS? Gaining my nine GCSEs
BIGGEST DRESSING DOWN YOU'VE RECEIVED? From my dad when I was 14. I went for a two during the second over of the match and only just made it in. The very next ball I tried to do the same and was run out by the same fielder a good four yards short
SURPRISING FACT? I'm a Swansea City FC fan
TWITTER FEED: @TomKohlerCadmor

JACK LEACH LHB SLA

SOMERSET

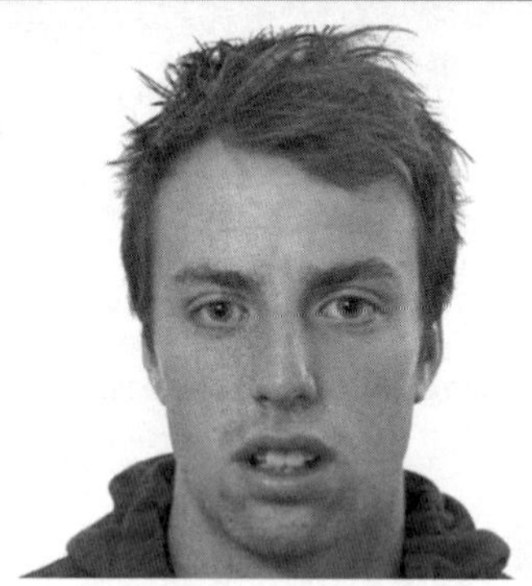

FULL NAME: Matthew Jack Leach
BORN: June 22, 1991, Taunton, Somerset
SQUAD NO: 17
HEIGHT: 6ft
NICKNAME: Leachy, Donkey, Snoz
EDUCATION: Trinity Primary School; Bishop Fox's Community School; Richard Huish College; Cardiff Metropolitan University
TEAMS: Cardiff MCCU, Dorset, Somerset, Somerset 2nd XI, Somerset Under-17s, Valley District Cricket Club
CAREER: First-class: 2012; List A: 2012

BEST BATTING: 0* Somerset vs Lancashire, Liverpool, 2012
BEST BOWLING: 2-37 Somerset vs Lancashire, Liverpool, 2012

WHO WOULD PLAY YOU IN A FILM OF YOUR LIFE? Will Ferrell… the film would be a comedy!
CAREER HIGHLIGHTS? Making my Championship debut last year against Lancashire. Playing the tour match against South Africa last year (and claiming the prize wicket of Hashim Amla!). Representing England at U15 level
BEST PLAYER IN COUNTY CRICKET? Graham Onions or Banger [Marcus Trescothick]
TIPS FOR THE TOP? The Overton brothers [Craig and Jamie], Chris Jones
DESERT ISLAND DISC? Project X Soundtrack
FAVOURITE TV? The Big Bang Theory
CRICKETING HEROES? Marcus Trescothick, Jacques Kallis, Steve Waugh
ACCOMPLISHMENTS? Achieving an Honours degree in Sports Psychology
WHEN YOU RETIRE? Become a sports psychologist for an elite sports team
SURPRISING FACT? I bowl with my left arm but throw with my right arm
FANTASY SLIP CORDON? Keeper: Dr Sheldon Cooper, 1st: Myself, 2nd: Karl Pilkington, 3rd: Jimmy Carr, Gully: Jack Whitehall
TWITTER FEED: @jackleach1991

Batting	Mat	Inns	NO	Runs	HS	Ave	SR	100	50	Ct	St
First-class	3	1	1	0	0*	-	0.00	0	0	0	0
List A	3	1	0	2	2	2.00	20.00	0	0	0	0
Bowling	**Inns**	**Balls**	**Runs**	**Wkts**	**BBI**	**BBM**	**Ave**	**Econ**	**SR**	**5w**	**10**
First-class	3	366	194	2	2/37	2/39	97.00	3.18	183.0	0	0
List A	3	114	90	1	1/30	1/30	90.00	4.73	114.0	0	0

JOE LEACH RHB RFM

FULL NAME: Joseph Leach
BORN: October 30, 1990, Stafford
SQUAD NO: 23
HEIGHT: 6ft 1in
NICKNAME: Hugh Jed
EDUCATION: Shrewsbury School; Leeds University
TEAMS: Leeds/Bradford MCCU, Shropshire, Staffordshire, Worcestershire, Worcestershire 2nd XI
CAREER: First-class: 2012; List A: 2012

BEST BATTING: 50 Worcestershire vs Lancashire, Worcester, 2012
BEST BOWLING: 4-73 Leeds/Bradford MCCU vs Surrey, The Oval, 2012

CAREER HIGHLIGHTS? Playing at Worcestershire and winning the National Knockout with Shrewsbury CC
CRICKETING HEROES? Jacques Kallis, Andrew Flintoff
BEST PLAYER IN COUNTY CRICKET? Being loyal, I'll have to say Alan Richardson
TIPS FOR THE TOP? Ben Slater and Luis Reece
WHEN RAIN STOPS PLAY? Taking the mickey out of Chris Russell or traipsing through Twitter
FAVOURITE TV? An Idiot Abroad
FAVOURITE FILM? The Hangover 2
DREAM HOLIDAY? Somewhere in the Caribbean
ACCOMPLISHMENTS? I can speak French (fairly well)
SURPRISING SKILL? I'm studying Philosophy at Leeds University
FANTASY SLIP CORDON? Keeper: Ricky Gervais, 1st: Al Murray, 2nd: Karl Pilkington, 3rd: Me
TWITTER FEED: @joeleach23

Batting	Mat	Inns	NO	Runs	HS	Ave	SR	100	50	Ct	St
First-class	7	13	0	159	50	12.23	36.89	0	1	2	0
List A	1	-	-	-	-	-	-	-	-	0	0
Bowling	**Inns**	**Balls**	**Runs**	**Wkts**	**BBI**	**BBM**	**Ave**	**Econ**	**SR**	**5w**	**10**
First-class	7	412	226	12	4/73	4/21	18.83	3.29	34.3	0	0
List A	1	24	47	0	-	-	-	11.75	-	0	0

STEVE LEACH LHB LB

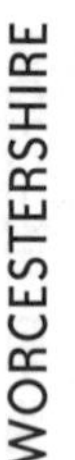

FULL NAME: Stephen Geoffrey Leach
BORN: November 19, 1993, Stafford
SQUAD NO: 30
HEIGHT: 6ft 2in
NICKNAME: Screech, Leachy, Scratch
EDUCATION: Shrewsbury School
TEAMS: Shropshire, Worcestershire 2nd XI
CAREER: Yet to make first-team debut

FAMILY TIES? My older brother Joe plays for Worcestershire as well as playing for Leeds/Bradford MCCU
CAREER HIGHLIGHTS? Playing for Worcestershire 2nd XI. Shrewsbury CC – Birmingham League Champions 2010, National Knockout winners 2011. Shrewsbury School – Silk Trophy winners, National T20 winners 2011
CRICKETING HEROES? Brian Lara, Marcus Trescothick, Matthew Hayden
NON-CRICKETING HEROES? Jonny Wilkinson, Muhammad Ali
BEST PLAYER IN COUNTY CRICKET? Bowler: Alan Richardson. Batsman: James Taylor – an old Shrewsbury School pupil
TIP FOR THE TOP? Ruaidhri Smith – a right-arm seam bowler and a right-handed middle order batsman. Roars is a teammate at school and is in the Glamorgan Academy. He is capable of swinging the ball both ways and can be a destructive batter
FAVOURITE TV? One Tree Hill
FAVOURITE FILM? Mean Girls – a second to none chick flick!
DREAM HOLIDAY? Cape Town
SURPRISING SKILL? I have a party trick where I can eat a Jaffa Cake, leaving the orange bit till last, without using my hands
GUILTY PLEASURES? Power naps – not sure how else I'd get through the day!
FANTASY SLIP CORDON? Keeper: Jack Whitehall (interesting accent and outstanding one-liners to keep everyone going through the day), 1st: Brian Blessed (would surely have some classic stories and the best sledges on the circuit), 2nd: Myself, 3rd: Gillian Zinser (actress in 90210), Gully: Benjamin Francis (my favourite artist at the moment, definitely worth a listen)
TWITTER FEED: @Screech71

JACK LEANING RHB RMF

FULL NAME: Jack Andrew Leaning
BORN: October 18, 1993, Bristol
SQUAD NO: 34
HEIGHT: 6ft
EDUCATION: Archbishop Holgate's School, York; York College
TEAMS: England Under-19s, Yorkshire, Yorkshire 2nd XI, Yorkshire Academy, Yorkshire Under-15s, Yorkshire Under-17s
CAREER: List A: 2012

NOTES: Son of former York City goalkeeper Andy, Leaning wrote himself into the Yorkshire record-books as a 14-year-old, when he hit an unbeaten 164 during the U14 squad's clash with Cheshire. Now 19, he joined hometown club York CC earlier this year, although he will hope to be playing as much as possible for the full Yorkshire side, having made his Yorkshire debut in a CB40 match last season. He won Yorkshire's Academy Player of the Year award last year

Batting	Mat	Inns	NO	Runs	HS	Ave	SR	100	50	Ct	St
List A	1	1	0	11	11	11.00	50.00	0	0	0	0
Bowling	**Inns**	**Balls**	**Runs**	**Wkts**	**BBI**	**BBM**	**Ave**	**Econ**	**SR**	**5w**	**10**
List A	1	-	-	-	-	-	-	-	-	-	-

ALEX LEES LHB LB

YORKSHIRE

FULL NAME: Alexander Zak Lees
BORN: April 14, 1993, Halifax, Yorkshire
SQUAD NO: 14
HEIGHT: 6ft 3in
NICKNAME: Leesy
EDUCATION: Holy Trinity Senior School
TEAMS: Yorkshire, Yorkshire 2nd XI, Yorkshire Academy, Yorkshire Under-17s
CAREER: First-class: 2010; List A: 2011

BEST BATTING: 38 Yorkshire vs Indians, Leeds, 2010

WHO WOULD PLAY YOU IN A FILM OF YOUR LIFE? Sean Lock
CAREER HIGHLIGHTS? Making my debut against India A in 2010
BEST PLAYER IN COUNTY CRICKET? Nick Compton
TIP FOR THE TOP? Matthew Fisher
IF YOU WEREN'T A CRICKETER? I'd be a teacher
DESERT ISLAND DISC? Mumford And Sons
FAVOURITE TV? Family Guy
CRICKETING HEROES? Brian Lara
ACCOMPLISHMENTS? I'm doing a Leeds half-marathon in May in memory of my late father
SURPRISING FACT? I like to do a bit of magic every now and then
FANTASY SLIP CORDON? Keeper: Sean Lock, 1st: Johnny Vegas, 2nd: James Bond, 3rd: Cheryl Cole, 4th: Batman, Gully: Gary Barlow
TWITTER FEED: @aleesy14

Batting	Mat	Inns	NO	Runs	HS	Ave	SR	100	50	Ct	St
First-class	2	2	0	38	38	19.00	35.18	0	0	0	0
List A	2	2	1	35	23	35.00	72.91	0	0	0	0
Bowling	**Inns**	**Balls**	**Runs**	**Wkts**	**BBI**	**BBM**	**Ave**	**Econ**	**SR**	**5w**	**10**
First-class	2	-	-	-	-	-	-	-	-	-	-
List A	2	-	-	-	-	-	-	-	-	-	-

JON LEWIS

RHB RM W9 MVP98

FULL NAME: Jonathan Lewis
BORN: August 26, 1975, Aylesbury, Buckinghamshire
SQUAD NO: 7
HEIGHT: 6ft 2in
NICKNAME: Lewy
EDUCATION: Churchfields School, Swindon
TEAMS: England, Gloucestershire, Surrey
CAREER: Test: 2006; ODI: 2005; T20I: 2005; First-class: 1995; List A: 1995; T20: 2003

BEST BATTING: 71 Gloucestershire vs Middlesex, Uxbridge, 2011
BEST BOWLING: 8-95 Gloucestershire vs Zimbabweans, Gloucester, 2000
COUNTY CAP: 1998 (Gloucestershire); BENEFIT YEAR: 2007 (Gloucestershire)

CAREER HIGHLIGHTS? Every time I played for England and all Gloucestershire one-day trophies
MOST MARKED CHARACTERISTIC? My calmness
BEST PLAYER IN COUNTY CRICKET? Marcus Trescothick
DESERT ISLAND DISC? Roberta Flack – The First Time Ever I Saw Your Face
FAVOURITE TV? The Masters golf tournament or the Ryder Cup
CRICKETING HEROES? Courtney Walsh, Richard Hadlee, Jack Russell
SURPRISING FACT? I have five kids
FANTASY SLIP CORDON? Keeper: Mick Jagger, 1st: Tiger Woods, 2nd: Rory McIlroy, 3rd: Paolo Di Canio
TWITTER FEED: @jonlew800

Batting	Mat	Inns	NO	Runs	HS	Ave	SR	100	50	Ct	St
Tests	1	2	0	27	20	13.50	60.00	0	0	0	0
ODIs	13	8	2	50	17	8.33	79.36	0	0	0	0
T20Is	2	2	1	1	1	1.00	25.00	0	0	1	0
First-class	241	346	69	4517	71	16.30		0	13	61	0
List A	222	127	45	918	54	11.19		0	1	41	0
Twenty20	56	37	9	353	43	12.60	125.62	0	0	10	0
Bowling	**Inns**	**Balls**	**Runs**	**Wkts**	**BBI**	**BBM**	**Ave**	**Econ**	**SR**	**5w**	**10**
Tests	1	246	122	3	3/68	3/122	40.66	2.97	82.0	0	0
ODIs	13	716	500	18	4/36	4/36	27.77	4.18	39.7	0	0
T20Is	2	42	55	4	4/24	4/24	13.75	7.85	10.5	0	0
First-class	241	43288	21603	829	8/95		26.05	2.99	52.2	35	5
List A	222	10024	7667	289	5/19	5/19	26.52	4.58	34.6	2	0
Twenty20	56	1146	1600	54	4/24	4/24	29.62	8.37	21.2	0	0

CHRIS LIDDLE RHB LMF

FULL NAME: Christopher John Liddle
BORN: February 1, 1984, Middlesbrough, Yorkshire
SQUAD NO: 11
HEIGHT: 6ft 4in
NICKNAME: Lids, Chuck
EDUCATION: Nunthorpe Comprehensive, Middlesborough; Teeside Tertiary College
TEAMS: Dhaka Gladiators, Leicestershire, Leicestershire 2nd XI, Sussex
CAREER: First-class: 2005; List A: 2006; T20: 2008

BEST BATTING: 53 Sussex vs Worcestershire, Hove, 2007
BEST BOWLING: 3-42 Leicestershire vs Somerset, Leicester, 2006

FAMILY TIES? My brother Andrew plays in the NYSD cricket league
CAREER HIGHLIGHTS? T20 debut. The 2011 season having previously missed the 2009 and 2010 seasons with injury
CRICKETING HEROES? Darren Gough, AB de Villiers, Marc Rosenberg
NON-CRICKETING HEROES? Jamie Redknapp
BEST PLAYER IN COUNTY CRICKET? Chris Nash
TIP FOR THE TOP? Luke Wells
IF YOU WEREN'T A CRICKETER? I'd be an electrician
WHEN RAIN STOPS PLAY? On my iPad or messing around with some teammates
FAVOURITE FILM? Snatch
FAVOURITE TV? An Idiot Abroad, Emmerdale
DREAM HOLIDAY? Sea apartment in the Maldives
SURPRISING SKILL? Occasional DJ for friends
GUILTY PLEASURES? Chocolate biscuits
FANTASY SLIP CORDON? Keeper: Karl Pilkington, 1st: Cheryl Cole, 2nd: Jamie Redknapp, 3rd: Mila Kunis, 4th: Me, Gully: Jessica Biel
TWITTER FEED: @chrisliddle11

Batting	Mat	Inns	NO	Runs	HS	Ave	SR	100	50	Ct	St
First-class	16	14	5	113	53	12.55	62.08	0	1	5	0
List A	39	12	2	60	15	6.00	71.42	0	0	12	0
Twenty20	44	11	6	45	16	9.00	67.16	0	0	13	0
Bowling	**Inns**	**Balls**	**Runs**	**Wkts**	**BBI**	**BBM**	**Ave**	**Econ**	**SR**	**5w**	**10**
First-class	16	1832	986	19	3/42	4/82	51.89	3.22	96.4	0	0
List A	39	1397	1368	50	5/18	5/18	27.36	5.87	27.9	1	0
Twenty20	44	827	1012	57	5/17	5/17	17.75	7.34	14.5	1	0

ARRON LILLEY RHB OB

FULL NAME: Arron Mark Lilley
BORN: April 1, 1991, Tameside, Lancashire
SQUAD NO: 19
HEIGHT: 6ft 1in
NICKNAME: Silly, Lils
EDUCATION: Mossley Hollins High School; Ashton Sixth Form
TEAMS: Lancashire, Lancashire 2nd XI, Lancashire Under-13s, Lancashire Under-15s, Lancashire Under-17s, Lancashire Under-19s
CAREER: List A: 2012

WHO WOULD PLAY YOU IN A FILM OF YOUR LIFE? Jim Carrey or David Beckham
CAREER HIGHLIGHTS? Signing my first professional contract for Lancashire and making my debut against Worcestershire in the CB40
SUPERSTITIONS? I always put my left pad on first
MOST MARKED CHARACTERISTIC? I'm an angry man
BEST PLAYER IN COUNTY CRICKET? Graeme Swann or Kevin Pietersen
TIPS FOR THE TOP? Alex Davies, Haseeb Hameed
IF YOU WEREN'T A CRICKETER? Physiotherapist or accountant
DESERT ISLAND DISC? Michael Bublé, so I could relax
FAVOURITE TV? TOWIE, The Undateables, Wild At Heart, Mr Selfridge
BIGGEST DRESSING DOWN YOU'VE RECEIVED? My first ever county 2nd XI game. We lost by two runs when we were cruising needing five to win with four wickets left and I was involved in the funniest run-out of my cricket career. The dressing room after the game was intense to say the least
CRICKETING HEROES? Shane Warne, Graeme Swann, Andrew Flintoff
NON-CRICKETING HEROES? Eddie Murphy, Jim Carrey, David Beckham
WHEN YOU RETIRE? Physio or sports accountant
SURPRISING FACT? I'm a mathematical genius
FANTASY SLIP CORDON? Keeper: Jim Carrey, 1st: Maxwell Bygraves, 2nd: Paddy O'Shea, 3rd: Saj Mahmood, 4th: Pixie Lott, Gully: Andrew Flintoff
TWITTER FEED: @Arronlilley20

Batting	Mat	Inns	NO	Runs	HS	Ave	SR	100	50	Ct	St
List A	1	-	-	-	-	-	-	-	-	-	-
Bowling	**Inns**	**Balls**	**Runs**	**Wkts**	**BBI**	**BBM**	**Ave**	**Econ**	**SR**	**5w**	**10**
List A	1	-	-	-	-	-	-	-	-	-	-

TIM LINLEY

RHB RFM W1

SURREY

FULL NAME: Timothy Edward Linley
BORN: March 23, 1982, Horsforth, Leeds
SQUAD NO: 12
HEIGHT: 6ft 3in
NICKNAME: Sheephead, Bambi
EDUCATION: St Mary's RC Comprehensive; Notre Dame Sixth Form College; Oxford Brookes University
TEAMS: Middlesex 2nd XI, Nottinghamshire 2nd XI, Oxford MCCU, Surrey, Surrey 2nd XI, Sussex, Sussex 2nd XI
CAREER: First-class: 2003; List A: 2009; T20: 2009

BEST BATTING: 42 Oxford UCCE vs Derbyshire, Oxford, 2005
BEST BOWLING: 6-57 Surrey vs Leicestershire, Leicester, 2011

WHO WOULD PLAY YOU IN A FILM OF YOUR LIFE? Anyone. If I've had a film made about me I have obviously achieved something with my life
CAREER HIGHLIGHTS? Gaining promotion to Division One with Surrey and taking my first five-wicket haul at The Oval in the County Championship vs Notts in 2012
SUPERSTITIONS? Always left pad on first. I never mess with Mother Cricket
MOST MARKED CHARACTERISTIC? Most people say I'm nice. I have no control over the tone and volume of my voice or laugh
BEST PLAYER IN COUNTY CRICKET? Nick Compton, Peter Trego
TIP FOR THE TOP? Stuart Meaker will play Test cricket in the next two seasons
FAVOURITE BOOK? The Alchemist by Paulo Coelho
SURPRISING FACT? I'm dyspraxic (look it up – it might explain a few things)

Batting	Mat	Inns	NO	Runs	HS	Ave	SR	100	50	Ct	St
First-class	42	59	14	393	42	8.73	33.67	0	0	14	0
List A	18	6	5	37	20*	37.00	78.72	0	0	2	0
Twenty20	7	2	0	9	8	4.50	112.50	0	0	2	0
Bowling	**Inns**	**Balls**	**Runs**	**Wkts**	**BBI**	**BBM**	**Ave**	**Econ**	**SR**	**5w**	**10**
First-class	42	6704	3370	133	6/57		25.33	3.01	50.4	5	1
List A	18	592	554	12	3/50	3/50	46.16	5.61	49.3	0	0
Twenty20	7	122	148	6	2/28	2/28	24.66	7.27	20.3	0	0

DAVID LLOYD RHB OB

FULL NAME: David Liam Lloyd
BORN: June 15, 1992, St Asaph, Flintshire
SQUAD NO: 14
TEAMS: Glamorgan, Glamorgan 2nd XI, Wales Minor Counties
CAREER: First-class: 2012

GLAMORGAN

BEST BATTING: 11* Glamorgan vs Kent, Cardiff, 2012

NOTES: Batsman who made his 2nd XI debut for Glamorgan in 2008 at the age of 16. Signed a professional contract in July 2012. Made a pair on first-class debut during the county's eight-wicket defeat to Yorkshire at Headingley, and followed that with another duck in the first innings of his second game, against Kent. Managed 11 not out in his fourth innings, before spending part of the winter training in Sri Lanka with the Global Cricket Academy. His place on the camp was funded by the Tom Maynard Trust Fund

Batting	Mat	Inns	NO	Runs	HS	Ave	SR	100	50	Ct	St
First-class	2	4	1	11	11*	3.66	29.72	0	0	0	0
Bowling	**Inns**	**Balls**	**Runs**	**Wkts**	**BBI**	**BBM**	**Ave**	**Econ**	**SR**	**5w**	**10**
First-class	2	-	-	-	-	-	-	-	-	-	-

ADAM LONDON

LHB OB

FULL NAME: Adam Brian London
BORN: October 12, 1988, Surrey
SQUAD NO: 19
HEIGHT: 5ft 8in
NICKNAME: Londers, Lon, Giggsy
EDUCATION: Ashford CofE; Bishop Wand CofE and Sixth Form
TEAMS: Middlesex, Middlesex 2nd XI
CAREER: First-class: 2009; List A: 2009

BEST BATTING: 77 Middlesex vs Northamptonshire, Northampton, 2010
BEST BOWLING: 1-15 Middlesex vs Oxford MCCU, Oxford, 2010

WHO WOULD PLAY YOU IN A FILM OF YOUR LIFE? Rowan Atkinson
CAREER HIGHLIGHTS? Scoring 68 for Middlesex at Lord's on my debut and being 12th man for England at Lord's in the Ashes
SUPERSTITIONS? Right pad on first
MOST MARKED CHARACTERISTIC? Moles!
BEST PLAYER IN COUNTY CRICKET? Joe Root
TIPS FOR THE TOP? Harry Podmore and Tom Helm
IF YOU WEREN'T A CRICKETER? I'd like to still be involved through coaching
DESERT ISLAND DISC? One Direction's latest album
FAVOURITE TV? Geordie Shore
BIGGEST DRESSING DOWN YOU'VE RECEIVED? Probably when I was doing 12th man for Middlesex at Leicester, when I was 18 or 19, and I dropped someone in it (I won't name names!). We had a poor day in the field and Toby Radford wasn't very happy! I won't tell the whole story...
CRICKETING HEROES? Maybe not heroes but I loved watching Graham Thorpe bat and now enjoy watching Alastair Cook
WHEN YOU RETIRE? I'd like to run my own business
SURPRISING FACT? I eat tomato sauce with near enough everything
TWITTER FEED: @londers19

Batting	Mat	Inns	NO	Runs	HS	Ave	SR	100	50	Ct	St
First-class	9	17	3	367	77	26.21	38.59	0	3	4	0
List A	3	1	0	3	3	3.00	30.00	0	0	0	0
Bowling	**Inns**	**Balls**	**Runs**	**Wkts**	**BBI**	**BBM**	**Ave**	**Econ**	**SR**	**5w**	**10**
First-class	9	96	54	1	1/15	1/15	54.00	3.37	96.0	0	0
List A	3	6	5	0	-	-	-	5.00	-	0	0

DAVID LUCAS

RHB LMF W1

FULL NAME: David Scott Lucas
BORN: August 19, 1978, Nottingham
SQUAD NO: 6
HEIGHT: 6ft 3in
NICKNAME: Muke, Lukey
EDUCATION: Djanogly City Academy, Nottingham
TEAMS: Lincolnshire, Northamptonshire, Nottinghamshire, Worcestershire, Yorkshire
CAREER: First-class: 1999; List A: 1999; T20: 2007

BEST BATTING: 60 Northamptonshire vs Leicestershire, Leicester, 2011
BEST BOWLING: 7-24 Northamptonshire vs Gloucestershire, Cheltenham, 2009
COUNTY CAP: 2009 (Northamptonshire)

WHO WOULD PLAY YOU IN A FILM OF YOUR LIFE? Daniel Craig
CAREER HIGHLIGHTS? Having a year out of the game, realising what I had, then being lucky enough to have another chance. Bowling four overs for four runs and taking four wickets against Derbyshire in a one-day game. Playing abroad in various countries. Spending time playing with and against great people throughout the season
MOST MARKED CHARACTERISTIC? Determined and selfless
BEST PLAYER IN COUNTY CRICKET? Marcus Trescothick
TIPS FOR THE TOP? George Edwards (Surrey) and Joe Root
IF YOU WEREN'T A CRICKETER? Working with my exterior cleaning business (Pristine Clean), coaching, working with animals
CRICKETING HEROES? Wasim Akram, Craig White, Chaminda Vaas, Steve Waugh, Damien Martyn
ACCOMPLISHMENTS? Setting up my business in 2006
WHEN YOU RETIRE? Pass on what I have learned over the years through coaching, further my business, have a holiday in the summer and get a dog
SURPRISING FACT? I played indoor cricket for England

Batting	Mat	Inns	NO	Runs	HS	Ave	SR	100	50	Ct	St
First-class	92	119	27	1664	60	18.08		0	2	17	0
List A	82	34	12	229	32*	10.40		0	0	22	0
Twenty20	30	7	4	16	5*	5.33	64.00	0	0	5	0
Bowling	**Inns**	**Balls**	**Runs**	**Wkts**	**BBI**	**BBM**	**Ave**	**Econ**	**SR**	**5w**	**10**
First-class	92	14249	8381	261	7/24		32.11	3.52	54.5	9	1
List A	82	3066	2951	94	5/48	5/48	31.39	5.77	32.6	1	0
Twenty20	30	476	612	21	3/19	3/19	29.14	7.71	22.6	0	0

MICHAEL LUMB

LHB RM R2 MVP46

FULL NAME: Michael John Lumb
BORN: February 12, 1980, Johannesburg, South Africa
SQUAD NO: 45
HEIGHT: 6ft
NICKNAME: Joe, Lumby, China, Slumdog
EDUCATION: St Stithians College
TEAMS: Deccan Chargers, England Lions, Hampshire, Nottinghamshire, Queensland, Rajasthan Royals, Sydney Sixers, Yorkshire
CAREER: T20I: 2010; First-class: 2000; List A: 2001; T20: 2003

BEST BATTING: 219 Hampshire vs Nottinghamshire, Nottingham, 2009
BEST BOWLING: 2-10 Yorkshire vs Kent, Canterbury, 2001
COUNTY CAPS: 2003 (Yorkshire); 2008 (Hampshire)

FAMILY TIES? Father Richard played for Yorkshire and uncle Tich played for Natal and South Africa
CAREER HIGHLIGHTS? It would have to be playing for England and winning the World T20, beating the Aussies in the final! Winning the C&G Trophy with Hampshire at Lord's
SUPERSTITIONS? Too many to mention, they call me Rain Man!
CRICKETING HEROES? Graham Thorpe, Darren Lehmann, Stephen Fleming, Craig White, Shane Warne, Jacques Kallis
NON-CRICKETING HEROES? Nelson Mandela
BEST PLAYER IN COUNTY CRICKET? Marcus Trescothick – no brainer!
FAVOURITE TV? Entourage, 24, CSI
FAVOURITE FILM? Man On Fire
FAVOURITE BOOK? Bringing Down The House
DREAM HOLIDAY? Any beach holiday
GUILTY PLEASURES? Chocolate and biltong

Batting	Mat	Inns	NO	Runs	HS	Ave	SR	100	50	Ct	St
T20Is	14	14	1	287	53*	22.07	128.69	0	2	5	0
First-class	150	251	15	8254	219	34.97		15	48	99	0
List A	174	168	11	4992	110	31.79	84.69	3	39	61	0
Twenty20	137	136	11	3083	124*	24.66	139.69	1	17	47	0
Bowling	**Inns**	**Balls**	**Runs**	**Wkts**	**BBI**	**BBM**	**Ave**	**Econ**	**SR**	**5w**	**10**
T20Is	14	-	-	-	-	-	-	-	-	-	-
First-class	150	330	255	6	2/10		42.50	4.63	55.0	0	0
List A	174	12	28	0	-	-	-	14.00	-	0	0
Twenty20	137	36	65	3	3/32	3/32	21.66	10.83	12.0	0	0

ADAM LYTH

LHB OB R1

FULL NAME: Adam Lyth
BORN: September 25, 1987, Whitby, Yorkshire
SQUAD NO: 9
HEIGHT: 5ft 9in
NICKNAME: Peanut, Lythy
EDUCATION: Caedmon Whitby Community College
TEAMS: England Lions, England Under-19s, Yorkshire, Yorkshire 2nd XI
CAREER: First-class: 2007; List A: 2006; T20: 2008

BEST BATTING: 248* Yorkshire vs Leicestershire, Leicester, 2012
BEST BOWLING: 1-12 Yorkshire vs Loughborough UCCE, Leeds, 2007
COUNTY CAP: 2010

WHO WOULD PLAY YOU IN A FILM OF YOUR LIFE? Bruce Willis
CAREER HIGHLIGHTS? Being the leading run-scorer in Division One in 2010. Receiving the PCA Young Player of the Year award in 2010. Being selected and playing for the England Lions. Playing for Yorkshire in the 2012 Champions League T20
BEST PLAYER IN COUNTY CRICKET? Marcus Trescothick
TIP FOR THE TOP? Azeem Rafiq
DESERT ISLAND DISC? The Script
FAVOURITE TV? Only Fools And Horses
CRICKETING HEROES? Graham Thorpe
NON-CRICKETING HEROES? David Beckham
ACCOMPLISHMENTS? Playing for Manchester City U15
WHEN YOU RETIRE? Umpire
FANTASY SLIP CORDON? Keeper: John Bishop, 1st: Charlize Theron, 2nd: Arsene Wenger, 3rd: Ian Poulter, Gully: Me

Batting	Mat	Inns	NO	Runs	HS	Ave	SR	100	50	Ct	St
First-class	65	104	2	3927	248*	38.50		5	29	57	0
List A	62	56	4	1457	109*	28.01	86.52	1	7	19	0
Twenty20	45	39	1	772	78	20.31	125.73	0	2	17	0
Bowling	**Inns**	**Balls**	**Runs**	**Wkts**	**BBI**	**BBM**	**Ave**	**Econ**	**SR**	**5w**	**10**
First-class	65	397	297	3	1/12	1/12	99.00	4.48	132.3	0	0
List A	62	18	14	0	-	-	-	4.66	-	0	0
Twenty20	45	9	14	0	-	-	-	9.33	-	0	0

MATT MACHAN LHB OB

FULL NAME: Matthew William Machan
BORN: February 15, 1991, Brighton, Sussex
SQUAD NO: 15
HEIGHT: 5ft 9in
NICKNAME: Mach
EDUCATION: Hurstpierpoint College; Brighton College
TEAMS: Scotland, Sussex, Sussex 2nd XI
CAREER: First-class: 2010; List A: 2010; T20: 2012

BEST BATTING: 99 Sussex vs Oxford MCCU, Oxford, 2011

CAREER HIGHLIGHTS? Making my 1st XI debuts for Sussex
CRICKETING HEROES? Andrew Hodd, Will Beer, David Warner
NON-CRICKETING HEROES? Gandhi
BEST PLAYER IN COUNTY CRICKET? Marcus Trescothick
TIPS FOR THE TOP? Ben Brown, Will Beer
IF YOU WEREN'T A CRICKETER? I'd be working for my dad
WHEN RAIN STOPS PLAY? Monopoly on iPad or dressing room golf
FAVOURITE TV? The Only Way Is Essex
FAVOURITE FILM? The Shawshank Redemption
FAVOURITE BOOK? Of Mice And Men
DREAM HOLIDAY? Cape Town
ACCOMPLISHMENTS? Yellow belt in judo
SURPRISING SKILL? Qualified personal trainer and nutritionist
GUILTY PLEASURES? Skittles, Lola Lo (bar in Brighton)
SURPRISING FACT? Used to play county rugby. Part-time garage DJ
FANTASY SLIP CORDON? Keeper: John Bishop, 1st: Jessica Wright, 2nd: Joey Essex, 3rd: Mike 'The Situation', Gully: Tinie Tempah
TWITTER FEED: @mattmachan

Batting	Mat	Inns	NO	Runs	HS	Ave	SR	100	50	Ct	St
First-class	5	6	0	191	99	31.83	69.70	0	2	0	0
List A	6	6	1	227	126*	45.40	96.59	1	1	2	0
Twenty20	8	8	0	61	22	7.62	75.30	0	0	4	0
Bowling	**Inns**	**Balls**	**Runs**	**Wkts**	**BBI**	**BBM**	**Ave**	**Econ**	**SR**	**5w**	**10**
First-class	5	6	4	0	-	-	-	4.00	-	0	0
List A	6	-	-	-	-	-	-	-	-	-	-
Twenty20	8	-	-	-	-	-	-	-	-	-	-

DARREN MADDY

RHB RM R4 MVP47

FULL NAME: Darren Lee Maddy
BORN: May 23, 1974, Leicester
SQUAD NO: 43
HEIGHT: 5ft 8in
NICKNAME: Roaster, Dazza, Madds, Mr C
EDUCATION: Roundhill, Thurmaston; Wreake Valley, Syston
TEAMS: England, Leicestershire, Warwickshire
CAREER: Test: 1999; ODI: 1998; T20I: 2007; First-class: 1994; List A: 1993; T20: 2003

BEST BATTING: 229* Leicestershire vs Loughborough UCCE, Leicester, 2003
BEST BOWLING: 5-37 Leicestershire vs Hampshire, Southampton, 2002
COUNTY CAPS: 1996 (Leicestershire); 2007 (Warwickshire); BENEFIT YEAR: 2006 (Leicestershire)

CAREER HIGHLIGHTS? Playing cricket for England in Tests, ODIs and T20Is, winning two Championships with Leicestershire in 1996 and 1998, winning two T20 Cups with Leicestershire in 2004 and 2006, captaining Warwickshire in 2007 and 2008, winning the CB40 with Warwickshire in 2010
CRICKETING HEROES? Ian Botham, David Gower
BEST PLAYER IN COUNTY CRICKET? Marcus Trescothick and Ian Bell
TIP FOR THE TOP? Chris Woakes
FAVOURITE TV? Luther
SURPRISING SKILL? I play the drums
TWITTER FEED: @DarrenMaddy

Batting	Mat	Inns	NO	Runs	HS	Ave	SR	100	50	Ct	St
Tests	3	4	0	46	24	11.50	24.21	0	0	4	0
ODIs	8	6	0	113	53	18.83	54.85	0	1	1	0
T20Is	4	4	0	113	50	28.25	141.25	0	1	1	0
First-class	281	455	31	13639	229*	32.16		27	62	289	0
List A	355	325	37	8939	167*	31.03		11	52	138	0
Twenty20	87	85	9	2238	111	29.44	131.41	1	13	40	0
Bowling	**Inns**	**Balls**	**Runs**	**Wkts**	**BBI**	**BBM**	**Ave**	**Econ**	**SR**	**5w**	**10**
Tests	3	84	40	0	-	-	-	2.85	-	0	0
ODIs	8	-	-	-	-	-	-	-	-	-	-
T20Is	4	18	26	3	2/6	2/6	8.66	8.66	6.0	0	0
First-class	281	15378	7898	252	5/37		31.34	3.08	61.0	5	0
List A	355	7247	6262	215	4/16	4/16	29.12	5.18	33.7	0	0
Twenty20	87	827	1096	49	3/10	3/10	22.36	7.95	16.8	0	0

WAYNE MADSEN RHB OB

FULL NAME: Wayne Lee Madsen
BORN: January 2, 1984, Durban, South Africa
SQUAD NO: 77
HEIGHT: 6ft
NICKNAME: Madders, Mads
EDUCATION: Highbury Prep School; Kearsney College; University of South Africa
TEAMS: Derbyshire, Derbyshire 2nd XI, KwaZulu-Natal
CAREER: First-class: 2004; List A: 2004; T20: 2010

BEST BATTING: 231* Derbyshire vs Northamptonshire, Northampton, 2012
BEST BOWLING: 3-45 KwaZulu-Natal vs Eastern Province, Port Elizabeth, 2008
COUNTY CAP: 2011

FAMILY TIES? My uncles, Trevor Madsen and Henry Fotheringham, played cricket for South Africa. Another uncle, Mike Madsen, and my cousin, Greg Fotheringham, both played first-class cricket in South Africa. My father Paddy played Natal Schools cricket
CAREER HIGHLIGHTS? Scoring 170* on debut for Derbyshire against Gloucestershire at Cheltenham in 2009
CRICKETING HEROES? Jonty Rhodes, Hansie Cronje, Shaun Pollock, Dale Benkenstein
NON-CRICKETING HEROES? Nelson Mandela, my grandfather Lionel Madsen
TIPS FOR THE TOP? James Taylor, Ross Whiteley, Tom Knight
IF YOU WEREN'T A CRICKETER? I'd be playing hockey or coaching sport. Might have had a stint as a game ranger
FAVOURITE FILM? Avatar
ACCOMPLISHMENTS? Playing 39 hockey Test matches for South Africa. Playing in the 2006 Commonwealth Games and the 2006 Hockey World Cup
SURPRISING FACTS? I'm one of 10 people in my family to represent South Africa at hockey, my right leg is shorter than my left by 1.5cm and I've shot a -4 round of 68 on a Championship golf course (when I was a student and playing regular golf!)

Batting	Mat	Inns	NO	Runs	HS	Ave	SR	100	50	Ct	St
First-class	80	140	9	4712	231*	35.96	48.37	13	21	68	0
List A	47	45	9	1291	75	35.86	82.86	0	10	34	0
Twenty20	27	26	3	510	61*	22.17	115.90	0	3	6	0
Bowling	**Inns**	**Balls**	**Runs**	**Wkts**	**BBI**	**BBM**	**Ave**	**Econ**	**SR**	**5w**	**10**
First-class	80	692	373	7	3/45		53.28	3.23	98.8	0	0
List A	47	102	74	5	2/18	2/18	14.80	4.35	20.4	0	0
Twenty20	27	-	-	-	-	-	-	-	-	-	-

STEVE MAGOFFIN LHB RFM W1 MVP17

FULL NAME: Steven James Magoffin
BORN: December 17, 1979, Corinda, Queensland, Australia
SQUAD NO: 64
HEIGHT: 6ft 4in
NICKNAME: Mags, Magsy, Emu
EDUCATION: Indooropilly High School, Brisbane
TEAMS: Leicestershire 2nd XI, Queensland, Surrey, Surrey 2nd XI, Sussex, Western Australia, Worcestershire
CAREER: First-class: 2004; List A: 2004; T20: 2006

BEST BATTING: 79 Western Australia vs Tasmania, Perth, 2008
BEST BOWLING: 8-47 Western Australia vs South Australia, Perth, 2006

FAMILY TIES? My older brother Chris played grade cricket in Brisbane
WHO WOULD PLAY YOU IN A FILM OF YOUR LIFE? George Clooney!
CAREER HIGHLIGHTS? Hitting the winning runs in the 2011/12 Sheffield Shield final for the Queensland Bulls. Touring South Africa for the second Test of Australia's tour – I didn't play but it was a great experience
MOST MARKED CHARACTERISTIC? Being particularly lanky!
BEST PLAYER IN COUNTY CRICKET? Chris Rogers
TIP FOR THE TOP? Luke Wells
IF YOU WEREN'T A CRICKETER? Not too sure – it's all I've done! But I'd love to be a chef
DESERT ISLAND DISC? Coldplay Live Tour 2012 or The 12th Man Box Set (very popular in Oz!)
FAVOURITE TV? Seinfeld
BIGGEST DRESSING DOWN YOU'VE RECEIVED? From former WA Warriors coach Wayne Clark for getting out to a "very part-time" spinner in the last over before the second new ball!
CRICKETING HEROES? Curtly Ambrose, Glenn McGrath, Mike Hussey
ACCOMPLISHMENTS? Becoming a father for the first time
TWITTER FEED: @magsy64

Batting	Mat	Inns	NO	Runs	HS	Ave	SR	100	50	Ct	St
First-class	88	124	33	1820	79	20.00	48.00	0	4	25	0
List A	51	29	19	225	24*	22.50	77.05	0	0	12	0
Twenty20	8	2	1	12	11*	12.00	171.42	0	0	1	0
Bowling	**Inns**	**Balls**	**Runs**	**Wkts**	**BBI**	**BBM**	**Ave**	**Econ**	**SR**	**5w**	**10**
First-class	88	17376	7719	304	8/47		25.39	2.66	57.1	10	1
List A	51	2556	2010	65	4/58	4/58	30.92	4.71	39.3	0	0
Twenty20	8	156	228	5	2/15	2/15	45.60	8.76	31.2	0	0

SAJ MAHMOOD RHB RFM

FULL NAME: Sajid Iqbal Mahmood
BORN: December 21, 1981, Bolton, Lancashire
SQUAD NO: 19
HEIGHT: 6ft 4in
NICKNAME: Saj, King
EDUCATION: Smithills School
TEAMS: England, England A, England Lions, Essex, Lancashire, Lancashire Cricket Board, Marylebone Cricket Club, Somerset, Western Australia
CAREER: Test: 2006; ODI: 2004; T20I: 2006; First-class: 2002; List A: 2002; T20: 2003

BEST BATTING: 94 Lancashire vs Sussex, Manchester, 2004
BEST BOWLING: 6-30 Lancashire vs Durham, Chester-le-Street, 2009
COUNTY CAP: 2007 (Lancashire)

CAREER HIGHLIGHTS? Playing for England and winning the County Championship
CRICKETING HEROES? Wasim Akram, Imran Khan
NON-CRICKETING HEROES? Muhammad Ali
BEST PLAYER IN COUNTY CRICKET? Oliver Newby
TIP FOR THE TOP? Karl Brown
IF YOU WEREN'T A CRICKETER? I'd have my own astrology business
WHEN RAIN STOPS PLAY? Drink cups of tea, play one hand-one bounce
FAVOURITE TV? Wildlife documentaries
ACCOMPLISHMENTS? Doing Level 11 on the bleep test
SURPRISING FACTS? Qualified sailor, I play the banjo, I'm a very good listener

Batting	Mat	Inns	NO	Runs	HS	Ave	SR	100	50	Ct	St
Tests	8	11	1	81	34	8.10	50.31	0	0	0	0
ODIs	26	15	4	85	22*	7.72	84.15	0	0	1	0
T20Is	4	2	2	1	1*	-	50.00	0	0	1	0
First-class	115	148	19	2036	94	15.78	68.97	0	9	26	0
List A	147	78	21	518	29	9.08		0	0	21	0
Twenty20	69	31	8	183	34	7.95	146.40	0	0	18	0
Bowling	**Inns**	**Balls**	**Runs**	**Wkts**	**BBI**	**BBM**	**Ave**	**Econ**	**SR**	**5w**	**10**
Tests	8	1130	762	20	4/22	6/130	38.10	4.04	56.5	0	0
ODIs	26	1197	1169	30	4/50	4/50	38.96	5.85	39.9	0	0
T20Is	4	84	155	3	1/31	1/31	51.66	11.07	28.0	0	0
First-class	115	16707	10396	323	6/30		32.18	3.73	51.7	9	2
List A	147	6473	5734	205	5/16	5/16	27.97	5.31	31.5	1	0
Twenty20	69	1450	1920	77	4/21	4/21	24.93	7.94	18.8	0	0

DAWID MALAN LHB LB R1 MVP19

FULL NAME: Dawid Johannes Malan
BORN: September 3, 1987, Roehampton
SQUAD NO: 29
HEIGHT: 6ft 1in
NICKNAME: AC, Mal
EDUCATION: Paarl Boys' High School; UNISA
TEAMS: Boland, Marylebone Cricket Club, Middlesex
CAREER: First-class: 2006; List A: 2006; T20: 2006

BEST BATTING: 143 Middlesex vs Derbyshire, Lord's, 2011
BEST BOWLING: 5-61 Middlesex vs Lancashire, Liverpool, 2012
COUNTY CAP: 2010

FAMILY TIES? Father [Dawid] played for Western Provence B and Northern Transvaal B, my brother [Charl] played for MCC Young Cricketers and Loughborough University
WHO WOULD PLAY YOU IN A FILM OF YOUR LIFE? Brad Pitt
CAREER HIGHLIGHTS? Scoring a century in the T20 Cup quarter-final in 2008 and going on to win the final. Winning Division Two of the County Championship in 2011
SUPERSTITIONS? Way too many
MOST MARKED CHARACTERISTIC? Determination
BEST PLAYER IN COUNTY CRICKET? Chris Rogers
TIP FOR THE TOP? Sam Robson
IF YOU WEREN'T A CRICKETER? I'd be studying or have qualified as a sports psychologist
DESERT ISLAND DISC? Train
CRICKETING HEROES? Gary Kirsten, Matthew Hayden
NON-CRICKETING HEROES? Tiger Woods
WHEN YOU RETIRE? Sports psychology
TWITTER FEED: @dmalan29

Batting	Mat	Inns	NO	Runs	HS	Ave	SR	100	50	Ct	St
First-class	81	139	10	4614	143	35.76	51.53	9	25	97	0
List A	65	65	6	1718	134	29.11	81.61	2	7	22	0
Twenty20	59	56	16	1217	103	30.42	117.58	1	2	13	0
Bowling	**Inns**	**Balls**	**Runs**	**Wkts**	**BBI**	**BBM**	**Ave**	**Econ**	**SR**	**5w**	**10**
First-class	81	2435	1591	38	5/61	5/61	41.86	3.92	64.0	1	0
List A	65	539	552	15	2/4	2/4	36.80	6.14	35.9	0	0
Twenty20	59	258	302	13	2/10	2/10	23.23	7.02	19.8	0	0

JOHNNY MARSDEN | RHB RFM

FULL NAME: Jonathan Marsden
BORN: April 7, 1993, Pembury, Kent
SQUAD NO: 29
EDUCATION: The King's School, Macclesfield
TEAMS: Derbyshire 2nd XI, Derbyshire Under-15s, Derbyshire Under-17s
CAREER: Yet to make first-team debut

NOTES: A member of the Derbyshire set-up since he was 15, Marsden went through the academy and into the 2nd XI, where he took 30 wickets in 22 matches over the 2011 and 2012 seasons. Yet to make his 1st XI debut for Derbyshire

HAMISH MARSHALL RHB RM R1 MVP95

FULL NAME: Hamish John Hamilton Marshall
BORN: February 15, 1979, Auckland, New Zealand
SQUAD NO: 9
HEIGHT: 5ft 7in
NICKNAME: Marshy
EDUCATION: Mahurangi College; King's College
TEAMS: New Zealand, Buckinghamshire, Gloucestershire, Northern Districts, Royal Bengal Tigers
CAREER: Test: 2000; ODI: 2003; T20I: 2005; First-class: 1999; List A: 1998; T20: 2005

BEST BATTING: 170 Northern Districts vs Canterbury, Rangiora, 2010
BEST BOWLING: 4-24 Gloucestershire vs Leicestershire, Leicester, 2009

FAMILY TIES? I have a twin brother [James] who has also played for New Zealand
WHO WOULD PLAY YOU IN A FILM OF YOUR LIFE? Will Ferrell
CAREER HIGHLIGHTS? Maiden Test century vs Australia in 2005
BEST PLAYER IN COUNTY CRICKET? Marcus Trescothick
TIPS FOR THE TOP? Moin Ashraf, Dan Housego, Chris Dent
DESERT ISLAND DISC? The Feelers – Best Of 1998-2008
CRICKETING HEROES? Richard Hadlee, Mark Waugh
NON-CRICKETING HEROES? Rory McIlroy, Roger Federer
WHEN YOU RETIRE? Coach or own a sushi bar
FANTASY SLIP CORDON? Keeper: Michael McIntyre, 1st: Me, 2nd: Rory McIlroy (he seems a top lad and there's always a need for golf chat), 3rd: Simon Cowell (he'd have some great stories and the two comedians will annoy him), Gully: Keith Lemon

Batting	Mat	Inns	NO	Runs	HS	Ave	SR	100	50	Ct	St
Tests	13	19	2	652	160	38.35	47.31	2	2	1	0
ODIs	66	62	9	1454	101*	27.43	73.06	1	12	18	0
T20Is	3	3	0	12	8	4.00	85.71	0	0	1	0
First-class	192	325	22	10824	170	35.72		20	56	104	0
List A	266	253	24	6472	122	28.26		6	43	101	0
Twenty20	81	79	6	1908	102	26.13	137.36	2	7	44	0
Bowling	**Inns**	**Balls**	**Runs**	**Wkts**	**BBI**	**BBM**	**Ave**	**Econ**	**SR**	**5w**	**10**
Tests	13	6	4	0	-	-	-	4.00	-	0	0
ODIs	66	-	-	-	-	-	-	-	-	-	-
T20Is	3	-	-	-	-	-	-	-	-	-	-
First-class	192	3499	1768	37	4/24		47.78	3.03	94.5	0	0
List A	266	284	295	4	2/21	2/21	73.75	6.23	71.0	0	0
Twenty20	81	6	14	0	-	-	-	14.00	-	0	0

DIMITRI MASCARENHAS RHB RM W1

FULL NAME: Adrian Dimitri Mascarenhas
BORN: October 30, 1977, Chiswick, Middlesex
SQUAD NO: 17
HEIGHT: 6ft 1in
NICKNAME: Dimi
EDUCATION: Trinity College, Perth
TEAMS: England, England Lions, Hampshire, Hampshire 2nd XI, Kings XI Punjab, Melbourne Stars, Otago, Rajasthan Royals, Rangpur Riders, Wellington
CAREER: ODI: 2007; T20I: 2007; First-class: 1996; List A: 1996; T20: 2003

BEST BATTING: 131 Hampshire vs Kent, Canterbury, 2006
BEST BOWLING: 6-25 Hampshire vs Derbyshire, Southampton, 2004
COUNTY CAP: 1998; **BENEFIT YEAR:** 2007

FAMILY TIES? Father and uncle played in Sri Lanka, both brothers are retired club cricketers
CRICKETING HEROES? Viv Richards, Malcolm Marshall
NON-CRICKETING HEROES? Michael Jordan
BEST PLAYER IN COUNTY CRICKET? Marcus Trescothick, Glen Chapple
TIPS FOR THE TOP? James Vince, Liam Dawson, Alex Hales
FAVOURITE TV? The Simpsons
FAVOURITE FILM? Lock Stock And Two Smoking Barrels
FAVOURITE BOOK? Breaking Vegas
DREAM HOLIDAY? Las Vegas
GUILTY PLEASURES? Ice cream and McDonald's
SURPRISING FACTS? I have a surprise piercing, I was a sprinter at school (100m, 200m, 400m) and I'm a couch potato
TWITTER FEED: @dimimascarenhas

Batting	Mat	Inns	NO	Runs	HS	Ave	SR	100	50	Ct	St
ODIs	20	13	2	245	52	22.27	95.33	0	1	4	0
T20Is	14	13	5	123	31	15.37	123.00	0	0	7	0
First-class	194	290	32	6454	131	25.01		8	23	76	0
List A	257	213	43	4260	79	25.05		0	27	63	0
Twenty20	114	92	26	1303	57*	19.74	129.00	0	3	26	0
Bowling	**Inns**	**Balls**	**Runs**	**Wkts**	**BBI**	**BBM**	**Ave**	**Econ**	**SR**	**5w**	**10**
ODIs	20	822	634	13	3/23	3/23	48.76	4.62	63.2	0	0
T20Is	14	252	309	12	3/18	3/18	25.75	7.35	21.0	0	0
First-class	194	28181	12640	446	6/25		28.34	2.69	63.1	17	0
List A	257	10935	7823	296	5/27	5/27	26.42	4.29	36.9	1	0
Twenty20	114	2281	2651	135	5/14	5/14	19.63	6.97	16.8	2	0

DAVID MASTERS RHB RMF W3 MVP59

FULL NAME: David Daniel Masters
BORN: April 22, 1978, Chatham, Kent
SQUAD NO: 9
HEIGHT: 6ft 4in
NICKNAME: Hod, Hoddy
EDUCATION: Fort Luton High
TEAMS: Essex, Kent, Leicestershire
CAREER: First-class: 2000; List A: 2000; T20: 2003

BEST BATTING: 119 Leicestershire vs Sussex, Hove, 2003
BEST BOWLING: 8-10 Essex vs Leicestershire, Southend, 2011
COUNTY CAPS: 2007 (Leicestershire); 2008 (Essex); BENEFIT YEAR: 2013 (Essex)

FAMILY TIES? My dad Kevin played for Kent and Surrey and my brother Daniel played for Leicestershire
WHO WOULD PLAY YOU IN A FILM OF YOUR LIFE? David Beckham
CAREER HIGHLIGHTS? Winning a Lord's final
SUPERSTITIONS? Too many to mention
BEST PLAYER IN COUNTY CRICKET? There are plenty. County cricket is in a good place
TIP FOR THE TOP? Reece Topley is going to be one to look out for
IF YOU WEREN'T A CRICKETER? Builder
DESERT ISLAND DISC? Whitney Houston's Greatest Hits
CRICKETING HEROES? Ian Botham
NON-CRICKETING HEROES? David Beckham and Sir Alex Ferguson
ACCOMPLISHMENTS? Getting married and having two wonderful children, Alfie and Harrison
FANTASY SLIP CORDON? Keeper: Paul Nixon, 1st: Sir Alex Ferguson, 2nd: Matt Walker, 3rd: David Beckham
TWITTER FEED: @DavehodMasters

Batting	Mat	Inns	NO	Runs	HS	Ave	SR	100	50	Ct	St
First-class	162	201	29	2438	119	14.17		1	6	52	0
List A	144	71	31	503	39	12.57		0	0	17	0
Twenty20	93	32	15	93	14	5.47	67.88	0	0	19	0
Bowling	**Inns**	**Balls**	**Runs**	**Wkts**	**BBI**	**BBM**	**Ave**	**Econ**	**SR**	**5w**	**10**
First-class	162	29756	13520	522	8/10		25.90	2.72	57.0	24	0
List A	144	5961	4486	139	5/17	5/17	32.27	4.51	42.8	2	0
Twenty20	93	1763	2180	68	3/7	3/7	32.05	7.41	25.9	0	0

GRAEME MCCARTER RHB RM

FULL NAME: Graeme John McCarter
BORN: October 10, 1992, Londonderry
SQUAD NO: 33
HEIGHT: 6ft 3in
NICKNAME: Macca, Gmac
EDUCATION: Foyle College
TEAMS: Ireland, Gloucestershire, Gloucestershire 2nd XI, Ireland Under-13s, Ireland Under-15s, Ireland Under-19s
CAREER: First-class: 2011; List A: 2012

BEST BATTING: 29* Gloucestershire vs Yorkshire, Bristol, 2012
BEST BOWLING: 1-47 Ireland vs Namibia, Belfast, 2011

WHO WOULD PLAY YOU IN A FILM OF YOUR LIFE? Liam Neeson
CAREER HIGHLIGHTS? Debut at Lord's for Gloucestershire on TV and my international debut
MOST MARKED CHARACTERISTIC? My accent
BEST PLAYER IN COUNTY CRICKET? Ian Bell
TIP FOR THE TOP? Jos Buttler
IF YOU WEREN'T A CRICKETER? Journalist
DESERT ISLAND DISC? Mud – Tiger Feet
FAVOURITE TV? King Of Queens
CRICKETING HEROES? Brett Lee
NON-CRICKETING HEROES? My mum and dad
ACCOMPLISHMENTS? Doing a bungee jump
WHEN YOU RETIRE? Travel
SURPRISING FACT? I've played badminton for Ireland
FANTASY SLIP CORDON? Keeper: James Corden, 1st: Me, 2nd: Jonty Rhodes, 3rd: Kevin Bridges
TWITTER FEED: @GraemeMcCarter

Batting	Mat	Inns	NO	Runs	HS	Ave	SR	100	50	Ct	St
First-class	2	2	1	39	29*	39.00	90.69	0	0	1	0
List A	2	-	-	-	-	-	-	-	-	0	0
Bowling	**Inns**	**Balls**	**Runs**	**Wkts**	**BBI**	**BBM**	**Ave**	**Econ**	**SR**	**5w**	**10**
First-class	2	228	157	1	1/47	1/90	157.00	4.13	228.0	0	0
List A	2	57	56	6	3/15	3/15	9.33	5.89	9.5	0	0

NEIL MCKENZIE RHB RM R1

FULL NAME: Neil Douglas McKenzie
BORN: November 24, 1975, Johannesburg, South Africa
SQUAD NO: 44
HEIGHT: 6ft
NICKNAME: Bertie
EDUCATION: King Edward VII; RAU, Johannesburg
TEAMS: South Africa, Durham, Gauteng, Hampshire, Lions, Northerns, Transvaal
CAREER: Test: 2000; ODI: 2000; T20I: 2006; First-class: 1995; List A: 1995; T20: 2004

HAMPSHIRE

BEST BATTING: 237 Hampshire vs Yorkshire, Southampton, 2011
BEST BOWLING: 2-13 Lions vs Eagles, Kimberley, 2007
COUNTY CAP: 2010 (Hampshire)

FAMILY TIES? Father Kevin played for North Eastern Transvaal and Transvaal
NOTES: Captained South African Schools and South Africa U19. South African Cricket Annual Cricketer of the Year in 2001. Part of a world record-breaking opening stand of 415 with Graeme Smith in the second Test against Bangladesh in Chittagong in 2008. Played a major role in Hampshire's one-day successes in 2012

Batting	Mat	Inns	NO	Runs	HS	Ave	SR	100	50	Ct	St
Tests	58	94	7	3253	226	37.39	42.00	5	16	54	0
ODIs	64	55	10	1688	131*	37.51	69.40	2	10	21	0
T20Is	2	1	1	7	7*	-	87.50	0	0	0	0
First-class	257	438	56	17423	237	45.60		48	81	229	0
List A	270	244	39	7754	131*	37.82		10	54	82	0
Twenty20	110	101	30	2468	89*	34.76	120.74	0	15	31	0
Bowling	**Inns**	**Balls**	**Runs**	**Wkts**	**BBI**	**BBM**	**Ave**	**Econ**	**SR**	**5w**	**10**
Tests	58	90	68	0	-	-	-	4.53	-	0	0
ODIs	64	46	27	0	-	-	-	3.52	-	0	0
T20Is	2	-	-	-	-	-	-	-	-	-	-
First-class	257	930	519	10	2/13		51.90	3.34	93.0	0	0
List A	270	255	248	4	2/19	2/19	62.00	5.83	63.7	0	0
Twenty20	110	24	34	1	1/4	1/4	34.00	8.50	24.0	0	0

STUART MEAKER RHB RF W1 MVP58

FULL NAME: Stuart Christopher Meaker
BORN: January 21, 1989, Pietermaritzburg, South Africa
SQUAD NO: 18
HEIGHT: 6ft
NICKNAME: Ten Bears
EDUCATION: Cranleigh School
TEAMS: England, England Lions, England Under-19s, Surrey, Surrey 2nd XI
CAREER: ODI: 2011; T20I: 2012; First-class: 2008; List A: 2008; T20: 2010

BEST BATTING: 94 Surrey vs Bangladeshis, The Oval, 2010
BEST BOWLING: 8-52 Surrey vs Somerset, The Oval, 2012

CAREER HIGHLIGHTS? Making my ODI debut against India
CRICKETING HEROES? Allan Donald, Dale Steyn
BEST PLAYER IN COUNTY CRICKET? Marcus Trescothick
TIP FOR THE TOP? Jason Roy
FAVOURITE TV? Family Guy
FAVOURITE FILM? Fight Club
FAVOURITE BOOK? Asterix And Obelix
DREAM HOLIDAY? Maldives
ACCOMPLISHMENTS? I played Pumba in the school play
SURPRISING SKILL? I can do a backflip
SURPRISING FACT? I cannot grow a moustache
FANTASY SLIP CORDON? Keeper: Will Ferrell, 1st: Michael McIntyre, 2nd: Robin Williams, 3rd: Peter Griffin, Gully: Me
TWITTER FEED: @SMeaker18

Batting	Mat	Inns	NO	Runs	HS	Ave	SR	100	50	Ct	St
ODIs	2	2	0	2	1	1.00	12.50	0	0	0	0
T20Is	2	-	-	-	-	-	-	-	-	1	0
First-class	43	55	7	777	94	16.18	38.16	0	4	6	0
List A	42	21	9	70	21*	5.83	51.47	0	0	8	0
Twenty20	22	5	3	27	17	13.50	150.00	0	0	9	0
Bowling	**Inns**	**Balls**	**Runs**	**Wkts**	**BBI**	**BBM**	**Ave**	**Econ**	**SR**	**5w**	**10**
ODIs	2	114	110	2	1/45	1/45	55.00	5.78	57.0	0	0
T20Is	2	47	70	2	1/28	1/28	35.00	8.93	23.5	0	0
First-class	43	6574	4025	145	8/52	11/167	27.75	3.67	45.3	8	1
List A	42	1469	1455	39	4/47	4/47	37.30	5.94	37.6	0	0
Twenty20	22	351	539	16	2/16	2/16	33.68	9.21	21.9	0	0

CRAIG MESCHEDE RHB RMF

FULL NAME: Craig Anthony Joseph Meschede
BORN: November 21, 1991, Johannesburg, South Africa
SQUAD NO: 26
EDUCATION: King's College, Taunton
TEAMS: Somerset, Somerset 2nd XI
CAREER: First-class: 2011; List A: 2011; T20: 2011

BEST BATTING: 62 Somerset vs Durham, Chester-le-Street, 2012
BEST BOWLING: 3-26 Somerset vs Durham, Chester-le-Street, 2012

NOTES: A hard-hitting allrounder. South African-born, but with a German father. Awarded a senior contract in June 2010. Impressed in the 2011 Caribbean T20, hitting 26 from just 11 balls against Combined Campuses and Colleges. Sachin Tendulkar was his maiden first-class wicket. Scored 53 from just 28 deliveries in a FL t20 victory against Glamorgan in 2011. Claimed nine wickets at 22 in last year's CB40, including 4-27 against Scotland

Batting	Mat	Inns	NO	Runs	HS	Ave	SR	100	50	Ct	St
First-class	12	15	2	321	62	24.69	55.44	0	2	3	0
List A	15	10	1	168	33	18.66	84.42	0	0	6	0
Twenty20	19	16	4	199	53	16.58	124.37	0	1	5	0
Bowling	**Inns**	**Balls**	**Runs**	**Wkts**	**BBI**	**BBM**	**Ave**	**Econ**	**SR**	**5w**	**10**
First-class	12	919	559	14	3/26	6/64	39.92	3.64	65.6	0	0
List A	15	378	358	14	4/27	4/27	25.57	5.68	27.0	0	0
Twenty20	19	87	121	6	3/9	3/9	20.16	8.34	14.5	0	0

CHRIS METTERS RHB SLA

FULL NAME: Christopher Liam Metters
BORN: September 12, 1990, Torquay, Devon
SQUAD NO: 35
HEIGHT: 6ft 1in
NICKNAME: Metts
EDUCATION: Coombeshead College, Newton Abbot
TEAMS: Devon, Essex 2nd XI, Minor Counties, Warwickshire, Warwickshire 2nd XI
CAREER: First-class: 2011; List A: 2011

BEST BATTING: 30 Warwickshire vs Hampshire, Southampton, 2011
BEST BOWLING: 6-65 Warwickshire vs Worcestershire, Birmingham, 2011

CAREER HIGHLIGHTS? Taking 6-65 on my Championship debut vs Worcestershire. Taking a five-fer live on Sky in the last game of the 2011 season against Hampshire
SUPERSTITIONS? Always put my left pad on first and if I do well in a certain piece of kit then I try to use it for as long as possible
CRICKETING HEROES? Always enjoyed watching Shane Warne bowl because he made something happen every time he came on
BEST PLAYER IN COUNTY CRICKET? Marcus Trescothick
TIP FOR THE TOP? Chris Woakes
IF YOU WEREN'T A CRICKETER? Probably working for my dad as a painter and decorator
WHEN RAIN STOPS PLAY? Playing games or trying to annoy people to keep myself occupied
FAVOURITE TV? I like most comedy shows – Only Fools And Horses is a classic!
FAVOURITE FILM? The Business
DREAM HOLIDAY? Las Vegas
TWITTER FEED: @metters7

Batting	Mat	Inns	NO	Runs	HS	Ave	SR	100	50	Ct	St
First-class	10	12	5	167	30	23.85	39.66	0	0	15	0
List A	3	2	0	3	2	1.50	30.00	0	0	1	0
Bowling	**Inns**	**Balls**	**Runs**	**Wkts**	**BBI**	**BBM**	**Ave**	**Econ**	**SR**	**5w**	**10**
First-class	10	1330	695	29	6/65	8/186	23.96	3.13	45.8	2	0
List A	3	108	94	2	2/41	2/41	47.00	5.22	54.0	0	0

JAIK MICKLEBURGH RHB RM

FULL NAME: Jaik Charles Mickleburgh
BORN: March 30, 1990, Norwich, Norfolk
SQUAD NO: 32
HEIGHT: 5ft 10in
NICKNAME: Juddy
EDUCATION: Earsham Primary; Bungay Middle; Bungay High School
TEAMS: England Under-19s, Essex, Essex 2nd XI, Mid West Rhinos, Norfolk
CAREER: First-class: 2008; List A: 2010; T20: 2010

BEST BATTING: 174 Essex vs Durham, Chester-le-Street, 2010

CAREER HIGHLIGHTS? Record partnership with James Foster [339 vs Durham, 2010]
CRICKETING HEROES? Darren Gough
NON-CRICKETING HEROES? Rafa Nadal, David Beckham
TIPS FOR THE TOP? Adam Wheater, Reece Topley, Tymal Mills
BEST PLAYER IN COUNTY CRICKET? Marcus Trescothick
IF YOU WEREN'T A CRICKETER? Utility warehouse distributor
WHEN RAIN STOPS PLAY? Watching the clouds to see where the next batch is coming from
FAVOURITE TV? The Only Way Is Essex
FAVOURITE FILM? Saving Private Ryan
FAVOURITE BOOK? The Slight Edge
DREAM HOLIDAY? Mauritius
FANTASY SLIP CORDON? Keeper: James Foster, 1st: Wentworth Miller, 2nd: David Beckham, 3rd: Torrie Wilson, Gully: Jamie T
TWITTER FEED: @JaikMickleburgh

Batting	Mat	Inns	NO	Runs	HS	Ave	SR	100	50	Ct	St
First-class	57	103	1	2694	174	26.41	42.85	4	13	44	0
List A	16	13	3	365	73	36.50	77.00	0	2	7	0
Twenty20	15	10	4	154	47*	25.66	100.00	0	0	8	0
Bowling	**Inns**	**Balls**	**Runs**	**Wkts**	**BBI**	**BBM**	**Ave**	**Econ**	**SR**	**5w**	**10**
First-class	57	78	50	0	-	-	-	3.84	-	0	0
List A	16	-	-	-	-	-	-	-	-	-	-
Twenty20	15	-	-	-	-	-	-	-	-	-	-

JAMES MIDDLEBROOK RHB OB W1 MVP48

FULL NAME: James Daniel Middlebrook
BORN: May 13, 1977, Leeds, Yorkshire
SQUAD NO: 7
HEIGHT: 6ft 1in
NICKNAME: Minders, Midhouse, Midi, Dog, Doggy, Brook
EDUCATION: Earsham Primary; Bungay Middle; Bungay High School
TEAMS: Essex, Northamptonshire, Yorkshire
CAREER: First-class: 1998; List A: 1998; T20: 2004

BEST BATTING: 127 Essex vs Middlesex, Lord's, 2007
BEST BOWLING: 6-82 Yorkshire vs Hampshire, Southampton, 2000
COUNTY CAPS: 2003 (Essex); 2011 (Northamptonshire)

FAMILY TIES? My father played local Leeds and Bradford league cricket for Pudsey Congs CC and also managed the Yorkshire indoor cricket school for 11 years
WHO WOULD PLAY YOU IN A FILM OF YOUR LIFE? Daniel Craig
CAREER HIGHLIGHTS? Playing at Lord's. Being part of a winning team at Essex in one-day cricket and getting to a final and winning the Pro40
SUPERSTITIONS? I always mark my run-up the same way and turn to my mark the same way. I put my pads and kit on the same way every time
BEST PLAYER IN COUNTY CRICKET? James Foster
TIPS FOR THE TOP? Joe Root, Jonny Bairstow, Alex Wakely
DESERT ISLAND DISC? Michael Jackson – Man In The Mirror
FAVOURITE TV? Homes Under The Hammer
BIGGEST DRESSING DOWN YOU'VE RECEIVED? Probably from Ronnie Irani
CRICKETING HEROES? John Emburey, Ian Botham, Shane Warne, Mark Waugh
FANTASY SLIP CORDON? Keeper: Ayrton Senna, 1st: Jeremy Clarkson, 2nd: James Bond, 3rd: Me, Gully: Eddie Murphy
TWITTER FEED: @midders07

Batting	Mat	Inns	NO	Runs	HS	Ave	SR	100	50	Ct	St
First-class	187	267	41	6242	127	27.61		9	24	92	0
List A	177	119	39	1563	57*	19.53		0	1	48	0
Twenty20	84	57	17	524	43	13.10	114.66	0	0	18	0
Bowling	**Inns**	**Balls**	**Runs**	**Wkts**	**BBI**	**BBM**	**Ave**	**Econ**	**SR**	**5w**	**10**
First-class	187	29956	15503	408	6/82		37.99	3.10	73.4	11	1
List A	177	6253	4869	138	4/27	4/27	35.28	4.67	45.3	0	0
Twenty20	84	1204	1523	39	3/13	3/13	39.05	7.58	30.8	0	0

CRAIG MILES RHB RM

FULL NAME: Craig Neil Miles
BORN: July 20, 1994, Swindon, Wiltshire
SQUAD NO: 34
HEIGHT: 6ft 4in
NICKNAME: Miler, Milo, Jedward
EDUCATION: Bradon Forest School, Swindon; Filton College, Bristol
TEAMS: Gloucestershire, Gloucestershire 2nd XI
CAREER: First-class: 2011; List A: 2011

BEST BATTING: 19 Gloucestershire vs Northamptonshire, Bristol, 2011
BEST BOWLING: 2-80 Gloucestershire vs Northamptonshire, Bristol, 2009
COUNTY CAP: 2011

FAMILY TIES? My brother [Adam] plays for Cardiff MCCU
WHO WOULD PLAY YOU IN A FILM OF YOUR LIFE? Jim Carrey
CAREER HIGHLIGHTS? Gloucestershire 1st XI debut and dismissing Ravi Bopara with my first ball in List A cricket
MOST MARKED CHARACTERISTIC? Height or Johnny Bravo-like quiff
BEST PLAYER IN COUNTY CRICKET? Peter Trego
TIPS FOR THE TOP? Gareth Roderick, Matt Taylor
DESERT ISLAND DISC? Drake – Take Care
FAVOURITE TV? Geordie Shore
CRICKETING HEROES? Andrew Flintoff, Brett Lee
ACCOMPLISHMENTS? Reaching the National Basketball Finals in Year 9 with my secondary school
WHEN YOU RETIRE? I'd like to still be involved in cricket through coaching
SURPRISING FACT? I'm the fourth youngest player to play for Gloucestershire (the youngest since the war)
FANTASY SLIP CORDON? Keeper: Lee Evans, 1st: Jim Carrey, 2nd: Myself, 3rd: Tim Cahill, Gully: Drake (rapper)
TWITTER FEED: @CMiles34

Batting	Mat	Inns	NO	Runs	HS	Ave	SR	100	50	Ct	St
First-class	1	2	0	24	19	12.00	25.80	0	0	0	0
List A	2	-	-	-	-	-	-	-	-	0	0
Bowling	**Inns**	**Balls**	**Runs**	**Wkts**	**BBI**	**BBM**	**Ave**	**Econ**	**SR**	**5w**	**10**
First-class	1	114	80	2	2/80	2/80	40.00	4.21	57.0	0	0
List A	2	66	63	2	2/32	2/32	31.50	5.72	33.0	0	0

TYMAL MILLS RHB LF

ESSEX

FULL NAME: Tymal Solomon Mills
BORN: August 12, 1992, Dewsbury, Yorkshire
SQUAD NO: 5
HEIGHT: 6ft 1in
NICKNAME: T, Tyrone, Tyson
EDUCATION: Mildenhall Upper; University of East London
TEAMS: England Lions, England Under-19s, Essex, Essex 2nd XI, Suffolk
CAREER: First-class: 2011; List A: 2011; T20: 2012

BEST BATTING: 20* Essex vs Yorkshire, Chelmsford, 2012
BEST BOWLING: 4-25 Essex vs Glamorgan, Cardiff, 2012

WHO WOULD PLAY YOU IN A FILM OF YOUR LIFE? No question, Denzel Washington
CAREER HIGHLIGHTS? Being selected for the England Lions tour to Bangladesh in January 2012 and taking a wicket on debut
SUPERSTITIONS? Have to lick and rub my fingers before I bowl – more of a bad habit than a superstition!
MOST MARKED CHARACTERISTIC? My pace I guess, either that or my annoying bark every time I bowl
BEST PLAYER IN COUNTY CRICKET? Chris Woakes
TIPS FOR THE TOP? Ben Foakes, Reece Topley, Luke Wells
DESERT ISLAND DISC? Kanye West and Jay-Z – Watch The Throne
FAVOURITE TV? New Girl, Prison Break, Lost
WHEN YOU RETIRE? I'd like to go into the media
SURPRISING FACT? Two of my toes on each foot haven't grown since I was young and actually do nothing! It means I'm not the most stable but it makes for interesting viewing...
FANTASY SLIP CORDON? Keeper: Mr Eko, 1st: Denzel Washington, 2nd: Me, 3rd: Eva Mendes, Gully: Jennifer Aniston
TWITTER FEED: @tmills15

Batting	Mat	Inns	NO	Runs	HS	Ave	SR	100	50	Ct	St
First-class	12	16	6	49	20*	4.90	30.81	0	0	7	0
List A	12	5	3	3	2*	1.50	23.07	0	0	0	0
Twenty20	1	1	1	3	3*	-	60.00	0	0	0	0
Bowling	**Inns**	**Balls**	**Runs**	**Wkts**	**BBI**	**BBM**	**Ave**	**Econ**	**SR**	**5w**	**10**
First-class	12	1166	666	21	4/25	4/34	31.71	3.42	55.5	0	0
List A	12	437	407	9	2/40	2/40	45.22	5.58	48.5	0	0
Twenty20	1	6	8	0	-	-	-	8.00	-	0	0

TOM MILNES RHB RFM

FULL NAME: Thomas Patrick Milnes
BORN: October 6, 1992, Stourbridge, Worcestershire
SQUAD NO: 8
HEIGHT: 6ft 1in
NICKNAME: Milner
EDUCATION: Heart of England School
TEAMS: England Under-17s, England Under-19s, Warwickshire, Warwickshire 2nd XI
CAREER: First-class: 2011

BEST BATTING: 24 Warwickshire vs Durham, Chester-le-Street, 2012
BEST BOWLING: 4-15 Warwickshire vs Durham MCCU, Durham University, 2011

CAREER HIGHLIGHTS? Being part of the 2012 Championship-winning squad, making my Championship debut and signing my first professional contract
MOST MARKED CHARACTERISTIC? Being very keen! And ginger
IF YOU WEREN'T A CRICKETER? Probably working in a shop
DESERT ISLAND DISC? Oasis – Definitely Maybe
FAVOURITE TV? Alan Partridge
CRICKETING HEROES? Andrew Flintoff, James Anderson, Dale Steyn
ACCOMPLISHMENTS? Passing my driving test and getting some grades at school
WHEN YOU RETIRE? Either coach or set up a business
SURPRISING FACT? I used to play football for Aston Villa and I love doing impressions
FANTASY SLIP CORDON? Keeper: Alan Partridge, 1st: Liam Gallagher, 2nd: Andrew Flintoff, 3rd: Myself, Gully: James Corden
TWITTER FEED: @TPMilnes8

Batting	Mat	Inns	NO	Runs	HS	Ave	SR	100	50	Ct	St
First-class	5	4	1	63	24	21.00	49.21	0	0	0	0
Bowling	**Inns**	**Balls**	**Runs**	**Wkts**	**BBI**	**BBM**	**Ave**	**Econ**	**SR**	**5w**	**10**
First-class	5	366	241	9	4/15	4/39	26.77	3.95	40.6	0	0

WORCESTERSHIRE

DARYL MITCHELL RHB RM R2 MVP29

FULL NAME: Daryl Keith Henry Mitchell
BORN: November 25, 1983, Badsey, nr Evesham
SQUAD NO: 27
HEIGHT: 5ft 10in
NICKNAME: Mitch, Touc
EDUCATION: Prince Henry's Evesham; University College, Worcester
TEAMS: Mountaineers, Worcestershire, Worcestershire 2nd XI
CAREER: First-class: 2005; List A: 2005; T20: 2005

BEST BATTING: 298 Worcestershire vs Somerset, Taunton, 2009
BEST BOWLING: 4-49 Worcestershire vs Yorkshire, Leeds, 2009

FAMILY TIES? Dad played club cricket and coaches Worcestershire Young Cricketers U13s
CAREER HIGHLIGHTS? Winning the CB40 in 2011. Scoring 298 against Somerset at Taunton
CRICKETING HEROES? Ian Botham, Graeme Hick
BEST PLAYER IN COUNTY CRICKET? Marcus Trescothick
TIP FOR THE TOP? Alexei Kervezee
IF YOU WEREN'T A CRICKETER? PE teacher
WHEN RAIN STOPS PLAY? Playing Perudo or Football Manager
FAVOURITE TV? Shameless, Match Of The Day
FAVOURITE FILM? Dumb And Dumber
FAVOURITE BOOK? Paul McGrath's autobiography
ACCOMPLISHMENTS? BSc Sports Studies. Won loads of football and darts trophies when I was younger. Played for Aston Villa's School of Excellence as a kid
FANTASY SLIP CORDON? Keeper: Tiger Woods (he'd have a few stories and maybe the odd golf tip), 1st: Paul McGrath (favourite Villa player), 2nd: Me (always stand at second slip), 3rd: Ian Botham (cricketing hero), Gully: Rhod Gilbert (bit of comedy for the long days in the dirt!)
TWITTER FEED: @mitchwccc

Batting	Mat	Inns	NO	Runs	HS	Ave	SR	100	50	Ct	St
First-class	97	179	21	5925	298	37.50	43.20	12	26	136	0
List A	79	66	14	1539	92	29.59	81.25	0	8	29	0
Twenty20	73	51	14	734	45	19.83	115.95	0	0	27	0
Bowling	**Inns**	**Balls**	**Runs**	**Wkts**	**BBI**	**BBM**	**Ave**	**Econ**	**SR**	**5w**	**10**
First-class	97	1401	710	17	4/49		41.76	3.04	82.4	0	0
List A	79	1702	1623	41	4/42	4/42	39.58	5.72	41.5	0	0
Twenty20	73	983	1282	49	4/11	4/11	26.16	7.82	20.0	0	0

STEPHEN MOORE

RHB RM R4 MVP60

FULL NAME: Stephen Colin Moore
BORN: November 4, 1980, Johannesburg, South Africa
SQUAD NO: 6
HEIGHT: 6ft
NICKNAME: Mandy, Rog, Circles
EDUCATION: St Stithians College, South Africa; Exeter University
TEAMS: England Lions, Lancashire, Marylebone Cricket Club, Sussex 2nd XI, Worcestershire
CAREER: First-class: 2003; List A: 2003; T20: 2003

BEST BATTING: 246 Worcestershire vs Derbyshire, Worcester, 2005
BEST BOWLING: 1-13 Worcestershire vs Lancashire, Worcester, 2004
COUNTY CAP: 2011 (Lancashire)

CAREER HIGHLIGHTS? Winning the Championship with Lancashire in 2011, scoring a hundred against the Australians for England Lions at New Road, Worcester, and playing in a Lord's final in 2004
CRICKETING HEROES? Steve Waugh, Jacques Kallis
NON-CRICKETING HEROES? Roger Federer, Rafa Nadal
BEST PLAYER IN COUNTY CRICKET? Marcus Trescothick
TIP FOR THE TOP? Simon Kerrigan
IF YOU WEREN'T A CRICKETER? Engineer
FAVOURITE FILM? The Prestige
FAVOURITE BOOK? Rainbow Six
DREAM HOLIDAY? The African bush
ACCOMPLISHMENTS? Achieving a Masters degree in Electronic Engineering
SURPRISING SKILL? I play alto saxophone and a little guitar
FANTASY SLIP CORDON? Keeper: Roger Federer, 1st: Kate Beckinsale, 2nd: Michael McIntyre, 3rd: Myself, Gully: Professor Brian Cox
TWITTER FEED: @stephen_moore6

Batting	Mat	Inns	NO	Runs	HS	Ave	SR	100	50	Ct	St
First-class	143	258	19	8762	246	36.66	57.01	17	41	72	0
List A	128	123	12	3417	118	30.78	75.64	5	22	35	0
Twenty20	88	82	10	2002	83*	27.80	130.76	0	13	25	0
Bowling	**Inns**	**Balls**	**Runs**	**Wkts**	**BBI**	**BBM**	**Ave**	**Econ**	**SR**	**5w**	**10**
First-class	143	342	321	5	1/13		64.20	5.63	68.4	0	0
List A	128	41	53	1	1/1	1/1	53.00	7.75	41.0	0	0
Twenty20	88	-	-	-	-	-	-	-	-	-	-

EOIN MORGAN LHB RM R1

FULL NAME: Eoin Joseph Gerard Morgan
BORN: September 10, 1986, Dublin
SQUAD NO: 7
HEIGHT: 5ft 10in
NICKNAME: Moggie, Morgs
EDUCATION: Catholic University School, Dublin
TEAMS: England, Ireland, Bangalore Royal Challengers, England A, Ireland A, Ireland Under-19s, Kolkata Knight Riders, Middlesex, Middlesex 2nd XI, Sir Paul Getty's XI
CAREER: Test: 2010; ODI: 2006; T20I: 2009; First-class: 2004; List A: 2003; T20: 2006

BEST BATTING: 209* Ireland vs UAE, Abu Dhabi, 2007
BEST BOWLING: 2-24 Middlesex vs Nottinghamshire, Lord's, 2007
COUNTY CAP: 2008

TWITTER FEED: @Eoin16
NOTES: Switched his allegiance from Ireland to England in April 2009 after he was named in England's 30-man provisional squad for the 2009 World T20. Made his ODI for his adopted nation against West Indies in May 2009 at Bristol and his T20I debut a month later in the shock defeat to the Netherlands at Lord's. Test debut followed against Bangladesh in May 2010 and he struck a maiden century in his third match – 130 vs Pakistan at Trent Bridge. Scored his second Test century vs India, again at Trent Bridge, in 2011. Dropped from England's Test side after the 2012 away series vs Pakistan but recalled for the tour to India in November, although he did not feature in the Test series. Hit 71* from 36 balls in a losing cause against West Indies in the World T20 last year. Awarded a central contract by England last September. Has captained England in ODI and T20I cricket

Batting	Mat	Inns	NO	Runs	HS	Ave	SR	100	50	Ct	St
Tests	16	24	1	700	130	30.43	54.77	2	3	11	0
ODIs	94	88	18	2739	115	39.12	85.40	4	17	37	0
T20Is	35	34	10	871	85*	36.29	132.16	0	4	19	0
First-class	76	123	14	3763	209*	34.52	51.31	9	18	61	1
List A	182	167	29	5309	161	38.47	87.08	9	31	60	0
Twenty20	101	92	17	2070	85*	27.60	131.26	0	9	46	0
Bowling	**Inns**	**Balls**	**Runs**	**Wkts**	**BBI**	**BBM**	**Ave**	**Econ**	**SR**	**5w**	**10**
Tests	16	-	-	-	-	-	-	-	-	-	-
ODIs	94	-	-	-	-	-	-	-	-	-	-
T20Is	35	-	-	-	-	-	-	-	-	-	-
First-class	76	97	83	2	2/24	2/24	41.50	5.13	48.5	0	0
List A	182	42	49	0	-	-	-	7.00	-	0	0
Twenty20	101	-	-	-	-	-	-	-	-	-	-

CHARLIE MORRIS RHB RFM

FULL NAME: Charles Andrew John Morris
BORN: July 6, 1992, Hereford
SQUAD NO: 31
HEIGHT: 6ft
EDUCATION: King's College, Taunton; Oxford Brookes University
TEAMS: Devon, Oxford MCCU, MCC Universities
CAREER: First-class: 2012

BEST BATTING: 7 Oxford MCCU vs Worcestershire, Oxford, 2012
BEST BOWLING: 2-7 Oxford MCCU vs Worcestershire, Oxford, 2012

NOTES: Promising young fast bowler. Represented Oxford MCCU, Devon and the MCC Universities during the 2012 season. Morris is the first player groomed by Devon's new development structure for the first-class game. Currently studying at Oxford Brookes University but signed a summer contract with Worcestershire for 2013

Batting	Mat	Inns	NO	Runs	HS	Ave	SR	100	50	Ct	St
First-class	2	3	0	8	7	2.66	11.94	0	0	1	0
Bowling	**Inns**	**Balls**	**Runs**	**Wkts**	**BBI**	**BBM**	**Ave**	**Econ**	**SR**	**5w**	**10**
First-class	2	371	206	4	2/7	3/64	51.50	3.33	92.7	0	0

GORDON MUCHALL RHB RM

DURHAM

FULL NAME: Gordon James Muchall
BORN: November 2, 1982, Newcastle upon Tyne
SQUAD NO: 24
HEIGHT: 6ft 1in
NICKNAME: Muchy
EDUCATION: Durham School
TEAMS: Durham
CAREER: First-class: 2002; List A: 2002; T20: 2003

BEST BATTING: 219 Durham vs Kent, Canterbury, 2006
BEST BOWLING: 3-26 Durham vs Yorkshire, Headingley, 2003
COUNTY CAP: 2005

FAMILY TIES? Granddad played for Northumberland, brother Paul plays at Gloucestershire, brother Matthew plays for Northumberland and dad Arthur plays for Durham Over 50s
CAREER HIGHLIGHTS? Winning the Championship twice with Durham
CRICKETING HEROES? Mike Hussey, Robin Smith, Dale Benkenstein
NON-CRICKETING HEROES? Jonny Wilkinson
BEST PLAYER IN COUNTY CRICKET? Marcus Trescothick
TIPS FOR THE TOP? Hayden and Rory Mustard, Jack and Luke Benkenstein, Adam Muchall, Mitchell Killeen, Luca Di Venuto, Charlie Harmison
IF YOU WEREN'T A CRICKETER? Coaching or personal trainer
WHEN RAIN STOPS PLAY? 500. Card school. Or some fitness
FAVOURITE TV? None at the minute, but loved 24 and Prison Break
FAVOURITE FILM? Forrest Gump, The Shawshank Redemption, Old School, Wedding Crashers
DREAM HOLIDAY? Caribbean
ACCOMPLISHMENTS? My son Adam
SURPRISING FACT? The last game of rugby I ever played was at Twickenham

Batting	Mat	Inns	NO	Runs	HS	Ave	SR	100	50	Ct	St
First-class	137	237	11	6537	219	28.92	53.84	11	33	93	0
List A	117	107	19	2953	101*	33.55		1	18	43	0
Twenty20	65	54	12	1071	64*	25.50	107.53	0	4	24	0
Bowling	**Inns**	**Balls**	**Runs**	**Wkts**	**BBI**	**BBM**	**Ave**	**Econ**	**SR**	**5w**	**10**
First-class	137	896	617	15	3/26		41.13	4.13	59.7	0	0
List A	117	168	144	1	1/15	1/15	144.00	5.14	168.0	0	0
Twenty20	65	12	8	1	1/8	1/8	8.00	4.00	12.0	0	0

PAUL MUCHALL RHB RMF

FULL NAME: Paul Bernard Muchall
BORN: March 17, 1987, Newcastle-upon-Tyne
SQUAD NO: 11
HEIGHT: 6ft 2in
NICKNAME: Muchy
EDUCATION: Durham School
TEAMS: Durham 2nd XI, Durham Under-17s, Gloucestershire, Gloucestershire 2nd XI, Kent, Kent 2nd XI, Marylebone Cricket Club Young Cricketers, Minor Counties Under-25s, Northumberland
CAREER: First-class: 2012; List A: 2010

BEST BATTING: 23 Gloucestershire vs Kent, Canterbury, 2012
BEST BOWLING: 2-60 Gloucestershire vs Essex, Chelmsford, 2012

FAMILY TIES? Granddad played minor counties for Northumberland. Brother Gordon plays for Durham, and my other brother Matthew plays for Northumberland
WHO WOULD PLAY YOU IN A FILM OF YOUR LIFE? Gerard Butler
CAREER HIGHLIGHTS? Signing with Gloucestershire in 2012
SUPERSTITIONS? Left pad goes on first
BEST PLAYER IN COUNTY CRICKET? Graham Onions
TIP FOR THE TOP? Ben Stokes
IF YOU WEREN'T A CRICKETER? Personal trainer
DESERT ISLAND DISC? Florence And The Machine – Ceremonials
FAVOURITE TV? Misfits
CRICKETING HEROES? Malcolm Marshall, Steve Waugh, Dale Steyn
NON-CRICKETING HEROES? Jamie Oliver, Morgan Freeman
SURPRISING FACT? I am 1/16th French
FANTASY SLIP CORDON? Keeper: Ricky Gervais (funny man that will always bring something entertaining to the game), 1st: Me, 2nd: Natalie Portman (got to have her, she is one of my favourites), 3rd: Jesus (because I don't think he could do anything wrong), Gully: Steve Waugh (because he is one of the best captains there has ever been)
TWITTER FEED: @muchdawg14

Batting	Mat	Inns	NO	Runs	HS	Ave	SR	100	50	Ct	St
First-class	4	7	2	82	23	16.40	38.49	0	0	1	0
List A	2	2	0	22	22	11.00	56.41	0	0	1	0
Bowling	**Inns**	**Balls**	**Runs**	**Wkts**	**BBI**	**BBM**	**Ave**	**Econ**	**SR**	**5w**	**10**
First-class	4	236	218	2	2/60	2/60	109.00	5.54	118.0	0	0
List A	2	36	58	1	1/34	1/34	58.00	9.66	36.0	0	0

STEVEN MULLANEY RHB RM

FULL NAME: Steven John Mullaney
BORN: November 19, 1986, Warrington, Cheshire
SQUAD NO: 5
HEIGHT: 5ft 10in
NICKNAME: Mull, Cadet Mahoney
EDUCATION: St Mary's RC High School, Astley
TEAMS: England Under-19s, Lancashire, Lancashire 2nd XI, Nottinghamshire
CAREER: First-class: 2006; List A: 2006; T20: 2006

BEST BATTING: 165* Lancashire vs Durham UCCE, Durham, 2007
BEST BOWLING: 4-31 Nottinghamshire vs Essex, Nottingham, 2010

WHO WOULD PLAY YOU IN A FILM OF YOUR LIFE? Hugh Jackman
CAREER HIGHLIGHTS? Breaking into the 1st XI at Notts
MOST MARKED CHARACTERISTIC? Blue moon tattoed on my inner thigh
BEST PLAYER IN COUNTY CRICKET? Harry Gurney
TIPS FOR THE TOP? George Bacon, Ben Kitt
IF YOU WEREN'T A CRICKETER? PE teacher
DESERT ISLAND DISC? Westlife – Swear It Again
FAVOURITE TV? Coronation Street
CRICKETING HEROES? Andrew Flintoff, VVS Laxman
NON-CRICKETING HEROES? Gary Barlow, Dominic Healy
WHEN YOU RETIRE? Coaching
SURPRISING FACT? I toured France with England U15 rugby league team
FANTASY SLIP CORDON? Keeper: Joe Hart, 1st: Kylie Minogue, 2nd: Johnny Vegas, 3rd: Luke Fletcher, Gully: Tess Daly
TWITTER FEED: @Mull05

Batting	Mat	Inns	NO	Runs	HS	Ave	SR	100	50	Ct	St
First-class	39	64	6	1809	165*	31.18	61.28	2	10	30	0
List A	42	31	4	513	61	19.00	92.10	0	2	21	0
Twenty20	45	28	9	328	53	17.26	128.62	0	1	19	0
Bowling	**Inns**	**Balls**	**Runs**	**Wkts**	**BBI**	**BBM**	**Ave**	**Econ**	**SR**	**5w**	**10**
First-class	39	1674	882	16	4/31	4/48	55.12	3.16	104.6	0	0
List A	42	1250	1050	37	3/13	3/13	28.37	5.04	33.7	0	0
Twenty20	45	780	976	34	4/19	4/19	28.70	7.50	22.9	0	0

DAVID MURPHY RHB WK

FULL NAME: David Murphy
BORN: June 24, 1989, Welwyn Garden City, Hertfordshire
SQUAD NO: 19
HEIGHT: 6ft 1in
NICKNAME: Murph
EDUCATION: Richard Hale School; Loughborough University
TEAMS: Scotland, Loughborough MCCU, Loughborough UCCE, Northamptonshire, Northamptonshire 2nd XI
CAREER: First-class: 2009; List A: 2010; T20: 2010

BEST BATTING: 79 Northamptonshire vs Glamorgan, Northampton, 2011

WHO WOULD PLAY YOU IN A FILM OF YOUR LIFE? Robert Downey Jr
CAREER HIGHLIGHTS? Scoring 69 not out on my first-class debut. Getting to the T20 quarter-finals in 2010. Getting some good appreciation from David Lloyd in my first game on Sky Sports. Breaking the highest score for Northants Academy in the Northants Premiership
MOST MARKED CHARACTERISTIC? Ambition
BEST PLAYER IN COUNTY CRICKET? Marcus Trescothick
TIPS FOR THE TOP? Rob Newton, David Willey
DESERT ISLAND DISC? Jack Johnson – In Between Dreams
FAVOURITE TV? Family Guy
BIGGEST DRESSING DOWN YOU'VE RECEIVED? One of the many I received from the cricketing legend that was Graham Dilley which resulted in lots of laps of Loughborough cricket pitch
CRICKETING HEROES? Steve Waugh, Jack Russell
ACCOMPLISHMENTS? Achieving a 2:1 in my Politics and Business Management degree from Loughborough, with a 1st in my dissertation
WHEN YOU RETIRE? Probably something in line with my Politics degree
FANTASY SLIP CORDON? Keeper: Me, 1st: Stephen Peters (always got something to offer in the slips), 2nd: Nelson Mandela, 3rd: Frankie Boyle, Gully: Steve Waugh

Batting	Mat	Inns	NO	Runs	HS	Ave	SR	100	50	Ct	St
First-class	33	45	10	1035	79	29.57	43.81	0	8	88	5
List A	19	14	8	148	31*	24.66	88.62	0	0	9	4
Twenty20	20	11	4	87	20	12.42	114.47	0	0	8	3
Bowling	**Inns**	**Balls**	**Runs**	**Wkts**	**BBI**	**BBM**	**Ave**	**Econ**	**SR**	**5w**	**10**
First-class	33	6	3	0	-	-	-	3.00	-	0	0
List A	19	-	-	-	-	-	-	-	-	-	-
Twenty20	20	-	-	-	-	-	-	-	-	-	-

TIM MURTAGH LHB RFM W4 MVP23

FULL NAME: Timothy James Murtagh
BORN: August 2, 1981, Lambeth, London
SQUAD NO: 34
HEIGHT: 6ft 1in
NICKNAME: Murts, Brows, Jack
EDUCATION: John Fisher School; St Mary's University
TEAMS: England Under-19s, Ireland, British Universities, Middlesex, Middlesex 2nd XI, Surrey
CAREER: ODI: 2012; T20I: 2012; First-class: 2000; List A: 2000; T20: 2003

BEST BATTING: 74* Surrey vs Middlesex, The Oval, 2004
BEST BOWLING: 7-82 Middlesex vs Derbyshire, Derby, 2009
COUNTY CAP: 2008 (Middlesex)

FAMILY TIES? Uncle [Andy] played for Hampshire in the 70s and brother [Chris] played for Surrey. My dad played for the Beckenham Merlins
CAREER HIGHLIGHTS? Gaining international honours with Ireland, getting capped at Middlesex, winning the T20 Cup in 2008 and bowling a ball above 80mph in a televised game
MOST MARKED CHARACTERISTIC? My eyebrows and banter
TIPS FOR THE TOP? Toby Roland-Jones, Tom Helm, Ravi Patel, Ross Whiteley
BIGGEST DRESSING DOWN YOU'VE RECEIVED? I got called a "hairy-faced dingo" by Andrew Symonds many years ago
SURPRISING FACT? The house that I grew up in was bought off the Butcher family back in the 80s. My brother Chris and I slept in the same bedroom that Mark and Gary Butcher had done before us. All four of us represented Surrey
TWITTER FEED: @tjmurtagh

Batting	Mat	Inns	NO	Runs	HS	Ave	SR	100	50	Ct	St
ODIs	2	1	0	15	15	15.00	53.57	0	0	0	0
T20Is	1	1	0	3	3	3.00	60.00	0	0	1	0
First-class	130	180	55	2828	74*	22.62		0	10	38	0
List A	129	84	31	629	35*	11.86		0	0	34	0
Twenty20	79	34	11	204	40*	8.86	105.69	0	0	18	0
Bowling	**Inns**	**Balls**	**Runs**	**Wkts**	**BBI**	**BBM**	**Ave**	**Econ**	**SR**	**5w**	**10**
ODIs	2	48	39	0	-	-	-	4.87	-	0	0
T20Is	1	12	9	0	-	-	-	4.50	-	0	0
First-class	130	21309	11870	426	7/82		27.86	3.34	50.0	18	2
List A	129	5648	4947	174	4/14	4/14	28.43	5.25	32.4	0	0
Twenty20	79	1548	2183	82	6/24	6/24	26.62	8.46	18.8	1	0

PHIL MUSTARD

LHB WK MVP21

FULL NAME: Philip Mustard
BORN: October 8, 1982, Sunderland, County Durham
SQUAD NO: 19
HEIGHT: 5ft 11in
NICKNAME: Colonel
EDUCATION: Usworth Comprehensive
TEAMS: England, Barisal Burners, Durham, Durham Cricket Board, England Under-19s, Mountaineers
CAREER: ODI: 2007; T20I: 2008; First-class: 2002; List A: 2000; T20: 2003

BEST BATTING: 130 Durham vs Kent, Canterbury, 2006

CAREER HIGHLIGHTS? Making my England debut in Sri Lanka, touring in 2007/08 and playing 10 ODIs. Winning our first trophy for Durham, the FP Trophy, in 2007, and then following up with two Championship victories in 2008 and 2009. Being asked to captain Durham in the middle of 2010
SUPERSTITIONS? A little one when I go out to bat: I always look high to my left. Not sure why, but it happens
BEST PLAYER IN COUNTY CRICKET? Marcus Trescothick
IF YOU WEREN'T A CRICKETER? Probably selling things, which wouldn't be exciting but it would be a job
WHEN RAIN STOPS PLAY? Playing cards, reading newspapers, every now and then the gym
FAVOURITE TV? An Idiot Abroad
DREAM HOLIDAY? Brazil
ACCOMPLISHMENTS? Bringing up my two boys
GUILTY PLEASURES? Crisps
TWITTER FEED: @colonel19

Batting	Mat	Inns	NO	Runs	HS	Ave	SR	100	50	Ct	St
ODIs	10	10	0	233	83	23.30	92.46	0	1	9	2
T20Is	2	2	0	60	40	30.00	162.16	0	0	0	0
First-class	148	228	28	6130	130	30.65	64.18	6	35	486	17
List A	153	138	8	4037	143	31.05		7	24	153	38
Twenty20	128	121	7	2725	97*	23.90	126.21	0	14	61	29
Bowling	**Inns**	**Balls**	**Runs**	**Wkts**	**BBI**	**BBM**	**Ave**	**Econ**	**SR**	**5w**	**10**
ODIs	10	-	-	-	-	-	-	-	-	-	-
T20Is	2	-	-	-	-	-	-	-	-	-	-
First-class	148	-	-	-	-	-	-	-	-	-	-
List A	153	-	-	-	-	-	-	-	-	-	-
Twenty20	128	-	-	-	-	-	-	-	-	-	-

JIGAR NAIK RHB OB

FULL NAME: Jigar Kumar Hakumatrai Naik
BORN: August 10, 1984, Leicester
SQUAD NO: 22
HEIGHT: 6ft 2in
NICKNAME: Jiggles, Jigga, Jiggly
EDUCATION: Nottingham Trent University; Loughborough University
TEAMS: Colombo Cricket Club, Leicestershire, Leicestershire 2nd XI, Leicestershire Cricket Board, Loughborough UCCE
CAREER: First-class: 2006; List A: 2003; T20: 2008

BEST BATTING: 109* Leicestershire vs Derbyshire, Leicester, 2009
BEST BOWLING: 7-96 Leicestershire vs Surrey, The Oval, 2010

WHO WOULD PLAY YOU IN A FILM OF YOUR LIFE? Harold and Kumar
CAREER HIGHLIGHTS? Taking 7-96 against Surrey at The Oval. Scoring my maiden Championship hundred. Topping the national bowling averages in 2010. Leading wicket-taker for Leicestershire in the Championship in 2011, along with 550 runs. Getting selected for Potential England Performance Player group
MOST MARKED CHARACTERISTIC? My long fingers
TIPS FOR THE TOP? Shiv Thakor, Joe Root, Josh Cobb
IF YOU WEREN'T A CRICKETER? Systems engineer
DESERT ISLAND DISC? Bollywood's Greatest Hits
FAVOURITE TV? 24, Prison Break, Awake
CRICKETING HEROES? Sachin Tendulkar, Robert Croft, Erapalli Prasanna and Claude Henderson
ACCOMPLISHMENTS? Getting my Masters degree and getting married to my beautiful wife Dipa
WHEN YOU RETIRE? I'll relax
SURPRISING FACT? I play the tabla (Indian instrument)
TWITTER FEED: @jigarnaik

Batting	Mat	Inns	NO	Runs	HS	Ave	SR	100	50	Ct	St
First-class	43	67	16	1205	109*	23.62	39.43	1	3	20	0
List A	28	19	8	100	18	9.09		0	0	4	0
Twenty20	18	7	5	16	7*	8.00	94.11	0	0	4	0
Bowling	**Inns**	**Balls**	**Runs**	**Wkts**	**BBI**	**BBM**	**Ave**	**Econ**	**SR**	**5w**	**10**
First-class	43	5957	3351	104	7/96	8/133	32.22	3.37	57.2	3	0
List A	28	1055	941	22	3/21	3/21	42.77	5.35	47.9	0	0
Twenty20	18	276	348	11	3/3	3/3	31.63	7.56	25.0	0	0

DIRK NANNES RHB LF

FULL NAME: Dirk Peter Nannes
BORN: May 16, 1976, Melbourne, Australia
SQUAD NO: TBC
HEIGHT: 6ft 2in
NICKNAME: Diggler
EDUCATION: Wesley College, Melbourne
TEAMS: Australia, Netherlands, Canterbury, Delhi Daredevils, Lions, Melbourne Renegades, Middlesex, Mountaineers, Nottinghamshire, Royal Challengers Bangalore, Surrey, Sylhet Royals, Victoria
CAREER: ODI: 2009; T20I: 2009; First-class: 2006; List A: 2006; T20: 2007

BEST BATTING: 31* Victoria vs South Australia, Adelaide, 2007
BEST BOWLING: 7-50 Victoria vs Queensland, 2008
COUNTY CAP: 2008 (Middlesex)

TWITTER FEED: @dirk_nannes
NOTES: Freelance T20 specialist. Joins Glamorgan having previously appeared for Middlesex, Nottinghamshire and Surrey. Former mogul racer who competed in alpine skiing World Cup competition. Started playing club cricket in 1999, and made his first-class debut for Victoria in 2006 at the age of 29. Part of the Dutch side that beat England in the 2009 World T20, but switched allegiance to Australia after two games for the Netherlands. Has retired from first-class and List A cricket to concentrate on T20, and he appears in almost every T20 tournament around the world. Columnist for All Out Cricket magazine

Batting	Mat	Inns	NO	Runs	HS	Ave	SR	100	50	Ct	St
ODIs	1	1	0	1	1	1.00	50.00	0	0	0	0
T20Is	17	5	3	22	12*	11.00	122.22	0	0	1	0
First-class	23	24	8	108	31*	6.75	33.12	0	0	7	0
List A	32	10	5	18	5*	3.60	40.90	0	0	2	0
Twenty20	176	32	25	57	12*	8.14	89.06	0	0	26	0
Bowling	**Inns**	**Balls**	**Runs**	**Wkts**	**BBI**	**BBM**	**Ave**	**Econ**	**SR**	**5w**	**10**
ODIs	1	42	20	1	1/20	1/20	20.00	2.85	42.0	0	0
T20Is	17	366	459	28	4/18	4/18	16.39	7.52	13.0	0	0
First-class	23	4139	2327	93	7/50	11/95	25.02	3.37	44.5	2	1
List A	32	1737	1396	47	4/38	4/38	29.70	4.82	36.9	0	0
Twenty20	176	3799	4566	210	5/40	5/40	21.74	7.21	18.0	1	0

ESSEX

GRAHAM NAPIER RHB RFM MVP37

FULL NAME: Graham Richard Napier
BORN: January 6, 1980, Colchester, Essex
SQUAD NO: 17
HEIGHT: 5ft 9in
NICKNAME: George, Napes
EDUCATION: Gilberd School, Colchester
TEAMS: Central Districts, England Lions, Essex, Essex 2nd XI, Essex Cricket Board, Mumbai Indians, Wellington
CAREER: First-class: 1997; List A: 1997; T20: 2003

BEST BATTING: 196 Essex vs Surrey, Croydon, 2011
BEST BOWLING: 6-53 Essex vs Surrey, Chelmsford, 2011
COUNTY CAP: 2003; **BENEFIT YEAR:** 2012

WHO WOULD PLAY YOU IN A FILM OF YOUR LIFE? Russell Crowe
CAREER HIGHLIGHTS? Testing myself against the world's best and scoring some runs. Winning the FP Trophy. Scoring 152*, including 16 sixes, in a T20 match. Being included in England's World T20 squad. Playing in the IPL for Mumbai Indians
SUPERSTITIONS? I always like to have lamb the evening before I bat
BEST PLAYER IN COUNTY CRICKET? Marcus Trescothick
TIPS FOR THE TOP? Reece Topley, Ben Foakes
IF YOU WEREN'T A CRICKETER? A photographer or a chef – potentially both
DESERT ISLAND DISC? Elton John's Greatest Hits
FAVOURITE TV? Africa by David Attenborough, Top Gear
CRICKETING HEROES? Graham Gooch, Viv Richards, Freddie Flintoff, Alastair Cook
NON-CRICKETING HEROES? Winston Churchill
WHEN YOU RETIRE? Play a lot of golf, not have to work too much and get plenty of sunshine!
FANTASY SLIP CORDON? Keeper: Russell Crowe, 1st: Winston Churchill, 2nd: Natalie Imbruglia, 3rd: Micky Flanagan, Gully: Elton John
TWITTER FEED: @Graham_Napier

Batting	Mat	Inns	NO	Runs	HS	Ave	SR	100	50	Ct	St
First-class	122	166	33	4068	196	30.58		5	21	46	0
List A	217	164	20	2660	79	18.47		0	13	50	0
Twenty20	86	67	8	897	152*	15.20	142.83	1	0	24	0
Bowling	**Inns**	**Balls**	**Runs**	**Wkts**	**BBI**	**BBM**	**Ave**	**Econ**	**SR**	**5w**	**10**
First-class	122	16317	9857	283	6/53		34.83	3.62	57.6	7	0
List A	217	7411	6468	248	6/29	6/29	26.08	5.23	29.8	1	0
Twenty20	86	1844	2257	106	4/10	4/10	21.29	7.34	17.3	0	0

BRENDAN NASH

LHB LM

FULL NAME: Brendan Paul Nash
BORN: December 14, 1977, Attadale, Australia
SQUAD NO: 40
HEIGHT: 5ft 8in
NICKNAME: Bubba
TEAMS: West Indies, Jamaica, Kent, Queensland, West Indies A
CAREER: Test: 2008; ODI: 2008; First-class: 2001; List A: 2001; T20: 2008

BEST BATTING: 207 Jamaica vs Trinidad and Tobago, St Augustine, 2011
BEST BOWLING: 2-7 Jamaica vs Combined Campuses and Colleges, Kingston, 2008

WHO WOULD PLAY YOU IN A FILM OF YOUR LIFE? Denzel Washington
CAREER HIGHLIGHTS? Playing Test cricket and winning a series against England
SUPERSTITIONS? I put my right pad on first
IF YOU WEREN'T A CRICKETER? I'd be running a business or being a golf pro on a resort somewhere
FAVOURITE TV? Two And A Half Men (the old ones)
CRICKETING HEROES? Allan Border, Sir Garfield Sobers
NON-CRICKETING HEROES? Michael Jordan, Tiger Woods
FANTASY SLIP CORDON? Keeper: Master Yoda (because he would catch everything), 1st: Michael Jordan (I would ask him how he had the drive to succeed for himself and in a team environment), 2nd: Sir Garfield Sobers (to pick his brains about the game), 3rd: Tiger Woods (I'd ask how he handles the pressure he faces everyday), Gully: Hugh Hefner (because he would have some great stories to tell)

Batting	Mat	Inns	NO	Runs	HS	Ave	SR	100	50	Ct	St
Tests	21	33	0	1103	114	33.42	43.28	2	8	6	0
ODIs	9	7	3	104	39*	26.00	73.75	0	0	1	0
First-class	102	168	24	5487	207	38.10		12	22	38	0
List A	71	50	13	1121	71	30.29		0	6	22	0
Twenty20	7	5	1	69	26	17.25	106.15	0	0	0	0
Bowling	**Inns**	**Balls**	**Runs**	**Wkts**	**BBI**	**BBM**	**Ave**	**Econ**	**SR**	**5w**	**10**
Tests	21	492	247	2	1/21	1/21	123.50	3.01	246.0	0	0
ODIs	9	294	224	5	3/56	3/56	44.80	4.57	58.8	0	0
First-class	102	1441	652	21	2/7		31.04	2.71	68.6	0	0
List A	71	780	547	15	4/20	4/20	36.46	4.20	52.0	0	0
Twenty20	7	24	40	1	1/32	1/32	40.00	10.00	24.0	0	0

CHRIS NASH RHB OB R2 MVP4

FULL NAME: Christopher David Nash
BORN: May 19, 1983, Cuckfield, Sussex
SQUAD NO: 23
HEIGHT: 6ft
NICKNAME: Nashy, Nashdog, Knocker, Spidey, Hairpiece
EDUCATION: Heron Way; Tanbridge House; Collyer's Sixth Form; Loughborough University
TEAMS: England Lions, Loughborough MCCU, Otago, Sussex, Sussex 2nd XI
CAREER: First-class: 2002; List A: 2006; T20: 2006

BEST BATTING: 184 Sussex vs Leicestershire, Leicester, 2010
BEST BOWLING: 4-12 Sussex vs Glamorgan, Cardiff, 2010
COUNTY CAP: 2008

FAMILY TIES? My brother played 2nd XI cricket for Sussex before losing the ability to bowl
WHO WOULD PLAY YOU IN A FILM OF YOUR LIFE? Luke Wright
CAREER HIGHLIGHTS? Winning the Championship in 2007 and T20 in 2009; my county cap in 2008; winning the Pro40 in 2009; playing for England Lions in 2011 and being part of the EPP in 2010. Being named Sussex vice-captain from 2013
MOST MARKED CHARACTERISTIC? My biceps
TIPS FOR THE TOP? Philip Hudson, Ryan Leverton, Richard Hawkes, Ben Nash Jr and Luke Marshall
DESERT ISLAND DISC? Kenny Loggins – Danger Zone
FAVOURITE TV? Two And A Half Men
CRICKETING HEROES? Luke Wright, Mark Nash, John Barclay, Dr John Dew, Les Lenham
NON-CRICKETING HEROES? Les Lenham, Will Ferrell, Maverick and Goose
WHEN YOU RETIRE? I'll sit in a deckchair and watch Sussex!
SURPRISING FACT? I spent the holidays selling Xmas trees at my local garden centre when I was 19
TWITTER FEED: @chrisnash23

Batting	Mat	Inns	NO	Runs	HS	Ave	SR	100	50	Ct	St
First-class	111	190	13	6646	184	37.54	58.20	13	33	50	0
List A	75	71	2	2253	124*	32.65	90.88	2	14	17	0
Twenty20	86	80	13	1584	80*	23.64	117.85	0	7	30	0
Bowling	**Inns**	**Balls**	**Runs**	**Wkts**	**BBI**	**BBM**	**Ave**	**Econ**	**SR**	**5w**	**10**
First-class	111	3302	1904	59	4/12		32.27	3.45	55.9	0	0
List A	75	985	871	34	4/40	4/40	25.61	5.30	28.9	0	0
Twenty20	86	529	621	31	4/7	4/7	20.03	7.04	17.0	0	0

OLIVER NEWBY RHB RFM

FULL NAME: Oliver James Newby
BORN: August 26, 1984, Blackburn, Lancashire
SQUAD NO: 8
HEIGHT: 6ft 5in
NICKNAME: Newbz, News
EDUCATION: Ribblesdale High School; Myerscough College
TEAMS: Gloucestershire, Lancashire, Lancashire Cricket Board, Nottinghamshire
CAREER: First-class: 2003; List A: 2003; T20: 2003

BEST BATTING: 38* Nottinghamshire vs Kent, Nottingham, 2004
BEST BOWLING: 5-69 Gloucestershire vs Northamptonshire, Bristol, 2008

FAMILY TIES? Father played club cricket
WHY CRICKET? Travelling the world playing sport
TIP FOR THE TOP? Jordan Clark
IF YOU WEREN'T A CRICKETER? I'd be looking for a rich widow
WHEN RAIN STOPS PLAY? Winding up Tom Smith for being bald and Glen Chapple for being old, ginger and rubbish at golf
FAVOURITE TV? Pointless
FAVOURITE FILM? Blades Of Glory
DREAM HOLIDAY? Thailand

Batting	Mat	Inns	NO	Runs	HS	Ave	SR	100	50	Ct	St
First-class	48	42	11	313	38*	10.09	41.18	0	0	8	0
List A	31	17	10	116	36*	16.57	92.80	0	0	3	0
Twenty20	13	5	2	15	6*	5.00	83.33	0	0	3	0
Bowling	**Inns**	**Balls**	**Runs**	**Wkts**	**BBI**	**BBM**	**Ave**	**Econ**	**SR**	**5w**	**10**
First-class	48	6055	3887	118	5/69		32.94	3.85	51.3	1	0
List A	31	1033	1081	31	5/35	5/35	34.87	6.27	33.3	1	0
Twenty20	13	178	238	7	2/34	2/34	34.00	8.02	25.4	0	0

ROB NEWTON RHB LB

FULL NAME: Robert Irving Newton
BORN: January 18, 1990, Taunton, Somerset
SQUAD NO: 21
HEIGHT: 5ft 8in
NICKNAME: Ewok, KOTL
EDUCATION: Framlingham College
TEAMS: Northamptonshire, Northamptonshire 2nd XI
CAREER: First-class: 2010; List A: 2009; T20: 2010

BEST BATTING: 119* Northamptonshire vs Derbyshire, Northampton, 2012

WHO WOULD PLAY YOU IN A FILM OF YOUR LIFE? Warwick Davis
CAREER HIGHLIGHTS? Scoring a hundred in both innings of a first-class game. Taking the new ball
BEST PLAYER IN COUNTY CRICKET? Darren Stevens
TIP FOR THE TOP? James Sales
IF YOU WEREN'T A CRICKETER? I'd be drinking the profits at my own bar
DESERT ISLAND DISC? Baha Men – Who Let The Dogs Out?
FAVOURITE TV? Entourage
CRICKETING HEROES? Ajaz Akhtar
NON-CRICKETING HEROES? Hank Moody, Vincent Chase
FANTASY SLIP CORDON? Keeper: Jack Brooks, 1st: Me, 2nd: Ben Howgego, 3rd: Gav Baker

Batting	Mat	Inns	NO	Runs	HS	Ave	SR	100	50	Ct	St
First-class	27	45	4	1586	119*	38.68	68.03	5	6	7	0
List A	21	20	0	484	66	24.20	95.84	0	1	2	0
Twenty20	14	13	1	178	38	14.83	108.53	0	0	0	0
Bowling	**Inns**	**Balls**	**Runs**	**Wkts**	**BBI**	**BBM**	**Ave**	**Econ**	**SR**	**5w**	**10**
First-class	27	13	19	0	-	-	-	8.76	-	0	0
List A	21	-	-	-	-	-	-	-	-	-	-
Twenty20	14	-	-	-	-	-	-	-	-	-	-

MARCUS NORTH LHB OB

FULL NAME: Marcus James North
BORN: July 28, 1979, Melbourne, Australia
SQUAD NO: 12
HEIGHT: 6ft 1in
NICKNAME: Snorks
EDUCATION: Kent Street Senior High School, Perth
TEAMS: Australia, Australia A, Derbyshire, Durham, Gloucestershire, Hampshire, Lancashire, Perth Scorchers, Western Australia
CAREER: Test: 2009; ODI: 2009; T20I: 2009; First-class: 1999; List A: 1999; T20: 2004

BEST BATTING: 239* Western Australia vs Victoria, Perth, 2006
BEST BOWLING: 6-55 Australia vs Pakistan, Lord's, 2010
COUNTY CAP: 2007 (Gloucestershire)

TWITTER FEED: @Marcus_North
NOTES: Glamorgan's captain in both FL t20 and YB40 for 2013. Joined the county in 2012 as overseas player after leading Perth Scorchers to the first Big Bash League final earlier in the year. Stepped down as Western Australia captain in October 2012. Made a century on Test debut for Australia against South Africa at The Wanderers in 2009. Hit two centuries in the 2009 Ashes against England. Scored 900 runs in the 2008 season for Gloucestershire

Batting	Mat	Inns	NO	Runs	HS	Ave	SR	100	50	Ct	St
Tests	21	35	2	1171	128	35.48	48.14	5	4	17	0
ODIs	2	2	0	6	5	3.00	31.57	0	0	1	0
T20Is	1	1	0	20	20	20.00	95.23	0	0	0	0
First-class	188	327	28	12338	239*	41.26		34	63	141	0
List A	158	148	17	4608	134*	35.17		8	31	54	0
Twenty20	63	55	10	1137	70	25.26	107.97	0	3	18	0
Bowling	**Inns**	**Balls**	**Runs**	**Wkts**	**BBI**	**BBM**	**Ave**	**Econ**	**SR**	**5w**	**10**
Tests	21	1258	591	14	6/55	6/55	42.21	2.81	89.8	1	0
ODIs	2	18	16	0	-	-	-	5.33	-	0	0
T20Is	1	-	-	-	-	-	-	-	-	-	-
First-class	188	11055	5563	136	6/55		40.90	3.01	81.2	2	0
List A	158	2618	2214	69	4/26	4/26	32.08	5.07	37.9	0	0
Twenty20	63	428	524	9	2/19	2/19	58.22	7.34	47.5	0	0

SAM NORTHEAST RHB OB MVP82

KENT

FULL NAME: Sam Alexander Northeast
BORN: October 16, 1989, Ashford, Kent
SQUAD NO: 17
HEIGHT: 5ft 11in
NICKNAME: North, Bam, Nick Knight
EDUCATION: Harrow
TEAMS: England Under-15s, England Under-19s, Harrow School, Kent, Kent 2nd XI
CAREER: First-class: 2007; List A: 2007; T20: 2010

BEST BATTING: 176 Kent vs Loughborough MCCU, Canterbury, 2011
COUNTY CAP: 2012

CRICKET MOMENTS TO FORGET? Not scoring many runs in my first two appearances at Lord's in the Eton vs Harrow match
SUPERSTITIONS? I put my right pad on first
CRICKETERS PARTICULARLY ADMIRED? Graham Thorpe, Steve Waugh
TIP FOR THE TOP? Alex Blake
OTHER SPORTS PLAYED? Rackets, squash, cross-country running, football, rugby
OTHER SPORTS FOLLOWED? Football (Spurs), rugby (Bath)
FAVOURITE BAND? Starsailor, Snow Patrol, Florence And The Machine
RELAXATIONS? Fishing, gardening and playing rackets
TWITTER FEED: @sanortheast

Batting	Mat	Inns	NO	Runs	HS	Ave	SR	100	50	Ct	St
First-class	58	103	4	3240	176	32.72	51.95	6	17	31	0
List A	34	28	3	665	69	26.60	74.05	0	5	9	0
Twenty20	28	21	7	355	60	25.35	118.72	0	1	8	0
Bowling	**Inns**	**Balls**	**Runs**	**Wkts**	**BBI**	**BBM**	**Ave**	**Econ**	**SR**	**5w**	**10**
First-class	58	42	10	0	-	-	-	1.42	-	0	0
List A	34	-	-	-	-	-	-	-	-	-	-
Twenty20	28	-	-	-	-	-	-	-	-	-	-

LIAM NORWELL RHB RMF

FULL NAME: Liam Connor Norwell
BORN: December 27, 1991, Bournemouth, Dorset
SQUAD NO: 24
HEIGHT: 6ft 3in
NICKNAME: Pasty, Landry
EDUCATION: Redruth School and Sixth Form
TEAMS: Gloucestershire, Gloucestershire 2nd XI
CAREER: First-class: 2011; List A: 2012; T20: 2012

BEST BATTING: 26 Gloucestershire vs Middlesex, Bristol, 2011
BEST BOWLING: 6-46 Gloucestershire vs Derbyshire, Bristol, 2011
COUNTY CAP: 2011

CAREER HIGHLIGHTS? Taking 6-46 on my first-class debut and making my T20 debut in a victory over Somerset
SUPERSTITIONS? I never shave during a four-day game and always wear two pairs of socks when bowling
MOST MARKED CHARACTERISTIC? Ginger hair and fairly large feet
BEST PLAYER IN COUNTY CRICKET? Will Gidman
TIPS FOR THE TOP? Joe Root, Craig Miles, Chris Dent
IF YOU WEREN'T A CRICKETER? Going through university most probably or still working in Card Factory
DESERT ISLAND DISC? Metallica – Enter Sandman
ACCOMPLISHMENTS? Winning multiple championships at youth age-group levels with Redruth Rugby. Getting through my A-Levels with three passes. Having the record on the basketball machine at the Hollywood Bowl arcade in Cribbs Causeway (at the time of writing)
WHEN YOU RETIRE? I'd like to be a teacher or possibly a superhero
TWITTER FEED: @LCNorwell24

Batting	Mat	Inns	NO	Runs	HS	Ave	SR	100	50	Ct	St
First-class	12	16	6	96	26	9.60	23.02	0	0	3	0
List A	3	1	1	1	1*	-	33.33	0	0	0	0
Twenty20	4	1	1	1	1*	-	50.00	0	0	0	0
Bowling	**Inns**	**Balls**	**Runs**	**Wkts**	**BBI**	**BBM**	**Ave**	**Econ**	**SR**	**5w**	**10**
First-class	12	1686	973	34	6/46	8/74	28.61	3.46	49.5	2	0
List A	3	114	129	8	6/52	6/52	16.12	6.78	14.2	1	0
Twenty20	4	78	123	4	2/41	2/41	30.75	9.46	19.5	0	0

NIALL O'BRIEN

LHB LB WK

FULL NAME: Niall John O'Brien
BORN: November 8, 1981, Dublin
SQUAD NO: 81
HEIGHT: 5ft 8in
NICKNAME: Nobi, Solano
EDUCATION: Marian College, Dublin
TEAMS: Ireland, Ireland Under-19s, Kent, Khulna Royal Bengals, Leicestershire, Marylebone Cricket Club, Northamptonshire, Rangpur Riders
CAREER: ODI: 2006; T20I: 2008; First-class: 2004; List A: 2003; T20: 2004

BEST BATTING: 182 Northamptonshire vs Glamorgan, Cardiff, 2012
BEST BOWLING: 1-4 Kent v Cambridge UCCE, Cambridge, 2006
COUNTY CAP: 2011 (Northamptonshire)

FAMILY TIES? My dad captained Ireland and my brother [Kevin] is an Ireland teammate. All my older brothers played senior club cricket for Railway Union in Dublin and my sister played for Ireland Women U23
WHO WOULD PLAY YOU IN A FILM OF YOUR LIFE? Colin Farrell – we are both from the same neighbourhood in Dublin
CAREER HIGHLIGHTS? My county debuts for Kent and Northants. My Ireland debut. Wins over Pakistan in 2007, Bangladesh in 2009 and England in 2011. Playing in five World Cups (T20 and ODI). Being able to play a sport I love for a career with some great friends
MOST MARKED CHARACTERISTIC? I'm an energetic character and a happy-go-lucky type of guy
BEST PLAYER IN COUNTY CRICKET? Chris Woakes – a top allrounder
TIP FOR THE TOP? Josh Cobb
TWITTER FEED: @niallnobiobrien

Batting	Mat	Inns	NO	Runs	HS	Ave	SR	100	50	Ct	St
ODIs	51	51	5	1215	72	26.41	67.57	0	8	38	7
T20Is	20	19	1	335	50	18.61	97.66	0	1	11	8
First-class	110	169	20	5317	182	35.68	56.20	11	23	300	31
List A	144	123	16	3081	121	28.79	76.26	1	20	120	31
Twenty20	96	82	11	1568	84	22.08	112.40	0	5	48	29
Bowling	**Inns**	**Balls**	**Runs**	**Wkts**	**BBI**	**BBM**	**Ave**	**Econ**	**SR**	**5w**	**10**
ODIs	51	-	-	-	-	-	-	-	-	-	-
T20Is	20	-	-	-	-	-	-	-	-	-	-
First-class	110	18	19	2	1/4	1/4	9.50	6.33	9.0	0	0
List A	144	-	-	-	-	-	-	-	-	-	-
Twenty20	96	-	-	-	-	-	-	-	-	-	-

GRAHAM ONIONS RHB RFM W4 MVP13

FULL NAME: Graham Onions
BORN: September 9, 1982, Gateshead
SQUAD NO: 9
HEIGHT: 6ft 2in
NICKNAME: Bunny, Wills
EDUCATION: St Thomas More RC School, Blaydon
TEAMS: England, England Lions, Durham, Durham Cricket Board, Marylebone Cricket Club
CAREER: Test: 2009; ODI: 2009; First-class: 2004; List A: 2003; T20: 2004

DURHAM

BEST BATTING: 41 Durham vs Yorkshire, Headingley, 2007
BEST BOWLING: 9-67 Durham vs Nottinghamshire, Trent Bridge, 2012

FAMILY TIES? My uncle used to play
WHO WOULD PLAY YOU IN A FILM OF YOUR LIFE? Russell Crowe
CAREER HIGHLIGHTS? My Test debut, taking nine wickets against Notts and the Test match against West Indies in 2012 after my serious back injury
SUPERSTITIONS? I lick my fingers before I bowl
MOST MARKED CHARACTERISTIC? My accent
BEST PLAYER IN COUNTY CRICKET? Joe Root
TIP FOR THE TOP? Ben Stokes
IF YOU WEREN'T A CRICKETER? I'd be struggling! Maybe a PE teacher
DESERT ISLAND DISC? T-Spoon – Sex On The Beach
FAVOURITE TV? 24
CRICKETING HEROES? Darren Gough, Dale Steyn
TWITTER FEED: @BunnyOnions

Batting	Mat	Inns	NO	Runs	HS	Ave	SR	100	50	Ct	St
Tests	9	10	7	30	17*	10.00	30.92	0	0	0	0
ODIs	4	1	0	1	1	1.00	50.00	0	0	1	0
First-class	100	131	46	1092	41	12.84	52.70	0	0	22	0
List A	65	25	7	120	19	6.66	71.85	0	0	9	0
Twenty20	37	12	5	61	31	8.71	107.01	0	0	9	0
Bowling	**Inns**	**Balls**	**Runs**	**Wkts**	**BBI**	**BBM**	**Ave**	**Econ**	**SR**	**5w**	**10**
Tests	9	1606	957	32	5/38	7/102	29.90	3.57	50.1	1	0
ODIs	4	204	185	4	2/58	2/58	46.25	5.44	51.0	0	0
First-class	100	16974	9866	361	9/67		27.32	3.48	47.0	16	3
List A	65	2713	2342	70	3/39	3/39	33.45	5.17	38.7	0	0
Twenty20	37	774	871	27	3/25	3/25	32.25	6.75	28.6	0	0

WORCESTERSHIRE

JACOB ORAM

LHB RMF

FULL NAME: Jacob David Philip Oram
BORN: July 28, 1978, Palmerston North, New Zealand
SQUAD NO: TBC
HEIGHT: 6ft 5in
TEAMS: New Zealand, Central Districts, Chennai Super Kings, Chittagong Kings, Rajasthan Royals, Uva Next, Worcestershire
CAREER: Test: 2002; ODI: 2001; T20I: 2005; First-class: 1997; List A: 1997; T20: 2005

BEST BATTING: 155 Central Districts vs Canterbury, Christchurch, 1999
BEST BOWLING: 6-45 Central Districts vs Northern Districts, Hamilton, 2006

NOTES: Retired from Test cricket in 2009 after making 33 appearances. One of six New Zealanders to have scored 1,000 ODI runs and taken 100 ODI wickets. His 101* against Australia in 2007 was, at the time, a record for the fastest ever ODI century by a New Zealander. Will join Thilan Samaraweera as Worcestershire's overseas player for the FL t20, arriving in time for the Royals' first match of the campaign against Glamorgan on June 28

Batting	Mat	Inns	NO	Runs	HS	Ave	SR	100	50	Ct	St
Tests	33	59	10	1780	133	36.32	50.38	5	6	15	0
ODIs	160	116	15	2434	101*	24.09	86.61	1	13	51	0
T20Is	36	30	7	474	66*	20.60	139.82	0	2	12	0
First-class	85	136	18	3992	155	33.83		8	18	36	0
List A	245	189	20	4328	127	25.60		3	23	78	0
Twenty20	99	81	16	1074	66*	16.52	126.50	0	4	35	0
Bowling	**Inns**	**Balls**	**Runs**	**Wkts**	**BBI**	**BBM**	**Ave**	**Econ**	**SR**	**5w**	**10**
Tests	33	4964	1983	60	4/41	6/63	33.05	2.39	82.7	0	0
ODIs	160	6911	5047	173	5/26	5/26	29.17	4.38	39.9	2	0
T20Is	36	546	793	19	3/33	3/33	41.73	8.71	28.7	0	0
First-class	85	10670	4158	155	6/45		26.82	2.33	68.8	3	0
List A	245	9481	6896	228	5/26	5/26	30.24	4.36	41.5	2	0
Twenty20	99	1707	2228	77	5/14	5/14	28.93	7.83	22.1	1	0

CRAIG OVERTON RHB RMF

FULL NAME: Craig Overton
BORN: April 10, 1994, Barnstaple, Devon
SQUAD NO: 12
HEIGHT: 6ft 6in
NICKNAME: Goober
EDUCATION: West Buckland School
TEAMS: Devon, Devon Under-11s, Devon Under-13s, Devon Under-15s, Devon Under-17s, Devon Under-19s, Devon Under-21s, England Lions, England Under-19s, Somerset, Somerset 2nd XI
CAREER: First-class: 2012; List A: 2012

BEST BATTING: 50 Somerset vs Durham, Taunton, 2012
BEST BOWLING: 4-38 Somerset vs Durham, Chester-le-Street, 2012

FAMILY TIES? My father played minor county cricket for Devon and my twin brother Jamie also plays for Somerset
WHO WOULD PLAY YOU IN A FILM OF YOUR LIFE? Christian Bale
CAREER HIGHLIGHTS? Making my debut for Somerset. Representing my country at the U19 World Cup
SUPERSTITIONS? Always left pad on first
MOST MARKED CHARACTERISTIC? Being a twin
BEST PLAYER IN COUNTY CRICKET? Peter Trego
TIPS FOR THE TOP? Tom Helm, Mathew Dunn, Tymal Mills
IF YOU WEREN'T A CRICKETER? I've just finished school so I would either be on a gap year or in my first year at university
DESERT ISLAND DISC? Calvin Harris – Drinking From The Bottle
BIGGEST DRESSING DOWN YOU'VE RECEIVED? Being taken to see the ICC panel after the World Cup quarter-final against South Africa
CRICKETING HEROES? Andrew Flintoff, Dale Steyn
NON-CRICKETING HEROES? Muhammad Ali
ACCOMPLISHMENTS? Achieving 3 A-Levels
WHEN YOU RETIRE? Become a cricket pundit
TWITTER FEED: @craigoverton12

Batting	Mat	Inns	NO	Runs	HS	Ave	SR	100	50	Ct	St
First-class	7	8	1	75	50	10.71	52.08	0	1	4	0
List A	7	7	1	69	20	11.50	82.14	0	0	3	0
Bowling	**Inns**	**Balls**	**Runs**	**Wkts**	**BBI**	**BBM**	**Ave**	**Econ**	**SR**	**5w**	**10**
First-class	7	679	363	12	4/38	6/87	30.25	3.20	56.5	0	0
List A	7	324	262	4	2/30	2/30	65.50	4.85	81.0	0	0

JAMIE OVERTON RHB RMF

FULL NAME: Jamie Overton
BORN: April 10, 1994, Barnstaple, Devon
SQUAD NO: 11
HEIGHT: 6ft 5in
NICKNAME: Goober, J
EDUCATION: West Buckland School
TEAMS: Devon, Devon Under-13s, Devon Under-14s, Devon Under-15s, Devon Under-17s, England Under-19s, Somerset, Somerset 2nd XI
CAREER: First-class: 2012; List A: 2012

BEST BATTING: 34* Somerset vs Surrey, The Oval, 2012
BEST BOWLING: 2-61 Somerset vs Durham, Taunton, 2012

FAMILY TIES? My dad played for Devon and my twin brother [Craig] also plays for Somerset
WHO WOULD PLAY YOU IN A FILM OF YOUR LIFE? Daniel Craig
CAREER HIGHLIGHTS? Receiving my contract from Somerset in 2012
SUPERSTITIONS? Always put my left pad on first. Always wear a jumper when batting
MOST MARKED CHARACTERISTIC? Being a twin
BEST PLAYER IN COUNTY CRICKET? Nick Compton
TIPS FOR THE TOP? Tom Helm, Tymal Mills, Matt Dunn
IF YOU WEREN'T A CRICKETER? I would be at university studying Sports Science
DESERT ISLAND DISC? Rihanna – Unapologetic
FAVOURITE TV? Eastenders
BIGGEST DRESSING DOWN YOU'VE RECEIVED? Getting a warning from the ICC in the U19 World Cup
CRICKETING HEROES? James Anderson, Andrew Flintoff
NON-CRICKETING HEROES? Rory McIlroy
WHEN YOU RETIRE? I would like to become a coach or a teacher
SURPRISING FACT? I play my club cricket at the same club as the late David Shepherd
FANTASY SLIP CORDON? Keeper: Me, 1st: Rory McIlroy, 2nd: Jack Whitehall, 3rd: Chris Ashton, Gully: Jamie Laing
TWITTER FEED: @JamieOverton

Batting	Mat	Inns	NO	Runs	HS	Ave	SR	100	50	Ct	St
First-class	3	4	2	55	34*	27.50	91.66	0	0	1	0
List A	3	3	2	19	10	19.00	63.33	0	0	0	0
Bowling	**Inns**	**Balls**	**Runs**	**Wkts**	**BBI**	**BBM**	**Ave**	**Econ**	**SR**	**5w**	**10**
First-class	3	396	229	6	2/61	3/106	38.16	3.46	66.0	0	0
List A	3	102	100	6	4/42	4/42	16.66	5.88	17.0	0	0

WILL OWEN RHB RFM

FULL NAME: William Thomas Owen
BORN: September 2, 1988, St Asaph, Flintshire
SQUAD NO: 34
HEIGHT: 6ft
NICKNAME: Swillo
EDUCATION: Prestatyn High School
TEAMS: Glamorgan, Glamorgan 2nd XI, Wales Minor Counties
CAREER: First-class: 2007; List A: 2010; T20: 2010

BEST BATTING: 69 Glamorgan vs Derbyshire, Derby, 2011
BEST BOWLING: 5-124 Glamorgan vs Middlesex, Cardiff, 2011

CAREER HIGHLIGHTS? Five-wicket haul on one-day debut against the Unicorns. Maiden first-class fifty against Derby in 2011
CRICKETING HEROES? Being a Welsh lad growing up watching the 2005 Ashes series, it's got to be Simon Jones
BEST PLAYER IN COUNTY CRICKET? Marcus Trescothick is a prize scalp
TIP FOR THE TOP? Andrew Salter
IF YOU WEREN'T A CRICKETER? Policeman
WHEN RAIN STOPS PLAY? On the pool table in our dressing room, the time flies by!
FAVOURITE TV? Eastbound And Down
FAVOURITE FILM? Cool Runnings
FAVOURITE BOOK? Anything written by Robert G Barrett
DREAM HOLIDAY? Barbados on a beach
GUILTY PLEASURES? Chocolate cookies
FANTASY SLIP CORDON? Keeper: Will Bragg, 1st: Ricky Gervais, 2nd: Michael McIntyre, 3rd: Darren Hughes
TWITTER FEED: @swillo88

Batting	Mat	Inns	NO	Runs	HS	Ave	SR	100	50	Ct	St
First-class	16	18	6	225	69	18.75	68.59	0	1	3	0
List A	21	10	4	53	12	8.83	81.53	0	0	2	0
Twenty20	12	1	0	8	8	8.00	114.28	0	0	0	0
Bowling	**Inns**	**Balls**	**Runs**	**Wkts**	**BBI**	**BBM**	**Ave**	**Econ**	**SR**	**5w**	**10**
First-class	16	2086	1548	40	5/124	6/61	38.70	4.45	52.1	1	0
List A	21	639	633	32	5/49	5/49	19.78	5.94	19.9	1	0
Twenty20	12	183	277	8	3/21	3/21	34.62	9.08	22.8	0	0

TONY PALLADINO

RHB RMF W2 MVP91

FULL NAME: Antonio Paul Palladino
BORN: June 29, 1983, London
SQUAD NO: 28
HEIGHT: 5ft 11in
NICKNAME: Dino, Italian Stallion, Pallas
EDUCATION: Anglia Polytechnic University
TEAMS: Namibia, British Universities, Cambridge MCCU, Derbyshire, Essex, Essex 2nd XI, Essex Cricket Board
CAREER: First-class: 2003; List A: 2003; T20: 2005

BEST BATTING: 106 Derbyshire vs Australia A, Derby, 2012
BEST BOWLING: 7-53 Derbyshire vs Kent, Derby, 2012

CAREER HIGHLIGHTS? The 2012 season. Winning Division Two of the County Championship with Derbyshire in 2012. Taking a hat-trick vs Leicestershire in 2012. First-class hundred vs Australia A 2012. All my first-class five-wicket hauls, but in particular my career best 7-53 vs Kent 2012. Bowler of the tournament at Zimbabwe Stanbic T20 competition in 2010 for Namibia Desert Vipers
MOST MARKED CHARACTERISTIC? I hate losing so I would say I have a never-say-die attitude
TIPS FOR THE TOP? Ross Whiteley, Chris Wright, Toby Roland-Jones
IF YOU WEREN'T A CRICKETER? Cage fighter or cliff diving champion
DESERT ISLAND DISC? Oasis – (What's the Story) Morning Glory?
BIGGEST DRESSING DOWN YOU'VE RECEIVED? A while ago from Graham Gooch because I kept bowling leg stump half volleys at Darren Bicknell
SURPRISING FACT? Before joining Derbyshire I nearly applied for a job as a bin man. Luckily, Derbyshire came along and saved me
FANTASY SLIP CORDON? Keeper: David Brent (legend), 1st: Me, 2nd: Ian Botham (hero), 3rd: Ted McMinn (great banter), Gully: David Wainwright (funny man)
TWITTER FEED: @Apalladino28

Batting	Mat	Inns	NO	Runs	HS	Ave	SR	100	50	Ct	St
First-class	82	109	26	1205	106	14.51	47.51	1	4	25	0
List A	41	23	5	162	31	9.00	82.23	0	0	4	0
Twenty20	16	5	3	21	8*	10.50	87.50	0	0	2	0
Bowling	**Inns**	**Balls**	**Runs**	**Wkts**	**BBI**	**BBM**	**Ave**	**Econ**	**SR**	**5w**	**10**
First-class	82	12834	6804	225	7/53		30.24	3.18	57.0	8	0
List A	41	1524	1377	39	4/32	4/32	35.30	5.42	39.0	0	0
Twenty20	16	287	347	22	4/21	4/21	15.77	7.25	13.0	0	0

MONTY PANESAR

LHB SLA W6 MVP50

FULL NAME: Mudhsuden Singh Panesar
BORN: April 25, 1982, Luton, Bedfordshire
SQUAD NO: 7
HEIGHT: 6ft 1in
EDUCATION: Bedford Modern School, Stopsley High School, Luton, Bedfordshire; Loughborough University
TEAMS: England, British Universities, England Lions, Lions, Loughborough MCCU, Marylebone Cricket Club, Northamptonshire, Sussex, Sussex 2nd XI
CAREER: Test: 2006; ODI: 2007; T20I: 2007; First-class: 2001; List A: 2002; T20: 2006

BEST BATTING: 46* Sussex vs Middlesex, Hove, 2010
BEST BOWLING: 7-60 Sussex vs Somerset, Taunton, 2012
COUNTY CAPS: 2006 (Northamptonshire); 2010 (Sussex)

NOTES: His first Test wicket was Sachin Tendulkar. Claimed a five-wicket haul (and eight wickets in all) in his first Ashes Test, at Perth in 2006. Helped secure an improbable draw in the first Ashes Test at Cardiff in 2009, batting with James Anderson for 37 minutes to deny Australia. Moved to Sussex after 10 years at Northamptonshire ahead of the 2010 season. Took 14 wickets in two matches against Pakistan in the UAE on his return to England's Test side in January 2012

Batting	Mat	Inns	NO	Runs	HS	Ave	SR	100	50	Ct	St
Tests	45	60	20	213	26	5.32	31.64	0	0	9	0
ODIs	26	8	3	26	13	5.20	28.57	0	0	3	0
T20Is	1	1	0	1	1	1.00	50.00	0	0	0	0
First-class	174	218	70	1268	46*	8.56	34.00	0	0	35	0
List A	84	29	13	141	17*	8.81	56.17	0	0	14	0
Twenty20	31	7	2	7	3*	1.40	46.66	0	0	3	0
Bowling	**Inns**	**Balls**	**Runs**	**Wkts**	**BBI**	**BBM**	**Ave**	**Econ**	**SR**	**5w**	**10**
Tests	45	11268	5190	159	6/37	11/210	32.64	2.76	70.8	12	2
ODIs	26	1308	980	24	3/25	3/25	40.83	4.49	54.5	0	0
T20Is	1	24	40	2	2/40	2/40	20.00	10.00	12.0	0	0
First-class	174	39823	18017	596	7/60		30.22	2.71	66.8	32	5
List A	84	3701	2865	81	5/20	5/20	35.37	4.64	45.6	1	0
Twenty20	31	618	758	27	3/14	3/14	28.07	7.35	22.8	0	0

MATTHEW PARDOE LHB LM

WORCESTERSHIRE

FULL NAME: Matthew Graham Pardoe
BORN: January 5, 1991, Stourbridge, Worcestershire
SQUAD NO: 19
HEIGHT: 6ft 1in
EDUCATION: Haybridge High School and Sixth Form College
TEAMS: Southern Rocks, Worcestershire, Worcestershire 2nd XI
CAREER: First-class: 2011; List A: 2011; T20: 2013

BEST BATTING: 90 Southern Rocks vs Mashonaland Eagles, Masvingo, 2013
BEST BOWLING: 2-34 Mountaineers vs Southern Rocks, Mutare, 2013

CAREER HIGHLIGHTS? My first-class and List A debuts, scoring 74 vs Notts and being part of the Worcestershire team who maintained Division One status in 2011
SUPERSTITIONS? Sometimes, but they change all the time
CRICKETING HEROES? Graeme Hick, Matthew Hayden and Marcus Trescothick
NON-CRICKETING HEROES? Rafael Nadal, Tiger Woods
BEST PLAYER IN COUNTY CRICKET? Marcus Trescothick
TIPS FOR THE TOP? Ben Stokes and James Taylor
IF YOU WEREN'T A CRICKETER? I'd be a Geography teacher or work on the family farm
WHEN RAIN STOPS PLAY? Snoozing, eating and chatting
FAVOURITE TV? Dr Who
FAVOURITE FILM? Gladiator
FAVOURITE BOOK? A Brief History Of Time by Stephen Hawking
DREAM HOLIDAY? The Caribbean
ACCOMPLISHMENTS? County swimming, and dancing at national competition in Blackpool
SURPRISING SKILL? Ballroom dancing
GUILTY PLEASURES? Michael Buble and sweets
SURPRISING FACT? I have seen every episode of Dr Who that has ever been shown

Batting	Mat	Inns	NO	Runs	HS	Ave	SR	100	50	Ct	St
First-class	28	53	2	1051	90	20.60	36.49	0	6	15	0
List A	3	3	0	69	42	23.00	66.99	0	0	2	0
Twenty20	1	1	0	1	1	1.00	100.00	0	0	-	-
Bowling	**Inns**	**Balls**	**Runs**	**Wkts**	**BBI**	**BBM**	**Ave**	**Econ**	**SR**	**5w**	**10**
First-class	28	164	100	2	2/34	2/34	50.00	3.65	82.0	0	0
List A	3	-	-	-	-	-	-	-	-	-	-
Twenty20	1	-	-	-	-	-	-	-	-	-	-

STEPHEN PARRY RHB SLA

FULL NAME: Stephen David Parry
BORN: January 12, 1986, Manchester
SQUAD NO: 4
HEIGHT: 6ft
NICKNAME: Pazza
EDUCATION: Audenshaw High School, Greater Manchester
TEAMS: Cumberland, England Lions, Lancashire, Lancashire 2nd XI
CAREER: First-class: 2007; List A: 2009; T20: 2009

BEST BATTING: 2 Lancashire vs Durham, Manchester, 2009
BEST BOWLING: 5-23 Lancashire vs Durham UCCE, Durham University, 2007

CAREER HIGHLIGHTS? Playing for Lancashire and England Lions
CRICKETING HEROES? Shane Warne
NON-CRICKETING HEROES? Muhammad Ali
BEST PLAYER IN COUNTY CRICKET? Marcus Trescothick
TIP FOR THE TOP? Jos Buttler
IF YOU WEREN'T A CRICKETER? Fishing or travelling the world
WHEN RAIN STOPS PLAY? Relaxing or working on my game
FAVOURITE TV? Sky Sports News
FAVOURITE FILM? Hangover, Man On Fire
DREAM HOLIDAY? Barbados
ACCOMPLISHMENTS? Running a marathon
SURPRISING SKILL? Elite table-tennis player
GUILTY PLEASURES? San Carlo for a meal and a bottle of Sancerre white wine
TWITTER FEED: @SDParry86

Batting	Mat	Inns	NO	Runs	HS	Ave	SR	100	50	Ct	St
First-class	3	2	0	3	2	1.50	10.34	0	0	1	0
List A	46	20	5	171	31	11.40	76.00	0	0	11	0
Twenty20	51	14	8	53	11	8.83	103.92	0	0	7	0
Bowling	**Inns**	**Balls**	**Runs**	**Wkts**	**BBI**	**BBM**	**Ave**	**Econ**	**SR**	**5w**	**10**
First-class	3	523	256	9	5/23	5/46	28.44	2.93	58.1	1	0
List A	46	1954	1665	54	4/21	4/21	30.83	5.11	36.1	0	0
Twenty20	51	1122	1264	59	4/23	4/23	21.42	6.75	19.0	0	0

JEETAN PATEL RHB OB W1 MVP20

WARWICKSHIRE

FULL NAME: Jeetan Shashi Patel
BORN: May 7, 1980, Wellington, New Zealand
SQUAD NO: 5
HEIGHT: 5ft 11in
NICKNAME: Jeets
TEAMS: New Zealand, New Zealand XI, Warwickshire, Wellington
CAREER: Test: 2006; ODI: 2005; T20I: 2005; First-class: 2000; List A: 1999; T20: 2005

BEST BATTING: 120 Warwickshire vs Yorkshire, Birmingham, 2009
BEST BOWLING: 7-75 Warwickshire vs Somerset, Taunton, 2012

NOTES: Took 5-145 on debut for Wellington against Auckland in 1999/00. Made New Zealand Test debut in Cape Town against South Africa in April 2006 and took 3-117 in 42 overs, dismissing Graeme Smith, Boeta Dippenaar and AB de Villiers. Took Test-best figures of 5-110 against West Indies in Napier in 2008. Overseas player for Warwickshire in 2009, 2011 and 2012, taking 51 first-class wickets at 22.76 last year

Batting	Mat	Inns	NO	Runs	HS	Ave	SR	100	50	Ct	St
Tests	19	30	7	276	27*	12.00	46.46	0	0	12	0
ODIs	39	13	7	88	34	14.66	58.66	0	0	12	0
T20Is	11	4	1	9	5	3.00	64.28	0	0	4	0
First-class	137	174	48	2566	120	20.36		1	11	59	0
List A	130	66	22	420	34	9.54		0	0	44	0
Twenty20	80	25	7	77	12	4.27	96.25	0	0	24	0
Bowling	**Inns**	**Balls**	**Runs**	**Wkts**	**BBI**	**BBM**	**Ave**	**Econ**	**SR**	**5w**	**10**
Tests	19	4723	2520	52	5/110	6/151	48.46	3.20	90.8	1	0
ODIs	39	1804	1513	42	3/11	3/11	36.02	5.03	42.9	0	0
T20Is	11	199	269	16	3/20	3/20	16.81	8.11	12.4	0	0
First-class	137	26900	13290	341	7/75		38.97	2.96	78.8	13	1
List A	130	6133	4732	131	4/16	4/16	36.12	4.62	46.8	0	0
Twenty20	80	1541	1903	79	4/27	4/27	24.08	7.40	19.5	0	0

RAVI PATEL RHB SLA

FULL NAME: Ravi Hasmukh Patel
BORN: August 4, 1991, Harrow, Middlesex
SQUAD NO: 36
HEIGHT: 5ft 10in
NICKNAME: Rav, Ravster
EDUCATION: Merchant Taylors' School, Northwood; Loughborough University
TEAMS: Loughborough MCCU, Middlesex, Middlesex 2nd XI
CAREER: First-class: 2010; List A: 2010

BEST BATTING: 20 Middlesex vs Lancashire, Lord's, 2012
BEST BOWLING: 4-72 Middlesex vs Lancashire, Lord's, 2012

FAMILY TIES? My dad played university cricket in India and club cricket in England
WHO WOULD PLAY YOU IN A FILM OF YOUR LIFE? Mike 'The Situation' from Jersey Shore
CAREER HIGHLIGHTS? Playing against Australia for Middlesex in a one-day game at Lord's in 2010. Making my County Championship debut vs Warwickshire at Edgbaston in 2012. Playing for England U15-18
MOST MARKED CHARACTERISTIC? I'm always up for having a good time
BEST PLAYER IN COUNTY CRICKET? Tim Murtagh
TIPS FOR THE TOP? Ryan Higgins and Harry Podmore from Middlesex
IF YOU WEREN'T A CRICKETER? I'd be studying to be an economist
DESERT ISLAND DISC? The Game – The Documentary
FAVOURITE TV? Jersey Shore
BIGGEST DRESSING DOWN YOU'VE RECEIVED? Turning up an hour late to a fitness test last year due to my alarm not going off. Our strength and conditioning coach Luke Woodhouse gave me a ticking off
CRICKETING HEROES? Pragyan Ojha, Murali Kartik, Monty Panesar
NON-CRICKETING HEROES? Cristiano Ronaldo, Will Smith, Dr Dre
WHEN YOU RETIRE? I'd like to get into the property and catering business
TWITTER FEED: @ravi36patel

Batting	Mat	Inns	NO	Runs	HS	Ave	SR	100	50	Ct	St
First-class	7	11	5	88	20	14.66	43.78	0	0	3	0
List A	1	-	-	-	-	-	-	-	-	0	0
Bowling	**Inns**	**Balls**	**Runs**	**Wkts**	**BBI**	**BBM**	**Ave**	**Econ**	**SR**	**5w**	**10**
First-class	7	1312	724	26	4/72	8/198	27.84	3.31	50.4	0	0
List A	1	30	38	0	-	-	-	7.60	-	0	0

SAMIT PATEL

RHB SLA R1 MVP31

NOTTINGHAMSHIRE

FULL NAME: Samit Rohit Patel
BORN: November 30, 1984, Leicester
SQUAD NO: 21
HEIGHT: 5ft 8in
NICKNAME: Sarnie, Slippery
EDUCATION: Worksop College
TEAMS: England, England Lions, England Under-19s, Nottinghamshire
CAREER: Test: 2012; ODI: 2008; T20I: 2011; First-class: 2002; List A: 2002; T20: 2003

BEST BATTING: 176 Nottinghamshire vs Gloucestershire, Bristol, 2007
BEST BOWLING: 7-68 Nottinghamshire vs Hampshire, Southampton, 2011
COUNTY CAP: 2008

FAMILY TIES? My dad played league cricket and my brother [Akhil] played for Notts for two years
CAREER HIGHLIGHTS? Making my ODI and Test debuts. Taking five wickets against South Africa at The Oval and scoring 70 off 40 balls at Chandigarh against India. Scoring 68 against Sri Lanka in the World T20
BEST PLAYER IN COUNTY CRICKET? Chris Read
TIPS FOR THE TOP? Sam Billings and Joe Root
DESERT ISLAND DISC? Chesney Hawkes – I Am The One And Only
FAVOURITE TV? Fawlty Towers, Only Fools And Horses
NON-CRICKETING HEROES? Tiger Woods and Mary Dawson
WHEN YOU RETIRE? Become a coach of a first-class team and then an international team

Batting	Mat	Inns	NO	Runs	HS	Ave	SR	100	50	Ct	St
Tests	5	7	0	109	33	15.57	42.41	0	0	2	0
ODIs	36	22	7	482	70*	32.13	93.23	0	1	7	0
T20Is	18	14	2	189	67	15.75	109.24	0	1	3	0
First-class	112	175	13	6316	176	38.98	62.54	14	36	62	0
List A	167	141	23	3728	114	31.59	82.24	2	19	41	0
Twenty20	111	100	18	2047	84*	24.96	123.98	0	13	30	0
Bowling	**Inns**	**Balls**	**Runs**	**Wkts**	**BBI**	**BBM**	**Ave**	**Econ**	**SR**	**5w**	**10**
Tests	5	606	257	4	2/27	2/36	64.25	2.54	151.5	0	0
ODIs	36	1187	1091	24	5/41	5/41	45.45	5.51	49.4	1	0
T20Is	18	252	321	7	2/6	2/6	45.85	7.64	36.0	0	0
First-class	112	12008	6175	157	7/68		39.33	3.08	76.4	3	1
List A	167	5145	4522	148	6/13	6/13	30.55	5.27	34.7	2	0
Twenty20	111	1843	2213	79	3/11	3/11	28.01	7.20	23.3	0	0

STEVEN PATTERSON RHB RMF W1 MVP84

FULL NAME: Steven Andrew Patterson
BORN: October 3, 1983, Beverley, Humberside
SQUAD NO: 17
HEIGHT: 6ft 4in
NICKNAME: Patto, Dead Man
EDUCATION: Malet Lambert School; St Mary's Sixth Form College; Leeds University
TEAMS: Yorkshire, Yorkshire 2nd XI, Yorkshire Cricket Board
CAREER: First-class: 2005; List A: 2003; T20: 2009

BEST BATTING: 53 Yorkshire vs Sussex, Hove, 2011
BEST BOWLING: 5-50 Yorkshire vs Essex, Scarborough, 2010
COUNTY CAP: 2012

CAREER HIGHLIGHTS? First five-fer vs Essex at Scarborough in 2010
TIPS FOR THE TOP? Jonny Bairstow and Joe Root
FAVOURITE FILM? The Shawshank Redemption
DREAM HOLIDAY? Skiing in the Alps
GUILTY PLEASURES? Chocolate
CRICKETING HEROES? Glenn McGrath, Allan Donald
FAVOURITE BAND? Coldplay
NOTES: Patterson enjoyed the best season of his career in 2012 when his 48 Championship wickets at 20.81 were double the amount taken by any other White Rose bowler. His tally over the last three seasons now stands at 119 wickets

Batting	Mat	Inns	NO	Runs	HS	Ave	SR	100	50	Ct	St
First-class	56	64	20	660	53	15.00	32.51	0	1	11	0
List A	49	19	15	111	25*	27.75		0	0	6	0
Twenty20	26	5	3	5	3*	2.50	50.00	0	0	4	0
Bowling	**Inns**	**Balls**	**Runs**	**Wkts**	**BBI**	**BBM**	**Ave**	**Econ**	**SR**	**5w**	**10**
First-class	56	8496	4272	141	5/50	8/94	30.29	3.01	60.2	2	0
List A	49	2091	1780	61	6/32	6/32	29.18	5.10	34.2	1	0
Twenty20	26	545	785	24	4/30	4/30	32.70	8.64	22.7	0	0

DAVID PAYNE LHB LFM

FULL NAME: David Alan Payne
BORN: February 15, 1991, Poole, Dorset
SQUAD NO: 14
HEIGHT: 6ft 2in
NICKNAME: Sid, Payney
EDUCATION: Lytchett Matravers Primary; Lytchett Minster Secondary
TEAMS: Dorset, England Development XI, England Under-19s, Gloucestershire, Gloucestershire 2nd XI
CAREER: First-class: 2011; List A: 2009; T20: 2010

BEST BATTING: 62 Gloucestershire vs Glamorgan, Bristol, 2011
BEST BOWLING: 6-26 Gloucestershire vs Leicestershire, Bristol, 2011
COUNTY CAP: 2011

CAREER HIGHLIGHTS? Making my first-class debut and taking a five-wicket haul. Breaking Gloucestershire's record for best bowling figures in a one-day game. Going to the U19 World Cup
MOST MARKED CHARACTERISTIC? Haircut
TIP FOR THE TOP? Tymal Mills
DESERT ISLAND DISC? Usher – Confessions
FAVOURITE TV? Take Me Out
CRICKETING HEROES? Freddie Flintoff
NON-CRICKETING HEROES? David Beckham
ACCOMPLISHMENTS? Being on AFC Bournemouth's Academy and playing at Old Trafford football ground
WHEN YOU RETIRE? Start my own clothing line
FANTASY SLIP CORDON? Keeper: David Beckham, 1st: Myself, 2nd: Pixie Lott, 3rd: Hayden Panettiere, Gully: Ricky Gervais
TWITTER FEED: @sidpayne7

Batting	Mat	Inns	NO	Runs	HS	Ave	SR	100	50	Ct	St
First-class	22	31	9	330	62	15.00	40.74	0	1	7	0
List A	25	11	9	30	13	15.00	62.50	0	0	7	0
Twenty20	14	7	2	16	10	3.20	84.21	0	0	0	0
Bowling	**Inns**	**Balls**	**Runs**	**Wkts**	**BBI**	**BBM**	**Ave**	**Econ**	**SR**	**5w**	**10**
First-class	22	2954	1802	64	6/26	9/96	28.15	3.66	46.1	2	0
List A	25	965	933	45	7/29	7/29	20.73	5.80	21.4	1	0
Twenty20	14	246	353	18	3/20	3/20	19.61	8.60	13.6	0	0

STEPHEN PETERS RHB LB R4

FULL NAME: Stephen David Peters
BORN: December 10, 1978, Harold Wood, Essex
SQUAD NO: 11
HEIGHT: 5ft 11in
NICKNAME: Pedro, Geezer
EDUCATION: Coopers Coburn Company School
TEAMS: Essex, Marylebone Cricket Club, Northamptonshire, Worcestershire
CAREER: First-class: 1996; List A: 1996; T20: 2003

NORTHAMPTONSHIRE

BEST BATTING: 222 Northamptonshire vs Glamorgan, Swansea, 2011
BEST BOWLING: 1-19 Essex vs Oxford UCCE, Chelmsford, 1999
COUNTY CAP: 2007 (Northamptonshire); BENEFIT YEAR: 2013 (Northamptonshire)

WHO WOULD PLAY YOU IN A FILM OF YOUR LIFE? George Clooney
CAREER HIGHLIGHTS? Winning U19 World Cup with England in 1998. Any hundred I score. Winning the Benson & Hedges Cup with Essex in 1998
SUPERSTITIONS? Habits more than superstitions. I did have loads but binned them
MOST MARKED CHARACTERISTIC? Moody, stubborn and terrible jokes
BEST PLAYER IN COUNTY CRICKET? Graham Onions
TIP FOR THE TOP? Rob Newton
DESERT ISLAND DISC? Nickelback
FAVOURITE TV? Gavin And Stacey
BIGGEST DRESSING DOWN YOU'VE RECEIVED? No dressing downs as such but plenty of disagreements! Matthew Hayden gave me an hour long serve once when batting
NON-CRICKETING HEROES? Paolo Di Canio
SURPRISING FACT? I'm an international fly fisherman
FANTASY SLIP CORDON? Keeper: Kate Beckinsale, 1st: Natalie Imbruglia, 2nd: Halle Berry, 3rd: My wife
TWITTER FEED: @PedroBenefit

Batting	Mat	Inns	NO	Runs	HS	Ave	SR	100	50	Ct	St
First-class	226	382	30	12433	222	35.32		29	59	180	0
List A	171	158	10	3345	107	22.60		2	20	46	0
Twenty20	24	20	3	300	61*	17.64	98.36	0	1	7	0
Bowling	**Inns**	**Balls**	**Runs**	**Wkts**	**BBI**	**BBM**	**Ave**	**Econ**	**SR**	**5w**	**10**
First-class	226	35	31	1	1/19		31.00	5.31	35.0	0	0
List A	171	-	-	-	-	-	-	-	-	-	-
Twenty20	24	-	-	-	-	-	-	-	-	-	-

ALVIRO PETERSEN RHB OB R1

SOMERSET

FULL NAME: Alviro Nathan Petersen
BORN: November 25, 1980, Port Elizabeth, South Africa
SQUAD NO: TBC
HEIGHT: 5ft 10in
NICKNAME: Viro
TEAMS: South Africa, Essex, Glamorgan, Lions, North West, Northerns, Titans
CAREER: Test: 2010; ODI: 2006; T20I: 2010; First-class: 2000; List A: 2000; T20: 2004

BEST BATTING: 210 Glamorgan vs Surrey, The Oval, 2011
BEST BOWLING: 2-7 Northerns vs Easterns, Benoni, 2002
COUNTY CAP: 2011 (Glamorgan)

NOTES: Hit 80 against Zimbabwe in his second ODI. Made his Test debut in February 2010, against India at Kolkata, scoring exactly 100 in his first innings, becoming only the third South African to score a century on Test debut. Skippered Glamorgan in 2011. He returned to the South African side in 2012, scoring a hundred against Sri Lanka in January, and was selected as Graeme Smith's opening partner in the Test series that took place in New Zealand in March of the same year. His most recent Test match ton (106) came against the same opposition in January 2013 at Cape Town. Made 235 runs at 21 in seven Championship matches for Essex last season. Will play for Somerset from the start of the season until the end of July

Batting	Mat	Inns	NO	Runs	HS	Ave	SR	100	50	Ct	St
Tests	24	43	2	1589	182	38.75	50.86	5	5	19	0
ODIs	17	15	1	437	80	31.21	83.23	0	4	3	0
T20Is	2	2	0	14	8	7.00	73.68	0	0	1	0
First-class	157	277	14	10353	210	39.36		31	41	123	0
List A	148	142	10	4497	145*	34.06		7	27	52	0
Twenty20	73	68	9	1658	84*	28.10	121.02	0	13	39	0
Bowling	**Inns**	**Balls**	**Runs**	**Wkts**	**BBI**	**BBM**	**Ave**	**Econ**	**SR**	**5w**	**10**
Tests	24	114	62	1	1/2	1/2	62.00	3.26	114.0	0	0
ODIs	17	6	7	0	-	-	-	7.00	-	0	0
T20Is	2	-	-	-	-	-	-	-	-	-	-
First-class	157	1160	612	11	2/7		55.63	3.16	105.4	0	0
List A	148	346	311	7	2/48	2/48	44.42	5.39	49.4	0	0
Twenty20	73	175	191	8	1/5	1/5	23.87	6.54	21.8	0	0

MARK PETTINI RHB RM R1 MVP85

FULL NAME: Mark Lewis Pettini
BORN: August 7, 1983, Brighton, Sussex
SQUAD NO: 24
HEIGHT: 5ft 11in
NICKNAME: Swampy
EDUCATION: Hills Road Sixth Form College; Cardiff University
TEAMS: England Under-19s, Essex, Mountaineers
CAREER: First-class: 2001; List A: 2001; T20: 2003

ESSEX

BEST BATTING: 208* Essex vs Derbyshire, Chelmsford, 2006
BEST BOWLING: 1-72 Essex vs Leicestershire, Leicester, 2012
COUNTY CAP: 2006

CRICKETERS PARTICULARLY ADMIRED? Graham Gooch, Andy Flower, Ronnie Irani
TIPS FOR THE TOP? Adam Wheater, Tom Westley
OTHER SPORTS PLAYED? Darts
OTHER SPORTS FOLLOWED? Football (Liverpool)
FAVOURITE BAND? The White Stripes, Foo Fighters, Editors
RELAXATIONS? Fishing, surfing, travelling, music
CAREER HIGHLIGHTS? Winning two Pro40 titles with Essex. Being made Essex captain in 2007, and winning the FP Trophy in 2008

Batting	Mat	Inns	NO	Runs	HS	Ave	SR	100	50	Ct	St
First-class	128	216	32	6327	208*	34.38	47.37	7	40	87	0
List A	140	129	10	3357	144	28.21	85.63	6	21	52	0
Twenty20	89	85	5	2101	87	26.26	126.56	0	13	32	0
Bowling	**Inns**	**Balls**	**Runs**	**Wkts**	**BBI**	**BBM**	**Ave**	**Econ**	**SR**	**5w**	**10**
First-class	128	132	263	1	1/72	1/72	263.00	11.95	132.0	0	0
List A	140	-	-	-	-	-	-	-	-	-	-
Twenty20	89	-	-	-	-	-	-	-	-	-	-

BEN PHILLIPS RHB RMF

NOTTINGHAMSHIRE

FULL NAME: Ben James Phillips
BORN: September 30, 1974, Lewisham, London
SQUAD NO: 13
HEIGHT: 6ft 6in
NICKNAME: Bennyphil, Bus
EDUCATION: Langley Park School, Beckenham
TEAMS: Kent, Northamptonshire, Nottinghamshire, Somerset
CAREER: First-class: 1996; List A: 1996; T20: 2003

BEST BATTING: 100* Kent vs Lancashire, Manchester, 1997
BEST BOWLING: 6-29 Northamptonshire vs Cambridge UCCE, Cambridge, 2006
COUNTY CAP: 2005 (Northamptonshire)

WHO WOULD PLAY YOU IN A FILM OF YOUR LIFE? Gerard Butler
MOST MARKED CHARACTERISTIC? My tattoos
BEST PLAYER IN COUNTY CRICKET? Marcus Trescothick
TIPS FOR THE TOP? Jos Buttler, Adam Tillcock
IF YOU WEREN'T A CRICKETER? Barista
DESERT ISLAND DISC? Haircut 100 – Young At Heart
FAVOURITE TV? Oz Aerobics
CRICKETING HEROES? Glenn McGrath and Jason Gillespie
ACCOMPLISHMENTS? Competing in triathlons
WHEN YOU RETIRE? Personal trainer/fitness coach
SURPRISING FACT? I don't drink alcohol
FANTASY SLIP CORDON? Keeper: Kerry Ann Louise, 1st: Steffan Jones, 2nd: Marcus Trescothick, 3rd: Kirsty Gallagher, Gully: Ali Brown
TWITTER FEED: @bennyphil13

Batting	Mat	Inns	NO	Runs	HS	Ave	SR	100	50	Ct	St
First-class	123	171	31	2938	100*	20.98		1	15	37	0
List A	137	85	29	1042	51*	18.60		0	1	37	0
Twenty20	63	39	11	438	41*	15.64	134.35	0	0	19	0
Bowling	**Inns**	**Balls**	**Runs**	**Wkts**	**BBI**	**BBM**	**Ave**	**Econ**	**SR**	**5w**	**10**
First-class	123	17122	8101	270	6/29		30.00	2.83	63.4	5	0
List A	137	5556	4623	153	4/25	4/25	30.21	4.99	36.3	0	0
Twenty20	63	1281	1723	62	4/18	4/18	27.79	8.07	20.6	0	0

TIM PHILLIPS

LHB SLA

FULL NAME: Timothy James Phillips
BORN: March 13, 1981, Cambridge
SQUAD NO: 23
HEIGHT: 6ft 1in
NICKNAME: Pips
EDUCATION: Felsted School; Durham University
TEAMS: Durham MCCU, England Under-19s, Essex, Essex 2nd XI, Essex Cricket Board
CAREER: First-class: 1999; List A: 1999; T20: 2006

BEST BATTING: 89 Essex vs Worcestershire, Worcester, 2005
BEST BOWLING: 5-41 Essex vs Derbyshire, Chelmsford, 2006
COUNTY CAP: 2006

FAMILY TIES? Father played in the Manchester leagues and then some serious village cricket, brother Nick represented Essex to U16 level
CAREER HIGHLIGHTS? Representing England at the U19 World Cup in 2000, earning my 1st XI cap at Essex in 2006, winning one-day trophies with Essex
CRICKETING HEROES? Brian Lara and Graham Thorpe for batting, Phil Tufnell and Daniel Vettori for bowling
NON-CRICKETING HEROES? Michael Johnson for his unique and amazing technique. He also wrote a great book called Slaying The Dragon. And Jack White (The White Stripes) – serious guitar player!
BEST PLAYER IN COUNTY CRICKET? Marcus Trescothick
TIPS FOR THE TOP? Adam Wheater and Reece Topley
FAVOURITE FILM? Enemy At The Gates
FAVOURITE BOOK? Catcher In The Rye by JD Salinger
DREAM HOLIDAY? Cape Town
ACCOMPLISHMENTS? Completing a degree at Durham University
TWITTER FEED: @timphillips23

Batting	Mat	Inns	NO	Runs	HS	Ave	SR	100	50	Ct	St
First-class	73	103	16	1789	89	20.56		0	7	48	0
List A	70	39	16	403	58*	17.52		0	1	21	0
Twenty20	58	31	15	289	57*	18.06	125.65	0	1	28	0
Bowling	**Inns**	**Balls**	**Runs**	**Wkts**	**BBI**	**BBM**	**Ave**	**Econ**	**SR**	**5w**	**10**
First-class	73	9600	5798	122	5/41		47.52	3.62	78.6	1	0
List A	70	2234	1914	78	5/28	5/28	24.53	5.14	28.6	3	0
Twenty20	58	903	1128	52	4/22	4/22	21.69	7.49	17.3	0	0

KEVIN PIETERSEN RHB OB R3

FULL NAME: Kevin Peter Pietersen
BORN: June 27, 1980, Pietermaritzburg, South Africa
SQUAD NO: 24
HEIGHT: 6ft 4in
NICKNAME: KP, Kelves, Kapes, Kev
EDUCATION: Maritzburg College; UNISA
TEAMS: England, Deccan Chargers, Delhi Daredevils, Dolphins, Hampshire, KwaZulu-Natal, Natal, Nottinghamshire, Royal Challengers Bangalore, Surrey
CAREER: Test: 2005; ODI: 2004; T20I: 2005; First-class: 1997; List A: 1999; T20: 2003

BEST BATTING: 254* Nottinghamshire vs Middlesex, Nottingham, 2002
BEST BOWLING: 4-31 Nottinghamshire vs Durham UCCE, Nottinghham, 2003
COUNTY CAPS: 2002 (Nottinghamshire); 2005 (Hampshire)

NOTES: Began his career as a bowling allrounder. Left South Africa in 2000. Scored three centuries in his second ODI series, against South Africa in 2004. Reached 1,000 ODI runs in 21 innings, equalling Viv Richard's record. Scored an Ashes-winning 158 at The Oval in 2005. Only Don Bradman made more runs in his first 25 Tests. England captain (2008-2009). Averages 57.12 in 17 Ashes Tests. Dropped for disciplinary issues following a stunning 149 at Headingley. Scored 186 against India in his second Test back, in November 2012

Batting	Mat	Inns	NO	Runs	HS	Ave	SR	100	50	Ct	St
Tests	92	158	8	7414	227	49.42	62.98	22	29	54	0
ODIs	132	121	16	4369	130	41.60	86.75	9	24	39	0
T20Is	36	36	5	1176	79	37.93	141.51	0	7	14	0
First-class	197	323	22	15016	254*	49.88		47	63	141	0
List A	249	229	34	8041	147	41.23		15	45	84	0
Twenty20	84	82	12	2402	103*	34.31	137.10	1	13	35	0
Bowling	**Inns**	**Balls**	**Runs**	**Wkts**	**BBI**	**BBM**	**Ave**	**Econ**	**SR**	**5w**	**10**
Tests	92	1287	869	10	3/52	4/78	86.90	4.05	128.7	0	0
ODIs	132	400	370	7	2/22	2/22	52.85	5.55	57.1	0	0
T20Is	36	30	53	1	1/27	1/27	53.00	10.60	30.0	0	0
First-class	197	6383	3722	73	4/31		50.98	3.49	87.4	0	0
List A	249	2390	2122	41	3/14	3/14	51.75	5.32	58.2	0	0
Twenty20	84	384	514	17	3/33	3/33	30.23	8.03	22.5	0	0

NEIL PINNER RHB OB

FULL NAME: Neil Douglas Pinner
BORN: September 28, 1990, Wordsley, Stourbridge, Worcestershire
SQUAD NO: 20
HEIGHT: 6ft
NICKNAME: Pins, Besty
EDUCATION: RGS Worcester
TEAMS: Worcestershire, Worcestershire 2nd XI
CAREER: First-class: 2011; List A: 2011

BEST BATTING: 82 Worcestershire vs Lancashire, Worcester, 2012

CAREER HIGHLIGHTS? Selection for England U15, one-day and first-class debuts for Worcestershire in the 2011 season
SUPERSTITIONS? I tap the boundary rope or line with my bat on the way out to the middle
CRICKETING HEROES? I used to love watching Michael Vaughan bat when he was in form, but my biggest hero would be Graeme Hick. I spent a lot of time watching him bat at New Road when I was growing up
NON-CRICKETING HEROES? Vincent Chase
BEST PLAYER IN COUNTY CRICKET? Alan Richardson or Marcus Trescothick
TIPS FOR THE TOP? Ben Stokes, James Taylor, Aneesh Kapil
WHEN RAIN STOPS PLAY? I spend a lot of time listening to music or trying very hard to complete The Sun crossword! I also enjoy a game of Stickman Golf against other members of the squad
FAVOURITE TV? Entourage – while in Adelaide I watched all eight series in about three weeks (I had a lot of spare time!)
FAVOURITE FILM? Anchorman
DREAM HOLIDAY? I'd love to tour America one day
ACCOMPLISHMENTS? 100 per cent completion of Call of Duty: MW3 (again, a lot of spare time while in Adelaide)
GUILTY PLEASURES? I enjoy a good sing-song when I'm fairly sure no one can hear me
TWITTER FEED: @Neil_Pinner

Batting	Mat	Inns	NO	Runs	HS	Ave	SR	100	50	Ct	St
First-class	5	8	0	132	82	16.50	37.07	0	1	2	0
List A	14	13	0	202	37	15.53	73.72	0	0	3	0
Bowling	**Inns**	**Balls**	**Runs**	**Wkts**	**BBI**	**BBM**	**Ave**	**Econ**	**SR**	**5w**	**10**
First-class	5	24	13	0	-	-	-	3.25	-	0	0
List A	14	24	27	0	-	-	-	6.75	-	0	0

STEFFAN PIOLET

RHB RM

FULL NAME: Steffan Andreas Piolet
BORN: August 8, 1988, Redhill, Surrey
SQUAD NO: 6
HEIGHT: 6ft 1in
NICKNAME: Squiff, Piles
EDUCATION: Warden Park School; Central Sussex College
TEAMS: Sussex 2nd XI, Warwickshire, Worcestershire 2nd XI
CAREER: First-class: 2009; List A: 2009; T20: 2009

BEST BATTING: 26* Warwickshire vs Durham UCCE, Durham University, 2009
BEST BOWLING: 6-17 Warwickshire vs Durham UCCE, Durham University, 2009

CAREER HIGHLIGHTS? Winning one-day trophies with Warwickshire, scoring hundreds in 2nd XI
SUPERSTITIONS? They vary
CRICKETING HEROES? Jacques Kallis
NON-CRICKETING HEROES? Dave Grohl, Glenn Hoddle
BEST PLAYER IN COUNTY CRICKET? Marcus Trescothick
TIP FOR THE TOP? Ateeq Javid
IF YOU WEREN'T A CRICKETER? I'd be selling something!
WHEN RAIN STOPS PLAY? Get on the iPhone, probably Facebook or Twitter
FAVOURITE TV? Entourage
FAVOURITE FILM? Gran Torino, Old School
DREAM HOLIDAY? Vegas all the way!
SURPRISING SKILL? I can copy any accent in the world easily!
GUILTY PLEASURES? Dancing, even though I'm terrible at it
SURPRISING FACTS? I'm half Norwegian. My birthday was 8/8/88, I was born at 8am and weighed eight pounds. I can't stand chewing gum
TWITTER FEED: @Spiolet14

Batting	Mat	Inns	NO	Runs	HS	Ave	SR	100	50	Ct	St
First-class	3	5	1	47	26*	11.75	39.49	0	0	3	0
List A	25	10	4	115	39	19.16	106.48	0	0	5	0
Twenty20	41	11	4	93	26*	13.28	103.33	0	0	11	0
Bowling	**Inns**	**Balls**	**Runs**	**Wkts**	**BBI**	**BBM**	**Ave**	**Econ**	**SR**	**5w**	**10**
First-class	3	342	182	13	6/17	10/43	14.00	3.19	26.3	1	1
List A	25	797	734	23	4/31	4/31	31.91	5.52	34.6	0	0
Twenty20	41	804	886	38	3/25	3/25	23.31	6.61	21.1	0	0

LIAM PLUNKETT RHB RFM W3

FULL NAME: Liam Edward Plunkett
BORN: April 6, 1985, Middlesbrough
SQUAD NO: 28
HEIGHT: 6ft 3in
NICKNAME: Pudsy
EDUCATION: Nunthorpe Comprehensive
TEAMS: England, Dolphins, Durham, Durham 2nd XI, Durham Cricket Board, England Lions, England Under-19s
CAREER: Test: 2005; ODI: 2005; T20I: 2006; First-class: 2003; List A: 2003; T20: 2003

BEST BATTING: 107* Durham vs Durham MCCU, Durham University, 2011
BEST BOWLING: 6-63 Durham vs Worcestershire, Chester-le-Street, 2009

CAREER HIGHLIGHTS? England debut
CRICKETING HEROES? Glenn McGrath
OTHER SPORTS PLAYED? Swimming, golf
OTHER SPORTS FOLLOWED? Football (Middlesbrough, Arsenal)
NOTES: Plunkett agreed a three-year deal with Yorkshire in October in the same week they signed Jack Brooks. Plagued by Achilles problems, he played just one match in the County Championship last season, against Somerset in May. He became only the second player to record a five-wicket haul on his Championship debut for Durham, 5-53 vs Yorkshire at Headingley, 2003. Represented England U19 that same year, and received the NBC Denis Compton Award for the most promising young Durham player in 2003 and 2005. He made his senior Test debut in November 2005 vs Pakistan at Lahore and his home Test debut in 2006 against Sri Lanka at Lord's

Batting	Mat	Inns	NO	Runs	HS	Ave	SR	100	50	Ct	St
Tests	9	13	2	126	44*	11.45	39.62	0	0	3	0
ODIs	29	25	10	315	56	21.00	83.33	0	1	7	0
T20Is	1	-	-	-	-	-	-	-	-	0	0
First-class	107	146	28	2645	107*	22.41		1	12	64	0
List A	118	79	28	945	72	18.52	89.91	0	2	25	0
Twenty20	63	35	16	345	41	18.15	127.30	0	0	13	0
Bowling	**Inns**	**Balls**	**Runs**	**Wkts**	**BBI**	**BBM**	**Ave**	**Econ**	**SR**	**5w**	**10**
Tests	9	1538	916	23	3/17	6/60	39.82	3.57	66.8	0	0
ODIs	29	1363	1321	39	3/24	3/24	33.87	5.81	34.9	0	0
T20Is	1	24	37	1	1/37	1/37	37.00	9.25	24.0	0	0
First-class	107	16815	10192	321	6/63		31.75	3.63	52.3	8	1
List A	118	4902	4427	139	4/15	4/15	31.84	5.41	35.2	0	0
Twenty20	63	1077	1393	45	5/31	5/31	30.95	7.76	23.9	1	0

HARRY PODMORE RHB RMF

FULL NAME: Harry William Podmore
BORN: July 23, 1994, Queen Charlotte Hospital, Hammersmith, Middlesex
SQUAD NO: 23
EDUCATION: Twyford High School
TEAMS: Middlesex 2nd XI, Middlesex Under-15s, Middlesex Under-17s
CAREER: Yet to make first-team debut

TWITTER FEED: @harrypod16
NOTES: A promising young seamer and graduate of the Middlesex Academy, Podmore joined the club at the age of 14. He is on the MCC Young Cricketers staff for 2013 but has also been registered by Middlesex and will be available for 2nd XI fixtures and first team action if required. He finished the 2012 season strongly, taking match figures of 7-137 vs Sussex at Horsham in a 2nd XI Championship fixture, and likens his style of bowling to that of teammate Steven Finn

RICKY PONTING RHB RM

FULL NAME: Ricky Thomas Ponting
BORN: December 19, 1974, Launceston, Tasmania, Australia
SQUAD NO: TBC
HEIGHT: 5ft 8in
NICKNAME: Punter
EDUCATION: Mowbray Primary; Brooks Senior High School, Launceston
TEAMS: Australia, ICC World XI, Kolkata Knight Riders, Somerset, Surrey, Tasmania
CAREER: Test: 1995; ODI: 1995; T20I: 2005; First-class: 1992; List A: 1992; T20: 2004

BEST BATTING: 257 Australia vs India, Melbourne, 2003
BEST BOWLING: 2-10 Australians vs Mumbai, Mumbai, 2001

NOTES: Second-highest Test match run-scorer ever, behind Sachin Tendulkar. Became the most successful captain in Test history when he passed Steve Waugh's 41 wins after victory in the 2009 Boxing Day Test. In the same match he overtook Shane Warne's record for most wins as an individual (92). Led Australia to 34 consecutive World Cup wins. Only Australian captain to lose three Ashes series. Retired from international cricket after the Perth Test against South Africa in December 2012. Signed for Surrey in February. Will be available for four Championship matches, two YB40 games and the FL t20 group stages

Batting	Mat	Inns	NO	Runs	HS	Ave	SR	100	50	Ct	St
Tests	168	287	29	13378	257	51.85	58.72	41	62	196	0
ODIs	375	365	39	13704	164	42.03	80.39	30	82	160	0
T20Is	17	16	2	401	98*	28.64	132.78	0	2	8	0
First-class	282	482	60	23417	257	55.49		79	104	300	0
List A	453	443	53	16344	164	41.90		34	99	194	0
Twenty20	30	29	3	713	98*	27.42	121.05	0	4	12	0
Bowling	**Inns**	**Balls**	**Runs**	**Wkts**	**BBI**	**BBM**	**Ave**	**Econ**	**SR**	**5w**	**10**
Tests	168	587	276	5	1/0	1/0	55.20	2.82	117.4	0	0
ODIs	375	150	104	3	1/12	1/12	34.66	4.16	50.0	0	0
T20Is	17	-	-	-	-	-	-	-	-	-	-
First-class	282	1482	802	14	2/10		57.28	3.24	105.8	0	0
List A	453	349	269	8	3/34	3/34	33.62	4.62	43.6	0	0
Twenty20	30	12	23	1	1/11	1/11	23.00	11.50	12.0	0	0

WILLIAM PORTERFIELD LHB OB

FULL NAME: William Thomas Stuart Porterfield
BORN: September 6, 1984, Londonderry
SQUAD NO: 10
HEIGHT: 5ft 11in
NICKNAME: Purdy, Porty
EDUCATION: Strabane Grammar School; Leeds Metropolitan University
TEAMS: Ireland, Gloucestershire, Marylebone Cricket Club, Warwickshire
CAREER: ODI: 2006; T20I: 2008; First-class: 2006; List A; 2006; T20: 2008

BEST BATTING: 175 Gloucestershire vs Worcestershire, Cheltenham, 2010
BEST BOWLING: 1-29 Ireland vs Jamaica, Spanish Town, 2010

CAREER HIGHLIGHTS? Playing in the World Cup, captaining Ireland
BEST PLAYER IN COUNTY CRICKET? Marcus Trescothick
TIP FOR THE TOP? Paul Stirling
IF YOU WEREN'T A CRICKETER? Maybe a farmer
WHEN RAIN STOPS PLAY? Anything that kills a bit of time
FAVOURITE TV? Two And A Half Men
FAVOURITE FILM? The Guard
FANTASY SLIP CORDON? Keeper: Frankie Boyle, 1st: Jimmy Carr, 2nd: John Bishop, 3rd: Kerry Katona
TWITTER FEED: @purdy34

Batting	Mat	Inns	NO	Runs	HS	Ave	SR	100	50	Ct	St
ODIs	60	60	3	1752	112*	30.73	67.17	5	8	30	0
T20Is	30	29	3	475	56*	18.26	115.57	0	1	11	0
First-class	77	129	5	3708	175	29.90	46.30	4	23	88	0
List A	141	140	6	4470	112*	33.35	73.37	6	27	61	0
Twenty20	81	80	4	1679	83	22.09	124.00	0	9	34	0
Bowling	**Inns**	**Balls**	**Runs**	**Wkts**	**BBI**	**BBM**	**Ave**	**Econ**	**SR**	**5w**	**10**
ODIs	60	-	-	-	-	-	-	-	-	-	-
T20Is	30	-	-	-	-	-	-	-	-	-	-
First-class	77	108	138	2	1/29	1/29	69.00	7.66	54.0	0	0
List A	141	-	-	-	-	-	-	-	-	-	-
Twenty20	81	-	-	-	-	-	-	-	-	-	-

MIKE POWELL

RHB OB R5

FULL NAME: Michael John Powell
BORN: February 3, 1977, Abergavenny, Monmouthshire
SQUAD NO: 14
HEIGHT: 6ft 1in
NICKNAME: Powelly
EDUCATION: Crickhowell Secondary School; Pontypool School
TEAMS: Glamorgan, Glamorgan 2nd XI, Kent
CAREER: First-class: 1997; List A: 1997; T20: 2003

BEST BATTING: 299 Glamorgan vs Gloucestershire, Cheltenham, 2006
BEST BOWLING: 2-39 Glamorgan vs Oxford UCCE, Oxford, 1999
COUNTY CAP: 2000 (Glamorgan); BENEFIT YEAR: 2011 (Glamorgan)

FAMILY TIES? Dad [John] and uncle [Mike] both played for Abergavenny
SUPERSTITIONS? None
OTHER SPORTS FOLLOWED? Rugby (Cardiff)
FAVOURITE BAND? Stereophonics or the Manic Street Preachers
FAVOURITE FOOD? Pizza
FAVOURITE FILM? Dumb And Dumber
PROUDEST MOMENT? Coming back from injury in 2007
LOOKALIKE? Heath Ledger

Batting	Mat	Inns	NO	Runs	HS	Ave	SR	100	50	Ct	St
First-class	229	379	37	13156	299	38.46		27	67	136	0
List A	204	193	20	4665	114*	26.96		1	25	79	0
Twenty20	44	41	4	844	68*	22.81	116.41	0	5	16	0
Bowling	**Inns**	**Balls**	**Runs**	**Wkts**	**BBI**	**BBM**	**Ave**	**Econ**	**SR**	**5w**	**10**
First-class	229	164	132	2	2/39		66.00	4.82	82.0	0	0
List A	204	24	26	1	1/26	1/26	26.00	6.50	24.0	0	0
Twenty20	44	-	-	-	-	-	-	-	-	-	-

TOM POYNTON RHB WK

DERBYSHIRE

FULL NAME: Thomas Poynton
BORN: November 25, 1989, Burton-on-Trent, Staffordshire
SQUAD NO: 23
HEIGHT: 5ft 10in
NICKNAME: TP, Poynts
EDUCATION: John Taylor High School; Repton School
TEAMS: Derbyshire, Derbyshire 2nd XI, England Under-19s
CAREER: First-class: 2007; List A: 2007; T20: 2007

BEST BATTING: 106 Derbyshire vs Northamptonshire, Northampton, 2012
BEST BOWLING: 2-96 Derbyshire vs Glamorgan, Cardiff, 2010

WHO WOULD PLAY YOU IN A FILM OF YOUR LIFE? Al Pacino. The Godfather, Scent Of A Woman and Scarface – I don't have to say any more
CAREER HIGHLIGHTS? Winning the County Championship Division Two title with Derbyshire in 2012 and scoring my maiden first-class hundred in the same year
MOST MARKED CHARACTERISTIC? Action Man scar on my left cheek
BEST PLAYER IN COUNTY CRICKET? Shivnarine Chanderpaul
TIPS FOR THE TOP? Peter Burgoyne, Harvey Hosein
IF YOU WEREN'T A CRICKETER? Stockbroker
BIGGEST DRESSING DOWN YOU'VE RECEIVED? Murali Kartik on my debut when I was 17 after appealing for a caught behind against him
CRICKETING HEROES? Adam Gilchrist, Martin Guptill, Usman Khawaja
NON-CRICKETING HEROES? Ted McMinn – currently our kit man at Derbyshire but a Derby and Rangers legend and all-round inspiring bloke
ACCOMPLISHMENTS? Three A grades in my A-Levels. I never went on to further education
SURPRISING FACTS? I'm a wine and food connoisseur. I once sponsored 24 meerkats at Twycross Zoo. I'm a petrol head

Batting	Mat	Inns	NO	Runs	HS	Ave	SR	100	50	Ct	St
First-class	21	28	4	498	106	20.75	37.08	1	2	54	3
List A	17	10	2	124	40	15.50	96.87	0	0	11	3
Twenty20	9	5	2	20	8*	6.66	71.42	0	0	6	5
Bowling	**Inns**	**Balls**	**Runs**	**Wkts**	**BBI**	**BBM**	**Ave**	**Econ**	**SR**	**5w**	**10**
First-class	21	48	96	2	2/96	2/96	48.00	12.00	24.0	0	0
List A	17	-	-	-	-	-	-	-	-	-	-
Twenty20	9	-	-	-	-	-	-	-	-	-	-

RYAN PRINGLE RHB OB

FULL NAME: Ryan David Pringle
BORN: April 4, 1992, Sunderland, County Durham
SQUAD NO: 17
HEIGHT: 6ft 2in
NICKNAME: Rhino
EDUCATION: Hetton Comprehensive School; Durham Sixth Form Centre; Sunderland University
TEAMS: Durham, Durham 2nd XI, Northumberland
CAREER: List A: 2012

FAMILY TIES? Dad played a little bit but I'm the first family member to take cricket seriously
WHO WOULD PLAY YOU IN A FILM OF YOUR LIFE? The Rock
CAREER HIGHLIGHTS? 1st XI CB40 debut vs Hampshire
SUPERSTITIONS? I always put my left pad on before my right pad
MOST MARKED CHARACTERISTIC? Very large bum
BEST PLAYER IN COUNTY CRICKET? Keaton Jennings
TIPS FOR THE TOP? Graham Clark, Paul Coughlin, Usman Arshad
IF YOU WEREN'T A CRICKETER? Pursuing a career as a PE teacher
DESERT ISLAND DISC? Drake – Take Care
FAVOURITE TV? Entourage
CRICKETING HEROES? Ricky Ponting
NON-CRICKETING HEROES? My granddad
ACCOMPLISHMENTS? Successfully passing my first year of university
WHEN YOU RETIRE? Play golf
SURPRISING FACT? There was a clip of me running through Newcastle Airport which was used on the news when I was five
FANTASY SLIP CORDON? Keeper: Lil Wayne, 1st: Peter Griffin; 2nd: Me, 3rd: Ricky Ponting, Gully: David Beckham. (I feel there's a good mix of people to make you laugh, entertain you and have meaningful chats about cricket with)

Batting	Mat	Inns	NO	Runs	HS	Ave	SR	100	50	Ct	St
List A	1	-	-	-	-	-	-	-	-	0	0
Bowling	**Inns**	**Balls**	**Runs**	**Wkts**	**BBI**	**BBM**	**Ave**	**Econ**	**SR**	**5w**	**10**
List A	1	-	-	-	-	-	-	-	-	-	-

MATT PRIOR

RHB WK R3

FULL NAME: Matthew James Prior
BORN: February 26, 1982, Johannesburg, South Africa
SQUAD NO: 13
HEIGHT: 5ft 11in
EDUCATION: Brighton College, East Sussex
TEAMS: England, England A, England Lions, England Under-19s, Sussex, Sussex Cricket Board, Victoria
CAREER: Test: 2007; ODI: 2004; T20I: 2007; First-class: 2001; List A: 2000; T20: 2003

BEST BATTING: 201* Sussex vs Loughborough UCCE, Hove, 2004
COUNTY CAP: 2003; **BENEFIT YEAR:** 2012

WHO WOULD PLAY YOU IN A FILM OF YOUR LIFE? Jason Statham. Because he is part of the baldy, beardy group
MOST MARKED CHARACTERISTIC? The beard. Is that a characteristic?
DESERT ISLAND DISC? Album: Now That's What I Call Music 21. Song: Mr Bojangles. I love the Robbie Williams version
BIGGEST DRESSING DOWN YOU'VE RECEIVED? Peter Moores at Tunbridge Wells in 2001. We lost and hadn't played well and he went round the whole squad, one by one, and basically abused every single player. It was a thing of beauty
TWITTER FEED: @MattPrior13

Batting	Mat	Inns	NO	Runs	HS	Ave	SR	100	50	Ct	St
Tests	62	92	15	3326	131*	43.19	62.95	6	24	173	13
ODIs	68	62	9	1282	87	24.18	76.76	0	3	71	8
T20Is	10	8	2	127	32	21.16	127.00	0	0	6	3
First-class	219	332	37	11854	201*	40.18	67.24	26	69	547	41
List A	220	202	18	5052	144	27.45		4	28	186	31
Twenty20	83	77	5	1867	117	25.93	143.28	1	11	44	6
Bowling	**Inns**	**Balls**	**Runs**	**Wkts**	**BBI**	**BBM**	**Ave**	**Econ**	**SR**	**5w**	**10**
Tests	62	-	-	-	-	-	-	-	-	-	-
ODIs	68	-	-	-	-	-	-	-	-	-	-
T20Is	10	-	-	-	-	-	-	-	-	-	-
First-class	219	-	-	-	-	-	-	-	-	-	-
List A	220	-	-	-	-	-	-	-	-	-	-
Twenty20	83	-	-	-	-	-	-	-	-	-	-

LUKE PROCTER LHB RMF

FULL NAME: Luke Anthony Procter
BORN: June 24, 1988, Oldham, Lancashire
SQUAD NO: 2
HEIGHT: 5ft 11in
EDUCATION: Counthill School, Oldham
TEAMS: Cumberland, Lancashire, Lancashire 2nd XI, Marylebone Cricket Club Young Cricketers
CAREER: First-class: 2010; List A: 2009; T20: 2011

BEST BATTING: 89 Lancashire vs Sussex, Hove, 2011
BEST BOWLING: 7-71 Lancashire vs Surrey, Liverpool, 2012

CAREER HIGHLIGHTS? Winning the County Championship
SUPERSTITIONS? Putting my right pad on first
CRICKETING HEROES? Marcus Trescothick
TIP FOR THE TOP? Simon Kerrigan
IF YOU WEREN'T A CRICKETER? I'd not be doing a lot
WHEN RAIN STOPS PLAY? I listen to music and chat to the lads
FAVOURITE TV? Take Me Out
FAVOURITE FILM? Happy Gilmore
FAVOURITE BOOK? The Twilight series
DREAM HOLIDAY? Las Vegas
GUILTY PLEASURES? Chocolate
TWITTER FEED: @vvsprocter

Batting	Mat	Inns	NO	Runs	HS	Ave	SR	100	50	Ct	St
First-class	24	36	4	986	89	30.81	38.97	0	3	2	0
List A	18	14	5	252	97	28.00	85.13	0	2	4	0
Twenty20	19	10	5	85	25*	17.00	91.39	0	0	5	0
Bowling	**Inns**	**Balls**	**Runs**	**Wkts**	**BBI**	**BBM**	**Ave**	**Econ**	**SR**	**5w**	**10**
First-class	24	1756	1045	38	7/71	8/79	27.50	3.57	46.2	2	0
List A	18	396	421	11	3/29	3/29	38.27	6.37	36.0	0	0
Twenty20	19	116	176	8	3/22	3/22	22.00	9.10	14.5	0	0

RICHARD PYRAH RHB RM

YORKSHIRE

FULL NAME: Richard Michael Pyrah
BORN: November 1, 1982, Dewsbury, Yorkshire
SQUAD NO: 27
HEIGHT: 6ft
NICKNAME: RP, Pyro, Iceman
EDUCATION: Ossett High School
TEAMS: Yorkshire, Yorkshire Cricket Board
CAREER: First-class: 2004; List A: 2001; T20: 2005

BEST BATTING: 134* Yorkshire vs Loughborough MCCU, Leeds, 2010
BEST BOWLING: 5-58 Yorkshire vs Nottinghamshire, Leeds, 2011
COUNTY CAP: 2010

CAREER HIGHLIGHTS? Receiving my 1st XI cap, scoring 117 vs Lancashire after we were 45-8
CRICKETING HEROES? Jacques Kallis, Sachin Tendulkar
NON-CRICKETING HEROES? My family
BEST PLAYER IN COUNTY CRICKET? Marcus Trescothick
TIPS FOR THE TOP? Joe Root, Jonny Bairstow
IF YOU WEREN'T A CRICKETER? I'd be some sort of businessman
FAVOURITE TV? EastEnders, One Born Every Minute
FAVOURITE FILM? Dumb And Dumber
FAVOURITE BOOK? The Beano comics!
DREAM HOLIDAY? Barbados
ACCOMPLISHMENTS? Having twins with my girlfriend
SURPRISING SKILL? I can down a bottle of VK in one second
GUILTY PLEASURES? Golf and babysitting my kids
SURPRISING FACT? I played for Sheffield Wednesday as a youngster
FANTASY SLIP CORDON? Keeper: Me, 1st: My dog Charlie, 2nd: Tiger Woods, 3rd: Mila Kunis
TWITTER FEED: @pyrah27

Batting	Mat	Inns	NO	Runs	HS	Ave	SR	100	50	Ct	St
First-class	37	48	5	1186	134*	27.58	55.13	3	5	15	0
List A	93	62	15	930	69	19.78		0	2	33	0
Twenty20	74	50	15	406	35	11.60	111.23	0	0	26	0
Bowling	**Inns**	**Balls**	**Runs**	**Wkts**	**BBI**	**BBM**	**Ave**	**Econ**	**SR**	**5w**	**10**
First-class	37	3200	1901	47	5/58		40.44	3.56	68.0	1	0
List A	93	2896	2778	110	5/50	5/50	25.25	5.75	26.3	1	0
Twenty20	74	1284	1620	79	5/16	5/16	20.50	7.57	16.2	1	0

ROB QUINEY LHB RM

FULL NAME: Robert John Quiney
BORN: August 20, 1982, Brighton, Australia
SQUAD NO: 2
HEIGHT: 6ft 3in
TEAMS: Australia, Auckland, Melbourne Stars, Rajasthan Royals, Victoria
CAREER: Test: 2012; First-class: 2007; List A: 2006; T20: 2006

BEST BATTING: 153 Victoria vs Tasmania, Hobart, 2010
BEST BOWLING: 2-22 Victoria vs Western Australia, Melbourne, 2007

NOTES: Top-order Australian batsman signed initially for the first half of the season. Made his Test debut against South Africa in November, bagging a pair in his second match. He has played for Victoria since 2006 and appeared for Rajasthan Royals in the IPL in 2009, and Melbourne Stars in the 2011 Big Bash. Was named Australia's Domestic Player of the Year in 2011

Batting	Mat	Inns	NO	Runs	HS	Ave	SR	100	50	Ct	St
Tests	2	3	0	9	9	3.00	40.90	0	0	5	0
First-class	57	97	8	3150	153	35.39	54.50	7	16	46	0
List A	60	55	3	1975	122	37.98	96.67	3	14	34	0
Twenty20	60	57	2	921	97	16.74	113.98	0	5	28	0
Bowling	**Inns**	**Balls**	**Runs**	**Wkts**	**BBI**	**BBM**	**Ave**	**Econ**	**SR**	**5w**	**10**
Tests	2	150	29	0	-	-	-	1.16	-	0	0
First-class	57	924	425	3	2/22	2/32	141.66	2.75	308.0	0	0
List A	60	120	121	0	-	-	-	6.05	-	0	0
Twenty20	60	6	13	0	-	-	-	13.00	-	0	0

AZEEM RAFIQ

RHB OB MVP56

FULL NAME: Azeem Rafiq
BORN: February 27, 1991, Karachi, Pakistan
SQUAD NO: 30
HEIGHT: 5ft 10in
NICKNAME: Raffa
EDUCATION: Holgate School Sports College; Barnsley College
TEAMS: England Under-15s, England Under-17s, England Under-19s, Derbyshire, Yorkshire, Yorkshire 2nd XI
CAREER: First-class: 2009; List A: 2009; T20: 2008

BEST BATTING: 100 Yorkshire vs Worcestershire, Worcester, 2009
BEST BOWLING: 5-50 Yorkshire vs Essex, Chelmsford, 2012

WHO WOULD PLAY YOU IN A FILM OF YOUR LIFE? Jackie Chan
CAREER HIGHLIGHTS? Playing in T20 Finals Day and the Champions League T20, and getting promoted to Division One
MOST MARKED CHARACTERISTIC? Confidence
BEST PLAYER IN COUNTY CRICKET? Graham Onions
TIPS FOR THE TOP? Ben Stokes, Adam Lyth
DESERT ISLAND DISC? Gangnam Style
FAVOURITE TV? Premier League Darts
BIGGEST DRESSING DOWN YOU'VE RECEIVED? I was banned for a month for a Twitter outburst
CRICKETING HEROES? Michael Vaughan, Anthony McGrath
NON-CRICKETING HEROES? Ryan Giggs
WHEN YOU RETIRE? Something in business or the media
FANTASY SLIP CORDON? Keeper: Megan Fox, 1st: Me, 2nd: Steven Patterson, 3rd: Ryan Giggs, Gully: Tiger Woods
TWITTER FEED: @AzeemRafiq30

Batting	Mat	Inns	NO	Runs	HS	Ave	SR	100	50	Ct	St
First-class	21	23	3	491	100	24.55	54.55	1	2	8	0
List A	17	11	6	111	34*	22.20	84.73	0	0	7	0
Twenty20	41	17	9	71	21*	8.87	85.54	0	0	17	0
Bowling	**Inns**	**Balls**	**Runs**	**Wkts**	**BBI**	**BBM**	**Ave**	**Econ**	**SR**	**5w**	**10**
First-class	21	3350	1759	51	5/50	8/115	34.49	3.15	65.6	1	0
List A	17	606	532	13	3/22	3/22	40.92	5.26	46.6	0	0
Twenty20	41	858	1079	35	3/15	3/15	30.82	7.54	24.5	0	0

HARRY RAMSDEN LHB OB

FULL NAME: Henry Douglas Ramsden
BORN: November 11, 1992, Wandsworth, London
SQUAD NO: 12
HEIGHT: 6ft 4in
NICKNAME: H, Raaaaambo
EDUCATION: Oundle School
TEAMS: Essex 2nd XI, Hertfordshire
CAREER: Yet to make first-team debut

CAREER HIGHLIGHTS? Playing for ESCA at Lord's
CRICKETING HEROES? Brian Lara, Stuart Broad, Alastair Cook
NON-CRICKETING HEROES? Jonny Wilkinson, Steve Gerrard
BEST PLAYER IN COUNTY CRICKET? Marcus Trescothick
TIPS FOR THE TOP? Ben Foakes, Tymal Mills
IF YOU WEREN'T A CRICKETER? I'd be studying
WHEN RAIN STOPS PLAY? Sleeping or listening to music
FAVOURITE TV? Top Gear
FAVOURITE FILM? The Other Guys
DREAM HOLIDAY? Beach holiday in Tanzania with fishing involved
SURPRISING FACT? I'm a sleep walker, a sleep talker and my real name is Henry
FANTASY SLIP CORDON?: Keeper: James Corden, 1st: Mila Kunis, 2nd: Me, 3rd: Graeme Swann, Gully: Megan Fox
TWITTER FEED: @HRamsden150

GURMAN RANDHAWA

LHB SLA

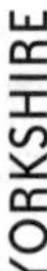

FULL NAME: Gurman Singh Randhawa
BORN: January 15, 1992, Huddersfield, Yorkshire
SQUAD NO: 25
HEIGHT: 5ft 10in
NICKNAME: Gurm
EDUCATION: Huddersfield New College
TEAMS: England Under-19s, Yorkshire 2nd XI, Yorkshire Academy, Yorkshire Under-13s, Yorkshire Under-14s, Yorkshire Under-15s, Yorkshire Under-17s
CAREER: First-class: 2011

BEST BATTING: 5 Yorkshire vs Durham MCCU, Durham University, 2011
BEST BOWLING: 2-54 Yorkshire vs Durham MCCU, Durham University, 2011

CAREER HIGHLIGHTS? Playing for England U19, Academy Player of the Year in 2009 and 2010
CRICKETING HEROES? Daniel Vettori, Graham Thorpe
NON-CRICKETING HEROES? Mario Balotelli
BEST PLAYER IN COUNTY CRICKET? Marcus Trescothick
TIP FOR THE TOP? Moin Ashraf
IF YOU WEREN'T A CRICKETER? Tennis player
WHEN RAIN STOPS PLAY? Tiger Woods PGA Tour
FAVOURITE TV? Super Sunday
FAVOURITE FILM? Gladiator
FAVOURITE BOOK? Herschelle Gibbs' autobiography
DREAM HOLIDAY? Barbados
TWITTER FEED: @Gurm1

Batting	Mat	Inns	NO	Runs	HS	Ave	SR	100	50	Ct	St
First-class	1	1	0	5	5	5.00	23.80	0	0	0	0
Bowling	**Inns**	**Balls**	**Runs**	**Wkts**	**BBI**	**BBM**	**Ave**	**Econ**	**SR**	**5w**	**10**
First-class	1	126	62	2	2/54	2/62	31.00	2.95	63.0	0	0

BOYD RANKIN LHB RMF W1

FULL NAME: William Boyd Rankin
BORN: July 5, 1984, Derry
SQUAD NO: 30
HEIGHT: 6ft 7in
NICKNAME: Boydo, Pierre
EDUCATION: Strabane Grammar School; Harper Adams University College
TEAMS: Ireland, Derbyshire, England Lions, Ireland Under-19s, Warwickshire
CAREER: ODI: 2007; T20I: 2009; First-class: 2007; List A: 2006; T20: 2009

BEST BATTING: 43 ICC Combined XI vs England XI, Dubai, 2012
BEST BOWLING: 5-16 Warwickshire vs Essex, Birmingham, 2010

CAREER HIGHLIGHTS? Playing for Ireland in World Cups. Beating Pakistan and England are my highlights
CRICKETING HEROES? I watched Curtly Ambrose and Glenn McGrath while I was growing up and have tried to emulate them
NON-CRICKETING HEROES? Big fan of George Best
BEST PLAYER IN COUNTY CRICKET? Marcus Trescothick
TIPS FOR THE TOP? Paul Stirling of Middlesex is a real talent, best striker of a cricket ball I have seen
IF YOU WEREN'T A CRICKETER? I would be back home in Ireland on the family farm
FAVOURITE FILM? Gladiator
DREAM HOLIDAY? Somewhere in the Caribbean – great beaches, rum and friendly people
ACCOMPLISHMENTS? Higher diploma in Agricultural Mechanisation
TWITTER FEED: @boydrankin

Batting	Mat	Inns	NO	Runs	HS	Ave	SR	100	50	Ct	St
ODIs	37	16	11	35	7*	7.00	33.33	0	0	6	0
T20Is	15	3	2	13	7*	13.00	81.25	0	0	6	0
First-class	54	64	26	313	43	8.23	40.33	0	0	18	0
List A	73	27	16	67	9	6.09	39.88	0	0	10	0
Twenty20	24	6	4	16	7*	8.00	84.21	0	0	8	0
Bowling	**Inns**	**Balls**	**Runs**	**Wkts**	**BBI**	**BBM**	**Ave**	**Econ**	**SR**	**5w**	**10**
ODIs	37	1700	1391	43	3/32	3/32	32.34	4.90	39.5	0	0
T20Is	15	354	364	17	3/20	3/20	21.41	6.16	20.8	0	0
First-class	54	7873	4908	175	5/16	8/115	28.04	3.74	44.9	6	0
List A	73	3029	2535	86	4/34	4/34	29.47	5.02	35.2	0	0
Twenty20	24	534	497	28	4/9	4/9	17.75	5.58	19.0	0	0

ADIL RASHID RHB LB W2

FULL NAME: Adil Usman Rashid
BORN: February 17, 1988, Bradford, Yorkshire
SQUAD NO: 3
HEIGHT: 5ft 9in
NICKNAME: Dilly, Dilo, Rash
EDUCATION: Heaton School, Bradford; Bellevue Sixth Form College, Bradford
TEAMS: England, England Lions, England Under-19s, Marylebone Cricket Club, South Australia, Yorkshire, Yorkshire 2nd XI
CAREER: ODI: 2009; T20I: 2009; First-class: 2006; List A: 2006; T20: 2008

BEST BATTING: 157* Yorkshire vs Lancashire, Leeds, 2009
BEST BOWLING: 7-107 Yorkshire vs Hampshire, Southampton, 2008
COUNTY CAP: 2008

CAREER HIGHLIGHTS? Playing for England
CRICKETING HEROES? Sachin Tendulkar, Shane Warne
NON-CRICKETING HEROES? Muhammad Ali
BEST PLAYER IN COUNTY CRICKET? Marcus Trescothick
TIP FOR THE TOP? Moin Ashraf
IF YOU WEREN'T A CRICKETER? Taxi driver
FAVOURITE TV? Friends
FAVOURITE FILM? Scarface
DREAM HOLIDAY? Barbados
TWITTER FEED: @AdilRashid03

Batting	Mat	Inns	NO	Runs	HS	Ave	SR	100	50	Ct	St
ODIs	5	4	1	60	31*	20.00	111.11	0	0	2	0
T20Is	5	2	1	10	9*	10.00	52.63	0	0	0	0
First-class	99	137	24	3709	157*	32.82		4	23	47	0
List A	74	50	14	553	43	15.36	77.99	0	0	26	0
Twenty20	69	39	11	346	36*	12.35	98.29	0	0	17	0
Bowling	**Inns**	**Balls**	**Runs**	**Wkts**	**BBI**	**BBM**	**Ave**	**Econ**	**SR**	**5w**	**10**
ODIs	5	204	191	3	1/16	1/16	63.66	5.61	68.0	0	0
T20Is	5	84	120	3	1/11	1/11	40.00	8.57	28.0	0	0
First-class	99	17554	10306	296	7/107	11/114	34.81	3.52	59.3	16	1
List A	74	2817	2413	76	4/38	4/38	31.75	5.13	37.0	0	0
Twenty20	69	1379	1748	80	4/20	4/20	21.85	7.60	17.2	0	0

OLLIE RAYNER RHB OB

FULL NAME: Oliver Philip Rayner
BORN: November 1, 1985, Fallingbostel, Germany
SQUAD NO: 2
HEIGHT: 6ft 5in
NICKNAME: Mervin, Rocket, Morag, Kalvin, Donk
EDUCATION: St Bede's, Eastbourne
TEAMS: Middlesex, Sussex, Sussex 2nd XI, Sussex Cricket Board
CAREER: First-class: 2006; List A: 2006; T20: 2006

BEST BATTING: 143* Middlesex vs Nottinghamshire, Nottingham, 2012
BEST BOWLING: 5-49 Sussex vs Hampshire, Arundel, 2008

CAREER HIGHLIGHTS? I was fortunate enough to be with Sussex through a very fruitful period regarding trophies. A ton on debut, and winning Division Two of the County Championship whilst on loan to Middlesex in 2011
CRICKETING HEROES? Freddie Flintoff, Chris Gayle, Adam Blackburn, Richard Smith
NON-CRICKETING HEROES? Kelly Brook, Harry Potter, the Top Gear crew
BEST PLAYER IN COUNTY CRICKET? Marcus Trescothick
TIPS FOR THE TOP? Sam Robson, Jonny Bairstow
IF YOU WEREN'T A CRICKETER? Used car salesman, toy boy or a stay at home dad
WHEN RAIN STOPS PLAY? Either just being a general pest, playing backgammon or doing my crossword
FAVOURITE TV? Downton Abbey, Top Gear, The Simpsons, Family Guy
FAVOURITE FILM? Any Harry Potter, Dodgeball
DREAM HOLIDAY? Maldives. I would also like to visit the West Indies
GUILTY PLEASURES? I'm a Harry Potter nut
FANTASY SLIP CORDON? Keeper: Peter Griffin, 1st: Alan Sugar, 2nd: Me, 3rd: Rihanna, Gully: Simon Cowell
TWITTER FEED: @Ollie2rayner

Batting	Mat	Inns	NO	Runs	HS	Ave	SR	100	50	Ct	St
First-class	63	79	17	1650	143*	26.61	53.71	2	9	72	0
List A	32	24	12	320	61	26.66	97.26	0	1	11	0
Twenty20	39	24	8	228	41*	14.25	108.57	0	0	10	0
Bowling	**Inns**	**Balls**	**Runs**	**Wkts**	**BBI**	**BBM**	**Ave**	**Econ**	**SR**	**5w**	**10**
First-class	63	9183	4483	126	5/49	8/96	35.57	2.92	72.8	3	0
List A	32	1020	974	23	2/20	2/20	42.34	5.72	44.3	0	0
Twenty20	39	683	796	24	5/18	5/18	33.16	6.99	28.4	1	0

CHRIS READ

RHB WK R3 MVP28

FULL NAME: Christopher Mark Wells Read
BORN: August 10, 1978, Paignton, Devon
SQUAD NO: 7
HEIGHT: 5ft 8in
NICKNAME: Reados, Readie
EDUCATION: Torquay Boys' Grammar School; University of Bath; Loughborough University
TEAMS: England, Devon, Gloucestershire, Nottinghamshire
CAREER: Test: 1999; ODI: 2000; T20I: 2006; First-class: 1998; List A: 1995; T20: 2004

BEST BATTING: 240 Nottinghamshire vs Essex, Chelmsford, 2007
COUNTY CAP: 1999 (Nottinghamshire); BENEFIT YEAR: 2009 (Nottinghamshire)

CAREER HIGHLIGHTS? Winning the County Championship twice
SUPERSTITIONS? Anything to keep the cricketing gods onside!
CRICKETING HEROES? Ian Botham, Ian Healy, Jack Russell
NON-CRICKETING HEROES? Sebastian Loeb
BEST PLAYER IN COUNTY CRICKET? Marcus Trescothick
TIP FOR THE TOP? Jos Buttler
IF YOU WEREN'T A CRICKETER? Racing and roadtesting cars or living the dream as a rock star
FAVOURITE TV? Top Gear
FAVOURITE BOOK? Redwall – my son is named after a character in the book
DREAM HOLIDAY? Barbados
ACCOMPLISHMENTS? Running the NYC marathon

Batting	Mat	Inns	NO	Runs	HS	Ave	SR	100	50	Ct	St
Tests	15	23	4	360	55	18.94	39.47	0	1	48	6
ODIs	36	24	7	300	30*	17.64	73.17	0	0	41	2
T20Is	1	1	0	13	13	13.00	118.18	0	0	1	0
First-class	274	412	69	12707	240	37.04		21	70	804	45
List A	285	230	60	4910	135	28.88		2	20	271	64
Twenty20	83	72	27	1203	58*	26.73	122.50	0	1	41	18
Bowling	**Inns**	**Balls**	**Runs**	**Wkts**	**BBI**	**BBM**	**Ave**	**Econ**	**SR**	**5w**	**10**
Tests	15	-	-	-	-	-	-	-	-	-	-
ODIs	36	-	-	-	-	-	-	-	-	-	-
T20Is	1	-	-	-	-	-	-	-	-	-	-
First-class	274	96	90	0	-	-	-	5.62	-	0	0
List A	285	-	-	-	-	-	-	-	-	-	-
Twenty20	83	-	-	-	-	-	-	-	-	-	-

DAN REDFERN LHB OB

FULL NAME: Daniel James Redfern
BORN: April 18, 1990, Shrewsbury
SQUAD NO: 19
HEIGHT: 5ft 11in
NICKNAME: Redders, Reddog
EDUCATION: Adams' Grammar School
TEAMS: Derbyshire, Derbyshire 2nd XI, England Under-19s
CAREER: First-class: 2007; List A: 2006; T20: 2008

BEST BATTING: 133 Derbyshire vs Hampshire, Southampton, 2012
BEST BOWLING: 1-7 Derbyshire vs Warwickshire, Birmingham, 2008

FAMILY TIES? Father, grandfather, brother, uncles and cousins played local cricket at Leycett
CAREER HIGHLIGHTS? Scoring 63* to win the National T20 Club Final at Chelmsford in 2011
SUPERSTITIONS? Always have to turn over my left shoulder at the end of my run-up
NON-CRICKETING HEROES? Andrew Flintoff, Ian Botham
TIP FOR THE TOP? James Taylor
IF YOU WEREN'T A CRICKETER? Probably playing golf
WHEN RAIN STOPS PLAY? Sleeping mostly, The Sun crossword, inventing stupid games to occupy ourselves
FAVOURITE TV? 24
FAVOURITE FILM? Robin Hood – the Disney version!
FAVOURITE BOOK? Bad Luck And Trouble by Lee Child
DREAM HOLIDAY? Elbow Quay, Bahamas
ACCOMPLISHMENTS? Building a table at school and actually getting into university
SURPRISING SKILL? Relatively good at technical things, such as fixing and building
GUILTY PLEASURES? Mr Bean, Mamma Mia!
FANTASY SLIP CORDON? Keeper: Lee Evans, 1st: Rowan Atkinson, 2nd: Me, 3rd: Frankie Boyle, 4th: Steven Spielberg, Gully: Alan Davies

Batting	Mat	Inns	NO	Runs	HS	Ave	SR	100	50	Ct	St
First-class	62	101	7	2961	133	31.50	54.00	2	21	31	0
List A	40	33	1	602	57*	18.81	72.70	0	2	10	0
Twenty20	4	4	0	24	13	6.00	77.41	0	0	1	0
Bowling	**Inns**	**Balls**	**Runs**	**Wkts**	**BBI**	**BBM**	**Ave**	**Econ**	**SR**	**5w**	**10**
First-class	62	564	341	6	1/7	2/15	56.83	3.62	94.0	0	0
List A	40	232	193	5	2/10	2/10	38.60	4.99	46.4	0	0
Twenty20	4	-	-	-	-	-	-	-	-	-	-

LUIS REECE LHB LM

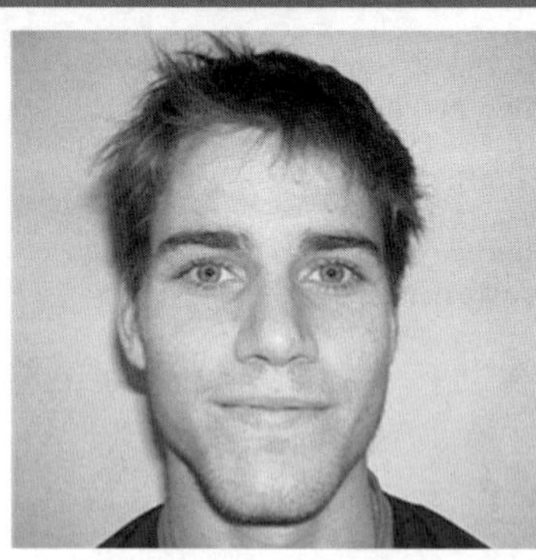

FULL NAME: Luis Michael Reece
BORN: August 4, 1990, Taunton, Somerset
SQUAD NO: 21
EDUCATION: St Michael's School; Myerscough College, Bilsborrow; Leeds Metropolitan University
TEAMS: Lancashire 2nd XI, Leeds/Bradford MCCU, Unicorns
CAREER: First-class: 2012; List A: 2011

BEST BATTING: 60 Leeds/Bradford MCCU vs Yorkshire, Leeds, 2012
BEST BOWLING: 3-25 Leeds/Bradford MCCU vs Yorkshire, Leeds, 2012

NOTES: A left-arm seamer and top order batsman, Reece played for both the Unicorns and Lancashire's 2nd XI last season, and has studied at Leeds Metropolitan University. He made his first-class debut for Leeds/Bradford MCCU in a friendly match against Surrey at The Oval on March 31-April 2, 2012, scoring 34 runs across two innings and claiming match figures of 2-69 against a strong Surrey line-up. He has recently signed a professional deal with Lancashire, having previously been on a scholarship contract

Batting	Mat	Inns	NO	Runs	HS	Ave	SR	100	50	Ct	St
First-class	2	4	0	134	60	33.50	52.75	0	1	1	0
List A	20	18	4	348	59	24.85	84.26	0	1	5	0
Bowling	**Inns**	**Balls**	**Runs**	**Wkts**	**BBI**	**BBM**	**Ave**	**Econ**	**SR**	**5w**	**10**
First-class	2	204	120	5	3/25	3/51	24.00	3.52	40.8	0	0
List A	20	404	418	6	4/35	4/35	69.66	6.20	67.3	0	0

MIKE REED RHB RFM

FULL NAME: Michael Thomas Reed
BORN: September 10, 1988, Leicester
SQUAD NO: 35
HEIGHT: 6ft 7in
NICKNAME: Frank, Denis Stracqualursi, Trigger, Long, Marouane Fellaini
EDUCATION: De Lisle Catholic Science College; Cardiff University
TEAMS: Cardiff MCCU, Glamorgan, Glamorgan 2nd XI, Wales Minor Counties
CAREER: First-class: 2012

GLAMORGAN

BEST BATTING: 5* Glamorgan vs Derbyshire, Derby, 2012
BEST BOWLING: 3-39 Glamorgan vs Kent, Cardiff, 2012

FAMILY TIES? Brother [Dominic] was part of 2011 Unicorns squad
CAREER HIGHLIGHTS? Signing for Glamorgan, playing against first-class counties for Cardiff MCCU
CRICKETING HEROES? Brett Lee, Steve Harmison, Andrew Flintoff
NON-CRICKETING HEROES? Martin O'Neill
BEST PLAYER IN COUNTY CRICKET? Marcus Trescothick
TIPS FOR THE TOP? James Harris, Joe Root
IF YOU WEREN'T A CRICKETER? Plugging numbers
FAVOURITE TV? Prison Break
FAVOURITE FILM? Blood Diamond
FAVOURITE BOOK? Any decent autobiography
DREAM HOLIDAY? Seychelles
ACCOMPLISHMENTS? Getting a Maths degree
GUILTY PLEASURES? Chocolate raisins
SURPRISING FACT? I have a large scar on my back from my time in Australia

Batting	Mat	Inns	NO	Runs	HS	Ave	SR	100	50	Ct	St
First-class	4	7	2	18	5*	3.60	18.75	0	0	0	0
Bowling	**Inns**	**Balls**	**Runs**	**Wkts**	**BBI**	**BBM**	**Ave**	**Econ**	**SR**	**5w**	**10**
First-class	4	528	310	8	3/39	4/91	38.75	3.52	66.0	0	0

GLAMORGAN

GARETH REES

LHB LM R2

FULL NAME: Gareth Peter Rees
BORN: April 8, 1985, Swansea
SQUAD NO: 28
HEIGHT: 6ft 2in
NICKNAME: Gums
EDUCATION: Coedcae Comprehensive; Coleg Sir Gar; Bath University
TEAMS: Glamorgan, Glamorgan 2nd XI, Wales Minor Counties
CAREER: First-class: 2006; List A: 2003; T20: 2009

BEST BATTING: 154 Glamorgan vs Surrey, The Oval, 2009
COUNTY CAP: 2009

CAREER HIGHLIGHTS? Being capped by Glamorgan. Having the pleasure of sitting next to Dean Cosker in the Glamorgan changing room
SUPERSTITIONS? No, there is no such thing as luck
CRICKETING HEROES? Brian Lara – best ever player to watch
NON-CRICKETING HEROES? Alan Turing
BEST PLAYER IN COUNTY CRICKET? Marcus Trescothick
TIPS FOR THE TOP? James Harris – best young bowler on the circuit. James Taylor – best young batter going around.
IF YOU WEREN'T A CRICKETER? Working in finance or consulting hopefully. Possibly a chef or model
FAVOURITE FILM? Braveheart, Pulp Fiction
DREAM HOLIDAY? The Whitsundays, Australia
ACCOMPLISHMENTS? Always felt getting a 1st in my degree was my biggest accomplishment
GUILTY PLEASURES? Just genuine hard work at the gym...
FANTASY SLIP CORDON? Keeper: Russell Howard, 1st: Ricky Gervais, 2nd: Me, 3rd: Albert Einstein
TWITTER FEED: @garethprees28

Batting	Mat	Inns	NO	Runs	HS	Ave	SR	100	50	Ct	St
First-class	92	159	8	4950	154	32.78	47.89	11	27	74	0
List A	44	42	6	1317	123*	36.58		3	9	12	0
Twenty20	27	26	5	350	38	16.66	105.74	0	0	7	0
Bowling	**Inns**	**Balls**	**Runs**	**Wkts**	**BBI**	**BBM**	**Ave**	**Econ**	**SR**	**5w**	**10**
First-class	92	31	25	0	-	-	-	4.83	-	0	0
List A	44	3	2	0	-	-	-	4.00	-	0	0
Twenty20	27	12	25	0	-	-	-	12.50	-	0	0

JAMES REGAN RHB WK

FULL NAME: James Alan Regan
BORN: May 30, 1994, Frimley, Surrey
SQUAD NO: 19
HEIGHT: 5ft 10in
NICKNAME: Reags
EDUCATION: King's College, Taunton
TEAMS: Hampshire Under-15s, Somerset 2nd XI
CAREER: First-class: 2012

CAREER HIGHLIGHTS? Playing against South Africa in a tour match and making my first-class debut
SUPERSTITIONS? I scratch the pitch six times when taking guard
MOST MARKED CHARACTERISTIC? My kindness
BEST PLAYER IN COUNTY CRICKET? Marcus Trescothick
TIPS FOR THE TOP? Jos Buttler, Stuart Meaker, Joe Root
DESERT ISLAND DISC? Justin Bieber – As Long As You Love Me
FAVOURITE TV? Geordie Shore
CRICKETING HEROES? Adam Gilchrist, Kevin Pietersen
NON-CRICKETING HEROES? David Beckham
ACCOMPLISHMENTS? My GCSE results, living in Australia and playing semi-pro football
WHEN YOU RETIRE? Become a coach or trainer/physio
SURPRISING FACT? I listen to Justin Bieber to relax before batting
FANTASY SLIP CORDON? Keeper: Me, 1st: David Beckham, 2nd: Cristiano Ronaldo, 3rd: Megan Fox, Gully: Cheryl Cole
TWITTER FEED: @reganja23

Batting	Mat	Inns	NO	Runs	HS	Ave	SR	100	50	Ct	St
First-class	1	-	-	-	-	-	-	-	-	0	0
Bowling	**Inns**	**Balls**	**Runs**	**Wkts**	**BBI**	**BBM**	**Ave**	**Econ**	**SR**	**5w**	**10**
First-class	1	-	-	-	-	-	-	-	-	-	-

ABDUR REHMAN LHB SLA

FULL NAME: Abdur Rehman
BORN: March 1, 1980, Sialkot, Pakistan
SQUAD NO: TBC
HEIGHT: 6ft
TEAMS: Pakistan, Gujranwala Cricket Association, Habib Bank Limited, Pakistan A, Pakistan Cricket Board Blues, Pakistan Cricket Board XI, Pakistan Under-19s, Punjab Stallions, Sialkot, Sialkot Stallions, Somerset
CAREER: Test: 2007; ODI: 2006; T20I: 2007; First-class: 1998; List A: 1999; T20: 2005

BEST BATTING: 96 Habib Bank Ltd vs National Bank of Pakistan, Multan, 2006
BEST BOWLING: 9-65 Somerset vs Worcestershire, Taunton, 2012

NOTES: Had to wait until he was 26 for his first international cap, an ODI against the West Indies at Faisalabad. Returned match figures of 8-210 (4-105 in both innings) on Test debut, but played just once more before being dropped for three years. Reached 50 Test wickets in his 11th Test. Claimed 19 wickets in Pakistan's 3-0 series win against England in the UAE in 2012. Took 27 wickets in just four Championship matches in 2012, including a career best 9-65 against Worcestershire. This season he will be available for the second half of the season, including the end of the FL t20 campaign and five Championship matches

Batting	Mat	Inns	NO	Runs	HS	Ave	SR	100	50	Ct	St
Tests	17	22	3	289	60	15.21	42.68	0	1	6	0
ODIs	25	18	5	104	31	8.00	52.52	0	0	5	0
T20Is	7	4	2	15	7	7.50	88.23	0	0	6	0
First-class	127	172	19	2613	96	17.07		0	12	56	0
List A	128	89	23	923	50	13.98		0	1	28	0
Twenty20	46	18	5	131	21	10.07	104.80	0	0	22	0
Bowling	**Inns**	**Balls**	**Runs**	**Wkts**	**BBI**	**BBM**	**Ave**	**Econ**	**SR**	**5w**	**10**
Tests	17	5354	2301	81	6/25	8/92	28.40	2.57	66.0	2	0
ODIs	25	1344	949	21	2/20	2/20	45.19	4.23	64.0	0	0
T20Is	7	150	174	11	2/7	2/7	15.81	6.96	13.6	0	0
First-class	127	28092	12217	470	9/65		25.99	2.60	59.7	23	5
List A	128	6780	4828	183	6/16	6/16	26.38	4.27	37.0	1	0
Twenty20	46	1041	1137	57	3/17	3/17	19.94	6.55	18.2	0	0

GEORGE RHODES RHB RM

FULL NAME: George Harry Rhodes
BORN: October 26, 1993, Worcester
SQUAD NO: 34
HEIGHT: 5ft 11in
NICKNAME: Rhodesy, Jnr Bump
EDUCATION: Chase Technology College; Worcester University
TEAMS: Worcestershire 2nd XI, Worcestershire Academy
CAREER: Yet to make first-team debut

FAMILY TIES? My father Steve Rhodes played professional cricket for 22 years, including playing for England. My grandfather [Billy] also played professional cricket
SUPERSTITIONS? No, I don't believe in all that rubbish!
CRICKETING HEROES? Alan Richardson (I'd best stay loyal), he's an absolute professional in every sense of the word
BEST PLAYER IN COUNTY CRICKET? Marcus Trescothick, easy question!
TIP FOR THE TOP? Alex Milton
IF YOU WEREN'T A CRICKETER? I'd have been a footballer or maybe a landscape gardener
FAVOURITE TV? The Inbetweeners, exactly my type of comedy
DESERT ISLAND DISC? Bob Marley – Don't Worry Be Happy
WHEN YOU RETIRE? Finally go on a summer holiday – I'm thinking Barbados
ACCOMPLISHMENTS? I was conkers champion at Rushwick CofE Primary School between 2002 and 2004
SURPRISING FACT? I always wanted to be a wicketkeeper but was never allowed!
FANTASY SLIP CORDON? Keeper: Keith Lemon, 1st: Lee Evans, 2nd Karl Pilkington, 3rd: Megan Fox, Gully: Eddie Murphy
TWITTER FEED: @Ghrhodes

HAMPSHIRE

HAMZA RIAZUDDIN RHB RMF

FULL NAME: Hamza Riazuddin
BORN: December 19, 1989, Hendon, Middlesex
SQUAD NO: 38
HEIGHT: 5ft 11in
NICKNAME: Riaz
EDUCATION: Bradfield College
TEAMS: England Under-19s, Hampshire, Hampshire 2nd XI
CAREER: First-class: 2008; List A: 2008; T20: 2008

BEST BATTING: 55* Hampshire vs Loughborough MCCU, Southampton, 2012
BEST BOWLING: 5-61 Hampshire vs Glamorgan, Cardiff, 2012

FAMILY TIES? My dad played minor counties
WHO WOULD PLAY YOU IN A FILM OF YOUR LIFE? Me. I'm a great actor
CAREER HIGHLIGHTS? Taking five-fer and winning the match at Glamorgan. Captaining England U19. Being part of three titles for Hampshire over the past five years
TIPS FOR THE TOP? Chris Wood, James Vince, Michael Roberts
IF YOU WEREN'T A CRICKETER? Going wild somewhere in the Southern Hemisphere
DESERT ISLAND DISC? Ed Sheeran
FAVOURITE TV? Any series with David Attenborough
CRICKETING HEROES? Kevin Pietersen, Imran Khan
NON-CRICKETING HEROES? Lionel Messi, Jamie Foxx, Che Guevara, Malcolm X
ACCOMPLISHMENTS? Three A grades at A-Level
WHEN YOU RETIRE? Open up a revolutionary business
SURPRISING FACT? I'm a clean freak
FANTASY SLIP CORDON? Keeper: Chris Rock, 1st: Me, 2nd: Will Smith, 3rd: Jessica Alba, 4th: Alicia Keys, Gully: James Corden
TWITTER FEED: @hamzariazuddin

Batting	Mat	Inns	NO	Runs	HS	Ave	SR	100	50	Ct	St
First-class	8	9	2	130	55*	18.57	58.82	0	1	1	0
List A	23	9	3	72	23*	12.00	77.41	0	0	7	0
Twenty20	17	6	3	24	13*	8.00	88.88	0	0	2	0
Bowling	**Inns**	**Balls**	**Runs**	**Wkts**	**BBI**	**BBM**	**Ave**	**Econ**	**SR**	**5w**	**10**
First-class	8	936	469	17	5/61	6/81	27.58	3.00	55.0	1	0
List A	23	864	737	16	3/37	3/37	46.06	5.11	54.0	0	0
Twenty20	17	348	417	21	4/15	4/15	19.85	7.18	16.5	0	0

ALAN RICHARDSON RHB RMF W4 MVP36

FULL NAME: Alan Richardson
BORN: May 6, 1975, Newcastle-under-Lyme, Staffordshire
SQUAD NO: 9
HEIGHT: 6ft 2in
NICKNAME: Richo
EDUCATION: Alleyne's High School, Stone; Stafford College
TEAMS: Derbyshire, Middlesex, Staffordshire, Warwickshire, Worcestershire
CAREER: First-class: 1995; List A: 1995; T20: 2004

BEST BATTING: 91 Warwickshire vs Hampshire, Birmingham, 2002
BEST BOWLING: 8-46 Warwickshire vs Sussex, Birmingham, 2002
COUNTY CAPS: 2002 (Warwickshire); 2005 (Middlesex)

CAREER HIGHLIGHTS? Being capped by Warwickshire and Middlesex, being promoted with Worcestershire in 2010 and being named one of five Wisden Cricketers of the Year in 2011
MOST MARKED CHARACTERISTIC? Bandy legs or my voice, you decide
BEST PLAYER IN COUNTY CRICKET? Marcus Trescothick or Andre Adams
TIPS FOR THE TOP? Tom Kohler-Cadmore, Tom Fell, Steve Leach and Josh Renshaw
IF YOU WEREN'T A CRICKETER? I'd be a PE teacher
DESERT ISLAND DISC? Maximo Park – Our Earthly Pleasures
FAVOURITE TV? Wilfred, Entourage and The Great British Bake Off
BIGGEST DRESSING DOWN YOU'VE RECEIVED? Vikram Solanki to the team, Cardiff 2010. Brutal
CRICKETING HEROES? Angus Fraser
NON-CRICKETING HEROES? Glenn Whelan, John Eustace, Mark Stein, Wayne Biggins, Vince Overson and Ricardo Fuller
ACCOMPLISHMENTS? Surviving Daryl Mitchell's stag do
WHEN YOU RETIRE? Spend my life on a beach
TWITTER FEED: @alricho21

Batting	Mat	Inns	NO	Runs	HS	Ave	SR	100	50	Ct	St
First-class	153	176	73	1067	91	10.35		0	1	46	0
List A	64	28	18	105	21*	10.50		0	0	14	0
Twenty20	11	2	1	6	6*	6.00	60.00	0	0	2	0
Bowling	**Inns**	**Balls**	**Runs**	**Wkts**	**BBI**	**BBM**	**Ave**	**Econ**	**SR**	**5w**	**10**
First-class	153	29642	13639	500	8/46		27.27	2.76	59.2	18	2
List A	64	2806	2199	62	5/35	5/35	35.46	4.70	45.2	1	0
Twenty20	11	228	268	10	3/13	3/13	26.80	7.05	22.8	0	0

MICHAEL RICHARDSON RHB WK

FULL NAME: Michael John Richardson
BORN: October 4, 1986, Port Elizabeth, South Africa
SQUAD NO: 18
HEIGHT: 5ft 11in
NICKNAME: Richie, Chelsea, Rory
EDUCATION: Rondebosch Boys' High School; Stonyhurst College; Nottingham University
TEAMS: Durham, Durham 2nd XI, Marylebone Cricket Club Young Cricketers
CAREER: First-class: 2010; List A: 2012

BEST BATTING: 73* Durham vs Yorkshire, Headingley, 2011

FAMILY TIES? My dad is Dave Richardson [former South Africa wicketkeeper now ICC general manager]
CAREER HIGHLIGHTS? Signing for Durham and my debuts in the different formats
SUPERSTITIONS? Yes, a few. I don't like batting on Nelson is an obvious one
MOST MARKED CHARACTERISTIC? Laid-back and often late
TIPS FOR THE TOP? Chris Woakes, Ben Stokes
IF YOU WEREN'T A CRICKETER? Working in finance
DESERT ISLAND DISC? Kings Of Leon
FAVOURITE TV? Revenge
CRICKETING HEROES? Brian Lara, Neil McKenzie
TWITTER FEED: @richo18howu

Batting	Mat	Inns	NO	Runs	HS	Ave	SR	100	50	Ct	St
First-class	11	17	1	353	73*	22.06	43.52	0	3	40	1
List A	2	1	0	45	45	45.00	70.31	0	0	1	0
Bowling	**Inns**	**Balls**	**Runs**	**Wkts**	**BBI**	**BBM**	**Ave**	**Econ**	**SR**	**5w**	**10**
First-class	11	-	-	-	-	-	-	-	-	-	-
List A	2	-	-	-	-	-	-	-	-	-	-

ADAM RILEY RHB OB

FULL NAME: Adam Edward Nicholas Riley
BORN: March 23, 1992, Sidcup, Kent
SQUAD NO: 33
HEIGHT: 6ft 2in
NICKNAME: Riles, Rilo, Sherman, Ed Sheeran, Ginge
EDUCATION: Beths Grammar School, Bexley; Loughborough University
TEAMS: Kent, Kent 2nd XI, Loughborough MCCU
CAREER: First-class: 2011; List A: 2011; T20: 2011

BEST BATTING: 18 Loughborough MCCU vs Nottinghamshire, Nottingham, 2012
BEST BOWLING: 5-76 Kent vs Loughborough MCCU, Canterbury, 2011

WHO WOULD PLAY YOU IN A FILM OF YOUR LIFE? Karl Pilkington
CAREER HIGHLIGHTS? My 1st XI debut in all formats and playing against India at Canterbury
MOST MARKED CHARACTERISTIC? I'm a quick learner
BEST PLAYER IN COUNTY CRICKET? James Taylor
TIPS FOR THE TOP? Daniel Bell-Drummond, Sam Northeast, Sam Billings
IF YOU WEREN'T A CRICKETER? I'd be a failing student
DESERT ISLAND DISC? Adele – 21
FAVOURITE TV? Derek
CRICKETING HEROES? Shane Warne
NON-CRICKETING HEROES? Dean Kiely, Clive Mendonca, Alan Curbishley
ACCOMPLISHMENTS? Leading Charlton Athletic to European glory on Football Manager
WHEN YOU RETIRE? I'd like to become a coach
SURPRISING FACT? I am very ticklish!
FANTASY SLIP CORDON? Keeper: Karl Pilkington, 1st: Me, 2nd: Jack Dee, 3rd: Michael McIntyre, Gully: Will Ferrell (how funny would the sledging be?!)
TWITTER FEED: @AdamRiley92

Batting	Mat	Inns	NO	Runs	HS	Ave	SR	100	50	Ct	St
First-class	13	15	4	55	18	5.00	19.57	0	0	6	0
List A	8	1	1	3	3*	-	42.85	0	0	2	0
Twenty20	4	1	1	5	5*	-	125.00	0	0	0	0
Bowling	**Inns**	**Balls**	**Runs**	**Wkts**	**BBI**	**BBM**	**Ave**	**Econ**	**SR**	**5w**	**10**
First-class	13	1428	960	23	5/76	5/76	41.73	4.03	62.0	1	0
List A	8	240	216	5	2/32	2/32	43.20	5.40	48.0	0	0
Twenty20	4	72	95	3	2/15	2/15	31.66	7.91	24.0	0	0

MICHAEL RIPPON RHB SLC

FULL NAME: Michael James Rippon
BORN: September 14, 1991, Cape Town, South Africa
SQUAD NO: 14
HEIGHT: 6ft
NICKNAME: Rips
EDUCATION: Rondebosch Boys' High School, Cape Town
TEAMS: Cape Cobras, Sussex, Sussex 2nd XI, Western Province, Western Province Under-19s
CAREER: First-class: 2011; List A: 2011; T20: 2011

BEST BATTING: 40 Western Province vs KwaZulu-Natal Inland, Pietermaritzburg, 2011
BEST BOWLING: 3-34 Western Province vs KwaZulu-Natal Inland, Pietermaritzburg, 2011

CAREER HIGHLIGHTS? Making my Cape Cobras and Sussex debuts
BEST PLAYER IN COUNTY CRICKET? Luke Wright
TIPS FOR THE TOP? Harry Finch and Callum Jackson
IF YOU WEREN'T A CRICKETER? I'd be studying
DESERT ISLAND DISC? Eminem – Lose Yourself
FAVOURITE TV? Two And A Half Men, Family Guy, The Simpsons, Modern Family
CRICKETING HEROES? Jacques Kallis, Brad Hogg, Shane Warne
NON-CRICKETING HEROES? Arnold Schwarzenegger and Usain Bolt
WHEN YOU RETIRE? Travel the world and take up new hobbies
SURPRISING FACTS? I'm not a fan of cold weather and I hate spiders; it's too bad that cold weather brings in rain spiders! I bowl and write left-handed, but bat and play golf right-handed. I was born in Cape Town but lived in the Netherlands for four years when I was a kid
FANTASY SLIP CORDON? Keeper: Usain Bolt, 1st: Zoolander, 2nd: Bobby Fresh, 3rd: Magneto, Gully: Mr Anderson
TWITTER FEED: @michaelrippon19

Batting	Mat	Inns	NO	Runs	HS	Ave	SR	100	50	Ct	St
First-class	3	2	0	40	40	20.00	56.33	0	0	1	0
List A	1	1	0	10	10	10.00	66.66	0	0	1	0
Twenty20	15	2	1	3	3*	3.00	60.00	0	0	2	0
Bowling	**Inns**	**Balls**	**Runs**	**Wkts**	**BBI**	**BBM**	**Ave**	**Econ**	**SR**	**5w**	**10**
First-class	3	447	272	6	3/34	4/49	45.33	3.65	74.5	0	0
List A	1	48	44	0	-	-	-	5.50	-	0	0
Twenty20	15	246	332	15	4/23	4/23	22.13	8.09	16.4	0	0

MICHAEL ROBERTS RHB OB

FULL NAME: Michael David Tudor Roberts
BORN: March 13, 1989, Oxford
SQUAD NO: 13
HEIGHT: 6ft 6in
NICKNAME: Robbo, Punter
EDUCATION: Oratory School; Bath University
TEAMS: Berkshire, Hampshire 2nd XI, Middlesex 2nd XI, Unicorns
CAREER: List A: 2012

FAMILY TIES? My dad played for Cambridge University 3rd XI once
WHO WOULD PLAY YOU IN A FILM OF YOUR LIFE? Tom Hardy or Christian Bale
CAREER HIGHLIGHTS? Signing with Hampshire after four years at university. Scoring 97* at Lord's in the 2011 Minor Counties Trophy final. Scoring 205 in a minor counties game. Leading run-scorer in the 2nd XI Championship in 2012
SUPERSTITIONS? I can't use a bat that hasn't been given a girl's name
MOST MARKED CHARACTERISTIC? Ambitious
BEST PLAYER IN COUNTY CRICKET? Michael Carberry
TIPS FOR THE TOP? James Vince, Jake George
DESERT ISLAND DISC? Recurring Dream: The Very Best Of Crowded House
FAVOURITE TV? Fawlty Towers
BIGGEST DRESSING DOWN YOU'VE RECEIVED? No particular occasion but Henley captain Bjorn Mordt loves a dummy spit when he loses
CRICKETING HEROES? Greg Blewett, Ricky Ponting, Michael Atherton, David Barnes
NON-CRICKETING HEROES? Carl Sagan, Valentino Rossi, Andre Agassi, Ollie Berger
ACCOMPLISHMENTS? 2:1 degree in Languages and Politics from Bath University. Raising money for charity running half marathons. 170 checkout twice. A highest break of 27 on a full-size snooker table
WHEN YOU RETIRE? Join the PGA Tour, win the FEDEX Cup, and then make wine in the south of France
SURPRISING FACT? I speak French and Italian fluently
FANTASY SLIP CORDON? Keeper: Amber Heard, 1st: Silvio Berlusconi, 2nd: Jimi Hendrix, 3rd: Me, 4th: Jay-Z, Gully: Lieutenant Colonel Bill Kilgore

Batting	Mat	Inns	NO	Runs	HS	Ave	SR	100	50	Ct	St
List A	1	1	0	4	4	4.00	22.22	0	0	1	0
Bowling	**Inns**	**Balls**	**Runs**	**Wkts**	**BBI**	**BBM**	**Ave**	**Econ**	**SR**	**5w**	**10**
List A	1	-	-	-	-	-	-	-	-	-	-

ANGUS ROBSON RHB

FULL NAME: Angus James Robson
BORN: February 19, 1992, Darlinghurst, Sydney, Australia
SQUAD NO: 8
HEIGHT: 5ft 9in
NICKNAME: Gus, Robbo
EDUCATION: Marcellin College, Randwick; Australian College of Physical Education
TEAMS: Gloucestershire 2nd XI, Leicestershire 2nd XI, New South Wales Under-19s
CAREER: Yet to make first-team debut

FAMILY TIES? My father [Jim] played 2nd XI for Worcestershire and captained Australian Universities. My brother [Sam] plays for Middlesex
WHO WOULD PLAY YOU IN A FILM OF YOUR LIFE? Adam Sandler
CAREER HIGHLIGHTS? Being signed by Leicestershire
MOST MARKED CHARACTERISTIC? I'm energetic
BEST PLAYER IN COUNTY CRICKET? Steve Finn
TIPS FOR THE TOP? Chris Russell, Jonathan Inglis
IF YOU WEREN'T A CRICKETER? Playing another sport
DESERT ISLAND DISC? Coldplay – Mylo Xyloto
FAVOURITE TV? One Tree Hill
BIGGEST DRESSING DOWN YOU'VE RECEIVED? It came from an U10s coach when I threw a bat!
CRICKETING HEROES? Ian Bell, Michael Clarke, Mike Atherton
NON-CRICKETING HEROES? Jonny Wilkinson, Ryan Gosling
ACCOMPLISHMENTS? Progressing through a Physical Education degree
WHEN YOU RETIRE? I'd like to be a teacher or a sports journalist
SURPRISING FACT? I've been told I'm a good dancer!
FANTASY SLIP CORDON? Keeper: Adam Sandler, 1st: Kate Beckinsale, 2nd: Chris Martin, 3rd: Myself, Gully: Tom DeLonge

SAM ROBSON RHB LB

FULL NAME: Sam David Robson
BORN: July 1, 1989, Paddington, Sydney, Australia
SQUAD NO: 12
HEIGHT: 6ft
NICKNAME: Robbo
EDUCATION: Marcellin College, Randwick
TEAMS: Australia Under-19s, Eastern Suburbs, Middlesex, Middlesex 2nd XI, New South Wales Under-19s, Sydney South East, University of New South Wales
CAREER: First-class: 2009; List A: 2008; T20: 2011

BEST BATTING: 204 Middlesex vs Oxford MCCU, Oxford, 2010

FAMILY TIES? My father [Jim] captained Australian Universities vs England in 1979 and also played for Worcestershire 2nd XI. My brother Angus is currently on the staff at Leicestershire
WHO WOULD PLAY YOU IN A FILM OF YOUR LIFE? Jim Carrey
CAREER HIGHLIGHTS? Winning Division Two of the Championship with Middlesex in 2011 and a 200-run opening partnership with Andrew Strauss at Lord's vs Leicestershire in 2011
MOST MARKED CHARACTERISTIC? Dodgy haircut
BEST PLAYER IN COUNTY CRICKET? Nick Compton
TIPS FOR THE TOP? Toby Roland-Jones, Tom Helm, Angus Robson
DESERT ISLAND DISC? The Naked And Famous album
FAVOURITE TV? Seinfeld, 666 Park Avenue
CRICKETING HEROES? Michael Slater, Mike Atherton, Shane Warne
WHEN YOU RETIRE? I'd like to be a journalist
SURPRISING FACT? I like doing pencil drawings and sketches
FANTASY SLIP CORDON? Keeper: Happy Gilmore, 1st: Shane Warne, 2nd: Jerry Seinfeld, 3rd: Cosmo Cramer, 4th: Jessica Biel, Gully: Billy Madison

Batting	Mat	Inns	NO	Runs	HS	Ave	SR	100	50	Ct	St
First-class	43	77	5	2671	204	37.09	48.14	5	12	44	0
List A	7	5	0	168	65	33.60	75.33	0	1	3	0
Twenty20	4	4	2	53	28*	26.50	103.92	0	0	2	0
Bowling	**Inns**	**Balls**	**Runs**	**Wkts**	**BBI**	**BBM**	**Ave**	**Econ**	**SR**	**5w**	**10**
First-class	43	59	47	0	-	-	-	4.77	-	0	0
List A	7	-	-	-	-	-	-	-	-	-	-
Twenty20	4	-	-	-	-	-	-	-	-	-	-

GLOUCESTERSHIRE

GARETH RODERICK RHB WK

FULL NAME: Gareth Hugh Roderick
BORN: August 28, 1991, Durban, South Africa
SQUAD NO: 27
HEIGHT: 6ft
NICKNAME: Roders
EDUCATION: Maritzburg College
TEAMS: Gloucestershire 2nd XI, KwaZulu-Natal, KwaZulu-Natal Inland Under-19s, Northamptonshire 2nd XI
CAREER: First-class: 2011; List A: 2011; T20: 2011

BEST BATTING: 71* KwaZulu-Natal vs Boland, Chatsworth, 2011

WHO WOULD PLAY YOU IN A FILM OF YOUR LIFE? Justin Bieber
CAREER HIGHLIGHTS? Making my first-class debut and playing 12 first-class games in South Africa
MOST MARKED CHARACTERISTIC? I'm easy going
BEST PLAYER IN COUNTY CRICKET? Marcus Trescothick
TIPS FOR THE TOP? Joe Root, Quinton de Kock, Marchant de Lange
IF YOU WEREN'T A CRICKETER? I'd be working for my father's business
DESERT ISLAND DISC? John Mayer – Free Fallin'
BIGGEST DRESSING DOWN YOU'VE RECEIVED? When a representative coach caught me batting with my thigh pad on the outside of my longs. My ears were ringing from the screaming!
CRICKETING HEROES? Steve Waugh and Adam Gilchrist
WHEN YOU RETIRE? I will maybe look at coaching, either in South Africa or the UK
SURPRISING FACT? I was walking at eight months old but wet the bed till I was seven
FANTASY SLIP CORDON? Keeper: Jimmy Carr, 1st: Jim Jefferies, 2nd: Cartman from South Park, 3rd: Myself, Gully: Steve Waugh. A bunch of comedians plus Cartman would be a funny day in the field and it would be great to meet my cricketing hero Steve Waugh
TWITTER FEED: @Roders369

Batting	Mat	Inns	NO	Runs	HS	Ave	SR	100	50	Ct	St
First-class	12	17	5	452	71*	37.66	43.96	0	3	10	1
List A	4	3	0	52	26	17.33	101.96	0	0	2	1
Twenty20	4	3	0	48	32	16.00	104.34	0	0	1	0
Bowling	**Inns**	**Balls**	**Runs**	**Wkts**	**BBI**	**BBM**	**Ave**	**Econ**	**SR**	**5w**	**10**
First-class	12	-	-	-	-	-	-	-	-	-	-
List A	4	-	-	-	-	-	-	-	-	-	-
Twenty20	4	-	-	-	-	-	-	-	-	-	-

CHRIS ROGERS

LHB LB R6 MVP42

FULL NAME: Christopher John Llewellyn Rogers
BORN: August 31, 1977, Sydney, Australia
SQUAD NO: 1
HEIGHT: 5ft 11in
NICKNAME: Bucky
EDUCATION: Wesley College; Curtin University
TEAMS: Australia, Derbyshire, Leicestershire, Middlesex, Northamptonshire, Victoria, W Australia
CAREER: Test: 2008; First-class: 1998; List A: 1998; T20: 2005

MIDDLESEX

BEST BATTING: 319 Northamptonshire vs Gloucestershire, Northampton, 2006
BEST BOWLING: 1-16 Northamptonshire vs Leicestershire, Northampton, 2006
COUNTY CAPS: 2008 (Derbyshire); 2011 (Middlesex)

FAMILY TIES? My father John played for New South Wales
CAREER HIGHLIGHTS? Test debut in 2008 for Australia vs India. Scoring 209 against Australia for Leicestershire in 2005. Scoring 319 against Gloucestershire in 2006
CRICKETING HEROES? Allan Border, Steve Waugh
NON-CRICKETING HEROES? Michael Jordan, Cadel Evans, Jack Reacher
BEST PLAYER IN COUNTY CRICKET? Marcus Trescothick
TIPS FOR THE TOP? Sam Robson, Alex Hales
WHEN RAIN STOPS PLAY? Coffee and crosswords
FAVOURITE TV? Entourage
FAVOURITE FILM? American Pie 2
FAVOURITE BOOK? Power Of One
DREAM HOLIDAY? South America
ACCOMPLISHMENTS? Journalism degree
GUILTY PLEASURES? Motorway service Burger Kings

Batting	Mat	Inns	NO	Runs	HS	Ave	SR	100	50	Ct	St
Tests	1	2	0	19	15	9.50	70.37	0	0	1	0
First-class	229	405	29	18817	319	50.04		58	85	195	0
List A	154	150	14	5030	140	36.98		5	34	69	0
Twenty20	43	37	1	627	58	17.41	114.62	0	3	22	0
Bowling	**Inns**	**Balls**	**Runs**	**Wkts**	**BBI**	**BBM**	**Ave**	**Econ**	**SR**	**5w**	**10**
Tests	1	-	-	-	-	-	-	-	-	-	-
First-class	229	230	131	1	1/16	1/16	131.00	3.41	230.0	0	0
List A	154	24	26	2	2/22	2/22	13.00	6.50	12.0	0	0
Twenty20	43	-	-	-	-	-	-	-	-	-	-

TOBY ROLAND-JONES RHB RMF W1 MVP7

FULL NAME: Tobias Skelton Roland-Jones
BORN: January 29, 1988, Ashford, Middlesex
SQUAD NO: 21
EDUCATION: Hampton School; Leeds University
TEAMS: England Lions, Marylebone Cricket Club, Middlesex, Middlesex 2nd XI
CAREER: First-class: 2010; List A: 2010; T20: 2011

BEST BATTING: 52 Middlesex vs Sussex, Lord's, 2012
BEST BOWLING: 6-66 Middlesex vs Sussex, Hove, 2012
COUNTY CAP: 2012

TWITTER FEED: @tobyrj21
NOTES: Third highest wicket-taker in Division One of the County Championship in 2012, behind Graham Onions and Chris Wright, with 61 wickets at 19.13. Took his first 10-wicket match haul last season, returning figures of 10-118 vs Worcestershire at New Road. Rewarded with selection for the England Lions tour to Australia over the winter, taking 3-58 in the final match of the unofficial 'ODI' series against Australia A. Signed a five-year contract with Middlesex in October last year, keeping him at Lord's until the end of 2017. Middlesex's joint leading wicket-taker in 2010 with a haul of 36 at 19.60, despite only featuring in eight matches, including five-wicket hauls against Surrey and Worcestershire. Represented MCC against County Championship winners Nottinghamshire in March 2011, taking four wickets in the floodlit match in Abu Dhabi. Older brother Oliver has played for Middlesex 2nd XI and Leeds/Bradford MCCU

Batting	Mat	Inns	NO	Runs	HS	Ave	SR	100	50	Ct	St
First-class	31	43	10	559	52	16.93	47.90	0	1	9	0
List A	20	11	3	95	24	11.87	88.78	0	0	3	0
Twenty20	10	5	2	25	12	8.33	119.04	0	0	0	0
Bowling	**Inns**	**Balls**	**Runs**	**Wkts**	**BBI**	**BBM**	**Ave**	**Econ**	**SR**	**5w**	**10**
First-class	31	5101	2743	132	6/66	10/118	20.78	3.22	38.6	7	1
List A	20	862	807	34	3/24	3/24	23.73	5.61	25.3	0	0
Twenty20	10	216	298	13	4/25	4/25	22.92	8.27	16.6	0	0

JOE ROOT

RHB OB R1 MVP66

FULL NAME: Joseph Edward Root
BORN: December 30, 1990, Sheffield, Yorkshire
SQUAD NO: 5
HEIGHT: 6ft
NICKNAME: Milkybar Kid, PT
EDUCATION: King Ecgbert School; Worksop College
TEAMS: England, England Lions, England Under-19s, Yorkshire, Yorkshire 2nd XI, Yorkshire Academy, Yorkshire Under-17s
CAREER: Test: 2012; ODI: 2013; T20I: 2012; First-class: 2010; List A: 2009; T20: 2011

BEST BATTING: 222* Yorkshire vs Hampshire, Southampton, 2012
BEST BOWLING: 3-33 Yorkshire vs Warwickshire, Leeds, 2011
COUNTY CAP: 2012

CAREER HIGHLIGHTS? Getting promoted with Yorkshire, making all international debuts and winning a Test series in India
MOST MARKED CHARACTERISTIC? Baby features! Cheeky!
BEST PLAYER IN COUNTY CRICKET? Graham Onions or Marcus Trescothick
TIPS FOR THE TOP? Gary Ballance, Moin Ashraf, Ben Foakes
IF YOU WEREN'T A CRICKETER? I'd be trying to get into a university to study Art
CRICKETING HEROES? Michael Vaughan, Marcus Trescothick, Matthew Hayden
SURPRISING FACT? I auditioned for a Milkybar Kid advert when I was growing up and got into the last three but didn't get the job
FANTASY SLIP CORDON? The Pussycat Dolls
TWITTER FEED: @joeroot05

Batting	Mat	Inns	NO	Runs	HS	Ave	SR	100	50	Ct	St
Tests	1	2	1	93	73	93.00	32.63	0	1	0	0
ODIs	8	7	3	326	79*	81.50	86.47	0	3	4	0
T20Is	2	-	-	-	-	-	-	-	-	3	0
First-class	37	63	9	2108	222*	39.03	49.89	4	9	19	0
List A	35	33	6	1084	110*	40.14	80.59	1	7	13	0
Twenty20	29	23	4	410	65	21.57	113.88	0	1	12	0
Bowling	**Inns**	**Balls**	**Runs**	**Wkts**	**BBI**	**BBM**	**Ave**	**Econ**	**SR**	**5w**	**10**
Tests	1	6	5	0	-	-	-	5.00	-	0	0
ODIs	8	126	114	0	-	-	-	5.42	-	0	0
T20Is	2	12	15	1	1/15	1/15	15.00	7.50	12.0	0	0
First-class	37	903	515	8	3/33	3/33	64.37	3.42	112.8	0	0
List A	35	569	475	12	2/10	2/10	39.58	5.00	47.4	0	0
Twenty20	29	156	233	5	1/12	1/12	46.60	8.96	31.2	0	0

ADAM ROSSINGTON RHB WK

FULL NAME: Adam Matthew Rossington
BORN: May 5, 1993, Edgware, Middlesex
SQUAD NO: 17
HEIGHT: 6ft
NICKNAME: Rosso
EDUCATION: Mill Hill School
TEAMS: England Under-19s, Middlesex, Middlesex 2nd XI
CAREER: First-class: 2010; List A: 2012; T20: 2011

BEST BATTING: 29 Middlesex vs Warwickshire, Birmingham, 2012

WHO WOULD PLAY YOU IN A FILM OF YOUR LIFE? Gerard Butler
CAREER HIGHLIGHTS? Scoring a hundred for England U19 at Galle
SUPERSTITIONS? I always put my left pad on before my right
MOST MARKED CHARACTERISTIC? Determination
BEST PLAYER IN COUNTY CRICKET? Marcus Trescothick
TIPS FOR THE TOP? Shiv Thakor, Tom Helm
IF YOU WEREN'T A CRICKETER? I'd be playing golf
DESERT ISLAND DISC? Kanye West – Touch The Sky
FAVOURITE TV? EastEnders
BIGGEST DRESSING DOWN YOU'VE RECEIVED? From my dad, at various points
CRICKETING HEROES? Alec Stewart, Paul Weekes
NON-CRICKETING HEROES? Tiger Woods
ACCOMPLISHMENTS? Learning to cook
WHEN YOU RETIRE? Something involved in sport, coaching preferably
SURPRISING FACT? I can't ride a bike
FANTASY SLIP CORDON? Keeper: Myself, 1st: Lee Evans, 2nd: Ian Botham, 3rd: Kelly Brook, Gully: Tiger Woods
TWITTER FEED: @Rossington17

Batting	Mat	Inns	NO	Runs	HS	Ave	SR	100	50	Ct	St
First-class	5	8	0	67	29	8.37	28.75	0	0	11	1
List A	2	2	0	22	17	11.00	91.66	0	0	1	1
Twenty20	10	10	0	84	25	8.40	98.82	0	0	4	0
Bowling	**Inns**	**Balls**	**Runs**	**Wkts**	**BBI**	**BBM**	**Ave**	**Econ**	**SR**	**5w**	**10**
First-class	5	-	-	-	-	-	-	-	-	-	-
List A	2	-	-	-	-	-	-	-	-	-	-
Twenty20	10	-	-	-	-	-	-	-	-	-	-

ADAM ROUSE RHB WK

FULL NAME: Adam Paul Rouse
BORN: June 30, 1992, Harare, Zimbabwe
SQUAD NO: 20
HEIGHT: 5ft 10in
NICKNAME: Rousie
EDUCATION: Lilfordia School, Zimbabwe; Perins Community Sports College; Peter Symonds College
TEAMS: England Under-19s, Hampshire, Hampshire 2nd XI, Hampshire Cricket Board, Hampshire Under-15s, Leicestershire 2nd XI
CAREER: Yet to make first-team debut

FAMILY TIES? My brothers both played county level age-group cricket
CAREER HIGHLIGHTS? Representing England U19. Catching Kumar Sangakkara as substitute fielder for England vs Sri Lanka at the Ageas Bowl
SUPERSTITIONS? Left pad on first and I mark my guard often
MOST MARKED CHARACTERISTIC? Enthusiastic
BEST PLAYER IN COUNTY CRICKET? Varun Chopra
TIPS FOR THE TOP? Danny Briggs, James Vince, Michael Bates, Chris Wood, Scott Borthwick, Jonny Bairstow, Jos Buttler, Chris Woakes, Tymal Mills, Daniel Bell-Drummond, Sam Billings
IF YOU WEREN'T A CRICKETER? Rugby player or something to do with fitness
DESERT ISLAND DISC? Ed Sheeran – +
FAVOURITE TV? How I Met Your Mother
CRICKETING HEROES? Hashim Amla, AB de Villiers
ACCOMPLISHMENTS? I played rugby for London Irish Academy and represented Hampshire Rugby at age-group level
WHEN YOU RETIRE? Live in an exotic country and soak up the sun for the rest of my life
SURPRISING FACT? I was the youngest player ever to score a men's league century and appeared in the Wisden Cricketer for the achievement
FANTASY SLIP CORDON? Keeper: Me, 1st: James Corden (legend and funny), 2nd: Jonah Hill (hilarious), 3rd: Usain Bolt (fastest man alive), Gully: Bar Refaeli (stunning)
TWITTER FEED: @Rousie20

JASON ROY RHB RM

FULL NAME: Jason Jonathan Roy
BORN: July 21, 1990, Durban, South Africa
SQUAD NO: 20
HEIGHT: 6ft
NICKNAME: JRoy
EDUCATION: Whitgift School
TEAMS: Chittagong Kings, England Lions, Surrey, Surrey 2nd XI
CAREER: First-class: 2010; List A: 2008; T20: 2008

BEST BATTING: 106* Surrey vs Glamorgan, The Oval, 2011
BEST BOWLING: 2-29 Surrey vs Glamorgan, The Oval, 2011

CAREER HIGHLIGHTS? Winning the CB40 with Surrey, getting promoted back to Division One with Surrey, my maiden first-class hundred against Glamorgan and being the first Surrey player to score a T20 hundred
CRICKETING HEROES? Jacques Kallis and Chris Gayle
BEST PLAYER IN COUNTY CRICKET? Marcus Trescothick
TIPS FOR THE TOP? All the Surrey youngsters
IF YOU WEREN'T A CRICKETER? Professional surfer
WHEN RAIN STOPS PLAY? Chatting in the dressing room
FAVOURITE TV? Two And A Half Men
FAVOURITE FILM? The Hangover
DREAM HOLIDAY? Mauritius or the Caribbean
GUILTY PLEASURES? Watching TV whilst eating a tub of ice cream
FANTASY SLIP CORDON? Keeper: Will Ferrell, 1st: Vince Vaughn, 2nd: Owen Wilson, 3rd: Jason Roy, Gully: Spider-Man
TWITTER FEED: @JasonRoy20

Batting	Mat	Inns	NO	Runs	HS	Ave	SR	100	50	Ct	St
First-class	28	50	3	1437	106*	30.57	82.02	1	6	22	0
List A	37	35	2	819	131	24.81	106.36	2	5	13	0
Twenty20	54	51	2	1176	101*	24.00	137.54	1	6	27	0
Bowling	**Inns**	**Balls**	**Runs**	**Wkts**	**BBI**	**BBM**	**Ave**	**Econ**	**SR**	**5w**	**10**
First-class	28	62	62	2	2/29	2/43	31.00	6.00	31.0	0	0
List A	37	6	12	0	-	-	-	12.00	-	0	0
Twenty20	54	-	-	-	-	-	-	-	-	-	-

CHRIS RUSHWORTH RHB RMF MVP40

FULL NAME: Christopher Rushworth
BORN: July 11, 1986, Sunderland
SQUAD NO: 22
HEIGHT: 6ft 2in
NICKNAME: Rushy, Sponge
EDUCATION: Castle View Comprehensive
TEAMS: Durham, Northumberland
CAREER: First-class: 2010; List A: 2004; T20: 2011

BEST BATTING: 28 Durham vs Yorkshire, Chester-le-Street, 2010
BEST BOWLING: 5-38 Durham vs Sussex, Chester-le-Street, 2012

FAMILY TIES? My father played local cricket, brother Lee represented England and Durham at junior levels and my cousin Phil Mustard plays for Durham
CAREER HIGHLIGHTS? My first-class debut against Yorkshire at Headingley is the highlight so far but I'm sure winning trophies with Durham will overshadow that
CRICKETING HEROES? Loved watching the two South Africans Shaun Pollock and Allan Donald tear teams apart as a young bowler! Sheer aggression was exciting to watch
BEST PLAYER IN COUNTY CRICKET? It's hard not to say Marcus Trescothick as he consistently scores runs in every format of the game
TIPS FOR THE TOP? Ben Stokes and Scott Borthwick both have brilliant futures and I'm sure they will feature for England and be a great success
IF YOU WEREN'T A CRICKETER? No idea. Thankfully I've had the opportunities at Durham
WHEN RAIN STOPS PLAY? Usually cards or just general relaxing. Mitch Claydon finds a way to entertain the lads with his magic tricks!
FAVOURITE TV? Love watching sports, football takes up a lot of time on the box
DREAM HOLIDAY? I've spent a few years in Australia playing cricket and that's probably my ideal holiday destination. The weather is marvellous and the people are friendly
TWITTER FEED: @rushworth22

Batting	Mat	Inns	NO	Runs	HS	Ave	SR	100	50	Ct	St
First-class	21	28	10	248	28	13.77	62.78	0	0	3	0
List A	21	11	4	45	12*	6.42	70.31	0	0	2	0
Twenty20	19	3	2	2	2	2.00	66.66	0	0	4	0
Bowling	**Inns**	**Balls**	**Runs**	**Wkts**	**BBI**	**BBM**	**Ave**	**Econ**	**SR**	**5w**	**10**
First-class	21	2883	1613	64	5/38	7/83	25.20	3.35	45.0	3	0
List A	21	798	682	37	5/31	5/31	18.43	5.12	21.5	1	0
Twenty20	19	324	452	17	3/20	3/20	26.58	8.37	19.0	0	0

CHRIS RUSSELL RHB RMF

FULL NAME: Christopher James Russell
BORN: February 16, 1989, Newport, Isle of Wight
SQUAD NO: 18
HEIGHT: 6ft 1in
NICKNAME: Goober, Goobs, Spaniel
EDUCATION: Wroxall Primary School; Ventnor Middle School; Medina High School
TEAMS: Worcestershire, Worcestershire 2nd XI
CAREER: First-class: 2012; List A: 2010

BEST BATTING: 22 Worcestershire vs Middlesex, Worcester, 2012
BEST BOWLING: 4-43 Worcestershire vs Warwickshire, Birmingham, 2012

WHO WOULD PLAY YOU IN A FILM OF YOUR LIFE? Johnny Depp
CAREER HIGHLIGHTS? Playing against South Africa in a two-day tour match and making my first-class debut against Warwickshire
SUPERSTITIONS? I always put my left pad on first
TIPS FOR THE TOP? Ben Stokes, James Taylor and Danny Briggs
IF YOU WEREN'T A CRICKETER? Animation and illustration
DESERT ISLAND DISC? Ed Sheeran – +
FAVOURITE TV? Celebrity Juice
WHEN YOU RETIRE? Chill on a beach in the Caribbean
FANTASY SLIP CORDON? Keeper: Keith Lemon, 1st: Nelson Mandela, 2nd: David Beckham, 3rd: Myself, Gully: Rhod Gilbert
TWITTER FEED: @Chris18Russell

Batting	Mat	Inns	NO	Runs	HS	Ave	SR	100	50	Ct	St
First-class	6	10	2	83	22	10.37	41.91	0	0	2	0
List A	2	-	-	-	-	-	-	-	-	0	0
Bowling	**Inns**	**Balls**	**Runs**	**Wkts**	**BBI**	**BBM**	**Ave**	**Econ**	**SR**	**5w**	**10**
First-class	6	808	563	17	4/43	6/117	33.11	4.18	47.5	0	0
List A	2	54	68	1	1/23	1/23	68.00	7.55	54.0	0	0

DAVID SALES RHB RM R6

FULL NAME: David John Grimwood Sales
BORN: December 3, 1977, Carshalton, Surrey
SQUAD NO: 5
HEIGHT: 6ft
NICKNAME: Jumble, Car-boot
EDUCATION: Caterham School
TEAMS: Northamptonshire, Wellington
CAREER: First-class: 1996; List A: 1994; T20: 2003

BEST BATTING: 303* Northamptonshire vs Essex, Northampton, 1999
BEST BOWLING: 4-25 Northamptonshire vs Sri Lanka A, Northampton, 1999
COUNTY CAP: 1996; BENEFIT YEAR: 2007

NON-CRICKETING HEROES? Phil Taylor
BEST PLAYER IN COUNTY CRICKET? Stephen Peters
TIP FOR THE TOP? Alex Wakely
IF YOU WEREN'T A CRICKETER? Cricket coach, bricklayer
WHEN RAIN STOPS PLAY? Drink coffee and talk rubbish
FAVOURITE TV? I'm A Celebrity... Get Me Out Of Here!
FAVOURITE FILM? Any Given Sunday
FAVOURITE BOOK? Bravo Two Zero
DREAM HOLIDAY? Spain
ACCOMPLISHMENTS? My three boys
GUILTY PLEASURES? A cheeky Chinese and a few beers

Batting	Mat	Inns	NO	Runs	HS	Ave	SR	100	50	Ct	St
First-class	230	366	32	13118	303*	39.27		26	63	208	0
List A	258	245	35	7250	161	34.52		4	53	114	0
Twenty20	56	53	12	1209	78*	29.48	129.86	0	10	28	0
Bowling	**Inns**	**Balls**	**Runs**	**Wkts**	**BBI**	**BBM**	**Ave**	**Econ**	**SR**	**5w**	**10**
First-class	230	345	184	9	4/25		20.44	3.20	38.3	0	0
List A	258	84	67	0	-	-	-	4.78	-	0	0
Twenty20	56	12	23	1	1/10	1/10	23.00	11.50	12.0	0	0

ANDREW SALTER RHB OB

FULL NAME: Andrew Graham Salter
BORN: June 1, 1993, Haverfordwest, Pembrokeshire
SQUAD NO: 21
HEIGHT: 5ft 9in
NICKNAME: Salts
EDUCATION: Milford Haven Sixth Form College; Cardiff Metropolitan University
TEAMS: Cardiff MCCU, England Under-17s, England Under-19s, Glamorgan, Glamorgan 2nd XI, Wales Minor Counties
CAREER: First-class: 2012; List A: 2012

BEST BATTING: 21 Cardiff MCCU vs Warwickshire, Birmingham, 2012
BEST BOWLING: 3-134 Cardiff MCCU vs Somerset, Taunton, 2012

FAMILY TIES? My dad loved and played the sport for many years and my brother also enjoyed his experiences attached to cricket
WHO WOULD PLAY YOU IN A FILM OF YOUR LIFE? Mark Wahlberg
CAREER HIGHLIGHTS? Playing at Lord's and being selected as England U15 captain. Signing my first full contract for Glamorgan. Exploring the world while playing cricket
SUPERSTITIONS? Not really, although I always get padded up in the same order
MOST MARKED CHARACTERISTIC? Massive schnoz
BEST PLAYER IN COUNTY CRICKET? James Harris
TIPS FOR THE TOP? Dave Lloyd, Daniel Bell-Drummond, Mike Reed and Uzi Qureshi
IF YOU WEREN'T A CRICKETER? I'd be a guitarist busking outside St David's Hall
DESERT ISLAND DISC? Venga Boys – We Like To Party
CRICKETING HEROES? Robert Croft and James Salter
NON-CRICKETING HEROES? John Butler, Eric Clapton, Newton Faulkner and Tom Turner
WHEN YOU RETIRE? Follow Tom Turner and Jack Beddis touring the world
FANTASY SLIP CORDON? Keeper: Inspector Gadget (could come in handy), 1st: Will Ferrell ("when in Rome"), 2nd: Lucy Pinder (offers some intellectual knowledge of the game), 3rd: Usain Bolt (won't need a third man), Gully: Vinny Jones (he'd take sledging to a whole new level)
TWITTER FEED: @AndySalts

Batting	Mat	Inns	NO	Runs	HS	Ave	SR	100	50	Ct	St
First-class	2	4	3	41	21	41.00	32.28	0	0	1	0
List A	2	1	0	3	3	3.00	50.00	0	0	0	0
Bowling	**Inns**	**Balls**	**Runs**	**Wkts**	**BBI**	**BBM**	**Ave**	**Econ**	**SR**	**5w**	**10**
First-class	2	312	211	4	3/134	3/134	52.75	4.05	78.0	0	0
List A	2	96	90	3	2/41	2/41	30.00	5.62	32.0	0	0

THILAN SAMARAWEERA RHB OB

FULL NAME: Thilan Thusara Samaraweera
BORN: September 22, 1976, Colombo, Sri Lanka
SQUAD NO: TBC
HEIGHT: 5ft 9in
TEAMS: Sri Lanka, Colts Cricket Club, Kandurata, Sinhalese Sports Club, Sri Lanka A, Sri Lanka Board President's XI, Worcestershire
CAREER: Test: 2001; ODI: 1998; First-class: 1995; List A: 1995; T20: 2004

BEST BATTING: 231 Sri Lanka vs Pakistan, Karachi, 2009
BEST BOWLING: 6-55 Sri Lanka A vs Pakistan A, Dambulla, 2001

NOTES: Scored a century on Test debut for Sri Lanka against India in Colombo. Scored double centuries in consecutive Test matches against Pakistan before a bullet penetrated 12 inches into his left thigh during the terrorist attack on the Sri Lankan team in Pakistan in 2009. Samaraweera was signed by Worcestershire in February for the entire 2013 season and retired from international cricket the following month

Batting	Mat	Inns	NO	Runs	HS	Ave	SR	100	50	Ct	St
Tests	81	132	20	5462	231	48.76	46.92	14	30	45	0
ODIs	53	42	11	862	105*	27.80	69.29	2	0	17	0
First-class	256	367	66	14799	231	49.16		41	72	196	0
List A	178	132	36	3070	105*	31.97		2	16	60	0
Twenty20	21	20	2	537	71	29.83	134.92	0	5	3	0
Bowling	**Inns**	**Balls**	**Runs**	**Wkts**	**BBI**	**BBM**	**Ave**	**Econ**	**SR**	**5w**	**10**
Tests	81	1327	689	15	4/49	6/67	45.93	3.11	88.4	0	0
ODIs	53	702	542	11	3/34	3/34	49.27	4.63	63.8	0	0
First-class	256	17961	8366	357	6/55		23.43	2.79	50.3	15	2
List A	178	4751	3159	110	7/30	7/30	28.71	3.98	43.1	2	0
Twenty20	21	62	66	3	3/17	3/17	22.00	6.38	20.6	0	0

GURJIT SANDHU RHB LMF

FULL NAME: Gurjit Singh Sandhu
BORN: March 24, 1992, Isleworth, Middlesex
SQUAD NO: 92
HEIGHT: 6ft 4in
NICKNAME: Gurj
EDUCATION: Isleworth and Syon School
TEAMS: Middlesex, Middlesex 2nd XI
CAREER: First-class: 2011; List A: 2012

BEST BATTING: 8 Middlesex vs Sri Lankans, Uxbridge, 2011

CAREER HIGHLIGHTS? Making my first-class debut against Sri Lanka at Uxbridge
SUPERSTITIONS? My chain, I can't play without it. I feel naked when I don't have it around my neck
CRICKETING HEROES? Wasim Akram, Brian Lara
NON-CRICKETING HEROES? Dimitar Berbatov, Karl Pilkington, Batman
BEST PLAYER IN COUNTY CRICKET? Marcus Trescothick
TIP FOR THE TOP? James Taylor
FAVOURITE TV? The Fresh Prince Of Bel-Air
FAVOURITE FILM? Inception, Gladiator
DREAM HOLIDAY? Caribbean islands
ACCOMPLISHMENTS? Winning a Football Manager season with Brentford
GUILTY PLEASURES? Junk food
TWITTER FEED: @gurjitsandhu92

Batting	Mat	Inns	NO	Runs	HS	Ave	SR	100	50	Ct	St
First-class	1	2	1	15	8	15.00	51.72	0	0	0	0
List A	1	1	0	0	0	0.00	0.00	0	0	0	0
Bowling	**Inns**	**Balls**	**Runs**	**Wkts**	**BBI**	**BBM**	**Ave**	**Econ**	**SR**	**5w**	**10**
First-class	1	78	69	0	-	-	-	5.30	-	0	0
List A	1	36	28	3	3/28	3/28	9.33	4.66	12.0	0	0

RAMNARESH SARWAN RHB LB MVP65

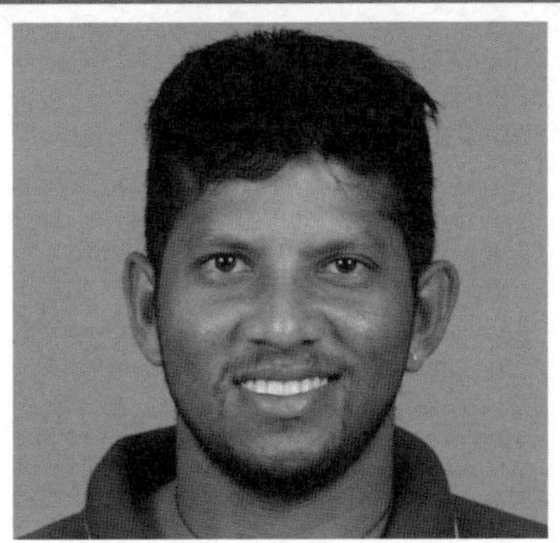

FULL NAME: Ramnaresh Ronnie Sarwan
BORN: June 23, 1980, Wakenaam Island, Essequibo, Guyana
SQUAD NO: 53
HEIGHT: 5ft 9in
NICKNAME: Ronnie
TEAMS: West Indies, Gloucestershire, Guyana, Kings XI Punjab, Leicestershire, Stanford Superstars
CAREER: Test: 2000; ODI: 2000; T20I: 2007; First-class: 1996; List A: 1996; T20: 2006

BEST BATTING: 291 West Indies vs England, Bridgetown, 2009
BEST BOWLING: 6-62 Guyana vs Leeward Islands, St John's, 2001
COUNTY CAP: 2005 (Gloucestershire)

NOTES: Sarwan was appointed as Leicestershire's new four-day captain in December 2012, replacing Matthew Hoggard. His recent recall to the West Indies ODI side means he is unlikely to be available for the whole season though, and he is expected to play the first five and last four County Championship fixtures. Australian batsman Joe Burns will provide cover in his absence. In 2012, his first season with Leicestershire, he scored 941 Championship runs, finishing just behind Hampshire's Jimmy Adams as Division Two's leading run-scorer. His international career saw him succeed Brian Lara as West Indies captain following the 2007 World Cup. He topped the batting averages in the 2008/09 Wisden Trophy against England, scoring 626 runs at an average of 104.33. He fell out of favour in 2011 but returned to the ODI side in February, making 120* vs Zimbabwe in his second game back

Batting	Mat	Inns	NO	Runs	HS	Ave	SR	100	50	Ct	St
Tests	87	154	8	5842	291	40.01	46.79	15	31	53	0
ODIs	179	167	33	5802	120*	43.29	75.79	5	38	45	0
T20Is	18	16	3	298	59	22.92	104.19	0	2	7	0
First-class	208	352	25	12882	291	39.39		33	68	144	0
List A	257	243	41	8300	120*	41.08		11	48	67	0
Twenty20	65	61	5	1071	70	19.12	105.30	0	5	21	0
Bowling	**Inns**	**Balls**	**Runs**	**Wkts**	**BBI**	**BBM**	**Ave**	**Econ**	**SR**	**5w**	**10**
Tests	87	2022	1163	23	4/37	7/96	50.56	3.45	87.9	0	0
ODIs	179	581	586	16	3/31	3/31	36.62	6.05	36.3	0	0
T20Is	18	12	10	2	2/10	2/10	5.00	5.00	6.0	0	0
First-class	208	4350	2328	56	6/62		41.57	3.21	77.6	1	0
List A	257	1130	1001	35	5/10	5/10	28.60	5.31	32.2	1	0
Twenty20	65	18	22	2	2/10	2/10	11.00	7.33	9.0	0	0

IAN SAXELBY

RHB RMF MVP77

FULL NAME: Ian David Saxelby
BORN: May 22, 1989, Nottingham
SQUAD NO: 21
HEIGHT: 6ft 2in
NICKNAME: Sax, Bugler, Piece
EDUCATION: Tuxford School; Oakham School
TEAMS: England Under-19s, Gloucestershire, Gloucestershire 2nd XI, Nottinghamshire 2nd XI
CAREER: First-class: 2008; List A: 2009; T20: 2009

BEST BATTING: 60* Gloucestershire vs Northamptonshire, Northampton, 2009
BEST BOWLING: 6-48 Gloucestershire vs Leicestershire, Cheltenham, 2012

FAMILY TIES? Two uncles [Kevin and Mark] played professionally. Father played England School Boys and 2nd XI
WHO WOULD PLAY YOU IN A FILM OF YOUR LIFE? Rupert Grint
CAREER HIGHLIGHTS? Playing for England U19 and my first professional contract
SUPERSTITIONS? Pads always go on the same way and I sit in the same place if someone is scoring runs
MOST MARKED CHARACTERISTIC? Excellent banter
IF YOU WEREN'T A CRICKETER? Engineer
DESERT ISLAND DISC? Coldplay – X&Y
FAVOURITE TV? Anything David Attenborough-based and Top Gear
CRICKETING HEROES? Richard Hadlee, Clive Rice, Curtly Ambrose, Courtney Walsh, Brian Lara
NON-CRICKETING HEROES? Martin Johnson
ACCOMPLISHMENTS? England U16 rugby and academic grades
FANTASY SLIP CORDON? Keeper: Jeremy Clarkson, 1st Me, 2nd: David Attenborough, 3rd: James Bond
TWITTER FEED: @saxelby21

Batting	Mat	Inns	NO	Runs	HS	Ave	SR	100	50	Ct	St
First-class	38	55	17	626	60*	16.47	42.84	0	1	12	0
List A	17	8	3	30	7*	6.00	55.55	0	0	0	0
Twenty20	20	10	3	24	7*	3.42	60.00	0	0	3	0
Bowling	**Inns**	**Balls**	**Runs**	**Wkts**	**BBI**	**BBM**	**Ave**	**Econ**	**SR**	**5w**	**10**
First-class	38	5515	3264	106	6/48	10/142	30.79	3.55	52.0	3	1
List A	17	604	651	22	4/31	4/31	29.59	6.46	27.4	0	0
Twenty20	20	411	545	23	4/16	4/16	23.69	7.95	17.8	0	0

JOE SAYERS

LHB OB R1

FULL NAME: Joseph John Sayers
BORN: November 5, 1983, Leeds, Yorkshire
SQUAD NO: 22
HEIGHT: 5ft 11in
NICKNAME: Squirrel
EDUCATION: St Mary's RC Comprehensive School; Worcester College; Oxford University
TEAMS: England Lions, England Under-19s, Oxford MCCU, Oxford University, Yorkshire
CAREER: First-class: 2002; List A: 2003; T20: 2005

BEST BATTING: 187 Yorkshire vs Kent, Tunbridge Wells, 2007
BEST BOWLING: 3-15 Yorkshire vs Durham MCCU, Durham University, 2011
COUNTY CAP: 2007

WHO WOULD PLAY YOU IN A FILM OF YOUR LIFE? Ed Harris
CAREER HIGHLIGHTS? Playing for England Lions against Australia at Canterbury in 2009
BEST PLAYER IN COUNTY CRICKET? Marcus Trescothick
TIP FOR THE TOP? Moin Ashraf
IF YOU WEREN'T A CRICKETER? Working in finance in the City perhaps
DESERT ISLAND DISC? Miles Davis – My Funny Valentine
FAVOURITE TV? Grand Designs
CRICKETING HEROES? Mike Atherton, Steve Waugh, Mike Brearley
WHEN YOU RETIRE? Work in corporate banking in Leeds
FANTASY SLIP CORDON? Keeper: Peter Kay, 1st: Michael Parkinson, 2nd: Barack Obama, 3rd: Me, Gully: Dalai Lama
TWITTER FEED: @Joe_Sayers

Batting	Mat	Inns	NO	Runs	HS	Ave	SR	100	50	Ct	St
First-class	102	170	13	5374	187	34.22	38.20	11	28	59	0
List A	28	28	2	516	62	19.84	59.44	0	4	2	0
Twenty20	12	9	0	172	44	19.11	120.27	0	0	2	0
Bowling	**Inns**	**Balls**	**Runs**	**Wkts**	**BBI**	**BBM**	**Ave**	**Econ**	**SR**	**5w**	**10**
First-class	102	361	178	6	3/15	3/15	29.66	2.95	60.1	0	0
List A	28	60	79	1	1/31	1/31	79.00	7.90	60.0	0	0
Twenty20	12	-	-	-	-	-	-	-	-	-	-

OWAIS SHAH

RHB OB R8

FULL NAME: Owais Alam Shah
BORN: October 22, 1978, Karachi, Pakistan
SQUAD NO: 3
HEIGHT: 6ft 1in
NICKNAME: Ace
EDUCATION: Isleworth and Syon School
TEAMS: England, Cape Cobras, Delhi Daredevils, Dhaka Gladiators, England Lions, Essex, Hobart Hurricanes, Kochi Tuskers Kerala, Kolkata Knight Riders, Middlesex, Rajasthan Royals, Wellington
CAREER: Test: 2006; ODI: 2001; T20I: 2007; First-class: 1996; List A: 1995; T20: 2003

BEST BATTING: 203 Middlesex vs Derbyshire, Southgate, 2001
BEST BOWLING: 3-33 Middlesex vs Gloucestershire, Bristol, 1999
COUNTY CAP: 2000 (Middlesex); **BENEFIT YEAR:** 2008 (Middlesex)

CAREER HIGHLIGHTS? My Test debut against India in Mumbai in 2006
OTHER SPORTS FOLLOWED? Football (I like to watch Manchester United)
CRICKETERS PARTICULARLY ADMIRED? Viv Richards, Sachin Tendulkar, Mark Waugh
NOTES: Captained England U19 to victory in the 1997/98 U19 World Cup in South Africa. Cricket Writers' Young Player of the Year for 2001. Made his Test debut in the third Test vs India at Mumbai in March 2006, scoring 88. His first and only ODI century came six years later against India at The Oval (107* from 95 balls). Made 98 from 89 balls in an ODI vs South Africa at Centurion in September 2007. Bought by Delhi Daredevils for IPL 2009, and by Kolkata Knight Riders a year later. Signed for Rajasthan Royals for IPL 2012 following a run to the semi-finals of the Big Bash League with Hobart Hurricanes. Has recently appeared for Dhaka Gladiators in the Bangladesh Premier League

Batting	Mat	Inns	NO	Runs	HS	Ave	SR	100	50	Ct	St
Tests	6	10	0	269	88	26.90	41.90	0	2	2	0
ODIs	71	66	6	1834	107*	30.56	78.67	1	12	21	0
T20Is	17	15	1	347	55*	24.78	122.18	0	1	5	0
First-class	245	417	37	16050	203	42.23		44	78	190	0
List A	355	335	43	10374	134	35.52		14	67	123	0
Twenty20	175	167	40	4345	84	34.21	128.36	0	24	63	0
Bowling	**Inns**	**Balls**	**Runs**	**Wkts**	**BBI**	**BBM**	**Ave**	**Econ**	**SR**	**5w**	**10**
Tests	6	30	31	0	-	-	-	6.20	-	0	0
ODIs	71	193	184	7	3/15	3/15	26.28	5.72	27.5	0	0
T20Is	17	-	-	-	-	-	-	-	-	-	-
First-class	245	2254	1493	26	3/33		57.42	3.97	86.6	0	0
List A	355	924	910	27	4/11	4/11	33.70	5.90	34.2	0	0
Twenty20	175	57	78	5	2/26	2/26	15.60	8.21	11.4	0	0

AJMAL SHAHZAD

RHB RFM MVP69

FULL NAME: Ajmal Shahzad
BORN: July 27, 1985, Huddersfield, Yorkshire
SQUAD NO: 1
HEIGHT: 6ft
NICKNAME: Ajy, AJ
EDUCATION: Bradford Grammar School; Woodhouse Grove School; Bradford University; Leeds Metropolitan University
TEAMS: England, England Lions, Lancashire, Yorkshire
CAREER: Test: 2010; ODI: 2010; T20I: 2010; First-class: 2006; List A: 2004; T20: 2006

BEST BATTING: 88 Yorkshire vs Sussex, Hove, 2009
BEST BOWLING: 5-51 Yorkshire vs Durham, Chester-le-Street, 2010
COUNTY CAP: 2010 (Yorkshire)

WHO WOULD PLAY YOU IN A FILM OF YOUR LIFE? Mackenzie Crook
MOST MARKED CHARACTERISTIC? My hair
TIPS FOR THE TOP? Joe Root, Hassan Azad
DESERT ISLAND DISC? Psy – Gangnam Style
FAVOURITE TV? PhoneShop
BIGGEST DRESSING DOWN YOU'VE RECEIVED? Reprimanded for scuffing the pitch against Warwickshire. Fined £750
CRICKETING HEROES? Imran Khan, Wasim Akram, Waqar Younis, Shoaib Akhtar
ACCOMPLISHMENTS? Qualified for British Olympic badminton squad
WHEN YOU RETIRE? Wedding photographer
TWITTER FEED: @AJShahzad

Batting	Mat	Inns	NO	Runs	HS	Ave	SR	100	50	Ct	St
Tests	1	1	0	5	5	5.00	41.66	0	0	2	0
ODIs	11	8	2	39	9	6.50	65.00	0	0	4	0
T20Is	3	1	1	0	0*	-	0.00	0	0	1	0
First-class	59	77	21	1323	88	23.62	42.87	0	3	9	0
List A	57	37	10	356	59*	13.18	94.17	0	1	14	0
Twenty20	27	18	5	133	20	10.23	127.88	0	0	6	0
Bowling	**Inns**	**Balls**	**Runs**	**Wkts**	**BBI**	**BBM**	**Ave**	**Econ**	**SR**	**5w**	**10**
Tests	1	102	63	4	3/45	4/63	15.75	3.70	25.5	0	0
ODIs	11	588	490	17	3/41	3/41	28.82	5.00	34.5	0	0
T20Is	3	66	97	3	2/38	2/38	32.33	8.81	22.0	0	0
First-class	59	9222	5273	155	5/51	8/121	34.01	3.43	59.4	3	0
List A	57	2613	2296	79	5/51	5/51	29.06	5.27	33.0	1	0
Twenty20	27	540	709	21	3/30	3/30	33.76	7.87	25.7	0	0

JACK SHANTRY LHB LM

FULL NAME: Jack David Shantry
BORN: January 29, 1988, Shrewsbury, Shropshire
SQUAD NO: 11
HEIGHT: 6ft 4in
NICKNAME: Shants, Mincer, Length
EDUCATION: Priory School; Shrewsbury Sixth Form College; Manchester University
TEAMS: Minor Counties U25, Shropshire, Worcestershire, Worcestershire 2nd XI
CAREER: First-class: 2009; List A: 2009; T20: 2010

BEST BATTING: 47* Worcestershire vs Yorkshire, Scarborough, 2011
BEST BOWLING: 5-49 Worcestershire vs Leicestershire, Leicester, 2010

FAMILY TIES? My brother [Adam] played for Northamptonshire, Warwickshire and Glamorgan before retiring due to injury in 2011. Dad played for Gloucestershire in the late 70s. Mum won 'most whites washed in a calendar year' in 1997
CAREER HIGHLIGHTS? Scoring 47* against Yorkshire in 2011. Watching Tim Bresnan fall to the ground in despair after myself and Alan Richardson skilfully dispatched the ball to all parts
SUPERSTITIONS? Never wear underpants on day four. Always seek new, innovative ways to put the batsman off his game. Always try to beat Matt Pardoe to the lunch queue. NB – not always possible
CRICKETING HEROES? Sohail Tanvir, Alastair Cook, James Anderson, Dale Steyn
NON-CRICKETING HEROES? Sam Harris, Christopher Hitchens, Richard Dawkins, the owner of Bushwackers
BEST PLAYER IN COUNTY CRICKET? You can't say yourself can you, it sounds arrogant! I'll say Marcus Trescothick. Or me
FAVOURITE TV? The Office, I'm Alan Partridge, Frozen Planet
DREAM HOLIDAY? The Caribbean
TWITTER FEED: @JackShantry

Batting	Mat	Inns	NO	Runs	HS	Ave	SR	100	50	Ct	St
First-class	27	36	12	282	47*	11.75	43.11	0	0	8	0
List A	40	14	9	71	18	14.20	77.17	0	0	8	0
Twenty20	36	8	5	11	6*	3.66	64.70	0	0	7	0
Bowling	**Inns**	**Balls**	**Runs**	**Wkts**	**BBI**	**BBM**	**Ave**	**Econ**	**SR**	**5w**	**10**
First-class	27	4646	2384	64	5/49	6/111	37.25	3.07	72.5	2	0
List A	40	1629	1631	57	4/32	4/32	28.61	6.00	28.5	0	0
Twenty20	36	760	932	43	4/33	4/33	21.67	7.35	17.6	0	0

ASHLEY SHAW

RHB LFM

FULL NAME: Stuart Ashley Shaw
BORN: April 15, 1991, Crewe, Cheshire
SQUAD NO: 22
HEIGHT: 5ft 10in
NICKNAME: Ash, Reem
EDUCATION: Shavington High School, Crewe
TEAMS: Kent, Kent 2nd XI
CAREER: First-class: 2011; List A: 2011; T20: 2010

BEST BATTING: 22* Kent vs Derbyshire, Canterbury, 2011
BEST BOWLING: 5-118 Kent vs Derbyshire, Canterbury, 2011

CAREER HIGHLIGHTS? Taking five-fer on debut in the County Championship
CRICKETING HEROES? Charl Langeveldt, David Balcombe
NON-CRICKETING HEROES? Floyd Mayweather Jr, Justin Bieber, Jack Wilshere
BEST PLAYER IN COUNTY CRICKET? Darren Stevens
IF YOU WEREN'T A CRICKETER? I'd be laying bricks
FAVOURITE TV? The Only Way Is Essex
FAVOURITE FILM? Adulthood
DREAM HOLIDAY? Malia
GUILTY PLEASURES? Big Brother
SURPRISING FACTS? I have a budgie named Dappy. There's a video of me singing on YouTube!
FANTASY SLIP CORDON? Keeper: David Seaman, 1st: Floyd Mayweather Jr, 2nd: Kelly Rowland, 3rd: Russell Brand, Gully: Me
TWITTER FEED: @stuashshaw

Batting	Mat	Inns	NO	Runs	HS	Ave	SR	100	50	Ct	St
First-class	4	5	3	50	22*	25.00	71.42	0	0	3	0
List A	6	5	3	8	4*	4.00	88.88	0	0	0	0
Twenty20	4	2	2	4	3*	-	133.33	0	0	2	0
Bowling	**Inns**	**Balls**	**Runs**	**Wkts**	**BBI**	**BBM**	**Ave**	**Econ**	**SR**	**5w**	**10**
First-class	4	487	400	11	5/118	6/175	36.36	4.92	44.2	1	0
List A	6	162	184	5	3/26	3/26	36.80	6.81	32.4	0	0
Twenty20	4	60	84	2	1/10	1/10	42.00	8.40	30.0	0	0

JACK SHEPPARD

RHB RFM

FULL NAME: Jack David Sheppard
BORN: December 29, 1992, Salisbury, Wiltshire
SQUAD NO: 27
TEAMS: England Under-19s, Hampshire 2nd XI, Hampshire Cricket Academy, Hampshire Under-17s
CAREER: Yet to make first-team debut

TWITTER FEED: @Jack_Sheppard29
NOTES: Newly signed Hampshire fast bowler who came through the club's academy. Previously impressed at the Bunbury U15 festival

CHARLIE SHRECK — RHB RFM W3

FULL NAME: Charles Edward Shreck
BORN: January 6, 1978, Truro, Cornwall
SQUAD NO: 19
HEIGHT: 6ft 7in
NICKNAME: Shrecker, Ogre, Stoat, Chough
EDUCATION: Truro School
TEAMS: Cornwall, Kent, Marylebone Cricket Club, Nottinghamshire, Wellington
CAREER: First-class: 2003; List A: 1999; T20: 2003

BEST BATTING: 19 Nottinghamshire vs Essex, Chelmsford, 2003
BEST BOWLING: 8-31 Nottinghamshire vs Middlesex, Nottingham, 2006
COUNTY CAP: 2006 (Nottinghamshire)

SUPERSTITIONS? None
CRICKETING HEROES? Viv Richards, Michael Holding, Ian Botham, Rob Key
MOMENT TO FORGET? Being run out off the last ball of the game against Shropshire while walking off – we lost!
FAVOURITE BAND? Catcha Fire or Black Seeds
FAVOURITE FOOD? Anything I've cooked
FAVOURTIE FILM? The Lives Of Others
QUOTE TO LIVE BY? "When I get sad, I stop being sad and be awesome instead. True story"
BEST CRICKETING MOMENT? Watching Andrew Parkin-Coates get Phil Mustard out after kicking the stumps down the wicket in his delivery stride
MOST ANNOYING HABIT? Not keeping the kitchen clean!
MOST LIKELY TO BE? First home on a night out
LOOKALIKE? Anyone with an awesome afro

Batting	Mat	Inns	NO	Runs	HS	Ave	SR	100	50	Ct	St
First-class	113	129	76	269	19	5.07	22.62	0	0	33	0
List A	52	19	12	45	9*	6.42		0	0	13	0
Twenty20	22	6	5	10	6*	10.00	62.50	0	0	4	0
Bowling	**Inns**	**Balls**	**Runs**	**Wkts**	**BBI**	**BBM**	**Ave**	**Econ**	**SR**	**5w**	**10**
First-class	113	22365	11948	399	8/31		29.94	3.20	56.0	21	2
List A	52	2309	2010	63	5/19	5/19	31.90	5.22	36.6	2	0
Twenty20	22	457	597	23	4/22	4/22	25.95	7.83	19.8	0	0

DOMINIC SIBLEY RHB OB

FULL NAME: Dominic Peter Sibley
BORN: September 5, 1995, Epsom, Surrey
SQUAD NO: TBC
HEIGHT: 6ft 3in
NICKNAME: Sibo, Sibbers
EDUCATION: Whitgift School
TEAMS: Surrey 2nd XI, Surrey Under-13s, Surrey Under-14s, Surrey Under-15s, Surrey Under-17s
CAREER: Yet to make first-team debut

FAMILY TIES? My dad played a bit of Surrey age-group cricket
WHO WOULD PLAY YOU IN A FILM OF YOUR LIFE? Colin Farrell
CAREER HIGHLIGHTS? Scoring a hundred for England U19 against South Africa at the age of 17. Getting a summer contract for Surrey on my 17th birthday. Scoring three double hundreds
SUPERSTITIONS? I always take my guard first ball I face of every over
MOST MARKED CHARACTERISTIC? Being lanky, apparently
BEST PLAYER IN COUNTY CRICKET? Marcus Trescothick
TIPS FOR THE TOP? Ben Duckett, Josh Shaw, Jack Scriven and Jack Winslade
IF YOU WEREN'T A CRICKETER? I'd be working harder at school than I am at the moment!
DESERT ISLAND DISC? Tyga – Well Done 3
FAVOURITE TV? Misfits
BIGGEST DRESSING DOWN YOU'VE RECEIVED? After a poor team performance in South Africa on a Surrey Academy tour
CRICKETING HEROES? Jacques Kallis, Sachin Tendulkar and Brian Lara
NON-CRICKETING HEROES? Muhammad Ali
ACCOMPLISHMENTS? I played a bit of rugby for Harlequins at age-group level. National independent school champions for football at Whitgift School
WHEN YOU RETIRE? I'd like to be a coach or a commentator
SURPRISING FACT? I don't like chocolate
FANTASY SLIP CORDON? Keeper: Mario Balotelli, 1st: Cheryl Cole, 2nd: Muhammad Ali, 3rd: Kim Kardashian, 4th: Myself, Gully: James Corden
TWITTER FEED: @DomSibley

RYAN SIDEBOTTOM LHB LFM W3

FULL NAME: Ryan Jay Sidebottom
BORN: January 15, 1978, Huddersfield, Yorkshire
SQUAD NO: 11
HEIGHT: 6ft 4in
NICKNAME: Siddy
EDUCATION: King James' Grammar School, Almondbury
TEAMS: England, Nottinghamshire, Yorkshire
CAREER: Test: 2001; ODI: 2001; T20I: 2007; First-class: 1997; List A: 1997; T20: 2003

BEST BATTING: 61 Yorkshire vs Worcestershire, Worcester, 2011
BEST BOWLING: 7-37 Yorkshire vs Somerset, Leeds, 2011
COUNTY CAPS: 2000 (Yorkshire); 2004 (Nottinghamshire); **BENEFIT YEAR:** 2010 (Nottinghamshire)

FAMILY TIES? My father [Arnie] played for Yorkshire and England
CAREER HIGHLIGHTS? Test hat-trick against New Zealand, World T20 winner in 2010
BEST PLAYER IN COUNTY CRICKET? Marcus Trescothick
TIPS FOR THE TOP? Jonny Bairstow, Joe Root
IF YOU WEREN'T A CRICKETER? I'd have been a footballer or maybe a landscape gardener
FAVOURITE TV? Game Of Thrones
FAVOURITE FILM? The Wolfman
SURPRISING SKILL? Canvas drawing
SURPRISING FACTS? I love birdwatching and collecting Steiff bears
TWITTER FEED: @RyanSidebottom

Batting	Mat	Inns	NO	Runs	HS	Ave	SR	100	50	Ct	St
Tests	22	31	11	313	31	15.65	34.66	0	0	5	0
ODIs	25	18	8	133	24	13.30	68.55	0	0	6	0
T20Is	18	1	1	5	5*	-	125.00	0	0	5	0
First-class	174	219	67	2145	61	14.11		0	3	52	0
List A	184	88	39	542	32	11.06		0	0	39	0
Twenty20	69	20	14	124	17*	20.66	106.89	0	0	22	0
Bowling	**Inns**	**Balls**	**Runs**	**Wkts**	**BBI**	**BBM**	**Ave**	**Econ**	**SR**	**5w**	**10**
Tests	22	4812	2231	79	7/47	10/139	28.24	2.78	60.9	5	1
ODIs	25	1277	1039	29	3/19	3/19	35.82	4.88	44.0	0	0
T20Is	18	367	437	23	3/16	3/16	19.00	7.14	15.9	0	0
First-class	174	30492	14268	561	7/37		25.43	2.80	54.3	24	3
List A	184	8130	6020	195	6/40	6/40	30.87	4.44	41.6	2	0
Twenty20	69	1457	1702	79	4/25	4/25	21.54	7.00	18.4	0	0

JOHN SIMPSON

LHB WK

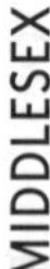

FULL NAME: John Andrew Simpson
BORN: July 13, 1988, Bury, Lancashire
SQUAD NO: 20
HEIGHT: 5ft 11in
NICKNAME: Simmo
EDUCATION: St Gabriel's RC High School
TEAMS: England Under-19s, Lancashire, Lancashire 2nd XI, Marylebone Cricket Club, Marylebone Cricket Club Young Cricketers, Middlesex, Middlesex 2nd XI
CAREER: First-class: 2009; List A: 2009; T20: 2009

BEST BATTING: 143 Middlesex vs Surrey, Lord's, 2011
COUNTY CAP: 2011

FAMILY TIES? My dad played Lancashire 2nd XI, England Amateurs and holds records in both Lancashire and Central Lancashire league cricket. My granddad and uncle played league cricket and my grandpa played in the Army. My cousin Ashley is on Lancashire's Academy and my other cousin Dominic is in Lancashire's age-group system
CAREER HIGHLIGHTS? Being capped by Middlesex in 2011, scoring my maiden first-class hundred for Middlesex and also winning Division Two of the Championship in 2011
MOST MARKED CHARACTERISTIC? Hard worker and very driven
BEST PLAYER IN COUNTY CRICKET? Marcus Trescothick
TIPS FOR THE TOP? Tom Helm, Ben Stokes
DESERT ISLAND DISC? Swedish House Mafia – Until One
FAVOURITE TV? The Simpsons, Family Guy, The Cleveland Show, Mock The Week, Take Me Out
SURPRISING FACT? My great-granddad and granddad both played rugby league for Great Britain and my dad played lacrosse for England
FANTASY SLIP CORDON? Keeper: Karl Pilkington, 1st: Charlie Sheen, 2nd: Candice Swanepoel, 3rd: Floyd Mayweather, Golf: Natalie Portman
TWITTER FEED: @JohnSimpson_88

Batting	Mat	Inns	NO	Runs	HS	Ave	SR	100	50	Ct	St
First-class	51	80	10	2039	143	29.12	47.64	2	10	157	8
List A	36	23	3	418	82	20.90	79.61	0	1	23	4
Twenty20	27	21	1	302	60*	15.10	117.96	0	1	13	6
Bowling	**Inns**	**Balls**	**Runs**	**Wkts**	**BBI**	**BBM**	**Ave**	**Econ**	**SR**	**5w**	**10**
First-class	51	-	-	-	-	-	-	-	-	-	-
List A	36	-	-	-	-	-	-	-	-	-	-
Twenty20	27	-	-	-	-	-	-	-	-	-	-

RAMMY SINGH RHB OB

FULL NAME: Ramanpreet Singh
BORN: February 19, 1993, Newcastle upon Tyne, Northumberland
SQUAD NO: 11
HEIGHT: 5ft 7in
NICKNAME: Loose Man
EDUCATION: Gosforth High School
TEAMS: Durham, Durham 2nd XI, England Under-19s, Northumberland
CAREER: First-class: 2012

BEST BATTING: 22 Durham vs Australia A, Chester-le-Street, 2012

WHY CRICKET? My dad's passion for the game
CAREER HIGHLIGHTS? Representing England U19, scoring back-to-back hundreds for the Durham Academy in 2011
CRICKETING HEROES? Sachin Tendulkar, Viv Richards, MS Dhoni
NON-CRICKETING HEROES? Bhagat Singh, Mahatma Gandhi, Manny Pacquiao
BEST PLAYER IN COUNTY CRICKET? Marcus Trescothick
TIPS FOR THE TOP? Ben Stokes, Jonny Bairstow
IF YOU WEREN'T A CRICKETER? Lawyer
FAVOURITE FILM? The Shawshank Redemption
FAVOURITE BOOK? Wolf Brother
DREAM HOLIDAY? Marbella
ACCOMPLISHMENTS? Charity work in India
GUILTY PLEASURES? The casino
SURPRISING FACT? I have a deep hatred for tomatoes

Batting	Mat	Inns	NO	Runs	HS	Ave	SR	100	50	Ct	St
First-class	1	2	0	34	22	17.00	73.91	0	0	1	0
Bowling	**Inns**	**Balls**	**Runs**	**Wkts**	**BBI**	**BBM**	**Ave**	**Econ**	**SR**	**5w**	**10**
First-class	1	-	-	-	-	-	-	-	-	-	-

BEN SLATER LHB OB

FULL NAME: Benjamin Thomas Slater
BORN: August 26, 1991, Chesterfield, Derbyshire
SQUAD NO: 26
HEIGHT: 5ft 11in
NICKNAME: Slats, Slatsy
EDUCATION: Netherthorpe School and Netherthorpe School Sixth Form; Leeds Metropolitan University
TEAMS: Leeds/Bradford UCCE, Derbyshire, Derbyshire 2nd XI, Southern Rocks
CAREER: First-class: 2012; List A: 2012; T20: 2012

BEST BATTING: 89 Southern Rocks vs Mashonaland Eagles, Harare, 2012

FAMILY TIES? Both my dad and granddad have played league cricket. My granddad was a league legend and played in successful Derbyshire Over 50 sides
WHO WOULD PLAY YOU IN A FILM OF YOUR LIFE? Ryan Gosling
CAREER HIGHLIGHTS? Scoring 100 not out for Leeds/Bradford UCCE against Warwickshire 1st XI. Playing for the Southern Rocks franchise in Zimbabwe and making my List A and T20 debuts whilst out there
BEST PLAYER IN COUNTY CRICKET? Nick Compton, Marcus Trescothick
TIPS FOR THE TOP? Joe Root, Dan Hodgson, Joe Leach, Alex Hughes
DESERT ISLAND DISC? 5ive – The Greatest Hits
FAVOURITE TV? Hawaii Five-O, Made In Chelsea, Geordie Shore
BIGGEST DRESSING DOWN YOU'VE RECEIVED? Every time we lost a game for Leeds/Bradford UCCE we used to get a big dressing down from coach Andrew Lawson
CRICKETING HEROES? Brian Lara, Alastair Cook
ACCOMPLISHMENTS? Getting a degree from Leeds Metropolitan
WHEN YOU RETIRE? I'd like to become a budding entrepreneur
FANTASY SLIP CORDON? Keeper: Chris Durham, 1st: Jack Whitehall, 2nd: David Beckham, 3rd: Tiger Woods, Gully: Kobe Bryant
TWITTER FEED: @BennySlats

Batting	Mat	Inns	NO	Runs	HS	Ave	SR	100	50	Ct	St
First-class	6	11	0	249	89	22.63	36.77	0	1	1	0
List A	5	4	0	98	46	24.50	52.40	0	0	1	0
Twenty20	4	4	0	138	57	34.50	105.34	0	1	0	0
Bowling	**Inns**	**Balls**	**Runs**	**Wkts**	**BBI**	**BBM**	**Ave**	**Econ**	**SR**	**5w**	**10**
First-class	6	9	28	0	-	-	-	18.66	-	0	0
List A	5	-	-	-	-	-	-	-	-	-	-
Twenty20	4	-	-	-	-	-	-	-	-	-	-

GRAEME SMITH LHB OB

FULL NAME: Graeme Craig Smith
BORN: February 1, 1981, Johannesburg, South Africa
SQUAD NO: TBC
HEIGHT: 6ft 3in
NICKNAME: Biff
TEAMS: South Africa, Africa XI, Cape Cobras, Gauteng, Hampshire Cricket Board, ICC World XI, Pune Warriors, Rajasthan Royals, Somerset, Surrey, Western Province
CAREER: Test: 2002; ODI: 2002; T20I: 2005; First-class: 2000; List A: 2000; T20: 2004

BEST BATTING: 311 Somerset vs Leicestershire, Taunton, 2005
BEST BOWLING: 2-145 South Africa vs West Indies, St John's, 2005
COUNTY CAP: 2005 (Somerset)

NOTES: Became South Africa captain aged just 22. Made back-to-back double hundreds in his 11th and 12th Tests. Led South Africa to their first series victory in Australia in 2009. Led the side to the No.1 Test ranking by beating England 2-0 in 2012. Reached 100 Tests as captain in February, against Pakistan at The Wanderers. Appointed as Surrey skipper on a three-year contract in November 2012. Will be available for all Surrey matches outside of international commitments

Batting	Mat	Inns	NO	Runs	HS	Ave	SR	100	50	Ct	St
Tests	110	192	12	8753	277	48.62	59.61	26	37	160	0
ODIs	189	186	10	6887	141	39.13	81.32	10	47	100	0
T20Is	33	33	2	982	89*	31.67	127.53	0	5	18	0
First-class	150	258	17	12021	311	49.87		35	48	218	0
List A	250	244	15	9155	141	39.97		14	66	130	0
Twenty20	81	81	6	2282	105	30.42	123.55	1	11	35	0
Bowling	**Inns**	**Balls**	**Runs**	**Wkts**	**BBI**	**BBM**	**Ave**	**Econ**	**SR**	**5w**	**10**
Tests	110	1418	885	8	2/145	2/145	110.62	3.74	177.2	0	0
ODIs	189	1026	951	18	3/30	3/30	52.83	5.56	57.0	0	0
T20Is	33	24	57	0	-	-	-	14.25	-	0	0
First-class	150	1786	1132	11	2/145		102.90	3.80	162.3	0	0
List A	250	1968	1796	47	3/30	3/30	38.21	5.47	41.8	0	0
Twenty20	81	96	148	4	3/23	3/23	37.00	9.25	24.0	0	0

GREG SMITH RHB RMF/OB

ESSEX

FULL NAME: Gregory Marc Smith
BORN: April 20, 1983, Johannesburg, South Africa
SQUAD NO: 83
HEIGHT: 5ft 9in
NICKNAME: Smudge
EDUCATION: St Stithians College; Future Fitness
TEAMS: Derbyshire, Derbyshire 2nd XI, Essex, Essex 2nd XI, Griqualand West, Mountaineers, South Africa Under-19s
CAREER: First-class: 2003; List A: 2003; T20: 2007

BEST BATTING: 165* Derbyshire vs Glamorgan, Derby, 2010
BEST BOWLING: 5-54 Derbyshire vs Northamptonshire, Chesterfield, 2010
COUNTY CAP: 2009 (Derbyshire)

FAMILY TIES? My dad used to be the financial advisor for the South African Cricket Board
WHO WOULD PLAY YOU IN A FILM OF YOUR LIFE? Ryan Gosling
CAREER HIGHLIGHTS? Getting my maiden first-class hundred and also getting to the final of the U19 World Cup in New Zealand
BEST PLAYER IN COUNTY CRICKET? Marcus Trescothick
TIPS FOR THE TOP? Reece Topley and Ben Foakes
IF YOU WEREN'T A CRICKETER? I would have hoped I'd have made it in the tennis world
DESERT ISLAND DISC? The Killers
CRICKETING HEROES? Jacques Kallis, Sachin Tendulkar
NON-CRICKETING HEROES? Roger Federer, Nelson Mandela
ACCOMPLISHMENTS? I'm a qualified gym instructor and nutritional advisor
WHEN YOU RETIRE? I'd like to stay in cricket and either coach or be part of the fitness and training regime of a club
FANTASY SLIP CORDON? Keeper: Ricky Gervais, 1st: Roger Federer, 2nd: Simon Pilkington, 3rd: Ari Gold (Entourage), Gully: Bear Grylls
TWITTER FEED: @smithyg83

Batting	Mat	Inns	NO	Runs	HS	Ave	SR	100	50	Ct	St
First-class	97	162	13	4617	165*	30.98	58.38	6	29	31	0
List A	88	87	7	1787	88	22.33	83.07	0	7	33	0
Twenty20	63	59	2	1162	100*	20.38	112.92	1	4	23	0
Bowling	**Inns**	**Balls**	**Runs**	**Wkts**	**BBI**	**BBM**	**Ave**	**Econ**	**SR**	**5w**	**10**
First-class	97	10454	5636	152	5/54		37.07	3.23	68.7	2	0
List A	88	2491	2339	67	4/53	4/53	34.91	5.63	37.1	0	0
Twenty20	63	718	928	41	5/17	5/17	22.63	7.75	17.5	2	0

GREG SMITH RHB LB

FULL NAME: Greg Phillip Smith
BORN: November 16, 1988, Leicester
SQUAD NO: 14
HEIGHT: 5ft 11in
EDUCATION: Oundle School; Durham University
TEAMS: Durham MCCU, Durham UCCE, England Under-19s, Leicestershire, Leicestershire 2nd XI
CAREER: First-class: 2008; List A: 2008; T20: 2012

BEST BATTING: 158* Leicestershire vs Gloucestershire, Leicester, 2010
BEST BOWLING: 1-64 Leicestershire vs Gloucestershire, Leicester, 2008

FAMILY TIES? My step-granddad [Peter Kelland] played for Sussex
WHO WOULD PLAY YOU IN A FILM OF YOUR LIFE? Gerard Butler
CAREER HIGHLIGHTS? Back-to-back Championship hundreds in 2010 and the T20 Cup and Champions League in 2011
MOST MARKED CHARACTERISTIC? I'm unpredictable
BEST PLAYER IN COUNTY CRICKET? Chris Woakes
TIP FOR THE TOP? Shiv Thakor
IF YOU WEREN'T A CRICKETER? I'd be a gunslinger day trader
DESERT ISLAND DISC? Asaf Avidan
FAVOURITE TV? Made In Chelsea
BIGGEST DRESSING DOWN YOU'VE RECEIVED? Foxy Fowler started a meeting with: "This is not a conversation. I'm going to say a few things and you're going to listen. You're not required to speak." Then gave me the hairdryer treatment
CRICKETING HEROES? Aravinda de Silva, David Gower
NON-CRICKETING HEROES? Olivier Giroud
SURPRISING FACT? I've created my own breed of apple
TWITTER FEED: @greg_smith14

Batting	Mat	Inns	NO	Runs	HS	Ave	SR	100	50	Ct	St
First-class	52	97	7	2596	158*	28.84	47.65	5	11	39	0
List A	21	21	2	321	58	16.89	66.45	0	1	9	0
Twenty20	8	8	0	115	23	14.37	115.00	0	0	1	0
Bowling	**Inns**	**Balls**	**Runs**	**Wkts**	**BBI**	**BBM**	**Ave**	**Econ**	**SR**	**5w**	**10**
First-class	52	36	73	1	1/64	1/64	73.00	12.16	36.0	0	0
List A	21	-	-	-	-	-	-	-	-	-	-
Twenty20	8	-	-	-	-	-	-	-	-	-	-

RUAIDHRI SMITH

RHB RM

FULL NAME: Ruaidhri Alexander James Smith
BORN: August 5, 1994, Glasgow, Lanarkshire
SQUAD NO: 20
TEAMS: Glamorgan 2nd XI, Scotland Under-19s, Wales Minor Counties
CAREER: Yet to make first-team debut

NOTES: Newly signed by Glamorgan on a development contract after coming through the youth set-up. Made a century (145* from 126 balls with 24 boundaries) on debut for Scotland U19 in March 2012 after they discovered he was born in Scotland. The allrounder was the fourth top wicket-taker at the U19 World Cup last August

TOM SMITH LHB RM

FULL NAME: Thomas Christopher Smith
BORN: December 26, 1985, Liverpool
SQUAD NO: 24
HEIGHT: 6ft 3in
NICKNAME: Smudger
EDUCATION: Parklands High School; Runshaw College
TEAMS: England Under-19s, Lancashire, Lancashire 2nd XI, Matabeleland Tuskers
CAREER: First-class: 2005; List A: 2005; T20: 2006

BEST BATTING: 128 Lancashire vs Hampshire, Southampton, 2010
BEST BOWLING: 6-46 Lancashire vs Yorkshire, Manchester, 2009
COUNTY CAP: 2010

CAREER HIGHLIGHTS? Winning the County Championship in 2011
CRICKETING HEROES? Brian Lara, Andrew Flintoff
BEST PLAYER IN COUNTY CRICKET? Marcus Trescothick
TIP FOR THE TOP? Jordan Clark
WHEN RAIN STOPS PLAY? I listen to music
FAVOURITE TV? Entourage
FAVOURITE FILM? Wedding Crashers
DREAM HOLIDAY? Thailand
GUILTY PLEASURES? Curry
TWITTER FEED: @Tcp24

Batting	Mat	Inns	NO	Runs	HS	Ave	SR	100	50	Ct	St
First-class	76	110	19	2454	128	26.96	45.63	3	13	82	0
List A	56	46	8	1155	117	30.39	89.12	2	7	15	0
Twenty20	69	63	12	1550	92*	30.39	116.71	0	8	30	0
Bowling	**Inns**	**Balls**	**Runs**	**Wkts**	**BBI**	**BBM**	**Ave**	**Econ**	**SR**	**5w**	**10**
First-class	76	9433	4831	150	6/46		32.20	3.07	62.8	2	0
List A	56	2066	1798	67	4/48	4/48	26.83	5.22	30.8	0	0
Twenty20	69	936	1211	38	3/12	3/12	31.86	7.76	24.6	0	0

TOM SMITH

RHB SLA

FULL NAME: Thomas Michael John Smith
BORN: August 29, 1987, Eastbourne, Sussex
SQUAD NO: 11
HEIGHT: 5ft 9in
NICKNAME: Smudge, Mooge
EDUCATION: Seaford Head Community College; Sussex Downs College
TEAMS: Middlesex, Middlesex 2nd XI, Surrey, Sussex, Sussex 2nd XI
CAREER: First-class: 2007; List A: 2006; T20: 2007

BEST BATTING: 33 Middlesex vs Derbyshire, Derby, 2010
BEST BOWLING: 3-38 Middlesex vs Derbyshire, Lord's, 2011

WHO WOULD PLAY YOU IN A FILM OF YOUR LIFE? Josh Holloway (Sawyer from Lost)
CAREER HIGHLIGHTS? Taking 5-24 in a T20 game at Lord's vs Kent
SUPERSTITIONS? No real superstitions but I like to be clean-shaven on day one of a match
MOST MARKED CHARACTERISTIC? My monotone voice
BEST PLAYER IN COUNTY CRICKET? Andrew Hodd (Yorkshire)
TIPS FOR THE TOP? Sam Robson and Tom Helm
IF YOU WEREN'T A CRICKETER? I qualified as a plumber after school, so I guess I would be doing that – not that I was very good at it!
FAVOURITE TV? Modern Family, Homeland, Silent Witness, Waking The Dead
BIGGEST DRESSING DOWN YOU'VE RECEIVED? Chris Adams gave me one once when he was captain of Sussex for giving away too many singles in the field!
CRICKETING HEROES? Shane Warne, Saqlain Mushtaq and Dan Vettori
WHEN YOU RETIRE? I completed my cricket coaching Level 3 last winter, so either a coaching job or I have also completed some work experience in the City for an investment management company, so that might be an avenue to explore after cricket
FANTASY SLIP CORDON? Keeper: Jack Whitehall, 1st: Me, 2nd: Shane Warne, 3rd: Sofia Vergara, Gully: Tiger Woods

Batting	Mat	Inns	NO	Runs	HS	Ave	SR	100	50	Ct	St
First-class	11	18	1	196	33	11.52	29.92	0	0	3	0
List A	33	12	1	176	65	16.00	74.26	0	1	16	0
Twenty20	42	21	15	146	36*	24.33	113.17	0	0	17	0
Bowling	**Inns**	**Balls**	**Runs**	**Wkts**	**BBI**	**BBM**	**Ave**	**Econ**	**SR**	**5w**	**10**
First-class	11	1369	851	12	3/38	4/107	70.91	3.72	114.0	0	0
List A	33	1122	1032	24	3/26	3/26	43.00	5.51	46.7	0	0
Twenty20	42	767	970	38	5/24	5/24	25.52	7.58	20.1	1	0

WILL SMITH RHB OB

FULL NAME: William Rew Smith
BORN: September 28, 1982, Luton, Bedfordshire
SQUAD NO: 2
HEIGHT: 5ft 9in
NICKNAME: Smudger, Jiggy
EDUCATION: Bedford School; Durham University
TEAMS: Bedfordshire, British Universities, Durham, Nottinghamshire
CAREER: First-class: 2002; List A: 2002; T20: 2003

BEST BATTING: 201* Durham vs Surrey, Guildford, 2008
BEST BOWLING: 3-34 Durham UCCE vs Leicestershire, Leicester, 2005

CAREER HIGHLIGHTS? Winning the County Championship with Durham 2008 and 2009, being Player of the Year in 2008 and captaining the club in 2009
CRICKETING HEROES? Mike Atherton, Graeme Fowler, Dale Benkenstein
TIPS FOR THE TOP? Scott Borthwick, Ben Stokes, Jos Buttler, Jonny Bairstow
IF YOU WEREN'T A CRICKETER? Professional gambler, pundit or journalist
WHEN RAIN STOPS PLAY? Relaxing, watching whatever sport is on TV
FAVOURITE TV? QI
FAVOURITE FILM? Top Gun
FAVOURITE BOOK? Any biography about great people
SURPRISING FACTS? I have a tattoo, I was a Latin scholar at school, I'm the best surfer yet to take up the sport...
FANTASY SLIP CORDON? Keeper: Myself (hugely underrated as a keeper), 1st: AP McCoy (the personification of dedication and bravery), 2nd: Stephen Fry (the wittiest, most intelligent man alive), 3rd: Bobby Robson (would have loved to meet him, don't know of one person who doesn't hold him in the highest regard), Gully: Inspector Gadget (he can use his go-go gadget arms to catch everything while the rest of us pay no attention)
TWITTER FEED: @WillSmith_2

Batting	Mat	Inns	NO	Runs	HS	Ave	SR	100	50	Ct	St
First-class	105	174	9	5115	201*	31.00	43.35	12	17	52	0
List A	79	70	5	1617	103	24.87	69.69	1	12	30	0
Twenty20	59	47	11	653	55	18.13	117.02	0	3	35	0
Bowling	**Inns**	**Balls**	**Runs**	**Wkts**	**BBI**	**BBM**	**Ave**	**Econ**	**SR**	**5w**	**10**
First-class	105	803	592	9	3/34		65.77	4.42	89.2	0	0
List A	79	95	96	4	2/22	2/22	24.00	6.06	23.7	0	0
Twenty20	59	95	132	1	1/31	1/31	132.00	8.33	95.0	0	0

VIKRAM SOLANKI

RHB OB R6 MVP92

FULL NAME: Vikram Singh Solanki
BORN: April 1, 1976, Udaipur, Rajasthan, India
SQUAD NO: TBC
HEIGHT: 6ft
NICKNAME: Vik
EDUCATION: Merridale Primary School; Regis School, Wolverhampton; Open University
TEAMS: England, Rajasthan, Worcestershire
CAREER: ODI: 2000; T20I: 2005; First-class: 1995; List A: 1993; T20: 2004

BEST BATTING: 270 Worcestershire vs Gloucestershire, Cheltenham, 2008
BEST BOWLING: 5-40 Worcestershire vs Middlesex, Lord's, 2004
COUNTY CAP: 1998 (Worcestershire); BENEFIT YEAR: 2007 (Worcestershire)

FAMILY TIES? My father played in India and my brother is a keen club cricketer
CAREER HIGHLIGHTS? Playing for England and captaining Worcestershire
SUPERSTITIONS? Many habits, but no superstitions
CRICKETING HEROES? Sachin Tendulkar, Graeme Hick, Wasim Akram
NON-CRICKETING HEROES? My father
BEST PLAYER IN COUNTY CRICKET? Marcus Trescothick
WHEN RAIN STOPS PLAY? You'll find me reading
FAVOURITE TV? House, Human Planet
FAVOURITE FILM? Gladiator
FAVOURITE BOOK? The Alchemist by Paulo Coelho
DREAM HOLIDAY? India, completing my Open University degree

Batting	Mat	Inns	NO	Runs	HS	Ave	SR	100	50	Ct	St
ODIs	51	46	5	1097	106	26.75	72.93	2	5	16	0
T20Is	3	3	0	76	43	25.33	124.59	0	0	3	0
First-class	297	501	32	16743	270	35.69		31	88	317	0
List A	382	353	29	10465	164*	32.29		15	60	151	0
Twenty20	67	65	1	1548	100	24.18	121.79	1	9	36	0
Bowling	**Inns**	**Balls**	**Runs**	**Wkts**	**BBI**	**BBM**	**Ave**	**Econ**	**SR**	**5w**	**10**
ODIs	51	111	105	1	1/17	1/17	105.00	5.67	111.0	0	0
T20Is	3	-	-	-	-	-	-	-	-	-	-
First-class	297	7105	4120	86	5/40		47.90	3.47	82.6	4	1
List A	382	1122	987	28	4/14	4/14	35.25	5.27	40.0	0	0
Twenty20	67	96	145	5	1/6	1/6	29.00	9.06	19.2	0	0

MATTHEW SPRIEGEL LHB OB

FULL NAME: Matthew Neil William Spriegel
BORN: March 4, 1987, Epsom, Surrey
SQUAD NO: 28
HEIGHT: 6ft 3in
NICKNAME: Spriegs
EDUCATION: Whitgift School; Loughborough University
TEAMS: Loughborough MCCU, Surrey, Surrey 2nd XI
CAREER: First-class: 2007; List A: 2008; T20: 2008

BEST BATTING: 108* Surrey vs Bangladeshis, The Oval, 2010
BEST BOWLING: 2-28 Surrey vs Hampshire, The Oval, 2008

WHO WOULD PLAY YOU IN A FILM OF YOUR LIFE? Sacha Baron Cohen
CAREER HIGHLIGHTS? Winning the CB40 with Surrey in 2011. Making my County Championship debut at my old school. Maiden first-class hundred
MOST MARKED CHARACTERISTIC? My monotonous voice
BEST PLAYER IN COUNTY CRICKET? Marcus Trescothick
TIPS FOR THE TOP? Jason Roy, Stuart Meaker, Brian Williams
DESERT ISLAND DISC? Otto Knows – Million Voices
FAVOURITE TV? Entourage, The Office
BIGGEST DRESSING DOWN YOU'VE RECEIVED? From a 2nd XI coach when I pulled the seat from under him when he was sitting down in front of everyone at lunch. He was not amused
CRICKETING HEROES? Alec Stewart, Graham Thorpe, Mark Butcher
NON-CRICKETING HEROES? Jonny Wilkinson
SURPRISING FACT? I got an A* in Japanese at GCSE
TWITTER FEED: @Spriegs

Batting	Mat	Inns	NO	Runs	HS	Ave	SR	100	50	Ct	St
First-class	35	57	3	1310	108*	24.25	42.40	3	3	24	0
List A	61	54	17	1438	86	38.86	84.19	0	10	29	0
Twenty20	45	34	13	365	53*	17.38	91.93	0	1	14	0
Bowling	**Inns**	**Balls**	**Runs**	**Wkts**	**BBI**	**BBM**	**Ave**	**Econ**	**SR**	**5w**	**10**
First-class	35	1429	859	19	2/28	2/28	45.21	3.60	75.2	0	0
List A	61	1643	1431	40	3/39	3/39	35.77	5.22	41.0	0	0
Twenty20	45	636	790	26	4/33	4/33	30.38	7.45	24.4	0	0

DARREN STEVENS RHB RM R2 MVP2

FULL NAME: Darren Ian Stevens
BORN: April 30, 1976, Leicester
SQUAD NO: 3
HEIGHT: 5ft 11in
NICKNAME: Stevo, Daz, Hoover, Steve
EDUCATION: John Cleveland College; Charles Keene College
TEAMS: Dhaka Gladiators, England Lions, Kent, Leicestershire, Otago
CAREER: First-class: 1997; List A: 1997; T20: 2003

BEST BATTING: 208 Kent vs Middlesex, Canterbury, 2009
BEST BOWLING: 7-21 Kent vs Surrey, Canterbury, 2011
COUNTY CAPS: 2002 (Leicestershire); 2005 (Kent)

FAMILY TIES? Dad and granddad played local club cricket in Leicestershire
WHO WOULD PLAY YOU IN A FILM OF YOUR LIFE? Mark Wahlberg
CAREER HIGHLIGHTS? Winning the T20 for Leicester in 2004, winning the T20 for Kent in 2007, winning the T20 for the Dhaka Gladiators in 2012
SUPERSTITIONS? I put my left pad on first
BEST PLAYER IN COUNTY CRICKET? Marcus Trescothick
TIPS FOR THE TOP? Sam Northeast, Joshua Cobb, Sam Billings, Anamul Haque Bijoy
IF YOU WEREN'T A CRICKETER? I wouldn't like to think!
DESERT ISLAND DISC? Snow Patrol – Eyes Open
CRICKETING HEROES? Sir Isaac Vivian Alexander Richards
NON-CRICKETING HEROES? George Digweed
WHEN YOU RETIRE? I'd like to buy and sell houses, maybe coach, or the ultimate would be to play professional golf
FANTASY SLIP CORDON? Keeper: Cheryl Tweedy, 1st: Me, 2nd: Angelina Jolie, 3rd: Keith Lemon, 4th: George Digweed, Gully: Alan 'Lord' Sugar
TWITTER FEED: @Stevo208

Batting	Mat	Inns	NO	Runs	HS	Ave	SR	100	50	Ct	St
First-class	202	327	20	10274	208	33.46		24	48	148	0
List A	247	229	25	6223	133	30.50		4	41	96	0
Twenty20	138	129	35	2811	77	29.90	132.97	0	12	48	0
Bowling	Inns	Balls	Runs	Wkts	BBI	BBM	Ave	Econ	SR	5w	10
First-class	202	10343	5109	170	7/21		30.05	2.96	60.8	3	1
List A	247	3210	2657	84	5/32	5/32	31.63	4.96	38.2	2	0
Twenty20	138	1092	1357	58	4/14	4/14	23.39	7.45	18.8	0	0

PAUL STIRLING RHB OB

FULL NAME: Paul Robert Stirling
BORN: September 3, 1990, Belfast
SQUAD NO: 39
HEIGHT: 5ft 10in
NICKNAME: The Hoover
EDUCATION: Belfast High School
TEAMS: Ireland, Ireland Under-13s, Ireland Under-15s, Ireland Under-17s, Ireland Under-19s, Ireland Under-23s, Middlesex, Sylhet Royals
CAREER: ODI: 2008; T20I: 2009; First-class: 2008; List A: 2008; T20: 2008

BEST BATTING: 107 Ireland vs Canada, Dublin, 2011
BEST BOWLING: 2-45 Ireland vs Jamaica, Spanish Town, 2010

FAMILY TIES? My brother [Richard] played in the U19 World Cup in Sri Lanka with Eoin Morgan as the skipper
WHO WOULD PLAY YOU IN A FILM OF YOUR LIFE? James Corden
CAREER HIGHLIGHTS? Scoring a hundred at Lord's
SUPERSTITIONS? Left pad before right and a Red Bull!
MOST MARKED CHARACTERISTIC? Terror accent
BEST PLAYER IN COUNTY CRICKET? Ed Joyce
TIP FOR THE TOP? Adam Rossington
DESERT ISLAND DISC? Nizlopi – JCB Song
CRICKETING HEROES? Ricky Ponting and Damien Martyn
SURPRISING FACT? I'm the only player to score three ODI centuries before turning 20
FANTASY SLIP CORDON? Keeper (standing up): Charles Colvile, 1st-5th: One Direction, Gully: Joey Barton, 2nd Gully: John Terry, Bowler: Dale Steyn
TWITTER FEED: @stirlo90

Batting	Mat	Inns	NO	Runs	HS	Ave	SR	100	50	Ct	St
ODIs	38	38	1	1448	177	39.13	96.21	4	6	20	0
T20Is	19	19	3	415	79	25.93	120.28	0	3	4	0
First-class	14	22	0	589	107	26.77	62.72	2	2	11	0
List A	78	77	3	2589	177	34.98	96.78	6	11	37	0
Twenty20	65	65	6	1536	82*	26.03	137.38	0	10	16	0
Bowling	**Inns**	**Balls**	**Runs**	**Wkts**	**BBI**	**BBM**	**Ave**	**Econ**	**SR**	**5w**	**10**
ODIs	38	937	692	20	4/11	4/11	34.60	4.43	46.8	0	0
T20Is	19	216	246	10	3/21	3/21	24.60	6.83	21.6	0	0
First-class	14	381	214	4	2/45	3/92	53.50	3.37	95.2	0	0
List A	78	1339	1064	31	4/11	4/11	34.32	4.76	43.1	0	0
Twenty20	65	534	611	23	3/20	3/20	26.56	6.86	23.2	0	0

BEN STOKES

LHB RM MVP11

FULL NAME: Benjamin Andrew Stokes
BORN: June 4, 1991, Christchurch, New Zealand
SQUAD NO: 38
HEIGHT: 6ft 1in
NICKNAME: Stokesy, Beast
EDUCATION: Cockermouth School
TEAMS: England, Durham, Durham 2nd XI, England Lions, England Under-19s
CAREER: ODI: 2011; T20I: 2011; First-class: 2010; List A: 2009; T20: 2010

BEST BATTING: 185 Durham vs Lancashire, Chester-le-Street, 2011
BEST BOWLING: 6-68 Durham vs Hampshire, Southampton, 2011

CAREER HIGHLIGHTS? Making my debut for England
SUPERSTITIONS? Left pad on first
CRICKETING HEROES? Herschelle Gibbs
BEST PLAYER IN COUNTY CRICKET? Marcus Trescothick, Dale Benkenstein
TIPS FOR THE TOP? Scott Borthwick, Jos Buttler, James Vince
WHEN RAIN STOPS PLAY? Sleeping, playing cards, Angry Birds
FAVOURITE TV? Friends, Scrubs
FAVOURITE FILM? Chopper
DREAM HOLIDAY? Ibiza
SURPRISING FACTS? Born in New Zealand and lived there for 12 years, my father played one Test match for New Zealand at rugby league and I was a right-handed batsman when I was younger
TWITTER FEED: @benstokes38

Batting	Mat	Inns	NO	Runs	HS	Ave	SR	100	50	Ct	St
ODIs	5	3	0	30	20	10.00	57.69	0	0	3	0
T20Is	2	1	0	31	31	31.00	134.78	0	0	0	0
First-class	44	70	5	2442	185	37.56		6	11	25	0
List A	42	38	4	873	150*	25.67	93.07	1	3	13	0
Twenty20	27	22	2	398	56	19.90	114.69	0	1	10	0
Bowling	**Inns**	**Balls**	**Runs**	**Wkts**	**BBI**	**BBM**	**Ave**	**Econ**	**SR**	**5w**	**10**
ODIs	5	-	-	-	-	-	-	-	-	-	-
T20Is	2	-	-	-	-	-	-	-	-	-	-
First-class	44	2872	1862	65	6/68	7/145	28.64	3.88	44.1	1	0
List A	42	480	432	23	4/29	4/29	18.78	5.40	20.8	0	0
Twenty20	27	144	190	7	2/14	2/14	27.14	7.91	20.5	0	0

OLLY STONE RHB RFM

FULL NAME: Oliver Peter Stone
BORN: October 9, 1993, Norwich, Norfolk
SQUAD NO: 9
HEIGHT: 6ft 2in
NICKNAME: Stoney
EDUCATION: Thorpe St Andrew High School; Moulton College
TEAMS: England Under-19s, Norfolk, Northamptonshire, Northamptonshire 2nd XI
CAREER: First-class: 2012; List A: 2012; T20: 2011

BEST BATTING: 26* Northamptonshire vs Yorkshire, Northampton, 2012
BEST BOWLING: 1-6 Northamptonshire vs Yorkshire, Northampton, 2012

WHO WOULD PLAY YOU IN A FILM OF YOUR LIFE? Owen Wilson
CAREER HIGHLIGHTS? Making my first-class debut and playing for England U19
MOST MARKED CHARACTERISTIC? My hair
TIPS FOR THE TOP? Gavin Griffiths, Dominic Sibley, Ben Duckett, Shiv Thakor
IF YOU WEREN'T A CRICKETER? I'd be at university
DESERT ISLAND DISC? Lighthouse Family
FAVOURITE TV? Soccer AM
CRICKETING HEROES? Paul Bradshaw
ACCOMPLISHMENTS? Passing my driving test
WHEN YOU RETIRE? I'd like to be a physio
SURPRISING FACT? David Willey is my third cousin
FANTASY SLIP CORDON? Keeper: Chris Gayle, 1st: Hulk Hogan, 2nd: James Corden, 3rd: Hugh Hefner, Gully: Nicky Jayne
TWITTER FEED: @OllyStone2

Batting	Mat	Inns	NO	Runs	HS	Ave	SR	100	50	Ct	St
First-class	3	3	1	47	26*	23.50	65.27	0	0	3	0
List A	8	6	3	10	7*	3.33	30.30	0	0	3	0
Twenty20	4	1	0	0	0	0.00	0.00	0	0	2	0
Bowling	**Inns**	**Balls**	**Runs**	**Wkts**	**BBI**	**BBM**	**Ave**	**Econ**	**SR**	**5w**	**10**
First-class	3	384	202	5	1/6	2/41	40.40	3.15	76.8	0	0
List A	8	190	184	2	1/12	1/12	92.00	5.81	95.0	0	0
Twenty20	4	30	38	2	2/26	2/26	19.00	7.60	15.0	0	0

MARK STONEMAN

LHB MVP71

FULL NAME: Mark Daniel Stoneman
BORN: June 26, 1987, Newcastle upon Tyne, Northumberland
SQUAD NO: 26
HEIGHT: 5ft 10in
NICKNAME: Rocky
EDUCATION: Whickham Comprehensive
TEAMS: Durham, Durham 2nd XI, England Under-19s
CAREER: First-class: 2007; List A: 2008; T20: 2010

BEST BATTING: 128 Durham vs Sussex, Hove, 2011

FAMILY TIES? Grandfather played and umpired, and father played
CAREER HIGHLIGHTS? Being part of two Championship winning squads
SUPERSTITIONS? Right pad goes on first
CRICKETING HEROES? My dad, Brian Lara, Michael Di Venuto
NON-CRICKETING HEROES? Billy Slater, Vincent Chase
BEST PLAYER IN COUNTY CRICKET? Marcus Trescothick
TIPS FOR THE TOP? Jonny Bairstow, Ben Stokes, Scott Borthwick
IF YOU WEREN'T A CRICKETER? I'd be a PE teacher
WHEN RAIN STOPS PLAY? Playing cards, reading magazines or annoying people
FAVOURITE TV? Entourage
FAVOURITE FILM? The Patriot
DREAM HOLIDAY? Las Vegas
GUILTY PLEASURES? Guinness, Southern Comfort and lemonade, pizza

Batting	Mat	Inns	NO	Runs	HS	Ave	SR	100	50	Ct	St
First-class	66	112	4	3006	128	27.83	48.46	4	16	43	0
List A	20	19	2	782	136*	46.00	94.67	3	3	6	0
Twenty20	3	3	0	85	46	28.33	100.00	0	0	1	0
Bowling	**Inns**	**Balls**	**Runs**	**Wkts**	**BBI**	**BBM**	**Ave**	**Econ**	**SR**	**5w**	**10**
First-class	66	-	-	-	-	-	-	-	-	-	-
List A	20	-	-	-	-	-	-	-	-	-	-
Twenty20	3	-	-	-	-	-	-	-	-	-	-

SCOTT STYRIS RHB RM

FULL NAME: Scott Bernard Styris
BORN: July 10, 1975, Brisbane, Australia
SQUAD NO: 56
HEIGHT: 5ft 10in
NICKNAME: Miley, The Rus
EDUCATION: Hamilton Boys' High School, Hamilton
TEAMS: New Zealand, Auckland, Chennai Super Kings, Deccan Chargers, Durham, Essex, Middlesex, Northern Districts, PCA Masters XI, Sussex, Sylhet Royals
CAREER: Test: 2002; ODI: 1999; T20I: 2005; First-class: 1994; List A: 1994; T20: 2005

BEST BATTING: 212* Northern Districts vs Otago, Hamilton, 2002
BEST BOWLING: 6-32 Northern Districts vs Otago, Gisborne, 2000
COUNTY CAP: 2006 (Middlesex)

NOTES: Distinguished limited overs career with more than 5,000 runs and 150 wickets for the Black Caps. He was awarded his Test cap on the eve of the Karachi Test in May 2002, but it was taken back when the match was cancelled because of a bomb blast. He had 10 years of domestic experience before he was awarded his Test cap. Having given up Test cricket in 2008, he announced his retirement from all international cricket in June 2011. Appeared for Sussex in the 2012 FL t20 where he smashed a record-breaking 37-ball century in the Sharks' victory over Gloucestershire. Signed for the 2013 edition of the FL t20 competition in October 2012

Batting	Mat	Inns	NO	Runs	HS	Ave	SR	100	50	Ct	St
Tests	29	48	4	1586	170	36.04	51.34	5	6	23	0
ODIs	188	161	23	4483	141	32.48	79.41	4	28	73	0
T20Is	31	29	2	578	66	21.40	119.66	0	1	8	0
First-class	128	213	20	6048	212*	31.33		10	30	102	0
List A	341	298	48	8330	141	33.32		6	57	130	0
Twenty20	159	145	22	3230	106*	26.26	137.09	2	11	42	0
Bowling	**Inns**	**Balls**	**Runs**	**Wkts**	**BBI**	**BBM**	**Ave**	**Econ**	**SR**	**5w**	**10**
Tests	29	1960	1015	20	3/28	3/44	50.75	3.10	98.0	0	0
ODIs	188	6114	4839	137	6/25	6/25	35.32	4.74	44.6	1	0
T20Is	31	309	349	18	3/5	3/5	19.38	6.77	17.1	0	0
First-class	128	12826	6446	204	6/32		31.59	3.01	62.8	9	1
List A	341	12072	9239	300	6/25	6/25	30.79	4.59	40.2	1	0
Twenty20	159	2399	3001	106	3/5	3/5	28.31	7.50	22.6	0	0

ARUL SUPPIAH RHB SLA R1 MVP79

FULL NAME: Arul Vivasvan Suppiah
BORN: August 30, 1983, Kuala Lumpur, Malaysia
SQUAD NO: 23
HEIGHT: 6ft
NICKNAME: Ruley, Ja Rule, Sinbad
EDUCATION: Millfield School; Exeter University
TEAMS: Somerset
CAREER: First-class: 2002; List A: 2002; T20: 2005

BEST BATTING: 156 Somerset vs Indians, Taunton, 2011
BEST BOWLING: 3-46 Somerset vs West Indies A, Taunton, 2002
COUNTY CAP: 2009; BENEFIT YEAR: 2013

WHO WOULD PLAY YOU IN A FILM OF YOUR LIFE? Will Smith
CAREER HIGHLIGHTS? Holding the world-record bowling figures in T20 cricket. Scoring 156 against India in July 2011
MOST MARKED CHARACTERISTIC? I'm charming!
BEST PLAYER IN COUNTY CRICKET? Marcus Trescothick
TIPS FOR THE TOP? Joe Root, James and Craig Overton, George Dockrell
IF YOU WEREN'T A CRICKETER? Working as a chef
DESERT ISLAND DISC? Adele – 21
FAVOURITE TV? The Big Bang Theory, Fawlty Towers
ACCOMPLISHMENTS? I'm a black tip belt holder in taekwando
WHEN YOU RETIRE? Teacher or accountant
SURPRISING FACT? I was the youngest player to have played cricket for Malaysia, aged 15
FANTASY SLIP CORDON? Keeper: Will Smith (coolest guy in the world), 1st: Eva Mendes (simply gorgeous!), 2nd: Steve Kirby (easy to wind him up), 3rd: Me, Gully: Michael McIntyre (to keep us entertained in the field)
TWITTER FEED: @arul_suppiah

Batting	Mat	Inns	NO	Runs	HS	Ave	SR	100	50	Ct	St
First-class	94	156	8	5026	156	33.95	49.73	8	29	54	0
List A	89	73	14	1622	80	27.49		0	9	34	0
Twenty20	82	53	17	472	32*	13.11	105.59	0	0	33	0
Bowling	**Inns**	**Balls**	**Runs**	**Wkts**	**BBI**	**BBM**	**Ave**	**Econ**	**SR**	**5w**	**10**
First-class	94	4653	2611	45	3/46		58.02	3.36	103.4	0	0
List A	89	1616	1496	46	4/39	4/39	32.52	5.55	35.1	0	0
Twenty20	82	647	785	41	6/5	6/5	19.14	7.27	15.7	1	0

GRAEME SWANN RHB OB W1

FULL NAME: Graeme Peter Swann
BORN: March 24, 1979, Northampton
SQUAD NO: 6
HEIGHT: 6ft 1in
NICKNAME: Chin, Swanny, G, Jimmy Hill
EDUCATION: Sponne School, Towcester
TEAMS: England, Northamptonshire, Nottinghamshire
CAREER: Test: 2008; ODI: 2000; T20I: 2008; First-class: 1998; List A: 1997; T20: 2003

BEST BATTING: 183 Northamptonshire vs Gloucestershire, Bristol, 2002
BEST BOWLING: 7-33 Northamptonshire vs Derbyshire, Northampton, 2003
COUNTY CAP: 1999 (Northamptonshire); BENEFIT YEAR: 2013 (Nottinghamshire)

CAREER HIGHLIGHTS? Being ignored for two sessions by Jimmy Anderson after letting a ball through my legs off his bowling at Lord's
NON-CRICKETING HEROES? Peter Beardsley, Alan Shearer, Noel Gallagher, Dame Kiri te Kanawa
TIPS FOR THE TOP? Scott Borthwick will be an Ashes winner. Alex Hales will one day score a double hundred in a T20 game. I know this because he told me after two sips of lager at the Notts Christmas party
GUILTY PLEASURES? I like listening to the back catalogue of Kylie Minogue in my car. I reduce the volume when driving through town centres or neighbourhoods where the queen of Australia isn't considered to be 'street' enough
TWITTER FEED: @Swannyg66

Batting	Mat	Inns	NO	Runs	HS	Ave	SR	100	50	Ct	St
Tests	50	60	10	1176	85	23.52	77.01	0	5	44	0
ODIs	76	46	12	484	34	14.23	90.63	0	0	28	0
T20Is	39	16	11	104	34	20.80	116.85	0	0	5	0
First-class	238	322	31	7473	183	25.68		4	36	182	0
List A	263	194	28	3134	83	18.87		0	14	87	0
Twenty20	80	54	15	791	90*	20.28	135.91	0	3	20	0
Bowling	**Inns**	**Balls**	**Runs**	**Wkts**	**BBI**	**BBM**	**Ave**	**Econ**	**SR**	**5w**	**10**
Tests	50	12709	6176	212	6/65	10/181	29.13	2.91	59.9	14	2
ODIs	76	3629	2744	101	5/28	5/28	27.16	4.53	35.9	1	0
T20Is	39	810	859	51	3/13	3/13	16.84	6.36	15.8	0	0
First-class	238	44073	21870	686	7/33		31.88	2.97	64.2	29	5
List A	263	10859	8028	301	5/17	5/17	26.67	4.43	36.0	3	0
Twenty20	80	1692	1851	98	3/13	3/13	18.88	6.56	17.2	0	0

SAM SWEENEY RHB RMF

FULL NAME: Samuel Alan Sweeney
BORN: March 15, 1990, Preston, Lancashire
SQUAD NO: 17
HEIGHT: 5ft 11in
NICKNAME: The Sweeney, Sweens, Sweendog
EDUCATION: Parklands High School, Chorley; Myerscough College, Manchester
TEAMS: Northamptonshire, Northamptonshire 2nd XI
CAREER: List A: 2011

FAMILY TIES? My dad was the local league sledger
CAREER HIGHLIGHTS? Getting a contract at Northants
SUPERSTITIONS? Last one out of the changing room
CRICKETING HEROES? Brett Lee, Rob Newton, Andrew Flintoff
NON-CRICKETING HEROES? Charlie Sheen, Robert De Niro
BEST PLAYER IN COUNTY CRICKET? Marcus Trescothick
TIP FOR THE TOP? James Taylor
WHEN RAIN STOPS PLAY? One hand-one bounce and sleeping
FAVOURITE TV? Geordie Shore
FAVOURITE FILM? Superbad
FAVOURITE BOOK? BFG
DREAM HOLIDAY? Benidorm
ACCOMPLISHMENTS? Signing for Bolton Wanders U12
SURPRISING SKILL? I can play the trombone
GUILTY PLEASURES? Terry's Chocolate Orange
FANTASY SLIP CORDON? Keeper: Sheldon from The Big Bang Theory, 1st: James Corden, 2nd: Peter Kay, 3rd: Alan from The Hangover

Batting	Mat	Inns	NO	Runs	HS	Ave	SR	100	50	Ct	St
List A	2	-	-	-	-	-	-	-	-	1	0
Bowling	**Inns**	**Balls**	**Runs**	**Wkts**	**BBI**	**BBM**	**Ave**	**Econ**	**SR**	**5w**	**10**
List A	2	30	48	0	-	-	-	9.60	-	0	0

JAMES SYKES

LHB SLA

FULL NAME: James Stuart Sykes
BORN: April 26, 1992, Huntingdon
SQUAD NO: 20
HEIGHT: 6ft 2in
NICKNAME: Sykesy
EDUCATION: St Ivo School
TEAMS: Cambridgeshire, Leicestershire, Leicestershire 2nd XI
CAREER: List A: 2012; T20: 2012

CAREER HIGHLIGHTS? Being offered a professional contract at Leicestershire
SUPERSTITIONS? I always put my right pad and right glove on first
CRICKETING HEROES? Shane Warne, Claude Henderson
NON-CRICKETING HEROES? Tom Hardy, Samuel L Jackson, Channing Tatum
BEST PLAYER IN COUNTY CRICKET? Chris Rogers
TIPS FOR THE TOP? Nathan Buck, Josh Cobb, Ned Eckersley, Alex Wyatt
IF YOU WEREN'T A CRICKETER? Ski season working as a chalet boy
WHEN RAIN STOPS PLAY? Listen to music, lots of talking, lots of sleeping
FAVOURITE TV? Hollyoaks, Geordie Shore, TOWIE
FAVOURITE FILM? Coach Carter, Any Given Sunday
FAVOURITE BOOK? The Beano
DREAM HOLIDAY? Switzerland
ACCOMPLISHMENTS? Passing my A-Levels
SURPRISING FACT? I can dance ballet (seriously)
GUILTY PLEASURES? Reality TV, McFlurrys, One Direction
FANTASY SLIP CORDON? Keeper: Michael Jordan, 1st: Tom Hardy, 2nd: Eminem, 3rd: Myself, Gully: Drake
TWITTER FEED: @Sykesy20

Batting	Mat	Inns	NO	Runs	HS	Ave	SR	100	50	Ct	St
List A	7	3	2	15	12*	15.00	68.18	0	0	1	0
Twenty20	1	1	1	2	2*	-	50.00	0	0	0	0
Bowling	**Inns**	**Balls**	**Runs**	**Wkts**	**BBI**	**BBM**	**Ave**	**Econ**	**SR**	**5w**	**10**
List A	7	234	194	7	3/39	3/39	27.71	4.97	33.4	0	0
Twenty20	1	24	24	2	2/24	2/24	12.00	6.00	12.0	0	0

SHAUN TAIT RHB RF

FULL NAME: Shaun William Tait
BORN: February 22, 1983, Bedford Park, Adelaide, Australia
SQUAD NO: TBC
HEIGHT: 6ft 3in
NICKNAME: Sloon
TEAMS: Australia, Australia A, Chittagong Kings, Durham, Essex, Glamorgan, Melbourne Renegades, Mid West Rhinos, Rajasthan Royals, South Australia, Wellington
CAREER: Test: 2005; ODI: 2007; T20I: 2007; First-class: 2002; List A: 2003; T20: 2005

BEST BATTING: 68 South Australia vs Victoria, Adelaide, 2006
BEST BOWLING: 7-29 South Australia vs Queensland, Brisbane, 2007

NOTES: The Bradman Young Cricketer of the Year in 2003/04, Tait made his Test debut at Trent Bridge during the 2005 Ashes series, with Marcus Trescothick becoming his first Test wicket. Took 23 wickets during Australia's victorious 2007 World Cup campaign; a year later he took an indefinite break away from the game, returning to focus solely on the limited overs formats. Following Australia's 2011 World Cup campaign he announced his decision to quit one-day cricket and play T20 matches only. One of the game's very fastest bowlers, Tait was clocked at 161.1kph in a 2010 ODI at Lord's – the second fastest recorded delivery of all time. Tait has been signed by Essex for the duration of their FL t20 campaign

Batting	Mat	Inns	NO	Runs	HS	Ave	SR	100	50	Ct	St
Tests	3	5	2	20	8	6.66	43.47	0	0	1	0
ODIs	35	7	5	25	11	12.50	86.20	0	0	8	0
T20Is	19	5	1	10	6	2.50	83.33	0	0	3	0
First-class	50	70	29	509	68	12.41	51.36	0	2	15	0
List A	98	35	19	109	22*	6.81	61.93	0	0	23	0
Twenty20	94	29	12	128	26	7.52	85.33	0	0	19	0
Bowling	**Inns**	**Balls**	**Runs**	**Wkts**	**BBI**	**BBM**	**Ave**	**Econ**	**SR**	**5w**	**10**
Tests	3	414	302	5	3/97	3/121	60.40	4.37	82.8	0	0
ODIs	35	1688	1461	62	4/39	4/39	23.56	5.19	27.2	0	0
T20Is	19	430	498	28	3/13	3/13	17.78	6.94	15.3	0	0
First-class	50	9263	5661	198	7/29		28.59	3.66	46.7	7	1
List A	98	4900	4171	178	8/43	8/43	23.43	5.10	27.5	3	0
Twenty20	94	2054	2612	126	5/32	5/32	20.73	7.62	16.3	1	0

JACK TAYLOR

RHB OB

FULL NAME: Jack Martin Robert Taylor
BORN: November 12, 1991, Banbury, Oxfordshire
SQUAD NO: 10
HEIGHT: 6ft
NICKNAME: Schlidd, Tails
EDUCATION: Chipping Norton School
TEAMS: Gloucestershire, Gloucestershire 2nd XI, Oxfordshire
CAREER: First-class: 2010; List A: 2011; T20: 2011

BEST BATTING: 63 Gloucestershire vs Glamorgan, Swansea, 2012
BEST BOWLING: 2-28 Gloucestershire vs Glamorgan, Swansea, 2012
COUNTY CAP: 2010

FAMILY TIES? Father and grandfather played minor counties for Oxfordshire. Brother [Matt] is also on the staff at Gloucestershire
WHO WOULD PLAY YOU IN A FILM OF YOUR LIFE? Ryan Gosling
CAREER HIGHLIGHTS? First-class debut vs Derbyshire at Bristol. T20 debut vs Somerset at Bristol and Man of the Match (4-16 and 38). Maiden first-class fifty vs Glamorgan at Swansea (61 off 45 balls). Playing alongside my little brother at the Cheltenham Festival vs Nottinghamshire
BEST PLAYER IN COUNTY CRICKET? Will Gidman – genuine allrounder, serious stats, top bloke
TIPS FOR THE TOP? Matt Taylor, Benny Howell
IF YOU WEREN'T A CRICKETER? Roundabout designer
DESERT ISLAND DISC? Drake – Take Care
CRICKETING HEROES? Muttiah Muralitharan, Jacques Kallis
NON-CRICKETING HEROES? One Direction
ACCOMPLISHMENTS? Passing my driving test first time
TWITTER FEED: @jacktaylor141

Batting	Mat	Inns	NO	Runs	HS	Ave	SR	100	50	Ct	St
First-class	8	14	1	273	63	21.00	67.24	0	1	4	0
List A	7	5	3	53	22*	26.50	165.62	0	0	1	0
Twenty20	10	10	1	53	38	5.88	84.12	0	0	2	0
Bowling	**Inns**	**Balls**	**Runs**	**Wkts**	**BBI**	**BBM**	**Ave**	**Econ**	**SR**	**5w**	**10**
First-class	8	1020	645	15	2/28	4/103	43.00	3.79	68.0	0	0
List A	7	250	207	9	3/37	3/37	23.00	4.96	27.7	0	0
Twenty20	10	139	178	8	4/16	4/16	22.25	7.68	17.3	0	0

JAMES TAYLOR

RHB LB R3 MVP94

NOTTINGHAMSHIRE

FULL NAME: James William Arthur Taylor
BORN: January 6, 1990, Nottingham
SQUAD NO: 4
HEIGHT: 5ft 6in
NICKNAME: Jimmy, Titch
EDUCATION: Shrewsbury School
TEAMS: England, England Lions, England Under-19s, Leicestershire, Nottinghamshire, Shropshire, Worcestershire 2nd XI
CAREER: Test: 2012; ODI: 2011; First-class: 2008; List A: 2008; T20: 2008

BEST BATTING: 237 Leicestershire vs Loughborough MCCU, Leicester, 2011
COUNTY CAP: 2009 (Leicestershire)

CRICKETERS PARTICULARLY ADMIRED? Sachin Tendulkar
TIP FOR THE TOP? Shiv Thakor
RELAXATIONS? Fishing, shooting, hunting
FAVOURITE BAND? The Pussycat Dolls
TWITTER FEED: @jamestaylor20
NOTES: Made England Test debut against South Africa at Headingley in 2012. Captained the England Lions winter tour to Australia in 2012/13, having captained them several times before. Made ODI debut against Ireland in 2011. Cricket Writers' Young Player of the Year in 2009. Joined Nottinghamshire for 2012 after four successful seasons with Leicestershire. Graduated from minor counties cricket with Shropshire and the academy at Worcestershire to the playing staff at Leicestershire. Represented England in 2008 U19 World Cup

Batting	Mat	Inns	NO	Runs	HS	Ave	SR	100	50	Ct	St
Tests	2	3	0	48	34	16.00	31.57	0	0	2	0
ODIs	1	1	0	1	1	1.00	12.50	0	0	0	0
First-class	81	134	19	5409	237	47.03		13	24	58	0
List A	73	69	13	2601	115*	46.44	80.77	6	15	12	0
Twenty20	57	50	15	1251	62*	35.74	116.69	0	6	16	0
Bowling	**Inns**	**Balls**	**Runs**	**Wkts**	**BBI**	**BBM**	**Ave**	**Econ**	**SR**	**5w**	**10**
Tests	2	-	-	-	-	-	-	-	-	-	-
ODIs	1	-	-	-	-	-	-	-	-	-	-
First-class	81	228	176	0	-	-	-	4.63	-	0	0
List A	73	138	170	5	4/61	4/61	34.00	7.39	27.6	0	0
Twenty20	57	74	100	2	1/10	1/10	50.00	8.10	37.0	0	0

ROBERT TAYLOR LHB LM

FULL NAME: Robert Meadows Lombe Taylor
BORN: December 21, 1989, Northampton
SQUAD NO: 10
HEIGHT: 6ft 3in
NICKNAME: Tayls, Robbie
EDUCATION: Harrow School; Loughborough University
TEAMS: Scotland, Harrow School, Leicestershire, Leicestershire 2nd XI, Loughborough MCCU, Northamptonshire 2nd XI
CAREER: First-class: 2010; List A: 2012; T20: 2012

BEST BATTING: 101* Loughborough MCCU vs Leicestershire, Leicester, 2011
BEST BOWLING: 5-91 Leicestershire vs Kent, Leicester, 2012

FAMILY TIES? My dad played club cricket in Northamptonshire and my brother Harry played for Stowe School
WHO WOULD PLAY YOU IN A FILM OF YOUR LIFE? Ryan Reynolds
CAREER HIGHLIGHTS? Hitting the winning runs off the last ball to win a CB40 game against Worcestershire
MOST MARKED CHARACTERISTIC? Wonky nose, red cheeks
BEST PLAYER IN COUNTY CRICKET? Gary Ballance
TIP FOR THE TOP? Shiv Thakor
IF YOU WEREN'T A CRICKETER? I'd be a full-time social golfer
DESERT ISLAND DISC? Kenny Rogers – The Gambler
CRICKETING HEROES? Mitchell Johnson, Mike Hussey
ACCOMPLISHMENTS? Getting my university degree and cycling from Land's End to John O'Groats for the charity SOBS
WHEN YOU RETIRE? Coaching, sports management
FANTASY SLIP CORDON? Keeper: Lee Evans, 1st: Michael McIntyre, 2nd: James Corden, 3rd: Me, Gully: Karl Pilkington
TWITTER FEED: @robtaylor1989

Batting	Mat	Inns	NO	Runs	HS	Ave	SR	100	50	Ct	St
First-class	12	20	1	399	101*	21.00	54.50	1	1	5	0
List A	9	9	3	106	29*	17.66	108.16	0	0	2	0
Twenty20	8	6	1	39	18*	7.80	105.40	0	0	4	0
Bowling	**Inns**	**Balls**	**Runs**	**Wkts**	**BBI**	**BBM**	**Ave**	**Econ**	**SR**	**5w**	**10**
First-class	12	1450	1142	26	5/91	5/91	43.92	4.72	55.7	1	0
List A	9	334	291	11	2/26	2/26	26.45	5.22	30.3	0	0
Twenty20	8	138	159	7	2/7	2/7	22.71	6.91	19.7	0	0

RYAN TEN DOESCHATE RHB RM

FULL NAME: Ryan Neil ten Doeschate
BORN: June 30, 1980, Port Elizabeth, South Africa
SQUAD NO: 27
HEIGHT: 5ft 11in
NICKNAME: Tendo
TEAMS: Netherlands, All Stars, Canterbury, Chittagong Kings, Essex, Impi, Kolkata Knight Riders, Mashonaland Eagles, Otago, Tasmania, Western Province
CAREER: ODI: 2006; T20I: 2008; First-class: 2003; List A: 2003; T20: 2003

BEST BATTING: 259* Netherlands vs Canada, Pretoria, 2006
BEST BOWLING: 6-20 Netherlands vs Canada, Pretoria, 2006
COUNTY CAP: 2006

CRICKETERS PARTICULARLY ADMIRED? Jacques Kallis, Kepler Wessels
OTHER SPORTS PLAYED? Rugby
OTHER SPORTS FOLLOWED? Football (Arsenal), rugby (Stormers)
FAVOURITE MUSICIAN? Phil Collins
RELAXATIONS? Golf, tennis, reading
TWITTER FEED: @rtendo27
NOTES: Netherlands international who won the inaugural ICC Associate ODI Player of the Year in 2007 and the ICC Affiliate Player of the Year award in 2010. Scored 686 runs at an average of 228.66 in the ICC Intercontinental Cup in 2006, recording four consecutive hundreds, including a competition record 259* vs Canada in Pretoria. Made a century (119) against England at Nagpur in the World Cup 2011, becoming the first batsman from the Netherlands to make a hundred in the World Cup finals, and a second century against Ireland at Kolkata

Batting	Mat	Inns	NO	Runs	HS	Ave	SR	100	50	Ct	St
ODIs	33	32	9	1541	119	67.00	87.70	5	9	13	0
T20Is	9	9	4	214	56	42.80	128.91	0	1	3	0
First-class	100	146	20	6035	259*	47.89		19	24	61	0
List A	147	120	35	3840	134*	45.17		7	22	45	0
Twenty20	168	150	30	3340	121*	27.83	134.08	2	13	61	0
Bowling	**Inns**	**Balls**	**Runs**	**Wkts**	**BBI**	**BBM**	**Ave**	**Econ**	**SR**	**5w**	**10**
ODIs	33	1580	1327	55	4/31	4/31	24.12	5.03	28.7	0	0
T20Is	9	204	241	12	3/23	3/23	20.08	7.08	17.0	0	0
First-class	100	8921	5904	174	6/20		33.93	3.97	51.2	7	0
List A	147	4243	3968	135	5/50	5/50	29.39	5.61	31.4	1	0
Twenty20	168	1374	1834	77	4/24	4/24	23.81	8.00	17.8	0	0

SEAN TERRY RHB OB

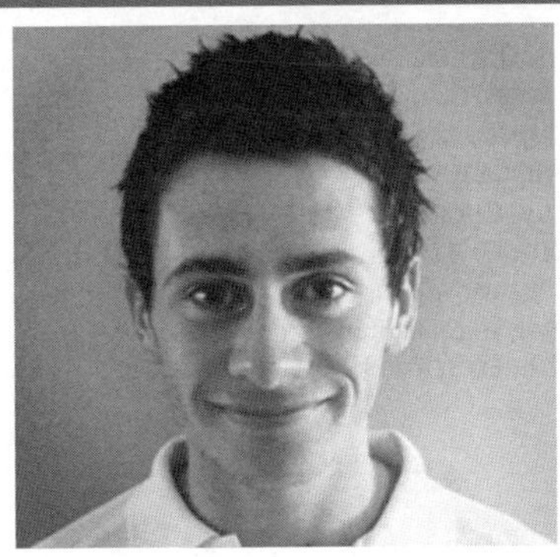

FULL NAME: Sean Paul Terry
BORN: August 1, 1991, Southampton, Hampshire
SQUAD NO: 10
HEIGHT: 5ft 11in
NICKNAME: Seany, ST
EDUCATION: Aquinas College, Perth
TEAMS: Derbyshire 2nd XI, Hampshire, Hampshire 2nd XI, Marylebone Cricket Club Young Cricketers
CAREER: First-class: 2012; List A: 2012

BEST BATTING: 59* Hampshire vs Loughborough MCCU, Southampton, 2012

FAMILY TIES? My dad [Paul] played for Hampshire
WHO WOULD PLAY YOU IN A FILM OF YOUR LIFE? Denzel Washington
CAREER HIGHLIGHTS? My debut for Hampshire and winning trophies with my club in Australia
SUPERSTITIONS? I put my left pad on first
BEST PLAYER IN COUNTY CRICKET? Michael Carberry
TIPS FOR THE TOP? Adam Rouse, Tom Barber (academy)
IF YOU WEREN'T A CRICKETER? Absolutely no idea
DESERT ISLAND DISC? Jay-Z – Black Album
FAVOURITE TV? Entourage
BIGGEST DRESSING DOWN YOU'VE RECEIVED? I've had too many in Australia to pick one
CRICKETING HEROES? My old man, Sachin, Michael Clarke and AB de Villiers
SURPRISING FACT? I was born in England, grew up in Australia and can play for Ireland
FANTASY SLIP CORDON? Keeper: Eddie Murphy, 1st: Michael Clarke, 2nd: Denzel Washington, 3rd: Myself, Gully: Sachin Tendulkar
TWITTER FEED: @sterry91

Batting	Mat	Inns	NO	Runs	HS	Ave	SR	100	50	Ct	St
First-class	4	5	1	93	59*	23.25	52.84	0	1	3	0
List A	1	-	-	-	-	-	-	-	-	0	0
Bowling	**Inns**	**Balls**	**Runs**	**Wkts**	**BBI**	**BBM**	**Ave**	**Econ**	**SR**	**5w**	**10**
First-class	4	-	-	-	-	-	-	-	-	-	-
List A	1	-	-	-	-	-	-	-	-	-	-

SHIV THAKOR

RHB RMF

FULL NAME: Shivsinh Jaysinh Thakor
BORN: October 22, 1993, Leicester
SQUAD NO: 57
HEIGHT: 5ft 11in
NICKNAME: Bob
EDUCATION: Uppingham School
TEAMS: England Under-17s, England Under-19s, Leicestershire, Leicestershire 2nd XI
CAREER: First-class: 2011; List A: 2011

BEST BATTING: 134 Leicestershire vs Loughborough MCCU, Leicester, 2011
BEST BOWLING: 3-57 Leicestershire vs Surrey, Leicester, 2011

FAMILY TIES? My father loves cricket and played from a very young age. His enthusiasm naturally rubbed off on me
CAREER HIGHLIGHTS? Making my first-class debut, scoring 134 and becoming the first county-born player to make a debut century for Leicestershire. Being named captain of England U19s
SUPERSTITIONS? A lot, far too many to name
MOST MARKED CHARACTERISTIC? I have an artistic and emotional flair that is often hidden under a shy and reserved nature
BEST PLAYER IN COUNTY CRICKET? Marcus Trescothick
TIPS FOR THE TOP? Olly Stone, Ben Duckett, Will Rogers, Aryan Patel, Dom Sibley
IF YOU WEREN'T A CRICKETER? At university studying PPE alongside playing cricket
DESERT ISLAND DISC? Simply Amazing
FAVOURITE TV? Made In Chelsea
CRICKETING HEROES? Sachin Tendulkar, Jacques Kallis
NON-CRICKETING HEROES? Achilles, Frankel, Ollie Mae, Secretariat
WHEN YOU RETIRE? I'd like to be able to look back at my career, smile, and be proud of what I achieved
SURPRISING FACT? I still have a teddy bear that goes everywhere with me
TWITTER FEED: @Thakor57

Batting	Mat	Inns	NO	Runs	HS	Ave	SR	100	50	Ct	St
First-class	9	15	3	617	134	51.41	51.97	1	4	2	0
List A	6	6	1	191	83*	38.20	93.17	0	2	0	0
Bowling	**Inns**	**Balls**	**Runs**	**Wkts**	**BBI**	**BBM**	**Ave**	**Econ**	**SR**	**5w**	**10**
First-class	9	306	233	7	3/57	3/57	33.28	4.56	43.7	0	0
List A	6	18	26	0	-	-	-	8.66	-	0	0

ALFONSO THOMAS RHB RFM MVP76

FULL NAME: Alfonso Clive Thomas
BORN: February 9, 1977, Cape Town, South Africa
SQUAD NO: 8
EDUCATION: Ravensmead Secondary School; Parrow High School, Cape Town
TEAMS: South Africa, Adelaide Strikers, Dhaka Gladiators, Dolphins, Lions, North West, Northerns, Perth Scorchers, Pune Warriors, Somerset, Staffordshire, Titans, Warwickshire, Western Province
CAREER: T20I: 2007; First-class: 1998; List A: 2000; T20: 2004

BEST BATTING: 119* North West vs Northerns, Centurion, 2002
BEST BOWLING: 7-54 Titans vs Cape Cobras, Newlands, 2005
COUNTY CAP: 2008 (Somerset)

NOTES: Came to prominence in the 2003/04 South African season, claiming 36 wickets in eight SuperSport Series matches for Titans. Replaced the injured Andre Nel in South Africa's Test squad to India in 2004. Made his international debut aged 30 in 2007, but signed with Somerset as a Kolpak player the following year. Leading wicket-taker in the 2010 FP t20 with 33 wickets, and took 109 wickets in all competitions that year. Claimed 33 Championship wickets at 22 from nine starts last season

Batting	Mat	Inns	NO	Runs	HS	Ave	SR	100	50	Ct	St
T20Is	1	-	-	-	-	-	-	-	-	0	0
First-class	129	179	34	3587	119*	24.73		2	12	33	0
List A	148	73	35	573	28*	15.07		0	0	30	0
Twenty20	176	59	30	358	30*	12.34	105.60	0	0	53	0
Bowling	**Inns**	**Balls**	**Runs**	**Wkts**	**BBI**	**BBM**	**Ave**	**Econ**	**SR**	**5w**	**10**
T20Is	1	24	25	3	3/25	3/25	8.33	6.25	8.0	0	0
First-class	129	23125	11235	419	7/54		26.81	2.91	55.1	20	2
List A	148	6250	5281	190	4/18	4/18	27.79	5.06	32.8	0	0
Twenty20	176	3559	4306	206	4/8	4/8	20.90	7.25	17.2	0	0

IVAN THOMAS

RHB RMF

FULL NAME: Ivan Alfred Astley Thomas
BORN: September 25, 1991, Greenwich, Kent
SQUAD NO: 5
HEIGHT: 6ft 4in
NICKNAME: Big Iv, Goober
EDUCATION: The John Roan School; University of Leeds
TEAMS: Kent 2nd XI, Kent Under-17s, Leeds/Bradford MCCU
CAREER: First-class: 2012

BEST BATTING: 11 Leeds/Bradford MCCU vs Yorkshire, Leeds, 2012
BEST BOWLING: 2-24 Leeds/Bradford MCCU vs Yorkshire, Leeds, 2012

WHO WOULD PLAY YOU IN A FILM OF YOUR LIFE? Damian Lewis or Michael C Hall
CAREER HIGHLIGHTS? Beating Sussex with Leeds/Bradford MCCU and making my county debut in 2012
SUPERSTITIONS? I always turn the same way at the top of my run-up
MOST MARKED CHARACTERISTIC? Ginger hair
BEST PLAYER IN COUNTY CRICKET? Marcus Trescothick
TIP FOR THE TOP? Daniel Bell-Drummond
IF YOU WEREN'T A CRICKETER? I'd be an international rap star
DESERT ISLAND DISC? Wu-Tang-Clan – Enter The Wu-Tang (36 Chambers)
FAVOURITE TV? The Wire
CRICKETING HEROES? Andrew Flintoff
NON-CRICKETING HEROES? Brendan Lynch
WHEN YOU RETIRE? I'd like to travel
SURPRISING FACTS? I've completed the Land's End to John O'Groats cycle, with the national three-peak walk and a Tough Mudder en route, raising money for CRY and Demelza
FANTASY SLIP CORDON? Keeper: Paul Merton, 1st: Ken Barlow, 2nd: David Brent, 3rd: Karl Pilkington
TWITTER FEED: @ivanthomas_5

Batting	Mat	Inns	NO	Runs	HS	Ave	SR	100	50	Ct	St
First-class	4	6	2	30	11	7.50	28.30	0	0	0	0
Bowling	**Inns**	**Balls**	**Runs**	**Wkts**	**BBI**	**BBM**	**Ave**	**Econ**	**SR**	**5w**	**10**
First-class	4	513	188	8	2/24	3/45	23.50	2.19	64.1	0	0

MIKE THORNELY RHB RM

FULL NAME: Michael Alistair Thornely
BORN: October 19, 1987, Camden, London
SQUAD NO: 7
HEIGHT: 6ft 1in
NICKNAME: Thorners, T-Bone, Major
EDUCATION: Brighton College
TEAMS: Kent 2nd XI, Leicestershire, Leicestershire 2nd XI, Mashonaland Eagles, Nottinghamshire 2nd XI, Somerset 2nd XI, Sussex, Sussex 2nd XI, Sussex Under-15s, Sussex Under-17s, Unicorns, Unicorns A
CAREER: First-class: 2007; List A: 2007; T20: 2012

BEST BATTING: 131 Leicestershire vs Glamorgan, Cardiff, 2012
BEST BOWLING: 2-14 Sussex vs Worcestershire, Hove, 2010

FAMILY TIES? My uncle played minor counties
WHO WOULD PLAY YOU IN A FILM OF YOUR LIFE? Tom Hanks, but probably more realistically Jason Statham or Bruce Willis!
CAREER HIGHLIGHTS? Winning Division Two of the County Championship with Sussex and scoring my first hundred on debut for Leicestershire
SUPERSTITIONS? I put my left pad on first
MOST MARKED CHARACTERISTIC? I've got a large forehead!
BEST PLAYER IN COUNTY CRICKET? Marcus Trescothick
TIP FOR THE TOP? Shiv Thakor
IF YOU WEREN'T A CRICKETER? Pilot
DESERT ISLAND DISC? Kenny Loggins – Danger Zone
FAVOURITE TV? Friends and Mock The Week
CRICKETING HEROES? Mark Waugh
NON-CRICKETING HEROES? @Bobs_Business, @OliWassell, @edfishclark, @stuiefinkelton
WHEN YOU RETIRE? Go on holiday in the summer and ski in the winter!
SURPRISING FACT? I was national long jump champion at 14
TWITTER FEED: @Thorners87

Batting	Mat	Inns	NO	Runs	HS	Ave	SR	100	50	Ct	St
First-class	28	50	2	1152	131	24.00	39.71	2	5	22	0
List A	34	32	1	926	105*	29.87	81.01	1	5	10	0
Twenty20	1	1	1	1	1*	-	100.00	0	0	0	0
Bowling	**Inns**	**Balls**	**Runs**	**Wkts**	**BBI**	**BBM**	**Ave**	**Econ**	**SR**	**5w**	**10**
First-class	28	390	250	7	2/14	2/14	35.71	3.84	55.7	0	0
List A	34	206	229	4	1/20	1/20	57.25	6.66	51.5	0	0
Twenty20	1	6	8	0	-	-	-	8.00	-	0	0

CALLUM THORP RHB RMF W1 MVP93

FULL NAME: Callum David Thorp
BORN: January 11, 1975, Mount Lawley, Perth, Australia
SQUAD NO: 36
HEIGHT: 6ft 3in
EDUCATION: Servite College
TEAMS: Durham, Western Australia
CAREER: First-class: 2003; List A: 2003; T20: 2005

BEST BATTING: 79* Durham vs MCC, Abu Dhabi, 2009
BEST BOWLING: 7-88 Durham vs Kent, Canterbury, 2008

CAREER HIGHLIGHTS? One-day final win for Wanneroo DCC, County Championship wins in 2008 and 2009 for Durham and my first-class debut for Western Australia
SUPERSTITIONS? All clothing and kit must be put on left side first
CRICKETING HEROES? Dennis Lillee, Viv Richards and Steve Waugh
NON-CRICKETING HEROES? Michael Jordan, Pele, Stefan Edberg and Carl Lewis
BEST PLAYER IN COUNTY CRICKET? Marcus Trescothick
TIPS FOR THE TOP? Ben Stokes and Scott Borthwick
WHEN RAIN STOPS PLAY? Sleep or harass the physio
FAVOURITE TV? Suits
FAVOURITE FILM? Gladiator
DREAM HOLIDAY? Maldives
GUILTY PLEASURES? Eating a slice of cake almost every day
FANTASY SLIP CORDON? Keeper: Billy Connolly, 1st: Me, 2nd: Michael Jordan, 3rd: Tiger Woods, Gully: Usain Bolt

Batting	Mat	Inns	NO	Runs	HS	Ave	SR	100	50	Ct	St
First-class	86	115	14	1507	79*	14.92	59.49	0	3	51	0
List A	42	28	9	323	52	17.00	99.69	0	1	8	0
Twenty20	9	6	0	63	13	10.50	114.54	0	0	1	0
Bowling	**Inns**	**Balls**	**Runs**	**Wkts**	**BBI**	**BBM**	**Ave**	**Econ**	**SR**	**5w**	**10**
First-class	86	13200	6398	249	7/88		25.69	2.90	53.0	9	1
List A	42	1897	1438	53	6/17	6/17	27.13	4.54	35.7	1	0
Twenty20	9	162	266	3	2/32	2/32	88.66	9.85	54.0	0	0

JAMES TOMLINSON

LHB LMF W1

FULL NAME: James Andrew Tomlinson
BORN: June 12, 1982, Winchester, Hampshire
SQUAD NO: 21
HEIGHT: 6ft 1in
NICKNAME: Tommo, T-bird
EDUCATION: Appleshaw; Harrow Way; Andover; Cricklade College; Cardiff University
TEAMS: British Universities, Cardiff MCCU, Hampshire, Hampshire 2nd XI, Hampshire Cricket Board, Wiltshire
CAREER: First-class: 2002; List A: 2000; T20: 2006

BEST BATTING: 42 Hampshire vs Somerset, Southampton, 2010
BEST BOWLING: 8-46 Hampshire vs Somerset, Taunton, 2008
COUNTY CAP: 2008

WHO WOULD PLAY YOU IN A FILM OF YOUR LIFE? Howard Keel or Errol Flynn
CAREER HIGHLIGHTS? Staying up in County Championship Division One in 2010. Taking 67 wickets in a season in 2008. Winning four out of the last five County Championship Division One games to stay up in 2008. Playing at Scarborough in 2011 (my family originate from there). Watching Hampshire win three one-day trophies at Lord's in 2005, 2009 and 2012. Taking 8-46 vs Somerset at Taunton in 2008. Taking 7-70 vs Somerset at Taunton in 2010. Playing alongside Shane Warne
MOST MARKED CHARACTERISTIC? I always have an opinion
BEST PLAYER IN COUNTY CRICKET? Chris Woakes. I'd like to see him bat up the order for Warwickshire and then progress to being England's allrounder in the Test team
TIP FOR THE TOP? Tom Barber – left-arm fast bowler in the Hampshire Academy
IF YOU WEREN'T A CRICKETER? Pond and nature reserve designer
DESERT ISLAND DISC? Clare Maguire – The Last Dance
FAVOURITE TV? Pointless, Spring/Summer/Autumn/Winterwatch
NON-CRICKETING HEROES? Chris Packham, Louis Smith, Bubba Watson
SURPRISING FACT? I like bird watching

Batting	Mat	Inns	NO	Runs	HS	Ave	SR	100	50	Ct	St
First-class	83	109	48	611	42	10.01	28.31	0	0	21	0
List A	27	14	5	34	14	3.77		0	0	3	0
Twenty20	2	1	0	5	5	5.00	125.00	0	0	0	0
Bowling	**Inns**	**Balls**	**Runs**	**Wkts**	**BBI**	**BBM**	**Ave**	**Econ**	**SR**	**5w**	**10**
First-class	83	14670	8439	248	8/46		34.02	3.45	59.1	10	1
List A	27	1089	910	29	4/47	4/47	31.37	5.01	37.5	0	0
Twenty20	2	42	48	1	1/20	1/20	48.00	6.85	42.0	0	0

REECE TOPLEY RHB LFM

ESSEX

FULL NAME: Reece James William Topley
BORN: February 21, 1994, Ipswich, Suffolk
SQUAD NO: 6
HEIGHT: 6ft 7in
EDUCATION: Royal Hospital School, Ipswich
TEAMS: England Lions, England Under-19s, Essex, Essex 2nd XI
CAREER: First-class: 2011; List A: 2011; T20: 2012

BEST BATTING: 9 Essex vs Derbyshire, Chelmsford, 2011
BEST BOWLING: 5-46 Essex vs Kent, Chelmsford, 2011

NOTES: Burst on the scene in 2011 aged 17 with 14 Championship wickets in his first three matches, including five-wicket hauls in each of his first two games against Kent and Middlesex. His season was truncated due to having to sit his summer exams (at the school where his father is a teacher; Don Topley was a first-class cricketer for Essex and Surrey, while Reece's uncle Peter was also a first-class cricketer). Made his England U19 debut against South Africa U19 in July 2011 and took 19 wickets in six matches at an average of 9.10 in the U19 World Cup 2012

Batting	Mat	Inns	NO	Runs	HS	Ave	SR	100	50	Ct	St
First-class	12	15	6	22	9	2.44	24.44	0	0	1	0
List A	5	2	0	21	19	10.50	63.63	0	0	0	0
Twenty20	9	2	2	1	1*	-	50.00	0	0	2	0
Bowling	**Inns**	**Balls**	**Runs**	**Wkts**	**BBI**	**BBM**	**Ave**	**Econ**	**SR**	**5w**	**10**
First-class	12	2010	1151	45	5/46	7/114	25.57	3.43	44.6	2	0
List A	5	193	190	7	4/46	4/46	27.14	5.90	27.5	0	0
Twenty20	9	192	246	17	3/19	3/19	14.47	7.68	11.2	0	0

JAMES TREDWELL LHB OB W1

FULL NAME: James Cullum Tredwell
BORN: February 27, 1982, Ashford, Kent
SQUAD NO: 15
HEIGHT: 5ft 11in
NICKNAME: Tredders, Pingu, Jimmy T
EDUCATION: Southlands Community Comprehensive
TEAMS: England, England A, England Lions, England Under-19s, Kent, Kent Cricket Board
CAREER: Test: 2010; ODI: 2010; T20I: 2012; First-class: 2001; List A: 2000; T20: 2003

BEST BATTING: 123* Kent vs New Zealanders, Canterbury, 2008
BEST BOWLING: 8-66 Kent vs Glamorgan, Canterbury, 2009
COUNTY CAP: 2007

FAMILY TIES? My father played a good level of club cricket for Ashford and Folkestone in the Kent League
CAREER HIGHLIGHTS? Being given the opportunity to play for England
MOST MARKED CHARACTERISTIC? My bald head
TIPS FOR THE TOP? Joe Root – he's already involved with England but there's plenty more from him. We have some good ones at Kent but I don't want to leave any out so I'm not going to name them all
FAVOURITE TV? The classic comedies: Black Adder, Only Fools And Horses etc
WHEN YOU RETIRE? Ideally I'd like to stay in cricket in some capacity but there are only so many positions to fill, so who knows!
SURPRISING FACT? I enjoy growing my own fruit and veg

Batting	Mat	Inns	NO	Runs	HS	Ave	SR	100	50	Ct	St
Tests	1	1	0	37	37	37.00	58.73	0	0	1	0
ODIs	14	8	4	45	16	11.25	42.85	0	0	5	0
T20Is	5	3	2	23	22	23.00	191.66	0	0	2	0
First-class	128	182	23	3599	123*	22.63	43.09	3	14	136	0
List A	188	126	43	1436	88	17.30		0	4	81	0
Twenty20	105	45	14	386	34*	12.45	109.34	0	0	33	0
Bowling	**Inns**	**Balls**	**Runs**	**Wkts**	**BBI**	**BBM**	**Ave**	**Econ**	**SR**	**5w**	**10**
Tests	1	390	181	6	4/82	6/181	30.16	2.78	65.0	0	0
ODIs	14	690	537	22	4/44	4/44	24.40	4.66	31.3	0	0
T20Is	5	96	133	3	1/20	1/20	44.33	8.31	32.0	0	0
First-class	128	22628	11621	335	8/66		34.68	3.08	67.5	11	3
List A	188	7720	6044	193	6/27	6/27	31.31	4.69	40.0	1	0
Twenty20	105	1992	2380	87	4/21	4/21	27.35	7.16	22.8	0	0

PETER TREGO

RHB RM W1 MVP1

FULL NAME: Peter David Trego
BORN: June 12, 1981, Weston-super-Mare, Somerset
SQUAD NO: 7
HEIGHT: 6ft
NICKNAME: Tregs, Darcy, Pedro Tregos, Pirate, Big Tone, Tony Dorigo
EDUCATION: Wyvern Comprehensive
TEAMS: England Lions, Central Districts, Herefordshire, Kent, Mashonaland Eagles, Middlesex, Somerset, Sylhet Royals
CAREER: First-class: 2000; List A: 1999; T20: 2003

BEST BATTING: 140 Somerset vs West Indies A, Taunton, 2002
BEST BOWLING: 6-59 Middlesex vs Nottinghamshire, Nottingham, 2005
COUNTY CAP: 2007 (Somerset)

WHO WOULD PLAY YOU IN A FILM OF YOUR LIFE? Johnny Depp
CAREER HIGHLIGHTS? County cap, England Lions tours, playing in the Champions League T20 twice with Somerset, fighting early on to keep my career alive and winning the PCA MVP in 2012
SUPERSTITIONS? Many, but mostly silly things like keeping the same sweatband for each different competition, same pants, batting socks – but washed regularly of course!
MOST MARKED CHARACTERISTIC? My tattoos
DESERT ISLAND DISC? Green Day – Welcome To Paradise
FAVOURITE TV? Match Of The Day, Hardcore Pawn (a reality programme about a pawn shop!)
BIGGEST DRESSING DOWN YOU'VE RECEIVED? All my memorable dressing downs happen at home!
NON-CRICKETING HEROES? George Best, David Beckham, Tiger Woods and still Lance Armstrong
SURPRISING FACT? My name is actually pronounced 'tree-go' not 'tray-go'
TWITTER FEED: @tregs140

Batting	Mat	Inns	NO	Runs	HS	Ave	SR	100	50	Ct	St
First-class	136	195	29	5805	140	34.96		9	36	60	0
List A	133	111	19	2270	147	24.67		2	10	39	0
Twenty20	114	104	13	2091	79	22.97	119.82	0	10	31	0
Bowling	**Inns**	**Balls**	**Runs**	**Wkts**	**BBI**	**BBM**	**Ave**	**Econ**	**SR**	**5w**	**10**
First-class	136	15314	9247	250	6/59		36.98	3.62	61.2	3	0
List A	133	4530	4258	136	5/40	5/40	31.30	5.63	33.3	2	0
Twenty20	114	1320	1872	64	4/27	4/27	29.25	8.50	20.6	0	0

CHRIS TREMLETT RHB RFM

FULL NAME: Christopher Timothy Tremlett
BORN: September 2, 1981, Southampton, Hampshire
SQUAD NO: 33
HEIGHT: 6ft 8in
NICKNAME: Goober, Trem, Twiggy
EDUCATION: Thornden Secondary School; Taunton's College, Southampton
TEAMS: England, ECB National Academy, England Lions, Hampshire, Surrey
CAREER: Test: 2007; ODI: 2005; T20I: 2007; First-class: 2000; List A: 2000; T20: 2004

BEST BATTING: 64 Hamphire vs Gloucestershire, Southampton, 2005
BEST BOWLING: 6-44 Hampshire vs Sussex, Hove, 2005
COUNTY CAP: 2004 (Hampshire)

FAMILY TIES? My father [Tim] played for Hampshire and England A and my grandfather [Maurice] played for Somerset and England
WHO WOULD PLAY YOU IN A FILM OF YOUR LIFE? Jaws from James Bond films
CAREER HIGHLIGHTS? Making my debuts for Hampshire, Surrey and England. Winning my first trophy in 2005 at Lord's. Winning the Ashes in 2010/11
MOST MARKED CHARACTERISTIC? Being very big and tall
BEST PLAYER IN COUNTY CRICKET? Michael Carberry
TIPS FOR THE TOP? Stuart Meaker and Joe Root
IF YOU WEREN'T A CRICKETER? Roof plasterer
SURPRISING FACT? I can hide a tennis ball in my mouth
TWITTER FEED: @ChrisTremlett33

Batting	Mat	Inns	NO	Runs	HS	Ave	SR	100	50	Ct	St
Tests	11	13	4	98	25*	10.88	42.42	0	0	4	0
ODIs	15	11	4	50	19*	7.14	56.17	0	0	4	0
T20Is	1	-	-	-	-	-	-	-	-	0	0
First-class	119	152	41	1979	64	17.82		0	7	32	0
List A	125	76	24	521	38*	10.01		0	0	26	0
Twenty20	50	17	7	77	13	7.70	100.00	0	0	5	0
Bowling	**Inns**	**Balls**	**Runs**	**Wkts**	**BBI**	**BBM**	**Ave**	**Econ**	**SR**	**5w**	**10**
Tests	11	2686	1311	49	6/48	8/150	26.75	2.92	54.8	2	0
ODIs	15	784	705	15	4/32	4/32	47.00	5.39	52.2	0	0
T20Is	1	24	45	2	2/45	2/45	22.50	11.25	12.0	0	0
First-class	119	20652	10805	391	6/44		27.63	3.13	52.8	9	0
List A	125	5787	4718	170	4/25	4/25	27.75	4.89	34.0	0	0
Twenty20	50	1059	1272	69	4/16	4/16	18.43	7.20	15.3	0	0

MARCUS TRESCOTHICK LHB RM R5

FULL NAME: Marcus Edward Trescothick
BORN: December 25, 1975, Keynsham, Somerset
SQUAD NO: 2
HEIGHT: 6ft 3in
NICKNAME: Banger, Tresco
EDUCATION: Sir Bernard Lovell School
TEAMS: England, Somerset
CAREER: Test: 2000; ODI: 2000; T20I: 2005; First-class: 1993; List A: 1993; T20: 2004

BEST BATTING: 284 Somerset vs Northamptonshire, Northampton, 2007
BEST BOWLING: 4-36 Somerset vs Young Australia, Taunton, 1995
COUNTY CAP: 1999; BENEFIT YEAR: 2008

NOTES: Made his Test debut against the West Indies at Old Trafford in 2000. Played his last Test against Pakistan at The Oval in 2006. Wisden Cricketer of the Year in 2005. PCA Player of the Year in 2000, 2009 and 2011. Has scored more ODI hundreds than any other Englishman. Topped 1,000 runs five years in a row between 2007 and 2011, amassing more than 7,500 runs. In an injury-hit season, he played just 16 times across all competitions in 2012, but still managed to pass 500 runs from nine Championship appearances

Batting	Mat	Inns	NO	Runs	HS	Ave	SR	100	50	Ct	St
Tests	76	143	10	5825	219	43.79	54.51	14	29	95	0
ODIs	123	122	6	4335	137	37.37	85.21	12	21	49	0
T20Is	3	3	0	166	72	55.33	126.71	0	2	2	0
First-class	293	502	29	20221	284	42.75		51	98	395	0
List A	351	336	28	11592	184	37.63		28	58	141	0
Twenty20	69	68	5	2151	108*	34.14	157.00	2	17	23	0
Bowling	**Inns**	**Balls**	**Runs**	**Wkts**	**BBI**	**BBM**	**Ave**	**Econ**	**SR**	**5w**	**10**
Tests	76	300	155	1	1/34	1/34	155.00	3.10	300.0	0	0
ODIs	123	232	219	4	2/7	2/7	54.75	5.66	58.0	0	0
T20Is	3	-	-	-	-	-	-	-	-	-	-
First-class	293	2704	1551	36	4/36		43.08	3.44	75.1	0	0
List A	351	2010	1644	57	4/50	4/50	28.84	4.90	35.2	0	0
Twenty20	69	-	-	-	-	-	-	-	-	-	-

JONATHAN TROTT RHB RM R6

FULL NAME: Ian Jonathan Leonard Trott
BORN: April 22, 1981, Cape Town, South Africa
SQUAD NO: 9
HEIGHT: 6ft
NICKNAME: Booger, Trotters, Trotty
EDUCATION: Rondebosch Boys' High School; Stellenbosch University
TEAMS: England, Boland, England Lions, Otago, South Africa A, South Africa Under-19s, Warwickshire, Western Province
CAREER: Test: 2009; ODI: 2009; T20I: 2007; First-class: 2000; List A: 2000; T20: 2003

BEST BATTING: 226 England vs Bangladesh, Lord's, 2010
BEST BOWLING: 7-39 Warwickshire vs Kent, Canterbury, 2003
COUNTY CAP: 2005

CRICKETING HEROES? Sachin Tendulkar, Adam Hollioake, Steve Waugh
WHEN RAIN STOPS PLAY? Music, watching sport
SURPRISING FACTS? I'm a San Francisco 49ers fan
NOTES: Represented South Africa A. Scored 245 on debut for Warwickshire 2nd XI. Hit 134 on County Championship debut for Warwickshire vs Sussex at Edgbaston in 2003. Made 119 on Test debut for England in the deciding match of the 2009 Ashes at The Oval. One of the four Wisden Cricketers of the Year for 2011. ICC Cricketer of the Year for 2011

Batting	Mat	Inns	NO	Runs	HS	Ave	SR	100	50	Ct	St
Tests	38	66	6	2970	226	49.50	46.76	8	13	17	0
ODIs	57	54	7	2379	137	50.61	75.40	3	20	12	0
T20Is	7	7	1	138	51	23.00	95.83	0	1	0	0
First-class	192	321	37	12840	226	45.21		31	62	170	0
List A	222	207	38	7903	137	46.76		14	55	66	0
Twenty20	77	72	16	2082	86*	37.17	114.90	0	13	18	0
Bowling	**Inns**	**Balls**	**Runs**	**Wkts**	**BBI**	**BBM**	**Ave**	**Econ**	**SR**	**5w**	**10**
Tests	38	582	341	3	1/5	1/5	113.66	3.51	194.0	0	0
ODIs	57	183	166	2	2/31	2/31	83.00	5.44	91.5	0	0
T20Is	7	-	-	-	-	-	-	-	-	-	-
First-class	192	4940	2807	58	7/39		48.39	3.40	85.1	1	0
List A	222	1552	1459	54	4/55	4/55	27.01	5.64	28.7	0	0
Twenty20	77	144	234	8	2/19	2/19	29.25	9.75	18.0	0	0

WARWICKSHIRE

JIM TROUGHTON — LHB SLA R1 MVP97

FULL NAME: Jamie Oliver Troughton
BORN: March 2, 1979, Camden, London
SQUAD NO: 24
HEIGHT: 5ft 11in
NICKNAME: Troughts
EDUCATION: Trinity School, Leamington Spa; Birmingham University
TEAMS: England, Warwickshire, Warwickshire Cricket Board
CAREER: ODI: 2003; First-class: 2001; List A: 1999; T20: 2003

BEST BATTING: 223 Warwickshire vs Hampshire, Birmingham, 2009
BEST BOWLING: 3-1 Warwickshire vs Cambridge UCCE, Cambridge, 2004
COUNTY CAP: 2001; **BENEFIT YEAR:** 2013

FAMILY TIES? Great grandfather [Henry Crighton] played for Warwickshire. Younger brother [Wigsy Troughton] played for Warwickshire youth and is a Stratford Panther
CAREER HIGHLIGHTS? Warwickshire debut and my first-team cap. Benson & Hedges Cup final in 2002. Playing for England. Championship winners in 2004 and 2012. CB40 finalists in 2010 and 2012. Captaining Warwickshire
CRICKETING HEROES? Graham Thorpe, Brian Lara
NON-CRICKETING HEROES? Eric Cantona and Ian Brown (Stone Roses)
IF YOU WEREN'T A CRICKETER? Actor, teacher or graphic designer
WHEN RAIN STOPS PLAY? Draw caricatures, do some reading or hit the gym
FAVOURITE TV? Dexter
DREAM HOLIDAY? Las Vegas, Cape Town or New York
SURPRISING SKILL? Guitar, drawing caricatures and movie-making
SURPRISING FACTS? I suffered from a form of epilepsy as a child. I come from a family of actors. I played youth football for Stoke City

Batting	Mat	Inns	NO	Runs	HS	Ave	SR	100	50	Ct	St
ODIs	6	5	1	36	20	9.00	47.36	0	0	1	0
First-class	156	242	20	7932	223	35.72	48.82	19	39	80	0
List A	161	143	16	3543	115*	27.89		2	21	61	0
Twenty20	88	81	9	1740	68*	24.16	122.53	0	10	36	0
Bowling	**Inns**	**Balls**	**Runs**	**Wkts**	**BBI**	**BBM**	**Ave**	**Econ**	**SR**	**5w**	**10**
ODIs	6	-	-	-	-	-	-	-	-	-	-
First-class	156	2357	1416	22	3/1		64.36	3.60	107.1	0	0
List A	161	736	644	25	4/23	4/23	25.76	5.25	29.4	0	0
Twenty20	88	96	127	6	2/10	2/10	21.16	7.93	16.0	0	0

MARK TURNER RHB RFM

FULL NAME: Mark Leif Turner
BORN: October 23, 1984, Sunderland
SQUAD NO: 6
HEIGHT: 6ft
NICKNAME: Tina, Beak
EDUCATION: Thornhill Comprehensive School, Sunderland
TEAMS: Derbyshire, Durham, England Under-19s, Somerset, Somerset 2nd XI
CAREER: First-class: 2005; List A: 2007; T20: 2005

BEST BATTING: 57 Somerset vs Derbyshire, Taunton, 2007
BEST BOWLING: 5-32 Derbyshire vs Northamptonshire, Northampton, 2011

FAMILY TIES? My brother Ian was a well-respected local cricket player. I played hours and hours of backyard cricket with him and my dad
WHO WOULD PLAY YOU IN A FILM OF YOUR LIFE? Peter Trego – a hero of mine and he would be able to pull off that big role. It could be his way in to acting when he hangs up his boots
CAREER HIGHLIGHTS? Playing in a Lord's final, even though it wasn't a great day personally. Two County Championship Division Two titles with Somerset and Derbyshire
MOST MARKED CHARACTERISTIC? People say I have a decent sized nose. I disagree
TIPS FOR THE TOP? Peter Burgoyne, Ross Whiteley
DESERT ISLAND DISC? Album: Maxwell's Urban Hang Suite. Song: Hot Natured – Benediction
BIGGEST DRESSING DOWN YOU'VE RECEIVED? That's easy. From Andrew Caddick for holding the ball cross seam while sharing the new ball with him. Not a happy man, understandable though. Absolute legend
ACCOMPLISHMENTS? Having a beautiful baby girl, Ivy, in December 2012
SURPRISING FACT? I met my wife Caroline 12 years ago while we were both working at Burger King. So romantic!
TWITTER FEED: @Tina2310

Batting	Mat	Inns	NO	Runs	HS	Ave	SR	100	50	Ct	St
First-class	23	26	12	245	57	17.50	64.98	0	1	10	0
List A	34	14	6	60	15*	7.50	61.22	0	0	6	0
Twenty20	41	12	5	29	11*	4.14	65.90	0	0	6	0
Bowling	**Inns**	**Balls**	**Runs**	**Wkts**	**BBI**	**BBM**	**Ave**	**Econ**	**SR**	**5w**	**10**
First-class	23	3080	2119	53	5/32		39.98	4.12	58.1	1	0
List A	34	1259	1300	50	4/36	4/36	26.00	6.19	25.1	0	0
Twenty20	41	709	1028	37	3/22	3/22	27.78	8.69	19.1	0	0

SURREY

FREDDIE VAN DEN BERGH RHB SLA

FULL NAME: Freddie Oliver Edward van den Bergh
BORN: June 14, 1992, Bickley, Kent
SQUAD NO: 15
HEIGHT: 6ft 3in
NICKNAME: Vanders
EDUCATION: Whitgift School; Durham University
TEAMS: Durham MCCU, Surrey, Surrey 2nd XI
CAREER: First-class: 2011

BEST BATTING: 16* Surrey vs Leeds/Bradford MCCU, The Oval, 2012
BEST BOWLING: 3-79 Surrey vs Cambridge MCCU, Cambridge, 2011

WHO WOULD PLAY YOU IN A FILM OF YOUR LIFE? Leonardo DiCaprio
CAREER HIGHLIGHTS? Making my first-class debut for Surrey with KP as captain and bowling well in the game, taking 3-79
MOST MARKED CHARACTERISTIC? Staying calm under pressure so I can hopefully make the right decision
BEST PLAYER IN COUNTY CRICKET? Marcus Trescothick
TIPS FOR THE TOP? Jason Roy and Stuart Meaker
IF YOU WEREN'T A CRICKETER? Studying at Durham University
DESERT ISLAND DISC? Anything from Mumford And Sons
FAVOURITE TV? Suits, Homeland, A League Of Their Own
BIGGEST DRESSING DOWN YOU'VE RECEIVED? After we lost to Cambridge in a first-class game we got a big dressing down from the coach
CRICKETING HEROES? Shane Warne and Freddie Flintoff
NON-CRICKETING HEROES? Bradley Wiggins and Jonny Wilkinson
ACCOMPLISHMENTS? Getting a place at Durham University
FANTASY SLIP CORDON? Keeper: James Corden (for entertainment value), 1st: Jack Whitehall, 2nd: Blake Lively, 3rd: Me, Gully: Harvey Spector (from Suits)
TWITTER FEED: @freddievdb15

Batting	Mat	Inns	NO	Runs	HS	Ave	SR	100	50	Ct	St
First-class	2	2	1	16	16*	16.00	50.00	0	0	0	0
Bowling	**Inns**	**Balls**	**Runs**	**Wkts**	**BBI**	**BBM**	**Ave**	**Econ**	**SR**	**5w**	**10**
First-class	2	282	148	4	3/79	3/79	37.00	3.14	70.5	0	0

KISHEN VELANI RHB RM

FULL NAME: Kishen Shailesh Velani
BORN: September 2, 1994, Newham, London
SQUAD NO: 8
HEIGHT: 5ft 11in
EDUCATION: Brentwood School
TEAMS: England Under-19s, Essex 2nd XI, Essex Under-13s, Essex Under-15s, Essex Under-17s
CAREER: Yet to make first-team debut

CRICKETING HEROES? Sachin Tendulkar
FAVOURITE FOOD? Chicken
NOTES: Essex Academy graduate who plays club cricket for Wanstead CC. First represented England U19 in July 2011 and has played 14 matches at that level with a highest score of 78, made against South Africa U19 in February of this year. Featured in two matches at the U19 World Cup last August

JAMES VINCE

RHB RM MVP55

FULL NAME: James Michael Vince
BORN: March 14, 1991, Cuckfield, Sussex
SQUAD NO: 14
HEIGHT: 6ft 2in
NICKNAME: Vincey
EDUCATION: Warminster School
TEAMS: England Lions, England Under-19s, Hampshire, Hampshire 2nd XI, Wiltshire
CAREER: First-class: 2009; List A: 2009; T20: 2010

BEST BATTING: 180 Hampshire vs Yorkshire, Scarborough, 2010

CAREER HIGHLIGHTS? Winning the T20 Cup and my first hundred for Hampshire
SUPERSTITIONS? I put my kit on in the same order every time
CRICKETING HEROES? Stephen Parry, Jimmy Adams, Neil McKenzie
BEST PLAYER IN COUNTY CRICKET? Marcus Trescothick
TIP FOR THE TOP? Jos Buttler
WHEN RAIN STOPS PLAY? Chill out and abuse Batesy [Michael Bates]
FAVOURITE TV? TOWIE
FAVOURITE FILM? Taken
DREAM HOLIDAY? Maldives
TWITTER FEED: @vincey14

Batting	Mat	Inns	NO	Runs	HS	Ave	SR	100	50	Ct	St
First-class	53	86	8	2460	180	31.53	59.76	5	7	36	0
List A	52	51	4	1714	131	36.46	93.50	2	8	16	0
Twenty20	51	48	6	1188	85*	28.28	124.92	0	7	39	0
Bowling	**Inns**	**Balls**	**Runs**	**Wkts**	**BBI**	**BBM**	**Ave**	**Econ**	**SR**	**5w**	**10**
First-class	53	110	67	0	-	-	-	3.65	-	0	0
List A	52	30	18	1	1/18	1/18	18.00	3.60	30.0	0	0
Twenty20	51	-	-	-	-	-	-	-	-	-	-

ADAM VOGES RHB SLA

FULL NAME: Adam Charles Voges
BORN: October 4, 1979, Subiaco, Perth, Australia
SQUAD NO: 3
HEIGHT: 6ft 1in
NICKNAME: Kenny, Hank, Vogesy
TEAMS: Australia, Australia A, Hampshire, Melbourne Stars, Nottinghamshire, Rajasthan Royals, Western Australia
CAREER: ODI: 2007; T20I: 2007; First-class: 2002; List A: 2004; T20: 2006

BEST BATTING: 180 Western Australia vs Tasmania, Hobart, 2007
BEST BOWLING: 4-92 Western Australia vs South Australia, Adelaide, 2007
COUNTY CAP: 2008 (Nottinghamshire)

TWITTER FEED: @acvoges
NOTES: Has signed with Middlesex for the duration of the FL t20, having had previous spells in county cricket with Hampshire and Nottinghamshire. Hit a 62-ball 100* for Western Australia vs New South Wales at Sydney in 2004/05 – his maiden one-day century and at the time the fastest one-day hundred in Australian domestic history. Scored his first ODI century for Australia vs West Indies in February of this year, making 112* from 106 balls to win the Man of the Match award and set up a 17-run win. Played for Rajasthan Royals in the 2010 IPL and has represented both Perth Scorchers and Melbourne Stars in the Big Bash League. Averaged 52.25 in last season's FL t20 for Nottinghamshire, with a top score of 70 coming against Yorkshire

Batting	Mat	Inns	NO	Runs	HS	Ave	SR	100	50	Ct	St
ODIs	17	16	6	532	112*	53.20	92.52	1	2	2	0
T20Is	7	5	2	139	51	46.33	121.92	0	1	3	0
First-class	129	219	28	7800	180	40.83	49.90	15	44	165	0
List A	147	142	34	4818	112*	44.61	79.95	5	37	59	0
Twenty20	107	99	17	2711	82*	33.06	131.98	0	12	46	0
Bowling	**Inns**	**Balls**	**Runs**	**Wkts**	**BBI**	**BBM**	**Ave**	**Econ**	**SR**	**5w**	**10**
ODIs	17	150	159	1	1/22	1/22	159.00	6.36	150.0	0	0
T20Is	7	12	5	2	2/5	2/5	2.50	2.50	6.0	0	0
First-class	129	2692	1439	42	4/92		34.26	3.20	64.0	0	0
List A	147	1506	1334	26	3/25	3/25	51.30	5.31	57.9	0	0
Twenty20	107	338	467	16	2/4	2/4	29.18	8.28	21.1	0	0

GRAHAM WAGG

RHB LM W2

FULL NAME: Graham Grant Wagg
BORN: April 28, 1983, Rugby, Warwickshire
SQUAD NO: 8
HEIGHT: 6ft
NICKNAME: Waggy
EDUCATION: Ashlawn High School, Rugby; Warwickshire College
TEAMS: Derbyshire, England A, England Under-19s, Warwickshire, Warwickshire Cricket Board
CAREER: First-class: 2002; List A: 2000; T20: 2003

BEST BATTING: 108 Derbyshire vs Northamptonshire, Northampton, 2008
BEST BOWLING: 6-35 Derbyshire vs Surrey, Derby, 2009
COUNTY CAP: 2007 (Derbyshire)

FAMILY TIES? My dad played 2nd XI cricket, minor counties, and a good standard of Premier League – he could bowl a heavy ball and hit a long ball – and my little man Brayden Wagg is just learning, so watch out for his name
CAREER HIGHLIGHTS? Getting my first contract at Warwickshire and playing for England Schools in all the age-groups
CRICKETING HEROES? Ian Botham, Allan Donald, Viv Richards
BEST PLAYER IN COUNTY CRICKET? Marcus Trescothick, without a doubt
TIPS FOR THE TOP? James Taylor, James Harris, Brayden Wagg
IF YOU WEREN'T A CRICKETER? Full-time dad I suppose
WHEN RAIN STOPS PLAY? Feet up, maybe a bit of poker
FAVOURITE TV? Banged Up Abroad
FAVOURITE FILM? Green Mile
DREAM HOLIDAY? Vegas with a winning lottery ticket to go nuts over there
SURPRISING SKILL? Dark horse on the snooker table
GUILTY PLEASURES? Eating too much in the winter

Batting	Mat	Inns	NO	Runs	HS	Ave	SR	100	50	Ct	St
First-class	91	130	12	2733	108	23.16	67.28	1	15	31	0
List A	92	76	10	1158	48*	17.54		0	0	24	0
Twenty20	56	47	10	606	62	16.37	126.25	0	1	16	0
Bowling	**Inns**	**Balls**	**Runs**	**Wkts**	**BBI**	**BBM**	**Ave**	**Econ**	**SR**	**5w**	**10**
First-class	91	15496	9175	281	6/35		32.65	3.55	55.1	9	1
List A	92	3451	3277	103	4/35	4/35	31.81	5.69	33.5	0	0
Twenty20	56	907	1190	44	3/23	3/23	27.04	7.87	20.6	0	0

JAMES WAINMAN RHB LM

FULL NAME: James Charles Wainman
BORN: January 25, 1993, Harrogate, Yorkshire
SQUAD NO: 15
HEIGHT: 6ft 3in
NICKNAME: Wainers
EDUCATION: Leeds Grammar School
TEAMS: Yorkshire 2nd XI, Yorkshire Academy, Yorkshire Under-14s, Yorkshire Under-15s, Yorkshire Under-17s
CAREER: Yet to make first-team debut

WHO WOULD PLAY YOU IN A FILM OF YOUR LIFE? Leonardo DiCaprio
CAREER HIGHLIGHTS? Signing my professional contract with Yorkshire, winning the League Cup with the Yorkshire Academy
SUPERSTITIONS? I always wear two pairs of socks
MOST MARKED CHARACTERISTIC? Teamwork
BEST PLAYER IN COUNTY CRICKET? Peter Trego
TIP FOR THE TOP? Alex Lees
IF YOU WEREN'T A CRICKETER? Student
FAVOURITE TV? Entourage
CRICKETING HEROES? Glenn McGrath, Dale Steyn, Morne Morkel
NON-CRICKETING HEROES? Nelson Mandela
WHEN YOU RETIRE? Do a season of skiing

DAVID WAINWRIGHT LHB SLA W1 MVP57

FULL NAME: David John Wainwright
BORN: March 21, 1985, Pontefract, Yorkshire
SQUAD NO: 21
HEIGHT: 5ft 9in
NICKNAME: Wainers
EDUCATION: Hemsworth High School; Hemsworth Arts and Community College; Loughborough University
TEAMS: England Lions, Derbyshire, Loughborough MCCU, Police Sports Club, Yorkshire
CAREER: First-class: 2004; List A: 2005; T20: 2007

BEST BATTING: 104* Yorkshire vs Sussex, Hove, 2008
BEST BOWLING: 6-33 Derbyshire vs Northamptonshire, Derby, 2012
COUNTY CAP: 2010 (Yorkshire)

FAMILY TIES? Grandfather played for Yorkshire schoolboys and was a slow left-arm bowler. Father played local cricket
WHO WOULD PLAY YOU IN A FILM OF YOUR LIFE? Will Smith
CAREER HIGHLIGHTS? Winning the County Championship Division Two title with Derbyshire in 2012. Representing England Lions. Scoring a first-class century at Scarborough
BEST PLAYER IN COUNTY CRICKET? Peter Trego
TIPS FOR THE TOP? Tom Knight, Peter Burgonye
DESERT ISLAND DISC? Will Smith – Big Willie Style
FAVOURITE TV? Family Guy
CRICKETING HEROES? Brian Charles Lara, Daniel Vettori
NON-CRICKETING HEROES? Steven Gerrard, Miguel Jimenez
SURPRISING FACT? I am a former world No.1 at Super Stick Golf
FANTASY SLIP CORDON? Keeper: Ian Shackelton (fantastic keeper), 1st: Peter Kay (for comedy value), 2nd: Me (in the thick of the cordon action), 3rd: Jacques Kallis (to teach us a thing or two about slip catching), Gully: James Corden (because no cordon is complete without James Corden)

Batting	Mat	Inns	NO	Runs	HS	Ave	SR	100	50	Ct	St
First-class	54	70	16	1465	104*	27.12	48.41	2	5	24	0
List A	60	28	17	191	26	17.36	72.34	0	0	19	0
Twenty20	31	10	7	38	15*	12.66	69.09	0	0	9	0
Bowling	**Inns**	**Balls**	**Runs**	**Wkts**	**BBI**	**BBM**	**Ave**	**Econ**	**SR**	**5w**	**10**
First-class	54	8990	4648	134	6/33		34.68	3.10	67.0	5	0
List A	60	2198	1780	47	3/26	3/26	37.87	4.85	46.7	0	0
Twenty20	31	557	646	26	3/6	3/6	24.84	6.95	21.4	0	0

ALEX WAKELY RHB RM

FULL NAME: Alex George Wakely
BORN: November 3, 1988, London
SQUAD NO: 8
HEIGHT: 6ft 2in
NICKNAME: Wakers, Al
EDUCATION: Bedford School
TEAMS: Bedfordshire, England Under-19s, Northamptonshire, Northamptonshire 2nd XI
CAREER: First-class: 2007; List A: 2005; T20: 2009

BEST BATTING: 113* Northamptonshire vs Glamorgan, Cardiff, 2009
BEST BOWLING: 2-62 Northamptonshire vs Somerset, Taunton, 2007
COUNTY CAP: 2012

FAMILY TIES? My father played minor counties. All of my family are very sporty and have various links to cricket
WHO WOULD PLAY YOU IN A FILM OF YOUR LIFE? Christian Bale
CAREER HIGHLIGHTS? Captaining England U19 in a World Cup. Scoring my first hundred
MOST MARKED CHARACTERISTIC? I drink too much Diet Coke
BEST PLAYER IN COUNTY CRICKET? Marcus Trescothick
TIPS FOR THE TOP? Olly Stone, Ben Duckett
IF YOU WEREN'T A CRICKETER? I constantly dream I am beating Tiger Woods on the golf course
DESERT ISLAND DISC? Daryl Hall and John Oates – You Make My Dreams
FAVOURITE TV? Suits
CRICKETING HEROES? Matthew Hayden, Ricky Ponting, Alastair Cook, David Ripley
WHEN YOU RETIRE? I'd like to work in marketing and PR
SURPRISING FACT? I play the piano and have a fascination with watch mechanics
FANTASY SLIP CORDON? Keeper: Will Ferrell, 1st: Prince Harry, 2nd: Adam Sandler, 3rd: Me, Gully: Zach Galifianakis

Batting	Mat	Inns	NO	Runs	HS	Ave	SR	100	50	Ct	St
First-class	64	101	4	2930	113*	30.20	45.60	2	19	38	0
List A	41	39	5	998	94	29.35	82.13	0	7	13	0
Twenty20	46	45	6	954	62	24.46	113.57	0	5	15	0
Bowling	**Inns**	**Balls**	**Runs**	**Wkts**	**BBI**	**BBM**	**Ave**	**Econ**	**SR**	**5w**	**10**
First-class	64	393	319	6	2/62	2/62	53.16	4.87	65.5	0	0
List A	41	132	107	5	2/14	2/14	21.40	4.86	26.4	0	0
Twenty20	46	12	29	0	-	-	-	14.50	-	0	0

MARK WALLACE

LHB WK R1 MVP87

FULL NAME: Mark Alexander Wallace
BORN: November 19, 1981, Abergavenny, Monmouthshire
SQUAD NO: 18
HEIGHT: 5ft 9in
NICKNAME: Gromit
EDUCATION: Crickhowell High School; Staffordshire University; University of Wales
TEAMS: Glamorgan, Wales Minor Counties
CAREER: First-class: 1999; List A: 1999; T20: 2003

BEST BATTING: 139 Glamorgan vs Surrey, The Oval, 2009
COUNTY CAP: 2003; BENEFIT YEAR: 2013

FAMILY TIES? Father still plays club cricket for Abergavenny and turns out for Wales Over 50s and 60s
CAREER HIGHLIGHTS? Winning one-day trophies and captaining Glamorgan
CRICKETING HEROES? Ian Healy, Alec Stewart, Steve James, Brendon McCullum, Justin Langer
NON-CRICKETING HEROES? Rory McIlroy, Harry Potter
BEST PLAYER IN COUNTY CRICKET? Steve Davies
TIPS FOR THE TOP? James Taylor, James Harris, Andrew Salter
IF YOU WEREN'T A CRICKETER? Journalist, student
WHEN RAIN STOPS PLAY? Reading, playing pool, talking rubbish
FAVOURITE TV? Spooks, EastEnders
FAVOURITE FILM? Harry Potter series, Blood Diamond, SWAT
FAVOURITE BOOK? Writers: JK Rowling, Bill Bryson, John Feinstein, Ed Smith, Steve James, Matthew Syed
SURPRISING FACT? Work as a rugby writer in the winter for Media Wales. Single handicap golfer
TWITTER FEED: @MarkWallace18

Batting	Mat	Inns	NO	Runs	HS	Ave	SR	100	50	Ct	St
First-class	199	318	26	8643	139	29.59		14	40	499	46
List A	176	141	28	2152	105	19.04		1	3	158	43
Twenty20	89	69	21	873	42*	18.18	128.38	0	0	37	21
Bowling	**Inns**	**Balls**	**Runs**	**Wkts**	**BBI**	**BBM**	**Ave**	**Econ**	**SR**	**5w**	**10**
First-class	199	6	3	0	-	-	-	3.00	-	0	0
List A	176	-	-	-	-	-	-	-	-	-	-
Twenty20	89	-	-	-	-	-	-	-	-	-	-

MAX WALLER RHB LB

FULL NAME: Max Thomas Charles Waller
BORN: March 3, 1988, Salisbury, Wiltshire
SQUAD NO: 10
HEIGHT: 6ft
NICKNAME: Steam Kat
EDUCATION: Millfield School; Bournemouth University
TEAMS: Dorset, Gloucestershire 2nd XI, Somerset, Somerset 2nd XI
CAREER: First-class: 2009; List A: 2009; T20: 2009

BEST BATTING: 28 Somerset vs Hampshire, Southampton, 2009
BEST BOWLING: 3-33 Somerset vs Cardiff MCCU, Taunton, 2012

FAMILY TIES? Dad is an MCC playing member
CAREER HIGHLIGHTS? Playing in the Champions League T20. Man of the Match in a Caribbean T20 match. Playing in Finals Day. First-class debut
SUPERSTITIONS? Like to have the ball in my hand before handing my hat and jumper to the umpire!
CRICKETING HEROES? Shane Warne, Jonty Rhodes
NON-CRICKETING HEROES? Ayrton Senna
BEST PLAYER IN COUNTY CRICKET? Marcus Trescothick
TIPS FOR THE TOP? Jamie Overton and Lewis Gregory
IF YOU WEREN'T A CRICKETER? Something business related or a failed artist!
FAVOURITE TV? MOTD, Take Me Out, The OC, Prison Break, Hawaii Five-O
DREAM HOLIDAY? Barbados
ACCOMPLISHMENTS? Having my paintings in an art shop (acrylics on canvas)
FANTASY SLIP CORDON? Keeper: Muhammad Ali (great hands!), 1st: Tiger Woods (get a few tips for my swing), 2nd: Shane Warne (has some great stories and obviously brilliant to talk to about bowling), 3rd: Me, Gully: Jimmy Carr (funniest man ever)
TWITTER FEED: @MaxTCWaller

Batting	Mat	Inns	NO	Runs	HS	Ave	SR	100	50	Ct	St
First-class	8	9	1	91	28	11.37	42.92	0	0	5	0
List A	30	11	7	43	13	10.75	59.72	0	0	9	0
Twenty20	35	8	3	7	3	1.40	33.33	0	0	14	0
Bowling	**Inns**	**Balls**	**Runs**	**Wkts**	**BBI**	**BBM**	**Ave**	**Econ**	**SR**	**5w**	**10**
First-class	8	840	493	10	3/33	3/57	49.30	3.52	84.0	0	0
List A	30	880	801	20	2/24	2/24	40.05	5.46	44.0	0	0
Twenty20	35	582	676	37	4/16	4/16	18.27	6.96	15.7	0	0

STEWART WALTERS RHB LB

FULL NAME: Stewart Jonathan Walters
BORN: June 25, 1983, Mornington, Australia
SQUAD NO: 26
HEIGHT: 6ft 1in
NICKNAME: Walts, Forrest
EDUCATION: Guildford Grammar School, Perth
TEAMS: Glamorgan, Glamorgan 2nd XI, Surrey, Surrey 2nd XI
CAREER: First-class: 2006; List A: 2005; T20: 2006

BEST BATTING: 188 Surrey vs Leicestershire, The Oval, 2009
BEST BOWLING: 1-4 Surrey vs Durham, Chester-le-Street, 2007

FAMILY TIES? Father, grandfather and grandmother all played at a high level
WHO WOULD PLAY YOU IN A FILM OF YOUR LIFE? William Wallace from Braveheart
CAREER HIGHLIGHTS? The hundreds I have scored, captaining Surrey and signing a contract with Glamorgan
SUPERSTITIONS? It used to be to put my right pad on first but for some reason I put the left one on first for one game and scored some runs, and guess what my new superstition is!
MOST MARKED CHARACTERISTIC? Determination
BEST PLAYER IN COUNTY CRICKET? Kevin Pietersen
TIPS FOR THE TOP? Joe Root, James Harris, Jim Allenby, Robert Croft
IF YOU WEREN'T A CRICKETER? Coaching cricket, fitness training
DESERT ISLAND DISC? Forever Young
CRICKETING HEROES? Dean Jones, Steve Waugh, Simon Katich
ACCOMPLISHMENTS? Becoming a father and husband
WHEN YOU RETIRE? Batting coach or strength and conditioning coach
SURPRISING FACT? I'm the biggest bat badger in the dressing room. I'm always cleaning my bats and fixing any little cracks – on my bats and others
TWITTER FEED: @stewiewalters

Batting	Mat	Inns	NO	Runs	HS	Ave	SR	100	50	Ct	St
First-class	55	91	7	2657	188	31.63	50.73	5	12	56	0
List A	67	61	10	1485	91	29.11	83.61	0	10	22	0
Twenty20	43	31	12	525	53*	27.63	111.94	0	1	28	0
Bowling	**Inns**	**Balls**	**Runs**	**Wkts**	**BBI**	**BBM**	**Ave**	**Econ**	**SR**	**5w**	**10**
First-class	55	432	245	3	1/4	1/9	81.66	3.40	144.0	0	0
List A	67	165	179	3	1/12	1/12	59.66	6.50	55.0	0	0
Twenty20	43	18	26	1	1/9	1/9	26.00	8.66	18.0	0	0

IAIN WARDLAW RHB RFM

FULL NAME: Iain Wardlaw
BORN: June 29, 1985, Dewsbury, Yorkshire
SQUAD NO: 7
HEIGHT: 6ft 3in
NICKNAME: Wardy
EDUCATION: Whitcliffe Mount School; Huddersfield University
TEAMS: Scotland, Yorkshire, Yorkshire 2nd XI
CAREER: First-class: 2011; List A: 2011; T20: 2011

BEST BATTING: 17* Yorkshire vs Hampshire, Leeds, 2012
BEST BOWLING: 1-37 Yorkshire vs Hampshire, Leeds, 2012

FAMILY TIES? My sister [Helen] played for Yorkshire and England Women
CAREER HIGHLIGHTS? First team debut vs Notts in T20
CRICKETING HEROES? Andrew Flintoff
BEST PLAYER IN COUNTY CRICKET? Marcus Trescothick
TIP FOR THE TOP? Jonny Bairstow
IF YOU WEREN'T A CRICKETER? Sales director
WHEN RAIN STOPS PLAY? Playing on iPad

Batting	Mat	Inns	NO	Runs	HS	Ave	SR	100	50	Ct	St
First-class	4	3	2	31	17*	31.00	58.49	0	0	2	0
List A	8	5	2	11	6*	3.66	61.11	0	0	1	0
Twenty20	7	-	-	-	-	-	-	-	-	0	0
Bowling	**Inns**	**Balls**	**Runs**	**Wkts**	**BBI**	**BBM**	**Ave**	**Econ**	**SR**	**5w**	**10**
First-class	4	468	368	4	1/37	2/119	92.00	4.71	117.0	0	0
List A	8	328	326	8	3/60	3/60	40.75	5.96	41.0	0	0
Twenty20	7	127	133	5	2/17	2/17	26.60	6.28	25.4	0	0

HUW WATERS RHB RMF

GLAMORGAN

FULL NAME: Huw Thomas Waters
BORN: September 26, 1986, Cardiff
SQUAD NO: 17
HEIGHT: 6ft 2in
NICKNAME: Muddy
EDUCATION: Llantarnam Comprehensive; Monmouth School; The Open University
TEAMS: Glamorgan, Wales Minor Counties
CAREER: First-class 2005; List A 2005; T20: 2010

BEST BATTING: 54 Glamorgan vs Surrey, Cardiff, 2011
BEST BOWLING: 7-53 Glamorgan vs Hampshire, Cardiff, 2012
COUNTY CAP: 2012

FAMILY TIES? Big Don [father] played for Usk in the old three counties bowling left-arm seam – he swears if Hawk-Eye had been in use back then he would have bagged many more scalps!
CAREER HIGHLIGHTS? Making my debut for Glamorgan, taking my first five-wicket haul and receiving my county cap last year
DESERT ISLAND DISC? The Killers – Hot Fuss
FAVOURITE TV? Homes Under The Hammer
BIGGEST DRESSING DOWN YOU'VE RECEIVED? Whenever I start pulling out the barn door
CRICKETING HEROES? My father and Glenn McGrath
NON-CRICKETING HEROES? Sir Alex Ferguson, Ryan Giggs
ACCOMPLISHMENTS? Renovating my flat – it took me the best part of a year but I got there in the end
WHEN YOU RETIRE? Hopefully become a PE teacher or carry on coaching within the game
FANTASY SLIP CORDON? Keeper: Peter Kay, 1st: Sir Alex Ferguson, 2nd: Myself, 3rd: Glenn McGrath, Gully: Karl Pilkington

Batting	Mat	Inns	NO	Runs	HS	Ave	SR	100	50	Ct	St
First-class	50	69	36	411	54	12.45	21.03	0	1	12	0
List A	22	8	3	24	8	4.80	42.10	0	0	3	0
Twenty20	4	2	2	11	11*	-	84.61	0	0	0	0
Bowling	**Inns**	**Balls**	**Runs**	**Wkts**	**BBI**	**BBM**	**Ave**	**Econ**	**SR**	**5w**	**10**
First-class	50	6498	3336	107	7/53		31.17	3.08	60.7	3	0
List A	22	816	844	14	3/47	3/47	60.28	6.20	58.2	0	0
Twenty20	4	85	118	3	3/30	3/30	39.33	8.32	28.3	0	0

LUKE WELLS LHB OB

FULL NAME: Luke William Peter Wells
BORN: December 29, 1990, Eastbourne, Sussex
SQUAD NO: 31
HEIGHT: 6ft 4in
NICKNAME: Rinser, Wellsy
EDUCATION: St Bede's School, Upper Dicker; Loughborough University
TEAMS: Colombo Cricket Club, England Under-19s, Sussex, Sussex 2nd XI
CAREER: First-class: 2010; List A: 2010; T20: 2011

BEST BATTING: 174 Sussex vs Yorkshire, Hove, 2011
BEST BOWLING: 2-28 Sussex vs Worcestershire, Horsham, 2011

FAMILY TIES? My father Alan played for Sussex, Kent and England and my uncle Colin played for Sussex, Derbyshire and England
CAREER HIGHLIGHTS? My debut hundred in a run chase against Durham and my hundred against Surrey in terrible conditions at Horsham that won the game
TIPS FOR THE TOP? Jos Buttler, Ben Stokes
IF YOU WEREN'T A CRICKETER? I'd be a History teacher
DESERT ISLAND DISC? Mumford And Sons – Babel
FAVOURITE TV? Family Guy, Prison Break
BIGGEST DRESSING DOWN YOU'VE RECEIVED? After getting stumped 10 minutes before lunch at Hove I got told to apologise to the rest of the team. I promptly refused!
CRICKETING HEROES? Chris Gayle, Sachin Tendulkar
NON-CRICKETING HEROES? Ricky Gervais, Stewie Griffin
WHEN YOU RETIRE? Coaching or teaching
FANTASY SLIP CORDON? Keeper: Ricky Gervais, 1st: Jesus, 2nd: Me, 3rd: Megan Fox, Gully: Stewie Griffin
TWITTER FEED: @luke_wells07

Batting	Mat	Inns	NO	Runs	HS	Ave	SR	100	50	Ct	St
First-class	33	56	6	1664	174	33.28	42.15	5	4	20	0
List A	6	3	0	28	17	9.33	73.68	0	0	1	0
Twenty20	1	1	0	3	3	3.00	50.00	0	0	0	0
Bowling	**Inns**	**Balls**	**Runs**	**Wkts**	**BBI**	**BBM**	**Ave**	**Econ**	**SR**	**5w**	**10**
First-class	33	474	297	5	2/28	2/33	59.40	3.75	94.8	0	0
List A	6	77	61	3	3/19	3/19	20.33	4.75	25.6	0	0
Twenty20	1	-	-	-	-	-	-	-	-	-	-

TOM WELLS RHB RMF

LEICESTERSHIRE

FULL NAME: Thomas Joshua Wells
BORN: March 15, 1993, Grantham, Lincolnshire
SQUAD NO: 19
HEIGHT: 6ft 2in
NICKNAME: Wellsy
EDUCATION: Beauchamp College
TEAMS: Leicestershire, Leicestershire 2nd XI
CAREER: List A: 2012

WHO WOULD PLAY YOU IN A FILM OF YOUR LIFE? Robert Downey Jnr
CAREER HIGHLIGHTS? Making my CB40 debut against Gloucestershire
SUPERSTITIONS? Left pad always on first
MOST MARKED CHARACTERISTIC? I'm energetic
BEST PLAYER IN COUNTY CRICKET? Nick Compton
TIPS FOR THE TOP? Ollie Freckingham, Rob Taylor (both Leicestershire)
IF YOU WEREN'T A CRICKETER? Ice road trucker
DESERT ISLAND DISC? Pitbull – Planet Pit
FAVOURITE TV? The Big Bang Theory
BIGGEST DRESSING DOWN YOU'VE RECEIVED? Playing a 2nd XI game against Derby last year I reverse-swept a ball to point after scoring about 35 off 10 balls hitting the ball straight. We needed three runs for the batting points with two wickets left and didn't end up getting them. The coach didn't say anything, but if looks could kill...
CRICKETING HEROES? Paul Nixon, Chris Gayle
NON-CRICKETING HEROES? My dad
ACCOMPLISHMENTS? Being part of a group that helped out under-privileged children in India by holding a sports day for them
SURPRISING FACT? I have to get my haircut weekly
FANTASY SLIP CORDON? Keeper: Paul Nixon (legend who has so much to talk about), 1st: Me (so I could be in between the blokes on the left and right of me), 2nd: Sheldon Cooper (I think he'd make the day go a lot faster), 3rd: Karl Pilkington (the greatest human alive), Gully: Michael McIntyre (just in case we need a few jokes)
TWITTER FEED: @t_wells15

Batting	Mat	Inns	NO	Runs	HS	Ave	SR	100	50	Ct	St
List A	1	1	0	4	4	4.00	133.33	0	0	0	0
Bowling	**Inns**	**Balls**	**Runs**	**Wkts**	**BBI**	**BBM**	**Ave**	**Econ**	**SR**	**5w**	**10**
List A	1	-	-	-	-	-	-	-	-	-	-

RIKI WESSELS RHB WK MVP67

FULL NAME: Matthew Hendrik Wessels
BORN: November 12, 1985, Marougudoore, Australia
SQUAD NO: 9
HEIGHT: 5ft 11in
NICKNAME: Blood, Weasel, Riki Bobby
EDUCATION: Woodridge College, Port Elizabeth; University of Northampton
TEAMS: Khulna Royal Bengals, Mid West Rhinos, Nondescripts Cricket Club, Northamptonshire, Nottinghamshire
CAREER: First-class: 2004; List A: 2005; T20: 2005

BEST BATTING: 199 Nottinghamshire vs Sussex, Hove, 2012
BEST BOWLING: 1-10 Mid West Rhinos vs Matabeleland Tuskers, Bulawayo, 2009

CAREER HIGHLIGHTS? That has to be my maiden first-class hundred, and the finals I've taken part in
CRICKETING HEROES? Michael Slater, Justin Langer
NON-CRICKETING HEROES? All the soldiers fighting currently, having lost a few friends to war myself
BEST PLAYER IN COUNTY CRICKET? Marcus Trescothick
TIPS FOR THE TOP? Chris Woakes, Alex Hales, Sam Wood
IF YOU WEREN'T A CRICKETER? Probably in the army on the front line
WHEN RAIN STOPS PLAY? iPad with a Will Ferrell film or avoiding Paul Franks and his bad banter
FAVOURITE FILM? Any Given Sunday
DREAM HOLIDAY? Zanzibar – heat, beaches and beer
ACCOMPLISHMENTS? Helping Macmillan Cancer UK raise money and helping people who need it more than myself
SURPRISING FACTS? I've bungee jumped at Vic Falls, I lived in Colombo for six months and I love hunting
TWITTER FEED: @RikiWessels

Batting	Mat	Inns	NO	Runs	HS	Ave	SR	100	50	Ct	St
First-class	112	185	15	6005	199	35.32	65.34	14	29	196	13
List A	110	103	9	2578	100	27.42	98.50	1	15	77	0
Twenty20	98	87	15	1930	86*	26.80	134.96	0	8	29	15
Bowling	**Inns**	**Balls**	**Runs**	**Wkts**	**BBI**	**BBM**	**Ave**	**Econ**	**SR**	**5w**	**10**
First-class	112	168	85	3	1/10	1/10	28.33	3.03	56.0	0	0
List A	110	49	48	1	1/0	1/0	48.00	5.87	49.0	0	0
Twenty20	98	-	-	-	-	-	-	-	-	-	-

TOM WESTLEY RHB OB MVP83

FULL NAME: Thomas Westley
BORN: March 13, 1989, Cambridge
SQUAD NO: 21
HEIGHT: 6ft 2in
NICKNAME: Wezzo
EDUCATION: HRSFC; Durham University
TEAMS: Cambridgeshire, England Under-19s, Essex, Essex 2nd XI, Marylebone Cricket Club
CAREER: First-class: 2007; List A: 2006; T20: 2010

BEST BATTING: 185 Essex vs Glamorgan, Colchester, 2012
BEST BOWLING: 4-55 Durham MCCU vs Durham, Durham University, 2010

FAMILY TIES? My dad dominates village cricket, as does my uncle. My brother bowls slow left-arm swing
WHO WOULD PLAY YOU IN A FILM OF YOUR LIFE? Ben Lawrence or Ben Matthews, definitely not Max Nolan or James Bunbury
CAREER HIGHLIGHTS? Captaining England U19, breaking into the Essex first team and Essex gaining promotion to Division One
BEST PLAYER IN COUNTY CRICKET? Obviously David Masters!
TIP FOR THE TOP? Reece Topley
IF YOU WEREN'T A CRICKETER? Something in the City
DESERT ISLAND DISC? Swedish House Mafia
FAVOURITE TV? Game Of Thrones
CRICKETING HEROES? Steve Waugh, Jacques Kallis
NON-CRICKETING HEROES? Thor
SURPRISING FACT? I was part of the first group of students in the UK to study Harry Potter academically
TWITTER FEED: @Westley21

Batting	Mat	Inns	NO	Runs	HS	Ave	SR	100	50	Ct	St
First-class	65	110	11	3003	185	30.33	49.66	5	15	36	0
List A	21	18	0	506	82	28.11	82.00	0	5	3	0
Twenty20	8	3	2	15	13	15.00	125.00	0	0	2	0
Bowling	**Inns**	**Balls**	**Runs**	**Wkts**	**BBI**	**BBM**	**Ave**	**Econ**	**SR**	**5w**	**10**
First-class	65	2405	1264	30	4/55	4/34	42.13	3.15	80.1	0	0
List A	21	144	118	4	1/9	1/9	29.50	4.91	36.0	0	0
Twenty20	8	12	13	1	1/7	1/7	13.00	6.50	12.0	0	0

IAN WESTWOOD LHB OB

FULL NAME: Ian James Westwood
BORN: July 13, 1982, Birmingham, Warwickshire
SQUAD NO: 22
HEIGHT: 5ft 7in
NICKNAME: Westy, Wezzo, Tot
EDUCATION: Wheelers Lane Boys' School; Solihull Sixth Form College
TEAMS: Warwickshire, Warwickshire Cricket Board
CAREER: First-class: 2003; List A: 2001; T20: 2005

BEST BATTING: 178 Warwickshire vs West Indies A, Birmingham, 2006
BEST BOWLING: 2-39 Warwickshire vs Hampshire, Southampton, 2009
COUNTY CAP: 2008

FAMILY TIES? Granddad was a member at Warwickshire. Brother played Warwickshire junior cricket
CAREER HIGHLIGHTS? Getting my county cap and being named club captain
CRICKETING HEROES? Stuart Eustace, Phil Stephenson, Vanraaj Padhaal
BEST PLAYER IN COUNTY CRICKET? Marcus Trescothick
TIPS FOR THE TOP? George and Isaac Maddy
IF YOU WEREN'T A CRICKETER? No idea!
WHEN RAIN STOPS PLAY? Playing iPhone games, eating, annoying the balding physio
FAVOURITE TV? House
FAVOURITE FILM? Old School
FAVOURITE BOOK? The Cricketers' Who's Who
DREAM HOLIDAY? Skegness
GUILTY PLEASURES? Sweets, Birmingham City FC

Batting	Mat	Inns	NO	Runs	HS	Ave	SR	100	50	Ct	St
First-class	108	183	18	5613	178	34.01	44.67	12	30	60	0
List A	59	49	9	928	65	23.20		0	3	6	0
Twenty20	38	27	12	342	49*	22.80	114.00	0	0	5	0
Bowling	**Inns**	**Balls**	**Runs**	**Wkts**	**BBI**	**BBM**	**Ave**	**Econ**	**SR**	**5w**	**10**
First-class	108	443	264	6	2/39		44.00	3.57	73.8	0	0
List A	59	252	215	3	1/28	1/28	71.66	5.11	84.0	0	0
Twenty20	38	54	91	5	3/29	3/29	18.20	10.11	10.8	0	0

ADAM WHEATER RHB WK

FULL NAME: Adam Jack Wheater
BORN: February 13, 1990, Whipps Cross, Essex
SQUAD NO: 31
HEIGHT: 5ft 6in
NICKNAME: Wheats
EDUCATION: Millfield School
TEAMS: Badureliya Sports Club, Cambridge MCCU, England Under-19s, Essex, Essex 2nd XI, Essex Under-17s, Hampshire, Matabeleland Tuskers
CAREER: First-class: 2008; List A: 2010; T20: 2009

BEST BATTING: 164 Essex vs Northamptonshire, Chelmsford, 2011
BEST BOWLING: 1-86 Essex vs Leicestershire, Leicester, 2012

WHO WOULD PLAY YOU IN A FILM OF YOUR LIFE? Frodo Baggins
CAREER HIGHLIGHTS? My career-best against Northants and having the opportunity to see the world through cricket
MOST MARKED CHARACTERISTIC? I'm argumentative
BEST PLAYER IN COUNTY CRICKET? Bowling: Dave Masters. Batting: Marcus Trescothick
TIPS FOR THE TOP? Reece Topley, Tymal Mills
IF YOU WEREN'T A CRICKETER? I'd find myself a very wealthy girlfriend I could sponge off
DESERT ISLAND DISC? At the moment it would be Snow Patrol's Greatest Hits
FAVOURITE TV? Jamie Oliver's cooking shows
CRICKETING HEROES? Alec Stewart, Nasser Hussain, Adam Gilchrist
ACCOMPLISHMENTS? I won a bottle of vodka at my local pub quiz
WHEN YOU RETIRE? I'll take a ski season in Canada
FANTASY SLIP CORDON? Keeper: Spider-Man (he's taking everyone's catches), 1st: Anthony Kiedis (he would have some stories to tell), 2nd: Micky Flanagan (just in case you had a long time in the field), 3rd: Shakira (to teach me Spanish)

Batting	Mat	Inns	NO	Runs	HS	Ave	SR	100	50	Ct	St
First-class	50	73	10	2463	164	39.09	71.99	3	17	76	1
List A	36	25	2	456	69	19.82	96.00	0	2	11	0
Twenty20	33	25	6	227	29	11.94	100.44	0	0	9	6
Bowling	**Inns**	**Balls**	**Runs**	**Wkts**	**BBI**	**BBM**	**Ave**	**Econ**	**SR**	**5w**	**10**
First-class	50	24	86	1	1/86	1/86	86.00	21.50	24.0	0	0
List A	36	-	-	-	-	-	-	-	-	-	-
Twenty20	33	-	-	-	-	-	-	-	-	-	-

CAMERON WHITE RHB LB R1

FULL NAME: Cameron Leon White
BORN: August 18, 1983, Bairnsdale, Australia
SQUAD NO: 4
HEIGHT: 6ft 1in
NICKNAME: Whitey, Bear
TEAMS: Australia, Australia A, Deccan Chargers, Melbourne Stars, Royal Challengers Bangalore, Somerset, Victoria
CAREER: Test: 2008; ODI: 2005; T20I: 2007; First-class: 2000; List A: 2001; T20: 2005

BEST BATTING: 260* Somerset vs Derbyshire, Derby, 2006
BEST BOWLING: 6-66 Victoria vs Western Australia, Melbourne, 2003
COUNTY CAP: 2006 (Somerset)

NOTES: White returns as one of Northants' overseas players for the FL t20 for a second season in succession. He was the youngest player to captain the state of Victoria and has also captained the Australian T20 side. He scored centuries in consecutive T20 matches for Somerset during the 2006 season, including 141* off 70 balls which held the record for the highest individual T20 score for almost two years until Brendon McCullum went past him

Batting	Mat	Inns	NO	Runs	HS	Ave	SR	100	50	Ct	St
Tests	4	7	2	146	46	29.20	44.24	0	0	1	0
ODIs	87	73	15	2037	105	35.12	80.48	2	11	37	0
T20Is	38	35	10	712	85*	28.48	133.58	0	3	21	0
First-class	127	214	27	7580	260*	40.53		17	34	133	0
List A	217	188	29	5344	126*	33.61	78.55	6	31	96	0
Twenty20	146	137	32	3197	141*	30.44	132.38	2	18	61	0
Bowling	**Inns**	**Balls**	**Runs**	**Wkts**	**BBI**	**BBM**	**Ave**	**Econ**	**SR**	**5w**	**10**
Tests	4	558	342	5	2/71	3/119	68.40	3.67	111.6	0	0
ODIs	87	331	351	12	3/5	3/5	29.25	6.36	27.5	0	0
T20Is	38	30	37	1	1/11	1/11	37.00	7.40	30.0	0	0
First-class	127	12573	7318	180	6/66		40.65	3.49	69.8	3	1
List A	217	3946	3541	97	4/15	4/15	36.50	5.38	40.6	0	0
Twenty20	146	424	630	25	4/10	4/10	25.20	8.91	16.9	0	0

NOTTINGHAMSHIRE

GRAEME WHITE RHB SLA

FULL NAME: Graeme Geoffrey White
BORN: April 18, 1987, Milton Keynes, Buckinghamshire
SQUAD NO: 87
HEIGHT: 5ft 11in
NICKNAME: Chalky, Whitey, Pony
EDUCATION: Stowe School, Buckingham
TEAMS: England Under-19s, Northamptonshire, Northamptonshire 2nd XI, Nottinghamshire
CAREER: First-class: 2006; List A: 2007; T20: 2007

BEST BATTING: 65 Northamptonshire vs Glamorgan, Colwyn Bay, 2007
BEST BOWLING: 4-72 Nottinghamshire vs Durham, Nottingham, 2011

IF YOU WEREN'T A CRICKETER? Bus driver
DESERT ISLAND DISC? Kings Of Leon – Sex On Fire
BIGGEST DRESSING DOWN YOU'VE RECEIVED? For playing the reverse sweep all the time
CRICKETING HEROES? Phil Tufnell, Bishan Bedi, Daniel Vettori
NON-CRICKETING HEROES? Olly Murs, Barack Obama
ACCOMPLISHMENTS? I won the Crazy Golf Championship in Skegness in 2010
WHEN YOU RETIRE? Social worker
FANTASY SLIP CORDON? Keeper: Paul Ince, 1st: Me, 2nd: Wayne Noon, 3rd: Beyonce, Gully: David Capel

Batting	Mat	Inns	NO	Runs	HS	Ave	SR	100	50	Ct	St
First-class	21	32	5	418	65	15.48	45.23	0	2	8	0
List A	35	20	8	161	39*	13.41	84.73	0	0	11	0
Twenty20	31	9	4	68	26*	13.60	115.25	0	0	11	0
Bowling	**Inns**	**Balls**	**Runs**	**Wkts**	**BBI**	**BBM**	**Ave**	**Econ**	**SR**	**5w**	**10**
First-class	21	2608	1493	34	4/72	7/89	43.91	3.43	76.7	0	0
List A	35	1065	952	36	5/35	5/35	26.44	5.36	29.5	1	0
Twenty20	31	395	522	21	3/22	3/22	24.85	7.92	18.8	0	0

WAYNE WHITE RHB RMF MVP32

FULL NAME: Wayne Andrew White
BORN: September 22, 1985, Derby
SQUAD NO: 25
HEIGHT: 6ft 3in
NICKNAME: Chalky, Sticks, Waz
EDUCATION: John Port School; Nottingham Trent University
TEAMS: Derbyshire, Derbyshire 2nd XI, Lancashire, Leicestershire
CAREER: First-class: 2005; List A: 2006; T20: 2009

BEST BATTING: 101* Leicestershire vs Derbyshire, Derby, 2010
BEST BOWLING: 5-54 Leicestershire vs Derbyshire, Derby, 2012

FAMILY TIES? Brother [Harry] is at the Derbyshire Academy
CAREER HIGHLIGHTS? Winning the T20 Cup and scoring my first hundred
CRICKETING HEROES? Mike Hendrick, Dominic Cork
BEST PLAYER IN COUNTY CRICKET? Marcus Trescothick
TIPS FOR THE TOP? Shiv Thakor, Liam Kinch
IF YOU WEREN'T A CRICKETER? Trying to be a footballer
WHEN RAIN STOPS PLAY? iPod, Football Manager, annoying everyone
FAVOURITE TV? 90210
FAVOURITE FILM? Saving Private Ryan, Gladiator
FAVOURITE BOOK? Cricketers' Who's Who
DREAM HOLIDAY? Grenada, Ibiza
ACCOMPLISHMENTS? Playing in the FA Cup, four years no claims on my car insurance
SURPRISING SKILL? DJ
GUILTY PLEASURES? Dunking biscuits
TWITTER FEED: @wayneAwhite

Batting	Mat	Inns	NO	Runs	HS	Ave	SR	100	50	Ct	St
First-class	62	100	13	2285	101*	26.26	51.23	1	12	20	0
List A	55	46	13	627	46*	19.00	84.38	0	0	13	0
Twenty20	48	36	15	345	26	16.42	113.11	0	0	23	0
Bowling	**Inns**	**Balls**	**Runs**	**Wkts**	**BBI**	**BBM**	**Ave**	**Econ**	**SR**	**5w**	**10**
First-class	62	7600	5003	139	5/54		35.99	3.94	54.6	4	0
List A	55	1744	1866	46	6/29	6/29	40.56	6.41	37.9	1	0
Twenty20	48	573	927	21	3/27	3/27	44.14	9.70	27.2	0	0

ROSS WHITELEY — LHB LM

FULL NAME: Ross Andrew Whiteley
BORN: September 13, 1988, Sheffield, Yorkshire
SQUAD NO: 44
HEIGHT: 6ft 2in
NICKNAME: Rossco, Pico, Brick
EDUCATION: Westfield School; Repton School; Leeds Metropolitan University
TEAMS: Derbyshire, Derbyshire 2nd XI
CAREER: First-class: 2008; List A: 2008; T20: 2011

BEST BATTING: 130* Derbyshire vs Kent, Derby, 2011
BEST BOWLING: 2-6 Derbyshire vs Hampshire, Derby, 2012

FAMILY TIES? Brother Adam played Derbyshire age-groups and 2nd XI cricket
CAREER HIGHLIGHTS? Maiden century at Northampton, signing my first professional contract
SUPERSTITIONS? Every time I am on strike I scrape my mark three times
CRICKETING HEROES? Martin Guptill, Shane Warne, Ben Hilfenhaus
NON-CRICKETING HEROES? Buddy Franklin – Hawthorn Hawks
TIPS FOR THE TOP? Will Beer, Tom Poynton, Greg Smith
IF YOU WEREN'T A CRICKETER? Playing some other form of sport
FAVOURITE BOOK? Sniper One
TWITTER FEED: @RossWhiteley44

Batting	Mat	Inns	NO	Runs	HS	Ave	SR	100	50	Ct	St
First-class	27	43	7	1198	130*	33.27	45.83	2	5	14	0
List A	19	16	2	197	40	14.07	71.11	0	0	6	0
Twenty20	17	16	7	266	40*	29.55	129.75	0	0	3	0
Bowling	**Inns**	**Balls**	**Runs**	**Wkts**	**BBI**	**BBM**	**Ave**	**Econ**	**SR**	**5w**	**10**
First-class	27	1681	1159	26	2/6	4/43	44.57	4.13	64.6	0	0
List A	19	144	144	3	1/17	1/17	48.00	6.00	48.0	0	0
Twenty20	17	36	46	2	1/12	1/12	23.00	7.66	18.0	0	0

OLLIE WILKIN RHB RMF

FULL NAME: Oliver Wilkin
BORN: April 6, 1992, Ealing, Middlesex
SQUAD NO: 30
HEIGHT: 6ft 3in
NICKNAME: Oli, O'z, Wilko
EDUCATION: Merchant Taylors' School; Loughborough University
TEAMS: Loughborough MCCU, Middlesex, Middlesex Under-15s, Middlesex Under-17s
CAREER: First-class: 2011; T20: 2012

BEST BATTING: 38 Loughborough MCCU vs Northamptonshire, Loughborough, 2011
BEST BOWLING: 2-63 Loughborough MCCU vs Kent, Canterbury, 2011

FAMILY TIES? My dad played a lot when he was younger but never professionally
WHO WOULD PLAY YOU IN A FILM OF YOUR LIFE? Keira Knightly or Orlando Bloom
CAREER HIGHLIGHTS? My first three T20 games in 2012
SUPERSTITIONS? I always turn over my left shoulder during my run-up when bowling
TIPS FOR THE TOP? James Taylor, Joe Root
DESERT ISLAND DISC? Dire Straits
FAVOURITE TV? 24
CRICKETING HEROES? Andrew Flintoff, Ian Botham
WHEN YOU RETIRE? I'd like to coach and fish
SURPRISING FACT? I have a phobia of shins
FANTASY SLIP CORDON? Keeper: Michael McIntyre, 1st: Brian Johnson, 2nd: Mark Knopfler, 3rd: Amber Heard, 4th: Frankie Boyle, Gully: Rowan Atkinson
TWITTER FEED: @oliwilkin

Batting	Mat	Inns	NO	Runs	HS	Ave	SR	100	50	Ct	St
First-class	3	6	0	138	38	23.00	57.26	0	0	1	0
Twenty20	3	3	1	38	28	19.00	122.58	0	0	4	0
Bowling	**Inns**	**Balls**	**Runs**	**Wkts**	**BBI**	**BBM**	**Ave**	**Econ**	**SR**	**5w**	**10**
First-class	3	300	213	4	2/63	2/63	53.25	4.26	75.0	0	0
Twenty20	3	24	20	4	3/12	3/12	5.00	5.00	6.0	0	0

DAVID WILLEY

LHB LFM MVP43

NORTHAMPTONSHIRE

FULL NAME: David Jonathan Willey
BORN: February 28, 1990, Northampton
SQUAD NO: 15
HEIGHT: 6ft 1in
NICKNAME: Willow, Wildman, Will
EDUCATION: Northampton School for Boys
TEAMS: England Under-19s, Northamptonshire, Northamptonshire 2nd XI
CAREER: First-class: 2009; List A: 2009; T20: 2009

BEST BATTING: 76 Northamptonshire vs Yorkshire, Northampton, 2012
BEST BOWLING: 5-29 Northamptonshire vs Gloucestershire, Northampton, 2011

FAMILY TIES? My dad [Peter] played a bit for Northants, Leicester and England
WHO WOULD PLAY YOU IN A FILM OF YOUR LIFE? Jack Bauer
CAREER HIGHLIGHTS? Playing in T20 Finals Day in 2009 and taking 10 wickets in a match vs Gloucestershire
SUPERSTITIONS? I put my left pad on first and turn right at the end of my run-up
MOST MARKED CHARACTERISTIC? Massive chin
TIP FOR THE TOP? Ben Duckett
DESERT ISLAND DISC? Bob Marley – Legend
FAVOURITE TV? 24
CRICKETING HEROES? Peter Willey
ACCOMPLISHMENTS? Cycling from Land's End to John O'Groats for Cancer Research UK
WHEN YOU RETIRE? Sit on a beach in Australia
FANTASY SLIP CORDON? Keeper: Jason Statham, 1st: Sylvester Stallone, 2nd: Arnold Schwarzenegger, 3rd: Jean Claude Van Damme, Gully: Jack Bauer
TWITTER FEED: @david_willey

Batting	Mat	Inns	NO	Runs	HS	Ave	SR	100	50	Ct	St
First-class	30	41	8	979	76	29.66	51.47	0	7	7	0
List A	37	28	4	423	74	17.62	85.28	0	2	13	0
Twenty20	48	30	12	268	30*	14.88	103.07	0	0	15	0
Bowling	**Inns**	**Balls**	**Runs**	**Wkts**	**BBI**	**BBM**	**Ave**	**Econ**	**SR**	**5w**	**10**
First-class	30	3750	2155	68	5/29	10/75	31.69	3.44	55.1	3	1
List A	37	918	873	22	3/49	3/49	39.68	5.70	41.7	0	0
Twenty20	48	515	637	32	3/9	3/9	19.90	7.42	16.0	0	0

ROBBIE WILLIAMS RHB RFM

FULL NAME: Robert Edward Morgan Williams
BORN: January 19, 1987, Pembury, Kent
SQUAD NO: 13
HEIGHT: 6ft
EDUCATION: Marlborough School; Durham University
TEAMS: Durham MCCU, Marylebone Cricket Club, Leicestershire, Middlesex, Middlesex 2nd XI
CAREER: First-class: 2007; List A: 2007; T20: 2010

BEST BATTING: 31 Durham UCCE vs Lancashire, Durham University, 2009
BEST BOWLING: 5-70 Durham UCCE vs Lancashire, Durham University, 2007

WHO WOULD PLAY YOU IN A FILM OF YOUR LIFE? Gene Wilder
CAREER HIGHLIGHTS? Winning the 2nd XI Trophy in 2007 and playing against Australia at Lord's
MOST MARKED CHARACTERISTIC? My feet
BEST PLAYER IN COUNTY CRICKET? Nick Compton
TIP FOR THE TOP? Tom Helm – Middlesex fast bowler
IF YOU WEREN'T A CRICKETER? Playing table-tennis
DESERT ISLAND DISC? The Very Best Of Supertramp
FAVOURITE TV? Family Guy
BIGGEST DRESSING DOWN YOU'VE RECEIVED? Something involving concierges...
CRICKETING HEROES? Dale Steyn, Malcolm Marshall
NON-CRICKETING HEROES? David Attenborough, Jamie Oliver
ACCOMPLISHMENTS? Obtaining a degree
SURPRISING FACT? I'm slightly metallic
FANTASY SLIP CORDON? Keeper: Michael McIntyre, 1st: Jamie Oliver, 2nd: Me, 3rd: Doctor Who, Gully: Sherlock Holmes

Batting	Mat	Inns	NO	Runs	HS	Ave	SR	100	50	Ct	St
First-class	9	15	5	119	31	11.90	35.95	0	0	4	0
List A	8	1	1	2	2*	-	28.57	0	0	1	0
Twenty20	2	-	-	-	-	-	-	-	-	0	0
Bowling	**Inns**	**Balls**	**Runs**	**Wkts**	**BBI**	**BBM**	**Ave**	**Econ**	**SR**	**5w**	**10**
First-class	9	1241	755	23	5/70	5/115	32.82	3.65	53.9	2	0
List A	8	251	325	2	2/60	2/60	162.50	7.76	125.5	0	0
Twenty20	2	24	55	0	-	-	-	13.75	-	0	0

GARY WILSON

RHB WK

SURREY

FULL NAME: Gary Craig Wilson
BORN: February 5, 1986, Dundonald
SQUAD NO: 14
HEIGHT: 5ft 9in
NICKNAME: Gaz, Wils, Suede
EDUCATION: Methodist College, Belfast
TEAMS: Ireland, Ireland Under-19s, Surrey, Surrey 2nd XI
CAREER: ODI: 2007; T20I: 2008; First-class: 2005; List A: 2006; T20: 2008

BEST BATTING: 125 Surrey vs Leicestershire, Leicester, 2010

CAREER HIGHLIGHTS? Playing in the World Cup and beating England, plus my maiden Championship and ODI hundreds
SUPERSTITIONS? Left pad first
CRICKETING HEROES? Alec Stewart
NON-CRICKETING HEROES? David Beckham, Sir Alex Ferguson
BEST PLAYER IN COUNTY CRICKET? Marcus Trescothick
TIPS FOR THE TOP? Jason Roy, Paul Stirling
IF YOU WEREN'T A CRICKETER? Probably a fireman or policeman
WHEN RAIN STOPS PLAY? On the internet, thinking about where I can play golf next
FAVOURITE TV? Spooks, The Apprentice, TOWIE
DREAM HOLIDAY? Zanzibar
GUILTY PLEASURES? Haribo sweets, Sensations crisps
SURPRISING FACTS? I have the biggest head in the changing room in terms of volume and I played Ulster Schools rugby
TWITTER FEED: @gwilson14

Batting	Mat	Inns	NO	Runs	HS	Ave	SR	100	50	Ct	St
ODIs	39	38	4	953	113	28.02	75.27	1	6	23	7
T20Is	27	23	3	431	41*	21.55	89.79	0	0	14	1
First-class	30	46	4	1178	125	28.04		1	6	53	1
List A	97	85	7	1801	113	23.08	69.34	1	12	62	18
Twenty20	66	54	14	983	54*	24.57	105.58	0	3	33	7
Bowling	**Inns**	**Balls**	**Runs**	**Wkts**	**BBI**	**BBM**	**Ave**	**Econ**	**SR**	**5w**	**10**
ODIs	39	-	-	-	-	-	-	-	-	-	-
T20Is	27	-	-	-	-	-	-	-	-	-	-
First-class	30	66	46	0	-	-	-	4.18	-	0	0
List A	97	-	-	-	-	-	-	-	-	-	-
Twenty20	66	-	-	-	-	-	-	-	-	-	-

CHRIS WOAKES RHB RMF W2 MVP25

FULL NAME: Christopher Roger Woakes
BORN: March 2, 1989, Birmingham, Warwickshire
SQUAD NO: 19
HEIGHT: 6ft 1in
NICKNAME: Woaksy, Woako, Wiz, GB
EDUCATION: Barr Beacon School
TEAMS: England, England Lions, England Under-19s, Herefordshire, Marylebone Cricket Club, Warwickshire, Wellington
CAREER: ODI: 2011; T20I: 2011; First-class: 2006; List A: 2007; T20: 2008

BEST BATTING: 136* Warwickshire vs Hampshire, Birmingham, 2010
BEST BOWLING: 7-20 Warwickshire vs Hampshire, Birmingham, 2011
COUNTY CAP: 2009

CAREER HIGHLIGHTS? Winning the CB40 in 2010 with Warwickshire. Making my debut for England in Australia in January 2011
CRICKETING HEROES? Jacques Kallis
NON-CRICKETING HEROES? Paul 'God' McGrath
BEST PLAYER IN COUNTY CRICKET? Marcus Trescothick
TIP FOR THE TOP? Tom Milnes
IF YOU WEREN'T A CRICKETER? I'd be just finishing university and struggling to find a job! I am very lucky to be doing something I love
WHEN RAIN STOPS PLAY? Eat, relax, or play a silly game called Tit!
FAVOURITE TV? An Idiot Abroad or A League Of Their Own
FAVOURITE FILM? Gladiator, The Hangover, Old School
FAVOURITE BOOK? Paul McGrath's autobiography
TWITTER FEED: @crwoakes19

Batting	Mat	Inns	NO	Runs	HS	Ave	SR	100	50	Ct	St
ODIs	11	8	4	92	33*	23.00	74.19	0	0	4	0
T20Is	3	3	2	37	19*	37.00	123.33	0	0	1	0
First-class	73	96	26	2678	136*	38.25		6	10	36	0
List A	76	47	17	568	49*	18.93	87.38	0	0	16	0
Twenty20	56	30	18	361	55*	30.08	139.92	0	1	26	0
Bowling	**Inns**	**Balls**	**Runs**	**Wkts**	**BBI**	**BBM**	**Ave**	**Econ**	**SR**	**5w**	**10**
ODIs	11	512	463	15	6/45	6/45	30.86	5.42	34.1	1	0
T20Is	3	60	94	2	1/29	1/29	47.00	9.40	30.0	0	0
First-class	73	12679	6493	254	7/20	11/97	25.56	3.07	49.9	12	3
List A	76	2950	2673	80	6/45	6/45	33.41	5.43	36.8	1	0
Twenty20	56	1042	1417	55	4/21	4/21	25.76	8.15	18.9	0	0

CHRIS WOOD RHB LMF MVP61

FULL NAME: Christopher Philip Wood
BORN: June 27, 1990, Basingstoke, Hampshire
SQUAD NO: 25
HEIGHT: 6ft 3in
NICKNAME: Woody
EDUCATION: Amery Hill Secondary School; Alton College
TEAMS: England Under-19s, Hampshire, Hampshire 2nd XI
CAREER: First-class: 2010; List A: 2010; T20: 2010

BEST BATTING: 105* Hampshire vs Leicestershire, Leicester, 2012
BEST BOWLING: 5-41 Hampshire vs Loughborough MCCU, Southampton, 2012

CAREER HIGHLIGHTS? Winning the 2010 T20 competition
SUPERSTITIONS? I always put my right shoe on before the left
CRICKETING HEROES? Freddie Flintoff
NON-CRICKETING HEROES? David Beckham
BEST PLAYER IN COUNTY CRICKET? Marcus Trescothick
TIPS FOR THE TOP? James Vince, James Taylor, Ben Stokes
IF YOU WEREN'T A CRICKETER? Dustbin man
WHEN RAIN STOPS PLAY? Listening to music, playing on my phone, or playing poker
FAVOURITE TV? A League Of Their Own
FAVOURITE FILM? Snatch
DREAM HOLIDAY? Las Vegas
ACCOMPLISHMENTS? I played in the FA Cup
SURPRISING FACT? I trialled for Chelsea FC
FANTASY SLIP CORDON? Keeper: Kelly Brook, 1st: Katy Perry, 2nd: Cheryl Cole, 3rd: Kim Kardashian, Gully: Delta White
TWITTER FEED: @CWoody27

Batting	Mat	Inns	NO	Runs	HS	Ave	SR	100	50	Ct	St
First-class	21	30	2	651	105*	23.25	67.95	1	2	5	0
List A	34	16	4	79	16	6.58	72.47	0	0	10	0
Twenty20	44	12	5	59	18	8.42	96.72	0	0	15	0
Bowling	**Inns**	**Balls**	**Runs**	**Wkts**	**BBI**	**BBM**	**Ave**	**Econ**	**SR**	**5w**	**10**
First-class	21	3226	1643	63	5/41	7/49	26.07	3.05	51.2	2	0
List A	34	1341	1238	55	5/22	5/22	22.50	5.53	24.3	1	0
Twenty20	44	844	1160	42	3/26	3/26	27.61	8.24	20.0	0	0

MARK WOOD RHB RMF

FULL NAME: Mark Andrew Wood
BORN: January 11, 1990, Ashington, Northumberland
SQUAD NO: 33
HEIGHT: 6ft
NICKNAME: Woody
EDUCATION: Ashington High School; Newcastle College
TEAMS: Durham, Durham 2nd XI, Durham Academy, Northumberland
CAREER: First-class: 2011; List A: 2011

BEST BATTING: 48 Durham vs Sri Lanka A, Chester-le-Street, 2011
BEST BOWLING: 5-78 Durham vs Nottinghamshire, Nottingham, 2012

FAMILY TIES? My uncle Neil Wood played minor counties cricket for Northumberland
WHO WOULD PLAY YOU IN A FILM OF YOUR LIFE? Vinnie Jones
CAREER HIGHLIGHTS? Taking 5-78 against Notts at Trent Bridge in 2012. County debut against Durham University
BEST PLAYER IN COUNTY CRICKET? Graham Onions
TIP FOR THE TOP? Ben Stokes
IF YOU WEREN'T A CRICKETER? Studying to be a school teacher
DESERT ISLAND DISC? Kasabian – Empire
FAVOURITE TV? Game Of Thrones
BIGGEST DRESSING DOWN YOU'VE RECEIVED? From academy coach John Windows every week, sometimes twice a week or more
CRICKETING HEROES? Graham Onions, Steve Harmison, Ian Botham
NON-CRICKETING HEROES? Lennox Lewis, David Beckham
ACCOMPLISHMENTS? Degree in Sports Management and Development
WHEN YOU RETIRE? Teach sport
SURPRISING FACTS? I was in the Newcastle United FC Academy. I am an AFC Wimbledon fan
TWITTER FEED: @MAWood33

Batting	Mat	Inns	NO	Runs	HS	Ave	SR	100	50	Ct	St
First-class	5	9	1	194	48	24.25	56.39	0	0	6	0
List A	5	3	1	7	5	3.50	53.84	0	0	4	0
Bowling	**Inns**	**Balls**	**Runs**	**Wkts**	**BBI**	**BBM**	**Ave**	**Econ**	**SR**	**5w**	**10**
First-class	5	622	411	19	5/78	5/97	21.63	3.96	32.7	1	0
List A	5	156	125	5	3/32	3/32	25.00	4.80	31.2	0	0

SAM WOOD LHB OB

FULL NAME: Samuel Kenneth William Wood
BORN: April 3, 1993, Nottingham
SQUAD NO: 23
HEIGHT: 6ft
NICKNAME: Woody, Swood, Gorm
EDUCATION: Colonel Frank Seely School; West Nottinghamshire College; South Nottinghamshire College
TEAMS: England Under-19s, Nottinghamshire, Nottinghamshire 2nd XI, Nottinghamshire Under-17s
CAREER: First-class: 2011; List A: 2011

BEST BATTING: 45 Nottinghamshire vs Surrey, The Oval, 2012
BEST BOWLING: 3-64 Nottinghamshire vs Surrey, The Oval, 2012

CAREER HIGHLIGHTS? Representing England U19, making my debut for Notts in one-day and four-day cricket, signing my first professional contract
CRICKETING HEROES? Marcus Trescothick, Mike Hussey, Brian Lara
NON-CRICKETING HEROES? Muhammad Ali
BEST PLAYER IN COUNTY CRICKET? Andre Adams
TIPS FOR THE TOP? Tom Rowe, Simon Webster
IF YOU WEREN'T A CRICKETER? I'd be going to university
WHEN RAIN STOPS PLAY? Listen to music, put the feet up
FAVOURITE TV? Coronation Street, The Inbetweeners
FAVOURITE FILM? Man On Fire
FAVOURITE BOOK? Muhammad Ali's autobiography
DREAM HOLIDAY? Abu Dhabi
SURPRISING FACT? I made my Notts Premier League debut when I was 10 for Blidworth
FANTASY SLIP CORDON? Keeper: Peter Kay, 1st: Michael Hall, 2nd: Megan Fox, 3rd: Luke Fletcher, Gully: Myself
TWITTER FEED: @SamWood33

Batting	Mat	Inns	NO	Runs	HS	Ave	SR	100	50	Ct	St
First-class	2	2	0	47	45	23.50	39.83	0	0	0	0
List A	4	3	0	8	8	2.66	47.05	0	0	2	0
Bowling	**Inns**	**Balls**	**Runs**	**Wkts**	**BBI**	**BBM**	**Ave**	**Econ**	**SR**	**5w**	**10**
First-class	2	192	92	3	3/64	3/84	30.66	2.87	64.0	0	0
List A	4	66	72	3	2/24	2/24	24.00	6.54	22.0	0	0

BEN WRIGHT RHB RM

FULL NAME: Ben James Wright
BORN: December 5, 1987, Preston, Lancashire
SQUAD NO: 29
HEIGHT: 5ft 11in
NICKNAME: Bej, Keller
EDUCATION: Cowbridge Comprehensive
TEAMS: England Under-19s, Glamorgan, Wales Minor Counties
CAREER: First-class: 2006; List A: 2006; T20: 2007

BEST BATTING: 172 Glamorgan vs Gloucestershire, Cardiff, 2007
BEST BOWLING: 1-14 Glamorgan vs Essex, Chelmsford, 2007
COUNTY CAP: 2011

CAREER HIGHLIGHTS? Scoring a hundred vs Middlesex at Lord's
CRICKETING HEROES? Andrew Flintoff, Matthew Maynard
NON-CRICKETING HEROES? Jonny Wilkinson
BEST PLAYER IN COUNTY CRICKET? Marcus Trescothick
TIP FOR THE TOP? Andrew Salter
IF YOU WEREN'T A CRICKETER? Fitness trainer
WHEN RAIN STOPS PLAY? Annoying people
FAVOURITE TV? Eastbound And Down
FAVOURITE FILM? Wedding Crashers
FAVOURITE BOOK? Jonny Wilkinson's autobiography
DREAM HOLIDAY? Hawaii
ACCOMPLISHMENTS? Playing rugby at U16 level for Wales
GUILTY PLEASURES? Pizza
TWITTER FEED: @bej29w

Batting	Mat	Inns	NO	Runs	HS	Ave	SR	100	50	Ct	St
First-class	63	103	7	2648	172	27.58	50.57	5	11	31	0
List A	63	57	7	1153	79	23.06	71.39	0	6	12	0
Twenty20	34	29	10	433	55*	22.78	105.86	0	1	11	0
Bowling	**Inns**	**Balls**	**Runs**	**Wkts**	**BBI**	**BBM**	**Ave**	**Econ**	**SR**	**5w**	**10**
First-class	63	270	167	2	1/14	1/14	83.50	3.71	135.0	0	0
List A	63	132	126	1	1/19	1/19	126.00	5.72	132.0	0	0
Twenty20	34	24	22	1	1/16	1/16	22.00	5.50	24.0	0	0

CHRIS WRIGHT — RHB RFM W1 MVP6

FULL NAME: Christopher Julian Clement Wright
BORN: July 14, 1985, Chipping Norton, Oxfordshire
SQUAD NO: 31
HEIGHT: 6ft 3in
NICKNAME: Wrighty, Baron, Almunia
EDUCATION: Eggars Grammar School, Alton
TEAMS: British Universities, Cambridge MCCU, England Lions, Essex, Tamil Union Cricket and Athletic Club, Warwickshire
CAREER: First-class: 2004; List A: 2004; T20: 2004

BEST BATTING: 77 Essex vs Cambridge MCCU, Cambridge, 2011
BEST BOWLING: 6-22 Essex vs Leicestershire, Leicester, 2008

CAREER HIGHLIGHTS? Winning the County Championship in 2012 and the FP Trophy in 2008
MOST MARKED CHARACTERISTIC? My awesome lid!
BEST PLAYER IN COUNTY CRICKET? Chris Woakes
DESERT ISLAND DISC? Linkin Park – Hybrid Theory
ACCOMPLISHMENTS? Two lovely children
FANTASY SLIP CORDON? Keeper: Me, 1st: Phil Edwards, 2nd: Tony Palladino, 3rd: Gareth James, Gully: Matt Hooper
TWITTER FEED: @ChrisWright1985

Batting	Mat	Inns	NO	Runs	HS	Ave	SR	100	50	Ct	St
First-class	79	98	25	1353	77	18.53	51.97	0	5	15	0
List A	85	35	16	215	42	11.31	79.92	0	0	15	0
Twenty20	43	10	6	22	6*	5.50	115.78	0	0	8	0
Bowling	**Inns**	**Balls**	**Runs**	**Wkts**	**BBI**	**BBM**	**Ave**	**Econ**	**SR**	**5w**	**10**
First-class	79	12811	7728	224	6/22		34.50	3.61	57.1	6	0
List A	85	3293	3018	84	4/20	4/20	35.92	5.49	39.2	0	0
Twenty20	43	854	1261	39	4/24	4/24	32.33	8.85	21.8	0	0

LUKE WRIGHT RHB RMF MVP49

FULL NAME: Luke James Wright
BORN: March 7, 1985, Grantham, Lincolnshire
SQUAD NO: 10
HEIGHT: 6ft
NICKNAME: Wrighty
EDUCATION: Belvoir High School; Ratcliffe College; Loughborough University
TEAMS: England, Dhaka Gladiators, England Lions, Impi, Leicestershire, Melbourne Stars, Pune Warriors, Sussex, Wellington
CAREER: ODI: 2007; T20I: 2007; First-class: 2003; List A: 2002; T20: 2004

BEST BATTING: 155* Sussex vs MCC, Lord's, 2008
BEST BOWLING: 5-65 Sussex vs Derbyshire, Derby, 2010
COUNTY CAP: 2007

FAMILY TIES? My father is a very keen cricketer – he's a Level 2 coach – and my brother played for Leicestershire
SUPERSTITIONS? Too many to mention
CRICKETING HEROES? Jacques Kallis, Andrew Flintoff
NOTES: Has won the Denis Compton Medal three times. Scored exactly 100 on his first-class debut for Sussex, against Loughborough UCCE – both the bowler (Chris Nash) and the catcher (Monty Panesar) who dismissed him are now teammates at Sussex. England's leading run-scorer at last year's ICC World T20

Batting	Mat	Inns	NO	Runs	HS	Ave	SR	100	50	Ct	St
ODIs	46	35	4	701	52	22.61	89.29	0	2	17	0
T20Is	42	36	3	649	99*	19.66	138.08	0	3	13	0
First-class	79	114	16	3460	155*	35.30	64.49	9	18	36	0
List A	155	122	20	2723	125	26.69		4	7	45	0
Twenty20	151	132	13	3131	117	26.31	146.10	2	14	44	0
Bowling	**Inns**	**Balls**	**Runs**	**Wkts**	**BBI**	**BBM**	**Ave**	**Econ**	**SR**	**5w**	**10**
ODIs	46	1020	863	15	2/34	2/34	57.53	5.07	68.0	0	0
T20Is	42	276	369	14	2/24	2/24	26.35	8.02	19.7	0	0
First-class	79	7439	4397	111	5/65		39.61	3.54	67.0	3	0
List A	155	4569	4023	104	4/12	4/12	38.68	5.28	43.9	0	0
Twenty20	151	1572	2189	68	3/17	3/17	32.19	8.35	23.1	0	0

ALEX WYATT RHB RMF

FULL NAME: Alexander Charles Frederick Wyatt
BORN: July 23, 1990, Roehampton
SQUAD NO: 16
HEIGHT: 6ft 7in
NICKNAME: Waz
EDUCATION: Oakham School; Open University
TEAMS: Leicestershire, Leicestershire 2nd XI
CAREER: First-class: 2009; List A: 2009; T20: 2009

BEST BATTING: 8 Leicestershire vs Yorkshire, Scarborough, 2012
BEST BOWLING: 3-35 Leicestershire vs Hampshire, Leicester, 2012

WHO WOULD PLAY YOU IN A FILM OF YOUR LIFE? John Krasinski – better looking version of myself
CAREER HIGHLIGHTS? My 1st XI debuts in all three formats, taking 3-14 in a T20 game against Durham and milking Wayne White for 68 in club cricket
MOST MARKED CHARACTERISTIC? Besides my height, being cool, calm and collected...
TIPS FOR THE TOP? Shiv Thakor, Josh Cobb
IF YOU WEREN'T A CRICKETER? Working in far off countries and travelling the world
DESERT ISLAND DISC? Bob Marley – Legend
CRICKETING HEROES? Glenn McGrath
NON-CRICKETING HEROES? Besides my parents and grandparents, David Attenborough
ACCOMPLISHMENTS? Twelve GCSEs and three A-Levels at Oakham School, Gold Duke of Edinburgh Award and four years no claims on my car insurance
SURPRISING FACT? I have Grade 3 on the piano and used to play the trumpet
FANTASY SLIP CORDON? Keeper: The Hulk (great hands), 1st: Stewart Francis (great one-liners), 2nd: Steve Carell (comedy genius), 3rd: Me, Gully: Usain Bolt (wouldn't need a third man)
TWITTER FEED: @acfwyatt

Batting	Mat	Inns	NO	Runs	HS	Ave	SR	100	50	Ct	St
First-class	12	13	5	28	8	3.50	37.33	0	0	2	0
List A	12	5	3	13	9*	6.50	72.22	0	0	2	0
Twenty20	2	-	-	-	-	-	-	-	-	1	0
Bowling	**Inns**	**Balls**	**Runs**	**Wkts**	**BBI**	**BBM**	**Ave**	**Econ**	**SR**	**5w**	**10**
First-class	12	1632	887	29	3/35	4/65	30.58	3.26	56.2	0	0
List A	12	380	410	10	2/36	2/36	41.00	6.47	38.0	0	0
Twenty20	2	42	36	3	3/14	3/14	12.00	5.14	14.0	0	0

MICHAEL YARDY

LHB SLA R2 MVP51

FULL NAME: Michael Howard Yardy
BORN: November 27, 1980, Pembury, Kent
SQUAD NO: 20
HEIGHT: 6ft
NICKNAME: Yards, Paolo, Moo Moo
EDUCATION: William Parker School, Hastings
TEAMS: England, England Lions, Central Districts, Sussex, Sussex Cricket Board
CAREER: ODI: 2006; T20I: 2006; First-class: 2000; List A: 1999; T20: 2004

BEST BATTING: 257 Sussex vs Bangladeshis, Hove, 2005
BEST BOWLING: 5-83 Sussex vs Bangladeshis, Hove, 2005
COUNTY CAP: 2005

CAREER HIGHLIGHTS? The successes with Sussex. Winning the World T20 in 2010
CRICKETING HEROES? Graham Gooch, Michael Atherton, Alec Stewart, Graham Thorpe
NON-CRICKETING HEROES? Paolo Di Canio, Paul Gascoigne
BEST PLAYER IN COUNTY CRICKET? Marcus Trescothick
IF YOU WEREN'T A CRICKETER? Doing a proper job
WHEN RAIN STOPS PLAY? Reading, irritating people
FAVOURITE TV? Outnumbered
FAVOURITE FILM? Snatch
FAVOURITE BOOK? Tony Cascarino's autobiography
DREAM HOLIDAY? Maldives
SURPRISING SKILL? Very sweet left foot
GUILTY PLEASURES? West Ham United

Batting	Mat	Inns	NO	Runs	HS	Ave	SR	100	50	Ct	St
ODIs	28	24	8	326	60*	20.37	69.06	0	2	10	0
T20Is	14	8	5	96	35*	32.00	133.33	0	0	8	0
First-class	155	258	25	8797	257	37.75		18	44	148	0
List A	195	167	29	3391	98*	24.57		0	22	74	0
Twenty20	99	77	28	1080	76*	22.04	104.44	0	2	36	0
Bowling	**Inns**	**Balls**	**Runs**	**Wkts**	**BBI**	**BBM**	**Ave**	**Econ**	**SR**	**5w**	**10**
ODIs	28	1332	1075	21	3/24	3/24	51.19	4.84	63.4	0	0
T20Is	14	276	299	11	2/19	2/19	27.18	6.50	25.0	0	0
First-class	155	3531	2078	28	5/83		74.21	3.53	126.1	1	0
List A	195	5993	5050	132	6/27	6/27	38.25	5.05	45.4	1	0
Twenty20	99	1873	2014	78	3/21	3/21	25.82	6.45	24.0	0	0

ED YOUNG RHB SLA

FULL NAME: Edward George Christopher Young
BORN: May 21, 1989, Chertsey, Surrey
SQUAD NO: 30
HEIGHT: 6ft 1in
NICKNAME: EY
EDUCATION: Wellington College; Oxford Brookes University
TEAMS: Gloucestershire, Gloucestershire 2nd XI, Oxford MCCU, Unicorns
CAREER: First-class: 2009; List A: 2010; T20: 2011

BEST BATTING: 133 Oxford MCCU vs Lancashire, Oxford, 2011
BEST BOWLING: 2-23 Gloucestershire vs Kent, Canterbury, 2012
COUNTY CAP: 2010

CAREER HIGHLIGHTS? Scoring my maiden first-class hundred vs Lancashire for Oxford MCCU in April 2011. Bowling in tandem in T20 with Muttiah Muralitharan was a fantastic privilege
SUPERSTITIONS? Left pad on first
CRICKETING HEROES? Marcus Trescothick, Daniel Vettori, Shane Warne, Chris Gayle
NON-CRICKETING HEROES? Michael Jordan, Jason Bourne, Barney Stinson (suit up!)
BEST PLAYER IN COUNTY CRICKET? Marcus Trescothick
TIPS FOR THE TOP? Ross Whiteley, Greg Smith
IF YOU WEREN'T A CRICKETER? I would try and see as much of the world as I could
FAVOURITE TV? How I Met Your Mother
DREAM HOLIDAY? Cape Town, Sydney or Barbados
ACCOMPLISHMENTS? Getting a degree in Anthropology/Sociology
SURPRISING SKILL? I can moonwalk...
FANTASY SLIP CORDON? Keeper: Lee Evans (he's a very funny man and has a great work rate), 1st: Morgan Freeman (great actor, great voice), 2nd: Me (just so I am in the middle), 3rd: Mr Motivator (obvious reasons), Gully: Michael McIntyre (just because he is a hero!)

Batting	Mat	Inns	NO	Runs	HS	Ave	SR	100	50	Ct	St
First-class	20	30	5	844	133	33.76	53.75	1	5	11	0
List A	31	22	5	230	50	13.52	84.55	0	1	9	0
Twenty20	22	16	2	103	28	7.35	106.18	0	0	0	0
Bowling	**Inns**	**Balls**	**Runs**	**Wkts**	**BBI**	**BBM**	**Ave**	**Econ**	**SR**	**5w**	**10**
First-class	20	1720	1033	15	2/23	3/41	68.86	3.60	114.6	0	0
List A	31	1229	1027	27	3/25	3/25	38.03	5.01	45.5	0	0
Twenty20	22	420	441	15	2/14	2/14	29.40	6.30	28.0	0	0

Additional *Yorkshire Bank 40* Teams

SCOTLAND
FORMED: 1980
HOME GROUNDS: Citylets Grange, Edinburgh; Citylets Titwood, Glasgow
ONE-DAY NAME: Scottish Saltires
CAPTAIN: Gordon Drummond
HEAD COACH: Peter Steindl
2012 RESULTS: CB40 7/7 in Group B

THE NETHERLANDS
FORMED: 1883
HOME GROUNDS: Sportpark Het Schootsveld, Deventer; Sportpark Thurlede, Schiedam; Hazelaarweg, Rotterdam; Boscawen Park, Truro; VRA Ground, Amstelveen
CAPTAIN: Peter Borren
HEAD COACH: Peter Drinnen
2012 RESULTS: CB40 4/7 in Group A

UNICORNS
FORMED: 2010
HOME GROUNDS: Sir Paul Getty's Ground, Wormsley; Queen's Park, Chesterfield; Garon Park, Southend-on-Sea; Boscawen Park, Truro
CAPTAIN: TBC
HEAD COACH: TBC
2012 RESULTS: CB40 7/7 in Group C

SCOTLAND CB40 AVERAGES 2012

	Mat	Inns	NO	Runs	HS	Ave	SR	100	50	4s	6s
PL Mommsen	11	9	2	271	67	38.71	77.87	0	1	20	4
J Symes	11	9	1	294	110	36.75	83.28	1	1	27	6
CS MacLeod	11	11	2	226	58*	25.11	72.43	0	1	23	2
DF Watts	2	1	0	25	25	25.00	62.50	0	0	1	0
R Flannigan	7	6	2	93	38	23.25	93.00	0	0	8	2
RD Berrington	10	8	1	157	43*	22.42	70.08	0	0	13	2
MA Parker	7	2	1	21	11*	21.00	105.00	0	0	2	0
S Sharif	1	1	0	20	20	20.00	74.07	0	0	3	0
RM Haq	11	7	2	92	53*	18.40	76.66	0	1	7	1
EF Chalmers	3	3	0	52	38	17.33	50.00	0	0	2	0
JH Davey	10	10	1	142	44*	15.77	59.66	0	0	12	1
G Goudie	3	3	0	32	21	10.66	114.28	0	0	1	2
CD Wallace	11	8	2	42	16	7.00	65.62	0	0	5	0
JH Stander	2	2	0	12	6	6.00	63.15	0	0	1	0
FRJ Coleman	2	1	0	5	5	5.00	45.45	0	0	0	0
GD Drummond	9	4	1	11	6	3.66	33.33	0	0	1	0
AC Evans	8	3	1	3	2*	1.50	37.50	0	0	0	0
MM Iqbal	2	1	0	0	0	0.00	0.00	0	0	0	0

Batting & Fielding

	Overs	Mdns	Runs	Wkts	BBI	Ave	Econ	SR	4w	5w
RM Haq	67.5	0	320	13	3/42	24.61	4.71	31.3	0	0
MA Parker	28.0	1	151	6	2/31	25.16	5.39	28.0	0	0
GD Drummond	36.3	0	201	4	2/28	50.25	5.50	54.7	0	0
AC Evans	36.0	1	203	2	1/21	101.50	5.63	108.0	0	0
J Symes	43.4	1	271	6	3/31	45.16	6.20	43.6	0	0
S Sharif	4.0	0	25	1	1/25	25.00	6.25	24.0	0	0
PL Mommsen	17.0	0	109	2	1/14	54.50	6.41	51.0	0	0
RD Berrington	25.0	0	161	3	2/37	53.66	6.44	50.0	0	0
JH Davey	45.4	1	302	8	3/22	37.75	6.61	34.2	0	0
G Goudie	15.0	0	101	4	3/44	25.25	6.73	22.5	0	0

Bowling

Catches/Stumpings:
8 MacLeod, Wallace (inc 2st), 3 Symes, 2 Drummond, Mommsen, Davey, 1 Haq, Parker, Evans, Berrington, Flannigan, Stander

THE NETHERLANDS CB40 AVERAGES 2012

Batting & Fielding

	Mat	Inns	NO	Runs	HS	Ave	SR	100	50	4s	6s
SJ Myburgh	9	9	2	346	77	49.42	109.84	0	3	42	11
CJ Borgas	9	9	2	287	61*	41.00	89.96	0	2	22	6
TLW Cooper	9	8	0	261	68	32.62	87.00	0	2	26	1
MR Swart	11	11	0	306	102	27.81	95.92	1	1	24	9
Mudassar Bukhari	11	10	2	168	39	21.00	109.09	0	0	14	6
TJ Heggelman	6	4	3	20	14*	20.00	74.07	0	0	1	0
TN de Grooth	4	4	0	72	36	18.00	84.70	0	0	6	1
W Barresi	11	9	1	118	30	14.75	92.18	0	0	14	1
T van der Gugten	9	5	2	32	15*	10.66	100.00	0	0	1	2
PM Seelaar	11	7	2	45	28	9.00	68.18	0	0	1	2
TGJ Gruijters	10	7	1	51	32	8.50	57.30	0	0	3	1
DLS van Bunge	1	1	0	7	7	7.00	58.33	0	0	0	0
PW Borren	10	8	1	46	15	6.57	53.48	0	0	3	0
Shahbaz Bashir	1	1	0	5	5	5.00	35.71	0	0	1	0
MAA Jamil	5	3	2	3	3*	3.00	21.42	0	0	0	0
ES Szwarczynski	2	2	0	4	2	2.00	25.00	0	0	0	0
LV van Beek	1	1	0	2	2	2.00	50.00	0	0	0	0
WL Coetsee	1	1	0	1	1	1.00	50.00	0	0	0	0

Bowling

	Overs	Mdns	Runs	Wkts	BBI	Ave	Econ	SR	4w	5w
MAA Jamil	27.3	2	116	7	4/24	16.57	4.21	23.5	1	0
PM Seelaar	64.0	0	298	12	4/42	24.83	4.65	32.0	1	0
WL Coetsee	6.0	0	31	0	-	-	5.16	-	0	0
Shahbaz Bashir	6.4	0	36	1	1/36	36.00	5.40	40.0	0	0
T van der Gugten	53.5	5	307	9	3/29	34.11	5.70	35.8	0	0
PW Borren	33.2	0	201	4	2/30	50.25	6.03	50.0	0	0
TGJ Gruijters	11.0	0	67	0	-	-	6.09	-	0	0
MR Swart	61.0	1	390	11	4/40	35.45	6.39	33.2	1	0
Mudassar Bukhari	66.3	0	426	13	3/29	32.76	6.40	30.6	0	0
TJ Heggelman	12.1	0	80	2	1/20	40.00	6.57	36.5	0	0
CJ Borgas	3.0	0	21	0	-	-	7.00	-	0	0
TLW Cooper	12.1	0	94	2	1/18	47.00	7.72	36.5	0	0
LV van Beek	6.0	0	57	1	1/57	57.00	9.50	36.0	0	0

Catches/Stumpings:
7 Barresi, 6 Cooper, 4 Gruijters, 3 Jamil, Seelaar, Swart, Borgas, 2 Borren, Heggelman, Myburgh, 1 van der Gugten, Bukhari

UNICORNS CB40 AVERAGES 2012

Batting & Fielding

	Mat	Inns	NO	Runs	HS	Ave	SR	100	50	4s	6s
LE Beaven	11	8	7	90	25*	90.00	73.77	0	0	4	2
PR Hindmarch	2	1	0	50	50	50.00	102.04	0	1	8	1
KA Parsons	11	11	3	254	58	31.75	71.14	0	1	14	6
TJ New	11	11	1	308	83*	30.80	67.99	0	1	24	1
LM Reece	11	11	2	233	59	25.88	81.18	0	1	16	4
LJ Hill	2	2	0	35	35	17.50	58.33	0	0	3	0
RG Querl	10	8	1	122	44	17.42	96.82	0	0	12	3
JE Ord	10	10	0	167	52	16.70	60.72	0	1	14	4
JR Levitt	3	3	0	42	17	14.00	58.33	0	0	4	0
RJJ Woolley	4	4	1	42	28*	14.00	71.18	0	0	5	0
SP Cheetham	8	4	2	28	20*	14.00	73.68	0	0	4	0
BL Wadlan	9	8	0	101	41	12.62	78.90	0	0	16	0
V Tripathi	6	6	1	63	19	12.60	45.98	0	0	4	0
CM Park	4	3	0	32	17	10.66	61.53	0	0	3	0
MA Thornely	5	5	0	51	20	10.20	66.23	0	0	6	0
WW Lee	8	5	1	19	11	4.75	45.23	0	0	0	1
MDT Roberts	1	1	0	4	4	4.00	22.22	0	0	0	0
JRA Campbell	3	3	0	8	6	2.66	26.66	0	0	0	0
DM Wheeldon	2	1	0	2	2	2.00	20.00	0	0	0	0

Bowling

	Overs	Mdns	Runs	Wkts	BBI	Ave	Econ	SR	4w	5w
BL Wadlan	38.0	2	171	4	2/37	42.75	4.50	57.0	0	0
RJJ Woolley	25.2	0	135	2	2/25	67.50	5.32	76.0	0	0
RG Querl	61.2	4	343	12	4/41	28.58	5.59	30.6	1	0
LE Beaven	57.0	1	320	5	2/23	64.00	5.61	68.4	0	0
SP Cheetham	44.0	3	264	5	2/34	52.80	6.00	52.8	0	0
WW Lee	42.4	1	275	7	3/50	39.28	6.44	36.5	0	0
PR Hindmarch	11.0	0	71	1	1/35	71.00	6.45	66.0	0	0
LM Reece	37.1	1	246	1	1/15	246.00	6.61	223.0	0	0
DM Wheeldon	8.0	0	61	1	1/9	61.00	7.62	48.0	0	0
MA Thornely	2.0	0	18	0	-	-	9.00	-	0	0

Catches/Stumpings:
6 New (inc 2st), 3 Beaven, Reece, Tripathi, 2 Parsons, 1 Cheetham, Lee, Park, Roberts

Scotland

RICHIE BERRINGTON

RHB RMF

SCOTLAND

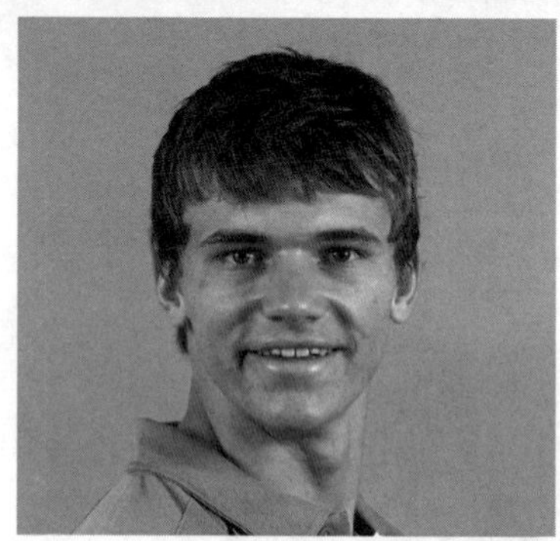

FULL NAME: Richard Douglas Berrington
BORN: April 3, 1987, Pretoria, South Africa
SQUAD NO: 44
HEIGHT: 6ft
NICKNAME: Richie, Berro
EDUCATION: Greenock Academy
TEAMS: Scotland, Scotland Under-19s
CAREER: ODI: 2008; T20I: 2008; First-class: 2007; List A: 2007; T20: 2008

BEST BATTING: 110 Scotland vs UAE, Sharjah, 2012
BEST BOWLING: 3-13 Scotland vs Kenya, Nairobi, 2010

CAREER HIGHLIGHTS? Receiving my first and 50th caps for Scotland. Beating India A at Titwood and scoring my first hundred for Scotland is a day I will always remember. Our win against Ireland in 2011 was also pretty special
CRICKETING HEROES? Growing up, Shaun Pollock and Jonty Rhodes. Both great players who always gave everything and Jonty was inspirational in the field
BEST PLAYER IN COUNTY CRICKET? Kyle Coetzer
TIP FOR THE TOP? Ben Stokes
FAVOURITE TV? MasterChef
FAVOURITE FILM? Gladiator
FAVOURITE BOOK? Shane Warne – Spun Out
DREAM HOLIDAY? The Maldives
GUILTY PLEASURES? Chocolate
FANTASY SLIP CORDON? Keeper: Herschelle Gibbs, 1st: Neil McCallum, 2nd: Katherine Jenkins, 3rd: Myself, Gully: Kanye West

Batting	Mat	Inns	NO	Runs	HS	Ave	SR	100	50	Ct	St
ODIs	21	19	1	396	84	22.00	80.98	0	3	11	0
T20Is	13	11	1	256	100	25.60	134.73	1	0	2	0
First-class	11	19	2	509	110	29.94	41.89	1	2	13	0
List A	60	54	3	1276	106	25.01	75.81	1	7	23	0
Twenty20	26	24	2	529	100	24.04	128.39	1	2	7	0
Bowling	**Inns**	**Balls**	**Runs**	**Wkts**	**BBI**	**BBM**	**Ave**	**Econ**	**SR**	**5w**	**10**
ODIs	21	620	488	11	2/14	2/14	44.36	4.72	56.3	0	0
T20Is	13	154	179	9	2/13	2/13	19.88	6.97	17.1	0	0
First-class	11	892	500	18	3/13	3/39	27.77	3.36	49.5	0	0
List A	60	1364	1245	33	4/47	4/47	37.72	5.47	41.3	0	0
Twenty20	26	359	450	17	2/12	2/12	26.47	7.52	21.1	0	0

CALVIN BURNETT LHB RMF

FULL NAME: Calvin Gary Burnett
BORN: October 23, 1990, Dundee
SQUAD NO: 33
HEIGHT: 6ft 1in
NICKNAME: Calv, Clive, Justin
EDUCATION: University of Abertay, Dundee
TEAMS: Scotland, Scotland Under-13s, Scotland Under-15s, Scotland Under-17s, Scotland Under-19s
CAREER: List A: 2011

FAMILY TIES? My father used to captain his club and my uncle was capped for Scotland
WHO WOULD PLAY YOU IN A FILM OF YOUR LIFE? Ryan Reynolds
CAREER HIGHLIGHTS? Gaining my first cap at The Oval was pretty special, as well as winning the league for my club in 2010
SUPERSTITIONS? I like to put my pads on first when padding up. I also can't receive the ball from the umpire after a wicket because that is bad luck!
MOST MARKED CHARACTERISTIC? Shyness
BEST PLAYER IN COUNTY CRICKET? Graeme Smith
TIP FOR THE TOP? Sam Billings
DESERT ISLAND DISC? Adele – 19
FAVOURITE TV? Breaking Bad, Californication, Friday Night Lights, Modern Family
CRICKETING HEROES? They were Flintoff and Vaughan, now they're Marcus Trescothick and Herschelle Gibbs
NON-CRICKETING HEROES? Matthew Parker and Calvin Harris
ACCOMPLISHMENTS? Surviving a lads' holiday
WHEN YOU RETIRE? I'd like to be a teacher
SURPRISING FACT? I love rom-coms
FANTASY SLIP CORDON? Keeper: Matthew Parker, 1st: Myself, 2nd: Phil from Modern Family, 3rd Herschelle Gibbs, Gully: LeBron James
TWITTER FEED: @calvgburnett

Batting	Mat	Inns	NO	Runs	HS	Ave	SR	100	50	Ct	St
List A	3	3	2	52	31*	52.00	104.00	0	0	0	0
Bowling	Inns	Balls	Runs	Wkts	BBI	BBM	Ave	Econ	SR	5w	10
List A	3	108	125	0	-	-	-	6.94	-	0	0

EWAN CHALMERS RHB RM

FULL NAME: Ewan Fraser Chalmers
BORN: October 19, 1989, Edinburgh
SQUAD NO: 7
HEIGHT: 6ft
NICKNAME: Chubby
EDUCATION: George Watson's College; University of St Andrews; Heriot-Watt University
TEAMS: Scotland, Scotland Under-13s, Scotland Under-15s
CAREER: First-class: 2009; List A: 2010

BEST BATTING: 67 Scotland vs Afghanistan, Ayr, 2010

FAMILY TIES? My dad played amateur club cricket in Edinburgh and introduced me to the game
WHO WOULD PLAY YOU IN A FILM OF YOUR LIFE? Ewan McGregor
CAREER HIGHLIGHTS? Making my debut for Scotland against Canada in 2009 and scoring my first international century at Lord's against the MCC in 2011
MOST MARKED CHARACTERISTIC? Chubby cheeks
BEST PLAYER IN COUNTY CRICKET? Kyle Coetzer
TIP FOR THE TOP? Calvin Burnett
IF YOU WEREN'T A CRICKETER? Club rep in Malia
DESERT ISLAND DISC? Take That – Never Forget
FAVOURITE TV? The Apprentice
CRICKETING HEROES? Jacques Kallis
NON-CRICKETING HEROES? Chris Hoy
ACCOMPLISHMENTS? Getting a degree in Maths
WHEN YOU RETIRE? Travel the world
SURPRISING FACT? I can play the bagpipes
FANTASY SLIP CORDON? Keeper: Usain Bolt, 1st: Myself, 2nd: Michael McIntyre, 3rd: Barack Obama, 4th: Will Ferrell, Gully: Michael Buble
TWITTER FEED: @EFChubby

Batting	Mat	Inns	NO	Runs	HS	Ave	SR	100	50	Ct	St
First-class	5	10	1	170	67	18.88	38.28	0	1	6	0
List A	8	8	0	134	50	16.75	59.55	0	1	0	0
Bowling	**Inns**	**Balls**	**Runs**	**Wkts**	**BBI**	**BBM**	**Ave**	**Econ**	**SR**	**5w**	**10**
First-class	5	-	-	-	-	-	-	-	-	-	-
List A	8	-	-	-	-	-	-	-	-	-	-

GORDON DRUMMOND RHB RMF

FULL NAME: Gordon David Drummond
BORN: April 21, 1980, Meigle, Perthshire
SQUAD NO: 24
HEIGHT: 6ft
NICKNAME: Big Toby
EDUCATION: Blairgowrie High School; Telford College; Edinburgh Napier University
TEAMS: Scotland, Scotland A
CAREER: ODI: 2007; T20I: 2008; First-class: 2007; List A: 2007; T20: 2008

BEST BATTING: 52 Scotland vs Canada, Aberdeen, 2009
BEST BOWLING: 3-18 Scotland vs Kenya, Nairobi, 2010

CAREER HIGHLIGHTS? Playing in the T20 World Cup in England and being part of Kyle Coetzer's amazing catch in the game against South Africa
CRICKETING HEROES? I loved Ian Botham as a kid and used to watch Botham's Ashes over and over again. I was amazed with how one man could have such an effect on a series
BEST PLAYER IN COUNTY CRICKET? Marcus Trescothick
TIPS FOR THE TOP? Ben Stokes and James Vince
FAVOURITE TV? Celebrity Juice
FAVOURITE FILM? Bloodsport – Jean-Claude Van Damme is a legend
ACCOMPLISHMENTS? I scored a three-minute hat-trick in amateur football. Honest!
SURPRISING SKILL? Purple belt in kickboxing
GUILTY PLEASURES? Chocolate and beer
FANTASY SLIP CORDON? Keeper: Shane Warne, 1st: David Attenborough, 2nd: Keith Lemon, 3rd: Gazza, Gully: Me
TWITTER FEED: @Drummo639

Batting	Mat	Inns	NO	Runs	HS	Ave	SR	100	50	Ct	St
ODIs	26	16	7	207	35*	23.00	93.24	0	0	4	0
T20Is	13	7	0	54	35	7.71	83.07	0	0	0	0
First-class	11	14	0	187	52	13.35	46.05	0	1	5	0
List A	71	49	13	402	35*	11.16	75.56	0	0	13	0
Twenty20	22	13	2	102	35	9.27	100.99	0	0	1	0
Bowling	**Inns**	**Balls**	**Runs**	**Wkts**	**BBI**	**BBM**	**Ave**	**Econ**	**SR**	**5w**	**10**
ODIs	26	1143	816	24	4/41	4/41	34.00	4.28	47.6	0	0
T20Is	13	264	319	13	3/20	3/20	24.53	7.25	20.3	0	0
First-class	11	1494	562	16	3/18	3/44	35.12	2.25	93.3	0	0
List A	71	2744	2215	52	4/41	4/41	42.59	4.84	52.7	0	0
Twenty20	22	420	495	24	3/20	3/20	20.62	7.07	17.5	0	0

RYAN FLANNIGAN RHB RM

SCOTLAND

FULL NAME: Ryan Flannigan
BORN: June 30, 1988, Kelso
SQUAD NO: 88
HEIGHT: 6ft
NICKNAME: Pieman
EDUCATION: Edenside Primary School; Kelso High School; Edinburgh Napier University
TEAMS: Scotland, Scotland Under-19s
CAREER: ODI: 2010; T20I: 2012; First-class: 2010; List A: 2010; T20: 2011

BEST BATTING: 102 Scotland vs Namibia, Windhoek, 2011

FAMILY TIES? Uncle [Jack Kerr] played 55 times for Scotland. Father [Ian] captained and played for Kelso CC for many years
CAREER HIGHLIGHTS? Maiden first-class century in Namibia for Scotland. Playing for my country at Test venues in England. Travelling the world
TIPS FOR THE TOP? Jos Buttler, Ben Stokes
WHEN RAIN STOPS PLAY? Listening to my iPod or annoying the boys
FAVOURITE TV? The Inbetweeners, Gavin And Stacey, Entourage
ACCOMPLISHMENTS? Honours degree in Sport Science. Nine golf trophies in one season at Kelso Golf Club
SURPRISING SKILL? My singing voice isn't too shabby
GUILTY PLEASURES? Indian food
FANTASY SLIP CORDON? Keeper: Alan from The Hangover (wearing his satchel), 1st: Tiger Woods (to compare stories), 2nd: Charlie Sheen (also to compare tales), 3rd: John Terry (more tales), 4th: Me
TWITTER FEED: @flanners_man88

Batting	Mat	Inns	NO	Runs	HS	Ave	SR	100	50	Ct	St
ODIs	1	1	0	0	0	0.00	0.00	0	0	0	0
T20Is	4	4	1	38	18	12.66	115.15	0	0	0	0
First-class	4	7	0	238	102	34.00	42.12	1	1	3	0
List A	18	17	2	227	39	15.13	67.96	0	0	4	0
Twenty20	7	5	1	48	18	12.00	109.09	0	0	0	0
Bowling	**Inns**	**Balls**	**Runs**	**Wkts**	**BBI**	**BBM**	**Ave**	**Econ**	**SR**	**5w**	**10**
ODIs	1	-	-	-	-	-	-	-	-	-	-
T20Is	4	-	-	-	-	-	-	-	-	-	-
First-class	4	-	-	-	-	-	-	-	-	-	-
List A	18	-	-	-	-	-	-	-	-	-	-
Twenty20	7	-	-	-	-	-	-	-	-	-	-

GORDON GOUDIE RHB RFM

FULL NAME: Gordon Goudie
BORN: August 12, 1987, Aberdeen
SQUAD NO: 16
HEIGHT: 6ft
NICKNAME: Goudz
EDUCATION: Bankhead Academy, Aberdeen
TEAMS: Scotland, Scotland Under-19s
CAREER: ODI: 2008; T20I: 2010; First-class: 2005; List A: 2004; T20: 2010

BEST BATTING: 44* Scotland vs Netherlands, Deventer, 2010
BEST BOWLING: 4-58 Scotland vs Ireland, Aberdeen, 2009

CAREER HIGHLIGHTS? Taking five wickets in an ODI vs Australia. Receiving my 50th cap for Scotland
SUPERSTITIONS? My left pad always goes on before the right one
BEST PLAYER IN COUNTY CRICKET? Nick Compton
TIP FOR THE TOP? Freddie Coleman
IF YOU WEREN'T A CRICKETER? Anything but working in an office with a suit on!
DESERT ISLAND DISC? Something chilled out like Bob Marley
FAVOURITE TV? Celebrity Juice
BIGGEST DRESSING DOWN YOU'VE RECEIVED? Probably after getting bowled out for 20-odd in the U19 World Cup in Bangladesh in 2004 – naughty boy nets followed straight after
CRICKETING HEROES? Darren Gough, Andrew Flintoff, Dale Steyn
WHEN YOU RETIRE? I would still like to be involved in the game in some sort of way
SURPRISING FACT? I played football for Dundee United until the age of 15
TWITTER FEED: @Goudz16

Batting	Mat	Inns	NO	Runs	HS	Ave	SR	100	50	Ct	St
ODIs	15	10	3	57	17*	8.14	77.02	0	0	5	0
T20Is	3	3	1	14	6*	7.00	107.69	0	0	1	0
First-class	10	11	2	129	44*	14.33	61.42	0	0	4	0
List A	54	39	12	295	45	10.92	100.68	0	0	16	0
Twenty20	10	9	1	75	26	9.37	163.04	0	0	1	0
Bowling	**Inns**	**Balls**	**Runs**	**Wkts**	**BBI**	**BBM**	**Ave**	**Econ**	**SR**	**5w**	**10**
ODIs	15	675	548	23	5/73	5/73	23.82	4.87	29.3	1	0
T20Is	3	42	81	1	1/29	1/29	81.00	11.57	42.0	0	0
First-class	10	1190	560	21	4/58	8/119	26.66	2.82	56.6	0	0
List A	54	2218	2089	77	5/73	5/73	27.12	5.65	28.8	1	0
Twenty20	10	168	262	5	1/17	1/17	52.40	9.35	33.6	0	0

MAJID HAQ LHB OB

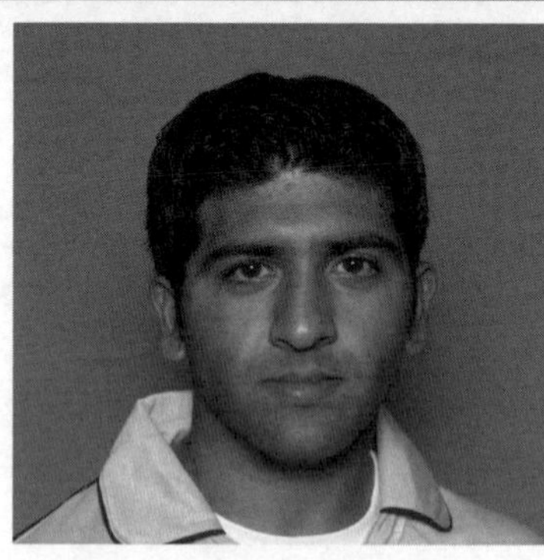

FULL NAME: Rana Majid Haq Khan
BORN: February 11, 1983, Paisley, Renfrewshire
SQUAD NO: 77
HEIGHT: 5ft 11in
NICKNAME: Maj, Haky, Panther, Crazy
EDUCATION: Toehold Primary; South Primary; Castlehead High; Reid Kerr College; University of the West of Scotland (Paisley Campus)
TEAMS: Scotland
CAREER: ODI: 2006; T20I: 2007; First-class: 2004; List A: 2003; T20: 2007

BEST BATTING: 120* Scotland vs Netherlands, Aberdeen, 2011
BEST BOWLING: 6-32 Scotland vs Namibia, Windhoek, 2011

FAMILY TIES? My uncles played club level, my cousin Omer Hussain was a former Scotland player and my five little cousins aged from 12-17 are starring in club cricket for Ferguslie CC
CAREER HIGHLIGHTS? Playing in World Cups and beating Bangladesh last year in a T20 international
BEST PLAYER IN COUNTY CRICKET? Owais Shah
TIPS FOR THE TOP? Paul Stirling, James Taylor, James Vince, Jos Buttler
IF YOU WEREN'T A CRICKETER? Working as an accountant
DESERT ISLAND DISC? Tracy Chapman – Fast Car
CRICKETING HEROES? They were: Brian Lara, Saeed Anwar, Saqlain Mushtaq. They are: Saeed Ajmal, Chris Gayle, Mahela Jayawardene
NON-CRICKETING HEROES? Muhammad Ali, Brian Laudrup, Lionel Messi
ACCOMPLISHMENTS? Obtaining a BA (Hons) in Accountancy
SURPRISING FACT? I have batted from No.1 to No.11 in the Scotland batting order!
TWITTER FEED: @MajidHaq

Batting	Mat	Inns	NO	Runs	HS	Ave	SR	100	50	Ct	St
ODIs	32	25	1	445	71	18.54	63.93	0	3	6	0
T20Is	13	10	6	64	21*	16.00	67.36	0	0	4	0
First-class	16	24	5	587	120*	30.89	51.90	1	1	7	0
List A	112	80	17	1194	71	18.95	66.51	0	5	11	0
Twenty20	26	15	9	116	27*	19.33	85.29	0	0	9	0
Bowling	Inns	Balls	Runs	Wkts	BBI	BBM	Ave	Econ	SR	5w	10
ODIs	32	1601	1215	40	4/28	4/28	30.37	4.55	40.0	0	0
T20Is	13	270	299	18	3/22	3/22	16.61	6.64	15.0	0	0
First-class	16	3102	1166	49	6/32	9/118	23.79	2.25	63.3	2	0
List A	112	4776	3888	104	4/28	4/28	37.38	4.88	45.9	0	0
Twenty20	26	562	615	34	3/12	3/12	18.08	6.56	16.5	0	0

MONEEB IQBAL RHB LB

FULL NAME: Moneeb Mohammed Iqbal
BORN: February 28, 1986, Glasgow
SQUAD NO: 2
HEIGHT: 5ft 5in
EDUCATION: Woodside Secondary School, Glasgow; Hillhead High School, Glasgow; Anniesland College, Glasgow
TEAMS: Scotland, Durham
CAREER: ODI: 2009; T20I: 2012; First-class: 2006; List A: 2002; T20: 2012

BEST BATTING: 42 Scotland vs Afghanistan, Alloway, 2010
BEST BOWLING: 4-36 Durham vs Oxford UCCE, Oxford, 2006

NOTES: Became the youngest player ever to represent Scotland when he made his debut against Leicestershire at the age of 16 in 2002. Played for Scotland in both the 2002 and 2004 U19 World Cups, scoring 67 in a win over Nepal in the latter. Studied at Durham University, where he attended the Centre of Cricketing Excellence, and played a handful of 1st XI matches for Durham, taking two wickets on his County Championship debut against Kent in 2006. Made his ODI debut against Ireland in a World Cup qualifier in 2009

Batting	Mat	Inns	NO	Runs	HS	Ave	SR	100	50	Ct	St
ODIs	10	10	3	156	63	22.28	56.31	0	1	1	0
T20Is	2	-	-	-	-	-	-	-	-	1	0
First-class	6	12	3	110	42	12.22	36.06	0	0	2	0
List A	21	19	4	316	67	21.06	57.45	0	2	3	0
Twenty20	3	1	1	1	1*	-	100.00	0	0	1	0
Bowling	**Inns**	**Balls**	**Runs**	**Wkts**	**BBI**	**BBM**	**Ave**	**Econ**	**SR**	**5w**	**10**
ODIs	10	258	249	4	2/35	2/35	62.25	5.79	64.5	0	0
T20Is	2	36	48	2	2/15	2/15	24.00	8.00	18.0	0	0
First-class	6	636	529	13	4/36	4/107	40.69	4.99	48.9	0	0
List A	21	516	450	5	2/35	2/35	90.00	5.23	103.2	0	0
Twenty20	3	54	75	2	2/15	2/15	37.50	8.33	27.0	0	0

MICHAEL LEASK

RHB OB

FULL NAME: Michael Alexander Leask
BORN: October 29, 1990, Aberdeen
SQUAD NO: TBC
HEIGHT: 6ft 2in
NICKNAME: Leasky
EDUCATION: Dyce Academy; Aberdeen College
TEAMS: Scotland Under-13s, Scotland Under-15s, Scotland Under-17s, Scotland Under-19s
CAREER: Yet to make first-team debut

FAMILY TIES? My father Ian played until the age of 58 for the local team Stoneywood-Dyce
WHO WOULD PLAY YOU IN A FILM OF YOUR LIFE? Jim Carrey – because he is a fun-loving guy in all his films, much like me
CAREER HIGHLIGHTS? The trip to South Africa in October of 2012, in particular playing against Kolkata Knight Riders and the Highveld Lions
SUPERSTITIONS? At my home club I always have the same spot in the changing room
MOST MARKED CHARACTERISTIC? The fact that I am always a very bubbly character
BEST PLAYER IN COUNTY CRICKET? Nick Compton – because of just how clinical he was at the start of last season
TIP FOR THE TOP? Sam Billings – having watched him play on TV he looks a good player
IF YOU WEREN'T A CRICKETER? Working in the banking industry
DESERT ISLAND DISC? U2 – U218 Singles
FAVOURITE TV? Sherlock – it's very clever and keeps you on edge the whole time you are watching it
BIGGEST DRESSING DOWN YOU'VE RECEIVED? When I holed out to long on when we needed three to win
CRICKETING HEROES? Jacques Kallis – because he is just a truly great allrounder
NON-CRICKETING HEROES? Nelson Mandela and David Attenborough
WHEN YOU RETIRE? Play golf at some of the best courses in the world
SURPRISING FACT? I was an uncle three times over by the time I was 15
FANTASY SLIP CORDON? Keeper: Jimmy Carr, 1st: James Corden, 2nd: Myself, 3rd: Karl Pilkington, Gully: Graeme Swann

CALUM MACLEOD

RHB RMF

FULL NAME: Calum Scott MacLeod
BORN: November 15, 1988, Glasgow
SQUAD NO: 10
HEIGHT: 6ft 2in
NICKNAME: Cloudy
EDUCATION: Hillpark School
TEAMS: Scotland, Scotland Under-19s, Warwickshire, Warwickshire 2nd XI
CAREER: ODI: 2008; T20I: 2009; First-class: 2007; List A: 2008; T20: 2009

BEST BATTING: 26 Warwickshire vs Durham UCCE, Durham University, 2009
BEST BOWLING: 4-66 Scotland vs Canada, Aberdeen, 2009

WHO WOULD PLAY YOU IN A FILM OF YOUR LIFE? Liam Neeson
CAREER HIGHLIGHTS? My first Scotland cap, opening the bowling in the World T20 and my first century for Scotland
SUPERSTITIONS? I keep them to myself!
BEST PLAYER IN COUNTY CRICKET? Graham Onions
TIP FOR THE TOP? Young Scottish pace bowler Gavin Main
IF YOU WEREN'T A CRICKETER? Sports psychologist
DESERT ISLAND DISC? Dire Straits – Brothers In Arms
CRICKETING HEROES? Glenn McGrath and Sachin Tendulkar
WHEN YOU RETIRE? Move somewhere warmer with a golf course on my doorstep
SURPRISING FACT? I once presented a Scottish Gaelic TV show called De A Nis
FANTASY SLIP CORDON? Keeper: Tiger Woods, 1st: Sherlock Holmes, 2nd: Me, 3rd: Emma Watson, Gully: Mark Knopfler
TWITTER FEED: @calummacleod640

Batting	Mat	Inns	NO	Runs	HS	Ave	SR	100	50	Ct	St
ODIs	9	8	2	179	99*	29.83	73.36	0	1	4	0
T20Is	7	6	0	138	57	23.00	135.29	0	2	2	0
First-class	7	7	2	93	26	18.60	48.18	0	0	5	0
List A	37	33	5	573	99*	20.46	75.59	0	2	19	0
Twenty20	17	16	1	465	104*	31.00	140.06	1	3	6	0
Bowling	**Inns**	**Balls**	**Runs**	**Wkts**	**BBI**	**BBM**	**Ave**	**Econ**	**SR**	**5w**	**10**
ODIs	9	138	139	3	2/46	2/46	46.33	6.04	46.0	0	0
T20Is	7	30	56	0	-	-	-	11.20	-	0	0
First-class	7	413	214	11	4/66	6/102	19.45	3.10	37.5	0	0
List A	37	360	338	8	2/38	2/38	42.25	5.63	45.0	0	0
Twenty20	17	30	56	0	-	-	-	11.20	-	0	0

PRESTON MOMMSEN RHB OB

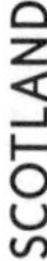

FULL NAME: Preston Luke Mommsen
BORN: October 14, 1987, Durban, South Africa
SQUAD NO: 1
HEIGHT: 5ft 8in
NICKNAME: P
EDUCATION: Hilton College; Gordonstoun; University of Reading
TEAMS: Scotland, Kent 2nd XI, Leicestershire, Leicestershire 2nd XI, Northamptonshire 2nd XI, Scotland A
CAREER: ODI: 2010; T20I: 2012; First-class: 2010; List A: 2010; T20: 2011

BEST BATTING: 102 Scotland vs Namibia, Windhoek, 2011
BEST BOWLING: 3-67 Scotland vs Netherlands, Aberdeen, 2011

FAMILY TIES? Heath Streak is my cousin and Norman Featherstone is my uncle
WHO WOULD PLAY YOU IN A FILM OF YOUR LIFE? Leonardo DiCaprio
CAREER HIGHLIGHTS? Beating Bangladesh in a T20 last year
MOST MARKED CHARACTERISTIC? My work ethic
BEST PLAYER IN COUNTY CRICKET? Nick Compton
IF YOU WEREN'T A CRICKETER? Property investment and management
DESERT ISLAND DISC? Any U2 album
FAVOURITE TV? Homes Under The Hammer
CRICKETING HEROES? Michael Clarke
NON-CRICKETING HEROES? Barack Obama
WHEN YOU RETIRE? Run my own business providing property solutions
SURPRISING FACT? I played for South African Schools in 2004 and 2005
TWITTER FEED: @PrestonMommsen

Batting	Mat	Inns	NO	Runs	HS	Ave	SR	100	50	Ct	St
ODIs	11	11	0	209	80	19.00	51.73	0	1	4	0
T20Is	5	5	1	72	26	18.00	114.28	0	0	4	0
First-class	7	12	0	226	102	18.83	42.00	1	0	10	0
List A	43	40	7	995	81*	30.15	75.78	0	4	23	0
Twenty20	17	15	3	279	39	23.25	119.74	0	0	11	0
Bowling	**Inns**	**Balls**	**Runs**	**Wkts**	**BBI**	**BBM**	**Ave**	**Econ**	**SR**	**5w**	**10**
ODIs	11	126	105	6	3/26	3/26	17.50	5.00	21.0	0	0
T20Is	5	114	132	3	1/23	1/23	44.00	6.94	38.0	0	0
First-class	7	252	170	4	3/67	3/67	42.50	4.04	63.0	0	0
List A	43	516	471	16	3/26	3/26	29.43	5.47	32.2	0	0
Twenty20	17	298	368	13	3/12	3/12	28.30	7.40	22.9	0	0

SAFYAAN SHARIF RHB RMF

FULL NAME: Safyaan Mohammed Sharif
BORN: May 24, 1991, Huddersfield
SQUAD NO: 50
HEIGHT: 6ft 2in
NICKNAME: Saf
EDUCATION: Buckhaven High School
TEAMS: Scotland, Scotland Under-15s, Scotland Under-17s, Scotland Under-19s
CAREER: ODI: 2011; T20I: 2012; First-class: 2011; List A: 2011; T20: 2011

BEST BATTING: 11 Scotland vs Namibia, Windhoek, 2011
BEST BOWLING: 3-27 Scotland vs UAE, Sharjah, 2012

CAREER HIGHLIGHTS? My Scotland debut against the Netherlands
IF YOU WEREN'T A CRICKETER? I'd be a footballer
DESERT ISLAND DISC? Nusrat Fateh Ali Khan
FAVOURITE TV? Soccer AM
CRICKETING HEROES? Wasim Akram
NON-CRICKETING HEROES? Mohammed Sharif (my dad)
WHEN YOU RETIRE? Businessman or coach

Batting	Mat	Inns	NO	Runs	HS	Ave	SR	100	50	Ct	St
ODIs	3	2	2	10	9*	-	43.47	0	0	1	0
T20Is	2	-	-	-	-	-	-	-	-	0	0
First-class	2	2	1	11	11	11.00	47.82	0	0	2	0
List A	12	8	4	55	20	13.75	64.70	0	0	1	0
Twenty20	11	3	1	33	13*	16.50	137.50	0	0	1	0
Bowling	**Inns**	**Balls**	**Runs**	**Wkts**	**BBI**	**BBM**	**Ave**	**Econ**	**SR**	**5w**	**10**
ODIs	3	120	119	5	4/27	4/27	23.80	5.95	24.0	0	0
T20Is	2	48	51	2	1/20	1/20	25.50	6.37	24.0	0	0
First-class	2	348	194	5	3/27	5/88	38.80	3.34	69.6	0	0
List A	12	448	401	13	4/27	4/27	30.84	5.37	34.4	0	0
Twenty20	11	214	244	14	3/29	3/29	17.42	6.84	15.2	0	0

JAN STANDER

RHB RMF

FULL NAME: Jan Hendrik Stander
BORN: January 4, 1982, Port Elizabeth, South Africa
SQUAD NO: 31
HEIGHT: 5ft 8in
NICKNAME: Simba
EDUCATION: Daniel Pienaar THS; Nelson Mandela Metropolitan University; PE Technikon
TEAMS: Scotland, Eastern Province Academy XI, Scotland Lions
CAREER: ODI: 2009; T20I: 2009; First-class: 2009; List A: 2009; T20: 2009

BEST BATTING: 64 Scotland vs Canada, Aberdeen, 2009
BEST BOWLING: 3-43 Scotland vs Canada, Aberdeen, 2009

WHO WOULD PLAY YOU IN A FILM OF YOUR LIFE? Matt Damon
CAREER HIGHLIGHTS? Playing in the 2009 World T20 against New Zealand and South Africa. Being part of the first Scotland team to beat a full member [Bangladesh in 2012]
MOST MARKED CHARACTERISTIC? I plan everything
BEST PLAYER IN COUNTY CRICKET? Marcus Trescothick
TIPS FOR THE TOP? Matthew Cross, Omar Afridi
IF YOU WEREN'T A CRICKETER? I'd work in biomechanics
DESERT ISLAND DISC? Bob Marley
FAVOURITE TV? Love a bit of The X Factor and CSI
CRICKETING HEROES? Hansie Cronje
NON-CRICKETING HEROES? Nelson Mandela
ACCOMPLISHMENTS? My beautiful wife and family
FANTASY SLIP CORDON? Keeper: Usain Bolt, 1st: Chris Gayle, 2nd: Jacques Kallis, 3rd: Hansie Cronje, Gully: Tiger Woods

Batting	Mat	Inns	NO	Runs	HS	Ave	SR	100	50	Ct	St
ODIs	5	5	1	44	22*	11.00	58.66	0	0	1	0
T20Is	11	11	2	94	45	10.44	104.44	0	0	2	0
First-class	1	2	0	64	64	32.00	49.61	0	1	0	0
List A	23	22	3	308	80*	16.21	70.64	0	1	6	0
Twenty20	22	21	4	405	116*	23.82	148.35	1	1	5	0
Bowling	**Inns**	**Balls**	**Runs**	**Wkts**	**BBI**	**BBM**	**Ave**	**Econ**	**SR**	**5w**	**10**
ODIs	5	150	166	6	2/25	2/25	27.66	6.64	25.0	0	0
T20Is	11	81	156	3	2/24	2/24	52.00	11.55	27.0	0	0
First-class	1	180	91	5	3/43	5/91	18.20	3.03	36.0	0	0
List A	23	865	821	24	4/41	4/41	34.20	5.69	36.0	0	0
Twenty20	22	171	278	5	2/24	2/24	55.60	9.75	34.2	0	0

CRAIG WALLACE RHB WK

FULL NAME: Craig Donald Wallace
BORN: June 27, 1990, Dundee
SQUAD NO: 18
HEIGHT: 5ft 10in
NICKNAME: Smilo
EDUCATION: Dundee High School; Edinburgh University
TEAMS: Scotland, Scotland Under-15s, Scotland Under-17s, Scotland Under-19s
CAREER: ODI: 2012; T20I: 2012; List A: 2011; T20: 2011

FAMILY TIES? My father used to play for Meigle CC back in the day
WHO WOULD PLAY YOU IN A FILM OF YOUR LIFE? Samuel L Jackson
CAREER HIGHLIGHTS? Playing and beating Bangladesh in an official international
SUPERSTITIONS? Yes, I have a lot but I don't like to give them away as they might not work
MOST MARKED CHARACTERISTIC? Being happy and cheeky and playing the game with a smile on my face
BEST PLAYER IN COUNTY CRICKET? James Taylor or Joe Root
DESERT ISLAND DISC? Mumford And Sons – Sigh No More
FAVOURITE TV? Strike Back
CRICKETING HEROES? AB de Villiers
ACCOMPLISHMENTS? Playing for Dundee United youth football team
WHEN YOU RETIRE? Become a PE teacher
SURPRISING FACT? I have been run over by a forklift and lived to tell the tale
FANTASY SLIP CORDON? Keeper: Me, 1st: Usain Bolt, 2nd: AB de Villiers, 3rd: Chris Gayle
TWITTER FEED: @Wally_smilo18

Batting	Mat	Inns	NO	Runs	HS	Ave	SR	100	50	Ct	St
ODIs	1	-	-	-	-	-	-	-	-	1	1
T20Is	4	3	2	14	7*	14.00	140.00	0	0	3	2
List A	17	12	2	100	40	10.00	57.14	0	0	10	3
Twenty20	13	10	7	76	24*	25.33	133.33	0	0	5	5
Bowling	**Inns**	**Balls**	**Runs**	**Wkts**	**BBI**	**BBM**	**Ave**	**Econ**	**SR**	**5w**	**10**
ODIs	1	-	-	-	-	-	-	-	-	-	-
T20Is	4	-	-	-	-	-	-	-	-	-	-
List A	17	-	-	-	-	-	-	-	-	-	-
Twenty20	13	-	-	-	-	-	-	-	-	-	-

The
Netherlands

RAHIL AHMED RHB WK

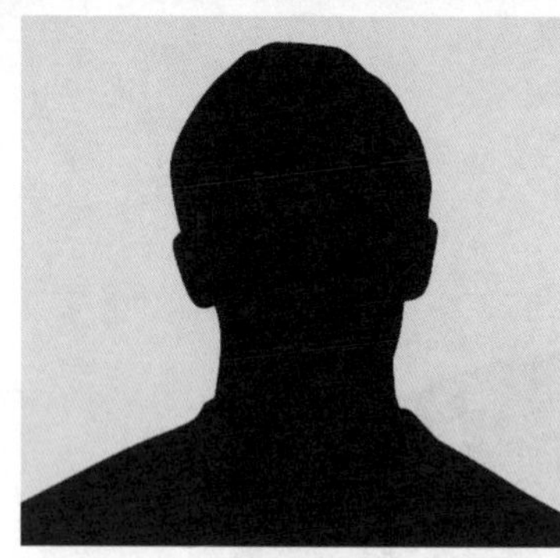

FULL NAME: Rahil Ahmed
BORN: January 3, 1994, Netherlands
SQUAD NO: TBC
TEAMS: Netherlands Under-13s, Netherlands Under-15s
CAREER: Yet to make first-team debut

TWITTER FEED: @iamrahilahmed
NOTES: A highly-regarded wicketkeeper-batsman who has captained the Netherlands at youth level, Ahmed played a key role in the Netherlands' success at the European U19 Challenge Series 2012 in the Channel Islands, which saw them register sizeable victories over both Jersey and Guernsey. Made his debut for the Netherlands' A team against France on June 29, 2012 at Sportpark Thurlede No 2, Schiedam, scoring 8 runs off 28 deliveries during a comfortable 35-run victory for the home side. He, along with several other Netherlands cricketers, is sponsored by Aedos Cricket

WESLEY BARRESI RHB OB WK

FULL NAME: Wesley Barresi
BORN: May 3, 1984, Johannesburg, South Africa
SQUAD NO: 2
HEIGHT: 6ft
NICKNAME: Pepe
EDUCATION: SBHS; Ekurhuleni East Campus College
TEAMS: Netherlands, Easterns, Easterns Under-15s, Easterns Under-19s, Easterns Under-23s
CAREER: ODI: 2010; T20I: 2012; First-class: 2004; List A: 2004; T20: 2012

BEST BATTING: 81 Netherlands vs Zimbabwe XI, Amstelveen, 2010

CAREER HIGHLIGHTS? Helping the Netherlands secure their first ever ODI victory against a full ICC member [Scotland] in Glasgow, scoring 65* off 43 balls
SUPERSTITIONS? I do have a couple but won't mention them. You just never know what the opposition will get up to with that kind of information
MOST MARKED CHARACTERISTIC? My positivity
TIPS FOR THE TOP? James Gruijters and Matthijs Luten
IF YOU WEREN'T A CRICKETER? Working as a DJ around the world and producing my own music, but probably still trying to be a professional cricketer
BIGGEST DRESSING DOWN YOU'VE RECEIVED? I get one almost every game! It's pretty hard to pinpoint one occasion
WHEN YOU RETIRE? I'll be a DJ and produce my own music
SURPRISING FACT? I'm Italian and I've never put a foot in the country
FANTASY SLIP CORDON? Keeper: Adam Gilchrist, 1st: Me, 2nd: Adriana Lima, 3rd: Eric Cartman, Gully Adam Sandler
TWITTER FEED: @Pepe_Barezi

Batting	Mat	Inns	NO	Runs	HS	Ave	SR	100	50	Ct	St
ODIs	21	20	2	508	67	28.22	71.85	0	4	9	6
T20Is	6	6	0	41	14	6.83	68.33	0	0	4	0
First-class	12	22	0	395	81	17.95	47.93	0	3	19	1
List A	55	52	5	1117	97*	23.76	73.14	0	6	38	6
Twenty20	15	13	1	128	45*	10.66	87.67	0	0	6	1
Bowling	**Inns**	**Balls**	**Runs**	**Wkts**	**BBI**	**BBM**	**Ave**	**Econ**	**SR**	**5w**	**10**
ODIs	21	18	20	0	-	-	-	6.66	-	0	0
T20Is	6	-	-	-	-	-	-	-	-	-	-
First-class	12	12	3	0	-	-	-	1.50	-	0	0
List A	55	18	20	0	-	-	-	6.66	-	0	0
Twenty20	15	-	-	-	-	-	-	-	-	-	-

SHAHBAZ BASHIR RHB RFM

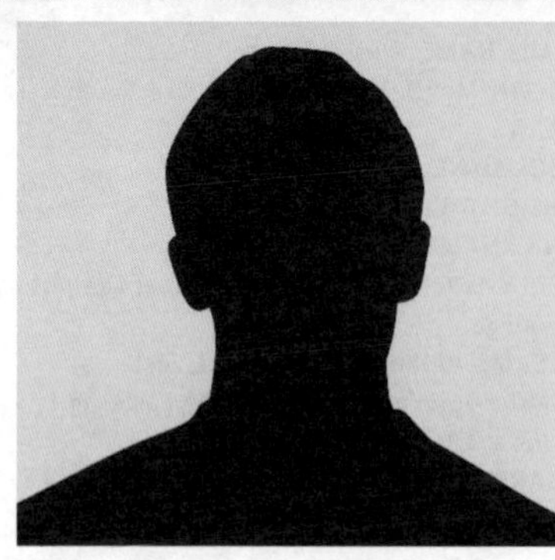

FULL NAME: Shahbaz Bashir
BORN: December 27, 1983, Lahore, Pakistan
SQUAD NO: TBC
TEAMS: Netherlands, Pakistan Cricket Board Greens
CAREER: First-class: 2012; List A: 2002

BEST BATTING: 102 Netherlands vs UAE, Deventer, 2012
BEST BOWLING: 1-5 Netherlands vs UAE, Deventer, 2012

NOTES: Made his List A debut for Pakistan Cricket Boards Greens in the Super League One-Day Ramadan Cup 2002/03, opening the batting and scoring 30 runs off 84 deliveries. Qualifies for Netherlands on residency grounds. Became the first Netherlands batsman to score a century on first-class debut when he made 102 off 157 balls from No.5 in the drawn ICC Intercontinental Cup match against the United Arab Emirates at Sportpark Het Schootsveld, Deventer. A useful right-arm seamer, his only List A wicket to date came in the the 2012 CB40 match against Leicestershire Foxes at the VRA Ground, Amstelveen, when he dismissed Mike Thornely for 86

Batting	Mat	Inns	NO	Runs	HS	Ave	SR	100	50	Ct	St
First-class	1	1	0	102	102	102.00	64.96	1	0	0	0
List A	4	3	0	35	30	11.66	33.98	0	0	2	0
Bowling	**Inns**	**Balls**	**Runs**	**Wkts**	**BBI**	**BBM**	**Ave**	**Econ**	**SR**	**5w**	**10**
First-class	1	54	5	1	1/5	1/5	5.00	0.55	54.0	0	0
List A	4	52	55	1	1/36	1/36	55.00	6.34	52.0	0	0

PETER BORREN — RHB RM

FULL NAME: Peter William Borren
BORN: August 21, 1983, Christchurch, New Zealand
SQUAD NO: 83
HEIGHT: 5ft 10in
NICKNAME: Scrappy, Coco
TEAMS: Netherlands, Canterbury Under-19s, Netherlands A, New Zealand Under-19s
CAREER: ODI: 2006; T20I: 2008; First-class: 2006; List A: 2006; T20: 2008

BEST BATTING: 109 Netherlands vs Scotland, Deventer, 2010
BEST BOWLING: 3-21 Netherlands vs Afghanistan, Amstelveen, 2009

FAMILY TIES? My brother and dad play backyard cricket
CAREER HIGHLIGHTS? Playing India in Delhi in front of a full house. Beating England at Lord's
MOST MARKED CHARACTERISTIC? I get pretty upset at bad fielding
BEST PLAYER IN COUNTY CRICKET? Marcus Trescothick
TIPS FOR THE TOP? Mahesh Hans, Alexei Kervezee
FAVOURITE TV? Great British Bake Off, anything with Mary Berry
CRICKETING HEROES? Martin Crowe, Darron Reekers, Michael Goldstein
NON-CRICKETING HEROES? My auntie Sylvia
ACCOMPLISHMENTS? Fat man/skinny man party trick
WHEN YOU RETIRE? PGA Seniors Tour
FANTASY SLIP CORDON? Keeper: Sergio Garcia, 1st: Seve Ballesteros, 2nd: Miguel Ángel Jiménez, 3rd: Me, Gully: José Maria Olazábal
TWITTER FEED: @dutchiepdb

Batting	Mat	Inns	NO	Runs	HS	Ave	SR	100	50	Ct	St
ODIs	51	44	4	815	96	20.37	79.35	0	4	24	0
T20Is	16	14	2	173	37*	14.41	94.02	0	0	12	0
First-class	17	30	0	932	109	31.06	58.46	2	3	19	0
List A	98	83	11	1466	96	20.36	78.85	0	6	38	0
Twenty20	26	22	5	295	45	17.35	97.35	0	0	15	0
Bowling	**Inns**	**Balls**	**Runs**	**Wkts**	**BBI**	**BBM**	**Ave**	**Econ**	**SR**	**5w**	**10**
ODIs	51	1787	1480	46	4/32	4/32	32.17	4.96	38.8	0	0
T20Is	16	298	344	11	2/19	2/19	31.27	6.92	27.0	0	0
First-class	17	2373	1223	31	3/21	4/54	39.45	3.09	76.5	0	0
List A	98	3415	2862	84	4/32	4/32	34.07	5.02	40.6	0	0
Twenty20	26	460	525	19	3/14	3/14	27.63	6.84	24.2	0	0

MUDASSAR BUKHARI RHB RMF

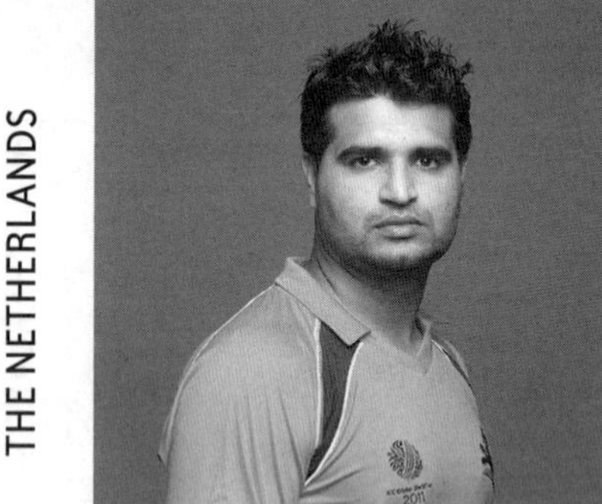

FULL NAME: Mudassar Bukhari
BORN: December 26, 1983, Gujrat, Pakistan
SQUAD NO: 7
HEIGHT: 6ft
TEAMS: Netherlands, Netherlands A
CAREER: ODI: 2007; T20I: 2008; First-class: 2007; List A: 2006; T20: 2008

BEST BATTING: 66* Netherlands vs Canada, King City, 2007
BEST BOWLING: 6-43 Netherlands vs Afghanistan, Sharjah, 2012

NOTES: Moved from Pakistan at the age of 14 along with his family. Plays club cricket in Amsterdam. First came to the Netherlands selectors' attention when he appeared for a KNCB Invitation XI against a Denmark XI at Sportpark Maarschalkerweerd, Utrecht, in 2007. Made his ODI debut against Canada in Toronto on July 3, 2007, bowling first change and claiming figures of 3-24 from eight overs. His top List A score of 84 came against Canada during the 2009 World Cup Qualifiers, while his highest ODI score of 71 came off 114 deliveries against Ireland at Belfast in 2007. Recorded his best first-class bowling figures in the ICC Intercontinental Cup match against Afghanistan at the Sharjah Cricket Association Stadium on April 2-4, 2012, claiming six of the first seven wickets to fall in Afghanistan's first innings

Batting	Mat	Inns	NO	Runs	HS	Ave	SR	100	50	Ct	St
ODIs	39	29	4	465	71	18.60	77.24	0	2	5	0
T20Is	14	11	3	87	28*	10.87	126.08	0	0	2	0
First-class	10	18	2	363	66*	22.68	69.54	0	3	1	0
List A	86	70	12	1238	84	21.34	88.87	0	5	13	0
Twenty20	24	18	5	139	28*	10.69	119.82	0	0	3	0
Bowling	**Inns**	**Balls**	**Runs**	**Wkts**	**BBI**	**BBM**	**Ave**	**Econ**	**SR**	**5w**	**10**
ODIs	39	1724	1280	46	3/17	3/17	27.82	4.45	37.4	0	0
T20Is	14	238	293	14	4/33	4/33	20.92	7.38	17.0	0	0
First-class	10	1603	787	30	6/43	7/113	26.23	2.94	53.4	2	0
List A	86	3642	2976	103	4/32	4/32	28.89	4.90	35.3	0	0
Twenty20	24	429	488	21	4/33	4/33	23.23	6.82	20.4	0	0

TOM COOPER RHB OB

FULL NAME: Tom Lexley William Cooper
BORN: November 26, 1986, Wollongong, Australia
SQUAD NO: 26
HEIGHT: 6ft 1in
NICKNAME: Coops
EDUCATION: University of NSW
TEAMS: Netherlands, Australia Under-19s, New South Wales Institute of Sport, New South Wales Second XI, South Australia, Adelaide Strikers, Melbourne Renegades
CAREER: ODI: 2010; T20I: 2012; First-class: 2008; List A: 2008; T20: 2008

BEST BATTING: 203* South Australia vs New South Wales, Sydney, 2011
BEST BOWLING: 1-2 Australia A vs England Lions, Manchester, 2012

NOTES: Qualifies for the Netherlands through his Dutch mother. Represented Australia at the 2006 U19 World Cup, making 104 against South Africa. Made his first-class debut for Western Australia against South Australia at Adelaide in November 2008. Made his List A debut against the same opponents at the same venue three days later, scoring 53 off 67 deliveries from the top of the order. Impressed with a brutal 160* for the Prime Minister's XI against the touring West Indians at Canberra in February 2010, a knock that contained six sixes and 14 fours. Made his ODI debut against Scotland at Rotterdam on June 15, 2010, and notched a half-century, a feat he then repeated in his next two ODIs. Scored his maiden first-class double-hundred – 203* off 291 deliveries – against New South Wales at Sydney in November 2011. Dismissed Stuart Meaker in the England Lions vs Australia A match at Old Trafford on August 7-10, 2012, to record his best first-class bowling figures. Switched from the Adelaide Strikers to the Melbourne Renegades for the 2012/13 BBL, during which he played nine matches and scored 149 runs at an average of 29.80

Batting	Mat	Inns	NO	Runs	HS	Ave	SR	100	50	Ct	St
ODIs	20	19	2	916	101	53.88	71.00	1	8	10	0
T20Is	6	6	0	123	60	20.50	125.51	0	1	3	0
First-class	27	47	3	1338	203*	30.40	51.66	1	8	18	0
List A	85	81	9	2862	126*	39.75	78.38	4	20	43	0
Twenty20	50	43	8	714	60	20.40	126.82	0	3	17	0
Bowling	**Inns**	**Balls**	**Runs**	**Wkts**	**BBI**	**BBM**	**Ave**	**Econ**	**SR**	**5w**	**10**
ODIs	20	415	332	12	3/11	3/11	27.66	4.80	34.5	0	0
T20Is	6	60	71	0	-	-	-	7.10	-	0	0
First-class	27	499	332	5	1/2	2/97	66.40	3.99	99.8	0	0
List A	85	524	447	14	3/11	3/11	31.92	5.11	37.4	0	0
Twenty20	50	138	134	4	2/8	2/8	33.50	5.82	34.5	0	0

TOM DE GROOTH RHB OB

FULL NAME: Tom Nico de Grooth
BORN: May 14, 1979, The Hague, Netherlands
SQUAD NO: 99
HEIGHT: 5ft 10in
NICKNAME: TdG
TEAMS: Netherlands, HCC
CAREER: ODI: 2006; T20I: 2008; First-class: 2004; List A: 2005; T20: 2008

BEST BATTING: 196 Netherlands vs Bermuda, Amstelveen, 2007
BEST BOWLING: 1-2 Netherlands vs Canada, Rotterdam, 2009

WHO WOULD PLAY YOU IN A FILM OF YOUR LIFE? My older brother. He is a director/actor and very much part of the theatre scene in the Netherlands
CAREER HIGHLIGHTS? Taking part in two World Cups and obviously the win against England at Lord's in the 2009 ICC World T20. Scoring 196 in a first-class game against Bermuda. Travelling and seeing the world. Cricket has taken me to places I may never have been able to go to otherwise
MOST MARKED CHARACTERISTIC? Stubbornness
DESERT ISLAND DISC? Pearl Jam – Rearview Mirror
CRICKETING HEROES? I grew up watching Sir Ian Botham play when cricket was still shown in the Netherlands on the BBC
NON-CRICKETING HEROES? Roger Federer. He's able to just stay himself while being such a massive sports icon
SURPRISING FACT? At one time I wanted to become a speed skater
TWITTER FEED: @tomdegrooth

Batting	Mat	Inns	NO	Runs	HS	Ave	SR	100	50	Ct	St
ODIs	33	31	4	472	97	17.48	62.18	0	1	6	0
T20Is	13	11	5	143	49	23.83	110.00	0	0	4	0
First-class	20	35	1	892	196	26.23		1	5	7	0
List A	70	64	7	996	97	17.47	65.05	0	3	10	0
Twenty20	21	15	5	159	49	15.90	95.78	0	0	5	0
Bowling	**Inns**	**Balls**	**Runs**	**Wkts**	**BBI**	**BBM**	**Ave**	**Econ**	**SR**	**5w**	**10**
ODIs	33	6	2	1	1/2	1/2	2.00	2.00	6.0	0	0
T20Is	13	-	-	-	-	-	-	-	-	-	-
First-class	20	45	36	1	1/2	1/2	36.00	4.80	45.0	0	0
List A	70	42	34	3	2/32	2/32	11.33	4.85	14.0	0	0
Twenty20	21	-	-	-	-	-	-	-	-	-	-

DANIEL DORAM LHB SLA

FULL NAME: Daniel Tarric Doram
BORN: October 30, 1997, St Maarten
SQUAD NO: TBC
HEIGHT: 6ft 7in
TEAMS: Netherlands Under-15s, Netherlands Under-17s, Netherlands Under-19s
CAREER: Yet to make first-team debut

NOTES: Spotted by former Dutch allrounder Ron Elferlink in his native St Maarten, Doram was brought to the Netherlands on a scholarship and plays club cricket for VOC Rotterdam. Has produced several memorable spells at youth level, prompting KNCB high performance coach Roland Lefebvre to tip him for big things: "When he bowled his first ball I knew he was something special. His height makes him different from other slow bowlers, and together with his unerring accuracy makes him very difficult to play. He represented the Dutch Lions at U15 level and within a matter of weeks had progressed through the U17s to the U19 team. There was not a single match when he got hit. His return of 1-4 off 10 overs against Ireland in the European U15 Championship was a truly memorable spell."

JAMES GRUIJTERS RHB

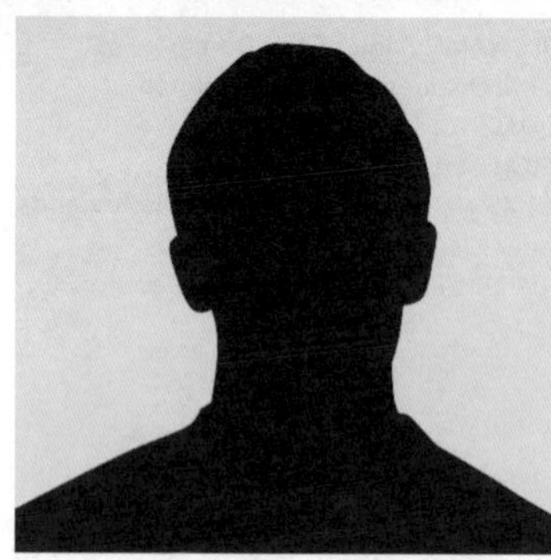

FULL NAME: James FM Gruijters
BORN: August 9, 1993, Den Haag, Netherlands
SQUAD NO: TBC
HEIGHT: 6ft
NICKNAME: Jimmy G
EDUCATION: Segbroek College
TEAMS: Netherlands Under-13s, Netherlands Under-15s
CAREER: Yet to make first-team debut

FAMILY TIES? My three brothers played cricket at the local club. We all played together in an U18 tournament one year. One brother [Tim] plays for the national side and was a youth player for Warwickshire. Our father played occasional recreational cricket and is now an umpire in the NL league. Mother is English and crazy about cricket
WHO WOULD PLAY YOU IN A FILM OF YOUR LIFE? Hugh Grant
CAREER HIGHLIGHTS? U15 calypso tour in West Indies. Taking 4-42 in 10 overs vs Pakistan. In the same tour I used Chanderpaul's locker at the Guyana stadium
SUPERSTITIONS? Wearing the right underwear
MOST MARKED CHARACTERISTIC? My dark red hair
BEST PLAYER IN COUNTY CRICKET? As a Dutchman I would have to say Ryan ten Doeschate. He has done really well for Essex in the last couple of years
TIPS FOR THE TOP? Sebastian Braat, Vivian Kingma
IF YOU WEREN'T A CRICKETER? Studying for my degree in Small Business and Retail Management, and working part-time as a gardener
DESERT ISLAND DISC? James Blunt – You're Beautiful
FAVOURITE TV? Sky Sports – just listening to whatever David Lloyd has to say
BIGGEST DRESSING DOWN YOU'VE RECEIVED? For getting undressed during the end of match team talk
CRICKETING HEROES? I would love to be able to bat like Rahul Dravid when he was in top form. It really looked as if nobody would be able to get him out
NON-CRICKETING HEROES? Lord Alan Sugar
ACCOMPLISHMENTS? Getting my school leaving diploma and finally passing my driving test (third time!)
WHEN YOU RETIRE? I would like to set up my own company

TIM GRUIJTERS RHB RM

FULL NAME: Timothy George Johannus Gruijters
BORN: August 28, 1991, The Hague, Netherlands
SQUAD NO: 51
HEIGHT: 6ft 2in
NICKNAME: Clifford, The Big Red, Buckets
EDUCATION: Segbroek College; Birmingham Metropolitan College
TEAMS: Netherlands, Netherlands Under-19s
CAREER: ODI: 2010; T20I: 2012; First-class: 2012; List A: 2010; T20: 2012

BEST BATTING: 3 Netherlands vs Afghanistan, Sharjah, 2012

FAMILY TIES? My brother James Gruijters plays for the Netherlands A team
WHO WOULD PLAY YOU IN A FILM OF YOUR LIFE? Brad Pitt. He looks relaxed and the ladies like him
CAREER HIGHLIGHTS? Scoring 148 in 65 balls in the Birmingham League and being in the squad during the 2009 ICC World T20 win against England
MOST MARKED CHARACTERISTIC? My hair and smile
BEST PLAYER IN COUNTY CRICKET? Darren Stevens. Experienced player who can win you a game at any stage
TIP FOR THE TOP? James Gruijters. A good, young batsman who has scored runs for every team he has played for recently
BIGGEST DRESSING DOWN YOU'VE RECEIVED? After we didn't qualify for the last World T20 there was a huge dressing down, but it was deserved
SURPRISING FACT? I played hockey for South Holland in the Netherlands. When I was in Birmingham I even played for Great Britain Colleges
TWITTER FEED: @TimGruijters

Batting	Mat	Inns	NO	Runs	HS	Ave	SR	100	50	Ct	St
ODIs	4	4	1	68	32	22.66	58.62	0	0	2	0
T20Is	4	3	2	35	21*	35.00	129.62	0	0	0	0
First-class	2	3	0	4	3	1.33	18.18	0	0	0	0
List A	18	15	4	145	32	13.18	53.11	0	0	10	0
Twenty20	8	5	2	46	21*	15.33	97.87	0	0	1	0
Bowling	**Inns**	**Balls**	**Runs**	**Wkts**	**BBI**	**BBM**	**Ave**	**Econ**	**SR**	**5w**	**10**
ODIs	4	120	79	2	2/37	2/37	39.50	3.95	60.0	0	0
T20Is	4	36	30	1	1/5	1/5	30.00	5.00	36.0	0	0
First-class	2	6	3	0	-	-	-	3.00	-	0	0
List A	18	246	195	4	2/37	2/37	48.75	4.75	61.5	0	0
Twenty20	8	60	52	3	2/11	2/11	17.33	5.20	20.0	0	0

TOM HEGGELMAN RHB RM

FULL NAME: Thomas Josephus Heggelman
BORN: January 16, 1987, Schiedam, Netherlands
SQUAD NO: 87
HEIGHT: 6ft
NICKNAME: Heggles
EDUCATION: Johan Cruyff University
TEAMS: Netherlands, Excelsior'20, Netherlands A, Netherlands Under-15s, Netherlands Under-17s, Netherlands Under-19s, Netherlands Under-23s
CAREER: ODI: 2010; First-class: 2010; List A: 2010; T20: 2012

BEST BATTING: 59 Netherlands vs Afghanistan, Sharjah, 2012
BEST BOWLING: 1-27 Netherlands vs Afghanistan, Sharjah, 2012

CAREER HIGHLIGHTS? Every opportunity I've been given to wear the orange jersey. Topklasse champions with my club team Excelsior'20 in 2009 and 2012. Scoring 128 against Denmark for Netherlands A in 2010. Scoring 59 vs Afghanistan in 2012 in European Championship Division 1
IF YOU WEREN'T A CRICKETER? Focus more on my university studies
DESERT ISLAND DISC? Tracy Chapman's Greatest Hits
FAVOURITE TV? All the sports channels
CRICKETING HEROES? Michael Clarke, Andrew Symonds, Allan Donald, Ricky Ponting, Wesley Barresi, Andrew Flintoff
WHEN YOU RETIRE? Travel the world and chill
FANTASY SLIP CORDON? Keeper: Spike, 1st: Todd, 2nd: Freddie Klokker, 3rd: Me, 4th: Mark 'Ice' Cleary, 5th: Ed Cowan, Gully: Michael Clarke

Batting	Mat	Inns	NO	Runs	HS	Ave	SR	100	50	Ct	St
ODIs	5	5	0	27	22	5.40	31.76	0	0	1	0
First-class	3	5	1	157	59	39.25	50.15	0	1	2	0
List A	22	15	5	72	22	7.20	39.13	0	0	5	0
Twenty20	2	-	-	-	-	-	-	-	-	0	0
Bowling	**Inns**	**Balls**	**Runs**	**Wkts**	**BBI**	**BBM**	**Ave**	**Econ**	**SR**	**5w**	**10**
ODIs	5	102	86	5	3/29	3/29	17.20	5.05	20.4	0	0
First-class	3	120	81	1	1/27	1/27	81.00	4.05	120.0	0	0
List A	22	325	302	9	3/29	3/29	33.55	5.57	36.1	0	0
Twenty20	2	6	17	0	-	-	-	17.00	-	0	0

AHSAN MALIK RHB RMF

FULL NAME: Malik Ahsan Ahmad Jamil
BORN: August 29, 1989, Rotterdam, Netherlands
SQUAD NO: 17
HEIGHT: 6ft 1in
TEAMS: Netherlands
CAREER: ODI: 2011; T20I: 2012; First-class: 2011; List A: 2011; T20: 2012

BEST BATTING: 4* Netherlands vs Afghanistan, Sharjah, 2012
BEST BOWLING: 2-32 Netherlands vs Afghanistan, Sharjah, 2012

NOTES: Only took up cricket at the age of 16. Plays club cricket for Rotterdam CC. Made his ODI debut on June 29, 2011, against Scotland at Mannofield Park, Aberdeen, during the ICC World Cricket League Championship 2011/12, returning figures of 0-45 off eight overs with the new ball. Made his T20I debut on March 13, 2012, against Canada in Dubai during the World T20 Qualifiers 2011/12, claiming figures of 2-18 off 2.4 overs. On July 26, 2012, batting at No.11, he sealed a one-wicket T20I victory over Bangaldesh by hitting the last ball of the match – the first ball he faced – for four

Batting	Mat	Inns	NO	Runs	HS	Ave	SR	100	50	Ct	St
ODIs	5	1	1	0	0*	-	-	0	0	0	0
T20Is	4	1	1	4	4*	-	400.00	0	0	2	0
First-class	2	3	3	9	4*	-	16.36	0	0	1	0
List A	12	4	3	3	3*	3.00	21.42	0	0	4	0
Twenty20	10	5	4	10	4*	10.00	111.11	0	0	2	0
Bowling	**Inns**	**Balls**	**Runs**	**Wkts**	**BBI**	**BBM**	**Ave**	**Econ**	**SR**	**5w**	**10**
ODIs	5	228	155	4	3/38	3/38	38.75	4.07	57.0	0	0
T20Is	4	80	109	6	2/18	2/18	18.16	8.17	13.3	0	0
First-class	2	210	95	3	2/32	3/44	31.66	2.71	70.0	0	0
List A	12	471	303	13	4/24	4/24	23.30	3.85	36.2	0	0
Twenty20	10	170	217	11	2/18	2/18	19.72	7.65	15.4	0	0

DOMINIC MICHAEL LHB RM

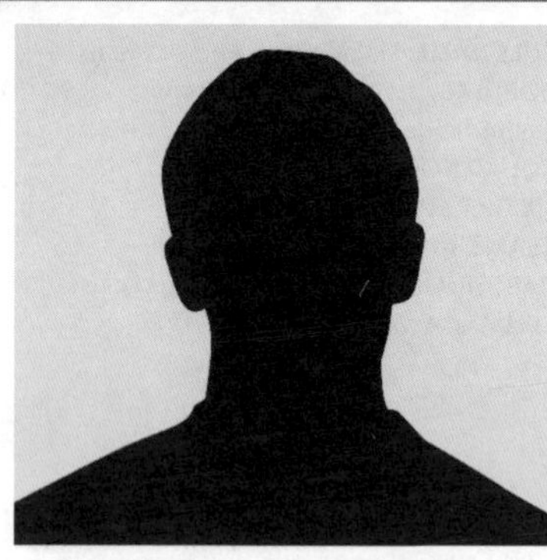

FULL NAME: Dominic Peter Michael
BORN: October 8, 1987, Brisbane, Australia
SQUAD NO: TBC
TEAMS: Queensland, Queensland Under-23s
CAREER: First-class: 2013; List A: 2013

BEST BATTING: 41 Queensland vs Victoria, Melbourne, 2013

NOTES: A top order batsman who has been one of the leading run-scorers in Queensland grade cricket for several seasons now, Michael – whose mother hails from Western Samoa and whose father is Greek Cypriot – has signed on to be the Netherlands' overseas pro for the 2013 campaign. Having broken into the Queensland 1st XI during the latter stages of the 2012/13 season – his first-class debut coming in an eight-wicket defeat to Victoria at Melbourne – Michael is widely touted as a batsman to watch on the Australian domestic circuit. He is captain of Northern Suburbs DCC, the same club side that Australian internationals James Hopes and Nathan Hauritz and West Indian international Brendan Nash play for

Batting	Mat	Inns	NO	Runs	HS	Ave	SR	100	50	Ct	St
First-class	1	2	0	41	41	20.50	26.97	0	0	0	0
List A	1	1	1	30	30*	-	150.00	0	0	1	0
Bowling	**Inns**	**Balls**	**Runs**	**Wkts**	**BBI**	**BBM**	**Ave**	**Econ**	**SR**	**5w**	**10**
First-class	1	30	14	0	-	-	-	2.80	-	0	0
List A	1	-	-	-	-	-	-	-	-	-	-

STEPHAN MYBURGH LHB OB

FULL NAME: Stephanus Johannes Myburgh
BORN: February 28, 1984, Pretoria, South Africa
SQUAD NO: 97
HEIGHT: 5ft 11in
NICKNAME: Stef, Uzzi, Mybs
EDUCATION: PBHS
TEAMS: Netherlands, KwaZulu-Natal Inland, Northerns
CAREER: ODI: 2011; T20I: 2012; First-class: 2006; List A: 2006; T20: 2011

BEST BATTING: 59 KwaZulu-Natal Inland vs Gauteng, Johannesburg, 2012

FAMILY TIES? My brother [Johann] is a professional player who has played for Durham and Hampshire
WHO WOULD PLAY YOU IN A FILM OF YOUR LIFE? Chad Michael Murray
CAREER HIGHLIGHTS? Representing Holland at the World Cup Qualifiers and making my international debut
MOST MARKED CHARACTERISTIC? Sarcasm
TIP FOR THE TOP? Devon Conway
DESERT ISLAND DISC? Lady Antebellum
FAVOURITE TV? Friends and White Collar
CRICKETING HEROES? Matthew Hayden, Andrew Hudson, Johann Myburgh
NON-CRICKETING HEROES? Jean de Villiers and Cesc Fabregas
SURPRISING FACTS? I'm a huge country music fan – it's all I listen to before I go out to bat. I enjoy creating websites. I studied Engineering and Finance and I'm busy with my third year studying Theology
TWITTER FEED: @StephanMyburgh

Batting	Mat	Inns	NO	Runs	HS	Ave	SR	100	50	Ct	St
ODIs	4	4	0	89	56	22.25	75.42	0	1	1	0
T20Is	4	4	0	73	36	18.25	100.00	0	0	1	0
First-class	15	21	2	350	59	18.42	80.83	0	1	12	0
List A	37	37	4	1106	105	33.51	91.10	1	9	8	0
Twenty20	15	15	1	368	68	26.28	115.72	0	3	3	0
Bowling	**Inns**	**Balls**	**Runs**	**Wkts**	**BBI**	**BBM**	**Ave**	**Econ**	**SR**	**5w**	**10**
ODIs	4	-	-	-	-	-	-	-	-	-	-
T20Is	4	-	-	-	-	-	-	-	-	-	-
First-class	15	60	42	0	-	-	-	4.20	-	0	0
List A	37	55	34	2	2/30	2/30	17.00	3.70	27.5	0	0
Twenty20	15	-	-	-	-	-	-	-	-	-	-

PIETER SEELAAR RHB SLA

FULL NAME: Pieter Marinus Seelaar
BORN: July 2, 1987, Schiedam, Netherlands
SQUAD NO: 8
HEIGHT: 6ft
NICKNAME: Charlie, Saucy, Vuvu, Woody
EDUCATION: Hogeschool, Rotterdam
TEAMS: Netherlands, Hermes DVS
CAREER: ODI: 2006; T20I: 2008; First-class: 2006; List A: 2005; T20: 2008

BEST BATTING: 81* Netherlands vs Zimbabwe XI, Amstelveen, 2010
BEST BOWLING: 5-57 Netherlands vs Kenya, Amstelveen, 2008

WHO WOULD PLAY YOU IN A FILM OF YOUR LIFE? Charlie Sheen
CAREER HIGHLIGHTS? ICC World T20 victory vs England in 2009 and playing India at the 2011 World Cup
SUPERSTITIONS? Putting my right pad on standing up and my left pad on sitting down
MOST MARKED CHARACTERISTIC? Arrogance and spontaneity
BEST PLAYER IN COUNTY CRICKET? Chris Nash
TIP FOR THE TOP? Paul Stirling
IF YOU WEREN'T A CRICKETER? Model
DESERT ISLAND DISC? Jay-Z and Kanye West – Watch The Throne
FAVOURITE TV? Californication, Two And A Half Men (with Charlie Sheen)
CRICKETING HEROES? Harro Seelaar, Michael Swart, Remco Borrani
FANTASY SLIP CORDON? Keeper: Richie, 1st: Me, 2nd: Charlie Sheen, 3rd: Conan the Barbarian, Gully: Kim Kardashian
TWITTER FEED: @seelaar8

Batting	Mat	Inns	NO	Runs	HS	Ave	SR	100	50	Ct	St
ODIs	33	20	10	95	34*	9.50	53.67	0	0	11	0
T20Is	15	5	2	14	9*	4.66	93.33	0	0	7	0
First-class	15	25	5	323	81*	16.15	43.70	0	1	4	0
List A	80	45	20	249	34*	9.96	53.77	0	0	28	0
Twenty20	25	10	5	41	12	8.20	80.39	0	0	10	0
Bowling	**Inns**	**Balls**	**Runs**	**Wkts**	**BBI**	**BBM**	**Ave**	**Econ**	**SR**	**5w**	**10**
ODIs	33	1525	1191	36	3/22	3/22	33.08	4.68	42.3	0	0
T20Is	15	318	329	19	4/19	4/19	17.31	6.20	16.7	0	0
First-class	15	2085	1205	30	5/57	5/57	40.16	3.46	69.5	1	0
List A	80	3484	2762	80	4/42	4/42	34.52	4.75	43.5	0	0
Twenty20	25	510	542	24	4/19	4/19	22.58	6.37	21.2	0	0

MICHAEL SWART RHB OB

FULL NAME: Michael Richard Swart
BORN: October 1, 1982, Subiaco, Perth, Australia
SQUAD NO: 25
HEIGHT: 5ft 11in
NICKNAME: Banksy, Swarta
TEAMS: Netherlands, Lombard XI, Western Australia, Western Australia Under-17s, Western Australia Under-19s
CAREER: ODI: 2011; T20I: 2012; First-class: 2010; List A: 2010; T20: 2010

BEST BATTING: 104 Western Australia vs Victoria, Perth, 2010
BEST BOWLING: 1-0 Western Australia vs Victoria, Perth, 2010

WHO WOULD PLAY YOU IN A FILM OF YOUR LIFE? Steve Irwin
CAREER HIGHLIGHTS? Playing for Western Australia and the Netherlands. Scoring a Sheffield Shield hundred vs Victoria at the WACA would have to be the most memorable
MOST MARKED CHARACTERISTIC? Bowling pace off a spinner's run-up
BEST PLAYER IN COUNTY CRICKET? Ramnaresh Sarwan
TIP FOR THE TOP? Stephen Parry
BIGGEST DRESSING DOWN YOU'VE RECEIVED? After my first Sheffield Shield innings I got pulled into a room by our coach Tom Moody and told to stop taking on the short ball because I wasn't Ricky Ponting
CRICKETING HEROES? David Boon. Anyone that can drink 52 cans of beer on a plane demands respect
NON-CRICKETING HEROES? My older brother – best fisherman around
TWITTER FEED: @mickyswart

Batting	Mat	Inns	NO	Runs	HS	Ave	SR	100	50	Ct	St
ODIs	6	6	1	140	52	28.00	67.96	0	1	2	0
T20Is	6	6	0	158	61	26.33	123.43	0	2	1	0
First-class	12	21	0	621	104	29.57	46.83	1	4	4	0
List A	34	34	1	711	102	21.54	74.52	1	4	13	0
Twenty20	17	17	1	430	61	26.87	113.75	0	5	3	0
Bowling	**Inns**	**Balls**	**Runs**	**Wkts**	**BBI**	**BBM**	**Ave**	**Econ**	**SR**	**5w**	**10**
ODIs	6	162	147	1	1/21	1/21	147.00	5.44	162.0	0	0
T20Is	6	126	137	5	2/18	2/18	27.40	6.52	25.2	0	0
First-class	12	150	100	3	1/0	1/0	33.33	4.00	50.0	0	0
List A	34	860	815	19	4/40	4/40	42.89	5.68	45.2	0	0
Twenty20	17	339	342	16	3/31	3/31	21.37	6.05	21.1	0	0

ERIC SZWARCZYNSKI RHB RM

FULL NAME: Eric Stefan Szwarczynski
BORN: February 13, 1983, Vanderbijlpark, South Africa
SQUAD NO: 13
HEIGHT: 6ft
NICKNAME: Turtle
EDUCATION: Anna van Rijn College; Erasmus University of Rotterdam; Open University
TEAMS: Netherlands
CAREER: ODI: 2006; T20I: 2008; First-class: 2005; List A: 2006; T20: 2008

BEST BATTING: 93 Netherlands vs Kenya, Nairobi, 2010
BEST BOWLING: 2-24 Netherlands vs Canada, King City, 2007

CAREER HIGHLIGHTS? Playing in two World Cups and making my maiden century at Hove in 2011
SUPERSTITIONS? Always put my gear on in the same order
CRICKETING HEROES? Jonty Rhodes and Andrew Hudson
NON-CRICKETING HEROES? Gary Player
IF YOU WEREN'T A CRICKETER? Hopefully making money playing golf
WHEN RAIN STOPS PLAY? Reading
FAVOURITE TV? The Big Bang Theory
FAVOURITE FILM? The Road To Redemption
FAVOURITE BOOK? The Sword Of Truth
DREAM HOLIDAY? Any tropical island
GUILTY PLEASURES? I have a bit of a sweet tooth

Batting	Mat	Inns	NO	Runs	HS	Ave	SR	100	50	Ct	St
ODIs	35	34	2	825	84*	25.78	68.63	0	7	6	0
T20Is	10	9	0	188	45	20.88	97.91	0	0	2	0
First-class	16	26	1	502	93	20.08		0	3	5	0
List A	72	69	2	1394	111	20.80	66.92	1	10	17	0
Twenty20	12	11	0	238	45	21.63	97.14	0	0	3	0
Bowling	**Inns**	**Balls**	**Runs**	**Wkts**	**BBI**	**BBM**	**Ave**	**Econ**	**SR**	**5w**	**10**
ODIs	35	-	-	-	-	-	-	-	-	-	-
T20Is	10	-	-	-	-	-	-	-	-	-	-
First-class	16	136	98	3	2/24	2/25	32.66	4.32	45.3	0	0
List A	72	36	32	0	-	-	-	5.33	-	0	0
Twenty20	12	-	-	-	-	-	-	-	-	-	-

DAAN VAN BUNGE RHB LB

FULL NAME: Daan Lodewjk Samuel van Bunge
BORN: October 19, 1982, Leidschendam, Voorburg, Netherlands
SQUAD NO: TBC
HEIGHT: 6ft 4in
NICKNAME: Bungey
TEAMS: Netherlands, Voorburg CC
CAREER: ODI: 2002; T20I: 2008; First-class: 2004; List A: 2002; T20: 2004

BEST BATTING: 98* Netherlands vs Canada, Rotterdam, 2009
BEST BOWLING: 4-163 Netherlands vs Canada, Pretoria, 2006

CAREER HIGHLIGHTS? The 2003 World Cup in South Africa was amazing. I top-scored with 62 vs India in the opening match and took three wickets against England. Also the ICC World T20 win against England at Lord's in 2009 was spectacular. And my 98* of 300 balls against Canada in the Intercontinental Cup to save the game with two wickets in hand
SUPERSTITIONS? I never kill little animals or bugs when I see them crawling on the pitch/crease. I always gently put them on the side. I believe for some reason that the bad karma of killing them will turn around on me and I'll lose my wicket soon after
BEST PLAYER IN COUNTY CRICKET? Ryan ten Doeschate
TIPS FOR THE TOP? Saqib Zulfiqar, Reinier Kalis
BIGGEST DRESSING DOWN YOU'VE RECEIVED? At the 2003 World Cup I missed the bus for practice the day before we played Pakistan at Boland Park. Our coach Emerson Trottman was furious. As a 19-year-old there was nothing I could do apart from just sit there and take it all in
TWITTER FEED: @DvB1982

Batting	Mat	Inns	NO	Runs	HS	Ave	SR	100	50	Ct	St
ODIs	32	27	1	564	80	21.69	65.12	0	3	11	0
T20Is	10	9	2	60	24	8.57	78.94	0	0	4	0
First-class	10	17	2	351	98*	23.40	37.66	0	2	13	0
List A	61	54	5	1348	137	27.51		1	7	24	0
Twenty20	14	12	2	144	76	14.40	108.27	0	1	4	0
Bowling	**Inns**	**Balls**	**Runs**	**Wkts**	**BBI**	**BBM**	**Ave**	**Econ**	**SR**	**5w**	**10**
ODIs	32	319	321	11	3/16	3/16	29.18	6.03	29.0	0	0
T20Is	10	12	14	1	1/14	1/14	14.00	7.00	12.0	0	0
First-class	10	891	563	20	4/163		28.15	3.79	44.5	0	0
List A	61	540	541	17	3/16	3/16	31.82	6.01	31.7	0	0
Twenty20	14	18	21	1	1/14	1/14	21.00	7.00	18.0	0	0

PAUL VAN MEEKEREN RHB RFM

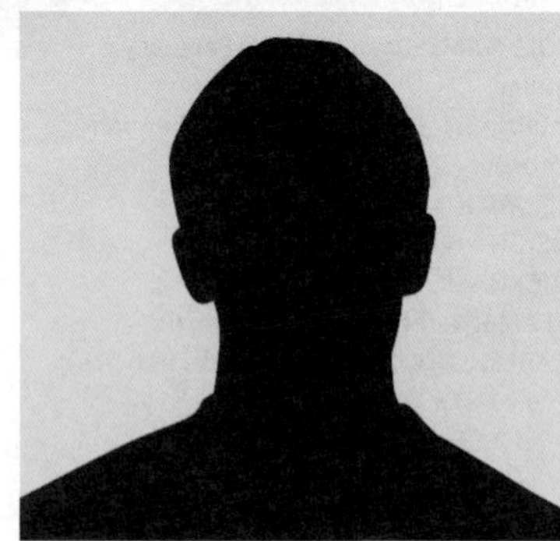

FULL NAME: Paul Adriaan van Meekeren
BORN: January 15, 1993, Amsterdam, Netherlands
SQUAD NO: TBC
HEIGHT: 6ft 5in
NICKNAME: Krusty
TEAMS: Netherlands Under-13s, Netherlands Under-15s, Netherlands Under-19s
CAREER: Yet to make first-team debut

FAMILY TIES? My father played the game
WHO WOULD PLAY YOU IN A FILM OF YOUR LIFE? Jim Carrey
CAREER HIGHLIGHTS? Named Player of the Tournament at the European Championships
MOST MARKED CHARACTERISTIC? Sociability
BEST PLAYER IN COUNTY CRICKET? Owais Shah
IF YOU WEREN'T A CRICKETER? I'd be a student
DESERT ISLAND DISC? Andy Grammer – Keep Your Head Up
FAVOURITE TV? Lucky Luke
BIGGEST DRESSING DOWN YOU'VE RECEIVED? Batting at No.11, under strict instructions not to get out, I went down to sweep and got given lbw. During lunch the coach had a go at me
CRICKETING HEROES? Brett Lee
NON-CRICKETING HEROES? Dennis Bergkamp
TWITTER FEED: @paulvanmeekeren

Unicorns
*At the time of writing Unicorns had not
announced a squad for the 2013 season

England
Women

ENGLAND WOMEN

CAPTAIN: Charlotte Edwards
COACH: Mark Lane

2013 FIXTURES

Only Ashes Test
England Women v Australia Women
August 11-15
Sir Paul Getty's Ground, Wormsley

1st ODI
England Women v Australia Women
August 20
Lord's, London

2nd ODI
England Women v Australia Women
August 23
The BrightonandHoveJobs.com County Ground, Hove

3rd ODI
England Women v Australia Women
August 25
The BrightonandHoveJobs.com County Ground, Hove

1st T20I
England Women v Australia Women
August 27
The Essex County Ground, Chelmsford

2nd T20I
England Women v Australia Women
August 29
Ageas Bowl, Southampton

3rd T20I
England Women v Australia Women
August 31
Emirates Durham ICG, Chester-le-Street

TAMMY BEAUMONT RHB WK

FULL NAME: Tamsin Tilley Beaumont
BORN: March 11, 1991, Dover, Kent
SQUAD NO: 12
HEIGHT: 5ft 3in
NICKNAME: Tampy
EDUCATION: Sir Roger Manwood's School; Loughborough University
TEAMS: Diamonds, England Women, Kent Women
CAREER: ODI: 2009; T20I: 2009

WHO WOULD PLAY YOU IN A FILM OF YOUR LIFE? Anne Hathaway – I wish I had her legs!
CAREER HIGHLIGHTS? Coming back from 2-0 down in an ODI series last summer against India to win 3-2, showing a lot of character as a team in the process. Also winning every game on our tour of New Zealand last year
SUPERSTITIONS? I wouldn't say I have any superstitions but my teammates would probably comment on how I push my pads down before every ball I face, but that's more to do with them being slightly too big!
BEST PLAYER IN COUNTY CRICKET? Charlotte Edwards still strikes fear into the eyes of opposition attacks
TIP FOR THE TOP? Nat Sciver from Surrey is a hard-hitting right-hander who can produce a good spell with the ball too
DESERT ISLAND DISC? Ed Sheeran – + or Adele – 21. Neither of those two get old
FAVOURITE TV? The Big Bang Theory
BIGGEST DRESSING DOWN YOU'VE RECEIVED? My old university coach, the late Graham Dilley, once gave me a dressing down the week before the start of the season about not living up to my potential and how I was indulging in university life too much. I think it had the desired effect as by the end of the university competition I had scored six hundreds in eight games!
ACCOMPLISHMENTS? Getting a 2:1 in Chemistry and Sports Science from Loughborough University. I surprised even myself because in my final year I was only in England for about half of the year and touring for the rest of it
TWITTER FEED: @Tammy_Beaumont

Batting	Mat	Inns	NO	Runs	HS	Ave	SR	100	50	Ct	St
ODIs	17	12	3	174	44	19.33	41.23	0	0	6	4
T20Is	23	10	2	57	17*	7.12	60.00	0	0	5	4
Bowling	**Inns**	**Balls**	**Runs**	**Wkts**	**BBI**	**BBM**	**Ave**	**Econ**	**SR**	**5w**	**10**
ODIs	17	-	-	-	-	-	-	-	-	-	-
T20Is	23	-	-	-	-	-	-	-	-	-	-

ARRAN BRINDLE RHB RM

FULL NAME: Arran Brindle
BORN: November 23, 1981, Keighley, Yorkshire
SQUAD NO: 77
HEIGHT: 5ft 6in
NICKNAME: Enid
EDUCATION: Skipton Girls' High School; Loughborough University
TEAMS: England Women, Lancashire Women, Sussex Women
CAREER: Test: 2001; ODI: 1999; T20I: 2005

BEST TEST BATTING: 101* England vs Australia, Hove, 2005

CAREER HIGHLIGHTS? Being part of the England team that beat the Aussies in an ODI for the first time in 12 years in 2005 and winning the Ashes the same year. And winning two quadrangular series on my return to the side in 2011
SUPERSTITIONS? I always put my left pad on first
MOST MARKED CHARACTERISTIC? Attention to detail
BEST PLAYER IN COUNTY CRICKET? Sarah Taylor and Charlotte Edwards
TIP FOR THE TOP? Amy Jones
IF YOU WEREN'T A CRICKETER? Teacher
DESERT ISLAND DISC? Pitbull – Give Me Everything Tonight, or Roxette – Fading Like A Flower
FAVOURITE TV? Murder In Paradise
CRICKETING HEROES? Graeme Hick and Mark Ramprakash
NON-CRICKETING HEROES? Andre Agassi
ACCOMPLISHMENTS? Being a mum
FANTASY SLIP CORDON? Keeper: Peter Schmeichel, 1st: David Beckham, 2nd: Me, 3rd: Dawn French
TWITTER FEED: @brindlecricket

Batting	Mat	Inns	NO	Runs	HS	Ave	SR	100	50	Ct	St
Tests	9	16	2	423	101*	30.21		1	2	4	0
ODIs	80	76	13	1668	107*	26.47		1	9	36	0
T20Is	27	23	9	297	42*	21.21	97.37	0	0	7	0
Bowling	**Inns**	**Balls**	**Runs**	**Wkts**	**BBI**	**BBM**	**Ave**	**Econ**	**SR**	**5w**	**10**
Tests	9	18	14	0	-	-	-	4.66	-	0	0
ODIs	80	846	637	31	3/0	3/0	20.54	4.51	27.2	0	0
T20Is	27	387	332	20	3/11	3/11	16.60	5.14	19.3	0	0

KATHERINE BRUNT RHB RFM

FULL NAME: Katherine Helen Brunt
BORN: July 2, 1985, Barnsley
SQUAD NO: 26
HEIGHT: 5ft 8in
NICKNAME: Nunny
TEAMS: England Women, Diamonds, Yorkshire Women
CAREER: Test: 2004; ODI: 2005; T20I: 2005

BEST TEST BATTING: 52 England vs Australia, Worcester, 2005
BEST TEST BOWLING: 6-69 England vs Australia, Worcester, 2009

NOTES: Brunt has a reputation as one of the fastest bowlers in women's cricket and is also a useful hitter from the lower order. She made her international debut at the age of 19 in 2004 and a year later helped England win the Ashes for the first time in 42 years. In 2006 she was named alongside Andrew Flintoff as one of two England Cricketers of the Year and was shortlisted for the Women's Player of the Year award by the ICC. Back injuries interrupted her career and she missed the 2007/08 Ashes before returning to play a key role in England's triumphant 2009, which saw them lift the 50-over World Cup and World T20. Her figures of 5-25 in an ODI against South Africa at Lord's in 2008 remain the best ever recorded at the ground, by a man or woman

Batting	Mat	Inns	NO	Runs	HS	Ave	SR	100	50	Ct	St
Tests	7	8	3	101	52	20.20	29.70	0	1	2	0
ODIs	70	30	9	205	21*	9.76	81.02	0	0	16	0
T20Is	39	18	10	97	35	12.12	102.10	0	0	10	0
Bowling	**Inns**	**Balls**	**Runs**	**Wkts**	**BBI**	**BBM**	**Ave**	**Econ**	**SR**	**5w**	**10**
Tests	7	1403	576	30	6/69	9/111	19.20	2.46	46.7	2	0
ODIs	70	3436	1877	88	5/18	5/18	21.32	3.27	39.0	3	0
T20Is	39	846	680	38	3/6	3/6	17.89	4.82	22.2	0	0

HOLLY COLVIN RHB SLA

FULL NAME: Holly Louise Colvin
BORN: September 7, 1989, Chichester, Sussex
SQUAD NO: 10
HEIGHT: 5ft 1in
NICKNAME: Monkey, Colin, Michelle
EDUCATION: Brighton College; Durham University
TEAMS: England Women, New South Wales Women, Rubies, Sussex Women
CAREER: Test: 2005; ODI: 2006; T20I: 2007

BEST TEST BATTING: 21 England vs Australia, Sydney, 2011
BEST TEST BOWLING: 3-42 England vs Australia, Bowral, 2008

WHO WOULD PLAY YOU IN A FILM OF YOUR LIFE? Charlize Theron – if only I looked like her!
CAREER HIGHLIGHTS? Hitting the winning runs in the 2009 Women's World Cup final and beating the Aussies 4-0 in an ODI series in 2009. It was the first whitewash against Australia in over 40 years
MOST MARKED CHARACTERISTIC? Independence
TIP FOR THE TOP? Joe Root
IF YOU WEREN'T A CRICKETER? Hopefully working for a big events management company
DESERT ISLAND DISC? John Mayer – Where The Light Is
FAVOURITE TV? Revenge
CRICKETING HEROES? Daniel Vettori
ACCOMPLISHMENTS? My exam grades, winning Telegraph School Pupil of the Year in 2006
WHEN YOU RETIRE? Start a family
SURPRISING FACT? I'm classically trained at the guitar
FANTASY SLIP CORDON? Keeper: Will Smith, 1st: Joshua Jackson, 2nd: Miranda Hart, 3rd: Me, Gully: Greg James
TWITTER FEED: @hollycolvin10

Batting	Mat	Inns	NO	Runs	HS	Ave	SR	100	50	Ct	St
Tests	5	7	3	59	21	14.75	20.20	0	0	1	0
ODIs	66	25	14	166	29	15.09	69.16	0	0	17	0
T20Is	43	10	3	56	17*	8.00	75.67	0	0	18	0
Bowling	**Inns**	**Balls**	**Runs**	**Wkts**	**BBI**	**BBM**	**Ave**	**Econ**	**SR**	**5w**	**10**
Tests	5	727	382	13	3/42	4/78	29.38	3.15	55.9	0	0
ODIs	66	3319	1986	88	4/20	4/20	22.56	3.59	37.7	0	0
T20Is	43	971	823	59	4/9	4/9	13.94	5.08	16.4	0	0

CHARLOTTE EDWARDS RHB LB

FULL NAME: Charlotte Marie Edwards
BORN: December 17, 1979, Huntingdon
SQUAD NO: 23
HEIGHT: 5ft 9in
NICKNAME: Lottie
EDUCATION: Ramsey Abbey School
TEAMS: East Anglia Women, England Women, Kent Women, Northern Districts Women
CAREER: Test: 1996; ODI: 1997; T20I: 2004

BEST TEST BATTING: 117 England vs New Zealand, Scarborough, 2004
BEST TEST BOWLING: 2-28 England vs Australia, Harrogate, 1998

FAMILY TIES? My dad, uncle and brother all played minor counties for Huntingdonshire and club cricket for Ramsey CC
CAREER HIGHLIGHTS? Winning the World Cup in Sydney in 2009 and the World T20 in England in the same year
MOST MARKED CHARACTERISTIC? I'm passionate
BEST PLAYER IN COUNTY CRICKET? Sarah Taylor
TIPS FOR THE TOP? Amy Jones and Nat Sciver
IF YOU WEREN'T A CRICKETER? I'd be in the police
DESERT ISLAND DISC? Take That's Greatest Hits
CRICKETING HEROES? Steve Waugh and Belinda Clark
NON-CRICKETING HEROES? Steffi Graf
ACCOMPLISHMENTS? Raising money for Macmillan nurses after sadly losing my dad to cancer
WHEN YOU RETIRE? Coaching
FANTASY SLIP CORDON? Keeper: Miranda, 1st: David Beckham, 2nd: Steffi Graf, 3rd: Steve Waugh, Gully: Gary Barlow
TWITTER FEED: @Lottie2323

Batting	Mat	Inns	NO	Runs	HS	Ave	SR	100	50	Ct	St
Tests	19	35	4	1522	117	49.09		4	8	9	0
ODIs	167	156	20	5075	173*	37.31		8	38	41	0
T20Is	61	59	9	1599	76*	31.98	108.48	0	6	10	0
Bowling	**Inns**	**Balls**	**Runs**	**Wkts**	**BBI**	**BBM**	**Ave**	**Econ**	**SR**	**5w**	**10**
Tests	19	1112	570	12	2/28	2/54	47.50	3.07	92.6	0	0
ODIs	167	1627	1174	54	4/30	4/30	21.74	4.32	30.1	0	0
T20Is	61	288	311	9	3/21	3/21	34.55	6.47	32.0	0	0

ENGLAND WOMEN

GEORGIA ELWISS

RHB RMF

FULL NAME: Georgia Amanda Elwiss
BORN: May 31, 1991, Wolverhampton, Staffordshire
SQUAD NO: 34
HEIGHT: 5ft 8in
NICKNAME: Gg, Paddy
EDUCATION: Wolverhampton Girls' High School; Loughborough University
TEAMS: England Women, Emeralds, Sapphires, Staffordshire Women, Sussex Women
CAREER: ODI: 2011; T20I: 2011

WHO WOULD PLAY YOU IN A FILM OF YOUR LIFE? Miranda!
CAREER HIGHLIGHTS? Making my debut in South Africa and winning the Player of the Series award last summer against India
MOST MARKED CHARACTERISTIC? Maybe that I'm hardworking?
BEST PLAYER IN COUNTY CRICKET? Sarah Taylor, without a doubt!
TIPS FOR THE TOP? Nat Sciver and Amy Jones
IF YOU WEREN'T A CRICKETER? A singer on Broadway perhaps? I wish!
DESERT ISLAND DISC? Emeli Sande's album
FAVOURITE TV? Grey's Anatomy – it's an emotional rollercoaster!
CRICKETING HEROES? I used to love Allan Donald! I used to write him letters and everything. How lame! From the women's side Lucy Pearson was always the person I looked up to and I was very fortunate to be able to play along side her a few times
ACCOMPLISHMENTS? Does nearly doing a skydive count?
WHEN YOU RETIRE? I'd like to be a nutritionist and set up my own practice
SURPRISING FACT? I had to have my tongue sewn back together after falling down the stairs and biting it off
FANTASY SLIP CORDON? Keeper: Sarah Taylor (I have to say that!), 1st: Me (it's either Sarah's or Swanny's), 2nd: Graeme Swann, 3rd: Alan Carr (for a bit of comedy value), Gully: Inspector Gadget (those arms would fly around to catch anything!)
TWITTER FEED: @Gelwiss

Batting	Mat	Inns	NO	Runs	HS	Ave	SR	100	50	Ct	St
ODIs	10	2	1	12	10	12.00	50.00	0	0	2	0
T20Is	2	-	-	-	-	-	-	-	-	0	0
Bowling	**Inns**	**Balls**	**Runs**	**Wkts**	**BBI**	**BBM**	**Ave**	**Econ**	**SR**	**5w**	**10**
ODIs	10	504	277	11	3/17	3/17	25.18	3.29	45.8	0	0
T20Is	2	48	50	2	2/30	2/30	25.00	6.25	24.0	0	0

LYDIA GREENWAY LHB OB

FULL NAME: Lydia Sophie Greenway
BORN: August 6, 1985, Farnborough, Kent
SQUAD NO: 20
HEIGHT: 5ft 8in
NICKNAME: Lyd
TEAMS: England Women, Diamonds, Kent Women
CAREER: Test: 2003; ODI: 2003; T20I: 2004

BEST TEST BATTING: 70 England vs South Africa, Shenley, 2003

FAMILY TIES? My dad was 1st XI captain at our local club (Hayes CC, Kent). My brother and sister also played, along with my mum on a few occasions!
CAREER HIGHLIGHTS? Winning the Ashes back in 2005 and winning both the 50-over and World T20 Cups in 2009/10
BEST PLAYER IN COUNTY CRICKET? Nat Sciver – I've only seen her play a few times but she has got the potential to be a very good player
TIPS FOR THE TOP? Tas Farrant and Grace Gibbs. Two young girls from Kent who played for the senior team last season
IF YOU WEREN'T A CRICKETER? Maybe a PE teacher
DESERT ISLAND DISC? Scouting For Girls
FAVOURITE TV? Friends. Even when there are repeat episodes on they still make me laugh
BIGGEST DRESSING DOWN YOU'VE RECEIVED? The 2010 World T20 in the West Indies. It wasn't necessarily a dressing down, it was more disbelief at what had happened. It was a feeling of pure disappointment and sickness knowing we hadn't done ourselves and the people supporting us justice
CRICKETING HEROES? Marcus Trescothick and Adam Gilchrist
ACCOMPLISHMENTS? Cycling from London to Paris to raise money for the charity Breast Cancer Care

Batting	Mat	Inns	NO	Runs	HS	Ave	SR	100	50	Ct	St
Tests	10	17	1	284	70	17.75	30.43	0	2	13	0
ODIs	104	92	23	2125	125*	30.79	62.72	1	10	46	0
T20Is	54	49	15	837	61*	24.61	97.21	0	1	29	0
Bowling	**Inns**	**Balls**	**Runs**	**Wkts**	**BBI**	**BBM**	**Ave**	**Econ**	**SR**	**5w**	**10**
Tests	10	-	-	-	-	-	-	-	-	-	-
ODIs	104	-	-	-	-	-	-	-	-	-	-
T20Is	54	-	-	-	-	-	-	-	-	-	-

JENNY GUNN

RHB RMF

ENGLAND WOMEN

FULL NAME: Jennifer Louise Gunn
BORN: May 9, 1986, Nottingham
SQUAD NO: 24
HEIGHT: 5ft 10in
NICKNAME: Trigger
EDUCATION: South Nottingham College
TEAMS: England Women, Nottinghamshire Women, South Australia Women
CAREER: Test: 2004; ODI: 2004; T20I: 2004

BEST TEST BATTING: 41 England vs Australia, Worcester, 2009
BEST TEST BOWLING: 3-40 England vs Australia, Hove, 2005

CAREER HIGHLIGHTS? Winning two World Cups, the Ashes and playing in over 100 matches for my country
SUPERSTITIONS? When walking round the boundary I walk right for runs and left for wickets
MOST MARKED CHARACTERISTIC? Probably my bowling action. From certain angles I look like I throw the ball but I just have a lot of hyper-extension in my elbow
BEST PLAYER IN COUNTY CRICKET? Sarah Taylor. I'm just glad I play on the same team most of the time so I don't have to bowl at her
IF YOU WEREN'T A CRICKETER? Singing and dancing on the West End or a chef
DESERT ISLAND DISC? Classic Motown
NON-CRICKETING HEROES? My family, especially my dad [Bryn] who played a high level of football [for Nottingham Forest] and he gives me good advice. And Alan Shearer too
ACCOMPLISHMENTS? Getting my 50m swimming badge – I hate swimming!
WHEN YOU RETIRE? Go and live in Australia
SURPRISING FACT? I used to do tap, ballet and modern – I think it was for my family's entertainment though!
TWITTER FEED: @GunnJenny

Batting	Mat	Inns	NO	Runs	HS	Ave	SR	100	50	Ct	St
Tests	8	14	0	272	41	19.42	29.27	0	0	3	0
ODIs	107	86	21	1404	73	21.60	56.18	0	5	33	0
T20Is	61	44	8	570	69	15.83	102.51	0	1	42	0
Bowling	**Inns**	**Balls**	**Runs**	**Wkts**	**BBI**	**BBM**	**Ave**	**Econ**	**SR**	**5w**	**10**
Tests	8	1565	501	19	3/40	4/67	26.36	1.92	82.3	0	0
ODIs	107	4346	2718	97	5/31	5/31	28.02	3.75	44.8	1	0
T20Is	61	527	572	26	4/9	4/9	22.00	6.51	20.2	0	0

DANIELLE HAZELL RHB OB

FULL NAME: Danielle Hazell
BORN: May 13, 1988, Durham
SQUAD NO: 17
HEIGHT: 5ft 3in
NICKNAME: Pet
EDUCATION: Deerness Valley
TEAMS: England Women, Diamonds, Sapphires, Yorkshire Women
CAREER: Test: 2011; ODI: 2009; T20I: 2009

BEST TEST BATTING: 0 England vs Australia, Sydney, 2011
BEST TEST BOWLING: 2-32 England vs Australia, Sydney, 2011

WHO WOULD PLAY YOU IN A FILM OF YOUR LIFE? Rebel Wilson
CAREER HIGHLIGHTS? England debut in 2009 in the West Indies
MOST MARKED CHARACTERISTIC? Northern accent
BEST PLAYER IN COUNTY CRICKET? Jenny Gunn
IF YOU WEREN'T A CRICKETER? Property tycoon
DESERT ISLAND DISC? Maria McKee – Show Me Heaven
FAVOURITE TV? Neighbours
CRICKETING HEROES? Ricky Ponting
NON-CRICKETING HEROES? Alan Shearer
FANTASY SLIP CORDON? Keeper: Me, 1st: Peter Andre, 2nd: Gavin Henson, 3rd: Alan Shearer, Gully: My mam

Batting	Mat	Inns	NO	Runs	HS	Ave	SR	100	50	Ct	St
Tests	1	2	0	0	0	0.00	0.00	0	0	1	0
ODIs	24	14	3	158	24*	14.36	98.13	0	0	5	0
T20Is	35	17	4	113	18*	8.69	87.59	0	0	7	0
Bowling	**Inns**	**Balls**	**Runs**	**Wkts**	**BBI**	**BBM**	**Ave**	**Econ**	**SR**	**5w**	**10**
Tests	1	132	52	2	2/32	2/52	26.00	2.36	66.0	0	0
ODIs	24	1131	785	24	3/22	3/22	32.70	4.16	47.1	0	0
T20Is	35	803	721	43	4/12	4/12	16.76	5.38	18.6	0	0

AMY JONES

RHB WK

FULL NAME: Amy Jones
BORN: June 13, 1993, Sutton Coldfield, Warwickshire
SQUAD NO: 40
NICKNAME: Jonesy, Jonah
EDUCATION: Loughborough University
TEAMS: Diamonds, Emeralds, England Academy Women, England Under-19s Women, Warwickshire Women
CAREER: ODI: 2013

CRICKETING HEROES? Matt Prior
FAVOURITE TV? Miranda, Live At The Apollo
FAVOURITE FILM? Love Actually
DESERT ISLAND DISC? Gavin Degraw or Scouting For Girls
NOTES: Jones made her international bow at the 2013 World Cup, featuring in England's shock defeat to Sri Lanka in their tournament opener in place of the injured Sarah Taylor. She performed impressively despite the result, scoring 41 from 49 balls in a partnership of 83 with Jenny Gunn to take England to a respectable total of 238-8. She is in the process of completing a degree in Sports Science at Loughborough University and plays her club cricket for Walmley CC. In 2012, Jones scored 366 limited overs runs at 45.75, including an unbeaten hundred for the Emeralds against the Rubies

Batting	Mat	Inns	NO	Runs	HS	Ave	SR	100	50	Ct	St
ODIs	1	1	0	41	41	41.00	83.67	0	0	1	0
Bowling	**Inns**	**Balls**	**Runs**	**Wkts**	**BBI**	**BBM**	**Ave**	**Econ**	**SR**	**5w**	**10**
ODIs	1	-	-	-	-	-	-	-	-	-	-

HEATHER KNIGHT RHB RM

FULL NAME: Heather Clare Knight
BORN: December 26, 1990, Rochdale
SQUAD NO: 5
HEIGHT: 5ft 7in
NICKNAME: Trev
EDUCATION: Plymstock School; Cardiff University
TEAMS: Berkshire, Diamonds, England Academy Women, England Women, Rubies, Sapphires
CAREER: Test: 2011; ODI: 2010; T20I: 2010

BEST TEST BATTING: 19 England vs Australia, Sydney, 2011

WHO WOULD PLAY YOU IN A FILM OF YOUR LIFE? Miranda Hart
CAREER HIGHLIGHTS? Opening the batting in my debut Ashes Test match in Australia, winning the quadrangular T20 and ODI series with England in 2011
MOST MARKED CHARACTERISTIC? My webbed feet
BEST PLAYER IN COUNTY CRICKET? Peter Trego
IF YOU WEREN'T A CRICKETER? I'd work in business
DESERT ISLAND DISC? The Verve – Urban Hymns
FAVOURITE TV? MasterChef
CRICKETING HEROES? Marcus Trescothick, Steve Waugh
ACCOMPLISHMENTS? Somehow getting through university whilst being away with England for half the year
SURPRISING FACT? I'm secretly a northerner and was born in Rochdale (shhh…!)
FANTASY SLIP CORDON? Keeper: Stephen Fry (to reel off interesting facts), 1st: Me, 2nd: Michael McIntyre (to laugh at), 3rd: Frankie Boyle (to sledge), Gully: Ryan Reynolds (to stare at)
TWITTER FEED: @Heatherknight55

Batting	Mat	Inns	NO	Runs	HS	Ave	SR	100	50	Ct	St
Tests	1	2	0	21	19	10.50	35.00	0	0	2	0
ODIs	34	30	8	570	72	25.90	57.75	0	2	6	0
T20Is	8	7	1	44	13	7.33	78.57	0	0	3	0
Bowling	**Inns**	**Balls**	**Runs**	**Wkts**	**BBI**	**BBM**	**Ave**	**Econ**	**SR**	**5w**	**10**
Tests	1	12	12	0	-	-	-	6.00	-	0	0
ODIs	34	72	48	3	2/15	2/15	16.00	4.00	24.0	0	0
T20Is	8	-	-	-	-	-	-	-	-	-	-

LAURA MARSH RHB OB

FULL NAME: Laura Alexandra Marsh
BORN: December 5, 1986, Pembury, Kent
SQUAD NO: 7
HEIGHT: 5ft 5in
NICKNAME: Marshy, Boggy
EDUCATION: Brighton College; Loughborough University
TEAMS: England Development Squad Women, England Women, Rubies, Sapphires, Sussex Women
CAREER: Test: 2006; ODI: 2006; T20I: 2007

BEST TEST BATTING: 38 England vs Australia, Worcester, 2009
BEST TEST BOWLING: 3-44 England vs India, Leicester, 2006

FAMILY TIES? Both my dad and brother played but not at a representative level
CAREER HIGHLIGHTS? Winning ODI and T20 World Cups in 2009. Travelling to fantastic parts of the world and playing at amazing grounds. Playing with and meeting some great friends and teammates
MOST MARKED CHARACTERISTIC? Small head
BEST PLAYER IN COUNTY CRICKET? Nat Sciver
TIPS FOR THE TOP? Natasha Farrant – fast left-arm seamer who I play county cricket with at Kent. Nat Sciver – a hard-hitting allrounder and skilful bowler. Amy Jones – wicketkeeper-batsman and a natural talent
IF YOU WEREN'T A CRICKETER? Maybe a golfer but definitely something in sport
FAVOURITE TV? Homeland or Dexter
WHEN YOU RETIRE? Have a family
SURPRISING FACT? I was a national javelin champion when I was 13
FANTASY SLIP CORDON? Keeper: AB de Villiers (great bum), 1st: Myself (good view!), 2nd: David Beckham (hero), 3rd: Mark Lane (great banter and sledging would be priceless), Gully: Swanny (all-round comedy value)
TWITTER FEED: @lauramarsh7

Batting	Mat	Inns	NO	Runs	HS	Ave	SR	100	50	Ct	St
Tests	5	7	0	55	38	7.85	27.77	0	0	4	0
ODIs	67	39	7	467	67	14.59	66.52	0	1	13	0
T20Is	55	50	5	729	54	16.20	99.86	0	1	6	0
Bowling	**Inns**	**Balls**	**Runs**	**Wkts**	**BBI**	**BBM**	**Ave**	**Econ**	**SR**	**5w**	**10**
Tests	5	983	344	11	3/44	4/83	31.27	2.09	89.3	0	0
ODIs	67	3420	2207	80	5/15	5/15	27.58	3.87	42.7	1	0
T20Is	55	1231	1073	51	3/17	3/17	21.03	5.22	24.1	0	0

SUSIE ROWE RHB RM

FULL NAME: Susannah Elizabeth Rowe
BORN: April 14, 1987, Lewisham, London
SQUAD NO: TBC
HEIGHT: 5ft 6in
EDUCATION: Colfe's School; University of Maryland (USA)
TEAMS: England Women, Emeralds, Kent Women, Rubies
CAREER: ODI: 2011; T20I: 2010

CAREER HIGHLIGHTS? Coming into the squad at such a successful time for the team
MOST MARKED CHARACTERISTIC? I'm known in the team as a bit of a faffer!
BEST PLAYER IN COUNTY CRICKET? Charlotte Edwards
TIP FOR THE TOP? There's a young player I play with at Hayes CC and Kent called Tash Farrant who's our opening bowler. She's a hockey player like me and I think the athleticism she has from that combined with her natural cricketing talent could make her one to watch
IF YOU WEREN'T A CRICKETER? Playing hockey
DESERT ISLAND DISC? The latest Ministry Of Sound Annual
FAVOURITE TV? Friends
BIGGEST DRESSING DOWN YOU'VE RECEIVED? The look Katherine Brunt gave me when I threw four overthrows off her bowling going for a run out!
CRICKETING HEROES? Freddie Flintoff
NON-CRICKETING HEROES? My younger sister for raising her wonderful daughter while studying for a degree in Physiotherapy and playing National League hockey – she's superhuman! Oh, and she's not a bad sister either!
ACCOMPLISHMENTS? Represented England U16-U21 at hockey. Studied for a degree in Marketing while on a hockey scholarship at the University of Maryland in the USA. We won the National Championship three out of the four seasons I played there and I got to meet George Bush at the White House as a result
WHEN YOU RETIRE? Travel and get to see those countries that don't play cricket
TWITTER FEED: @susierowe6

Batting	Mat	Inns	NO	Runs	HS	Ave	SR	100	50	Ct	St
ODIs	1	-	-	-	-	-	-	-	-	0	0
T20Is	20	8	4	111	29*	27.75	111.00	0	0	4	0
Bowling	**Inns**	**Balls**	**Runs**	**Wkts**	**BBI**	**BBM**	**Ave**	**Econ**	**SR**	**5w**	**10**
ODIs	1	-	-	-	-	-	-	-	-	-	-
T20Is	20	-	-	-	-	-	-	-	-	-	-

NATALIE SCIVER RHB RM

FULL NAME: Natalie Sciver
BORN: August 30, 1992, Cobham, Surrey
SQUAD NO: TBC
NICKNAME: Scivs, Skiver
EDUCATION: Loughborough University
TEAMS: Emeralds, Rubies, Surrey Women
CAREER: Yet to make England debut

CRICKETING HEROES? Chris Gayle
DESERT ISLAND DISC? Chris Brown
FAVOURITE TV? Grey's Anatomy
FAVOURITE FILM? Bridget Jones
NOTES: Sciver made her county debut for Surrey in 2010 and was selected for the England Women's Academy last year. She is currently studying Sports and Exercise Sciences at Loughborough University. In 2012 she scored 209 limited overs runs at 69.66 with a best score of 67* against the Diamonds for the Emeralds. She is also a useful medium-pacer and has the potential to become a genuine allrounder

ANYA SHRUBSOLE RHB RFM

FULL NAME: Anya Shrubsole
BORN: December 7, 1991, Bath, Somerset
SQUAD NO: 41
HEIGHT: 5ft 11in
NICKNAME: Shrubby
EDUCATION: Hayesfield Girls' School; Loughborough University
TEAMS: England Women, Rubies, Somerset Women
CAREER: ODI: 2008; T20I: 2008

CAREER HIGHLIGHTS? Making my debut against South Africa, winning the World Cup in Australia in 2009 and taking for 5-11 against New Zealand
MOST MARKED CHARACTERISTIC? My knowledge of cricket
BEST PLAYER IN COUNTY CRICKET? Sarah Taylor, Marcus Trescothick
TIPS FOR THE TOP? Georgia Elwiss, Joe Root
IF YOU WEREN'T A CRICKETER? I'd still be at university doing Psychology
DESERT ISLAND DISC? Stevie Wonder – Songs In The Key Of Life
FAVOURITE TV? Friends
BIGGEST DRESSING DOWN YOU'VE RECEIVED? From my mother for throwing my bat when I got out when I was younger!
CRICKETING HEROES? Michael Holding, Aravinda de Silva
NON-CRICKETING HEROES? Sir Steve Redgrave, Nelson Mandela
WHEN YOU RETIRE? Settle down and get a job. Hopefully in Psychology but it depends on how the degree goes!
SURPRISING FACT? I play the flute pretty well
FANTASY SLIP CORDON? Keeper: Michael McIntyre, 1st: Myself, 2nd: Usain Bolt, 3rd: Bradley Wiggins, Gully: Iron Man
TWITTER FEED: @Anya_shrubsole

Batting	Mat	Inns	NO	Runs	HS	Ave	SR	100	50	Ct	St
ODIs	15	3	2	28	15*	28.00	63.63	0	0	7	0
T20Is	23	3	2	2	1*	2.00	50.00	0	0	8	0
Bowling	**Inns**	**Balls**	**Runs**	**Wkts**	**BBI**	**BBM**	**Ave**	**Econ**	**SR**	**5w**	**10**
ODIs	15	607	378	19	5/17	5/17	19.89	3.73	31.9	1	0
T20Is	23	432	443	30	5/11	5/11	14.76	6.15	14.4	1	0

SARAH TAYLOR RHB WK

FULL NAME: Sarah Jane Taylor
BORN: May 20, 1989, London Hospital, Whitechapel, London
SQUAD NO: 30
HEIGHT: 5ft 8in
NICKNAME: Squirt, Dave, Taylor
EDUCATION: Brighton College
TEAMS: England Development Squad Women, England Women, Emeralds, Rubies, Sussex Women
CAREER: Test: 2006; ODI: 2006; T20I: 2006

BEST TEST BATTING: 28 England vs India, Leicester, 2006

WHO WOULD PLAY YOU IN A FILM OF YOUR LIFE? Missy Peregrym. Probably unknown to most but she is in Rookie Blue
CAREER HIGHLIGHTS? The year 2009 as a whole: winning two World Cups and an ODI series against Australia, as well as retaining the Ashes. Scoring a hundred at Lord's
SUPERSTITIONS? I always have to put my left pad on first
MOST MARKED CHARACTERISTIC? My stupid voices!
TIP FOR THE TOP? Nat Sciver
IF YOU WEREN'T A CRICKETER? I'd be playing tennis, or at least trying to
DESERT ISLAND DISC? A Marianas Trench album. Or if it had to be one song then I would say Tidal Wave by Sub Focus
FAVOURITE TV? White Collar
CRICKETING HEROES? Graham Thorpe and Rebecca Rolls (New Zealand)
NON-CRICKETING HEROES? Steffi Graf – I used to play tennis and I just loved watching her play
FANTASY SLIP CORDON? Keeper: Myself, 1st: Fat Amy (from Pitch Perfect, would say random things), 2nd: Michael Clarke (great pair of hands), 3rd: Lee Evans (would make me laugh so much), Gully: David Attenborough (listening to his voice in person would be awesome!)
TWITTER FEED: @Sarah_Taylor30

Batting	Mat	Inns	NO	Runs	HS	Ave	SR	100	50	Ct	St
Tests	4	7	0	124	28	17.71	46.79	0	0	7	1
ODIs	77	71	8	2398	129	38.06	78.00	4	10	61	30
T20Is	46	44	7	1219	73	32.94	112.24	0	8	14	28
Bowling	**Inns**	**Balls**	**Runs**	**Wkts**	**BBI**	**BBM**	**Ave**	**Econ**	**SR**	**5w**	**10**
Tests	4	-	-	-	-	-	-	-	-	-	-
ODIs	77	-	-	-	-	-	-	-	-	-	-
T20Is	46	-	-	-	-	-	-	-	-	-	-

DANIELLE WYATT RHB OB

FULL NAME: Danielle Nicole Wyatt
BORN: April 22, 1991, Stoke-on-Trent, Staffordshire
SQUAD NO: 28
HEIGHT: 5ft 4in
NICKNAME: Dan, Danni, Waggy, Wag, Waggo
EDUCATION: St Peter's High School; Stoke-on-Trent Sixth Form College
TEAMS: Emeralds, England Women, Sapphires, Staffordshire Women
CAREER: ODI: 2010; T20I: 2010

FAMILY TIES? My dad plays cricket for my men's club Whitmore. My older brother Ryan used to play but quit when I started doing better than him and now my little brother Max plays for Whitmore and Staffordshire U14
WHO WOULD PLAY YOU IN A FILM OF YOUR LIFE? I don't think anyone could live my life! I never sit down!
CAREER HIGHLIGHTS? Beating Australia 4-1 in a T20 series in Australia with such an inexperienced team and beating Australia at Wormsley to retain our No.1 status in ODI cricket
SUPERSTITIONS? No, although if I do well in a game I'll wear the same socks the next game
MOST MARKED CHARACTERISTIC? I like to be known as a happy person who likes living life to the full! YOLO!
IF YOU WEREN'T A CRICKETER? Maybe a window cleaner or run my own car cleaning company. I love cleaning cars!
DESERT ISLAND DISC? Daniel Bedingfield – If You're Not The One
FAVOURITE TV? Coronation Street. I don't watch much TV but I love Corrie. I sit and watch it with my mum with a cuppa, without fail! It's a family tradition
NON-CRICKETING HEROES? David Beckham. I can't believe I can say I've actually met him as well!
WHEN YOU RETIRE? Get married, have kids and have my own restaurant on the beach
SURPRISING FACT? I fell out of a tree when I was 10 after watching Tarzan with my brother and broke my wrist and foot. Awkward!
TWITTER FEED: @Danni_Wyatt

Batting	Mat	Inns	NO	Runs	HS	Ave	SR	100	50	Ct	St
ODIs	26	23	3	368	40	18.40	67.15	0	0	3	0
T20Is	37	23	5	265	41	14.72	114.71	0	0	6	0
Bowling	**Inns**	**Balls**	**Runs**	**Wkts**	**BBI**	**BBM**	**Ave**	**Econ**	**SR**	**5w**	**10**
ODIs	26	678	570	23	3/7	3/7	24.78	5.04	29.4	0	0
T20Is	37	537	479	38	4/11	4/11	12.60	5.35	14.1	0	0

The Umpires

ROB BAILEY

NAME: Robert John Bailey
BORN: October 28, 1963, Biddulph
HEIGHT: 6ft 3in
NICKNAME: Bailers
APPOINTED TO FIRST-CLASS LIST: 2006
INTERNATIONAL PANEL: 2011-
ODIS UMPIRED: 3
T20IS UMPIRED: 5
COUNTIES AS PLAYER: Northamptonshire, Derbyshire
ROLE: Right-hand bat, off spin bowler
COUNTY DEBUT: 1982 (Northamptonshire), 2000 (Derbyshire)
TEST DEBUT: 1988
ODI DEBUT: 1985

NOTES: Officiated at T20 Cup Finals Day 2008, 2009, 2010, 2011 and 2012, including the final in the last three years

Batting	Mat	Inns	NO	Runs	HS	Ave	SR	100	50	Ct	St
Tests	4	8	0	119	43	14.87	36.50	0	0	0	0
ODIs	4	4	2	137	43*	68.50	69.89	0	0	1	0
First-class	374	628	89	21844	224*	40.52	-	47	111	272	0
List A	396	376	65	12076	153*	38.82	-	10	79	111	0

Bowling	Mat	Balls	Runs	Wkts	BBI	BBM	Ave	Econ	SR	5w	10
Tests	4	-	-	-	-	-	-	-	-	-	-
ODIs	4	36	25	0	-	-	-	4.16	-	0	0
First-class	374	9713	5144	121	5/54	-	42.51	3.17	80.2	2	0
List A	396	3092	2564	72	5/45	5/45	35.61	4.97	42.9	1	0

NEIL BAINTON

NAME: Neil Laurence Bainton
BORN: October 2, 1970, Romford, Essex
HEIGHT: 5ft 8in
APPOINTED TO FIRST-CLASS LIST: 2006
FAVOURITE GROUND? Colwyn Bay and Arundel. Most outgrounds are nice to go to
FIRST COUNTY PLAYER YOU GAVE OUT? I can't remember, but it was probably wrong!
CAREER HIGHLIGHT AS AN UMPIRE? Being appointed to the first-class list and my two Tests as fourth umpire

---

NOTES: Has been reserve umpire in two Tests, two ODIs and two T20Is, as well as umpiring in five women's ODIs and two women's T20Is

2013 RESERVE UMPIRE LIST

Paul Baldwin
Mike Burns
Ismail Dawood
Ben Debenham
Mark Eggleston
Russell Evans
Graham Lloyd
Paul Pollard
Billy Taylor
Alex Wharf

MARK BENSON

NAME: Mark Richard Benson
BORN: July 6, 1958, Shoreham, Sussex
HEIGHT: 5ft 10in
NICKNAME: Benny
APPOINTED TO FIRST-CLASS LIST: 2000
INTERNATIONAL PANEL: 2004-2006
ELITE PANEL: 2006-2010
TESTS UMPIRED: 27 (plus 9 as TV umpire)
ODIS UMPIRED: 72 (plus 25 as TV umpire)
T20IS UMPIRED: 19 (plus 6 as TV umpire)
COUNTY AS PLAYER: Kent
ROLE: Left-hand bat
COUNTY DEBUT: 1980
TEST DEBUT: 1986
ODI DEBUT: 1986

NOTES: Stood in the C&G Trophy final in 2003. Umpired in the 2007 World Cup and the 2007 ICC World T20, including the final

Batting	Mat	Inns	NO	Runs	HS	Ave	SR	100	50	Ct	St
Tests	1	2	0	51	30	25.50	31.48	0	0	0	0
ODIs	1	1	0	24	24	24.00	41.37	0	0	0	0
First-class	292	491	34	18387	257	40.23	-	48	99	140	0
List A	269	257	11	7838	119	31.86	-	5	53	68	0

Bowling	Mat	Balls	Runs	Wkts	BBI	BBM	Ave	Econ	SR	5w	10
Tests	1	-	-	-	-	-	-	-	-	-	-
ODIs	1	-	-	-	-	-	-	-	-	-	-
First-class	292	467	493	5	2/55	-	98.60	6.33	93.4	0	0
List A	269	-	-	-	-	-	-	-	-	-	-

MARTIN BODENHAM

NAME: Martin John Dale Bodenham
BORN: April 23, 1950, Brighton
HEIGHT: 6ft 1in
APPOINTED TO FIRST-CLASS LIST: 2009
COUNTY AS PLAYER: Played for Sussex in a number of 2nd XI Championship matches
ROLE: Right-hand bat; wicketkeeper

NOTES: He is the first man to referee in football's Premier League and umpire first-class cricket. As a ref, he was in charge of three FA Cup semi-finals and the League Cup final in 1997, as well as being reserve referee for the European Cup final between AC Milan and Barcelona in 1994. In his career he sent off Vinnie Jones for threatening to break an opponent's legs and gave Roy Keane a yellow card while he was going off on a stretcher. Umpired in three women's ODIs and five women's T20Is

NICK COOK

NAME: Nicholas Grant Billson Cook
BORN: June 17, 1956, Leicester
HEIGHT: 6ft
NICKNAME: Beast
APPOINTED TO FIRST-CLASS LIST: 2009
COUNTIES AS PLAYER: Leicestershire, Northamptonshire
ROLE: Right-hand bat, slow left-arm bowler
COUNTY DEBUT: 1978 (Leicestershire), 1986 (Northamptonshire)
TEST DEBUT: 1983
ODI DEBUT: 1984
RITUALS OR QUIRKS? I like to walk out to the left of my colleague
SOMETHING WE DON'T KNOW ABOUT YOU? I have two Siamese cats

NOTES: Officiated as TV umpire in the Clydesdale Bank 40 final at Lord's in 2011. Reserve umpire in one Test. Officiated in one women's Test, four women's ODIs and at the 2012 FL t20 Finals Day

Batting	Mat	Inns	NO	Runs	HS	Ave	SR	100	50	Ct	St
Tests	15	25	4	179	31	8.52	23.58	0	0	5	0
ODIs	3	-	-	-	-	-	-	-	-	2	0
First-class	356	365	96	3137	75	11.66	-	0	4	197	0
List A	223	89	36	491	23	9.26	-	0	0	74	0

Bowling	Mat	Balls	Runs	Wkts	BBI	BBM	Ave	Econ	SR	5w	10
Tests	15	4174	1689	52	6/65	11/83	32.48	2.42	80.2	4	1
ODIs	3	144	95	5	2/18	2/18	19.00	3.95	28.8	0	0
First-class	356	64460	25507	879	7/34	-	29.01	2.37	73.3	31	4
List A	223	10077	6812	200	4/22	4/22	34.06	4.05	50.3	0	0

NIGEL COWLEY

NAME: Nigel Geoffrey Charles Cowley
BORN: March 1, 1953, Shaftesbury
HEIGHT: 5ft 6in
APPOINTED TO FIRST-CLASS LIST: 2000
COUNTIES AS PLAYER: Hampshire, Glamorgan
ROLE: Right-hand bat, off spin bowler
COUNTY DEBUT: 1974 (Hampshire), 1990 (Glamorgan)

NOTES: Has stood as reserve umpire in four Tests and three ODIs and officiated in one women's ODI and one women's T20I

Batting	Mat	Inns	NO	Runs	HS	Ave	SR	100	50	Ct	St
First-class	271	375	62	7309	109*	23.35	-	2	36	105	0
List A	305	226	45	3022	74	16.69	-	0	5	69	0

Bowling	Mat	Balls	Runs	Wkts	BBI	BBM	Ave	Econ	SR	5w	10
First-class	271	32662	14879	437	6/48		34.04	2.73	74.7	5	0
List A	305	11704	8038	248	5/24	5/24	32.41	4.12	47.1	1	0

JEFF EVANS

NAME: Jeffrey Howard Evans
BORN: August 7, 1954, Llanelli
HEIGHT: 5ft 8in
APPOINTED TO FIRST-CLASS LIST: 2001

NOTES: Played league cricket in South Wales as a right-hand bat. Has stood as reserve umpire in four Tests, three ODIs and two T20Is

STEVE GALE

NAME: Stephen Clifford Gale
BORN: June 3, 1952, Shrewsbury
APPOINTED TO FIRST-CLASS LIST: 2011
WHAT'S YOUR FAVOURITE COUNTY GROUND? Durham
FIRST COUNTY PLAYER YOU GAVE OUT? Jim Troughton
RITUALS OR QUIRKS? I always count the number of deliveries with six pound coins
CAREER HIGHLIGHT AS AN UMPIRE? My first televised game, a full house between Lancashire and Yorkshire at Old Trafford

NOTES: Gale spent three seasons on the reserve list, following a playing career representing Shropshire in minor counties cricket between 1975 and 1987, before joining the full list in 2011. He umpired the Second XI Knockout final at Horsham and the Cockspur T20 Cup final at The Rose Bowl in 2010. Officiated in one women's ODI

Batting	Mat	Inns	NO	Runs	HS	Ave	SR	100	50	Ct	St
List A	5	5	0	156	68	31.20	0	1	0	0	0

Bowling	Mat	Balls	Runs	Wkts	BBI	BBM	Ave	Econ	SR	5w	10
List A	5	-	-	-	-	-	-	-	-	-	-

STEVE GARRATT

NAME: Steven Arthur Garratt
BORN: July 5, 1953, Nottingham
HEIGHT: 6ft 2in
NICKNAME: Trigger
APPOINTED TO FIRST-CLASS LIST: 2008
FAVOURITE GROUND? My favourite ground has to be Lord's, although the more traditional grounds such as Canterbury, Taunton and Worcester certainly have a special charm
SOMETHING WE DON'T KNOW ABOUT YOU? My nickname Trigger is a reference to the speed of my decision-making early in my career and NOT the character in Only Fools And Horses, although some may beg to differ...

NOTES: Garratt is a retired police officer

MICHAEL GOUGH

NAME: Michael Andrew Gough
BORN: December 18, 1979, Hartlepool
HEIGHT: 6ft 5in
NICKNAME: Goughy
APPOINTED TO FIRST-CLASS LIST: 2009
COUNTIES AS PLAYER: Durham
ROLE: Right-hand bat; off spin bowler
COUNTY DEBUT: 1998
SOMETHING WE DON'T KNOW ABOUT YOU? I'm a qualified football referee and a season ticket holder at Hartlepool United
FAVOURITE GROUND? Worcester
RITUALS AND QUIRKS? I step onto the pitch with my left foot first and my left foot is the first off the pitch

---

NOTES: Gough started umpiring in 2005 after retiring from the first-class game; he was appointed to the ECB reserve list in 2006. He is believed to be the youngest first-class umpire in the history of the game. In 2011 he officiated at T20 Finals Day at Edgbaston and was named PCA Umpire of the Year. Reserve umpire in one Test and two T20Is

Batting	Mat	Inns	NO	Runs	HS	Ave	SR	100	50	Ct	St
First-class	67	119	3	2952	123	25.44	-	2	15	57	0
List A	49	45	4	974	132	23.75	-	1	3	14	0

Bowling	Mat	Balls	Runs	Wkts	BBI	BBM	Ave	Econ	SR	5w	10
First-class	67	2486	1350	30	5/66	-	45.00	3.25	82.8	1	0
List A	49	1136	947	21	3/26	3/26	45.09	5.00	54.0	0	0

IAN GOULD

NAME: Ian James Gould
BORN: August 19, 1957, Taplow
HEIGHT: 5ft 7in
NICKNAME: Gunner
APPOINTED TO FIRST-CLASS LIST: 2002
INTERNATIONAL PANEL: 2006-
ELITE PANEL: 2010-
TESTS UMPIRED: 33
ODIS UMPIRED: 79
T20IS UMPIRED: 20
COUNTIES AS PLAYER: Middlesex, Sussex
ROLE: Left-hand bat, wicketkeeper
COUNTY DEBUT: 1975 (Middlesex), 1981 (Sussex)
ODI DEBUT: 1983

NOTES: Officiated at T20 Finals Day at Edgbaston in 2004 and at The Oval in 2005 – including standing in both finals – and again at Edgbaston in 2009. PCA Umpire of the Year 2005, 2007. Umpired in the 2007 World Cup. Stood in the FP Trophy final at Lord's in 2007

Batting	Mat	Inns	NO	Runs	HS	Ave	SR	100	50	Ct	St
ODIs	18	14	2	155	42	12.91	63.78	0	0	15	3
First-class	298	399	63	8756	128	26.05	-	4	47	536	67
List A	315	270	41	4377	88	19.11	-	0	20	242	37

Bowling	Mat	Balls	Runs	Wkts	BBI	BBM	Ave	Econ	SR	5w	10
ODIs	18	-	-	-	-	-	-	-	-	-	-
First-class	298	478	365	7	3/10	-	52.14	4.58	68.2	0	0
List A	315	20	16	1	1/0	1/0	16.00	4.80	20.0	0	0

PETER HARTLEY

NAME: Peter John Hartley
BORN: April 18, 1960, Keighley
HEIGHT: 6ft
NICKNAME: Jack
APPOINTED TO FIRST-CLASS LIST: 2003
INTERNATIONAL PANEL: 2006-
TESTS UMPIRED: 9 as TV umpire and 6 as reserve umpire
ODIS UMPIRED: 6
T20IS UMPIRED: 3
COUNTIES AS PLAYER: Warwickshire, Yorkshire, Hampshire
ROLE: Right-hand bat, right-arm fast-medium bowler
COUNTY DEBUT: 1982 (Warwickshire), 1985 (Yorkshire), 1998 (Hampshire)

NOTES: Officiated at T20 Finals Day in 2006 at Trent Bridge, including standing in the final. Umpired the FP Trophy final in 2007, the 2008 U19 World Cup final in Malaysia and the 2010 CB40 final

Batting	Mat	Inns	NO	Runs	HS	Ave	SR	100	50	Ct	St
First-class	232	283	66	4321	127*	19.91	-	2	14	68	0
List A	269	170	62	1765	83	16.34	-	0	4	46	0

Bowling	Mat	Balls	Runs	Wkts	BBI	BBM	Ave	Econ	SR	5w	10
First-class	232	37108	20635	683	9/41	-	30.21	3.33	54.3	23	3
List A	269	12636	-	-	-	-	-	-	-	-	-

RICHARD ILLINGWORTH

NAME: Richard Keith Illingworth
BORN: August 23, 1963, Greengates
HEIGHT: 5ft 11in
NICKNAME: Harry, Lucy
APPOINTED TO FIRST-CLASS LIST: 2006
INTERNATIONAL PANEL: 2009-
TESTS UMPIRED: 2
ODIS UMPIRED: 16
T20IS UMPIRED: 7
COUNTIES AS PLAYER: Worcestershire, Derbyshire
ROLE: Right-hand bat, slow left-arm bowler
COUNTY DEBUT: 1982 (Worcestershire), 2001 (Derbyshire)
TEST DEBUT: 1991
ODI DEBUT: 1991

NOTES: Officiated at T20 Finals Day at Edgbaston in 2011

Batting	Mat	Inns	NO	Runs	HS	Ave	SR	100	50	Ct	St
Tests	9	14	7	128	28	18.28	32.08	0	0	5	0
ODIs	25	11	5	68	14	11.33	57.14	0	0	8	0
First-class	376	435	122	7027	120*	22.45	-	4	21	161	0
List A	381	185	87	1458	53*	14.87	-	0	1	93	0

Bowling	Mat	Balls	Runs	Wkts	BBI	BBM	Ave	Econ	SR	5w	10
Tests	9	1485	615	19	4/96	6/150	32.36	2.48	78.1	0	0
ODIs	25	1501	1059	30	3/33	3/33	35.30	4.23	50.0	0	0
First-class	376	65868	26213	831	7/50	-	31.54	2.38	79.2	27	6
List A	381	16918	11157	412	5/24	5/24	27.08	3.95	41.0	2	0

TREVOR JESTY

NAME: Trevor Edward Jesty
BORN: June 2, 1948, Gosport
HEIGHT: 5ft 9in
NICKNAME: Jets
APPOINTED TO FIRST-CLASS LIST: 1994
TESTS UMPIRED: 4 as reserve umpire
ODIS UMPIRED: 3 as TV umpire and 1 as reserve umpire
T20IS UMPIRED: 1 as reserve umpire
COUNTIES AS PLAYER: Hampshire, Surrey, Lancashire
ROLE: Right-hand bat, right-arm medium bowler
COUNTY DEBUT: 1966 (Hampshire), 1985 (Surrey), 1988 (Lancashire)
ODI DEBUT: 1983

NOTES: Stood in the CB40 final at Lord's in 2011. Umpired in two women's Tests, three women's ODIs and six women's T20Is

Batting	Mat	Inns	NO	Runs	HS	Ave	SR	100	50	Ct	St
ODIs	10	10	4	127	52*	21.16	69.78	0	1	5	0
First-class	490	777	107	21916	248	32.71	-	35	110	265	1
List A	428	394	54	9216	166*	27.10	-	7	46	106	0

Bowling	Mat	Balls	Runs	Wkts	BBI	BBM	Ave	Econ	SR	5w	10
ODIs	10	108	93	1	1/23	1/23	93.00	5.16	108.0	0	0
First-class	490	36864	16075	585	7/75	-	27.47	2.61	63.0	19	0
List A	428	13309	9283	372	6/20	6/20	24.95	4.18	35.7	5	0

RICHARD KETTLEBOROUGH

NAME: Richard Allan Kettleborough
BORN: March 15, 1973, Sheffield
HEIGHT: 5ft 10in
NICKNAME: Ketts
APPOINTED TO FIRST-CLASS LIST: 2006
INTERNATIONAL PANEL: 2008-2011
ELITE PANEL: 2011-
TESTS UMPIRED: 12
ODIS UMPIRED: 28
T20IS UMPIRED: 9
COUNTIES AS PLAYER: Yorkshire, Middlesex
ROLE: Left-hand bat
COUNTY DEBUT: 1994 (Yorkshire), 1998 (Middlesex)

NOTES: Rates Trent Bridge and Scarborough as his favourite county grounds and always takes a picture of his children out to the middle with him. He describes his career highlight as an umpire as officiating in his first Test match between Sri Lanka and West Indies in Galle in 2010 and being appointed to the ICC Elite Panel

Batting	Mat	Inns	NO	Runs	HS	Ave	SR	100	50	Ct	St
First-class	33	56	6	1258	108	25.16	-	1	7	20	0
List A	21	16	4	290	58	24.16	-	0	1	6	0

Bowling	Mat	Balls	Runs	Wkts	BBI	BBM	Ave	Econ	SR	5w	10
First-class	33	378	243	3	2/26	-	81.00	3.85	126.0	0	0
List A	21	270	-	-	-	-	-	-	-	-	-

NIGEL LLONG

NAME: Nigel James Llong
BORN: February 11, 1969, Ashford, Kent
HEIGHT: 6ft
NICKNAME: Nidge
APPOINTED TO FIRST-CLASS LIST: 2002
INTERNATIONAL PANEL: 2004-2006 as TV umpire; 2006-present as full member
TESTS UMPIRED: 16
ODIS UMPIRED: 59
T20IS UMPIRED: 17
COUNTY AS PLAYER: Kent
ROLE: Left-hand bat, right-arm off spin bowler
COUNTY DEBUT: 1990

NOTES: Officiated at T20 Finals Day at Edgbaston in 2004, including standing in the final, and again in 2007, 2009 and 2010. Umpired at 2007 ICC World T20 in South Africa

First-class	68	108	11	3024	130	31.17	-	6	16	59	0
List A	136	115	24	2302	123	25.29	-	2	8	41	0
Bowling	**Mat**	**Balls**	**Runs**	**Wkts**	**BBI**	**BBM**	**Ave**	**Econ**	**SR**	**5w**	**10**
First-class	68	2273	1259	35	5/21	-	35.97	3.32	64.9	2	0
List A	136	1317	1210	40	4/24	4/24	30.25	5.51	32.9	0	0

JEREMY LLOYDS

NAME: Jeremy William Lloyds
BORN: November 17, 1954, Penang, Malaysia
HEIGHT: 5ft 11in
NICKNAME: Jerry
APPOINTED TO FIRST-CLASS LIST: 1998
INTERNATIONAL PANEL: 2002-2004 as TV umpire; 2004-2006
TESTS UMPIRED: 5
ODIS UMPIRED: 18
T20IS UMPIRED: 1
COUNTIES AS PLAYER: Somerset, Gloucestershire
ROLE: Left-hand bat, off spin bowler
COUNTY DEBUT: 1979 (Somerset), 1985 (Gloucestershire)

NOTES: Stood in the C&G final in 2006. Officiated at T20 Finals Day in 2007, 2008 and 2012

Batting	Mat	Inns	NO	Runs	HS	Ave	SR	100	50	Ct	St
First-class	267	408	64	10679	132*	31.04	-	10	62	229	0
List A	177	150	26	1982	73*	15.98	-	0	5	58	0

Bowling	Mat	Balls	Runs	Wkts	BBI	BBM	Ave	Econ	SR	5w	10
First-class	267	24175	12943	333	7/88	-	38.86	3.21	72.5	13	1
List A	177	1522	1129	26	3/14	3/14	43.42	4.45	58.5	0	0

NEIL MALLENDER

NAME: Neil Alan Mallender
BORN: August 13, 1961, Kirk Sandall
HEIGHT: 6ft
NICKNAME: Ghostie
APPOINTED TO FIRST-CLASS LIST: 1999
INTERNATIONAL PANEL: 2002-2004
TESTS UMPIRED: 3
ODIS UMPIRED: 22
COUNTIES AS PLAYER: Northamptonshire, Somerset
ROLE: Right-hand bat, right-arm fast-medium bowler
COUNTY DEBUT: 1980 (Northamptonshire), 1987 (Somerset)
TEST DEBUT: 1992

NOTES: PCA Umpire of the Year 2001, 2002, 2003, 2004, 2006, 2008. Stood in the 2003 World Cup. Describes his two favourite grounds, discounting Lord's, as Taunton and Chester-le-Street and loves to listen to rock/metal music before going out to umpire. Officiated at T20 Finals Day at Edgbaston in 2011, including the final, and stood at the CB40 final in 2012

Batting	Mat	Inns	NO	Runs	HS	Ave	SR	100	50	Ct	St
Tests	2	3	0	8	4	2.66	36.36	0	0	0	0
First-class	345	396	122	4709	100*	17.18	-	1	10	111	0
List A	325	163	75	1146	38*	13.02	-	0	0	60	0

Bowling	Mat	Balls	Runs	Wkts	BBI	BBM	Ave	Econ	SR	5w	10
Tests	2	449	215	10	5/50	8/122	21.50	2.87	44.9	1	0
First-class	345	53215	24654	937	7/27	-	26.31	2.77	56.7	36	5
List A	325	15488	9849	387	7/37	7/37	25.44	3.81	40.0	3	0

DAVID MILLNS

NAME: David James Millns
BORN: February 27, 1965, Clipstone
HEIGHT: 6ft 3in
NICKNAME: Rocket Man
APPOINTED TO FIRST-CLASS LIST: 2009
COUNTIES AS PLAYER: Nottinghamshire, Leicestershire
ROLE: Left-hand bat, right-arm fast bowler
COUNTY DEBUT: 1988 (Nottinghamshire), 1990 (Leicestershire)
SOMETHING WE DON'T KNOW ABOUT YOU? I spend my winters scuba diving, skiing and sailing

NOTES: Has stood as reserve umpire in two Tests, one ODI and one T20I

Batting	Mat	Inns	NO	Runs	HS	Ave	SR	100	50	Ct	St
First-class	171	203	63	3082	121	22.01	-	3	8	76	0
List A	91	49	26	338	39*	14.69	-	0	0	18	0

Bowling	Mat	Balls	Runs	Wkts	BBI	BBM	Ave	Econ	SR	5w	10
First-class	171	26571	15129	553	9/37	-	27.35	3.41	48.0	23	4
List A	91	3931	3144	83	4/26	4/26	37.87	4.79	47.3	0	0

STEVE O'SHAUGHNESSY

NAME: Steven Joseph O'Shaughnessy
BORN: September 9, 1961, Bury
APPOINTED TO FIRST-CLASS LIST: 2011
COUNTIES AS PLAYER: Lancashire, Worcestershire
ROLE: Right-hand bat, right-arm medium bowler
COUNTY DEBUT: 1980 (Lancashire), 1988 (Worcestershire)

NOTES: O'Shaughnessy started umpiring in 2007 and was appointed to the full list for the 2011 season

Batting	Mat	Inns	NO	Runs	HS	Ave	SR	100	50	Ct	St
First-class	112	181	28	3720	159*	24.31	-	5	16	57	0
List A	176	151	23	2999	101*	23.42	-	1	15	44	0

Bowling	Mat	Balls	Runs	Wkts	BBI	BBM	Ave	Econ	SR	5w	10
First-class	112	7179	4108	114	4/66	-	36.03	3.43	62.9	0	0
List A	176	5389	4184	115	4/17	4/17	36.38	4.65	46.8	0	0

TIM ROBINSON

NAME: Robert Timothy Robinson
BORN: November 21, 1958, Sutton-in-Ashfield
HEIGHT: 6ft
NICKNAME: Robbo, Chop
APPOINTED TO FIRST-CLASS LIST: 2007
TESTS UMPIRED: 5 as reserve umpire
ODIS UMPIRED: 2 as reserve umpire
T20IS UMPIRED: 4 as reserve umpire
COUNTY AS PLAYER: Nottinghamshire
ROLE: Right-hand batsman
COUNTY DEBUT: 1978
TEST DEBUT: 1984
ODI DEBUT: 1984

NOTES: TV umpire in the CB40 final in 2010 and stood in the CB40 final at Lord's in 2011. Umpired in six women's ODIs and two women's T20Is

Batting	Mat	Inns	NO	Runs	HS	Ave	SR	100	50	Ct	St
Tests	29	49	5	1601	175	36.38	41.62	4	6	8	0
ODIs	26	26	0	597	83	22.96	58.18	0	3	6	0
First-class	425	739	85	27571	220*	42.15	-	63	141	257	0
List A	397	386	40	11879	139	34.33	-	9	75	120	0

Bowling	Mat	Balls	Runs	Wkts	BBI	BBM	Ave	Econ	SR	5w	10
Tests	29	6	0	0	-	-	-	0.00	-	0	0
ODIs	26	-	-	-	-	-	-	-	-	-	-
First-class	425	259	289	4	1/22	-	72.25	6.69	64.7	0	0
List A	397	-	-	-	-	-	-	-	-	-	-

MARTIN SAGGERS

NAME: Martin John Saggers
BORN: May 23, 1972, King's Lynn
HEIGHT: 6ft 2in
NICKNAME: Saggs
APPOINTED TO FIRST-CLASS LIST: 2012
COUNTIES AS PLAYER: Durham, Kent
ROLE: Right-hand bat, right-arm fast-medium bowler
COUNTY DEBUT: 1996 (Durham), 1999 (Kent)
TEST DEBUT: 2003

NOTES: Retired from first-class cricket in 2009 and added to the reserve list of umpires in 2010

Batting	Mat	Inns	NO	Runs	HS	Ave	SR	100	50	Ct	St
Tests	3	3	0	1	1	0.33	3.33	0	0	1	0
First-class	119	147	43	1165	64	11.20	-	0	2	27	0
List A	124	68	34	313	34*	9.20	-	0	0	23	0
Twenty20	10	1	0	5	5	5.00	62.50	0	0	2	0

Bowling	Mat	Balls	Runs	Wkts	BBI	BBM	Ave	Econ	SR	5w	10
Tests	3	493	247	7	2/29	3/62	35.28	3.00	70.4	0	0
First-class	119	20676	10513	415	7/79	-	25.33	3.05	49.8	18	0
List A	124	5622	4229	166	5/22	5/22	25.47	4.51	33.8	2	0
Twenty20	10	186	256	6	2/14	2/14	42.66	8.25	31.0	0	0

GEORGE SHARP

NAME: George Sharp
BORN: March 12, 1950, West Hartlepool
HEIGHT: 5ft 11in
NICKNAME: Sharpie, Blunt, Razor
APPOINTED TO FIRST-CLASS LIST: 1992
INTERNATIONAL PANEL: 1996-2002
TESTS UMPIRED: 15 (plus 1 as TV umpire)
ODIS UMPIRED: 31 (plus 13 as TV umpire)
COUNTY AS PLAYER: Northamptonshire
ROLE: Right-hand bat, wicketkeeper
COUNTY DEBUT: 1968

NOTES: Stood in the 1997 and 2001 Ashes

Batting	Mat	Inns	NO	Runs	HS	Ave	SR	100	50	Ct	St
First-class	306	396	81	6254	98	19.85	-	0	21	565	90
List A	285	203	52	2377	51*	15.74	-	0	1	242	50

Bowling	Mat	Balls	Runs	Wkts	BBI	BBM	Ave	Econ	SR	5w	10
First-class	306	114	70	1	1/47	-	70.00	3.68	114.0	0	0
List A	285	-	-	-	-	-	-	-	-	-	-

PETER WILLEY

NAME: Peter Willey
BORN: December 6, 1949, Sedgefield
HEIGHT: 6ft 1in
NICKNAME: Will
APPOINTED TO FIRST-CLASS LIST: 1993
INTERNATIONAL PANEL: 1996-2003
TESTS UMPIRED: 25
ODIS UMPIRED: 34
COUNTIES AS PLAYER: Northamptonshire, Leicestershire
ROLE: Right-hand bat, off spin bowler
COUNTY DEBUT: 1966 (Northamptonshire), 1984 (Leicestershire)
TEST DEBUT: 1976
ODI DEBUT: 1977

NOTES: Stood in the 1999 and 2003 World Cups, in the 1999 Benson & Hedges Cup final and in the 2004 C&G Trophy final. Officiated at T20 Finals Day at The Oval in 2005 and Edgbaston in 2007, including standing in both finals. Willey is chairman of the First-Class Umpires'Association

Batting	Mat	Inns	NO	Runs	HS	Ave	SR	100	50	Ct	St
Tests	26	50	6	1184	102*	26.90	42.37	2	5	3	0
ODIs	26	24	1	538	64	23.39	62.92	0	5	4	0
First-class	559	918	121	24361	227	30.56	-	44	101	235	0
List A	458	436	43	11105	154	28.25	-	10	67	124	0

Bowling	Mat	Balls	Runs	Wkts	BBI	BBM	Ave	Econ	SR	5w	10
Tests	26	1091	456	7	2/73	2/73	65.14	2.50	155.8	0	0
ODIs	26	1031	659	13	3/33	3/33	50.69	3.83	79.3	0	0
First-class	559	58635	23400	756	7/37	-	30.95	2.39	77.5	26	3
List A	458	18520	11143	347	4/17	4/17	32.11	3.61	53.3	0	0

Roll *of*
Honour

LV= COUNTY CHAMPIONSHIP TABLES

Division One

Team	Mat	Won	Lost	Tied	Draw	Aban	Pts
Warwickshire	16	6	1	0	9	0	211
Somerset	16	5	1	0	10	0	187
Middlesex	16	5	4	0	7	0	172
Sussex	16	5	5	0	6	0	167
Nottinghamshire	16	4	2	0	10	0	163
Durham	16	5	5	0	5	1	157
Surrey	16	3	4	0	8	1	139
Lancashire	16	1	5	0	10	0	106
Worcestershire	16	1	8	0	7	0	96

Division Two

Team	Mat	Won	Lost	Tied	Draw	Aban	Pts
Derbyshire	16	6	2	0	8	0	194
Yorkshire	16	5	0	0	11	0	194
Kent	16	4	3	0	9	0	170
Hampshire	16	4	5	0	7	0	153
Essex	16	3	3	0	10	0	145
Glamorgan	16	3	6	0	6	1	131
Leicestershire	16	3	3	0	10	0	130
Northamptonshire	16	2	5	0	9	0	130
Gloucestershire	16	3	6	0	6	1	126

SURRIDGE

CLYDESDALE BANK 40

Group A							
Team	Mat	Won	Lost	Tied	N/R	Pts	Net RR
Lancashire	12	9	2	0	1	19	+0.050
Middlesex	12	6	3	1	2	15	+0.778
Gloucestershire	12	5	5	0	2	12	+0.995
Netherlands	12	5	6	0	1	11	-0.910
Essex	12	4	6	0	2	10	-0.185
Leicestershire	12	3	6	0	3	9	-0.732
Worcestershire	12	3	7	1	1	8	-0.011

Group B							
Team	Mat	Won	Lost	Tied	N/R	Pts	Net RR
Hampshire	12	7	3	0	2	16	+0.754
Surrey	12	6	3	0	3	15	+0.466
Somerset	12	6	4	0	2	14	+0.385
Nottinghamshire	12	6	5	0	1	13	+0.101
Durham	12	5	5	0	2	12	+0.262
Glamorgan	12	3	6	0	3	9	-0.971
Scotland	12	1	8	0	3	5	-1.359

Group C							
Team	Mat	Won	Lost	Tied	N/R	Pts	Net RR
Sussex	12	7	1	0	4	18	+1.012
Warwickshire	12	8	3	0	1	17	+0.660
Kent	12	7	2	0	3	17	+0.870
Derbyshire	12	4	5	0	3	11	-0.438
Yorkshire	12	4	7	0	1	9	+0.006
Northamptonshire	12	1	6	0	5	7	-0.568
Unicorns	12	1	8	0	3	5	-1.545

SEMI-FINALS

Lancashire v Warwickshire at Manchester – Sep 1, 2012: *Warwickshire won by 23 runs* Warwickshire 250/6 (40/40 ov); Lancashire 227 (39.4/40 ov)

Sussex v Hampshire at Hove – Sep 1, 2012: *Hampshire won by 8 wickets (with 42 balls remaining)* Sussex 219/8 (40/40 ov); Hampshire 222/2 (33/40 ov)

FINAL

Hampshire v Warwickshire at Lord's – Sep 15, 2012: *Hampshire won (lost fewer wickets)* Hampshire 244/5 (40/40 ov); Warwickshire 244/7 (40/40 ov)

PROBIZ
FOREIGN EXCHANGE
PROSTAR
Clydesdale Bank

FRIENDS LIFE T20

North Group

Team	Mat	Won	Lost	Tied	N/R	Pts	Net RR
Yorkshire	10	7	1	0	2	16	+0.863
Nottinghamshire	10	5	1	0	4	14	+1.877
Durham	10	4	4	1	1	10	-0.251
Lancashire	10	3	4	1	2	9	+0.106
Derbyshire	10	2	6	0	2	6	-0.561
Leicestershire	10	2	7	0	1	5	-1.352

South Group

Team	Mat	Won	Lost	Tied	N/R	Pts	Net RR
Sussex	10	6	1	0	3	15	+1.389
Hampshire	10	5	2	0	3	13	+0.693
Essex	10	5	4	0	1	11	-0.032
Kent	10	4	5	0	1	9	-0.465
Middlesex	10	3	7	0	0	6	-0.210
Surrey	10	3	7	0	0	6	-0.700

Midlands/Wales/West Group

Team	Mat	Won	Lost	Tied	N/R	Pts	Net RR
Somerset	10	5	2	0	3	13	+0.275
Gloucestershire	10	4	2	0	4	12	+0.248
Worcestershire	10	4	3	0	3	11	+0.578
Warwickshire	10	4	3	0	3	11	-0.033
Glamorgan	10	2	3	0	5	9	-0.708
Northamptonshire	10	1	7	0	2	4	-0.611

QUARTER-FINALS

Somerset vs Essex at Taunton – Jul 24, 2012: *Somerset won by 27 runs*
Somerset 175/6 (20/20 ov); Essex 148 (18.3/20 ov)

Sussex vs Gloucestershire at Hove – Jul 24, 2012: *Sussex won by 39 runs*
Sussex 230/4 (20/20 ov); Gloucestershire 191/8 (20/20 ov)

Yorkshire vs Worcestershire at Leeds – Jul 25, 2012: *Yorkshire won by 29 runs*
Yorkshire 212/5 (20/20 ov); Worcestershire 183/6 (20/20 ov)

Nottinghamshire vs Hampshire at Nottingham – Jul 25, 2012: *Hampshire won by 4 wickets (with 0 balls remaining)* Nottinghamshire 178/7 (20/20 ov); Hampshire 182/6 (20/20 ov)

SEMI-FINALS

Sussex v Yorkshire at Cardiff – Aug 25, 2012: *Yorkshire won by 36 runs*
Yorkshire 172/6 (20/20 ov); Sussex 136/8 (20/20 ov)

Hampshire v Somerset at Cardiff – Aug 25, 2012 : *Hampshire won by 6 wickets (with 6 balls remaining)*
Somerset 125/6 (20/20 ov); Hampshire 126/4 (19/20 ov)

FINAL

Yorkshire v Hampshire at Cardiff – Aug 25, 2012: *Hampshire won by 10 runs*
Hampshire 150/6 (20/20 ov); Yorkshire 140/8 (20/20 ov)

Friends

FIRST-CLASS BATTING AVERAGES *Minimum of 20 innings*

Name	Mat	Inns	NO	Runs	HS	Ave	BF	SR	100	50	0	4s	6s
NRD Compton	14	21	6	1494	236	99.60	3205	46.61	5	7	0	145	7
C Kieswetter	13	20	6	848	152	60.57	1231	68.88	2	3	2	111	15
JC Hildreth	17	26	3	1214	268	52.78	1783	68.08	4	5	1	164	2
JM Bairstow	15	21	2	972	182	51.15	1507	64.49	4	4	1	130	8
JHK Adams	15	27	6	1024	149	48.76	2291	44.69	3	4	1	141	3
BP Nash	16	24	5	908	132*	47.78	1589	57.14	3	4	0	98	1
CMW Read	17	26	4	1014	104*	46.09	1762	57.54	1	8	1	130	8
R Clarke	17	22	4	826	140	45.88	1287	64.18	3	3	2	97	14
MH Wessels	13	20	0	905	199	45.25	1268	71.37	3	1	1	131	4
RI Newton	13	20	3	751	119*	44.17	1088	69.02	3	2	2	91	9
AG Prince	15	24	1	1008	144	43.82	2030	49.65	2	8	0	84	5
GO Jones	16	20	4	677	88	42.31	1301	52.03	0	7	1	74	3
JE Root	18	26	3	964	222*	41.91	1582	60.93	3	3	3	123	3
RR Sarwan	14	25	2	941	117	40.91	1700	55.35	2	5	1	128	3
MJ Powell	17	21	4	695	134	40.88	1566	44.38	2	3	4	87	1
MA Wallace	16	24	5	775	122*	40.78	1202	64.47	3	1	4	87	3
J Allenby	15	22	4	733	125*	40.72	1267	57.85	2	3	0	76	11
IJ Westwood	13	20	1	771	120	40.57	1883	40.94	2	5	3	94	0
JD Middlebrook	15	22	4	714	121	39.66	1570	45.47	2	4	0	82	5
EC Joyce	14	24	3	829	108*	39.47	1849	44.83	2	5	1	110	4
V Chopra	18	28	1	1062	195	39.33	2168	48.98	3	5	4	140	1
DJG Sales	14	21	3	706	140	39.22	1390	50.79	2	3	1	91	0
MJ Lumb	15	25	0	971	171	38.84	2071	46.88	3	3	1	137	2
SJ Walters	14	23	2	813	159	38.71	1592	51.06	1	7	0	105	1
GS Ballance	17	20	4	617	121*	38.56	1261	48.92	1	2	0	79	4
DJ Redfern	17	25	3	848	133	38.54	1354	62.62	2	6	4	108	2
CJL Rogers	17	31	2	1108	173	38.20	1924	57.58	3	6	3	134	5
RWT Key	15	24	3	797	119	37.95	1694	47.04	1	5	1	92	0
CD Nash	17	28	2	984	162	37.84	1529	64.35	3	2	2	132	5
LWP Wells	15	21	2	713	127	37.52	1764	40.41	2	3	1	102	0
HJH Marshall	15	25	3	822	117*	37.36	1500	54.80	1	5	2	96	2
WL Madsen	17	27	2	928	231*	37.12	1790	51.84	3	3	2	109	0
WJ Durston	17	27	3	878	121	36.58	1384	63.43	2	4	0	108	13
JWA Taylor	18	28	4	875	163*	36.45	1835	47.68	3	1	1	104	2
JO Troughton	16	25	3	800	132	36.36	1790	44.69	2	5	1	79	7
SM Ervine	17	25	4	763	109*	36.33	1236	61.73	1	4	4	84	4
SD Peters	15	23	2	763	148	36.33	1663	45.88	2	3	2	82	2
AG Wakely	14	21	2	690	96	36.31	1466	47.06	0	5	1	74	4
SM Katich	15	23	2	738	196	35.14	1164	63.40	1	5	3	95	2
JL Denly	16	28	4	840	134*	35.00	1708	49.18	2	4	1	112	5
PD Trego	17	22	4	630	92	35.00	815	77.30	0	4	0	86	10
IA Cockbain	15	24	2	764	112	34.72	1709	44.70	1	5	2	102	1
AD Hales	16	26	1	857	155*	34.28	1496	57.28	2	4	2	128	1
JJ Cobb	14	23	1	752	105	34.18	1409	53.37	1	5	2	110	9
T Westley	17	25	2	786	185	34.17	1520	51.71	2	3	3	112	0
ML Pettini	16	23	4	644	92	33.89	1433	44.94	0	7	0	63	5
PD Collingwood	14	25	3	744	114	33.81	1482	50.20	1	4	0	96	2
NJ Dexter	13	23	2	701	125	33.38	1402	50.00	2	4	3	89	2
DJ Malan	17	27	0	897	140	33.22	1778	50.44	2	4	2	110	2
PJ Horton	17	27	4	742	137*	32.26	1794	41.36	2	2	4	95	0

FIRST-CLASS BOWLING AVERAGES *Minimum of 2000 balls*

Name	Mat	Overs	Mdns	Runs	Wkts	BBI	BBM	Ave	Econ	SR	5	10
G Onions	14	415.1	114	1061	72	9/67	11/95	14.73	2.55	34.5	5	3
DD Masters	14	395.3	119	941	53	7/60	7/60	17.75	2.37	44.7	4	0
AR Adams	12	344.3	63	1035	54	7/32	10/50	19.16	3.00	38.2	4	1
M Davies	15	368.3	129	699	36	5/27	7/58	19.41	1.89	61.4	1	0
TS Roland-Jones	15	405.0	87	1245	64	6/66	10/118	19.45	3.07	37.9	4	1
A Richardson	14	461.3	137	1113	57	6/47	10/128	19.52	2.41	48.5	4	1
SJ Magoffin	15	480.1	161	1143	57	7/34	9/50	20.05	2.38	50.5	2	0
KHD Barker	15	392.1	94	1166	56	6/40	10/70	20.82	2.97	42.0	5	1
SA Patterson	16	427.2	125	1115	53	5/77	8/94	21.03	2.60	48.3	1	0
MT Coles	17	400.1	51	1341	59	6/51	9/83	22.72	3.35	40.6	2	0
JS Patel	13	395.1	87	1161	51	7/75	8/114	22.76	2.93	46.4	4	0
MS Panesar	16	514.1	157	1227	53	7/60	13/137	23.15	2.38	58.2	2	1
CJC Wright	16	471.3	77	1562	67	5/24	9/89	23.31	3.31	42.2	2	0
J Allenby	15	359.3	80	992	42	4/39	5/54	23.61	2.75	51.3	0	0
TJ Murtagh	16	526.3	127	1455	61	5/37	6/68	23.85	2.76	51.7	2	0
SC Meaker	13	355.3	62	1225	51	8/52	11/167	24.01	3.44	41.8	3	1
G Chapple	15	394.5	101	1010	42	5/47	10/133	24.04	2.55	56.4	2	1
AP Palladino	16	499.4	107	1431	56	7/53	9/118	25.55	2.86	53.5	3	0
TD Groenewald	14	399.4	89	1086	42	5/29	5/29	25.85	2.71	57.0	1	0
DJ Balcombe	17	533.1	111	1671	64	8/71	11/119	26.10	3.13	49.9	3	1
BJ Phillips	14	345.3	105	841	32	4/33	5/62	26.28	2.43	64.7	0	0
JA Tomlinson	12	376.1	82	1131	43	5/69	6/105	26.30	3.00	52.4	2	0
CE Shreck	17	526.3	112	1544	58	5/41	9/140	26.62	2.93	54.4	2	0
GH Dockrell	11	340.5	80	996	35	6/27	8/62	28.45	2.92	58.4	2	0
WA White	16	349.0	41	1286	43	5/54	5/69	29.90	3.68	48.6	3	0
DJ Wainwright	17	565.5	141	1542	50	6/33	8/134	30.84	2.72	67.9	3	0
J Lewis	13	335.0	77	980	31	5/41	7/97	31.61	2.92	64.8	1	0
PD Trego	17	523.5	125	1609	50	5/53	7/115	32.18	3.07	62.8	2	0
SC Kerrigan	17	573.2	98	1674	50	6/59	7/122	33.48	2.91	68.8	1	0
DJ Willey	15	440.1	90	1474	43	5/39	8/92	34.27	3.34	61.4	1	0
JC Tredwell	15	371.0	99	912	26	3/35	5/118	35.07	2.45	85.6	0	0
JD Middlebrook	15	346.2	100	883	24	5/63	6/110	36.79	2.54	86.5	1	0
CW Henderson	12	390.1	82	1110	30	5/116	6/104	37.00	2.84	78.0	1	0
TT Bresnan	9	337.2	75	1071	28	5/81	8/141	38.25	3.17	72.2	1	0
JE Anyon	15	429.5	73	1646	42	5/36	6/134	39.19	3.82	61.4	2	0
LM Daggett	14	372.1	95	1218	27	4/76	4/67	45.11	3.27	82.7	0	0
DA Cosker	15	361.3	83	991	16	4/22	5/46	61.93	2.74	135.5	0	0

Cotton
BREWIN
DOLPHIN

FIRST-CLASS WICKETKEEPING *Minimum of 20 dismissals*

Name	Mat	Mat	Dis	Ct	St	Max Dis Mat	Dis/Inn
MD Bates	17	28	57	56	1	6 (6ct 0st)	2.035
GO Jones	16	27	52	52	0	5 (5ct 0st)	1.925
JA Simpson	14	27	48	43	5	5 (5ct 0st)	1.777
TR Ambrose	14	25	47	46	1	5 (5ct 0st)	1.880
P Mustard	15	26	46	46	0	4 (4ct 0st)	1.769
JS Foster	16	27	46	43	3	4 (4ct 0st)	1.703
MA Wallace	16	27	46	42	4	4 (4ct 0st)	1.703
CMW Read	17	29	46	45	1	4 (4ct 0st)	1.586
EJH Eckersley	16	21	43	40	3	6 (5ct 1st)	2.047
T Poynton	14	25	43	42	1	4 (4ct 0st)	1.720
BC Brown	14	25	41	38	3	6 (6ct 0st)	1.640
C Kieswetter	13	23	34	32	2	4 (3ct 1st)	1.478
BJM Scott	14	23	34	29	5	5 (3ct 2st)	1.478
GD Cross	16	26	34	31	3	4 (4ct 0st)	1.307
JN Batty	8	13	25	24	1	4 (4ct 0st)	1.923
D Murphy	10	15	25	23	2	4 (4ct 0st)	1.666
SM Davies	12	19	25	24	1	3 (3ct 0st)	1.315
MJ Prior	11	14	20	16	4	6 (5ct 1st)	1.428
JM Bairstow	15	15	19	19	0	4 (4ct 0st)	1.266
AJ Hodd	4	8	18	18	0	5 (5ct 0st)	2.250

FIRST-CLASS FIELDING *Minimum of 16 catches*

Name	Mat	Mat	Ct	Max	Ct/Inn
LA Dawson	17	28	37	4	1.321
MH Yardy	16	28	32	3	1.142
R Clarke	17	31	31	5	1.000
V Chopra	18	32	27	3	0.843
ME Trescothick	9	18	26	5	1.444
WJ Durston	17	30	26	3	0.866
DJ Malan	17	33	25	3	0.757
DKH Mitchell	17	27	23	3	0.851
SG Borthwick	14	25	21	2	0.840
WTS Porterfield	15	27	21	3	0.777
PD Collingwood	14	25	19	3	0.760
VS Solanki	14	23	18	3	0.782
AD Hales	16	27	18	2	0.666
PJ Horton	17	27	18	2	0.666
JC Hildreth	17	32	17	3	0.531
PA Jaques	15	25	16	4	0.640
JC Tredwell	15	25	16	2	0.640
GJ Batty	14	23	15	2	0.652
AG Prince	15	24	15	3	0.625
JHK Adams	15	25	15	2	0.600
SJ Croft	17	27	15	3	0.555
AWR Barrow	9	17	14	2	0.823

#	Name	County	Batting	Bowling	Field	Capt.	Wins	Pld	Pts	Average
1	Trego, Peter	Somerset	168.01	296.67	19	0	17.0	35	501	14.31
2	Stevens, Darren	Kent	176.58	232.37	16	0	15.0	36	441	12.24
3	Ali, Moeen	Worcs	205.90	208.70	11	0	8.0	36	434	12.04
4	Nash, Chris	Sussex	292.24	101.18	17	0	18.0	35	428	12.24
5	Barker, Keith	Warks	58.07	332.29	8	0	16.0	32	414	12.95
6	Wright, Chris	Warks	31.49	353.87	7	0	17.0	33	409	12.40
7	Roland-Jones, Tobias	Middx	48.09	347.24	4	0	10.0	27	409	15.16
8	Durston, Wes	Derbyshire	234.73	129.75	31	0	12.0	36	408	11.32
9	Croft, Steven	Lancs	287.51	55.37	41	3	13.0	37	400	10.81
10	Chapple, Glen	Lancs	70.47	301.45	6	10	10.0	28	398	14.21
11	Stokes, Benjamin	Durham	181.22	185.97	15	0	12.0	32	394	12.32
12	Clarke, Rikki	Warks	211.45	110.61	51	0	18.0	36	391	10.86
13	Onions, Graham	Durham	33.82	337.62	5	0	10.0	24	386	16.10
14	Chopra, Varun	Warks	331.32	-0.25	32	1	19.0	35	383	10.94
15	Ervine, Sean	Hants	168.84	166.15	14	0	21.0	41	371	9.04
16	Allenby, James	Glamorgan	148.87	197.25	13	2	8.0	27	370	13.70
17	Magoffin, Steven	Sussex	58.53	298.28	5	0	6.0	17	368	21.64
18	Batty, Gareth	Surrey	68.11	248.85	25	5	12.0	36	359	9.97
19	Malan, Dawid	Middx	280.00	32.36	31	0	14.0	36	357	9.93
20	Patel, Jeetan	Warks	40.71	284.05	13	0	15.0	31	353	11.38
21	Mustard, Phil	Durham	237.49	0.00	98	0	13.0	34	348	10.25
22	Dawson, Liam	Hants	114.52	164.14	41	0	21.0	39	341	8.74
23	Murtagh, Tim	Middx	64.39	260.83	7	0	5.0	19	337	17.75
24	Berg, Gareth	Middx	114.50	187.39	21	0	14.0	34	337	9.91
25	Woakes, Christopher	Warks	83.43	233.56	8	0	10.0	22	335	15.23
26	Davies, Mark	Kent	26.90	285.43	7	0	14.0	33	334	10.11
27	Hughes, Phillip	Worcs	315.43	0.00	7	0	7.0	27	329	12.20
28	Read, Christopher	Notts	214.18	0.00	84	10	15.0	35	323	9.23
29	Mitchell, Daryl	Worcs	197.50	77.44	30	8	8.0	36	321	8.91
30	Coles, Matthew	Kent	55.62	241.17	10	0	11.0	29	318	10.97
31	Patel, Samit	Notts	144.58	142.14	13	0	13.0	26	313	12.03
32	White, Wayne	Leics	114.90	180.40	6	0	7.0	33	309	9.36
33	Adams, James	Hants	250.13	1.66	23	12	20.0	38	307	8.07
34	Compton, Nick	Somerset	279.04	0.00	11	0	12.0	25	302	12.08
35	Hildreth, James	Somerset	257.16	-1.50	26	2	16.0	36	300	8.32
36	Richardson, Alan	Worcs	12.31	281.58	3	0	1.0	14	298	21.28
37	Napier, Graham	Essex	72.41	201.05	12	0	12.0	29	298	10.26
38	Groenewald, Timothy	Derbyshire	30.01	250.83	5	0	11.0	30	297	9.91
39	Foster, James	Essex	187.95	0.00	87	11	11.0	33	297	9.00
40	Rushworth, Christopher	Durham	16.88	262.32	3	0	12.0	21	294	14.01
41	Adams, Andre	Notts	25.70	255.75	8	0	4.0	12	293	24.45
42	Rogers, Christopher	Middx	264.89	0.00	14	4	10.0	28	293	10.46
43	Willey, David	Northants	99.28	180.23	9	0	3.0	31	292	9.42
44	Dexter, Neil	Middx	166.61	86.09	16	10	13.0	32	292	9.12
45	Davies, Steven	Surrey	168.17	0.00	111	0	10.0	34	289	8.50
46	Lumb, Michael	Notts	260.50	-0.65	14	0	14.0	32	288	9.00
47	Maddy, Darren	Warks	160.57	91.40	16	0	17.0	34	285	8.38
48	Middlebrook, James	Northants	112.58	162.39	4	0	4.0	33	284	8.60
49	Wright, Luke	Sussex	232.37	21.06	11	0	17.0	27	281	10.42
50	Panesar, Monty	Sussex	12.69	254.16	5	0	9.0	20	281	14.04

#	Name	County	Batting	Bowling	Field	Capt.	Wins	Pld	Pts	Average
51	Yardy, Michael	Sussex	134.14	80.96	34	13	18.0	35	280	8.00
52	Kieswetter, Craig	Somerset	206.75	7.95	56	0	9.0	22	280	12.71
53	Ballance, Gary	Yorks	230.64	-0.22	27	0	18.0	39	275	7.06
54	Gidman, William	Gloucs	78.97	183.30	4	0	6.0	18	273	15.15
55	Vince, James	Hants	230.69	-0.32	22	0	20.0	36	273	7.57
56	Rafiq, Azeem	Yorks	47.22	188.99	13	5	16.0	32	270	8.44
57	Wainwright, David	Derbyshire	47.50	198.88	12	0	11.0	30	270	9.00
58	Meaker, Stuart	Surrey	31.80	222.74	6	0	9.0	27	270	9.98
59	Masters, David	Essex	17.51	233.92	4	0	8.0	28	264	9.42
60	Moore, Stephen	Lancs	235.08	0.00	15	0	13.0	33	263	7.97
61	Wood, Christopher	Hants	50.40	183.41	8	0	20.0	33	262	7.95
62	Prince, Ashwell	Lancs	231.19	-0.40	21	0	10.0	27	262	9.70
63	Hales, Alex	Notts	228.23	0.00	19	0	14.0	32	261	8.16
64	Cobb, Joshua	Leics	195.40	38.93	13	3	8.0	31	259	8.35
65	Sarwan, Ramnaresh	Leics	243.31	-1.72	9	0	7.0	32	258	8.07
66	Root, Joseph	Yorks	206.72	15.76	19	0	15.0	34	257	7.56
67	Wessels, Matthew	Notts	210.78	4.84	26	0	13.0	32	255	7.96
68	Jaques, Phil	Yorks	218.47	0.00	17	0	18.0	37	254	6.87
69	Shahzad, Ajmal	Lancs	36.81	204.50	3	0	9.0	26	253	9.74
70	Denly, Joseph	Middx	221.11	2.65	14	0	11.0	32	249	7.77
71	Stoneman, Mark	Durham	226.71	0.00	12	0	10.0	24	249	10.36
72	Kartik, Murali	Surrey	22.19	212.98	6	0	7.0	25	248	9.93
73	Balcombe, David	Hants	40.26	200.10	3	0	4.0	16	248	15.47
74	de Bruyn, Zander	Surrey	168.09	54.38	11	0	12.0	35	245	7.01
75	Borthwick, Scott	Durham	65.58	143.86	21	0	14.0	33	244	7.41
76	Thomas, Alfonso	Somerset	21.10	198.30	5	7	13.0	24	244	10.18
77	Saxelby, Ian	Gloucs	27.54	200.05	5	0	10.0	24	243	10.11
78	Ambrose, Tim	Warks	155.96	0.00	73	0	12.0	24	241	10.04
79	Suppiah, Arul	Somerset	168.23	45.40	13	0	12.0	30	239	7.95
80	Carberry, Michael	Hants	214.98	3.64	7	0	12.0	25	238	9.50
81	Jones, Geraint	Kent	122.63	0.00	99	0	15.0	36	237	6.59
82	Northeast, Sam	Kent	211.12	0.00	11	0	14.0	31	237	7.64
83	Westley, Tom	Essex	179.82	38.16	10	0	8.0	29	236	8.14
84	Patterson, Steven	Yorks	22.48	203.86	3	0	6.0	19	236	12.41
85	Pettini, Mark	Essex	209.67	2.18	10	1	12.0	35	235	6.71
86	Crook, Steven	Middx	69.38	145.10	10	0	10.0	23	234	10.19
87	Wallace, Mark	Glamorgan	145.86	0.00	74	6	8.0	31	234	7.56
88	Joyce, Edmund	Sussex	202.19	0.00	14	6	11.0	24	233	9.72
89	Andrew, Gareth	Worcs	95.66	118.93	9	0	7.0	26	231	8.87
90	Fuller, James	Gloucs	55.41	160.99	4	0	9.0	22	230	10.45
91	Palladino, Antonio	Derbyshire	31.36	192.58	0	0	5.0	16	230	14.36
92	Solanki, Vikram	Worcs	189.89	0.00	31	0	8.0	33	229	6.94
93	Thorp, Callum	Durham	41.87	170.96	10	0	5.0	13	228	17.53
94	Taylor, James	Notts	202.67	-0.80	11	0	14.0	30	227	7.56
95	Marshall, Hamish	Gloucs	192.05	0.00	18	4	12.0	33	227	6.87
96	Anyon, James	Sussex	49.23	165.60	7	0	5.0	15	227	15.12
97	Troughton, Jamie	Warks	170.44	0.00	20	18	18.0	33	226	6.86
98	Lewis, Jon	Surrey	57.33	156.65	7	0	5.0	22	226	10.27
99	Katich, Simon	Hants	174.45	14.99	15	1	20.0	36	226	6.27
100	Dockrell, George	Somerset	11.12	193.91	11	0	9.0	23	225	9.78

jf
jellyfish